DEAF WOMEN of CANADA

A PROUD HISTORY AND EXCITING FUTURE

J. Robinson

Hilda M. Campbell

Stratiy

CAMPBELL, ROBINSON & STRATIY

Printed in Canada.   5   4   3   2   1

Duval House Publishing/Les Éditions Duval, Inc.
Head Office   Ontario Office
18228 - 102 Avenue   5 Graham Avenue
Edmonton, Alberta   Ottawa, Ontario
CANADA T5S 1S7   CANADA K1S 0B6
Telephone: 1-800-267-6187
Fax: (780) 482-7213
e-mail: duvalhouse@duvalhouse.com
website: www.duvalhouse.com

National Library of Canada Cataloguing in Publication Data

Campbell, Hilda Marian, 1927-
    Deaf women of Canada

    ISBN 1-55220-265-8

    1. Deaf women--Canada--Biography. I. Robinson, Jo-Anne, 1949- II.
Stratiy, Angela, 1947- III. Title.
HV2577.A3C35 2002   362.4'2'092271 C2002-910082-8

 Canada We acknowledge the financial support of the Government of Canada through the Book Publishing Industry Development Program (BPIDP) for our publishing activities.

CONTENTS

Canada is distinct because of its unique cultural mosaic. The heart and soul of Canada is found in all the races and diverse cultures that comprise this great country. Canadians do not subscribe to the 'melting pot' theory. We do not want all our various cultures to assimilate into the one majority. It is evident that Canadians take pride in their individual cultural heritages. It is important for us to retain each culture's customs, traditions and language within the wider scope of our community; thus, allowing for a colourful integration of all that we hold dear. Deaf women are just one tile found in Canada's cultural mosaic, but without them the true picture of Canada would be left incomplete.

Until now, not much had been written about Deaf women of Canada. Although they started out as seedlings in a forest of trees, the roots of these Deaf women grew strong. It is easy to see that all of the women written about in this book have stood tall and proud of their cultural heritage. From the mid 1800s to the present day, Deaf women across Canada, have accepted challenges and overcome obstacles. They have grown strong in the constant face of adversity and they have contributed to our knowledge and understanding of the world. Their anecdotes, stories and recounted histories help us understand the experiences and backgrounds of a colourful and spirited group.

Women like Charmaine Letourneau, who was the first Deaf person in Canada to be invested in Order of Canada, are strong leaders, capable of changing not only our country's image, but also the face of the world. To grow up in the twenty-first century will be a benefit to our children. They will have the opportunity to learn from, and emulate, the many role models in our society today. The profiles in this book will encourage them to look to Deaf women for leadership, support and advocacy. *Deaf Women of Canada* is a compilation of historical data, stories and events about a strong cultural group who have grown and excelled in areas such as business, politics, religion, sports, education, science, publishing and the arts. It is striking to see the variety of their accomplishments and the diversity of their interests and expertise which provide lessons we can learn from the many great Deaf women of Canada through the ages and today.

"Grow into your ideals so that life does not rob you of them." —Kettinger

The Canadian Cultural Society of the Deaf (CCSD) is committed to ensuring that we continue to rise to each and every challenge and to be proud of our accomplishments. In keeping with CCSD's commitment, *Deaf Women of Canada* beautifully illustrates how each one of us can achieve our dreams!

Helen Pizzacalla
CCSD President

ACKNOWLEDGEMENTS

In addition to the women who contributed their stories, we acknowledge with special thanks and appreciation, the assistance we received from the following individuals, institutes, and archives: Agnes Manchul, Anne McKercher, Antoine Mountain, Betty Halverson, Beverley Boudreau, Bill Fillmore, Bill Swanson, Billie Richardson, Brad Bice, Bruce Koskie, Carl Brown, Carole Sue Bailey, Caroline Ann Fritz, Celia May Baldwin, Chris Kenopic, Christina Dorschner, Christine Ayles, Christine Mitchell, Dale Birley, Danny Elliot, Darlene Karran, Donna Mason, Dr. Clifton Carbin, Corissa Ford, Dr. Deborah Bingham Van Broekhoven, Dr. Maureen Donald, Dr. Marty Taylor, Doreen Youngs, Donna Vann, Doris MacKillop, Dorothy Beam, Douglas Ferguson, Ed Curtis, Emma Foster, Elizabeth Doull, Ellie Provow, Flo Cates, Frank Gyle, Fred Drysdale, Gail Black, Georgina Lilley, Gerald Zimmer, Geraldine Buchanan, Gladys Baxter, Gordon Ayles, Gordon Slack, Gretchen Drummie, Heather McDonald, Helen Pizzacalla, Howard Nemeroff, Irvin MacDonald, Jacqueline Belmore, Jack Weldon, Jamie Menzies, Jamie MacDougall, Jan McConnell, Janice Drake, Jeannine Green, Joan Dale, Joan Drysdale, Joan Williams, Joanne Cripps, Joanne Stump, Joe McLaughlin, Joyanne Burdett, Jean Gardner, Judy Nadon-Yuen, Judy Shea, Juan Jaramillo, Kathy Dolby, Kathy Messervey, Kathy Schoenberg, Keith Dorschner, Kevin Klein, Laurel Ann Roberts, Laverne Foster, Lawrie McKeith, Leanor Vlug, Len Mitchell, Leslie Dunn, Lester Settle, Linda Koskie, Lois Birley, Lois Nickerson, Lucille Hutchinson, Lynn LeBlanc, Mack Buchanan, Macklin Youngs, Marguerite Pettypiece, Margaret Dunn, Mark Korol, Mary Jane MacKinnon McCool, Michael Maddison, Mike Olson, Monica Ruiz, Monique Boudreault, Nancy Hopkins, Nellie Shores, Pastor Don McQueen, Pauline Buchanan, Pauline Peikoff, Peter Hines, Philip Taylor, Professor Laurie Stanley-Blackwell, Professor Ron MacKinnon, Reverend Bob Rumball, Reverend Francis Gyle, Rick Zimmer, Rita Bomak, Robert Hutchinson, Robert St. Louis, Roxanne Whitting, Sally Austin, Silva Notland, Sister Elizabeth Kass, Sheila Carlin, Shirley Handley, Suzie Jacobs, Teresa Mihalik, the American Baptist Historical Society Valley Forge Archives Center, the Art Gallery of Ontario, the Canadian Cultural Society of the Deaf, the Canadian National Institute for the Blind Library, the Colchester Historical Society, the Family History Centre of Edmonton, the Family History Centre of Winnipeg, the Gallaudet Archives, the Halifax-Dartmouth Regional Municipal Library, the Manitoba Genealogical Society, the Manitoba School for the Deaf Archives, the Northern Images Gallery, the Nova Scotia Archives and Records Management, the National Archives of Canada, the Nova Scotia Legislative Library, the Provincial Archives of Alberta, the Sir James Whitney School for the Deaf Archives, the Staff of the Royal National Institute of the Deaf Library of London, the University of Alberta Special Collections, the University of Winnipeg Archives, the Winnipeg Community Centre of the Deaf, Thelma Durling, Theresa Kelly, Theresa Swedick, Tom Boroday, Vincent Elliott, Wendy McNutt, and William Edward Payne.

This book began in 1989 with the idea that a collective history of Deaf women and their contributions to their various communities should be recorded. It was a daunting thought and presented many difficulties, such as where to begin, how to collect information, and how to assemble the material. Now, in 2002, with the work completed, we can look back on twelve years of frustration, setbacks, thrills, and triumphs as the pieces of the jigsaw puzzle fell into place.

If those of us involved in creating this book have often felt unequal to the task, we have been constantly inspired and sustained by the women whose remarkable accomplishments have been revealed to us. Information about the daily lives and struggles of Deaf women is not easy to come by, mainly because, until recent decades, women were not considered to be makers of history, so documentation of their achievements has often been sketchy. In addition, selecting profiles for inclusion in this book was a monumental task and there are doubt-lessly many deserving Deaf women whose stories have been inadvertently omitted. To those women, we offer our sincere apologies, and to those who agreed to share their stories, we proffer our heartfelt thanks.

We owe an enormous debt of gratitude to many individuals. Without their contributions the publica-tion of this book would not have been possible. To the Canadian Cultural Society of the Deaf (CCSD), we are grateful for the grant of $50,000 to begin our research. To Helen Pizzacalla, President of CCSD, we owe thanks for her support, the use of the CCSD office in Edmonton, Alberta, and her contribution of the Foreword. We also offer our gratitude to CCSD staff members Caroline Anne Fritz and Shirley Handley who provided us with office assistance. We are indebted to those who served as provincial representatives: Leanor Vlug, Joanne Stump, Lucille Hutchinson, Joanne Cripps, Marguerite Pettypiece, Judy Shea, and Elizabeth Doull. These valiant women provided the "leg work" we needed, spending endless hours searching for information in archives, local records, and libraries. They examined transcripts, conducted interviews, found appropriate photographs, and, where none existed, they put their own cameras to use. They tracked down subjects to be profiled, verified information, and assisted with revisions and final approvals of the stories. What you read in this book was gleaned from reminiscences, letters, newspapers, resumes, school records, family lore, and records of organizations of the Deaf. Most of these materials were collected by the provincial representatives.

As our research progressed, we were delighted to find so many heroines we could call our own—magnificent Deaf women who confronted obstacles to their success with determination, intelligence, and optimistic vision. There is great satisfaction in the knowledge that their struggles to break down barriers are now recorded for posterity. Accuracy in the translation of documents from French to English for the women of Québec was a challenge which we hope has been satisfactorily met. We have attempted to cover every area of the nation, including all ten provinces as well as the northern territories. For many of the deceased women we have profiled, we owe thanks to their family members who provided us with informa-tion and photographs. Last, but not least, we thank Beverley Boudreau for her eye-catching cover design and Jamie Menzies for her guiding hand in facilitating the book's printing and publication.

It is our hope that this work will provide our readers with greater insight and understanding. We are confi-dent that this will inspire them.

ACHNEEPINESKUM, Lillian N.

1966–
Avid Athlete, Role Model for Aboriginal Deaf People, and Deaf Community Volunteer.

LILLIAN ACHNEEPINESKUM was born hearing into a hearing family at Geraldton, Ontario, east of Thunder Bay. She became Deaf at the age of two as a result of a severe bout of scarlet fever but it was quite some time before she was actually diagnosed as Deaf by a medical doctor. Her foster mother eventually took her to Toronto to be tested, and her audiogram soon indicated beyond doubt that Lillian was Deaf. This news left her foster parents feeling overwhelmed and depressed. She has no known Deaf relatives, but the early circumstances of her life precluded her having much knowledge of her family history. Lillian is the single mother of a young hearing daughter named Gabby Brynne. They currently make their home in Scarborough, Ontario.

Lillian's education began when she was five years old and decided to accompany her five-year-old nephew Deon to the local school in Nakima, which was run by nuns. When they found out she was Deaf, Lillian was assigned to a special teacher in a one-to-one program which, in theory, was perhaps a good idea. But, in fact, she was mostly ignored by all the staff and spent her time in the school library, learning virtually nothing. In those unenlightened days, she was treated as "retarded" because she was Deaf. It was assumed that she could not learn.

In due course, a social worker called on her parents to discuss her placement in a School for the Deaf. It took a great deal of convincing before her parents reluctantly agreed to allow her to go to Belleville to attend Sir James Whitney School for the Deaf when she was eight years old. She was at that time living on the Constance Lake Reserve, which had been named after one of her great aunts who had lived there. When she first arrived in Belleville she was frightened and apprehensive. Before long, however, she was learning Sign Language and was happy to finally have a means of communication. She soon began to participate in all types of sports and was very athletically inclined, a description that still applies to Lillian today.

After winning numerous sports awards as well as receiving academic recognition, she graduated in 1986 when she was twenty years old. She then went on to George Brown College and enrolled in a general arts and science program. She also briefly attended Gallaudet University.

What had the greatest impact on Lillian's life, however, was her involvement in the Deaf Community, which began in 2000 when she attended the Ontario Association of the Deaf's (OAD's) Convention. This was a real eye-opener for Lillian and she began to take an interest in her Deaf heritage. She is on the board of directors of OAD, is a superb role model to other Aboriginal Deaf persons, and serves as chairperson of OAD's committee on violence against women. She loves her constant contact with the Deaf Community. Her goal is to work for OAD. If funding can be obtained, Lillian would like to lead projects for the Deaf.

Besides her participation in sports, Lillian is interested in numerous other pastimes and hobbies.

ADAMSON (TURRIFF), Lily James

1864–1952
Dedicated Teacher of the Deaf and Tireless Worker in the Deaf Community.

Although very few of LILY TURRIFF's achievements were documented, it is known that her impact on the Deaf Community in Winnipeg, Manitoba, was significant. She was a true pioneer as an advocate for the Deaf people of her era, and a staunch supporter and proponent of the preservation of the Deaf Canadian heritage.

Lily's family emigrated from Scotland, and she was born in Little Metis, Québec. She came to Winnipeg in 1880 and became one of the few Deaf teachers who taught at the old Manitoba School for the Deaf in downtown Winnipeg, at the corner of Portage Avenue and Sherbrook Street. Records indicate that Lily spent thirty-two years as a teacher of the Deaf in Manitoba, from 1893 until 1926, most of them during Duncan W. McDermid's tenure as principal. Some of today's old-timers remember her fondly and recall that Mr. McDermid often visited her classroom to observe her teaching methods and to note the progress of her students. Lily subscribed to the philosophy that while speech and lipreading were important, mental development and language acquisition were even more crucial for Deaf children, and could best be achieved through manual methods of instruction. Her success as a teacher was renowned.

She married Alan Joseph Adamson in 1927, and had four stepsons—Justice J.E. Adamson, A.J. Adamson, Hebert Adamson and Gilbert Adamson—and two stepdaughters, Mrs. Lily Marganella and Miss Harrietta Adamson. In later years, she participated in every aspect of the establishment of the Winnipeg Community Centre of the Deaf (WCCD) and made considerable monetary donations to the organization.

WCCD was an outgrowth of several earlier "silent" organizations and served as a recreational centre during the week. On Sundays it was used as a place of worship. Lily was also actively involved in the Winnipeg Church of the Deaf. WCCD put out a newsletter regularly, and eventually the centre metamorphosed into the Kiwanis Centre of the Deaf. Today it is known as Deaf Centre Manitoba.

Lily passed away in Winnipeg on July 25, 1952. Lily (Turriff) Adamson's contributions to Deaf education in Manitoba and to the founding of WCCD were manifold and praiseworthy.

ANDERSON (HARRIS), Elaine Freda

1957–
Library Clerk, Bookkeeper, Cashier, and Rental Clerk.

ELAINE HARRIS was born Deaf, with some degree of physical disability, as a result of maternal rubella, in Winnipeg, Manitoba. At eight years of age, she was fitted with hearing-aids and given speech therapy at the Children's Hospital. She was also sent to Robertson School in the mainstream public school system, but was very unhappy and frustrated due to communication difficulties. She was then sent to Wellington Public School and placed in a class for Deaf children. Her frustration continued, however, because she was ostracized for her appearance and this prevented her from becoming socialized. Finally, from 1964 to 1976, she attended the Manitoba provincial School for the Deaf from which she graduated.

After graduation, Elaine enrolled at Gallaudet University in Washington, BC, but withdrew within the first month due to unbearable homesickness. She returned home to Winnipeg and took upgrading classes at Red River Community College.

Elaine's first employment was with the Freshwater Institute Library at the University of Manitoba as a library clerk, but she was laid off after six months. She then found work at a downtown hotel, the Royal Albert Arms, as a bookkeeper. After one year, she was laid off again. She was then offered a position at the Kiwanis Centre of the Deaf (now Deaf Centre Manitoba), as a cafeteria cashier. She worked there for over seven years while also doing part-time tutoring for ten months

with a client from the Society of Manitobans with Disabilities. In February of 1987 she began her present job at Deaf Centre Manitoba as a rental clerk and is pleased with her work there.

Elaine married Kenneth Anderson in 1999 and they are very happy together. Elaine likes being a stepmother to Kenneth's three adult children, Judith, Lizabeth, and Keith. She had always vowed never to marry, but now feels that her marriage to Kenneth has improved her entire outlook on life. She has started to become involved again in the Deaf Community, which she had first tried in early adulthood, but later abandoned. Since marrying Kenneth, she has served as secretary and as membership director for the Winnipeg Community Centre of the Deaf, and is actively involved with the executive of the Winnipeg Church of the Deaf as treasurer and member-at-large.

At her graduation ceremony in 1976, Elaine was the recipient of three coveted awards—Outstanding Student Citizenship Award from the National Fraternal Society of the Deaf, Daisy Smith Scholarship Award, and the Ralston Trophy for overall excellence as a student. These honours gave her confidence and pride in her accomplishments. She and Kenneth currently make their home in Winnipeg.

ANDERSON, Lisa Margit

1971–
Travel Counsellor, Member of a Deaf Rowing Team, Travel Columnist, and Workshop Planner.

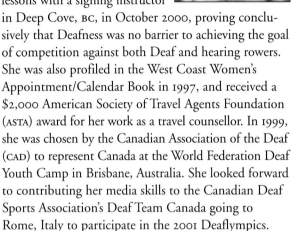

LISA ANDERSON was born profoundly Deaf into a hearing family in Victoria, British Columbia. Although she has no known Deaf relatives, she has a very famous hearing ancestor. Lisa is the great granddaughter of John Percy Page who organized and coached the world-renowned women's basketball team known as the Edmonton Commercial Grads in 1914. During the twenty-five-year period that followed, the team travelled and played internationally, winning 502 of the 522 games played. John Percy Page also entered politics and was MLA for Edmonton for eight years before he was appointed Lieutenant Governor of Alberta, a post he held until 1966. Lisa was only two years old at the time of his death at the age of eighty-five.

Lisa was educated in mainstream public schools in Victoria and eventually graduated from the University of Victoria with a BA degree in Geography in 1996. A year later she earned a certificate in Travel Counselling with a view to becoming an international travel agent for Deaf and hard-of-hearing Canadians.

Throughout her life, Lisa has had to cope with isolation and exclusion as a Deaf person in a hearing society. She has noted that Deaf people are constantly being told, "You can't do that," but they respond with, "Yes, we can," and then go ahead and do it. She has personally encountered and challenged many obstacles. With a supportive family and good teachers, she now believes that anything is possible. Lisa recognizes the need for young Deaf women to be role models for the current generation of Deaf girls growing up.

She has had many unique experiences that have contributed to her self-esteem and confidence, and have made her the successful, determined woman she is today. At the age of six, Lisa was a participant in a captivating Christmas play that attracted the local media. When she was nine, she received her Golden Hand Badge, her wings, and two certificates as a member of the 40th Victoria Brownie Pack. At fifteen, Lisa was told by teachers in the Deaf and hard-of-hearing support program in high school that she could not take the French language classes required by other academic students. She went ahead and took the classes and achieved an "A" grade in her first French course, proving the teachers were mistaken. At sixteen, she was able to facilitate communication between Deaf French and English students during a visit to Victoria by a group from the MacKay Centre for the Deaf in Montréal. At twenty-four years of age, she was one of three Deaf women to graduate from the University of Victoria. Their achievement was the result of several years of determined effort to make their way in a "hearing" university and in a predominantly "hearing" world.

Lisa was one of the first group of Deaf rowers to take lessons with a signing instructor in Deep Cove, BC, in October 2000, proving conclusively that Deafness was no barrier to achieving the goal of competition against both Deaf and hearing rowers. She was also profiled in the West Coast Women's Appointment/Calendar Book in 1997, and received a $2,000 American Society of Travel Agents Foundation (ASTA) award for her work as a travel counsellor. In 1999, she was chosen by the Canadian Association of the Deaf (CAD) to represent Canada at the World Federation Deaf Youth Camp in Brisbane, Australia. She looked forward to contributing her media skills to the Canadian Deaf Sports Association's Deaf Team Canada going to Rome, Italy to participate in the 2001 Deaflympics.

She was a travel columnist for the publication *Deaf Canada Today*, and *Newswaves for the Deaf and Hard of Hearing*, an American newspaper. Lisa had her own Deaf Travel Counselling agency for a year—Deafinitely Canadian Travel Services (DCTS)—and has had many opportunities over the past few years for extensive travel to such places as Australia and numerous countries in Europe. She then took advantage of an opportunity to become program coordinator for the Greater Vancouver Association of the Deaf (GVAD). In that capacity, she edited several newsletters, organized educational workshops with a wide variety of topics, planned recreational activities, and led a Deaf seniors' day tour to La Conner, Washington, to view the famous tulip fields. From 1995 to 1997 Lisa was president of the South Vancouver Island Deaf Women's Group (DWG), which offered peer support to women from the age of eighteen to seventy-five, and organized workshops on women's issues.

Currently, Lisa is working with the Deaf, Hard of Hearing and Deaf-Blind Well-Being Program as a workshop planner, coordinating mental health workshops such as stress management, understanding boundaries, and the highly successful "Gossip" workshop series. She now lives in Burnaby on the Lower Mainland, but often visits her family in Victoria.

This versatile and busy young woman has many interests and hobbies. In her spare time she reads, works at various crafts, travels, and enjoys rowing, rollerblading, and downhill skiing.

ANGNATUK, Pasha Levina

1968–

Advocate for the Deaf, Hairdresser, ASL Instructor, and Day-Care Worker.

PASHA ANGNATUK became Deaf at the age of nine months due to illness. She has no known Deaf relatives. Her hearing husband, Chesley Mesher, is an environmental researcher focusing on northern animals. They have three hearing sons—Henry, Bobby, and Matthew—and make their home at Kujjuaq in northern Québec.

As a child, Pasha attended the community school in Kujjuaq. At the age of eleven she was sent to the MacKay Centre for the Deaf in Montréal, where she remained until she was nineteen. She stayed in Montréal for one more year, attending Rosemount High School where she trained as a hairdresser. JoAnne Stump was Pasha's first Deaf teacher and remains her mentor to this day.

Since returning to her home community, Pasha has been actively involved in bringing greater public awareness to issues relating to Deafness. She has also had varied employment experiences, working at the Post Hotel restaurant and at Michel's Restaurant. She has taught ASL classes and currently works with the Head Start Program in a day-care centre that accepts both hearing and Deaf children, and where they use Sign Language. She would like to update her training to become a teacher in the day-care centre. She has obtained approval to hire an ASL interpreter but is faced with the problem of finding a qualified person who would be willing to move to the remote community of Kujjuaq.

Pasha is the only Deaf adult in her community, although there are several Deaf children. The people in the settlement use their own signs to communicate with her. She is fortunate to have a wonderful family. Her husband and sons all communicate well in ASL. As a family, they enjoy the adventures of camping out in the wilderness and would like to do it all year round. Pasha is very knowledgeable about the history of the Far North.

She is a talented craftswoman who does freelance custom work in arts, crafts, and sewing. When she and her family travel to Montréal, they love to go shopping, and have fun browsing around in all the big stores. Such opportunities do not exist in Kujjuaq, where residents use catalogues to order their needs from Montréal.

Although bringing about positive changes in the Far North is a difficult and slow process, Pasha Angnatuk has both the courage and determination to make good things happen that will benefit future generations of Deaf people in some of the remotest communities in Canada.

ANOBIS, Denise Catherine

1955–

Full-Time Deaf Letter Carrier for Canada Post.

DENISE ANOBIS was born with normal hearing into a hearing family in St. John's, Newfoundland. She became Deaf at ten months of age due to rubella. She has two Deaf relatives, a nephew and a niece. Her niece is currently attending Gallaudet University in Washington, BC. Denise's common-law spouse, Frank Leon Funk, who is an employee at Boeing in Winnipeg, is also Deaf. Denise has two hearing children—a son, Michael, living in St. John's, Newfoundland, and a daughter, Maria Rosa, who lives with her and Frank. Denise has two hearing brothers—Rene, who works as a Coast Guard radio operator in St. John's, and Henri, who served with the Canadian Forces from 1974 to 1995, and now works at Boeing. She also has two hearing sisters. Denise and Frank make their home in Winnipeg, Manitoba.

Denise was educated in several schools. Her first year, 1960–61, was spent at the MacKay School for the Deaf in Montréal, Québec. For the next three years, she attended the Interprovincial School for the Deaf in Amherst, Nova Scotia. From 1961 to 1964 she was at the Newfoundland School for the Deaf in St. John's, and finally, in her last year, she enrolled at the Ontario School for the Deaf in Milton, Ontario, where she took a keypunch course. During the early 1970s, Denise's mother was a vocal activist who fought the provincial government for the rights of Deaf graduates to enter vocational training programs with whatever supports they required.

When Denise joined the workforce, she was employed at the John Leckie factory in Toronto for a while before taking a position as a clerk with the government of Newfoundland's Department of Social Services in St. John's. In 1976 she was hired by Canada Post, working in the office in St. John's until 1984, when she was transferred to Toronto. Then she was transferred back to St. John's for five years, and eventually to Winnipeg, where she finally achieved a promotion to mail service courier-driver in 2000. Denise continued applying for further promotion and, at last, on 16 October 2000, she was granted her dream of becoming a full-time letter carrier, the first Deaf female to do so in Winnipeg.

While living in St. John's, Denise obtained a hearing-ear dog, Dee, through the Newfoundland Lion's Club, with the support and encouragement of her mother. At first she felt overwhelmed and over-protected by Dee, but they soon became working friends and partners. Sadly, Dee died in September of 2000, a major emotional loss for Denise.

Denise is involved in recreational and competitive Deaf curling, and is presently the treasurer of the Manitoba Deaf Curling Association. Formerly, she was treasurer of the Newfoundland Deaf Sports Association. In her leisure time, Denise's main interests are camping, fishing, walking, and participating in the Deaf Women's Curling League.

ARCHIBALD, Kathryn ("Kathy") Jennifer

1950–
Dog Lover Who Owns and Operates a Kennel, Breeds and Trains Dogs, and Raises Show Dogs.

KATHY ARCHIBALD was born in Montréal and adopted by loving and caring hearing parents when she was seven months old. When her Deafness was diagnosed, they took her to the John Tracey Clinic in Los Angeles for assessment and treatment recommendations. The family lived in Montréal, but spent every summer in Prince Edward Island where Kathy's grandparents lived. Her mother taught her to write, speak, and speechread without difficulty because Kathy was a highly motivated child with an abundance of natural curiosity. She currently makes her home in North River, Prince Edward Island.

In 1956 she was enrolled at the Montréal Oral School for the Deaf. Eight years later she transferred to a public school, which was a shock to her when she saw classrooms with thirty or more students seated in rows, instead of the familiar semi-circle of eight to ten Deaf students. She had no support other than her parents, and finally left school in frustration and disappointment.

She had always loved dogs so, in 1968, she entered the workforce, helping to bathe and dry dogs in a grooming parlour to which her mother had always taken their family poodle. That was the beginning of her very successful career with dogs. She learned and advanced quickly because word of her expertise at trimming and grooming dogs soon got around the community. In 1970, with the help of her parents, she established her own business in Dorval, near Montréal, and named it Kildrummy after an inn at which the family had stayed in Scotland. In 1969 she bought her first Shetland sheepdog, "Missy," and was invited to Montréal by Hazel Slaughter, an expert dog-trainer, to learn the art of instilling discipline and obedience in dogs. With these new skills, Kathy was able to expand her business to include an obedience school. She also learned the A to Zs of dog breeding so she could add another feature to the services offered by her business.

In 1972 she moved her business to Prince Edward Island, where her strongest family ties were, and built a kennel in the backyard of the family home. Once again, her clientele grew rapidly, and today many dog owners consider her facility the number-one dog kennel in the province. Many veterinarians recommend her to their clients. She regularly participates in dog shows, and has won numerous awards. She also sells her dogs to customers across Canada, from Newfoundland to British Columbia.

In 1998, realizing her parents would not be around forever to handle her telephone calls and messages, Kathy had a cochlear implant. The surgery was successful and Kathy is glad she had it done, but it has not altered her priorities. She still keeps in close touch with her friends from both the Deaf and the hearing worlds. In 2001, after thirty years as a member, she was awarded a life-time membership in the prestigious Canadian Kennel Club.

She attends meetings of the Prince Edward Island Hearing Impaired Association, and often meets her Deaf friends for coffee or a social evening.

In her leisure hours, when she is not at a dog show, Kathy enjoys being a guest speaker for Brownie packs. She teaches them about pets and how to care for them, and shows them basic Sign Language. She also loves to fish, play darts and bingo, go camping, and travel. Her philosophy of life is to follow your dreams and make them come true.

AUSTIN, Lynn Shelley
1967–
Pewter Finisher and Employment Trail-Blazer.

LYNN AUSTIN was born Deaf into a hearing family in Truro, Nova Scotia. She grew up on a berry farm in the Wentworth-Westchester area, north of Truro. From the age of twelve until she was eighteen, she spent her summers raking blueberries and picking strawberries. She has no known Deaf relatives and currently makes her home in Amherst, Nova Scotia.

Lynn's education began at the age of three and a half years when she entered the Interprovincial School for the Deaf at Amherst, at that time known as the Atlantic Provinces Resource Centre for the Hearing Handicapped (APRCHH), and since renamed the Atlantic Provinces Special Education Authority (APSEA). When she graduated in 1985, she took up dressmaking, in which she earned a certificate at the Atlantic Technological Vocational Centre in 1987.

In the same year (1987–88), Lynn participated in a Human Resources Development Canada (HRDC) Job Entry Program, attending weekly classroom instruction as well as receiving hands-on training with Seagull Pewter in Pugwash, Nova Scotia. This venture proved to be a wise step toward her present career.

The Seagull company produces a variety of giftware items including costume jewellery, plaques, lapel pins, ornaments, and bookmarks. Lynn has remained with them since her initial training period in 1987–88, thus providing a pioneering example for five other Deaf people who later joined the Seagull staff. None of the five is still working at Seagull Pewter, however, due to various reasons such as death, injury, and layoffs, so Lynn is now their only Deaf employee. Over the years, she has taken on several roles—as a packer, assembler, grinder, and finisher. She is currently a buffing finisher, applying the final touches to the production of each item and making the pewter smooth and shiny. In 1998 she was the proud recipient of a ten-year certificate of appreciation from the company, in recognition of her loyalty and dedication.

Apart from her working life, Lynn is an active member of the Border Association of the Deaf (BAD) which was founded and is run by Deaf people living on both sides of the border between Nova Scotia and New Brunswick. She has also played on a bowling team with the Eastern Bowling Association of the Deaf (EBAD).

When she is not busy with her work and her participation in the Deaf Community, Lynn enjoys walking, camping, skidooing, cross-country skiing, and travelling. She visited the Canadian Hearing Society's Annual Mayfest in Toronto in 2001.

BABAK (JAN), Agnes Emma
1923–
Printer's Assistant, Baker, Entrepreneur, and Business Partner.

AGNES JAN was born Deaf to hearing parents in LaFleche, Saskatchewan. She had a Deaf sister, Virginia Jan, and her late husband, William Babak (Bill), was also Deaf. Agnes has a hearing daughter, Faye Tomlinson, who has three hearing children. Construction of the Saskatchewan School for the Deaf in Saskatoon did not commence until Agnes was seven years old, so her education there did not begin until she was eight. She went on to graduate and entered the workforce. She currently makes her home in Saskatoon, Saskatchewan.

Agnes worked for some time at Modern Press in Saskatoon before marrying Bill Babak. Together, along with another partner, they bought the local bakery in Foam Lake, Saskatchewan. After a year they bought out their partner's share and set up their own independent business. The building was small so they decided to buy an adjacent lot when its owner died. In 1963 they built a new building that combined a bakery with a coffee shop. Their business thrived as their hearing customers were more than willing to write their orders rather than communicate them verbally. Bill and Agnes Babak were liked and respected by the entire community.

They hired two hearing staff members who served coffee and sold pastries at the front of the building while Agnes and Bill operated the bakery at the back. They also hired three hearing staff members to do the slicing and packaging, as well as the cleanup of all the equipment. The Babaks expanded their business to include three other nearby villages to which they delivered baked goods twice weekly.

The enterprise did so well that it was obviously an asset to the community and a source of pride and success for the Babaks for twenty years. Sadly, it ended with Bill Babak's death in 1980. He had been an avid curler and loved to golf. He was a member of the local Lions' Club, and Agnes joined the Lioness Club, the Women's Auxiliary, acting as its treasurer for three years. After Bill's death, Agnes continued to live in Foam Lake until 1989, when she decided to move to Saskatoon to be nearer her daughter, her grandchildren, and, eventually, her Deaf sister, Virginia, who had spent many years in Toronto, working at *Maclean's* magazine. When her health failed in 1991, Virginia moved to Saskatoon to live with Agnes. She enjoyed all types of crafts, but her health deteriorated rapidly and, after only four short months, she passed away, much to Agnes's sorrow.

Agnes enjoys her family and likes to socialize with her Deaf friends.

BAILEY, Carole Sue ("Sue")

1949–
Educator, ASL and Deaf Culture Specialist, Drama Director, Program Developer, Presenter, and Editor.

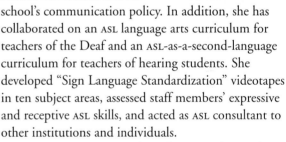

SUE BAILEY was born Deaf into a Deaf family in Birmingham, Alabama, in 1949. Besides Deaf parents, she also has two Deaf sisters, Linda Faye and Cheryl Ann, and Deaf aunts, uncles, and cousins who reside in the US. Sue has made her home in Edmonton, Alberta since 1976.

She was educated at two different schools, the Alabama School for the Deaf in Talladega and the Maryland School for the Deaf in Frederick. She received a Bachelor of Arts degree from Gallaudet University in 1975 and a Master's degree from Western Maryland College in 1976.

Her first professional employment was at Alberta College in Edmonton where she taught in an upgrading program for Deaf adults and held evening drama classes. In 1981 she began her present career at the Alberta School for the Deaf (ASD) where she has taught at all levels, mainly in the area of ASL and Deaf Studies. She has guided the production of many videotapes and school news broadcasts and has undertaken myriad extra duties which include taking charge of the annual ASD Student Conference, directing and producing a play entitled *Laurent Clerc: A Profile*, and coordinating a student trip to England and France.

Sue's strong grasp of the linguistic structures of ASL and her experience with Deaf Culture led to her leadership roles as developer and evaluator of ASL programs. She is a co-founder of the Grant MacEwan College Interpreter Training Program and the Canadian Cultural Society of the Deaf's "Deaf ASL Instructors of Canada." She has taught ASL courses at summer and evening sessions at the University of Alberta and Grant MacEwan College. She has also taught classes specifically designed for hearing parents of Deaf children and professionals working with the Deaf. She helped to develop ASD's Deaf Studies curriculum and the school's communication policy. In addition, she has collaborated on an ASL language arts curriculum for teachers of the Deaf and an ASL-as-a-second-language curriculum for teachers of hearing students. She developed "Sign Language Standardization" videotapes in ten subject areas, assessed staff members' expressive and receptive ASL skills, and acted as ASL consultant to other institutions and individuals.

As a Native signer, Sue has often served as a role model. In that capacity, she assisted in the production of *ASL In Canada: A Videodisc Dictionary* developed by the Canadian Cultural Society of the Deaf (CCSD) in co-operation with ACCESS TV network. Her most significant contribution to date, however, has been her involvement for over twenty years in the compiling and editing of *The Canadian Dictionary of ASL* to be published by University of Alberta Press. On this project, she played a major role, working alongside Kathy Dolby, Hilda Campbell, and Angela Stratiy. Sue has made many ASL and Deaf Culture presentations across Canada and is considered an authority on these subjects. She has also served in many capacities for CCSD and the Alberta Cultural Society of the Deaf (ACSD), organizing conferences, coordinating cultural events, and being the predominant figure in a host of drama presentations. Sue is regarded by her colleagues and students, as well as their parents, as an exemplary teacher. On 5 May 2001, Sue was one of twenty-two Alberta teachers presented with the provincial Excellence in Teaching Award at a gala event in Calgary.

In her spare time, Sue enjoys travelling and researching her family history. Her Deaf aunt, Maude Nelson, is a noted oil-painter of chinaware in Birmingham, Alabama, and her Deaf cousin, Edna Johnson, is very active in the field of Deafness in Chicago, Illinois. Since her arrival in Canada in 1976, Sue has become one of Canada's most notable Deaf women for her dedicated continuous promotion of ASL and Deaf Culture, both of which are very close to her heart. Her pleasant disposition and keen sense of humour make her a popular favourite among young and old alike in Edmonton's Deaf Community.

BALIS (CHAPIN), Sylvia Lee

1864–1950
Educator of Deaf Children and Compiler of a Significant Literary Work.

Although little is known of her early life, there is ample historical evidence that SYLVIA LEE BALIS (nee Chapin) was among the earliest Deaf teachers of Deaf students in Canada. Her entire teaching career was spent at what was then known as the Ontario Institution for the Education and Instruction of the Deaf and Dumb in Belleville. She was one of only fourteen Deaf teachers who taught at that institution from the time it was founded in 1870 until 1929 when she retired. There followed a period of forty years before the practise of hiring Deaf teachers was again resumed in 1969.

Sylvia's teaching career spanned nearly four decades from 1890 to 1929. Among her fellow Deaf teachers at Belleville, from 1890 to 1916, was the noted Deaf poet, James C. Balis, who wrote the acclaimed poem entitled *Do I Hear When I Dream?* in 1886.

In 1914, Gallaudet College in Washington, BC, conferred an honorary Master of Arts degree on Sylvia Balis, a prestigious distinction for a Canadian woman of that era. In 1901 Sylvia attended the 16th Convention of American Instructors of the Deaf from July 2nd to 8th in Buffalo, New York. During that conference she was appointed to chair a committee to select stories and illustrations for a children's book, aimed particularly toward young Deaf readers, a concept which was simple but highly effective. She spent a year gathering approximately 150 simple stories and drawings dealing with subjects familiar to Deaf children. Most of these short stories were gleaned from the children's columns of numerous issues of *Little Paper Family*, a small newspaper that was published by residential schools for Deaf children in Canada and the United States.

Sylvia's selections were eventually compiled into a 144-page book under the title *From Near and Far* and published in Toronto in 1902 by George M. Morgan and Company. The book has been read and enjoyed by generations of Deaf children.

Sylvia Lee (Chapin) Balis died in 1950 at the age of eighty-six after having made many significant contributions to the education of Deaf children in Canada.

BANCARZ, Sharon Ann

1948–
Intervenor, Deaf Interpreter and ASL Instructor, Rater and Coordinator.

SHARON BANCARZ, who prefers to be called "Shari," was born hearing in Melville, Saskatchewan, but became Deaf at ten months of age after a serious illness. She has an older Deaf sister. Her education was acquired at three different provincial Schools for the Deaf—Halifax, Nova Scotia, Belleville, Ontario, and Vancouver, BC.

As a young woman, Shari worked at several jobs—in a fish cannery, at a dry-cleaning establishment, and as a data-entry processor while often teaching ASL at night classes. In Vancouver she became involved in the project "Look–Listen–Learn" which was chaired by Maureen Donald. In that capacity she travelled to Prince George, Williams Lake, and Quesnel in northern BC to present workshops and forums. She was co-chair of three open forums: The Relationship Between the Deaf and Interpreting Communities, Ethical Practices Within the Interpreting Community, and Interpreters and the Deaf: A Cross-Cultural Relationship. She also chaired the open forum entitled The Deaf-Blind Speak Out.

While she lived in Vancouver, Shari was closely involved in every aspect of the Deaf Community, serving in various capacities with organizations such as the Western Canada Association of the Deaf, the Greater Vancouver Association of the Deaf, the BC Association of the Deaf-Blind, and the Dinsdale Information Service of Canada. She also hosted a TV program with Janice Jickels, Karen Foot, and Aastrid Flanjak-Evenson, directed by Vincent Kennedy, and was an ASL rater for the Canadian Cultural Society of the Deaf and the Association of Visual Language Interpreters of Canada.

When Shari moved to Toronto in 1990 she immersed herself in the Deaf Community there, working with the Ontario Association of the Deaf, the Canadian National Society of the Deaf-Blind, the Ontario Association of Sign Language Interpreters, and a number of consortiums and committees. Between 1990 and 1997. she worked for the Canadian Hearing Society in Sign Language Services and coordinated, as well as instructed, ASL programs in Oshawa, Brampton, and Toronto. She was also a job coach in Toronto and an intervenor/Deaf interpreter in Milton. In 1997 she went to Hamilton, Bermuda, to instruct interpreters and broaden their skills.

Throughout her life Shari has been a cheerful, positive individual who loves challenges, has a keen sense of humour, and sets a beautiful example for younger Deaf women as their mentor and guide. She loved her pet dog, a miniature Schnauser named Shonie (now deceased) whom she taught to recognize the fingerspelled word "w-a-l-k" which would send the dog into a wild frenzy of excitement. She even trained Shonie to smile!

In her leisure time, Shari expands her skills at crafts, bakes, and cooks, and enjoys drawing and writing poetry. Above all, she is always prepared to meet new challenges. She is well known across Canada for her many contributions toward creating equality and accessibility for the Deaf and the Deaf-Blind.

BASKERVILLE, Laureen Charada

1970–
Fourth-Generation Deaf Family Member, Teacher, Deaf Role Model, Volunteer, and Proud Baskerville.

LAUREEN BASKERVILLE was born Deaf to Deaf parents in Richmond Hill, Ontario. She has numerous Deaf relatives—her parents, James and Maureen Baskerville, her sister, Sally Langford, a niece, Trista Langford, her grandparents, Silas and Elise (nee Wilson) Baskerville (now deceased), and her great-aunt Beulah Wilson, also deceased. Her husband, Chris Kenopic, currently executive director of the Ontario Association of the Deaf, was also born Deaf. He and Laureen have two hearing daughters, Charada and Janna, and make their home in Georgetown, Ontario.

Laureen was educated at Sir James Whitney School for the Deaf in Belleville, Ontario, and after graduating, obtained a Bachelor's degree in Elementary Education from Gallaudet University in Washington, BC. She then went on to earn a diploma in Deaf Education from York University in Toronto, and a MSc degree in Deaf Education from Western Maryland College. She holds an Ontario Teacher's Certificate (primary and junior) and is a Deaf education specialist.

Laureen is currently teaching at the E.C. Drury School for the Deaf in Milton, Ontario. She had a wonderfully unique experience as an intern, teaching ten Deaf children in Embu, Kenya, in the summer of 1992 for three months. It was part of the Experience Placement Off-Campus (EPOC) program at Gallaudet University, and gave her an opportunity to learn Kenyan Sign Language (KSL).

The Baskerville family is well known throughout the Deaf community. Laureen's mother has been involved in many projects such as the *Freckles and Popper* video-tapes in which Laureen participated by doing the art activities. Laureen also appears in a Bi-Bi (bilingual and bicultural) video, and her Deaf niece Trista had a role in a movie entitled *Dead Silence*, in 1996, starring Marlee Matlin and James Garner. The family members are justifiably proud of their fifth-generation Deaf status.

Awards and honours Laureen has received include being chosen as Miss Deaf Ontario First Runner-Up, and Miss Deaf Canada First Runner-Up. She was the valedictorian at her graduation ceremony in 1988 and the Winter Carnival Snow Queen in the same year.

At Sir James Whitney School for the Deaf, she was selected to play the Virgin Mary in the school's famous Christmas Nativity Pageant. Both at Sir James Whitney School and at York University, Laureen was recognized for her outstanding achievements.

Her involvement in the Deaf Community has been mainly with the Ontario Association of the Deaf and the Ontario Cultural Society of the Deaf where she served two terms on the board. At E.C. Drury School for the Deaf, where she teaches, Laureen serves on many committees and contributes creatively and innovatively to the quality of education the school provides.

BASKERVILLE (MacDONALD), Maureen

1934–
Civil Servant, Automobile Assembler, Storyteller, Fundraiser, and Tireless Leader in the Deaf Community.

MAUREEN MACDONALD was born Deaf in Canada's capital city, Ottawa. Her husband James Silas Baskerville, son of Elsie and Silas Baskerville, is third-generation Deaf. Maureen and James moved to Toronto after their marriage, and they have five daughters, two of whom are fourth-generation Deaf—Sally Langford and Laureen Baskerville. Laureen is now married to a Deaf husband, Chris Kenopic, who is executive director of the Ontario Association of the Deaf and president of the Canadian Association of the Deaf. Laureen teaches at E.C. Drury School for the Deaf in Milton, Ontario. James and Maureen currently make their home in Richmond Hill, Ontario. They are blessed with eight wonderful grandchildren, four boys and four girls, ranging in age from twenty-six years to eight months. One of the girls, Trista, is fifth-generation Deaf.

Maureen attended the Belleville School for the Deaf for thirteen years, graduating in 1951. In her working life, she was employed in two very different occupations—for nine years as a federal civil servant in Ottawa and for twenty-eight years as an assembler in an automobile manufacturing plant in Aurora, Ontario. For a number of years, until all her girls were in school, she was a stay-at-home mother.

Even while she was working, Maureen was always a very active participant in the life of the Deaf Community. Since her retirement, she has continued to devote her time and energy to many projects, and her achievements over the years have been manifold. One of her most notable successes was the organization of two walka-thons that yielded $55,000 for the Bob Rumball Centre for the Deaf. She also chaired the Ontario Association of the Deaf's annual convention in Belleville when it successfully merged with the Cultural Society of the Deaf (now known as the Canadian Cultural Society of the Deaf). For eight years she was secretary for the Elderly Persons Centre and coordinator of the Gift Gallery at the Bob Rumball Centre.

Maureen is well known as a "Grandma Storyteller" at the E.C. Drury School for the Deaf, a job she loves. She was also one of five senior activity leaders for "Keeping the Hands in Motion," a project coordinated by Chris Kenopic. Several years ago, she served on the committee that helped to create the dictionary project sponsored by the Canadian Cultural Society of the Deaf, *The Canadian Dictionary of ASL*, which is now in the process of being published. In addition to these many involvements, Maureen was the story-teller for the four movie videos entitled *Freckles and Popper*. She and her husband, James, have also been very active in the Ontario Bowling Association and National Fraternal Society of the Deaf for many years, as well as with the York-Simcoe Silent Film Club. In addition, they contribute significantly to the Ontario Association of the Deaf (OAD), with James serving as treasurer and as a volunteer for the *OAD Newsletter*. They keep the *OAD Newsletter* records in their basement where James also attends to his financial duties as treasurer.

Maureen was honoured by the Canadian Association of the Deaf as Canadian Deaf Citizen of the Year in 1978, and by the National Fraternal Society of the Deaf in the same year. The town of Richmond Hill presented her with a "Good Citizen of the Deaf Community" award in 1982, and she has been recognized for her contributions to the E.C. Drury School and the Bob Rumball Centre for the Deaf.

Her peers view Maureen as a very happy person who is a good listener and is always prepared to go the extra mile in her dedication to the Deaf Community.

BASTIN (VARLEY), Joan Honour

1916–
Dancer, Land Army Girl, Canadian War Bride, and Retired Federal Civil Servant.

JOAN VARLEY was born hearing, to hearing parents, in London, England. At the age of three, she contracted a severe case of diphtheria and became Deaf as a result. She has no known Deaf relatives and her husband, Aubrey Archibald Bastin, a Canadian soldier who served overseas during World War II, was a hearing man. Joan has three adult hearing children, Sandra Johnson, Susan Bastin, and Sydney Varley. She currently makes her home in Victoria, BC.

Joan has many wonderful memories of her happy childhood and her youth in England, even though two world wars had occurred before she reached the age of thirty. Her father was sickly, and therefore unable to enlist in the military during World War I. Joan recalls visiting him in hospital where he died of pneumonia. She remembers the many young soldiers of that era, and the German Zeppelins that flew over her home. After her father's death, she was raised as an only child by her mother, whom she adored, and her aunt Gertie. The two women operated a hotel in London, and they did a splendid job of raising her in England during the interwar years.

Joan was sent to a private school and felt fortunate to have a well-trained, dedicated teacher who had gone to New York to learn how to reach Deaf children by the Alexander Graham Bell oral method. Joan, then eight years old, was her first pupil. Eventually there were twenty students, and Joan was very happy at her school. Sadly, she lost all contact with her classmates after she left. She did not learn to sign until she was fifty years old but has had many memorable experiences in both worlds, the Deaf and the hearing. As a senior, she attended an adult Deaf literacy program to improve her written English skills, and took great delight in writing stories about her childhood and adult life, which fascinated everyone who read them.

Joan recalls going on seaside holidays when she was in her teens and riding a patient horse named Jeppy. She loved to dance and was sent to ballet school, wearing tutus made by her mother. Above all, she loved attending ballet productions at Covent Garden, and was always beautifully attired in clothes designed and sewn by her mother. She recalls a red serge coat made from a leftover remnant of the uniforms worn by the Buckingham Palace guards. During World War II, Joan became a "land-army girl" and worked on a pig farm, helping in the fields and working with the livestock. She recalls the bombing and the destruction that forced her family to leave London in the early months of the war and settle in a rural village named Odiham. Many people from the army and airforce visited them while they lived there.

Aubrey was a Canadian soldier so, when they married in a lovely old Norman church in Odiham, Joan became a Canadian "war bride" who eventually joined many others on a Red Cross ship, *The Lady Nelson*, that brought them to their new country after the war ended. Joan then crossed the nation by train, from the east coast to the west, to be met by Aubrey and his family in Vancouver. They established their first home on Vancouver Island and Aubrey worked for the BC Power Commission, putting up power lines. Joan accompanied him on his trips around the island until their first child, a lovely wee daughter, Sandra, was born. Joan had two more fine girls, Susan and Sydney. The youngest, Sydney, took her mother's maiden name, Varley, as her surname when she was thirty years old.

Joan worked for twenty years at the Naval Supply Depot for the Department of National Defence in Victoria, retiring in 1978, almost five years after Aubrey died. She has many trophies and certificates attesting to her talents as a dancer, and now spends her time at the many hobbies and interests she enjoys. She is still the happy and caring person she was during her youth in England, and is loved and respected by all who know her.

BEAM (OUELLETTE), Dorothy Ellen

1918–
Volunteer, Public Speaker, Fundraiser, Teacher, and Dedicated Advocate for the Deaf.

DOROTHY ELLEN OUELLETTE was born Deaf to hearing parents in Ottawa, Ontario, near the end of World War I, during the widespread flu epidemic of 1918. In the aftermath and chaos resulting from these two historic events, she was adopted by Joseph and Mary Ouellette who were both hearing. Her first husband, John D. Angus, was Deaf and they had one hearing daughter, Eleanor Mary, whom they called "Mary." After separation and divorce, Dorothy married Harold Stanley M. Beam, now deceased, who was hearing, and they had two hearing children, a son, G. Timothy, and a daughter, Bonnie-Lea. Her grandchildren are all hearing and she has no known Deaf relatives.

Dorothy considers her early education to have been "hit and miss" until she met the late Miss Harriet Stirk, a trained teacher of the Deaf from the Belleville provincial school who set up a lip-reading class for Deaf and hard-of-hearing children in a public school in Ottawa. Dorothy was in her twelfth year at that time and is grateful to Miss Stirk for having guided her toward a high school diploma. In 1932 she was enrolled at the provincial School for the Deaf in Belleville where a strict "oral" policy was in practice. Although signing was forbidden, she quickly learned fingerspelling and the signs used by the senior students. Despite the policy of rigid oralism, many of the teachers used Dorothy to translate their verbal instruction into sign language for her nonverbal peers. Thus, she unwittingly became an interpreter long before interpreting was viewed as a profession. After graduating in 1934, she remained to take a business administration course and left the school in 1935.

Working at various office jobs and being an avid reader expanded her education and broadened her experience. She retired in 1983 after more than twenty-three years with the federal government and nearly twelve years in the private sector. Between jobs she was a stay-at-home mother for thirteen years while her children were growing up.

Dorothy has spent most of her adult life as a volunteer advocate for the Deaf, promoting sign language as the language of instruction for Deaf students, publicizing the need for Sign Language interpreters, raising funds, planning and coordinating projects in the Deaf Community, writing, editing, teaching, opening doors, and breaking down barriers. She has had many private talks with appropriate authorities and influenced changes in policies in the education system, fields of employment, the needs of Deaf seniors, and health care issues. She hand signs for the Deaf-Blind to help them enjoy church services and social events, and has offered to type or speak for those members of the Deaf congregation who need that sort of assistance.

She was often an invited speaker and has held several executive positions in the organizations of Ontario's Deaf Community. Dorothy became the second female president of the Ontario Association of the Deaf (OAD) in 1976, served as secretary in 1974 and again in 1982, as vice-president in 1984, and was editor of the OAD News. When OAD celebrated its 100th anniversary, it was Dorothy who wrote the history of the organization. The material was laid out by others and photographs were included in the printed copy. She was a founding member of ARCH and the Ontario Advisory Board for Interpreter Services, chairing the latter for several years. She has also been a fundraiser, one of her more notable feats being the establishment of a print shop in the Community Centre for the Deaf in Toronto. She taught advanced English in one of Toronto's vocational schools, providing night courses for three years. Her volunteer work also included assisting with the Parry Sound Camp whenever she was needed.

The list of Dorothy's awards and honours is a lengthy one—the Defty Award for Hymn Singing, the Hall of Fame award (Humanitarian) from the Canadian Cultural Society of the Deaf in 1978, a plaque of appreciation from the Ontario Association of the Deaf (Lifetime Membership) in 1980, the Deaf Woman of the Year Award from the Quota Club (both National and International) in 1982, the Canadian Association of the Deaf Citizen of the Year Award (Lifetime Membership), also in 1982, the Order of Ontario in 1989, an Outstanding Contributions plaque from the Canadian Hearing Society in 1997, plus framed acknowledgements from the Prime Minister, the Premier, the Town of Pickering and several MPPs on the occasion of her seventy-fifth birthday in 1993. Dorothy has been an active member of the Evangelical Church of the Deaf since 1936 and is a devout Christian.

Dorothy Beam was a real pioneer leading the crusade for Deaf rights in Canada and is widely recognized as a Canadian Deaf woman who rendered services of great distinction for the benefit of all Deaf Communities across the nation.

BEER (de MONTMORENCY), Jane Louise

1945–
Active Worker in the Deaf Community and Daughter of the Co-Founder of the Montréal Oral School for the Deaf.

JANE DE MONTMORENCY was born Deaf to hearing parents in Montréal, Québec, just after World War II ended. She has no known Deaf relatives, but her husband, Ivan Beer, is Deaf. They have an adult son, Robin, who is hearing.

Jane's father, William de Montmorency, was one of the co-founders of the Montréal Oral School for the Deaf in 1950. When it opened, Jane, at the age of five, was one of the five "pioneer" pupils. She was also a member of the school's first graduating class in 1962 and helped to celebrate its fiftieth anniversary in October 2000.

After graduating from high school and completing a two-week IBM course, she worked as a keypunch operator and office clerk. She has also worked as a library assistant and more recently was employed at a community college. Her husband, Ivan, is an employee of the Ford Motor Company.

Jane and Ivan make their home in St. Thomas, Ontario, and have been active members of the Deaf Community in London, Ontario. Jane has been particularly involved with the London Centre of the Deaf, serving on the board and various committees. She was recently elected director of recreation, a position she had previously held for many years.

In her spare time, Jane is an avid gardener and enjoys beautifying the yard of her home. People often stop to admire her garden and ask for gardening advice. She hopes to register for the City Garden Tour, which would put her home on the tour's circuit. People have been suggesting this to her for years, and she now feels ready to do so. She took a package garden tour to England in 2000 and visited many beautiful spots there, collecting rare perennials for her own garden. She and her husband are planning a trip to Belize to visit the Mayan ruins and have been to Europe twice, visiting historical museums while there.

BELL (JAMESON), Charlotte ("Lottie") Helen

1889–1970
First Deaf Female Manitoban to Attend Gallaudet College and First Canadian Liaison Officer for Gallaudet Alumni.

LOTTIE JAMESON was born Deaf in Tara, Ontario. Little is known about her childhood except that she attended the Manitoba Institution for the Deaf (which became the Manitoba School for the Deaf in 1913) in Winnipeg from 1893 until 1905. Records indicate that she graduated in 1905. She developed excellent English-language skills during her years in residence, in part because her father always corrected the errors in her letters home, and asked her to rewrite them and return the revised versions.

She was one of the first two Deaf Manitobans to attend Gallaudet College (now Gallaudet University) in Washington, BC, sharing that distinction with a young Deaf man named Archibald Wright. There is no doubt that she was the first Deaf female from Manitoba to attend Gallaudet College. Lottie studied there for two years, from 1907 to 1909, after attending the Kendall School's introductory class for a year (1906–1907). At that time in the history of Gallaudet College, the president was one of its founders, Edward Miner Gallaudet, PhD, LLD, and its patron was William Howard Taft, the President of the United States of America. Some of the courses offered were English, grammar, physics, trigonometry, chemistry, psychology, moral philosophy, political economics, American history, astronomy, and several languages. The student newspaper of the day was *The Buff and Blue*, which still exists today. Unfortunately, Lottie attended for only two years and did not complete a degree, nor did her male counterpart, Archibald Wright, but their attendance set a precedent for all future Deaf Manitobans to strive for higher education.

Eventually, Lottie Jameson married Walter Dake Bell, who was an American alumnus of Gallaudet College, class of 1911. When he told his mother he would marry a Canadian woman, she fainted. She was concerned about his relationship with a "Yankee" northerner, and it took

Walter a while to convince her that Canada was not "Yankee" territory. Walter came from Alabama, so the newlywed couple made their first home in Birmingham in that state. After six years in Alabama, Lottie and Walter moved to Canada, settling in Toronto, Ontario, in 1919. In 1928, they moved to Oshawa, Ontario. Lottie and Walter were faithful members of the Evangelical Church of the Deaf, and were responsible for founding a Deaf group in Oshawa to worship in one of the local churches. Walter was a tireless worker in his efforts to raise funds for the Ontario Deaf Youth Camp just south of Parry Sound. He organized many projects, both in Toronto and Oshawa, and through this labour of love, he managed to pay off a $25,000 mortgage on the camp.

Lottie and Walter were proud of their three children. Their only son, Jameson, a PhD graduate in Agronomy from Cornell University, worked in the Far East for the US State Department for more than thirty years. He received many international awards for his contributions to developing countries. Their daughter, Lillian, established a career in the field of education, and a second daughter, Margaret, made a career of volunteer work.

Lottie and Walter supported improved education for the Deaf. Lottie tutored numerous young students from the Belleville School for the Deaf (now Sir James Whitney School) during the summer vacations and gave assistance wherever it was needed.

On 10 December 1949, memorable because it was "Thomas Hopkins Gallaudet Day," the first Canadian chapter of the Gallaudet Alumni Association was established in Toronto, although its members were scattered across Canada. Charlotte Helen Bell (nee Jameson), who was sixty years old at the time, became the first liaison officer between the Toronto chapter and the alumni office in Washington, BC. Despite its significant place in Canadian Deaf history, that chapter is no longer active.

Lottie (Jameson) Bell died in Oshawa on 13 December 1970, at the age of eighty-two. She predeceased her husband by five years, Walter Dake Bell passing away in 1975.

They were an inspiration to their children, and left them with the motto, "Give back to the world, and always do your best." In their own way, Lottie and Walter did just that.

BENNETT, Catherine ("Cathy") Ruth

1968–
Teacher of the Deaf and ASL Specialist.

CATHY BENNETT was born Deaf into a hearing family in Springdale, Newfoundland. She has no known Deaf relatives, and currently makes her home in Colorado Springs, Colorado. Her hearing sister was a teacher assistant for the Deaf and hard-of-hearing in Bathurst, New Brunswick, for three years, and is presently a teacher assistant in a Deaf and hard-of-hearing class in a public school program in Victoria, British Columbia.

Cathy was educated at the Newfoundland School for the Deaf in Torbay, graduating in 1988. While in School, she was active in many sports and became a member of the Army Cadet Corps. She was one of several Deaf cadets to be honoured with a Duke of Edinburgh Award and a Canada Fitness Award. Throughout her cadet training, she proved to be an able learner on par with her hearing peers. She was also one of the first five Deaf cadets to attend Camp Argonaut, a two-week boot camp in Gagetown, New Brunswick. The other four were Michael Best, Wade Moores, Rosalind Chaffey, and Cathy Lushman. Their accompanying officers were Lt. Jack Jardine and Lt. Desmond McCarthy. They proved themselves capable and three received shadow ranks at the final inspection.

On graduating in 1988, Cathy enrolled at Gallaudet University in Washington, BC, earning a Bachelor of Arts degree in Communication Arts in 1993. Subsequently, she attended the Rochester Institute of Technology (RIT) in Rochester, New York, where she completed a Master of Arts degree in Deaf Education and ASL in 1999. From 1996 to 1999, Cathy taught ASL as a foreign language at a public school in Rochester, New York, and also at the University of Rochester while she worked on her graduate studies. In 1999, as a student teacher and ASL specialist, she worked at the Rochester School for the Deaf before moving to Colorado Springs to take up a position as an ASL specialist at the Colorado State School for the Deaf.

Cathy's involvement in the Deaf Community has been mostly associated with education matters. She consults with parents, teaches ASL classes in the community, makes ASL presentations for Colorado State, serves on committees related to ASL with a special focus on ASL and English literacy, develops curricula for her school, coordinates parent-awareness training in Deaf communication and Culture, as well as developing ASL curricula for hearing parents of Deaf children. In addition to these activities, Cathy has developed a summer ASL Immersion Week, trained ASL teachers, presented ASL workshops for teachers, and is responsible for ASL assessment of students. She is also active in the American Sign Language Teachers' Association of Colorado. In her leisure time, Cathy likes to rollerblade, cycle, hike, ski, and camp.

BERGBUSCH, Caroline Mary

1965–
Business Office Expert, Health Records Technician, and Certified Cook.

CAROLINE BERGBUSCH, the first child of Judith Hirst and Martin Bergbusch, was born Deaf due to maternal rubella. She was baptized as an infant in Regina's St. Paul's Lutheran Church by her paternal grandfather, Julius Bergbusch. Caroline has three younger brothers—Peter, Michael, and Philip—who are all hearing, and the family lives in Regina, Saskatchewan.

When Caroline was two years old the family lived in Ithaca, New York, while her father studied at Cornell University and she attended the Rochester School for the Deaf for one year. After returning to Regina, she received the rest of her education in mainstream programs at various public schools. She was in the last graduating class at Central Collegiate in 1985, when that school closed. That fall she enrolled in the preparatory program for the hearing impaired at Red River College in Winnipeg and two years later completed a commercial cooking program as a certified cook. Caroline then returned to Regina, did casual work in several restaurants and later found a permanent position in food services at Luther College, University of Regina.

In August of 1992, Caroline decided she wanted a more exciting and challenging career so she studied health records technology at the Wascana Campus of the Saskatchewan Institute of Applied Arts and Science Technology (SIAST). When she completed the course and became a certified health records technician, she was unable to find work in her chosen field so she took a position as a casual clerk with Victims' Services in the Saskatchewan Justice Department.

Caroline then acquired a Microcomputer Business Application Diploma at the Academy of Learning, working part-time at Luther College and Victims' Services. She also found casual employment as an ASL teaching aide at Balfour Collegiate. In November of 2000 she finally found the job of her dreams and began her current employment as medical accounts assessor for the Medical Services and Health Registration Department with Saskatchewan Health.

She is involved in the Deaf Community, serving as a board member for the Regina Association of the Deaf and as vice-president of the Saskatchewan Cultural Society of the Deaf. She also teaches ASL classes two nights per week.

In her leisure time, Caroline enjoys walking, swimming, playing darts, and shopping. Her favourite pastime is doing cross-stitch embroidery. She also likes sewing and other crafts. Being godmother to her two nieces, Samantha and Sarah, is one of her greatest pleasures.

BERNHARDT (BLACK), Shelley Marie

1951–

Miss Deaf Canada Pageant Participant, Arts and Crafts Medalist, Devoted Vounteer, and Postal Worker.

SHELLEY BLACK was born hearing into a hearing family at Churchill in northern Manitoba. At about eighteen months of age, she suffered a severe bout of spinal meningitis which left her hard of hearing. She was educated at the Ontario provincial School for the Deaf in Belleville from 1954 to 1960. She then attended the Saskatchewan provincial School for the Deaf in Saskatoon from 1960 to 1964. This was followed by three years in Great Falls, Montana, US. After returning to Canada, Shelley attended the Alberta provincial School for the Deaf in Edmonton where she remained until she graduated in 1971. Shelley's father is a retired Lieutenant Colonel of the Royal Canadian Air Force, as well as a retired manager of the Calgary Chamber of Commerce, a position he held for fifteen years. Her mother is an enthusiastic homemaker. The frequent changes of schools is typical for military families.

Shelley is married to Douglas R. Bernhardt who is Deaf, and they have twin sons, Casey and Gavin, who are both hard-of-hearing. The family currently makes its home in Calgary. Casey and Gavin graduated from high school in 1999 and are now working, but plan to attend college in the future.

Shelley has worked for the last thirteen years as a postal mechanic for the Canada Post Corporation. Her accomplishments are many and she is justly proud of her achievements.

She has always been a strong supporter of the Alberta Cultural Society of the Deaf and has been presented with many of their awards. In 1973 she was selected to be Miss Deaf Calgary. The following year she was a runner-up in the Miss Deaf Canada Pageant and, from 1980 to 1990, she won two gold medals—one for embroidery and the other for sewing. She won a Golden Defty in 1990 in home arts, and over the years has been awarded two gold, one silver, and one bronze medal for her songs. She always attends the National Deaf Festival of the Arts, several times acting as a judge for the Miss Deaf Canada pageant. Shelley has also co-chaired the Miss Deaf Canada pageant in Calgary.

Her contributions to the Deaf Community in Calgary are exemplary. As a member of the Calgary Association of the Deaf, she has served as vice-president and chief social director. In her spare time she enjoys many hobbies.

BERRETTE, Wanda Marie

1957–

Devout Religious Leader, One of the Founders of GOLD, and Interpreter-Facilitator for the Deaf and Deaf-Blind.

WANDA MARIE BERRETTE was born Deaf, the fourth of six children, with two brothers and three sisters, in a hearing family. She also has two nephews and five nieces. One of her brothers is now deceased. The cause of Wanda's Deafness is unknown and she has no other Deaf relatives of whom she is aware.

Wanda graduated from Gallaudet University in Washington, BC, with a Bachelor of Science degree in 1982. She is a life member of the Gallaudet Alumni Association and the Gallaudet University Delta Epsilon Sorority. In addition, she is a former member of the Halifax Association of the Deaf (HAD), and the Association of Visual Language Interpreters of Nova Scotia (AVLINS). Wanda is also a life member of the National Catholic Deaf Association (NCDA), Chapter 62, which is the Canadian section of the International Catholic Deaf Association (ICDA), for which she has

held offices at the local, national, and executive levels. Wanda moved to Sudbury, Ontario, in 1991 to take up a position as literary instructor-coordinator for the Canadian Hearing Society. She then became a member of the Sudbury Association of the Deaf, the Ontario Association of the Deaf, and one of the ten founders of GOLD (Goal: Literacy for Deaf People in Ontario), of which she is still a board member.

She was the assistant rector for the first Canadian Deaf Cursillo (#34) in October 1988, a spiritual retreat for Deaf Catholics. Wanda has assisted in coordinating and organizing weekend retreats and workshops for the Deaf congregation ever since. She was also instrumental in petitioning the Archbishop for a priest to work part-time with Catholics in the Deaf Community in Halifax.

In addition to her contributions to the religious community and GOLD, Wanda can be credited with numerous other achievements. She has been an interpreter and guide for Deaf-Blind persons, has advocated eloquently for Deaf rights, and has promoted greater public awareness of the needs of the Deaf and Deaf-Blind, especially in the area of interpreters/facilitators.

In 1990, for her many outstanding services to the Deaf Community, Wanda was presented with the prestigious John Blois Memorial "Woman of the Year" Award by the Halifax Association of the Deaf, an honour she richly deserves.

In her leisure hours, Wanda enjoys walking, swimming, travelling, and reading. She is an expert needlewoman who likes to sew, do counted cross-stitching, and embroidery.

BICKLE (STEVENS), Helen Joanne

1957–
Minister-in-Training, Outreach Worker, Deaf Advocate, and Pastoral Worker.

HELEN STEVENS was born Deaf into a hearing family in Toronto, Ontario. In 1978, she married a hearing man, Vern Bickle, and they have three children—Veronica, who is Deaf, and Beverly and George who are hearing. She has no known Deaf relatives, and currently makes her home with her family near Consecon, Ontario.

Helen was educated at the Metro School for the Deaf and Northern Secondary School in Toronto, Sir Oliver Mowat Collegiate Institute in West Hill, near Scarborough, and Centennial College in Scarborough, Ontario. She also earned a Small Business Office Automation certificate from Loyalist College. At present, she is a part-time student at Queen's University in Kingston, attending a program of theological studies with a view to becoming a lay pastoral minister.

After her youngest child started school in 1986, Helen took a part-time secretarial and bookkeeping position at the Ministry with the Deaf Church in Belleville, where she was part of the staff team with Reverend Karen Ptolemy-Stam and, later, Reverend Brad Ford. During a one-year hiatus between these two leaders, Helen kept the church active by recruiting guest ministers from across the province to preach on Sundays. The church was housed in the Bridge Street United Church but operated independently with its own chapel and office.

In 1996 Helen played a key role in merging the Ministry with the Deaf with the Holloway and Tabernacle United Churches. The new church became St. Matthew's United Church and Helen was hired as its Deaf pastoral worker, focusing on an outreach ministry within the Deaf community, the first nation-wide program of its kind for the United Church of Canada.

In 1999 she began her part-time theological studies at Queen's University while continuing to work part-time at St. Matthew's as a minister-in-training. She provides worship services twice monthly and works outside the church within the Deaf Community as an advocate and counsellor. Helen hopes to complete her studies in 2003. On a national level, she helped to establish and is currently the chairperson of the United Church of Canada Workgroup on Deaf Ministries, focusing on issues concerning Deaf ministries across Canada. Participating representatives are from Winnipeg, Belleville, Toronto, Halifax, and St. John's.

In addition to her church work, Helen is involved with the Canadian Hearing Society and other Ontario agencies for the disabled. She has also acted as president and treasurer, at different times, for the Belleville Association of the Deaf, and has served on the Sir James Whitney School for the Deaf Advisory Committee. The mandate of her present employment at St. Matthew's United Church is to provide pastoral care for Deaf members and their families in the Bay of Quinte area, including hospital and home visits as well as general advocacy for the Deaf. She is also involved in the social activities of the church community.

BIDERMAN, Beverly

1946–
Computer Programmer, Systems Analyst and Planner, Adaptive Technology Analyst, and Author.

BEVERLY BIDERMAN was born with a progressive genetic hearing loss inherited from her father's side of the family which resulted in her becoming profoundly Deaf during her teens. Her Deafness eventually led her into the field of technological research and authorship.

She acquired a liberal arts education, earning a BA degree in Sociology at Glendon College (York University) in Toronto and was hired as a computer programmer by the Crown Life Insurance Company in the late 1960s. There she received months of training and became deeply interested in the logic involved in writing computer programs and developing complex systems. She became an expert at problem solving and quickly earned promotions within the company, supervising and training programmers to develop intricate systems used by the insurance industry.

In 1973 Beverly left Crown Life for a position as a computer analyst with the government of Ontario. For the next two years she prepared feasibility studies, systems designs, and systems proposals for several government departments. In this position she was also able to hone her people skills and work as part of a cohesive team.

In 1975 she took a break from her career when she and her husband adopted a ten-week-old baby boy. She enjoyed being a stay-at-home mom. When her son reached school age she decided to reenter the work force.

In 1980 Beverly was hired by the University of Toronto to develop computer systems for the Records Department. Again, she advanced quickly through the ranks, holding key positions in computing and communications. One of these was as a planning analyst for the vice-president of computing and communications. In this capacity she carried out research and consulted with experts around the world before submitting a detailed proposal that resulted in the establishment of the Adaptive Technology Resource Centre located in the Robarts Library. The centre serves the needs of students, faculty members, and staff who are disabled. In 1996 she accepted a severance package from the university, although she stayed on as a consultant. She was then free to focus on her lifelong dream of becoming a writer.

Having acquired a cochlear implant in 1993, Beverly turned her attention to writing a book on the subject. The result was *Wired for Sound: A Journey Into Hearing,* in 1998. Her book combines memories of growing up Deaf with detailed discussion about the benefits and drawbacks of cochlear implantation. It also deals with the need for assertiveness on the part of Deaf individuals in order to create greater public awareness of Deafness. In recognition of the research that went into the book, and the balanced treatment of the issues of Deafness and cochlear implants, *Wired for Sound* was named an American Library Association Outstanding Title for 1999. It was also named a *Globe and Mail* Notable Book.

Beverly continues to follow through on her ambitions as a researcher and writer who focuses on disabilities. In addition to consulting work in adaptive technology, frequent speaking engagements, and writing, she is also vice-chair of the Canadian Hearing Society, an associate editor of *Contact*, the quarterly journal of the Cochlear Implant Association in Washington, BC, and serves on the board of directors of Voice for Hearing Impaired Children.

BIRD, Patti Lillian

1966–
Entrepreneur, Mentor, and Small-Business Role Model.

PATTI BIRD of the Cree Nation at Montréal Lake, Saskatchewan, became profoundly Deaf when she was three or four years old. She currently makes her home in Saskatoon, Saskatchewan, with her Deaf common-law partner, Craig Waldbillig. She has two children, Andy and Tamika, who are both hearing. Patti is the ninth of twelve children, one of three girls, and nine boys. Her youngest brother, Burton Bird, who is hard of hearing, is a hoop-dancer. An older brother, Richie Bird, has been Chief of the Montréal Lake Cree Nation since 1998. Her father, Allen Bird, now a senator in Ottawa, and her eldest brother, Roy H. Bird, are both former chiefs of Montréal Lake. Another brother, Bobby Bird, now deceased, was the third vice-chief of the Federation of Saskatchewan Indian Nations.

From preschool to grade twelve, Patti attended the Saskatchewan School for the Deaf in Saskatoon. She was the first of two Deaf Native students to graduate grade twelve in 1986. From 1990 to 1993 she was in a basic adult education program at Kelsey Institute to upgrade her academic skills. For the next two years she worked as a packer for Redi Chef Meat, happy to be gainfully employed after many years on welfare.

Around that time the Small Business Development Program for People with Disabilities was launched. Patti eagerly became involved and, to some extent, was at least partially responsible for its success. The program, a collaborative effort between federal and provincial agencies, devised a project which helped establish five new small businesses in Saskatoon. One of them was Patti's Saskatoon Doggy Wash and another was Craig Waldbillig's Silent Vending.

One of the aims of the project was that Patti would serve as a role model and mentor for other young people with disabilities, to show what they could do in order to become equally successful. She had excellent support from her family and friends and encouraging input from the business community. She enrolled in a course offered by Deaf and Hard of Hearing Services which helps Deaf people go into business. There she learned marketing strategies, book-keeping skills, and research techniques. After completing the course, she had to raise the money to establish her business. She reached out to the Deaf Community for support to transform a former beauty salon into an animal grooming parlour. Deaf people helped her paint and decorate the premises and install the washing tubs and grooming tables. Before long her business was thriving and she had built up a fairly large clientele.

Patti sees her entrepreneurship as helping to break down some of the barriers between the Deaf and the hearing communities. She serves clients from both groups and communicates with hearing people by writing and gesturing. As a Deaf single mother, Patti has achieved her lifelong dream of operating a small business. In doing so, she has become a role model and mentor for others. She is grateful for the innovative project that gave her this remarkable opportunity.

BIRLEY, Dawn Jani

1977–
Tae Kwon Do Champion and Specialist in Communication Arts.

DAWN JANI BIRLEY was born Deaf into a third-generation Deaf family in Regina, Saskatchewan. Her parents, both Deaf, are Dale and Susan Birley. She is the granddaughter of Marian Egger and William Birley, and step-granddaughter of Ralph Egger and Lois Birley, all of whom are Deaf. Dawn Jani also has a Deaf sister, Jodi, born in 1980, who is currently attending Gallaudet University.

Dawn Jani was educated in the mainstream public school system from the time she was enrolled in preschool at the age of three until her high school graduation in 1995. She was an outstanding student and a gifted athlete. On leaving high school she attended Gallaudet University in Washington, BC, where she earned, with distinction, a BA degree in Communication Arts. Dawn Jani was the first Canadian student to receive the title of "Homecoming

Queen" during her senior year (1998–99). She was also nominated twice for *Who's Who in American Universities and Colleges*.

When Dawn Jani was seven years old she watched a Bruce Lee movie that inspired her early interest in the martial arts. She focused on Tae Kwon Do with determination and perseverance until she reached the top middleweight division, competing in western Canada and also at the national and international championship levels. Her countless awards and medals attest to her prowess in this art and have won her recognition as Canada's representative in international competitions.

Dawn Jani was named Deaf World Sportswoman of the Year in 1997. Her ultimate goal was to be a member of Team Canada in the 2000 Olympics. She succeeded in breaking down some of the perceived barriers that have historically denied the Deaf access to major athletic competitions. Unfortunately, she developed health problems that prevented her from competing at the Olympics in Australia. Instead, she has taken time off to ponder her life's choices and is at present living and working in Norway, about three and a half hours northwest of Oslo. There, she teaches ASL and English and is responsible for extracurricular activities and outdoor education for the *skolegruppe* (children of parents attending her school to learn Sign Language).

She has many other interests and hopes to become a world traveller and adventurer and explore the farthest reaches of the globe. Since she is still a very young woman, she has a lifetime ahead of her in which to attain her goals.

BIRLEY (KRISMER), Lois Evelyn

1935–
Data-Entry Operator, Champion Curler, and Sports Enthusiast.

LOIS KRISMER was born profoundly Deaf in Abbey, Saskatchewan, and received her first three years of education at the provincial School for the Deaf in Saskatoon, where she learned ASL. She was then mainstreamed into public schools for the rest of her education and consequently lost her signing skills. After high school she took a business course in Saskatoon and worked as a filing clerk and typist for many years. Her lengthiest period of employment was with Modern Press, a large printing plant that was part of the circulation department of the Saskatchewan Wheat Pool. She enjoyed her work and liked the staff. Her many years there were very happy ones.

In 1974 Lois married her Deaf spouse, William Birley. They live in Regina where Lois has held various jobs with the Saskatchewan Wheat Pool, Sears, and the Saskatchewan government's Drug Plan Department as a data-entry operator. She retired from the workforce in 1987.

While living and working in Saskatoon, Lois became interested in the Deaf Community. She renewed her ASL skills and very soon became happily involved. For some time she was secretary of the Saskatoon Association of the Deaf and, after her marriage, was active in the Regina Association of the Deaf. Lois's interest in athletics and sports led her to the Saskatoon Deaf Athletic Club and the Saskatchewan Deaf Sports Association, in which she has been very active.

Her greatest pleasure is curling. For more than ten years Lois has played twice a week with the Wheat City Ladies' Curling Club. She was an ardent admirer of the late Olympic gold medalist curler, Sandra Schmirler. During the early 1970s, Lois participated in Deaf curling leagues and competed in many Western Canada Deaf Curling Association bonspiels, often winning cash prizes.

Since their retirement, Lois and her husband have motored across Canada and most states in the US. They have attended several conferences of the Deaf and a number of Deaf Curling Championship events. They are currently planning a trip to Europe.

In her leisure time, Lois enjoys her crafts, pets, and garden. She also is a winemaker and loves to cook.

BIRLEY (HUCHCROFT), Susan Gail

1951–
Office Worker, ASL Instructor, and Costume Designer.

SUSAN HUCHCROFT became Deaf at the age of eighteen months as a result of illness and/or the side-effects of medication. She was born in Vancouver, BC, and has hearing parents and four hearing brothers. She attended Jericho Hill School for the Deaf in Vancouver from 1955 until she graduated in 1970. She then went on to Gallaudet University in Washington, BC, majoring in social work.

After completing two years of the five-year program, she left Gallaudet and married Dale Edward Birley, who is hard of hearing but has many Deaf relatives. They settled in Saskatchewan where their two Deaf daughters, Dawn Jani and Jodi Lynn, were born. Susan attended the Saskatchewan Institute of Applied Science and Technology (SIAST), Wascana Campus, in Regina, Saskatchewan, to complete a three-month certificate program in data entry in 1979. This gave her the qualifications she needed to keypunch and verify thousands of batches of data over the next six years for Co-operator's Insurance.

Susan remained with Co-operator's until 1990. During her employment with the company she advanced from mailroom clerk to account clerk, maintaining more than 1,000 client files—coding, processing, verifying, and entering data into a mainframe computerized system. She also upgraded her qualifications at SIAST with a one-year program in office education which led to a new job with Revenue Canada in Regina for the next two years. She then took a seven-week training program to upgrade her computer skills and worked for the Royal Bank of Canada in their Processing Operation Centre.

From September 1997 to May 1998 she further upgraded her computer skills before securing a job with the Saskatchewan Property Management Corporation as an accounting clerk, with a large number of duties and responsibilities. She remained there for a year. Susan is currently living temporarily at her mother's home in Abbotsford, BC, where she is taking career and college preparatory classes at University College of the Fraser Valley. It is Susan's hope to enter Gallaudet University again to continue her pursuit of the degree which was interrupted nearly thirty years ago. This time, however, she is interested in ASL linguistics and Deaf studies. Meanwhile, her two Deaf daughters are both successful and doing well in their chosen careers, carving out special places for themselves as distinguished and well-respected Deaf Canadian women.

Susan enjoys various hobbies. When her girls were young, she was noted for her unique and specially designed birthday cakes. Her daughters encouraged Susan to set up a cake-decorating business. Her favourite pastime, however, is the creation of medieval and other types of costumes. She is a skilled seamstress and craftswoman and has produced many unique clothing items, ranging from ladies' suits and dresses to children's outfits. She has had a long-time dream to establish a costume business. Some day it might become a reality.

BLACK (ELASCHUK), Gail Margaret

1959–
Outstanding Employee and Volunteer in the Deaf Community.

GAIL ELASCHUK was born Deaf into a hearing family in Edmonton, Alberta, where she has lived all her life. She has no known Deaf relatives, but has a female Deaf roommate with whom she shares a home. Her son, Zachary (called Zak), is hearing and, at present, is a high school student. Her hearing sister is a graduate registered nurse who works with sick children at the Grey Nun's Hospital in southeast Edmonton.

Gail's education began at Windsor Park Elementary School which she attended from 1965 to 1969. It was a very frustrating experience for her because no signing was used in the strictly oral program offered there. Finally, her mother consulted their family doctor who recommended that Gail be sent to the Alberta provincial School for the Deaf (ASD) in south Edmonton. She was enrolled at once and attended ASD from 1969 to 1977. One of Gail's most pleasant and vivid memories of her years at ASD is the 1976–77 production of the film *Deafula*, in which she was one of the actors. It was produced by Jeff Jensen and Craig Loher, both ASD students, on a farm near Edmonton and involved thirty of their classmates.

After leaving school, Gail attended Alberta College for a while. She realizes now that her life had no focus at that time and that she lacked goals. As a result, she left college and entered the workforce, finding eclectic employment as a housekeeper and group-home worker, but eventually she became a Jane-of-all-trades for the Ackland's-Grainger Company, where she has continued to work for the last twenty-one years. Her duties there have varied from clerking in the mailroom and freight office, to being a courier and performing entry-level computer tasks. The company values her work ethic and loyalty and she has been recognized several times as its "Employee of the Month."

Gail's involvement as a volunteer in the Deaf Community began fairly recently with the Canadian

Deaf Festival held in Edmonton in July 2000. This was such an enriching experience that she was motivated to volunteer her assistance for a Deaf children's camp the following summer. This first Deaf summer camp in July 2001, held at Pigeon Lake, was a great success. Gail was a volunteer staff member representing the Edmonton Association of the Deaf (EAD) and Calgary Association of the Deaf (CAD). The attendees included thirty-seven Deaf children between the ages of six and fifteen. She received a Certificate of Appreciation from EAD for her work at the camp.

Gail now realizes what a wealth of knowledge and understanding of Deaf Culture she can gain by participating fully in the events of the Deaf Community. She looks forward to being of service and making many more significant contributions in the future.

BLUNDEN, Melba ("Mel")

1966–
Videographer and Aspiring Video and Filmmaker with a View to Deafness-Related Projects.

MELBA BLUNDEN was born Deaf in Glace Bay, Cape Breton Island, Nova Scotia. She has a Deaf sister and a Deaf brother, but the rest of her family and relatives are hearing. Melba grew up in Truro, Nova Scotia.

She attended day classes for Deaf students until grade six, when she was transferred to regular classrooms without an interpreter, although she had some tutoring help throughout those years. After graduating from grade twelve in 1987, she took a few years off before entering Saint Mary's University in Halifax, Nova Scotia. She graduated with a BA degree in Sociology in 1996.

After some soul searching and a few experiences with videography, she entered Nova Scotia Community College, Halifax Campus, to take a two-year Screen Arts Program in the fall of 2000, with a focus on the art of video and filmmaking. In May of 2001, as part of the program's work practicum, she developed a video for Northwood Centre, which had recently opened a floor for Deaf seniors. Melba expects to graduate from the program in 2002.

She is now working on developing Deafness-related video projects and hopes to establish a Deaf production company upon graduation and also to work in the film industry. Her plan is to involve the Deaf Community in the production of short films, videos, and other projects.

She has been a volunteer for some organizations, and is currently on the Association of Visual Language Interpreters of Canada (AVLIC) Halifax 2002 Conference Committee.

Melba was a board member for the Halifax Regional Board of Directors of the Society of Deaf and Hard of Hearing Nova Scotians (SDHHNS). She was at one time chairperson for the steering committee of the Deaf Workplace Education Project, and has served as president of the Nova Scotia Deaf Sports Association.

In her spare time, Melba enjoys night photography, drawing, reading, and analyzing films. She makes her home in Halifax.

Her videography credits are:

Camera/Editor/Director—Metro Deaf Literacy Network, developed ASL video for the Deaf Workplace Education Committee.

Scriptwriter/Assistant Editor/ASL Consultant— developed ASL CD-ROM *Human Resources Development Canada Labour Market Information.*

Production Manager/Scriptwriter/Signer— developed video *Deaf Literacy in Nova Scotia: An Evaluation Report* by Dr. Michael Rodda.

BOMAK (CHAIKOWSKI), Rita Elizabeth

1959–
Community Counsellor, Deaf Youth Leader and Advocate, ASL Instructor, and Champion Curler.

RITA CHAIKOWSKI was born Deaf to Deaf parents (Joseph and Marjorie Chaikowski) in Winnipeg, Manitoba. Her older sister, Sue Tebow, is Deaf and her brother, Randy, is hearing. Rita is married to a Deaf spouse, Kenneth Bomak. They live in Winnipeg with two Deaf daughters, Sally and Cathy, and two hearing sons, Gregory and Jonathon, in what Rita affectionately calls a "bilingual-bicultural household." This is Rita's second marriage, a very happy one, that has restored her self-esteem and confidence and helped her overcome the abuses suffered in her first marriage.

Rita was educated at the Manitoba School for the Deaf in Winnipeg and followed this up with a Deaf Training Program in human resources. She has been employed for thirteen years by the Society for Manitobans with Disabilities as a community counsellor. She attained her counselling certification through the Faculty of Continuing Education at the University of Manitoba. She has also worked as a Deaf interpreter, has taught life skills, promoted Deaf Culture, coordinated ASL immersion programs, facilitated parent skills training for Deaf parents, and has provided many individuals with counselling related to personal growth and development.

One of the accomplishments of which Rita is most proud is her participation, as a fourteen-year-old, in the 1975 Deaf Youth Camp held at Parry Sound, Ontario. It was the first time the camp was hosted by Canada and she met many new friends and learned important lessons that influenced her desire to become a leader in the Deaf Community. She was inspired by the camp because she was recognized for her leadership qualities. In 1998 she became the coordinator for the Manitoba Deaf Youth Camp at Camp Kakepitay, Vermillion Bay, Ontario.

Rita is best known, however, for her outstanding curling skills and her impressive record of medal victories. The following is a list of her triumphs in the Canadian Deaf Curling Championships since she was twenty years of age:

WOMEN'S TEAM:

1980	played second in Montréal	Gold Medal
1982	played third in Québec City	Gold Medal
1984	played third in Toronto	Bronze Medal
1985	skipped in Saskatoon	Gold Medal
1986	skipped in Ottawa	Gold Medal
1987	played third in Winnipeg	Silver Medal
1990	skipped in Halifax	Silver Medal
1991	played third in Banff	Silver Medal
1993	played third in Vancouver	Gold Medal
1994	played third in St. John's	Gold Medal

MIXED TEAM:

1997	played third in Portage La Prairie	Gold Medal
1998	played third in Winnipeg	Gold Medal
1999	played third in Edmonton	Gold Medal
2000	played 5th spare in St. John	Gold Medal
2001	played third in Whitehorse	Gold Medal

ALL-STAR WOMEN:

1982	played third
1985	skipped
1986	skipped
1987	played third
1994	played third

ALL-STAR MIXED:

1997	played third
1998	played third
2001	played third

Rita loves the challenge of competitive curling and is a talented and superior player. She is considered a national asset to Deaf curling in Canada.

Rita is also a strong member of the Deaf Community who is involved in its organizations and agencies, providing encouragement to Deaf youth, heading committees and projects. She is respected and honoured for her many contributions. She believes in self-sufficiency, development of self-esteem, and freedom from abuse for all Deaf women in Canada.

BORODAY (BLONDIN), Elaine Marie

1941–
Business Machines Expert and Dedicated Royal Bank Employee.

ELAINE BLONDIN was born Deaf to hearing parents in Barachois, Gaspé, Québec. She has no known Deaf relatives, but her husband, Thomas (Tom) Boroday, is Deaf. They have one adult son, William (Will), who is hearing. Elaine and Tom have some famous relatives—the well-known Canadian Senator, Gratton O'Leary, was related to Elaine's mother, and Mike Bossy, an NHL player for the New York Islanders, who was inducted into the Hockey Hall of Fame, is Tom's second cousin. Eddie Palchak, former trainer and equipment manager for the Montréal Canadiens, who retired with six Stanley Cup rings, is also Tom's cousin.

Elaine was educated at the Montréal Deaf Girls' High School on St. Denis Street from 1950 to 1959. She was a member of the Girl Guides and enjoyed the Centre Nôtre-Dame de Fatima camps for the Deaf in Vaudreuil, Québec.

In 1960, Elaine began her professional career at Chas. Cusson Ltd. where she worked until 1964. She was then employed at W. and F.P. Currie Ltd. for two years before leaving to have her son. In 1972, after being a stay-at-home mother for a few years, Elaine enrolled in a one-year training program to become a keypunch operator. She returned to the workforce in 1974 to take a position where she operated a bookkeeping machine as well as the postage machine for Wee Folks Diaper Service. In 1981 she joined the Royal Bank of Canada and worked there until 1997 when her department was merged with two others to form Symcor. She continued working for Symcor until her retirement in January 2001, after twenty years of dedicated service.

In 1996 Elaine was the recipient of a Performance Award Certificate from the Royal Bank. She also received a fifteen-year recognition pin and the Spirit of Excellence Award as well as quarterly winner certificates from Symcor in 1999.

Elaine has participated in Deaf curling bonspiels for many years. Between 1981 and 1990 she won numerous medals and prizes. She and her husband Tom, who worked as an architectural technician in computer-aided design and drafting for thirty-six years, moved to Toronto when he was transferred in 1994. They now make their home in Mississauga, Ontario.

BOTTLINGER (SHEDECK), Bernice Theresa

1930–
Homemaker, Historian, and Dedicated Worker for the Deaf.

BERNICE SHEDECK was born in Yukon, Oklahoma, US. She came to Canada as a landed immigrant in 1962 and became a Canadian citizen in 1970. She was married to Wayne Bottlinger in 1957 and together they raised three hearing daughters, who have since presented them with three hearing grandsons. Bernice has been actively involved in the Deaf Community in both Canada and the US all her life, holding many offices and serving in many different capacities.

Educated at the Oklahoma School for the Deaf and at Gallaudet University, Bernice had a wide variety of experiences and developed many interests. For five years (1945–50) she was a member of Future Homemakers of America, occupying the office of State Historian for Oklahoma. From 1950 to 1957 she was president of the Oklahoma City Silent Club and since 1954 she has been a member of the National Fraternal Society of the Deaf (NFSD). When Division #166 of NFSD was established in Vancouver in 1979, she became a charter member and has acted as recording secretary, correspondence secretary—Ye Scribe—and general historian. She has also worked on many committees of the Vancouver division.

Since 1964 Bernice has also been a hard-working member of the Greater Vancouver Association of the Deaf (GVAD). In this organization she has been a board member, secretary, cultural director, chair of the Sick Visiting Committee, a participant in seniors' activities such as dinners and tours, and has sat on the Grants Project Committee.

She is also a member of the British Columbia Cultural Society of the Deaf and a long-time member of Trinity Lutheran Church for the Deaf, serving on numerous committees for both.

Bernice and Wayne make their home in Burnaby, BC. Since her arrival in Canada, Bernice has made many significant contributions to Canadian Deaf Culture and to the Deaf Community of the Greater Vancouver area.

BOUDREAU, Beverley Anne

1954–
Deaf Canadian Artist, Illustrator, Graphic Designer, and World Traveller.

BEVERLEY BOUDREAU was born in Toronto, Ontario, and has lived in Windsor since 1986. In the intervening years she explored Canada from coast to coast and travelled the world. Her family roots in Antigonish County, Nova Scotia, date back more than 200 years, and most summers during her youth were spent there. After graduating from Alderwood Collegiate in Toronto and working for two years for the Canadian Red Cross as an educational materials designer, she headed to Vancouver where she lived for seven years, working and continuing her studies. After completing two years at Simon Fraser University, she turned her attention, full-time, to her fascination with art, earning a two-year diploma in Graphic and Communication Arts at Douglas (now Kwantlen) College. This has been her career focus ever since, interrupted only by a four-year break in the 1990s when she returned to university to take care of the unfinished business of completing a degree.

In fact, she completed two, during which time she and her ASL interpreters became familiar figures on the university campus. Her undergraduate degree was an Honours BA for which she received the university's highest distinction, the Governor-General's Medal, as the top graduating student in her class of more than 2,000. She went on to complete a graduate degree, a Master of Arts, funded by an Ontario government graduate scholarship. Her educational goals completed, Beverley returned to her career as a graphic designer and has a thriving freelance business in Windsor.

Her special areas of interest as a designer are the creation and production of book covers, corporate symbols and logotypes, advertising campaigns for public institutions such as schools and environmental groups, and the illustration of children's literature. She has also produced drawings and maps for scientific publications, and designed museum displays and postage stamps.

Travel has played an important role in Beverley's life. In addition to her Canadian coast-to-coast explorations, she has visited more than thirty countries, from Norway (her favourite) to Brazil and Japan, as well as more than half of the American states. From 1982 to 1986, she lived in Gaborone, the capital city of Botswana in southern Africa. This was the experience of a lifetime, creating opportunities to camp among the world's most stunning wildlife, to be the only non-African member of a national championship-winning softball team, and to teach art at the National School for the Deaf. While living in Botswana, Beverley visited the neighbouring African nations of South Africa, Zimbabwe, Malawi, Lesotho, Swaziland, Mauritius, and Kenya.

Beverley, who has a congenital, profound hearing loss, is a past president of the Windsor chapter of the Canadian Hearing Society and the 1980 recipient of a Golden Defty Award in painting and drawing from the Canadian Cultural Society of the Deaf. During her stint in British Columbia, the Vancouver Foundation of BC awarded her the prestigious William and Emily Ross Award. She is also a published author, most notably for her article on John Constable's nineteenth-century cloud paintings, and her Master's thesis which reported on her studies of wave processes along lake shorelines.

She lives in Windsor with her husband, John Corlett, a university professor and sport psychologist, and her Wheaten terrier, Max.

BOUDREAULT (ROUTHIER), Monique

1942–
Consultant, Interior Decorator, Teacher, and Developer of Educational Materials.

MONIQUE BOUDREAULT, Deaf since birth, has had an interesting and varied life with many enviable accomplishments. She is married to a Deaf spouse, Jacques Boudreault, and they have two sons—Patrick, who is Deaf, and David, who is hearing. The family resides in Sillery, Québec. Monique also has a Deaf sister, Thérèse, and a Deaf brother, Réal.

Although her formal education ended at the eleventh grade, she has furthered her knowledge and expanded her skills by attending adult education courses in language, culture, computer programs, written French, LSQ, and family education. These classes gave her the qualifications required to hold teaching positions, do consultative work, develop educational materials, and author an LSQ program manual. Also, in 1983, she acted as interior decorator for the Cité Joie, a centre for handicapped persons.

Since 1978 Monique has held a number of prestigious positions. She was employed at Boreal College in Sudbury, Ontario, as a teacher and developer of teaching aids and materials related to the interpreting of LSQ. She also acted as a consultant for the Ministry of Health and Social Services, Institut Raymond Dewar, Hospital Administrative Centre at Université Laval, and the Canadian Hearing Society. In addition, she worked for Service Handi "A" as a coordinator, instructor, and workshop presenter. It was while she held this position that she authored a program manual entitled: *La Sexualité en Langue des Signes Québécoise*.

From 1982 to 1990 Monique taught LSQ at Sainte-Foy Collège. In 1984–85 she did likewise at Université de Sherbrooke, and from 1985 to 1990 she taught for the Commission Scolaire Regionale Tardival. Throughout the 1990s she participated in many workshops related to teaching methods, computer programs, communication issues, health matters, and concerns specific to Francophone women. She has been active in several organizations, mainly the Collectif des Femmes Francophones du Nord-Est Ontarien, the Societe Culturelle Québécoise des Sourds, the Association de Curling des Sourds de Québec, and the Féderation Sportive des Sourds du Québec.

Her Deaf son, Patrick, interprets LSQ/ASL and has obtained a Master's degree in Linguistics. David, her hearing son, has completed a Master's degree in Environment. Her husband, Jacques, has a keen interest in Deaf history and is very active in the Association des Sourds de Québec. The family members are avid curlers, and do volunteer work for organizations of the Deaf, particularly in the field of sports. In 1986 Monique was the director of the Miss Deaf Canada Pageant. She has been awarded several trophies and medals for her outstanding contributions to Deaf Canadians.

Despite her extraordinarily busy life, she finds time to sew, ski, cycle, and travel. She also enjoys family camping expeditions, does aerobics and physical conditioning in water, and pursues an interest in art and painting. Her full and rewarding life provides inspiration to all Deaf women, but especially those whose languages are French and LSQ.

BOULE-DESROSIERS, Lucette

1924–
Former Sister of the Congregation of Our Lady of Seven Dolors, French-Language Instructor, Dedicated Advocate for the Deaf, Devoted Wife, Mother, and Grandmother.

LUCETTE BOULE was born hearing to hearing parents, the seventh of ten children (including seven girls and three boys) in Chicoutimi, Québec. At the age of five years she was stricken with a severe case of spinal meningitis, which resulted in her becoming profoundly Deaf. She grew quite skilful at speaking and reading lips despite the severity of her hearing loss. Lucette has no known Deaf relatives but is now married to a Deaf man, Oscar Desrosiers, and they have one adult child, a beautiful hearing daughter, Jeannine, and a young grandson, who have both been their greatest joy. Lucette and Oscar have lived in the province of Québec all their lives and, at present, reside in Anjou.

Lucette was educated in Montréal, where her family had moved in 1929. At the age of seven and a half years she was enrolled at L'Institution des Sourdes on St. Denis Street, a residential school for Deaf girls, the majority of whom were of

French-Canadian background, from which she graduated eleven years later. In 1968 Club Abbé de l'Epée voted her "Queen of Sports." The Institution des Sourdes was one of the projects of the Sisters of Providence, who taught and gave spiritual guidance to the Deaf pupils. In 2001, these Sisters celebrated the 150th anniversary of their work with the Deaf. Many of the Deaf girls who attended the institution were so impressed with the dedication of the Sisters who taught them that they aspired to take religious vows themselves. Lucette Boule was one of them. After staying at home with her parents for a year, and being unable to find employment, she decided, at the age of nineteen, to enter the religious life.

By that time, a community of Deaf Sisters had been established at the institution, and most of the postulants who entered the Congregation of Our Lady of Seven Dolors came from the student body of the school. This was a unique religious community because all the Sisters were Deaf, the only congregation of its kind in North America. Lucette was accepted into this community of Deaf Sisters and, in due course, made the profession of her vows. She became a teacher and taught all subjects to the Deaf girls at the institution, thus helping the hearing Sisters of Providence for seventeen years. After twenty years as a devoted Sister, working among Deaf people of all ages and serving as a French-language instructor during her free time, Lucette made the decision to withdraw from religious life and reenter the secular world. She moved to Québec City and worked in the Justice Department, reviewing passports and learning many new things

after her years of seclusion, especially regarding individual human rights and laws. She returned to Montréal and did secretarial work for the Adoption Bureau, from which she retired in 1996.

Lucette Boule married Oscar Desrosiers and a year later, when she was forty-five years old, gave birth to a lovely daughter who brought great happiness and spiritual enrichment into both of their lives. As a lay person, Lucette has been a dedicated and selfless volunteer in the Deaf Community. She was the founder of Centre Alpha Sourd (CAS), which offers classes for Deaf people in written French, and a co-founder of Centre de la Communauté Sourde de Montréal Metropolitan (CCSMM), where she offered her many talents and skills. She taught classes and was a strong proponent for Deaf literacy. On 16 January 2001 she was honoured with a certificate of appreciation, presented to her by Lise Thibault, Lieutenant Governor of the province of Québec, as a tribute to her many contributions. On 12 March 2001 she was awarded Centraide's Antoinette Robidoux prize, with a cheque for $5,000 presented to CCSMM on her behalf. This most-deserving woman has worked with the Deaf for more than sixty-six years.

Lucette has recently had to curtail her volunteering in order to devote her time to taking care of her ailing husband. Her hobbies include reading, walking, visiting cultural places, doing crossword puzzles, bowling, and travelling. She has taken cruises to Greece, the Antilles, Bermuda, the Gaspé, and the Caribbean. She is often referred to as "a big heart— a mother to Montréal's Deaf Community."

BOURQUE (GAGNE), Mary Joann

1960–
Data-Entry Operator, Deaf Interpreter, Aboriginal Deaf Role Model, and Advocate for the Deaf.

JOANN GAGNE was born hearing, the third child in a family of twelve in Dalhousie, New Brunswick, but became Deaf in infancy due to scarlet fever. She has two Deaf sisters and two Deaf brothers. Their mother was a Micmac Aboriginal and their father, a French-speaking Acadian. Joann currently has the status of an off-reserve member of the First Nation. Her Deaf husband is Paul Bourque, whose parents are French-speaking Acadians from a village near Miramichi, New Brunswick. Joann and Paul have two hearing children, Vanessa and Jason, and currently make their home in Saint John, where Paul works for the Workplace Health Safety and Compensation Commission of New Brunswick.

Joann's education began at the age of six at a mainstream elementary school in Charlo, New Brunswick. She was later transferred to the Interprovincial School for the Deaf in Amherst, Nova Scotia, along with her older brother, in 1969. All five Deaf Gagne siblings received their education there. Joann is satisfied with the level of learning that she received at that school. It was there that she made many lifelong friends and met her life partner. She identifies more readily with her Deaf peers than with her Aboriginal ancestry. Both cultures have had lengthy and difficult challenges to achieve equality in the larger society, so Joann is grateful for the shared strengths in her heritage.

She became a data-entry operator, graduating from the Atlantic Technological Vocational Centre (ATVC) in Amherst in 1979. She moved to Saint John and worked as a clerk for Tabufile for over two years, and then held several short-term positions before leaving the workforce in 1984 to become a full-time stay-at-home mother to her children for the next sixteen years.

In 1997 she organized a workshop which succeeded in creating greater public awareness of the Deaf Community and Culture in Saint John. There was a deplorable shortage of Deaf interpreters in the Saint John area at that time so, in 1999, Saint John Deaf and Hard of Hearing Services (SJDHHS) brought in Rita Bomak, a highly respected Community counsellor and Deaf interpreter from Winnipeg to train Deaf New Brunswickers for that type of work. Joann was the only applicant, so was able to go through the training process and learn the Code of Ethics with Rita in just four days. In February 2000 she became a professional Deaf interpreter, registered with the Association of Visual Language Interpreters of New Brunswick (AVLI–NB).

Joann mentors young Deaf girls, giving them a social identity through greater awareness of their language and culture. In today's education system they are mainstreamed and may have no exposure to their Deaf heritage. In 1999 the New Brunswick government's Social Policy Committee held a public hearing attended by about 150 people, including many who were Deaf. Joann was one of them. She capably presented a paper outlining the need for adequate funding of services, professional development for medical interpreters, a bilingual-bicultural-based literacy program, and a reinstatement of full social assistance for laid-off workers. The latter was successfully implemented.

Joann has held office with the Saint John Association of the Deaf (SJAD) and is on the board of directors for Saint John Deaf and Hard of Hearing Services. Apart from her work as a Deaf interpreter, she also provides day-care for preschool-aged Deaf children of hearing parents to give them a better language background when they enter school. For relaxation, she enjoys cooking, taking long walks, reading, going on outings with her family, and socializing with other Deaf people.

BOWMAN (CHARLEBOIS), Monique Denise Marie

1957–

Canada Post Coder and Letter Carrier (Possibly the first Deaf Female Letter Carrier in Canada).

MONIQUE CHARLEBOIS was born Deaf to hearing parents, Denis and Carmen Charlebois, in Shellbrook, Saskatchewan. She has a younger Deaf sister, Paulette Smith, a Deaf brother-in-law, Ray Smith, and two hard-of-hearing nephews, Corey and Duane Smith. Monique's husband, Glenn Bowman, a carpenter-installer by trade, is also Deaf, and they have four hearing children—Blair, Amy, Matthew, and Jessica. Monique's hearing sister, Lorraine, works with Deaf-Blind adults in a group-home setting. Monique, Glenn, and their family currently make their home in Saskatoon, Saskatchewan.

Monique has the interesting distinction of being a distant cousin of the historical Canadian Métis leader, Louis Riel, whose grandmother, Marie-Anne (Gaboury) Lagimodière, was one of the first white women on the western Canadian prairies. Her second youngest daughter, Julie Lagimodière, was Louis Riel's mother. Before her marriage, Monique's mother was Carmen Lagimodière, Riel's cousin, thrice removed.

Monique's Deafness, and that of her sister, was not diagnosed by doctors until she was two and Paulette

was a year old, but they believed that both children were Deaf at birth.

Monique was educated at the Saskatchewan School for the Deaf from preschool, in 1962, until her graduation in 1975. She was hired by Canada Post as a casual seasonal worker in December 1975. In January 1976 she advanced to a full-time position as a coder. Subsequently, she applied twice for a promotion to letter carrier, but was turned down on both occasions because of her Deafness. Monique appealed to her union and to the Human Rights Commission. They helped her fight this discriminatory policy of the Canada Post Corporation. In March 1980 she finally became a full-time letter carrier, and may have been the first Deaf woman in Canada to achieve this status.

In 1982 Monique married her Deaf spouse, Glenn Bowman, and, in due course, they became the proud parents of four hearing children. Monique left the workforce to concentrate on being a full-time housewife and mother but returned in 1997, on a casual, part-time basis.

Monique and Glenn are active members of Saskatoon's Deaf Community. They hold membership in the Saskatoon Association of the Deaf (SAD) and the Saskatchewan Cultural Society of the Deaf (SCSD). In 1980 Monique had the honour of being selected Miss

Deaf Saskatchewan at a pageant sponsored by the Canadian Cultural Society of the Deaf (CCSD) in Winnipeg.

In her leisure time, Monique enjoys crocheting and cross-stitching. She loves taking family camping trips every summer and is noted for her expertise at creating a variety of homemade soups.

BRIAN (HILL), Gloria Jean

1941–
Florist, Microfilm Technician, and Active Retiree.

It is not known exactly when GLORIA JEAN HILL became Deaf. She was born in Wetaskiwin, Alberta, to hearing parents and her mother taught school there for many years. She was sent to the Saskatchewan School for the Deaf in Saskatoon in 1946 at the age of five. Ten years later (in 1956) she was enrolled in the new Alberta School for the Deaf (ASD), which had just opened in Edmonton.

After graduating in 1959, Gloria worked as a florist in a downtown Edmonton flower shop. In 1961 she married William Jennings Brian (Bill), an American, who worked as a barber, a printer, and then as a travelling encyclopedia salesman. Together they raised two hearing children. In 1972, when both children were in school, she returned to the workforce, taking a job with the Alberta government as a microfilm technician in the Education Department. She enjoyed her work there and was honoured with an Alberta Education Award. At the time, she was the only Deaf person in her departent, but her hearing co-workers relied on her when it came to locating old school records. She developed an uncanny knack for turning them up very quickly whenever she was called upon to do so. After almost a quarter century of service with the government of Alberta, Gloria retired in 1996.

She loves her life as a retiree and is active in the Deaf Community as a volunteer. She was recognized for her contributions to the Edmonton Society for the

Deaf (EAD), when she was presented with their Member of the Year Award in 1998. She chaired the Bingo Committee from 1996 to 1998, when Bingo was the major fundraiser for EAD's building fund, and is still a loyal bingo volunteer, both for EAD and the Alberta Chapter of Registered Interpreters for the Deaf (ACRID). Gloria was chairperson of the Deaf Seniors' Club in Edmonton from 1998 to 2000, when she planned, organized and participated in countless activites. She feels privileged to be in excellent health, which enables her to remain actively involved and to gain new knowledge everyday. Most of all she enjoys helping other "Deafies."

Gloria's husband Bill has been a member of EAD since 1954, and Gloria joined the group in 1961. Both have been proclaimed Honorary Life Members. When she was a student at SSD, she began to read the magazine Reader's Digest, and that is still one of her favourite pasttimes. She also enjoys sewing and making clothes for her grandchildren, as well as doing cross-stitchery. Above all, she likes serving the Deaf Community and can often be found maintaining the new kitchen at the Edmonton Association of the Deaf Community Centre (EADCC). She is highly-valued and greatly respected by the rest of the membership.

BROOKER (HILLCOX), Audrey Bernice

1930–

Bookbinder, Office Employee, Domestic Engineer, and Doting Grandmother.

AUDREY HILLCOX was born Deaf to hearing parents in Winnipeg, Manitoba. Her family moved to Wapella, Saskatchewan, when she was a toddler. She has a Deaf brother, Clarence Hillcox, who is seven years her junior. Audrey married into a third-generation Deaf family when she wed Sidney Harold Brooker (Sid), more than forty years ago. Sid and his Deaf sister, Peggy Fee, both attended the British Columbia School for the Deaf and Blind and were outstanding athletes. In his later years, Sid was an avid golfer who took every possible opportunity to enjoy the game. Their Deaf daughter, Avonne, was born in New Westminster, BC, in 1966, and their Deaf granddaughter, Alexandria Sydney, in Austin, Texas, in 1998. Alexandria is now a fifth-generation Deaf member of the Brooker family. Sadly, Sid left them to play the ultimate round of golf when he passed away on 12 July 2001, and is greatly missed and fondly remembered by all who knew him. Audrey continues to reside in the family home in Port Moody, BC.

She attended the Saskatchewan School for the Deaf in Saskatoon as a residential student until she was seventeen, when she left to enter the workforce. She was employed in a book bindery and lived with her mother in Saskatoon. Eventually, she moved to Calgary and found work with a printing company. It was there that she met her future husband, Sid, through his Deaf sister, Peggy, at a Western Canada Association of the Deaf (WCAD) convention they were all attending in July of 1957.

When they married, on 17 May 1958, Audrey and Sid moved to Vancouver, BC, where they both worked for the Evergreen Printing Company (now Quebecor). Sid retired after thirty-four years with the company. Audrey left the company when she became pregnant with Avonne. She has spent most of her life since then as a mother and housewife, laughingly referring to herself as a most dedicated and energetic domestic engineer. However, when Avonne was old enough, Audrey did return to the workforce, spending eighteen years as an employee of the TB Veterans in downtown Vancouver

before her retirement in 1995. Although they both worked outside the home, Audrey and Sid focused most of their attention on their daughter, Avonne, who was the joy of their lives. They always loved and supported her unconditionally especially throughout the years when she was acquiring her university education and establishing her professional career.

Both Audrey and Sid were very active in the Deaf Community, mainly in the area of sports and athletics. Besides his noted prowess as a golfer, Sid was also an outstanding fastball pitcher, curler, basketball player, and coach. Audrey was proud of his achievements, particularly his induction to the NWAAD (Northwest Athletic Association of the Deaf) Hall of Fame. He coached the Canada Deaf Basketball team for the 1973 World Games of the Deaf held in Malmo, Sweden, and was named one of British Columbia's Most Outstanding Deaf Athletes.

Audrey and Sid greatly enjoyed their retirement. They loved to travel, often visiting Avonne and her family in Texas, and attending a variety of Deaf functions across Canada. They were members of the Greater Vancouver Association of the Deaf (GVAD), the Deaf Curling Club, the Deaf Golf Club, and the Happy Hands Club. Audrey is still involved with the Happy Hands Club, a social Deaf club in Vancouver, and looks forward to frequent visits from her beloved granddaughter, Alexandria, with whom she has much in common. They both love to munch on chocolates while they sit and watch Disney videos together. Sid's greatest pleasure also was Alexandria, his "little princess," with whom he had many profound discussions when he and Audrey were a pair of "Canadian Snowbirds" spending their winters in Texas. At present, Audrey is bravely adjusting to the enormous void in her life since Sid's untimely death after a of courageous seven-year battle with leukemia.

BROOKER-RUTOWSKI, Avonne Maureen

1966–
Deaf Educator of the Deaf, Proud Mother, and Outstanding Deaf-Canadian Role Model Living in the US.

AVONNE BROOKER was born Deaf to Deaf parents, Audrey Bernice Hillcox of Saskatoon and Sidney Harold Brooker of Calgary, in New Westminster, British Columbia. Her daughter, Alexandria Sydney, is a fifth-generation Deaf member of the Brooker family. Avonne has a Deaf husband, Paul Rutowski from Wisconsin, and their daughter was born in Texas in 1998. Little Alexandria is the joy of their lives and currently attends the preschool at the Texas School for the Deaf (TSD). She started attending the parent-infant program at TSD at the age of eighteen months. Avonne, Paul, and Alexandria make their home in Austin, Texas, where Avonne has worked at TSD for the last nine years. Avonne's mother, Audrey Brooker, resides in Port Moody, BC, and her father, the outstanding Canadian Deaf athlete whose greatest joy was golfing, Sid Brooker, passed away on 12 July 2001.

Avonne was raised in Port Moody and was enrolled at the Jericho Hill School for the Deaf (JHS) in Vancouver when she was only four and a half years old, remaining there until she reached high school. She then attended Kitsilano High School from 1981 until she graduated in 1985. She subsequently acquired a Bachelor of Arts degree in Psychology from Gallaudet University in Washington, BC, and a Master of Science degree in Deaf Education from Western Maryland College in Westminster, Maryland.

As an adult, Avonne has become an active member of various organizations and paraprofessional activities, including Phi Kappa Zeta, the Canadian Club, and head resident advisor of student life, among many others. Her middle name, Maureen, was chosen by her parents in honour of the highly respected and nationally beloved Deaf Canadian role model, Maureen Donald, who was a teacher at JHS. Avonne was born on her birthday. Maureen Donald, now in her eighties, was recently awarded an honorary Doctor of Laws degree by the University of British Columbia, for her outstanding contributions to the community. Avonne continues to be inspired by her.

At TSD, her present place of employment, Avonne has worn several different hats. Among the various responsibilities she has undertaken are her position as a language arts teacher, her mentorship for the STARS School Project, and her leadership in early childhood education. She has a passion for Deaf education and is closely involved with the study of bilingual-bicultural education for Deaf students. In the summer of 2001 she was appointed to the position of early childhood/ elementary principal at TSD. Uncannily, it was her father, shortly before his death in July, who told Avonne of this appointment, having gotten the news from the assistant superintendent of TSD before the official announcement was made.

Although Avonne is now residing far from her original roots in British Columbia, she vows she will always remain a true Canadian at heart. She and other Canadians who live in Austin make it a point to celebrate Canadian Thanksgiving every year in October as well as the American holiday in November. Her daughter, Alexandria, loves the white and red Canadian flag, and is always very excited about visiting her Canadian family in Port Moody. Avonne has acquired a host of wonderful friends in the United States, but she always looked upon her mother and father as her best friends, and is constantly grateful for the uncon-ditional love and support they gave her and her family. Before his death, Sid Brooker's greatest passions in life were golfing and spending time with his granddaughter. He and his wife Audrey spent their winters in Texas so they could be near Avonne, Paul, and Alexandria. Although her father's passing has created a great void in Avonne's life, she is grateful for her many wonderful memories of him, and for the challenges of the new job which will now fill her daily life.

BROPHY, Shannon

1963–
Swimming Champion and Aspiring Deaf Team Canada Swim Coach.

SHANNON BROPHY was born prematurely to hearing parents, Tony and Adele Brophy, in Edmonton, Alberta. She was Deaf at birth. Her entire family of five hearing brothers and one hearing sister are all strong competitive swimmers and water polo players who compete at the national level. She has no known Deaf relatives, and is now the single mother of two lovely hearing children, Sara and Darcy.

The entire Brophy family has a reputation in Edmonton as outstanding swimmers, and her father was instrumental in establishing the city's well-known Eastglen swim team. With such a strong family background of swimmers, Shannon was influenced by her parents and siblings to become a swimmer at a very early age. However, the adult influence that affected her most was that of Jo-Anne Robinson, a Deaf teacher at the Alberta School for the Deaf (ASD) in Edmonton. Jo-Anne was a champion swimmer herself, and was a powerful mentor in encouraging Shannon's involvement and training until the age of thirteen.

Shannon received her education at ASD from 1969 to 1981. When she graduated, she attended Grant MacEwan Community College (now Grant MacEwan College) until 1984, where she trained to become a rehabilitation/child care worker. Since completing her education, she has been employed for over sixteen years as a Sign Language instructor at the Associated Commercial Traveller's (ACT) Centre and other locations. She is also a team leader at Key Support Services.

Her swimming career began at the age of three, but she would have given it up at the age of nine had it not been for the encouragement and mentoring she received from Jo-Anne Robinson. She began to swim competitively at the age of six, and her efforts paid off. She participated in the World Summer Games for the Deaf in Malmo, Sweden, in 1973, capturing four bronze medals: in the 200-metre breaststroke, the 100-metre backstroke, the 100-metre butterfly, and the 4 x 100 freestyle relay. In 1977 she attended the World Summer Games for the Deaf in Bucharest, Romania, broke her own world record in the 200-metre breaststroke and won a gold medal. She also won silver medals in the 100-metre breaststroke and the 4 x 100 medley relay. That year the Canadian Deaf Sports Association (CDSA) presented her with a special award as Best Deaf Canadian Athlete. In 1981 she attended the World Summer Games for the Deaf in Cologne, Germany, where she captured two silver medals in the 100-metre breaststroke and 100-metre butterfly, as well as two bronze medals in the 200-metre breaststroke and 4 x 100 medley relay. Again, she was honoured by CDSA as Best Deaf Canadian Athlete. In addition, Shannon received a gold ring award from the Alberta Premier, and competed against hearing swimmers at both the provincial and national levels while at ASD, when she swam with the St. Joseph's Swim Team (a mainstream Edmonton high school) during the school year.

Shannon still swims in master competitions, and plays water polo for fun with master-level mixed teams. She is working on her qualifications to become a national-level swim coach, having now attained level II. Her goal is to some day become a swim coach for Team Canada in the World Games for the Deaf, and to establish a swim club for Deaf and hearing swimmers.

She has a full-time job and is a devoted mother to Sara and Darcy. In her spare time she likes to work at home improvements, play with the family's two mini long-haired daschunds, watch her children participate in community sports, and spend time with their large extended family (Sara and Darcy have twenty-seven cousins). Shannon is still the holder of the Canadian Deaf Record in four different swimming events.

BROSZEIT (ZIMMER), Cheryl Tina

1970–
Teacher, Consultant, Resource Worker, and Volunteer.

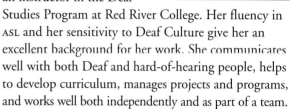

CHERYL ZIMMER was born Deaf into a Deaf family in Winnipeg, Manitoba. The Deaf members of her family include her parents (Lawrence and Diane Zimmer), three aunts and uncles (Dennis and Edith Zimmer, Donald and Vicki Zimmer, Robert and Susan Zimmer), three first cousins (Laurie, Dana, and Tammy Zimmer), several second cousins (Richard and Kyra Zimmer, Eugene and Diane Zimmer, Gerald and Gail Zimmer, Ron and Jean Hartogsveld, and Lucille Nickerson). Cheryl also has two Deaf third cousins (Cody and Jeremy Zimmer) and a Deaf husband, Brian Broszeit. Many of her Deaf relatives are employed in various services for the Deaf and have made significant contributions to Deaf Culture and the Deaf Community. Her uncle, Dennis Zimmer, influenced Boeing Canada to hire Deaf workers and helped to dispel many myths and misconceptions commonly held by the public about Deaf people in the workplace.

Cheryl attended the Manitoba School for the Deaf from 1976 to 1988 when she enrolled at Gallaudet University in Washington, BC. Eighteen months later she withdrew and returned to Winnipeg to take a job as a Deaf youth group coordinator. She also worked as a Deaf resource person, an ASL instructor, and an early learning consultant for Deaf and hard-of-hearing children.

From 1995 to 1999, Cheryl attended the University of Winnipeg, earning a Bachelor of Education degree.

She was one of the first Deaf people to achieve this goal at that university. She was also one of the first Deaf members of her family to get a higher education.

Cheryl is now employed as an instructor in the Deaf Studies Program at Red River College. Her fluency in ASL and her sensitivity to Deaf Culture give her an excellent background for her work. She communicates well with both Deaf and hard-of-hearing people, helps to develop curriculum, manages projects and programs, and works well both independently and as part of a team.

Her awards and honours include three academic plaques, six academic certificates, four citizenship certificates, two general scholarships, the Will Knutson Good Friend award, an academic award from Gallaudet, and a War Amputees' Scholarship from the University of Winnipeg.

She has increased her knowledge and improved her skills by attending many Deafness-related workshops and seminars and has been involved in many volunteer activities. Like all her Deaf relatives, Cheryl is a devoted promoter of ASL and Deaf Culture. In her spare time she enjoys crafts, reading, involvement in family events, the great outdoors, and camping.

BROWN (STEWART), Patricia ("Patsy") Anne

1939–
Library Cataloguer and Avid Gardener.

PATSY STEWART was born Deaf to hearing parents in Campbellton, New Brunswick, and grew up in nearby Dalhousie. She had a Deaf cousin, Marion Hamilton, and Patsy's late husband, Ian Brown, a newspaper photographer from Trail, BC, was also Deaf. There are no other known Deaf relatives in her family. Patsy and Ian made their home in Fredericton, New Brunswick.

Her Deaf cousin, Marion, was a student at the School for the Deaf in Halifax, Nova Scotia, from 1920 to 1931, and spent many years in Charlo, Bathurst, and Saint John, New Brunswick. Later, she was a resident of the Bob Rumball Centre for the Deaf in Toronto until her death in October 2001. Marion and Patsy both had Usher's Syndrome, and Patsy had declining vision for some years before she became Deaf-Blind at the age of forty-three.

She attended the MacKay School for the Deaf in Montréal for ten years before attending Gallaudet College (now Gallaudet University), in Washington, BC. She graduated with a Bachelor's degree in Library Science, with a minor in Education, in 1960. According to *Deaf Heritage in Canada* (Carbin, C.F., McGraw-Hill Ryerson, 1996), Patsy held the distinction of being the first female New Brunswicker to attend and graduate from Gallaudet. Armed with her new degree, Patsy found employment at the University of New Brunswick in Fredericton, where she worked as a library cataloguer for twenty-two years before her declining vision forced her into early retirement in 1982.

Patsy had been an amateur gardener, but after losing her sight, she became an expert gardener and enjoyed it immensely. She starts the growth process in her greenhouse and transplants the seedlings outdoors as soon as the weather allows. She enlists a friend to make the rows for her, but Patsy does all the planting and weeding herself. In the fall, she takes pleasure in harvesting her vegetables and keeps busy freezing, bottling, and pickling them. One of her specialties is green tomato chow.

Patsy and Ian were married in 1965. After thirty happy years together, she was widowed in 1995. She feels she owes Ian a great debt of gratitude for the way he encouraged and supported her gardening activities while her vision was failing. Gardening has become central to her life. She lives alone in her own home with her cats, Patches and Petunia, and manages her household quite capably. She goes to appointments and social events with her intervenors, using the manual two-hand alphabet. She uses a fan system similar to the flashing light signals used by Deaf people. The fans blow air onto her and alert her to the telephone or doorbell. Patsy's TTY has a Telebraille which gives her the independence of making her own telephone calls. In her leisure hours she enjoys reading, collecting recipes and jokes, knitting, and playing Scrabble. Patsy is known for her great sense of humour. In October 2001, Patsey was featured on the CBC TV program, *On the Road Again with Wayne Rostad*.

BRUNDSON, Gail Marie

1954–
ASL Instructor, Coordinator, and Counsellor.

GAIL BRUNDSON was born hearing into a hearing family in St. Thomas, Ontario, but became profoundly Deaf at the age of three. She received her basic education at Ontario provincial Schools for the Deaf in Belleville and Milton.

Gail now has a hearing partner, Kelly Adamski, and four Deaf children from a previous marriage. Her children range in age from fifteen to twenty-six years. Timothy, the eldest, works as a counsellor for Deaf and mentally delayed persons. Jennifer, who recently graduated from the Rochester Institute of Technology (RIT) with a BA degree in Social Work, now lives in California with her husband. Matthew is in his first year at Gallaudet University and Heather, the youngest, competed in the Deaf World Games as a member of the Women's Volleyball Team in Rome during the summer of 2001. The family lives in Milton.

After graduating from high school with honours in academics in 1972, Gail furthered her education and upgraded her qualifications by taking a number of courses in various fields of interest—banking/accounting, keypunch operating, business management and administration, computer training, social work, levels I and II of "Signing Naturally," the sociolinguistics of ASL, the social dynamics of Deaf Culture, and CPI/CPR certification in First-Aid. She also attended many lectures, seminars, and workshops which help her to meet the needs of her clients in her present position as the resource coordinator for PAH! (Mental Health Services for Deaf Children).

Gail's diverse skills and experience have qualified her to hold some very interesting jobs. She has been employed as an ASL instructor, a program supervisor, an educational assistant, and a program counsellor.

She is currently working toward a Child/Youth Worker Diploma to add to her resume and has had short-term experience in other areas as well—as a foster parent, an instructor in a Deaf literacy program, and a supervisor of summer camps for Deaf children sponsored by the Robarts School in London. Gail is proficient in office management and administration and has excellent computer skills.

Despite her heavy workload and her constant educational upgrading, Gail also finds time to participate fully in the Deaf Community as an active member of all the associations of the Deaf, locally, provincially, and nationally. She has been a representative on the E.C. Drury student council, the Committee for Deaf-Plus Ontarians, and the Ontario Deaf Education Review. In addition, she helped to develop a parents' kit to educate hearing parents of Deaf children.

For her work and dedication Gail has received three awards, a Deaf Woman of the Year award and two prizes at Deaf Cultural Festivals of the Arts as well as academic recognition at the Milton School for the Deaf from which she graduated.

Her hobbies are horseback riding, camping, swimming, quilting, motorcycling, and mountain biking. Her partner, Kelly, who was an ASL interpreter for ten years, is now a computer engineer and shares many of her interests.

BUCHANAN, Beverly Josephine

1964–
Collegiate Dean, Teacher, Presenter, Researcher, Volunteer, and World Traveller.

BEVERLY BUCHANAN was born Deaf to Deaf parents in Halifax, Nova Scotia. She has two Deaf sisters, Helen and Carolyn, and a hearing daughter, Amanda Josephine. She and Amanda currently make their home in Big Spring, Texas.

Beverly received her early education in Halifax and took her high school at a private facility, Armbrae Academy (formerly Halifax Ladies' College). She then earned a BA degree in Biology from Gallaudet University and a Master's degree in Deaf Education from Western Maryland College. She spent an additional year in a PhD program at Gallaudet and is now working toward a doctorate in Educational Leadership at Texas Tech University.

At present, Beverly is employed as Dean of Student Services at Southwest Collegiate Institute for the Deaf in Big Spring. She has had a varied and interesting employment record, beginning in 1981 when she held several student positions at Gallaudet. In her professional career she has been a residential advisor, a biology lab teacher, a volunteer for Voluntary Services Overseas (VSO) at the Sethsation School for the Deaf in Bangkok, Thailand, a Gallaudet research assistant, an international advisor for Gallaudet students, and a staff assistant at the Centre for Global Education.

She has many awards and honours to her credit. These include service awards, certificates of recognition, and a Staff Member of the Year award. Her achievements are numerous. She was part of the first Deaf team to cycle from Malaysia to Singapore and has cycled across the US with other Deaf cyclists from Norway, Germany, and Denmark. She was a staff trainer for the Youth Leadership Training Program in Singapore, Thailand, Malaysia, the Philippines, Myanmar, and Hong Kong from 1995 to 1999. In Seoul, Korea, in 1995, she gave a presentation on "How to Teach Deaf Children English as a Second Language" at the Asian Pacific Congress. In 1999 she gave a forty-five-minute powerpoint presentation at the World Federation of the Deaf in Brisbane, Australia, and attended the 3rd Thai Deaf Youth Leadership Camp in 2001.

Beverly considers her work in Thailand to have been the most rewarding part of her career and is particularly proud of her success in raising the funds to print 2,000 manual alphabet posters for Thai students learning English as a second language.

BUCHANAN (LAWRENCE) Geraldine ("Gerry") Bessie

1920–
Fur Finisher, Homemaker, and Lifetime Member of Two Organizations of the Deaf.

GERRY LAWRENCE was born into a hearing family in Windsor, Nova Scotia. She and her sister (now deceased) were both profoundly Deaf and were taken to Halifax to attend the School for the Deaf, where Gerry received her education from 1927 to 1938. She recalls that she won a gold medal in 1937 for general academic excellence, and enjoyed her sojourn at the school.

After graduating in 1938, she became a fur finisher and worked for Mitchell Furriers in Halifax from 1939 to 1945. In December of 1945, Gerry married Malcolm (Mack) Buchanan from Regina, Saskatchewan, who had attended the Saskatchewan School for the Deaf in Saskatoon from 1931 to 1938. Together they raised five children, three boys and two girls, who are now all middle-aged and have presented their parents with four grandsons and two granddaughters. Their children and

grandchildren are all hearing. Mack had a hearing sister who died in 1978 and a Deaf brother, Leonard, who died in 1990. Leonard and his wife, Polly, who is also Deaf, had three Deaf daughters, Helen, Carolyn, and Beverley. Helen lives in Nova Scotia with her hearing husband and two hearing sons. Beverley now lives in Texas with her hearing daughter. She has travelled widely and has worked in Thailand. Carolyn was a wonderful niece to Gerry and Mack, but her life was short. She died of cancer in 1997, a sad event for all the family. Gerry had twin sisters—Georgina, who was Deaf, and Christina, who is hearing. Georgina's husband Nairne was also Deaf but their son, Nolan, is hearing. Georgina and Nairne are deceased. Christina is a nurse and Gerry and Mack visit her often. She is a good sister to Gerry and a wonderful sister-in-law to Mack.

Eventually the Buchanans moved to Moncton where they currently make their home. Gerry continued to work as a fur finisher, spending forty-five years in that career. She and Mack have both been active members of the Deaf Community and, in 1991, she was granted a lifetime membership by the Moncton Association of the Deaf. In 1995 Gerry was again honoured by being presented the Eastern Canada Association of the Deaf Award which also included a lifetime membership. She had been a member for sixty-one years.

As a couple, Gerry and Mack have travelled to western Canada on several occasions to attend Deaf festivals and other events. They celebrated their fifty-fifth wedding anniversary in December 2000 and have many happy memories of their life together. They have taken two wonderful cruises—the first to the western Mediterranean in 1994, and the second in 1996, to the United Kingdom which they toured with some other Deaf people from Ontario.

Gerry's hobbies include homemaking, cooking, and knitting. She is also a TV soap opera fan and likes doing word search and other types of puzzles.

BUCHANAN (FORSYTHE), Josephine Pauline ("Polly")
1926–
Professional Weaver of Tartans, World Traveller, and Devoted Grandmother.

POLLY FORSYTHE was born hearing in Delhaven near Wolfville, Nova Scotia. She became Deaf at the age of three, as a result of scarlet fever, at the same time as her younger sister, Joyce, also became Deaf at nine months of age. Besides her Deaf sister, Joyce Forsythe Kay, who currently resides in Delhaven, Polly had three Deaf daughters: Helen Hilton, living in Halifax; Beverly Buchanan, living in Texas; and Carolyn Fitzgerald, deceased at the age of thirty-seven from breast cancer. Polly's husband, Leonard Buchanan, was Deaf and, although the late Carolyn's husband, Wade, and their three children are all hearing, Wade Fitzgerald has a Deaf sister, Linda Keating. Leonard Buchanan's Deaf brother, Malcolm, and his Deaf wife, Geraldine ("Gerry"), live in Moncton, New Brunswick.

Polly attended the Halifax School for the Deaf from 1938 to 1946. At that time the Gaelic College, also known as the Gaelic Foundation of Nova Scotia, approached Louise Fearon, weaving teacher at the Halifax School for the Deaf, asking her to recommend a Deaf girl to be trained in the art of weaving tartans. Miss Fearon gave them Polly's name. When she graduated at the age of twenty, in 1946, Polly's father took her by train to St. Ann's, near Baddeck, on Cape Breton Island, to begin her professional training as a weaver. Later in the same year, Polly's Deaf sister, Joyce, joined her at the renowned Gaelic College which specialized in tartan weaving, highland dancing, bagpipe music, and the study of the Gaelic language. The two sisters, who were the first Deaf trainees in the weaving program,

graduated from Gaelic College in December 1949.

During their training, a very memorable event took place. Joyce Forsythe had created an exquisitely beautiful tartan slumber rug, a 45" by 75" weaving which resembled a shawl, and was deemed to be of such superior workmanship that it was chosen as a gift for Princess Elizabeth when she and her husband, Prince Philip, toured Nova Scotia in November 1951. Angus MacDonald, who was premier of Nova Scotia at that time, presented the Royal Stuart tartan rug to Her Royal Highness, the Princess Elizabeth, who is now Elizabeth II, Queen of the United Kingdom and the Commonwealth. Her husband is now the Queen's Consort and Duke of Edinburgh. The rug was presented at a state dinner held by the government of Nova Scotia for the royal couple. This was probably one of the most unique national honours ever bestowed upon any Deaf Canadian.

Both Polly and Joyce continued their weaving after they were married. They worked from home for Nova Scotia Tartans while raising their families. They have since put their looms away and taken up other interests.

Today, Polly lives in Halifax and keeps busy with her daughter, Helen, and her grandchildren. She has also travelled around Europe and the US with Beverly, and was delighted to have an opportunity to visit Thailand when Beverly worked there.

BUCKLER (PECK), Krystal Joy

1966–
Entrepreneur, Businesswoman, and Jane-of-all-Trades.

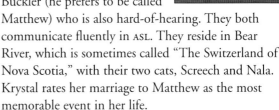

KRYSTAL PECK was born in Halifax and grew up in Bear River, Nova Scotia, where she still lives. She was hard-of-hearing from birth as a result of maternal rubella. More than her hearing was affected—she was also left with mild cerebral palsy in both legs, blindness in one eye, and asthma. She wore hearing-aids to get through elementary school in a mainstream program and reached grade nine. She left public school to acquire a trade and, as an adult, has upgraded her basic education to the tenth-grade level. Krystal comes from a large extended family, ranging in age from two to ninety-five, many on her father's side having natural musical talents. She learned to read music and play the piano. She has only one Deaf relative, a cousin, who was born Deaf due to her mother's ingestion of certain drugs during her pregnancy.

In 1984 Krystal entered the Atlantic Technological Vocational Centre in Amherst, Nova Scotia, to study data entry, and graduated from the program in 1986. It was during these two years that she learned to sign so she could communicate with her Deaf friends at the college. She took some teacher's aide training, sold Avon products door to door, trained as a general office clerk, volunteered at a gift shop, and undertook a two-week work assessment before finally deciding to become an entrepreneur.

Her hearing grandfather, Watson Peck, excelled in water sports and Boston Marathon runs, so he was well known in the community. Krystal is married to Gary Matthew Buckler (he prefers to be called Matthew) who is also hard-of-hearing. They both communicate fluently in ASL. They reside in Bear River, which is sometimes called "The Switzerland of Nova Scotia," with their two cats, Screech and Nala. Krystal rates her marriage to Matthew as the most memorable event in her life.

She manages her own business, Buckler's Maritime Deaf Connection, a mail-order company dealing in specialty gifts and items related to Deafness, ranging from hearing-aid batteries to Sign Language books. She contracts with Nova Scotian craftspersons to create a wide variety of specialty gift items. Krystal recently produced her first catalogue to which new products are regularly added.

Krystal keeps busy running her office, handling phone calls and orders, doing the accounting and banking, and working on her catalogue and website. In her spare time she enjoys her friends and works at many crafts.

BULL, Mary

1852–(date of death unknown)
Alumnus and Teacher of the Ontario Institution for the Deaf and Dumb, now Known as Sir James Whitney School for the Deaf.

MARY BULL was born with normal hearing to hearing parents, William and Joanna Bull, who had emigrated from England, and were farming at Berlin, Ontario, in the County of Waterloo at the time of her birth. As a teenager, Mary lost her hearing rather traumatically after being afflicted with a severe cold. The loss was nearly total and neither the local family doctor nor the Toronto specialist whom her parents consulted, was able to reverse her Deafness. She could hear very loud noises such as claps of thunder and was sometimes aware of human voices, but was unable to discriminate speech.

It was not until several years later that her parents were advised to refer Mary to the Ontario Institution for the Deaf and Dumb at Belleville (now Sir James Whitney School for the Deaf). There, she was assessed by staff and was found to be a bright, inquisitive girl who displayed practical and academic talents. Mary was deemed to have good mathematics and writing skills and was placed in a class of students who came to the Institute when they were nearly grown up. She was taught individually for the most part, in order to prepare her for suitable employment.

She began teaching in 1882 and, in due course, Mary Bull became a full-fledged "Monitorial" teacher. It was in 1884 that she was granted a full-time position at the Ontario Institution, her alma mater. She was one of three teachers assigned to preside over the second-grade students. The other two were Mrs. Terrill and Miss Maybee, and all were considered highly successful in their profession. Their sixty pupils were taught notation, addition, subtraction, and a little grammar, but most of the focus, as was common in all schools for the Deaf during that era, was on the development of speech and lipreading skills, with little regard for the many other subjects being taught to the students' hearing counterparts in public schools.

During her tenure at the Ontario Institution, Mary's supervisor was Robert Mathison, who took the title of superintendent rather than principal.

He had no experience with education, nor with the Deaf, but was popular and well respected by his colleagues and Ontario's Deaf Community. Many of the "Monitorial" teachers at the Institution would have attended Gallaudet College to become properly qualified, but were denied funding because of government concern as to who would employ them. Mary Bull continued her work at the school until 1920, after having spent nearly fifty years there as a pupil and staff member. Regrettably, no information regarding her death is known.

CAISSIE (CLAWSON), Mary Lou

1958–
Flower Arranger, Book Repairer, and Inductee to the Council of the Blind's "Book of Fame."

MARY LOU CLAWSON was born Deaf to hearing parents in Antigonish, Nova Scotia. She had a considerable vision loss at birth as well. After several corneal surgeries, she became Deaf-Blind in 1978 at the age of twenty. She has no known Deaf relatives but her husband, Kenneth Caissie, is a Deaf man from Bathurst, New Brunswick. Kenneth has a peripheral vision loss and, though his sight is narrowed, he retains partial vision. Mary Lou and Kenneth live in Halifax, Nova Scotia.

Mary Lou's education began in day classes for Deaf children in Halifax. She then briefly attended the Interprovincial School for the Deaf in Amherst, Nova Scotia, and the Montréal Oral School for the Deaf. Despite her failing vision, she worked for some time as a flower arranger, at which she excelled. As her vision worsened, she attended a CNIB training program in Saint John, New Brunswick. There, in addition to learning how to read and write Braille, she acquired orientation and mobility skills, and was taught such life skills as getting around the city without a guide, shopping, handling money, and communicating by using the British two-hand alphabet.

In 1980 she tried to learn to operate an OPTICON, but decided it was not for her. She explored various careers at the Atlantic Technological Vocational Centre and enjoyed being there with her Deaf friends. In the summer of 1981 she attended the Lake Joseph Camp in Ontario for Deaf and Deaf-Blind people. It was her first contact with other Deaf-Blind persons and inspired her to attend a New Brunswick camp as well.

In 1985, through a thirty-seven week CNIB/Silent Outreach (Deaf Employment Service)-sponsored Intervenors for Employment Project, Mary Lou was able to find permanent employment and come closer to enjoying the independence most people take for granted. Officials at Human Resources Development Canada (HRDC), which funded the project, were a little skeptical at first, but she learned to repair books at the Killam Library of Dalhousie University. When the library staff saw how capable she was at restoring and maintaining badly damaged and neglected old books, she was permanently hired, part-time, and continues to work there. In 1987 Mary Lou married Kenneth Caissie, a Deaf man who has Usher's Syndrome. They live in an apartment and wear pagers to alert them to all sounds. They manage well, with the assistance of intervenors thirty hours a week. They shop, do their own cooking, and participate socially. Mary Lou has developed the most amazing tactile skills and can identify different foods by weight, texture, and shape. She has battled with the provincial government for the right to have access to Deaf intervenors so she and her husband can be independent and enjoy social events.

Mary Lou is gregarious and outgoing and loves organized parties and church activities. She is fluent in all types of communication for the Deaf-Blind and can identify the signer by the feel of the hands and the style of signing. She is sensitive to the needs of others, and when a sighted person enters their apartment, she immediately turns on the lights.

Mary Lou is an active member of the Halifax Association of the Deaf, Society of Deaf and Hard of Hearing Nova Scotians, Canadian Council of the Blind, CNIB, and Canadian National Society of the Deaf-Blind. She has also served on the board of the Atlantic Ministry of the Deaf, then known as the Ecumenical

Ministry of the Deaf. She was the recipient of three very prestigious awards—one from the government of Nova Scotia on the thirty-ninth anniversary of the Universal Declaration of Human Rights in 1987; the second, in 1990, was the Nova Scotia League of Equal Opportunity Lifestyle Award; and in 1991, she was welcomed into the Council of the Blind's "Book of Fame." In each case, she was given recognition for her efforts, achievements, attitude, and determination.

In her leisure hours, Mary Lou enjoys corresponding with friends, either by mail or e-mail, reading Braille magazines, and playing cards and board games. Outdoors, she jogs, roller skates, and walks with her sighted guide. She also goes table bowling with Blind friends.

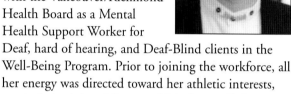

CAMERON, Marjorie Lillian

1960–
Outstanding Girl Guide, Avid Athlete, Champion Skier, Certified Ski Instructor, and Coach.

MARJORIE CAMERON was born with normal hearing in Chilliwack, British Columbia, the only daughter of hearing parents, Mavis and Donald Cameron, of Vernon, BC. She became Deaf at six months of age due to a high fever associated with pneumonia. She has two hearing brothers, Gray and Hu, who were her best friends and supporters when they were growing up in Vernon. Her family members were all enthusiastic skiers, and encouraged Marjorie to participate competitively from the age of fourteen. Her ex-husband, Russ Ward, who was also Deaf, was a competitive alpine skier. Marjorie and her elder brother, Gray, have taught many Deaf people to ski, and have been involved with several Canadian ski teams at World Winter Games for the Deaf. As a young girl, Marjorie was involved in the Girl Guides of Canada, and achieved the top award in 1975—the Canada Cord—as the only Deaf Guide in her troop. Marjorie currently makes her home in Vancouver with her two black and white kittens, both with normal hearing.

Although she has no known Deaf relatives, she does have a famous father—Lt. Colonel Donald Cameron (now deceased), was a great grandson of Sir Charles Tupper, one of Canada's Fathers of Confederation, and grandson of Major General Donald Cameron, commissioner of the Canadian Boundary. He was the Commanding Officer of the British Columbia Dragoons, who, at the age of twenty-two, was the youngest Major in the Canadian Army. He was in charge of taking the BC Dragoons' advance party overseas in 1941, and continued to serve with the regiment until 1944.

Marjorie was brought up orally, attending various mainstream public schools in Vernon, Chilliwack, Kelowna, and Vancouver, where the Oral Deaf program was incorporated into the regular curriculum. She has never attended a school for the Deaf and did not begin to learn ASL until she was nineteen years old and living in Vancouver. Although she has been employed in many fields, including data entry, picture framing, and sign making, she has worked for most of the past eight years with the Vancouver/Richmond Health Board as a Mental Health Support Worker for Deaf, hard of hearing, and Deaf-Blind clients in the Well-Being Program. Prior to joining the workforce, all her energy was directed toward her athletic interests, particularly alpine skiing, at which she excelled.

She began competitive skiing at the age of fourteen when she entered the 1975 North Okanagan Molstar alpine race for amateur girls and captured her first gold medal. Again, she was the only Deaf person among all the other competitors. She continued competing with hearing skiers for the next four years, receiving a gold medal at Vernon in 1976, third place on Mount Baldy in 1976, fourth place at Banff in 1976, second place in the North Okanagan Molstar Mixed Slalom in 1977, and first place in the Vernon area in 1979. Besides demonstrating her prowess as a skier, Marjorie also placed third in the North Okanagan Canoe Race in 1977, and first in a kayak race in 1978. In 1979 she obtained her Level 1 Ski Instructor Certificate from the Vernon Ski School. In the same year, she also experienced her first competition with Deaf skiers as a competitor at the 9th World Winter Games for the Deaf held in France, and came in fourth as an overall female alpine competitor. In 1980 she competed in the US Nationals for the Deaf at Steamboat, Colorado, winning first place as overall female alpine competitor. In the same year she also obtained her Ski Coach Certificate for Level 1 with a hearing group of trainees at Whistler, near Vancouver, and was named "Top British Columbia Deaf Athlete Between 1975 and 1980."

In 1981 Marjorie became a member of the Coaching Association of Canada, and took first place in the US World Cup at Big Sky, Montana, in 1982. She was the torchbearer at the Opening Ceremonies of the BC Summer Games held in Vernon in 1982, and was an invited, honoured guest at the retirement party for the well-known skier Dave Irwin, when he left the Canadian Olympic Ski Team that winter. At the 10th annual World Winter Games for the Deaf in Italy in 1983, she placed eighth among female alpine competitors, and in 1985, she came first in Disabled Skiing at Grouse Mountain, Vancouver. In addition, she won a cycling award, became a member of the Canadian Ski Instructor's Alliance, obtained her Ski Instructor's Certificate for Level II, and became the first Deaf alpine skier to qualify as a level II coach in the Canadian Ski Coaches' Federation. After a serious skiing accident which injured her left knee and necessitated several surgeries, she retired from competitive skiing.

Other recognitions Marjorie has received are the BC Association of the Deaf's Honours Achiever Award in 1998, and the Hughes Award for Access to Justice for her involvement in the production of the video *See You in Court*, that was jointly sponsored by the Law Courts Education Society of BC and the Greater Vancouver

Association of the Deaf (GVAD). She also received a plaque from the Western Institute for the Deaf and Hard of Hearing (WIDHH), recognizing her two years of service on their board of directors. Since 2001 she has been on the board of GVAD and the British Columbia Rainbow Alliance of the Deaf (BCRAD). In the Deaf Community, Marjorie enjoys such athletic activities as volleyball and slo-pitch with the Dogwood team.

In her winter leisure hours, Marjorie still does recreational skiing and loves outdoor camping and snow-shoeing. In the summer, she likes water-skiing, walking, cycling, canoeing, and kayaking. She works on her computer, collects First Nation and Eagle Art, and amuses her two resident kittens. She has three nephews—Tyler, Eric, and Sean—and one niece, Bryanne, all with normal hearing, who love to go snowboarding and downhill skiing. In 1999 Marjorie took snowboarding lessons at Vernon Silver Star with Bryanne and Sean, and continues to enjoy all the fun her family members have when they get together.

CAMPBELL (KUFFNER), Hilda Marian

1927–
Lifelong Educator and Advocate for the Deaf and Hard of Hearing.

HILDA KUFFNER was born in Europe and emigrated to Canada with her family when she was three years old. They settled in southern Saskatchewan, where some of her relatives still live today. She had five siblings—two sisters, Joanne and Stephanie (Ollie), both deceased, and three brothers, Philip (deceased), Bert, and Bill. She also has many nieces and nephews whom she appreciates and enjoys.

From birth, Hilda had a profound hearing loss. She battled her way through the hearing world but was over forty years of age before she could comfortably make the statement, "I am Deaf." This did not occur until she applied for a teaching position at the Alberta School for the Deaf (ASD) and was hired. Until then, she had struggled with the universal stigma attached to Deafness that prevented her from acknowledging the enormous difficulties she faced daily. She did not attend a school for the Deaf, nor any special program for Deaf students, and was not exposed to ASL until she taught at ASD.

She attended "Normal School" in Moose Jaw, Saskatchewan, which was one of only a few teacher training programs available to her at that time, and spent several years teaching in rural areas of the province while attending annual summer sessions at Regina College

to upgrade her teaching certificate and earn a Bachelor of Arts degree. She then took a position in Regina at Embury House, which was one of the earliest treatment centres in Canada for emotionally disturbed children, aged six to sixteen. There, she developed a keen interest in special needs education, which became her focus for the remainder of her teaching career.

Hilda was married to a hearing man, Donald Lorne Campbell (Don), and they had one daughter, Lawrie Patricia, now married to Hugh McKeith, and residing in Yellowknife, NWT, where she, too, is an educator. Lawrie was born in Winnipeg, Manitoba, where the Campbells resided for nearly twenty years. Hilda taught in West Kildonan, in the Norwood School Division, and at St. James Collegiate, at the junior and senior high school levels. She always chose to teach older students because she found young children virtually impossible to speechread. Meanwhile, she attended summer sessions at the Universities of Manitoba and Winnipeg, taking courses to supplement her teaching credentials and to apply to a BA degree. Because no support services of any kind existed in those days, she had to manage by speechreading what the instructors said, borrowing notes from her fellow students and reading far more extensively than everyone else in her class.

Her husband accepted a transfer to Edmonton, Alberta, and, when they moved, Hilda immediately enrolled to take further courses at the University of Alberta to complete a BA degree in English. Sadly, they had only been in Edmonton a very short time before her husband suffered a fatal heart attack on Christmas Day 1970. Hilda then became a single parent to her daughter who was twelve years old at the time. She taught in Strathcona County and in the Sturgeon School Division while continuing to attend summer and evening sessions at the University of Alberta, earning a BA, BEd, and a Graduate Diploma in Special Education. By that time, coping with her Deafness in the classroom had become so stressful that she applied to the Alberta School for the Deaf for a teaching position and was hired.

Teaching at ASD opened a whole new world of culture and language, and Hilda's work there became the most challenging and rewarding of her forty-seven-year career as an educator. She completed a Master's degree in Educational Psychology with specialization in Deaf Education and attended many workshops, seminars, and special lectures related to Deafness, ASL, and the concept of bilingual and bicultural education for Deaf students. Due to respiratory problems, she retired at the age of sixty-two. She has never been idle, however, serving on many committees and boards in an advisory capacity and working with hard-of-hearing adults for years, teaching speechreading and strategies for coping with adult-onset hearing loss. She was also vice-president and president of the Edmonton Hard of Hearing Association for Adults (EHHAA) for many years. This organization is now a part of the Edmonton Branch of the Canadian Hard of Hearing Association (CHHA). Hilda was part of the team that compiled *The Canadian Dictionary of ASL* to be published by the University of Alberta Press, a project that has been ongoing for over twenty years.

In her leisure time, Hilda is a voracious reader. She has authored numerous articles and is an enthusiastic walker and fitness buff. She enjoys travelling, social activities, and keeping in touch with dozens of her former students and her vast network of friends, both by letter and email. She is proud of her daughter's achievements and enjoys a wonderful relationship with her. Hilda considers her family and friends her greatest assets.

CAPNER (McINNES), Corinna ("Cori")

1970–
Mother, Churchworker, Pastor's Wife, and Helpmate.

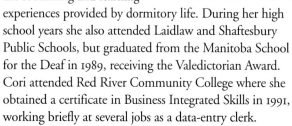

CORI MCINNES was born hearing in Winnipeg, Manitoba, and became Deaf at about three months of age, possibly due to ear inflammation or infection. It took almost two years of visiting various doctors across the country before she was diagnosed as Deaf. Meanwhile, she communicated with her family through home signs, gestures, and speechreading. Eventually, she was enrolled in a program to learn ASL, and spent a year at the Jericho Hill provincial School for the Deaf in Vancouver. Because the family moved around, she attended several other schools in Vancouver, Surrey, and New Westminster.

From 1977 to 1982, the family lived in Chetwynd in northern BC. Cori was sent to Dawson Creek where she attended Tremblay Public School in a program with another Deaf girl and teachers who used ASL. In August 1982 the family moved to Penticton, BC, where there was no suitable school program for Cori and she was frustrated and unhappy. They decided to move back to Manitoba and settled in the city of Brandon. In November 1982 Cori was enrolled at the Manitoba School for the Deaf in Winnipeg and a whole new world opened for her. She lived in residence for the next seven years and enjoyed the socializing and learning experiences provided by dormitory life. During her high school years she also attended Laidlaw and Shaftesbury Public Schools, but graduated from the Manitoba School for the Deaf in 1989, receiving the Valedictorian Award. Cori attended Red River Community College where she obtained a certificate in Business Integrated Skills in 1991, working briefly at several jobs as a data-entry clerk.

Cori met Edward Capner at the Manitoba School for the Deaf in 1985 and they dated for eight years before marrying in 1993. They have four children, Justin, Blake, Adrienne, and Shania. After spending several years in Minneapolis, Minnesota, while Edward completed his training for the church ministry, they live in Winnipeg where he is the pastor at Calvary Temple of the Deaf. Cori has held various jobs and now has a home-based Watkins business. She prefers to be at home with her children while they are growing up. Her goal, however, is to go back to school to obtain a university degree, although she is not yet certain what her area of study will be.

Cori's life as a mother of four young children and a pastor's wife is very busy, but has provided her with many opportunities to grow and expand her knowledge and experience. She enjoys reading her Bible and being involved in parish events. Her hobbies are knitting, crocheting, doing cross-stitch embroidery,

and baking. She has also always been interested in a variety of sports.

Her mother, stepfather, and two brothers now live in Red Deer, Alberta, so she sees them less often, but she keeps busy with so many new challenges that her days are filled to capacity. She has done some preaching from the pulpit, has taught Bible study classes and established a women's retreat for members of their congregation. Cori has many future goals in mind but has learned to rely on God's will for their fulfilment and to look to her personal saviour, Jesus Christ, for guidance. Meanwhile, she is happy raising her children and being a supportive helpmate to her husband.

CARLIN, Sheila Marie

1971–
Business Administrator, ASL Instructor, and Community Resource Development Officer.

SHEILA CARLIN was probably born Deaf, but her hearing loss was not diagnosed until she was fifteen months of age. Her parents, Eugene and Agnes Carlin, are hearing, as are her two older brothers, Brian and Kevin. There are no known Deaf relatives in the Carlin family, and it seems that Sheila was the first Deaf baby among them. She currently makes her home in Winnipeg, Manitoba where she was born and raised.

Because of her Deafness, Sheila's education began very early in life. At eighteen months, she was sent to a preschool operated by the Society for Crippled Children and Adults of Manitoba (now known as the Society for Manitobans with Disabilities). In keeping with the prevailing educational philosophy of the early 1970s, this early schooling involved speech therapy and the development of good listening skills, as well as constant encouragement to use her voice. Nevertheless, she was also introduced to Sign Language, although it was not ASL. Instead, Signing Exact English (SEE) was taught, based on oral syntax and grammar as well as English-language word order.

From kindergarten to the sixth grade, Sheila attended mainstream public schools in Winnipeg–Wellington, Gladstone, and Grosvenor. These schools offered special classes for Deaf students as well as an integrated program where Total Communication was used. This involved Deaf students being urged to interact with their hearing peers as much as possible. Subsequently, she was enrolled at the Manitoba School for the Deaf (MSD) for her junior and senior high school education. She also attended integrated classes at Laidlaw Junior High School and Shaftesbury High School while enrolled at MSD.

After graduating, Sheila obtained a Child Care Worker Certificate and spent the next two years working at Sign Talk Children's Centre which is housed in Deaf Centre Manitoba.

With strong support and encouragement from her family, she applied to Gallaudet University in Washington, BC, where she was accepted as a freshman in 1993. Her intention was to become a teacher of the Deaf, but when she entered university, she took a part-time job at a restaurant-bar called The Abbey. Because she enjoyed the work so much, it made her consider changing the focus of her program from teaching to business administration. She started in an entry-level position, but was soon promoted to supervisor and then manager. In her senior year at Gallaudet, she left The Abbey and took an administrative position as an auxiliary services liaison officer with Campus Auxiliary Services. In 1999 she graduated with a Bachelor of Science degree in Business Administration.

Sheila then returned home to Winnipeg and entered the workforce there, holding more than one administrative position at Deaf Centre Manitoba and the Catholic Church of the Deaf. She has also been an ASL intsructor in the Interpreter Training Program at Red River Community College and has taught ASL classes at Deaf Centre Manitoba. At present, she is employed as a community resource development officer for the Canadian Association of the Deaf and the board of directors at Deaf Centre Manitoba.

Sheila's hobbies and interests include collecting movies, reading books, and playing several sports.

CHAFFEY-JOHNSON, Rosalind Grace

1966–
Residential Counsellor-Liaison and Food/Nutrition Specialist.

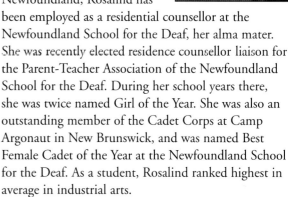

ROSALIND CHAFFEY was born Deaf to hearing parents in Corner Brook, Newfoundland. The cause of her Deafness is unknown but is likely hereditary because she has a Deaf brother, Anthony, and nine Deaf cousins. Her husband, Bryan V. Johnson, is Deaf, and they have a hearing daughter, Petra. Like Rosalind, Bryan is a graduate of Gallaudet University and is currently a staff member at the Newfoundland School for the Deaf in St. John's. He is a former director of the Canadian Association of the Deaf, former president of the Newfoundland Deaf Sports Association, current president of the Newfoundland Coordinating Council on Deafness, current sports director of the Newfoundland and Labrador Association of the Deaf, and host chairperson of the Deaf Canada Conference (DCC) 2002. Rosalind, Bryan, and Petra currently make their home in St. John's, Newfoundland.

Rosalind has a well-known hearing relative—her uncle Bud Hulan is a research scientist in nutrition, a professor at Memorial University of Newfoundland, a guest lecturer across Europe, and Liberal Minister of Agriculture, Food, and Fisheries for the government of Newfoundland and Labrador.

Rosalind was educated at the Newfoundland School for the Deaf in St. John's from 1971 to 1985. When she graduated, she attended the Gallaudet Alternative Preparatory Program in London, Ontario, for one year before entering Gallaudet University in Washington, BC, in 1986. She graduated with a Bachelor of Science degree in Food and Nutrition in 1993.

Since returning to Newfoundland, Rosalind has been employed as a residential counsellor at the Newfoundland School for the Deaf, her alma mater. She was recently elected residence counsellor liaison for the Parent-Teacher Association of the Newfoundland School for the Deaf. During her school years there, she was twice named Girl of the Year. She was also an outstanding member of the Cadet Corps at Camp Argonaut in New Brunswick, and was named Best Female Cadet of the Year at the Newfoundland School for the Deaf. As a student, Rosalind ranked highest in average in industrial arts.

She is involved in the local Deaf Community and she and Bryan participate in all its activities. She is also a member of the Delta Epsilon Sorority. While attending Gallaudet College (now Gallaudet University), she worked in the library, and at The Abbey, as well as being a residence assistant. In her leisure time, Rosalind enjoys cooking, reading, hiking, and doing needlepoint and tole painting. She likes to travel, especially to visit relatives.

CHAIKOWSKI (LALIBERTE), Marjorie Lorraine

1925–
Dedicated Housewife and Devoted Mother of Three.

MARJORIE LALIBERTE was born Deaf into a hearing family in Kenora, Ontario. She has two well known Deaf daughters, Rita Bomak and Susan Tebow, who are both profiled elsewhere in this book. Marjorie was also married to a Deaf man, Joseph Chaikowski. They had three children, a hearing son, Randy Chaikowski, and their two Deaf daughters, Sue and Rita, both noted curlers who have often competed at the national level in the Canadian Deaf Curling Championships. Marjorie is proud of her children and has seven hearing grandchildren whom she adores. Sadly, Joseph passed away in 1998, the year of their fifty-third wedding anniversary. They lived in Winnipeg, Manitoba, throughout their marriage, and Marjorie still resides there.

She attended the Ontario School for the Deaf, now Sir James Whitney School, in Belleville from 1932 to 1940. Despite incidents of abuse and educational neglect during the first four years, she has many good memories of her schooling in Belleville, particularly the lasting friendships she established and the opportunity to become fluent in ASL. In 1936 she was placed in a different program and her life changed dramatically. When the program closed in 1940, she returned home to Kenora and lived with her parents.

One summer, her parents took her to Winnipeg to visit her sister, and there she met her future husband,

Joseph Chaikowski, a Deaf man who worked at MacDonald Industries. They were married on 2 June 1945 and had fifty-three wonderfully happy years together. Marjorie was a splendid housekeeper throughout their marriage and a warm and loving mother to their three fine children.

She has been a member of the Winnipeg Community Centre of the Deaf since 1944, and has served as the centre's chairperson for the Women's Auxiliary Annual Tea and Bazaar. She also supports many other organizations and agencies of the Deaf in Winnipeg.

During her leisure time, Marjorie keeps herself busy with her many different interests and hobbies. She likes to go bowling with her Deaf friends and to play cards at the Deaf Seniors' Club. Most of all, though, she loves to watch curling, and tries to attend the Canadian Deaf Curling Championships every year to watch the games, particularly when her daughters, Sue and Rita, are competing.

CHAMPAGNE, Jeannette Laura

1956–
Therapeutic Youth Worker, Parent Aide, and ASL Instructor.

JEANNETTE CHAMPAGNE was born Deaf, an only girl among six siblings in a hearing family, in Edmonton, Alberta. Her youngest brother, Paul, is hard of hearing but, with the use of a hearing-aid, is fluent in spoken language. When Paul and Jeannette communicate, they rely mainly on speechreading. Jeannette spent most of her childhood growing up on a farm, as did her brothers. At the age of six she was enrolled in a special oral class where she mastered speech and auditory skills with the use of a hearing aid. She also attended another rural public school for a while before spending her teen years at the Alberta provincial School for the Deaf (ASD). Jeannette's hearing brother's wife, Janette, now resides in Victoria, BC, but was an ASL interpreter for the Deaf for about eight years. Her first few years as an interpreter were spent in Edmonton, Alberta, before she and her family moved to BC. Prior to her career, she was trained at Grant MacEwan College in Edmonton in 1990.

In 1974, after graduating from ASD, Jeannette participated in the Miss Deaf Canada Pageant and was chosen as first runner-up. In 1975 she entered Alberta College for two years of upgrading before enrolling at Gallaudet College (now University) in Washington, BC. After one year at Gallaudet, she put her education and career on hold while she married and became the mother of three fine sons—Leigh, Jason, and Mark—who are now all adults. When she was a young mother, she was diagnosed with encephalitis, a severe and sometimes fatal inflammation of the brain. Her recovery period lasted almost ten years. For part of that time, the family lived in the BC interior.

When her sons were older and she had fully regained her health, Jeannette was finally able to resume her education, acquiring a diploma in Social Work from Grant MacEwan Community College in Edmonton in 2000. Her training included two practicums, one of which she served at ASD, her alma mater. Her employment record has been varied—from Edmonton's Family Centre as a parent-aide and therapeutic youth worker, to providing enhancement of communication skills for Deaf parents of hearing children and hearing parents of Deaf children. In addition, Jeannette has worked at the Loseca Foundation in St. Albert, Alberta, and has earned recognition for her many volunteer commitments to Family Services, the Young Offenders' Centre, and the Alberta Association of the Disabled.

She is currently employed by the Family Centre, which offers a specialized service for the Deaf and hard of hearing. She also teaches ASL and Deaf Culture. In her free time, Jeannette enjoys reading, horticulture, outdoor activities such as camping, and sports. Above all, she loves to socialize and travel.

CHMIEL, Maryann Patricia

1953–
Canadian Theatre of the Deaf Performer and Residential Counsellor.

MARYANN CHMIEL was born hearing but became Deaf at the age of six months. She currently lives in St. Catherines, Ontario, with William H. Whyte (Bill), who is Deaf, and Bill's two daughters, Aimee and Ashleigh, who are both Deaf. Aimee hopes to pursue graduate studies at Gallaudet University in Washington, BC, and Ashleigh is at present a high school student.

Maryann attended the Ontario provincial School for the Deaf in Belleville from 1959 to 1966 before transferring to the newly opened provincial school in Milton (now known as the E.C. Drury School). After graduating she attended Gallaudet University for four years, majoring in Social Work, but was unable to complete her degree because of her commitment at that time to the Canadian Theatre of the Deaf.

Maryann was the first female performer in the first Canadian Theatre of the Deaf which was established in Vancouver, British Columbia, in the fall of 1976. She participated in its successful tour under the aegis of a Canada Works Project in 1977–78, when the company performed throughout the province of British Columbia. She was also the first Miss Deaf Ontario to compete in the Miss Deaf Canada Pageant in which she became the second runner-up in Vancouver in 1976.

Besides her work in Deaf theatre, Maryann has held several positions, working for the Vancouver Stock Exchange and at the Woodlands Institute for the Mentally Challenged. At present, she is employed as a residential counsellor at the E.C. Drury School for the Deaf, where she has been working with elementary school girls for the past ten years.

Maryann is an active member of the Deaf Community in St. Catharines and is currently the secretary of the Niagara Association of the Deaf.

CHOVAZ MCKINNON, Cathy Jean

1960–
First and Only Deaf Clinical Psychologist in Canada, Registered Nurse, Researcher, Presenter, and Published Author.

CATHY CHOVAZ was born hearing in Hamilton, Ontario, but became Deaf at the age of twenty-five. She has no known Deaf relatives. Cathy and her hearing husband, Scott McKinnon, have two hearing children, Emma and Aaron, whom they adopted in Romania. They currently make their home in London, Ontario.

Cathy was educated in mainstream public schools and attended the University of Western Ontario where she acquired three degrees: BScN, MEd, and PhD. She became the first and is still the only Deaf practicing clinical psychologist in Canada, and works exclusively with Deaf and hard-of-hearing clients. She presently consults to the Robarts School for the Deaf in London and has a small private practice.

Cathy has written and collaborated on numerous publications, journal articles, and abstracts. She is also in popular demand as a speaker and has presented many talks to a wide spectrum of audiences. She has been a manuscript reviewer and holds membership in several prestigious organizations: the London Psychological Association, the Canadian Psychological Association, the Canadian Hearing Society, the Council for Exceptional Children, and the Ontario Council for Mental Health and Deafness.

Cathy contends that mental health concerns present differently with Deaf persons than hearing people, possibly related to the fact that their social and environmental triggers differ from those of their hearing counterparts. Social isolation, lack of public understanding, and the many barriers to effective care and treatment may be contributing factors. There is still a considerable sense of mistrust among members of the Deaf Community regarding mental health issues. All of these circumstances make Cathy's work both sensitive and challenging.

She does not consider herself outstanding in any way and is grateful for the support and encouragement she received from a wide network of family and friends who helped her through difficult times while she battled serious illness. She also draws strength and hope from her abiding faith. She considers herself a most fortunate woman to have such a wonderful husband and two beautiful, delightful children who are the true focus of her life.

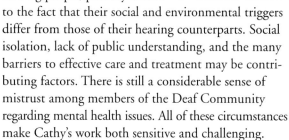

CHRISTENBERRY (PERKINS), Margaret Sarah

1932–
Typist, Word Processor, World Traveller, and Dedicated Church Worker.

MARGARET PERKINS was born Deaf to hearing parents at Henribourg, Saskatchewan, where she grew up on a farm. She was the third child in the family. Her hearing brother, Jack, lives in Nanaimo, British Columbia, and a Deaf sister, Julia, lives in Regina, Saskatchewan. She was married to a Deaf man, Robert Christenberry, an American fellow traveller whom she met on an overseas flight from New York to Copenhagen when she attended the Olympics for the Deaf in Helsinki, Finland, in 1961. She then took a conducted tour of ten countries in Europe with a group of thirty-nine people.

Margaret's formal education began when she was seven years old and her parents sent her to the Saskatchewan School for the Deaf in Saskatoon (SSD) in 1939. She recalls that her first teacher was Miss Molland and that Miss Melaven, later Mrs. Waleck, was her second teacher. One of her most vivid recollections of her years at SSD is the play they produced, *Snow White and the Seven Dwarfs*, for a Christmas concert. Margaret recalls wearing a bear costume and a mask for her role, and remembers fondly that Joyce Thompson was a perfect Snow White. Evidently, Emily Paulson was the talented creator of all the wonderful masks the students wore in the play. Margaret also recalls that Clare Hume was superintendent of SSD at the time of her graduation in 1951. She received an SSD senior ring in her last year, 1950–51.

After graduating, Margaret entered the workforce and found employment with the Early Mailing Service in Saskatoon, where she did typing and duplicating for three years. She then worked in the office at University Hospital in Saskatoon for the next ten years.

She and Robert Christenberry were married in St. James Anglican Church in Saskatoon on 24 June 1963 and made their first home in Santa Clara, California. Margaret learned to drive and took employment with the General Electric Company as a technical typist, switching to word processing when that technology came into use. In 1974 they bought their first home in San José, and this made it easier for her to commute to her job by car. Robert, who worked with IBM, was transferred to Charlotte, North Carolina, and they moved east in 1978. In 1981, Robert's mother died and they moved back to the west coast, where the climate suited them better, and lived in his mother's home in San Francisco. Margaret secured employment with IBM as a word processor in downtown San Francisco, where she worked for ten years until her retirement in 1990.

While Margaret lived and worked in Saskatoon, she was very much involved in the life of the Deaf Community there, particularly in the Western Canadian Association of the Deaf (WCAD). She assisted with its newsletter, *WCAD News*, and wrote a regular news column for the Saskatoon Association of the Deaf, reporting on their social, recreational, and political activities. She was considered a marvelous organizer of social events such as parties, box socials, whist drives, and unique fundraisers.

After their marriage, Margaret and Robert travelled extensively in Europe, Hawaii, Japan, and, of course, Canada, where she faithfully visited her parents every summer. Her most recent Canadian trip took her to the west coast in August 2001. Sadly, Robert passed away in November 1993 after several years of illness. Margaret keeps busy with her house and yard work and is a devoted member of her church, serving as its treasurer for twelve years. She also attends activities at the Deaf Seniors' Centre and does volunteer visiting with lonely, shut-in Deaf seniors, taking them out to lunches. This charming, vibrant woman is affectionately remembered by many of her Saskatchewan peers who are now scattered across the nation.

CHRISTIE (STEPHENSON), Rachel Madeleine

1897–1977
First Female President of the Western Canada Association of the Deaf.

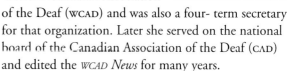

RACHEL STEPHENSON, who preferred to be called "Rae," was born in Saskatoon eight years before Saskatchewan became a province. She became Deaf at the age of six, after a series of bad colds and a serious case of mumps. She received her schooling at the Manitoba Institution for the Education of the Deaf and Dumb (1908 to 1913) in Winnipeg and at the Kendall School (1913 and 1914) in Washington, BC, before entering Gallaudet College. A year later she left Washington and returned home, where she enrolled at the University of Saskatchewan in Saskatoon to earn the required qualifications to become a teacher. After completing her degree in 1918, she taught for one year at the Manitoba School for the Deaf.

In 1921 Rae married a hearing man, Roy Christie, from Fredericton, New Brunswick. Roy had a BSc degree in forestry so the couple moved often, living on a number of forest reserves, including Hudson Bay, Big River, and Meadow Lake in northern Saskatchewan. After nearly thirty years of nomadic life in remote areas, the Christies finally settled in Prince Albert.

Living in an urban area for the first time in her married life enabled Rae to become involved in the Deaf Community as well as in patriotic and charitable organizations with hearing people. Her husband was promoted to the position of director of forestry for the Saskatchewan Department of Natural Resources and Rae immersed herself in community activities. She joined the IODE, the Royal Canadian Legion, the

Canadian Red Cross Society, and the McDermid Scholarship Foundation.

In the Deaf Community, she was the first woman to be elected president of the Western Canadian Association of the Deaf (WCAD) and was also a four- term secretary for that organization. Later she served on the national board of the Canadian Association of the Deaf (CAD) and edited the *WCAD News* for many years.

Roy Christie retired from his work in 1956 but, just five days after doing so, he died suddenly. There was nothing to keep Rae in Prince Albert so she moved to Winnipeg where there was a larger Deaf Community. She became very active in the Church of the Deaf, the Winnipeg Community Centre of the Deaf, the annual campaigns for the March of Dimes, and the Canadian Legion's Women's Auxiliary. Although she was kept very busy with these organizations, she found time to go snow-shoeing and to play tennis, football, and hockey. She was also an avid reader and sports fan.

When the Kiwanis Centre of the Deaf opened in 1975 (now renamed Deaf Centre Manitoba), Rae Christie was the first Deaf senior to become a resident. Seventeen months later, on 28 April 1977, she died peacefully in St. Boniface Hospital at the age of eighty. This versatile and interesting woman was respected by everyone, both Deaf and hearing, who knew about her life and work.

COGGINS (KNIGHT), Paula Joan

1971–
Student Assistant and Dormitory Counsellor.

PAULA KNIGHT was born hearing to hearing parents in St. John's, Newfoundland. She became Deaf at the age of two years due to illness. Paula has four Deaf cousins, but no other known Deaf relatives. Her husband, Curtis Coggins, a talented basketball player and computer expert, is Deaf. Paula and Curtis currently make their home in Mount Pearl, Newfoundland. Paula's mother, now deceased, was employed as a utility worker, switchboard operator, and food services worker for ten years at the Newfoundland School for the Deaf in St. John's.

Paula attended the Newfoundland School for the Deaf from 1974 to 1990. When she graduated she

enrolled at the National Technical Institute for the Deaf (NTID), a college of the Rochester Institute of Technology in Rochester, New York. When she began her studies there in 1990, she was one of the first four Canadian students to attend NTID. The other three were Lynn Winklemairer, Tammy Vaters, and Joanna Karp. In 1991 Paula decided to go to Gallaudet University in Washington, BC, to pursue an undergraduate degree. She graduated from Gallaudet in 1998 with a Bachelor of Science degree in Accounting.

At present, Paula works at the Newfoundland School for the Deaf. During the day she is a part-time student assistant and also works the night shift and some weekends as a part-time dormitory counsellor.

As a high school student, Paula excelled in mathematics and was the recipient of the Sir Michael and Lady Cashin Mathematics Award in 1987, 1988, 1989, and 1990. In 1989 she was selected as Deaf Female of the Year by the Newfoundland and Labrador Association of the Deaf. When she graduated in 1990, the Newfoundland School for the Deaf named her Outstanding Graduate.

Paula and Curtis were married on 23 June 2001. During her spare time, Paula enjoys reading novels, shopping, renting movies, and socializing with friends. Meanwhile, she is also pursuing her goal of becoming a teacher of the Deaf by investigating possible graduate study courses.

COLDWELL (JONES), Patricia Diana

1975–
Dedicated Army Cadet, Outstanding Athlete, Woodworker, and Skilled Embroiderer.

PATRICIA JONES was born Deaf to hearing parents in Corner Brook, Newfoundland. She is married to a Deaf man, Timothy Coldwell, from Gaspereau in the Annapolis Valley in Nova Scotia. Timothy has a Deaf cousin, but they have no other known Deaf relatives. After living for a few years in the Annapolis Valley, they now make their home in Halifax.

When she was in school, Patricia was active in Army Cadets and in many sports. In 1989 she attended the Canadian Foresters' Games in Vancouver and won the Best Female Athlete Award. She had joined the Army Cadet Corps while attending the Newfoundland School for the Deaf in St. John's. By 1994 she had attained the rank of Warrant Officer. In 1992 she received the Cadets' Merit of Excellence Award and, in 1993, the Best Senior Cadet Award. In 1994 she was one of the first six Deaf cadets who received the Duke of Edinburgh Award for Young Canadian Challenge Awards at the bronze level. The other five recipients were Joanne Dillon, Tammy Morgan, Loralee Butt, Deanna Emberley, and Donny Crocker.

She was also one of first four Deaf cadets to attend a six-week boot camp at Camp Argonaut in Gagetown, New Brunswick, in 1993. The other three were Deanna Emberley, Loralee Butt, and Donny Crocker. Prior to this, Deaf cadets had attended a two-week boot camp at Camp Argonaut in 1988, 1989, and 1990. Over the years, more than 240 Deaf cadets reaped the benefits of the Cadet program and many have gone on to leadership roles elsewhere. In 1988 Thomas Wiseman, a former cadet, became the first Deaf Civilian Instructor (CI) and Doreen Fowler became the first female cadet Commanding Officer. Patricia's cadet experience taught her many valuable lessons and provided her with an excellent background in life and leadership skills.

Following her graduation from the Newfoundland School for the Deaf, Patricia entered the Atlantic Technological Vocational Centre (ATVC) in Amherst, Nova Scotia, to take up a trade. She and a black Deaf woman were the first two Deaf females to enrol in a two-year carpentry program. When ATVC closed in 1995, they transferred to the Halifax campus of Nova Scotia Community College to complete their training. They were taught by a Deaf instructor, Mike Perrier, who is an outstanding carpenter. Patricia had always loved working with wood and had helped her brother-in-law build a house. She has also assisted her father-in-law in making wooden ironing boards, wooden deck chairs, shelves, and tables. After acquiring her carpentry certificate, Patricia had two short-term jobs in woodworking, but soon came to realize that such positions were scarce.

To earn a decent living, she took employment as an intervenor for a Deaf–Blind person. Later she found a job as an embroidery operator and continues to enjoy her work in that field. She has an unerring eye for details.

Patricia continues to be active in baseball, floor hockey, badminton, skiing, camping, and curling. She creates wood crafts as a hobby and in her leisure hours corresponds with her friends by mail and e-mail, surfs the Internet, and enjoys attending events in the Deaf Community. She hopes to study more carpentry, her first love, in the near future.

COLLINS (HAYDEN), Audrey Idella

1945–1998
Food-Service Worker and Loyal Member of the Deaf Community.

AUDREY HAYDEN was born Deaf to hearing parents in Badger, Newfoundland, on 31 August 1945. She was married to a Deaf spouse, Donald Collins, a talented woodcrafter and avid hobbyist with antique cars and boats. They had two hearing children, a daughter, Sharon Pardy, and a son, Stanford Collins, as well as two hearing grandsons, Madison and Hayden. Audrey's Deaf sister, Lois Birley, lives in Winnipeg, Manitoba, and two of her four Deaf brothers, Robert and Waldo Hayden, are also in Winnipeg. The third brother, David Hayden, lives in Calgary, Alberta, and the fourth one, Maxwell Hayden, lives in Badger, Newfoundland. Sharon Pardy is an ASL interpreter in Wolfville, Nova Scotia, and her husband, Larry Pardy, is an armed forces veteran who is studying for the ministry at Acadia University in Nova Scotia. Larry was formerly a volunteer at the Newfoundland School for the Deaf and still does freelance interpreting. Stanford Collins was recently appointed as a sales/marketing consultant for Cellular Network Systems and his wife, Faith Ann Collins, is a student in the Faculty of Education at Memorial University of Newfoundland in St. John's. Audrey and Donald Collins resided in St. John's throughout their marriage and raised their family there.

Because there was no School for the Deaf in Newfoundland during her childhood, Audrey was sent to Montréal, to the MacKay School for the Deaf, when she was ten years old, remaining there from 1955 to 1961. She was then transferred to the Interprovincial School for the Deaf in Amherst, Nova Scotia, where she continued her education until she was seventeen years old.

On leaving school and joining the workforce, Audrey found employment as a food-service worker at the Newfoundland School for the Deaf, which had opened in Torbay in 1965. She worked there for about three years before taking time off to have her children and be a stay-at-home mother. She returned to work at the Newfoundland School for the Deaf in Torbay from 1976 until 1987, when it was moved to St. John's. Audrey's dedicated service to the school's food department continued until 1995, when she had to leave for medical reasons. She was granted a Public Service Award for her nineteen years and eight months of loyal dedication by the provincial government of Newfoundland and Labrador.

During her adult years, before her health failed, Audrey was a loyal and active member of the Newfoundland/Labrador Association of the Deaf (NLAD), volunteering her services whenever possible. She was also a faithful attendee of the monthly Deaf Bible study meetings.

Audrey was an easygoing, friendly woman who loved ASL humour and comedy. Whenever others teased or joked with her, she displayed a trademark blush, even though she enjoyed it immensely. She was well known in the Deaf Community for her knitting skills, and the many beautiful garments she created. One of her favourite pastimes was knitting baby blankets. She loved playing a game of Skipbo every second Wednesday evening with six other Deaf women and was a loyal best friend to Evelyn Philpott, with whom she attended Dingo games, Deaf adult birthday parties, bridal showers, and baby showers. She collected interesting recipes and loved to bake and cook. Her other interests were walking and shopping.

Sadly, Audrey passed away, as a result of cancer, shortly before her fifty-third birthday on 11 July 1998, surrounded by her loving family. Her memory will always be preserved by her wide network of peers in the Deaf Community of St. John's.

CONRAD, Hendrika ("Sis")

1923–1996
Farmer, Culinary Expert, Seamstress, and Skilled Craftswoman.

Born HENDRIKA VISSCHER in Lemelereveld, The Netherlands, she and her younger sister contracted severe cases of spinal meningitis as they travelled to Alberta in 1929 with their family. Sadly, only Hendrika survived and the illness left her profoundly Deaf. Thus, at the tender age of six, she faced multiple challenges as a Dutch-speaking immigrant in a predominantly English-speaking nation and as a Deaf child in a hearing community with a different culture.

For several years Hendrika attended public school with her brothers in the Edmonton area. At the age of eleven, on the recommendation of a school super-intendent, she was sent to residential schools for the Deaf, first to Winnipeg and then to Saskatoon. She went happily and was educated until she turned eighteen, when she reluctantly left school to assist her parents on their farm. Later she found employment with Great Western Garments (GWG) as a seamstress.

In 1948 Hendrika married Blair Conrad. The young couple settled in the agricultural community of Sangudo, northwest of Edmonton, where they farmed for the next twenty-eight years. There, they also raised their three hearing children—Verna, now a pharmacist; Patty, an ASL interpreter, writer, and former interpreter-educator; and Gerry, a farmer and meat cutter.

During her life on the farm, Hendrika acquired a well-deserved reputation for her baking, gardening,

sewing and craftwork. She was especially skilled at quilting and spent long hours lovingly creating beautiful and artistic quilted products which were displayed at local fairs and exhibitions. The Conrads won trophies three times for "Top Farm Family" at the Mayerthorpe Fair. Hendrika also won widespread recognition for her baked goods, garden produce, and needlework displays.

Her achievements have always been a source of pride for the Conrad family. She was an extraordinary wife and mother, with a gentle nature and cheerful disposition admired by all who knew her.

In 1976 Blair and Hendrika retired to Salmon Arm, BC, where they enjoyed being involved in the Deaf community. Sadly, in 1988 Hendrika was diagnosed with Alzheimer's disease. They returned to Alberta in 1989 to be closer to their family and Hendrika spent her final years in a Stony Plain nursing home. Blair lived nearby and he and the family visited her regularly. Her cheerful attitude and loving nature remained constant despite her illness. On 22 July 1996, Hendrika passed away and was laid to rest in Sangudo.

COOK (McPHAIL), Annie Lavina

1878–1959
Teacher and Pioneer in Deaf Education.

ANNIE MCPHAIL was a Deaf woman who pioneered in the education of Deaf children in Canada. Born Deaf near Paris, Ontario, to Scottish immigrants, Hugh and Annie McPhail, she was the youngest in a family of six—four brothers and one sister, who were all hearing. Later the family moved to Hamilton, Ontario, and Annie, who was by then eight years old, was enrolled at the Ontario Institution for the Deaf and Dumb (now Sir James Whitney School for the Deaf) in Belleville in 1886. She proved to be a very bright child and a model student and, in 1894, she graduated at the top of her class. She then spent another two years at the Fanwood School for the Deaf in New York to prepare for entrance to Gallaudet College. Eventually, she became one of the first two female Deaf Canadians to be enrolled at and graduate from

Gallaudet College, which is now known as Gallaudet University in Washington, BC. Annie graduated in 1903 with a Bachelor of Arts degree.

Her teaching career began in 1904 at the Oregon School for Deaf Mutes in Salem, where she prepared senior pupils for entrance to Gallaudet. Her students were the first graduates of the Salem school ever to attend Gallaudet College. By then, her family had moved from Hamilton to Buffalo, New York, and Annie returned there to be married to Joseph Reginald Cook, who was also an alumnus of the Belleville Institution, and a teacher at the Manitoba School for the Deaf.

Annie's teaching career continued for nearly five decades in two other schools. She spent most of her professional life in Canada, teaching in the province of Manitoba. After she was married, she and her husband both taught at the Manitoba Institution for the Education of the Deaf and Dumb in Winnipeg. It became the Manitoba School for the Deaf (MSD) in 1913 and Annie McPhail Cook continued to teach there until 1940, although her husband had passed away in 1918, at the age of fifty. Annie was one of four teachers who came to MSD from the Oregon School in Salem. The other three were Candace MacPhail, Augusta Spaight, and Lily Turriff (Adamson), all of whom were influential in promoting the use of Sign Language in educating the Deaf.

During World War II the Manitoba School was taken over by the RCAF as a wireless training school and most students were sent to other provinces to be educated. Those who were residents of Winnipeg were sent to local day classes for which the location was constantly being changed. Dissatisfied with this haphazard arrangement, Annie accepted a position at the Pennsylvania School for the Deaf where she remained for the last six years of her professional career, from 1945 to 1951.

While living and working in Winnipeg, Annie edited a small monthly newsletter for the younger pupils, which she called *The Junior Echo*. For ten years she was president of the Ladies' Aid Society of the Winnipeg Community Centre Association (WCCA), later known as the WCCA Ladies' Auxiliary. During the formation of the Winnipeg Community Centre for the Deaf (WCCD) in 1937, she was on the Building Committee and then served on the Board of Trustees for the rest of her days in Winnipeg.

She was the sixth Deaf educator to be employed at the Manitoba School for the Deaf and is remembered for her outstanding skills as a teacher, as well as her many years of tireless work for the Winnipeg Community Centre of the Deaf. She was an inspiration to all who knew her, particularly her students.

Annie (McPhail) Cook died in 1959 at the age of eighty-one after forty-six years as an educator. In 1958, Rupert J.D. Williams wrote that her success as a teacher of the Deaf was unquestionably linked to her signing skills, which she combined with speech training in order to give the pupils a better understanding of the material to be learned. Annie was loved and respected by all whose lives she touched.

When the Deaf Centre Manitoba (DCM) came into being, several rooms were named in honour of special people. The Cook Room, which constitutes the cafeteria and dining area, was named after Annie Lavina (McPhail) Cook as a lasting tribute to her memory.

COOKE (WONG), Rosalind May Han

1960–
Teacher and Proud-to-be-Deaf Chinese-Canadian Working Mother of Two.

ROSALIND WONG was born Deaf into a hearing Chinese-Canadian family in Vancouver, British Columbia. She has no known Deaf relatives, but her husband, Anthony William Cooke, is Deaf. They have two hearing children, Liam Anthony and Jade Ashleigh. Anthony is presently employed as a child and family therapist with PAH! Mental Health Services for Deaf and Hard of Hearing Children and Youth in Milton, Ontario. The family currently lives in Mississauga, Ontario.

Rosalind started school at age three in the Sunny Hill Oral Pre-School Program at the Vancouver Oral Centre, where oral communication was fostered. She was one of its first graduates in 1966. She then attended a series of six different elementary schools where communication methods varied, but the emphasis was mainly on speech and cued speech. Some schools had both mainstream and self-contained classes for Deaf children. For her high school education, Rosalind attended Kitsilano Secondary School where total communication was practised in conjunction with Pidgin Signed English. She graduated with diplomas from both Kitsilano and the Jericho Hill School for the Deaf, where she was valedictorian, in 1979. Rosalind then attended Gallaudet University in Washington, BC, where she earned a BSc degree in Recreation and Leisure Studies in 1984. She followed this up with a Master of Arts degree in Special Education in 1988 from Hampton University in Hampton, Virginia. She then took basic qualification courses to obtain an Ontario Teacher's Certificate in 1999.

Rosalind's employment history is interesting and varied. She has worn many different hats—working with both children and adults in various capacities. She has been a supervisor, a counsellor, a project worker, a tutor, a program planner and coordinator, and a peer advisor. She has also taught ASL, been a student/supply/

substitute teacher, served as an educational and community consultant, worked as an instructor and counsellor-trainer, and is presently a teacher of the Deaf at E.C. Drury School in Milton, Ontario. She is now a contented, well-adjusted woman after an early life of experiencing what she calls "triple oppression"—being Deaf in a hearing society, being Chinese in a white society, and being a woman in a male-dominated society.

Rosalind was an outstanding scholar and a top student in high school and college. Her name regularly appeared on Honour Rolls and Dean's Lists. She was chosen Miss Deaf British Columbia, Miss Congeniality, and Miss Deaf Canada runner-up in 1980 by the Canadian Cultural Society of the Deaf. She was in the first class that graduated in Recreation and Leisure Studies at Gallaudet University, and was in the first group to receive the Canadian Hearing Society's Management Equity Training in 1991.

Rosalind was also the only Deaf Chinese–Canadian teacher on the staff at E.C. Drury School for a period of three years, before a Deaf Chinese-Trinidadian teacher transferred from Robarts School in London, Ontario, to the school in Milton.

She is proud of both of the cultures she represents, and is close to her hearing parents, two sisters, and a brother. In 1993 she travelled to the Orient to learn as much as she could about her Asian heritage. As a child, she was sometimes ashamed of her background because there were no Deaf-Chinese professionals to look upon as role models. Her parents came from different districts of China and speak different dialects of Mandarin, so she is enriched with Chinese cultures. She believes that people of different backgrounds and cultures should be encouraged to be proud of their heritage and to strive for success.

COPELAND (MacEACHERN), Ethelene Sadie Ellen

1942–
Medical Technologist and First Female Gallaudet Graduate from Prince Edward Island.

ETHELENE MACEACHERN is the hearing daughter of the late Colin and Margaret (Campbell) MacEachern. She became Deaf at the age of four years due to spinal meningitis. She grew up in the rural community of New Argyle, Prince Edward Island. The only Deaf student in the area, she was educated at a one-room country school near her farming village. There was only one teacher who taught grades one to ten, usually with only one to three students in each grade. During the autumn and spring months, she walked a mile each way, with short-cuts through a neighbouring farm, and sometimes she got a ride with a neighbour or the rural mailman. During the winter, she rode in a horse-drawn sleigh to and from school. Often, she and her classmates would huddle around the wood stove to keep warm in the bitterly cold winters. Those days are now just memories as students are bussed to new schools, and the old schoolhouse is used as a vacation home by American residents.

Ethelene eventually took her grade eleven, twelve, and first-year college courses at Prince of Wales College (PWC) in Charlottetown from 1959 to 1962. In 1969 the college merged with St. Dunstan's University, becoming the University of Prince Edward Island. She relied on lipreading and took notes in class. She enrolled at Gallaudet College, now Gallaudet University, in Washington, BC, and graduated with a Bachelor of Arts degree in Biology and a minor in Chemistry. She learned Sign Language at Gallaudet, and was the first native Prince Edward Islander to graduate. She also took part-time studies at the George Washington University School of Cytotechnology. In 1966–67 Ethelene trained as a medical technologist at the School of Medical Technology, Franklin County Public Hospital, in Greenfield, Massachusetts.

In August 1967 she married Barry L. Copeland, a hard-of-hearing graduate from the Pennsylvania School for the Deaf in Philadelphia. They have three hearing daughters, Elizabeth, Christine, and Connie. The eldest, Elizabeth, is an elementary teacher of the Deaf at the Pennsylvania School for the Deaf, currently on a one-year leave of absence to teach in Costa Rica. Previously, she taught at the North Carolina School for the Deaf. Barry and Ethelene have three grandchildren.

Ethelene is employed as a medical technologist at Quest Diagnostics in Baltimore, Maryland, in the Flow Cytometry Department. Earlier, she spent thirteen years at home raising her children. She has been a medical technologist for twenty years.

For leisure, she enjoys reading, sewing, needlework, gardening, taking walks, Bible study, church activities, and travelling to Canada, Pennsylvania, and Virginia. Ethelene and Barry make their home in Columbia, Maryland, and have a Shih-tzu dog, Winnie, who serves as their faithful follower and doorbell alarm.

CRAIG (MURPHY), Noreen Elizabeth

1931–
Businesswoman, Sports Enthusiast, and Assistant Cottage Renovator.

NOREEN MURPHY was born Deaf to hearing parents, in Montréal, Québec. She has two Deaf brothers, Edward and Gordon, three hearing brothers, and a Deaf husband, William R. Craig, who is a builder, carpenter, and sheet-metal worker. They have one adult hearing son, Colin. The Craigs currently reside in St. Laurent, Québec. Colin obtained a degree from McGill University in Montréal as an electrical engineer, and has worked for Kraft General Foods in Montréal since graduation. He is married to Cinzia Girelli, whom he met at a curling club, in 1998, and they have a daughter, Alexandra, of whom Noreen and William are very proud grandparents.

Noreen was educated at the MacKay School for the Deaf in Montréal (now known as the MacKay Centre of the Deaf), while her Deaf brothers, Edward and Gordon, attended the French School for the Deaf. Edward passed away in 1979. Gordon is married to a French wife, Suzanne, and they have two adult hearing children. After leaving MacKay School, Noreen studied computers at work and acquired remarkable skills in this field. Noreen's career has been interesting and includes work in the business offices of several large, well-known corporations. Shortly after leaving MacKay School, Noreen was surprised when she was hired by the first company to which she applied, Liquid Carbon, where she spent the next seven years. Eager to try a new challenge, she applied to Charles Cusson Equipment where three other Deaf girls were already employed (one of them was a niece of the president, Charles Cusson), and she worked there for five years. She then became a stay-at-home mother for eight years. When Noreen returned to the workforce, she was hired by Nortel Networks, where she remained for twenty-two years until her retirement.

Noreen has always been a keen sportswoman and enjoys curling, bowling, and skiing. She is involved in the Deaf Community and her lengthy business career makes her an excellent role model for young Deaf women entering the workforce.

Every summer for the past fifty years, Noreen has gone to a lovely summer cottage, "Bide-a-Wee," in the Laurentians, which has been in the Craig family for several generations and was inherited by Noreen's husband, William. Thanks to the hard work of their son Colin, the cottage has been modernized and renovated, but the installation of electricity is still to be done. Noreen keeps busy taking care of the garden and feeding all the beautiful birds that are attracted to the grounds. She and William cut wood for the fireplace, do painting, and other maintenance chores, but always have time to sit on their balcony and chat with their Deaf friends who visit them from all parts of Canada and the United States. They also enjoy travelling and have driven in their van throughout Canada and the US. Noreen says that office work was challenging but she works even harder in her retirement, helping William with renovations and the upkeep of their summer home.

Besides her sports activities in the Deaf Community, Noreen is involved in the Montréal Association of the Deaf, of which she and William are lifetime members. She attends almost every social event and has sung "O Canada" at most of them. She was a volunteer for the Canadian Cultural Society of the Deaf in 1979. Her hobbies are knitting, crocheting, and sewing. She has recently become a computer-owner and looks forward to surfing the Internet.

CRAWFORD, Isabel Alice Hartley

1865–1961
Baptist Missionary, Artist, and Author.

ISABEL CRAWFORD was born hearing into a devout Baptist family at Cheltenham, Ontario, the fourth and last child of a Scottish father, John Crawford, and an Irish mother, Louisa Crawford. She did not become Deaf until her late teens, as a result of a severe and lengthy illness. Her father, a Baptist minister, had emigrated to Canada in the early 1860s, and worked in a succession of parishes and Baptist colleges in Canada and North Dakota. Her mother, a recognized scholar, supervised Isabel's education. She spent her childhood surrounded by the gospel and culture, and helped her father in his church work. At the age of ten she was already expressing a keen interest in becoming a missionary. When she was eleven, she began to teach Sunday school classes.

Although she never formally graduated from high school, Isabel, under the tutelage of her parents, developed an agile mind and a quick, biting wit. Schooled at home and in her father's colleges, she was exposed to the best literature. The family's home was filled with books, art, and music, intellectual conversation, and a devotion to the church that played a significant role in shaping her personality and her goals in life. At the age of eighteen, Isabel moved with her family to Rapid City, Manitoba, where her father was serving a stint at the Prairie Baptist College. There, she became seriously ill and had to spend six months in bed. The records indicate that she was stricken with consumption. In accordance with her doctor's orders, she apparently consumed nothing but milk and the anti-malarial drug, quinine. Isabel believed that it was the milk that saved her life, the quinine that destroyed her hearing, and the after-effects of the consumption that plagued her health for the rest of her life. Although she was not an invalid, her health was never robust and on several occasions she checked herself into a sanatorium.

When Isabel recovered she spent the next six years with her family in North Dakota, teaching art classes and selling her paintings to raise money for her tuition to be trained as a missionary. Finally, when she had saved the required $300 fee, she entered the Baptist Missionary School in Chicago in 1891 and spent two years preparing for missionary service, graduating in 1893. She was then assigned by the Women's American Baptist Home Mission Society to minister to the Kiowa-Comanche-Apache Reservation in southwest Oklahoma. The reserve was considered one of the most important in the country because it was created by the 1867 Medicine Lodge Treaty and designated to receive "civilizing" through Christianity. Indeed, the plan was to make the Indian people living there indistinguishable from their white counterparts, except for the colour of their skin. At first she was strongly opposed to this assignment because it was a very difficult undertaking for her when she could neither speak nor hear their language and had to wear an acousticon into which the native people shouted. She constantly wore this device around her neck and referred to it as her "conversation tube." Before long, however, she learned to communicate in Indian Sign Language which most of the people understood.

Isabel began her missionary work at Elk Creek, but was later drawn to Saddle Mountain in the southeast part of Kiowa County, where the Kiowans referred to her as "Little Jesus Woman." She felt needed there, and a local mission society was formed for the purpose of establishing a church. She endured conditions that once again brought her to the edge of collapse, but in 1902 the cornerstone of the new church was laid. A television movie starring the Deaf Oscar-winning actor, Marlee Matlin, and depicting Isabel's Kiowan experiences, has been made under the title *Isabel Crawford of Saddle Mountain*.

Isabel remained with the Kiowans for fourteen years, teaching them to sew clothes, live in permanent houses, and grow crops and gardens. In 1906 she began travelling from one reservation to another in several states, preaching and teaching in speech and signs. She also returned to Canada and the northern United States to lecture.

Isabel learned to read lips and became quite proficient at it. In 1915 she wrote her first book, *Kiowa—A Story of a Blanket Indian Mission*, which was an account of her experiences among that tribe. She retired in 1930 and returned to Canada, settling in Grimsby, Ontario. There she lived with her two nieces while she wrote two more books, *A Jolly Journal* and *Joyful Journey*. When she died in a local nursing home in 1961, at the age of ninety-six, her remains were sent to Oklahoma to be interred in the Saddle Mountain Cemetery, as she had earlier promised the Kiowans, so that she could be near the people she loved. She was posthumously inducted into the Kiowa County Hall of Fame. What she and the Saddle Mountain Kiowans accomplished has become an integral part of a community-wide narrative of their history.

In 1998 the University of Nebraska Press published a book entitled *Kiowa: A Woman Missionary in Indian Territory*, based on Isabel Crawford's journal, with an introduction by Clyde Ellis, a noted authority on Oklahoma tribes. The book outlines her decade-long struggle to establish the Saddle Mountain Baptist Mission, which still exists. She and her assistant were the only white women at the isolated station in the Wichita Mountains, where their faith, endurance, and resourcefulness were tested daily. Her sensitivity to the history and culture of the Kiowan people was remarkable. To this day, Isabel Crawford is remembered with the greatest affection and kindness.

CRAWFORD (NAULT), Marie-Josée

1972–
Community Development Coordinator, Tutor, Residential Counsellor, Lifeguard, and Role Model.

MARIE-JOSÉE NAULT, known to her friends as MJ (or Josée), was born Deaf to hearing, French-speaking Acadian parents in Edmundston, New Brunswick. Her husband, Lee Crawford, is a wonderful hard-of-hearing man from Pictou County, Nova Scotia. They live in Dartmouth with their mini-dachshund, Oscar. MJ has no known Deaf relatives and the cause of her Deafness was never determined.

When she was a year old, her family moved to California, where her bilingual father was pursuing doctoral studies at the University of Southern California. When her Deafness was discovered, she was immediately sent to the renowned John Tracey Clinic in Los Angeles, where she was placed in an oral preschool program based on speech and speech reading, which was a challenging experience for her. The highlight of her stay was being photographed with the celebrated Hollywood couple, Robert Wagner and the now-deceased Natalie Wood, who were promoting the clinic's Women's Auxiliary at a fundraising event in 1975.

MJ's education path was never smooth nor simple. After a year in a primary public school in Sherbrooke, Québec, she was sent to the Montréal Oral School for the Deaf where she was dissatisfied with the program and unhappy with her boarding arrangements. As a result, she returned home to North Hatley, Québec, and attended a mainstream public school with the assistance of a resource person and tutor. Back in Edmundston, New Brunswick, for grades eleven and twelve, MJ relied on help from her family and an itinerant teacher who saw her every two weeks. Nevertheless, she did well, and graduated with several scholarships toward a university education.

Throughout her school life, MJ was exposed to a variety of experiences that had a profound impact on her developing personality. She was happily immersed in ASL and Deaf Culture when she attended a series of summer camps sponsored by the MacKay Centre. She also acquired a brief taste of Inuit culture through a five-day student-exchange project, which took her grade five/six class to Inukjuak, a village on the shore of Hudson's Bay, north of the 58th parallel. Another wonderful cultural experience was made possible through a later student exchange which took her grade eight class to Courtney, BC, on Vancouver Island and Expo '86 in Vancouver.

In a rather unusual step for a Deaf teenager, MJ took lifeguard training at the University of Sherbrooke in 1988, achieving the Bronze Cross and Bronze Medal. The course was given in French, so a good friend, who was also taking the course, helped to translate for MJ. It is quite likely that she was one of the first Deaf lifeguards in Québec. MJ worked as a lifeguard for three summers—one summer at a public pool and two summers at a camp sponsored by the Atlantic Ministry of the Deaf. She has proved to be a very capable and professional lifeguard with excellent leadership skills.

In 1991 MJ enrolled at Gallaudet University in Washington, BC, where she had further exposure to ASL and Deaf Culture that she valued greatly. She was also inspired by the *Bison Song*, which was sung in ASL at the Gallaudet football games. A year later she transferred to Saint Mary's University in Halifax and learned to use an ASL interpreter for her classes there. It was not easy but her efforts paid off and she received a Bachelor of Arts degree in Sociology. She had the honour of reading the citation in ASL to Gallaudet University President I. King Jordan, who was presented with an honorary Doctorate. Since early childhood, MJ has dreamed of becoming a teacher of the Deaf, and that is still one of her goals for the future.

MJ's employment experiences have been eclectic. She worked as a residential counsellor with the Atlantic Provinces Special Education Authority (APSEA) in Halifax, for five years. She was also an intervenor for

Deaf–Blind adults. In 2001 she trained to become a community resource worker in a community development training project sponsored by the Canadian Association of the Deaf. Recently, she was hired as a community development coordinator with the Deafness Advocacy Association Nova Scotia (DAANS). She was involved in organizing a Deaf Parents' Support Group in Halifax and has worked as a tutor. MJ was recently accepted into the Bachelor of Social Work

(BSW) program at the Maritime School of Social Work, part of Dalhousie University, and began part-time study in the fall of 2001.

In her free time, MJ enjoys camping, watching movies, cycling, travelling, tole painting, rollerblading, golfing, attending concerts, and surfing the Internet. In view of her youth and ambition, there will likely be further exciting chapters in MJ's life story.

CRIPPS (STEPHENS), Joanne Selena

1954–
Published Author and Co-Author, Canadian Deaf Heritage Director, Advocate for Deaf Children, Collaborator for the Ladder Awards®, and Spokeswoman on Related Deaf Issues.

JOANNE STEPHENS was born Deaf to hearing parents in Markdale, Ontario. She has two known Deaf relatives—a first cousin, Marvin Ferris, and a great-uncle, Austin Trudgeon. Her husband, James Cripps, is also Deaf. They have two hearing children, Jason and Jeri, and make their home in Cambridge, Ontario. Joanne's hearing sister, Mossie Stephens, works with Deaf students as a residential counsellor.

Joanne received her early education at the Ontario School for the Deaf, now known as Sir James Whitney School, in Belleville, Ontario. Since graduating from high school at E.C. Drury School for the Deaf in Milton, Ontario, she has furthered her education by completing numerous courses of study at the University of Waterloo, Sheridan College, Conestoga College, Gallaudet University, Lougheed Business College, the Ontario Ministry of Education and Training, the Ontario Ministry of Community and Social Services for Professional Development, and Centennial College. The subjects covered in these courses ranged from English and early childhood education to business/accounting and cross-cultural mediation.

Her first employment was as a filing clerk. She went on to become a residential counsellor, as well as an ASL instructor in 1980, and advanced to ESL instructor, Deaf Culture consultant, coordinator of summer family immersion programs, advocate for Child and Family Services at the ministry level, employment system review task force participant, supervisor of residential counsellors, and director of the Canadian Deaf Heritage Project for the Preservation and Expansion of ASL Literature and Deaf Literature. This was under the auspices of the Canadian Cultural Society of the Deaf (CCSD), and included instituting

the first Ladder Awards® for Deaf storytellers, authors, and illustrators.

Joanne Cripps is best known for her involvement in the Deaf Community as a volunteer, and for the various publications she has authored and co-authored. As a volunteer, she has raised funds for such worthwhile projects as the Canadian Deaf Festival '98, served on many boards and committees, acted as a consultant for the Bell Relay Service, represented CCSD at a bilingual-bicultural Deaf education conference in Sweden, helped found a Deaf club in Kitchener, Ontario, presented workshops and lectures, and was an ambassador for Deaf Canada at the World Federation of the Deaf Conference in Brisbane, Australia.

As an author and collaborator, her published works include *Quiet Journey: Understanding the Rights of Deaf Children*, a first-person account of growing up Deaf, published in 2000 by Ginger Press, and highly recommended reading for everyone living and working with Deaf children; *American Sign Language Literature and Deaf Literature Development* (with Anita Small); a feature article in *Feliciter*, Vol. 45, No. 5 (1999), which describes the Canadian Deaf Heritage Project; *Strategies for Deaf Presenters* (with Helen Pizzacalla); *You and Your Deaf Child* (with the Ontario Association of the Deaf and the Ontario Cultural Society of the Deaf), a parent information kit; and *Cross-Cultural Mediation* (with Helen Pizzacalla), a conflict resolution program for the culturally Deaf; plus contributions to other journals and newsletters. The outgrowth of the first Ladder Awards®, launched on 27 October 1999, was the production of the first anthology of ASL stories by Deaf Canadians produced in Canada, called *River of Hands: ASL Stories*. The anthology is available in VHS and CD–ROM and includes a documentary tracing the process of telling stories in ASL, in written form and with illustrations. The Ladder Awards® also led to the first children's storybook published in Canada by Second Story Press, written and illustrated by Deaf Canadians, *River of Hands: Deaf Heritage Stories*. This publication was chosen as the Best Choice Book in Canada by the Canadian Children's Book Centre. Prior to the initiation of this project, there had been virtually no published ASL literature or Deaf literature for either Deaf or hearing families to read and enjoy, which was Joanne's primary reason for collaborating with Anita Small to create such materials. Their joint effort has been well received by the Deaf Community.

Many of Joanne's successful ventures have received prestigious recognition. She participated in a VISION TV program called *Skylight* and was subsequently interviewed by Shelagh Rogers on CBC radio. In 1998 she was the recipient of a Canadian Deaf Festival Certificate of Appreciation and, in 1994 as well as 1997, she was awarded certificates of appreciation by the Association of Visual Language Interpreters of Canada (AVLIC). In

1998 CCSD presented her with an Outstanding Contribution Award and she was inducted into the Deaf Hall of Fame in 2000. Her husband, Jim Cripps, is credited with naming the Bell Relay Service in 1986.

Joanne's hobbies and personal interests include reading, travelling, skiing, quilting, and enjoying outings with her family, whenever she can find time in her busy life. She does not view herself as an activist but as a pursuer of rights and justice for everyone in both the Deaf and hearing worlds. She contends that natural Sign Language and Deaf Culture are the birthright of every Deaf child and person. While conceding that there are barriers and problems, Joanne is adamant that every individual is not only responsible for his or her own growth but for that of the community as well.

She loves challenges, new ideas, and innovative approaches to centuries-old problems. After presenting a workshop with Anita Small, someone likened her to a "catfish" that cleanses its habitat from germs because she encourages Deaf people to heal themselves. She thinks that being labelled a catfish is not a bad thing.

CUMMINGS, Carla Marie

1956–
Park Sign Painter, Outstanding Athlete, and Skilled Craftswoman.

CARLA CUMMINGS was born Deaf to hearing parents, Edison and Elizabeth (Sharpe) Cummings, in Fredericton, New Brunswick. Her two sisters are Elaine and Corinne, and her three brothers are Edward, Billy, and Bobby. All members of her family are hearing. She also has two hearing daughters, Sharlene and Gloria Canning, whose father, Tommy Canning, is hard of hearing. She has no known Deaf relatives and currently makes her home in Nackawic, New Brunswick, with her younger daughter, Gloria, who has been in remission after a two-and-a-half-year battle with leukemia. Sharlene, her older daughter, lives in Fredericton. Her sister Elaine formerly taught at the Interprovincial School for the Deaf in Amherst, now known as the Atlantic Provinces Special Education Authority (APSEA), where Carla received her early schooling.

Carla began her education at what was then known as the Interprovincial School for the Deaf and remained there for nine years before transferring to Nackawic Junior High School in 1971. She had no interpreter but her sister Corinne, and later two good friends, tutored her. She was very active in sports and won the Female Athlete of the Year trophy in 1974. The following year she entered Gallaudet University in Washington, BC,

where she studied for a year and a half. Nearly twenty years later, she received her Genereral Educational Development (GED) certificate.

Carla's parents owned a motel and she worked for them for a while. After being employed at a summer job in 1976 as a utility worker at Mactaquac Provincial Park, she was one of three women hired for full-time work, and is now the only one of the three still employed there. Her duties consist mainly of maintenance chores around the various campsites in the park. She enjoys the independence and self-motivation the job provides. Carla feels that being outdoors doing physical work is infinitely superior to sitting at an office desk all day. In 1988 she was promoted to sign painter and is now required to draft and stencil each sign, router the letters or symbols, sand the sign, and, finally, paint it. When she is not working on signs, she mows the lawns and performs other duties such as dressing up in an Easter Bunny costume for the annual Easter egg hunt. She has now been with the park for more than twenty-five years.

Her activities in the Deaf Community include being treasurer of the Fredericton Association of the Deaf (FAD) for four years and serving as chairperson of the Eastern Bowling Association of the Deaf's (EBAD's) Annual Tournament in Fredericton in 1992 and again in 1998. She was sports chairperson for three conventions hosted by the Eastern Canada Association of the Deaf (ECAD), and her bowling team has won several EBAD championships. She was the recipient of a plaque from FAD, honouring her work as treasurer.

Carla is skilled at crafts and enjoys cross-stitching, crocheting, sewing, and knitting dolls. She is planning to set up a homepage for her family's genealogy on the Internet.

CUNDY, Linda Jean

1952–
Educator, Administrator, Consultant, Athlete, Deaf Interpreter, Drama Performer and Producer, and Enthusiastic Worker for the Deaf Community.

Born LINDA JEAN HATRAK in LaPorte, Indiana, into a three-generation Deaf family, this gifted American woman chose to become a Canadian citizen after she married her Deaf husband, Robert M. Cundy from Ontario. They met at Gallaudet University and have always shared many interests, particularly sports such as golf and tennis. Linda and Rob have three hearing children: Kira, Larissa, and Nicholas, and are host parents to a Deaf boy, Damian.

Although most of Linda's relatives are Deaf, she has a hearing sister, Daphne Craft, who was at one time an interpreter coordinator at Purdue University and is currently an active interpreter in northern Indiana, and a cousin, Janet Maxwell, who interpreted for the White House/Senate in Washington, BC. Linda was educated at the Indiana School for the Deaf, graduating in 1970 as the class valedictorian. She attended Gallaudet University for four years, majoring in English with a minor in psychology. In 1974 she graduated with a BA degree and was listed in *Who's Who in American Universities and Colleges*. She took further education courses at California State University at Northridge (1973) and at the University of Alberta in Edmonton, eventually earning a Master's degree in Deaf Education in 1988. In 1998 she participated in a seven-week summer session in the ASL Specialist Program at Western Maryland College.

Residing in Edmonton, Alberta, Linda and her husband were fellow teachers for many years at the Alberta School for the Deaf, where Rob still teaches. Linda's professional career began in 1976. Since then she has taught classes ranging from the elementary level to high school for twenty-one years. She also acted as vice-principal for two years and is currently employed as an educational consultant for the Deaf and hard of hearing in Northern Alberta, a job she loves. Both Linda and her husband Rob are very active in the Deaf community.

Besides her role as a devoted wife and mother, Linda has played a vital part in the life of the Deaf community in Edmonton and has served on many boards and committees at the local, provincial, and national levels. For these contributions she has received two Awards of Excellence in community service related to the cultural aspects of the Deaf community and the interpreting community. In the field of sports, she placed fourth in mixed tennis at the World Summer Games of the Deaf in Cologne, Germany, in 1981 and generously contributed her time and expertise to the organizing of the World Winter Games for the Deaf held in Banff, Alberta, in 1991.

Among her many achievements, Linda will probably be most widely remembered as the co-director of *Across Canada in 91 Minutes*, produced in 1991, and as the originator of the ASL version of the national anthem, "O Canada," in 1984. She was also the founder of the Early Intervention Program for Hearing Children of Deaf Parents.

Other activities include service on the Premier's Council, direction and consultation for several productions at the Walterdale Theatre in Edmonton, and organizing the AVLIC 2000 Conference. In addition, she was secretary of the Edmonton Association of the Deaf when the purchase of the EAD Community Centre was made in 1999. Deaf communities in the city of Edmonton, the province of Alberta, and across Canada have benefited, culturally and educationally, from Linda's diverse skills and talents.

CUNNINGHAM, Joy

1955–
Finance Technician, Computer Expert, and ASL Instructor.

JOY CUNNINGHAM, who has lived most of her life in British Columbia, was born Deaf in Flin Flon, Manitoba. She was six months old before her parents realized that she could not hear. They were renovating their house and realized that none of the hammering and other loud noises seemed to startle their baby.

By the time Joy was six years old, the family had relocated to Abbotsford, BC. She was sent to Vancouver to attend the Jericho Hill Provincial School for the Deaf, where she lived in the dormitory but was able to go home on weekends and during the school holidays. Thus, she was able to make friends in both communities. During the school year she was part of the Jericho Hill swim club and during the summer holidays she participated in the swim club at home in Abbotsford, so she had the best of both worlds.

When she was twelve, Joy spent a year in off-campus mainstream classes, but returned to Jericho Hill until she was sixteen when she was sent to an off-campus public high school. She graduated in 1973. While at school, she worked at part-time summer jobs—babysitting and berrypicking—which not only gave her a bit of pocket money, but also helped to prepare her for the world of employment. She attended Vancouver City College to learn office and book-keeping procedures.

Joy's first job was with Correctional Services Canada at Regional Pacific Headquarters in Abbotsford, in the finance department, where she worked for twelve years.

In 1986 she was transferred to the Matsqui Institution and spent the next seven years working in finance there. She attended Fraser Valley College to upgrade her English and letter-writing skills, and at night she taught ASL classes in Abbotsford.

One of her co-workers, Wayne, encouraged her to learn the computer system at work. Joy took up his suggestion, which proved to be a wise decision. In 1993 she was transferred back to Regional Pacific Headquarters to begin a new job generating Imprest cheques on the computer. She jokingly claims that she became very popular among her colleagues because she was the staff member who prepared their paycheques. Joy and Wayne were married in 1991.

Her hearing daughter, Amanda, who is now a teenager, learned ASL as an infant and communicates easily with her mother. She is in high school, plays the flute, and is studying Japanese in anticipation of a trip to Japan in 2002. Wayne is a hearing man but is also fluent in ASL. He is now employed as a teaching assistant with the Mission School District. In his spare time, he enjoys creating wood carvings.

Joy has numerous hobbies. The ones she likes best are travelling, camping, crocheting, doing needlepoint, walking, and watching movies. She is also interested in pets and surfing the Internet.

CURTIS (HAYWARD), Bertha May (Honorary Doctor of Divinity)

1909–2001
Dedicated Parish Worker, Christian Worker, Ministerial Assistant, Camp Leader, Counsellor, and Educator.

BERTHA MAY HAYWARD was born hearing to hearing parents in North View, a small rural commu-nity five miles out of Plaster Rock, New Brunswick. She apparently became Deaf at two years of age due to a serious fall from a piece of furniture. She attended the New Brunswick School for the Deaf in Lancaster, which is now a suburb of Saint John, for two years, from 1916 to 1918. Subsequently, she attended and graduated from the Halifax School for the Deaf in Nova Scotia in 1925. Bertha had no known Deaf relatives and, although she was married briefly, she was widowed soon after. She then dedicated the rest of her long life to her church and the Deaf community.

After graduating and returning to her home province of New Brunswick, she held various jobs. Bertha's longest employment was as a sorter for Neilson's Company, a chocolate manufacturer, where she worked until her retirement. As a Christian worker, she spent most of her adult life serving as a volunteer for the Deaf Community, travelling around New Brunswick, visiting Deaf families, and seeking out unidentified Deaf persons. She was instrumental in developing a Christian ministry for Deaf people in New Brunswick. She also assisted the Reverend Francis Gyle and Reverend Waldo Grandy in various missions among the Deaf. For fifteen years Bertha accompanied Deaf children to religious summer camps, where they became familiar with Bible stories and lessons, and Christian songs were signed around the campfire. These camps were sponsored by the Ecumenical Ministry of the Deaf (EMD), now known as the Atlantic Ministry of the Deaf.

After the establishment of the EMD in 1972, following the appointment of Reverend Gyle as a full-time chaplain in 1973, Bertha became a volunteer assistant and, after her retirement from Neilson's in 1975, a full-time parish worker for the Deaf Community.

In addition to her leadership in the EMD summer camping programs and her parish work, Bertha was also a teacher of ASL and of religious education classes, a home visitor, a counsellor, and a member of the board of the Ecumenical Ministry of the Deaf.

She was the first Deaf woman in Canada to be awarded an honorary Doctorate by a Canadian university when she was granted a Doctor of Divinity degree by the Atlantic School of Theology at its eleventh convocation in Halifax on 30 April 1982. She was justifiably proud of this illustrious achievement and was widely respected by her peers, both Deaf and hearing, in the province of New Brunswick.

Those who recall Bertha from the summer camps remember her as an older woman who was willing to go anywhere and try anything, and as someone who loved children. Sometimes they worried about her possibly having a heart attack from her many exertions, but soon discovered that they were usually worn out long before she was. She was always delighted to be included in any gathering and to be among other Deaf people. They recall that her name sign was a '3-handshape' which was done in a 'v' or '/\' movement on the upper arm. No one is certain how it originated but there is some recollection that her father may have been in the military as the sign suggests a representation of a sergeant's stripes.

Throughout her lifetime, Bertha Curtis was a stellar role model and one of the finest examples of an ecumenical outreach worker in the Deaf Communities of Atlantic Canada. She died peacefully in October 2001. Her pioneering spirit and courage will always be an inspiration to future generations of Deaf Canadian women.

DAHL (FINNESTAD), Marilyn Olive

1931–
Registered Nurse, Researcher, Volunteer, and Advocate for Hard-of-Hearing and Late-Deafened Persons.

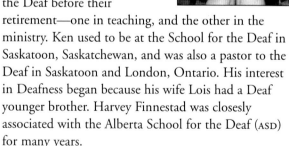

MARILYN FINNESTAD did not become Deaf until she was twenty years of age. She was born in Broderick, Saskatchewan. After graduating from high school, she became a registered nurse. She married Lloyd Dahl (now deceased) and they had two sons and a daughter who are now adults. She has four grandchildren.

Marilyn earned all her university credentials as a mature student, after losing her hearing. The lack of access for late-Deafened students in post-secondary education became a powerful motive for her to work for change while she completed a BSc degree in Nursing, a Master's degree in Communications, and a PhD in Interdisciplinary Graduate Studies.

She had broad experience in nursing and it soon became evident that she also possessed strong leadership skills when she became involved in volunteer consumer self-help advocacy. At present, she is the executive director of the Western Institute for the Deaf and Hard of Hearing, and makes her home in Vancouver, British Columbia. Her husband, Lloyd, was involved in pastoral care and teaching. After his retirement, he too became hard of hearing and started taking an active role in the Canadian Hard of Hearing Association (CHHA), of which Marilyn is a past president. Lloyd acted as president of the BC chapter for several years. Marilyn also has two cousins, Ken and Harvey Finnestad, who worked with the Deaf before their retirement—one in teaching, and the other in the ministry. Ken used to be at the School for the Deaf in Saskatoon, Saskatchewan, and was also a pastor to the Deaf in Saskatoon and London, Ontario. His interest in Deafness began because his wife Lois had a Deaf younger brother. Harvey Finnestad was closely associated with the Alberta School for the Deaf (ASD) for many years.

Marilyn was sixty-four years old when she completed her PhD, and decided to have a cochlear implant. It was successful and has restored 80 per cent of her hearing. Buoyed by this phenomenon, she accepted her current position and began a whole new career.

Marilyn is a published author with a variety of papers, journal articles, theses, resource manuals, and monographs to her credit. A few of her publications deal with nursing issues but most of them are related to the social, emotional, and psychological impact of adult hearing loss. She has given presentations, lectures, and workshops across Canada and abroad, and is often an invited speaker for national and international events.

As a volunteer, Marilyn has served in many capacities on different boards and committees. From 1986 to 1992 she was president of CHHA, where she was able to use her influence to appeal to governments and bureaucracies as well as families and individuals to create greater public awareness of the communication needs of those with hearing loss. She founded the CHHA national magazine, *Listen/Écoute*, and was also active in other areas—the BC Tel Relay Services, the Disability Resource Centre at the University of British Columbia (UBC), the Canadian Disability Rights Council, Mental Health Services for the Deaf and Hard of Hearing in the Greater Vancouver area, the International Federation of Hard of Hearing People, the Health Professionals Committee of CHHA, the Advisory Committee on Federal Policy Regarding

Communication Needs for the Deaf, Hard of Hearing and Deaf/Blind, the BC Elks Family Resource Centre, the editorship of the *Journal for the International Federation of Hard of Hearing People*, the BC chapter of CHHA, the executive of Hearing International, the Canadian Deaf and Hard of Hearing Forum, live captioning services in post-secondary education in BC, the creation of the Institute for Hearing Accessibility Research at UBC, as well as several other focus and study groups.

At one point Marilyn had her own weekly children's television show and was also involved in the production of two videos as writer and actor. She is a member of several professional organizations and has received at least a dozen prestigious awards and honours, including the Order of British Columbia, which cited her as "Canada's Foremost Advocate for the Hard of Hearing." Her name appears in *Who's Who Among Canadian Women* and a special award was named in her honour by CHHA, "The Marilyn Dahl Award of Merit."

DEER (PAULSON), Esther MeDora

1902–1988
Beloved Teacher of the Deaf, Talented Artist, and Writer.

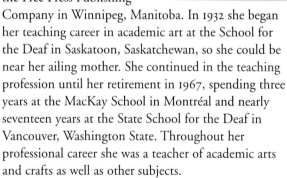

ESTHER PAULSON was born Deaf on a homestead at Harvey, North Dakota, US, in 1902. Her parents farmed there and at Ryder, North Dakota, until 1913, when her father moved the family to Mawer in south-central Saskatchewan to establish the Mawer Hardware Company. Esther had four hearing siblings—two sisters, Ledall and Jeanet, and two brothers, Enoch (Bud) and Arnold. While they lived in the US, Esther attended the North Dakota School for the Deaf at Devil's Lake, from 1909 to 1914. After moving to Canada she attended the Saskatchewan School for the Deaf in Regina for a year and the Manitoba School for the Deaf in Winnipeg for another year. The school in Regina was established in the former Parliament Building by a Deaf graduate of the Minnesota School for the Deaf and opened in 1913. Esther spent the year 1918–19 attending the local public school in Mawer with her sisters. Subsequently, she attended the Kendall School in Washington, BC, for two years, and Gallaudet College on the same campus for another two years. Esther's fondest memories were of the school in Regina, where her teacher was Thomas Rodwell, who was also the principal. He was an excellent instructor and Esther thought he was wonderful, as did all the other

students. He is fondly remembered by many alumni of both the Saskatchewan and Manitoba schools.

From 1924 to 1928 Esther worked as a ledger-keeper for the Free Press Publishing Company in Winnipeg, Manitoba. In 1932 she began her teaching career in academic art at the School for the Deaf in Saskatoon, Saskatchewan, so she could be near her ailing mother. She continued in the teaching profession until her retirement in 1967, spending three years at the MacKay School in Montréal and nearly seventeen years at the State School for the Deaf in Vancouver, Washington State. Throughout her professional career she was a teacher of academic arts and crafts as well as other subjects.

In 1944 Esther married Dewey H. Deer, whom she had first met at Gallaudet College in the early 1920s when he was on the college football squad. They renewed their acquaintance when they both taught at the State School for the Deaf in Washington from which she retired in 1967. In 1982 Esther and Dewey Deer drove from Olympia, Washington State, to attend the

Fiftieth Anniversary Celebration of the Saskatchewan School for the Deaf in Saskatoon. She had been one of the first teachers there, in 1932, and even though five decades had passed, she remembered every student she had taught—their faces, their names, and details of how they had behaved. She was an active member of many organizations of the Deaf on both sides of the border. While living in Saskatoon, she was one of the founding members of both the Saskatoon Association of the Deaf (SAD) and the Saskatoon Branch of the Western Canada Association of the Deaf (WCAD), with the initial meeting being held in her home on 10 May 1932.

Esther had outstanding artistic talents and enjoyed writing short articles based on local and family history. One of her family stories appeared in *Mawer Memories and Darmody Days*, compiled by the Mawer-Darmody Historical Society in 1984. Although she spent many

years living and working in the US, Esther Paulson Deer had put down very firm roots in western Canada and her writing reflects the fond memories she cherished of her life on the Canadian prairies. During the many years she lived in the United States, she continued to celebrate Dominion Day on the first of July.

Esther is remembered and loved by young and old alike, for many reasons. She had a rather flamboyant style of dressing and accessorizing her clothes that seemed to match her gregarious personality. Esther was someone who stood out in a crowd. She was curious and inquisitive, and was constantly learning as well as teaching. She was full of fun, yet serious when she needed to be. Esther Paulson Deer left a lasting imprint on many of today's leaders in Deaf Communities across Canada.

DEMIANYK (KOSKIE), Carol Elizabeth

1953–
Civil Servant, Stage Performer, Outstanding Curler, and Dart Team Member.

CAROL KOSKIE was born hard of hearing to Deaf parents, Elizabeth (Bessie) Sutherland and Anthony (Tony) Koskie, in Winnipeg, Manitoba. Both of her parents are now deceased. Although ASL was her first language, Carol received her entire education in the mainstream public school system, graduating from St. James Collegiate Institute in the west end of Winnipeg.

As a child, Carol participated in many events with her hearing friends—Sunday school, junior church choir, Explorers, and Canadian Girls in Training (CGIT) at St. James United Church. She also fondly recalls many winter walks along Ferry Road to the Bourkevale Community Club to go ice skating and tobogganing with her hearing peers.

In 1972 she began her first permanent job with the Queen's Printer for the province of Manitoba, where she worked for twenty-one years until the office closed. After being out of work for a few months, she again found a job with the Manitoba government, this time with the Department of Culture, Heritage, and Citizenship (under Statutory Publications). She has been employed there, full-time, since 1994. Carol and her Deaf husband, Donald Demianyk, make their home in Winnipeg, and have two children, Shawn and Jaclyn.

It was in 1973, when she was twenty years old, that Carol had her first experience with Deaf theatre when she performed in *Silent Shadows*, a series of fifty skits

directed by Angela Petrone (now Stratiy). Her love of acting, however, was not surpassed by her avid interest in the winter sport of curling, which she started at the age of fifteen, transferring from one Winnipeg Curling Club to another in order to gain more experience and enhance her skills. She is a former member of the Manitoba Ladies' Curling Association, the Winnipeg Deaf Curling Club, and the Manitoba Government Employees' Curling League. As a member of the Canadian Deaf Curling Association, she has won five All-Star championships, two gold medals, and five silver medals. In 1980 the city of Winnipeg presented her with the Outstanding Achievement Award for her curling accomplishments.

Carol is a long-time member of the Winnipeg Community Centre of the Deaf and the Winnipeg Church of the Deaf.. She also served on the board of Sign Talk Children's Centre for nine years. In 2000 she became a member of the Manitoba Provincial Deaf Women's Dart Team which competed in the 7th Canadian Deaf Dart Championships in London, Ontario.

Due to an injury that resulted from her falling on the ice, Carol's curling has been somewhat curtailed, but she still enjoys playing in selected bonspiels in Winnipeg and sometimes in rural Manitoba.

DeVILLE (STEWART), Gayle Anne

1934–
Educator, Evaluator, and ASL Specialist.

GAYLE STEWART was born in Regina, Saskatchewan. She has Deaf relatives—her brother, Jack Stewart; her uncle, Peter Stewart; and a second cousin, Donald Kidd. Her husband, John Louis DeVille, has been hard of hearing since birth. Their three children are all hearing.

Gayle entered the Saskatchewan School for the Deaf in Saskatoon in 1940, but remained there only half a year before transferring to Ontario. Five years later she returned to Saskatoon and graduated there in 1953. Her education includes a Bachelor of Science degree in Education from Gallaudet University, graduate studies at Eastern Kentucky University and Gallaudet University, and a Master of Education degree from Western Maryland College. Gayle was certified to teach high school social studies by the Kentucky Department of Education Certification Division.

Her working career began with summer office jobs in Saskatchewan and advanced to teaching positions at schools for the Deaf in South Carolina, Louisiana, Kentucky, and Rochester, New York. Currently, she is employed as a teacher of ASL and librarian at the Kentucky School for the Deaf. She has also been very active as an ASL instructor, proficiency evaluator, and interpreter evaluator. She is at present in charge of about twenty trained ASL instructors whom she assigns to teach ASL to faculty and staff members at her school, as well as to interested people in the community at large.

Gayle is the official certified Sign Communication Proficiency Interview (SCPI) coordinator responsible for seeing that all staff members at the Kentucky School for the Deaf are evaluated for their ASL skills by her SCPI team. She recently received an award of recognition for her lengthy service to the Kentucky Chapter Registry of Interpreters of the Deaf (KYRID). She also earned an ASLTA (ASL Teachers' Association) certificate which has been updated annually for the last six years. Besides her interest in ASL she has helped to develop curriculum guides for Deaf studies and communication skills for the Kentucky School for the Deaf.

Apart from her school duties, Gayle has been active in the Kentucky Association of the Deaf (KYAD), served on the state Advisory Board of Libraries and Archives, and is past-president of the Kentucky chapter of Gallaudet University Alumni Association (GUAA). She plays auction bridge every month with Deaf members of the Carrie J. McClure Bridge Club, founded in Danville, Kentucky, in 1933.

Gayle's husband has been a secondary school science teacher of the Deaf for many years.

DOBBIE (BRUCE), Wendy Kathleen

1965–
Sports Enthusiast, Office Clerk, and Certified ASL Instructor.

WENDY BRUCE, one of a pair of fraternal twins, came into the world on a cold January day in the nation's capital city, Ottawa. Her parents and sisters were all hearing, and Wendy's Deafness, due to rubella, was not discovered until she was eleven months old, when she was promptly fitted with hearing aids. Her twin sister is Heather. Wendy has no known Deaf relatives, but is married to a Deaf man, Christopher Dobbie. They have two hearing children, Camilla Sarah and Lance Alexander, and the family currently resides in Victoria, BC.

Wendy's father, the late Lou Bruce (1933–1985) was a professional football player who won the Most Valuable Player Award at the 1960 Grey Cup game. He played for the Ottawa Roughriders from 1956 to 1960 and was a personal friend of the notable Bob Rumball.

Her parents enrolled Wendy in a mainstream program when she was two and a half years old, at Centennial Public School, where she was happy among her Deaf friends until 1974, when she started fourth grade and was placed in a class where she was the only Deaf child. This had a profound effect on her and was the beginning of her struggle as an oralist. Academically, she did remarkably well, but her social life was sadly lacking due to communication barriers.

The worst came when she was twelve years old and her parents separated. Her mother, Janet, left Canada and moved to Paris, France, with Wendy's two sisters, while Wendy was placed in a boarding school in Toronto (Branksome Hall). Fortunately, she found great comfort in Kathleen, her paternal grandmother who was like a second mother to her. This relationship was so important to Wendy that she promised Kathleen she would never smoke and she has kept her word, something that makes her feel good.

After three years at Branksome Hall she returned to Ottawa to attend Lisgar Collegiate Institute (Class of 1984) with her twin sister. There she met a Deaf girl named Tanis Doe and her whole life changed. Tanis knew Sign Language and steered Wendy toward the Deaf Community where she renewed her acquaintance with many of her old friends from Centennial School. She started working as a counsellor at the Total Communication Day Camp (Ottawa) and even participated in the 1986 Miss Deaf Ontario Pageant, where she was the only mainstream-educated contestant among six culturally Deaf participants.

What helped to boost Wendy's confidence and self-esteem was her natural athletic ability, inherited from her father. She was a slalom skier, played basketball and volleyball for Branksome and Lisgar, played baseball and floor hockey with Deaf teams in Ottawa, and was a third on a Deaf curling team in Kingston in 1987. She also participated in the Deaf Canadian Slo-Pitch Tournament in Surrey, BC, in 1994.

After three years of studying biology at Queen's University in Kingston, Ontario, Wendy became engaged to Christopher Dobbie. They moved to BC in 1987 and were married in 1988. Their daughter was born at Maple Ridge, near Vancouver, the same year. They moved to Victoria in 1990 and Wendy worked as a Youth Intervenor until their son was born in 1991.

Since then she has held various jobs, working as a computer operator, secretary-librarian, and clerk for Income Security Programs (Canada Pension Plan), where she is still employed. Since 1994 she has taught ASL classes at Camosun and Malaspina Colleges and has obtained an ASL Instructor's Certificate for BC. She is a member of several organizations and was treasurer of the Deaf Women's Group of Vancouver Island for two years. Wendy's specific interests are sports, reading, cooking, and surfing the Internet.

DOBIE (MODIE), Patti A.

1950–
Community Advocate, Project Worker, Co-Writer and Producer, Presenter, and Community Mental Health Worker.

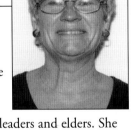

PATTI MODIE was born hearing into a hearing family in Ephrata, Washington, US. She became Deaf when she was five years old, due to influenza-meningitis. Her family moved to Red Deer, Alberta, when she was only a year old and then to Montréal, Québec. Later, they moved to Vancouver, British Columbia, where Patti still resides. There are no other known Deaf relatives in the family but Patti's husband, John Dobie, is Deaf. They have four hearing children, Liz, April, Matthew, and JoAnn, and two hearing grandchildren, Jennifer and Alexandria. Liz (Bates) is a married homemaker, April is a physical education major at Douglas College, Matthew's goal is to attend the Justice Institute in the Corrections Officer Program, and JoAnn is currently in high school.

Patti was educated at the MacKay School for the Deaf in Montréal and Jericho Hill School for the Deaf in Vancouver. She later attended Langara College in the Social Service Worker Program. As a child, she was fortunate to have Martha (Hawkins) Bodkin as a neighbour. Although she had developed signing skills quite naturally at MacKay School and at Jericho Hill, it was at Martha's home that she was introduced to Deaf Culture and was able to refine her ASL skills. At Martha's, Patti met most of the Deaf Community leaders and elders. She enjoyed visiting with Martha, just sitting and chatting in the evenings, throughout her youth.

When she graduated from Jericho Hill, Patti worked for the Royal Bank of Canada as an edit clerk and then at Jericho Hill School as a teacher's aide. She married John Dobie and left the workforce to raise their family. Patti obtained a certificate from the social workers' program at Langara College when her children were toddlers.

She was concerned about the limited access Deaf children have to information about sexual abuse, so she co-wrote and co-produced *Sharing Secrets*, a prevention video and user's guide for Deaf children and their families. Since then, she has served as a community advocate with the Canadian Panel on Violence Against Women, the Health Promotions Directorate Office, the Office of the Ombudsman, and several other advisory committees. Patti has been employed as a project worker with the Greater Vancouver Association of the Deaf (GVAD), as a support worker with the Deaf Children's Society of British Columbia, and is currently a community mental health worker for the Vancouver-Richmond Health Board.

Patti's involvement in the Deaf Community is extensive. She is presently serving as president of the board of directors for the Deaf Children's Society of BC and has been active in various capacities in the Western Institute for the Deaf, the Deaf Youth Program, the Canadian Association of the Deaf, the Northwest Athlete's Association of the Deaf, the Pacific Coast Bowler's Association, the City of Vancouver Committee for Disability Issues, the Program Advisory Committee for Vancouver Community College's Deaf Program, the Deaf/Deaf-Blind/Hard of Hearing Wellbeing Project, and the Medical Interpreters' Advisory Committee. She has edited the newsletter of the Greater Vancouver Association of the Deaf and captained the Deaf Women's Ten-Pin Bowling Team that broke all records in a tournament in Reno, Nevada. She enjoys giving psycho-educational presentations in the community and is a very busy woman in her field of employment. Her activities in the Deaf Community are often with the helping professions, as well as organizations and agencies of the Deaf.

She likes to spend time with her family and reduces her stress by swimming and playing Scrabble. Patti is also a member of the Deaf Rowing Club. Although she has devoted so much time to the Deaf Community, she considers her years as a young mother the best years of her life.

DODD, Barbara E.

1966–

Aspiring Professional Firefighter, Volunteer Public Educator, Caregiver, Researcher, and Advocate for Deaf Rights.

BARBARA DODD was born Deaf in Toronto, Ontario, into a Deaf family. Her Deafness is congenital, as she has Deaf parents, two Deaf grandparents, a Deaf sister, three Deaf children, and possibly other Deaf ancestors. Her hearing partner, Robert Smith, is a veteran Peel County police officer. They have four children—James, Brooks, and Zachary (Zak), who are Deaf, and Ashley, who is hearing. The family currently lives in Milton, Ontario.

Barbara received her high school education at Northern Secondary School in the mainstream public system, where the teachers used an FM system. She became so frustrated with mainstream oralism that she left school. She now realizes how fortunate her children are to have Deaf teachers. The rest of her education consisted mainly of courses, workshops, and seminars directed toward certification as a professional firefighter, achieved through Seneca College and the North York Fire department. She worked for four years as a secretary for the Unisys Company, was a counsellor at an Ontario Camp for Deaf Youth in Parry Sound, and, at present, is a volunteer worker in a fire prevention program where she lectures on fire and life safety issues related to the Deaf, hard of hearing, and hearing people as well.

In 1989, when she was twenty-three years old, Barbara was involved in a highly publicized and controversial abortion case which received intense media scrutiny and made headlines in the national press, including her appearance on the cover of Canada's national newsmagazine, *Maclean's* (31 July 1989). Since then, her life has changed greatly and she has become a loving mother, a housewife, a primary caregiver for her chronically ill Deaf mother, and, above all, has achieved the required training to qualify as a professional firefighter. Present rules and regulations prevent her from actually working as a firefighter, but she has spent many years trying to break down the barriers and the hearing world's preconceived notions about what Deaf people are capable of doing. She does not want her Deaf children to face the same prejudices and encourages young Deaf people to challenge unjust discrimination with courage and determination.

Barbara feels that because the dominant hearing society has no idea what Deaf people can really do, many Deaf persons sell themselves short. Nevertheless, despite feeling discriminated against, she insists on maintaining a positive attitude and looking on the bright side of life. Her research has revealed the existence of at least two active male Deaf firefighters, which has given her the courage to pursue her goal.

Her theory is that firefighting is almost exclusively based on good training, self-discipline, and exercising common sense and wise judgment—attributes which most Deaf people demonstrate in abundance. Hence, the legislated policies of the Occupational Health and Safety Act (OHSA) are biased and unfair. Therefore, she continues her crusade in challenging the law.

Within the Deaf Community, Barbara feels she is a relative newcomer as a director on the board of the Ontario Association of the Deaf, which has brought new meaning into her life in a bright and positive way. Being involved in the organization has given her a much better understanding of her rights and abilities and she hopes to influence the present generation of young Deaf women by providing them with a positive role model, so they will not feel intimidated or negative about themselves. She has created a website that tells her story and shows pictures from her firefighting training courses, making her better known in the Deaf Community.

Besides her regular volunteer work as an advocate for all Deaf persons, Barbara has some very special interests. She has filed an action complaint with the Ontario Human Rights Commission (OHRC) against a Toronto hotel, proposing that hotels in Ontario provide strobe lights for smoke detectors and fire alarms instead of portable kits which are unreliable since they only activate when a room is on fire but not when the building alarm is engaged. Her goal is to provide a more accessible and safer environment for everyone, but especially for those who cannot hear an alarm. She wants to be taken seriously by governments at both the local and provincial levels. Safety rights in a barrier-free setting is her number-one priority. She also serves as a representative of the Ontario Association of the Deaf (OAD) on the board of the Ontario Association of Sign Language Interpreters of Canada (OASLIC). In addition, she is a board director of OAD and the Canadian Hearing Society (CHS).

Her hobbies include hiking, rock climbing, camping, collecting porcelain figurines, and spending time with children. On 28 July 2001 she was one of eight performers for "Dancing Hands," co-sponsored by the Canadian Association of the Deaf (CAD) and the Canadian Cultural Society of the Deaf (CCSD) at the Sky Dome during a baseball game between the Toronto Blue Jays and the New York Yankees. Barbara and her fellow performers danced and signed during the singing of both the Canadian and American national anthems.

DOE, Ann-Marie Carlene

1982–
Student, Track and Field Champion, and Outstanding Athlete.

ANN-MARIE DOE was born Deaf in White River, Jamaica, and was adopted by her Canadian mother, Tanis Maureen Doe, when she was three years of age. She came to Canada when she was five. Ann-Marie had attended St. Christopher's School for the Deaf in Jamaica for two years before coming to Canada with her adoptive mother. Tanis was at that time an MSW student who had moved to Edmonton to do her practicum at Disabled Student Services at the University of Alberta in 1988.

Ann-Marie settled into her new life in Edmonton and was enrolled at the Alberta School for the Deaf, which she attended until she was ten years old. She and her mother then moved to the west coast and Ann-Marie spent the next three years at Jericho Hill School for the Deaf in Vancouver. When she was thirteen she had the experience of an American education for two years at the California School for the Deaf at Fremont. When she returned to Canada she was enrolled at the Burnaby South/Provincial School for the Deaf for two years, and is currently completing her final year of high school at the Belmont Public Secondary School in Victoria, BC.

Ann-Marie's foremost interest lies in the field of sports. She won several awards for her prowess at the schools she attended as well as a few from the western Canada tournaments of the Deaf which she was privileged to attend. Her greatest pride, however, is in her considerable achievement in track and field events. She is currently the holder of fourteen gold medals which she won at various BC Deaf sports events. She also had the honour of competing in Kentucky and Washington State.

Having spent her entire school life at schools for the Deaf, Ann-Marie is finding her education at Belmont Secondary School with an interpreter enjoyable but different and challenging. She has made many new friends among her hearing peers and communicates with some of them by e-mail. During the summer of 2000 she competed in the BC Deaf Games and won five gold medals.

In addition, she participated in the Summer Games of the Deaf in Kentucky and won in several categories other than track and field. Currently, she is training and looking forward to representing her school in the spring of 2001 at the Senior Island Track and Field Championships. If she is successful she hopes to represent Canada at the World Games of the Deaf in Rome in July 2001.

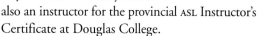

DOE, Tanis Maureen

(UNKNOWN)–
Action Sociologist, Educator, Researcher, and Community Consultant.

TANIS DOE lives in a small house on a lake at Langford, near Victoria, BC, with her teen-aged Deaf daughter, Ann-Marie, whom she adopted in Jamaica. They both keep very busy and are supportive of each other while enjoying their recently acquired home and making friends in their new community.

Tanis has achieved an impressive array of university credentials, beginning with a BA degree in Sociology and Political Science which she earned with distinction at Carleton University in Ontario in 1985. By 1989 she had completed her MSW degree in Social Policy and Administration, also at Carleton. Four years later, in 1993, she earned her PhD in the Sociology of Education at the University of Alberta in Edmonton.

While acquiring her extensive education, Tanis developed a wide variety of skills in several areas of expertise. She has worked in government and community liaison, is a published author of many professional treatises and monographs, has worked as an editor and website developer, planned and implemented many programs, raised funds, and acted as a trainer for specialists in the fields of violence prevention, disabilities, and employment. She organizes and promotes community outreach and is a skilled researcher and evaluator of social services and training practices. Her specialty is participatory research with marginalized populations, and her consulting company, DEW Research, has produced several reports and policy documents, as well as providing evaluation and consulting services both in Canada and the US. Currently, Tanis is instructing a course in disability studies for the School of Social Work at the University of Victoria and another, in research methods, at Royal Roads University. She is also an instructor for the provincial ASL Instructor's Certificate at Douglas College.

Tanis became Deaf at the age of twelve. She and her daughter have many "chosen" Deaf relatives but no known Deaf biological kinfolk. Eleanor McPeak was a grandmother mentor to Tanis, along with Marshall Wick. She was nominated by the Canadian Association of the Deaf for two special awards which she won—the Commemorative Award for Canada's 125th anniversary and the National Leadership Award given by the Coalition of Provincial Organizations of the Handicapped. She also received a doctoral fellowship award from the Social Sciences and Research Council and was once named "Youth of the Year" in Ottawa.

Tanis is in demand as a respected and knowledgeable presenter at conferences, workshops, and seminars and is the co-founder of several new groups, most of which deal with women's issues as well as Deafness-related ones. Perhaps her most significant achievement to date might be the careful nurturing and upbringing of her daughter which she has done with an abundance of loving care and innate wisdom.

DONALD, Maureen Mitchell

1917–
Educator, TV Host, Tireless Volunteer, and Deaf Community Leader.

MAUREEN DONALD was born in Saskatoon, Saskatchewan, the daughter of the chief of police in that city in 1917. She received her education in schools for the Deaf in Manitoba (1925–31) and Saskatchewan (1931–37). In 1945 she became the first Deaf teacher of Deaf children in British Columbia at the Jericho Hill Provincial School in Vancouver. She retired from her teaching career in 1978 after thirty-three years of dedicated service to Deaf students.

Retirement brought many new opportunities and experiences into Maureen's life. She became involved in the Western Institute of the Deaf, hosting their highly rated TV program *Show of Hands* for several years. Later, she participated in the *Look–Listen–Learn* project sponsored by the British Columbia Ministry of Education, which eventually led to the compiling and publishing of *The Directory of Programs and Services for the Deaf in British Columbia and Major Services Across Canada*.

Maureen also sat on the editorial board of the project *American Sign Language in Canada,* sponsored by the Canadian Cultural Society of the Deaf. In this capacity, she represented the Pacific Region in compiling *The Canadian Dictionary of ASL*, to be published by University of Alberta Press.

She has been a very active member of the British Columbia Society of the Deaf, where her main goal was to preserve Deaf Heritage and Culture in her province. Maureen has been a natural and highly respected leader in the Deaf community locally, provincially, and nationally, serving in many executive capacities. In 1990 she founded a local club for Deaf seniors, The Happy Hands Club, and in 1992 she coordinated the first Canadian Deaf Festival held in Richmond, BC. She has spent much of her leisure time updating *The Canadian Deaf Festival Handbook*, an invaluable resource for local and provincial chairpersons.

Maureen earned her first great distinction when she was nominated by Gallaudet University for honorary membership in the Phi Kappa Zeta sorority because she had been such an exemplary role model for all Deaf women in North America. Her greatest distinction, however, came on 24 November 2000 when she was awarded an Honorary Doctor of Laws degree by the University of British Columbia for her many contributions to the community.

Between her numerous projects, Maureen has found time to travel extensively in Asia, Europe, the United Kingdom, Australia, New Zealand, and the US. Her wide travels in Canada include visits to the Maritimes and Newfoundland.

Maureen's tireless and dedicated leadership has benefited all Deaf Canadians and her impact on the Deaf Community will be felt by future generations.

DOOLEY, Beverley Anne

1963–
Teacher, Preschool Director, Manager, and Able Spokeswoman for the Deaf.

BEVERLEY DOOLEY was born Deaf into a hearing family at a small cottage hospital in Bonavista, Newfoundland. She was the only Deaf child in her family and has no known Deaf relatives. She was raised with four hearing brothers and four hearing sisters, mainly by their father because their mother died when Beverley was only five years old. Beverley's husband, Danny Daniels, is Deaf, and they have three hearing children—Daniel, Jake, and Calista—who are all fluently bilingual in English and ASL. Danny works as an accounting clerk for the Canadian Hearing Society and is very active in Deaf sports. The family currently lives in Whitby, Ontario.

Beverley grew up in a close-knit, loving family in a small community where people looked out for each other. Her father, Jack Dooley, was a veteran of World War II. Because Newfoundland was not part of Canada in 1939, he enlisted in the British Navy and remained overseas for the duration of the war (1939 to 1945), even though he was wounded when the minesweeper on which he was serving hit a mine and sank in the North Sea. Jack was in and out of hospital for almost nine months while recovering from injuries and was given an honourable discharge, but he refused to leave the Navy and return to Canada until the war was won. He was awarded five medals at the conclusion of World War II. This experience reflected his philosophy: "Never start something you can't finish."

Beverley's family placed a lot of emphasis on education, and her father ensured that they all received a high school standing. Beverley's schooling began at the Newfoundland School for the Deaf in St. John's, where she attended from 1970 to 1982. This was a difficult decision for her father and brothers because they feared the future of a little Deaf girl couldn't possibly be very bright. Eventually they began to realize just how mistaken they had been. When she graduated from high school, Beverley moved to Toronto and enrolled at George Brown College, where she earned qualifications as a nursery aide in early childhood education. She graduated in 1986 and, later, in 1992, took management training with the Canadian Hearing Society.

Her employment record has been eclectic. She started out as a teacher and director of the Happy Hands Pre-School at the Bob Rumball Centre for the Deaf (BRCD) in Toronto, where she spent fifteen happy years. She always felt BRCD was her second home and she appreciated the welcoming warmth of the staff members and the positive atmosphere throughout the centre. Since then, Beverley has become very involved with the Ontario Association of the Deaf (OAD), the Ontario Interpreter Service Advisory Council, and the Interpreter Training Program Advisory Council at

George Brown College. At times, she has helped with such fundraising events as a twenty-four-hour rock-a-thon. She has learned a great deal about politics and how to raise public awareness about the accessibility needs of the Deaf. Her participation in the activities of OAD has taught her much and has fostered her maturation into a confident, knowledgeable, strong spokeswoman for the Deaf Community.

At present, Beverley works as a manager of the Interpreter and Sign Language Services, as well as the Community Development Program for the Canadian Hearing Society. She sees it as a challenge and a marvelous opportunity for personal growth. She is constantly learning and gaining greater understanding of the political processes through which she can best serve the Deaf Community. Providing the hearing society with accurate information about Deaf issues is her major focus.

Beverley is proud of who she is and the successes she has achieved. She credits her family with making it all possible, by providing her with the unconditional love, support, encouragement, and independence she needed when she was growing up in a difficult but happy period of her early life. They believed in her, and from their confidence in her, she developed her own philosophy of life: "Believe in yourself and have the passion to reach your career dreams."

DOULL, Elizabeth

1949–
Project Coordinator, Researcher, Educator, Consultant, Community Worker, and Avid Birder.

Born Deaf in Ottawa, ELIZABETH DOULL attended an oral program at Clarke School for the Deaf in Northampton, Massachusetts, day classes for Deaf students in Ottawa, and regular schools in Ottawa and Halifax. The best education she received was at Halifax Ladies' College, a private girls' school now known as Armbrae Academy, where classes were small, allowing more support from the teachers. She graduated in 1970, which made a big difference in her life. Without quality education and supportive teachers, she could never have achieved what she has. She also developed a lifelong love of learning that has broadened her interests. Interpreters and notetakers were unheard of in those days, so Deaf individuals like Elizabeth had to strive to succeed on their own.

When she was growing up she was active in the Girl Guides of Canada for eight years; one year with the Brownies, five years with the Girl Guides, and finally, two years with the Sea Rangers. She earned the Gold

Cord, the highest possible award offered to Girl Guides of her time. In her final year with the Guides, she was promoted to Company Leader, the third-highest rank after Captain and Lieutenant in a Guide Company. Elizabeth attended Guide Camps for five summers and had the prestigious honour of being selected as one of fourteen Rangers to represent Canada on a two-week trip to Mexico, including a week-long stay at the renowned World Guide Centre, "Our Cabana," in Cuernavaca, Mexico, with other Rangers and senior Girl Guides from different parts of the world, a memorable experience.

According to *Deaf Heritage in Canada* (C.F. Carbin, McGraw-Hill Ryerson, Ltd., 1996), Elizabeth was the first Deaf Nova Scotia woman to graduate from Gallaudet College (now Gallaudet University) in

Washington, BC, when she received a Bachelor of Arts degree in Sociology-Social Work in 1974. There, she enjoyed meeting interesting Deaf people from around the globe, and learned Sign Language. In addition to her BA, Elizabeth also earned a Bachelor of Social Work (BSW) degree from Dalhousie University in 1987 and a Master's degree in Adult Education (MEd) from Mount Saint Vincent University in 1999, both of which she found worthwhile and essential to her professional career.

In 1972, while she was a Gallaudet student, she found summer employment back in Nova Scotia, as a counsellor with "Summer Sounds," a recreational program geared toward Deaf and hard-of-hearing children. This was her first exposure to the signs of the Maritime region, used by Deaf Maritime students, and she was immensely fascinated. In fact, she documented signs in illustrations and notes long before the advent of videotaping.

After a brief stint of studying and working in the field of cartography, Elizabeth realized her heart was still with Deaf people, so she returned to her first love when a job became available in 1976. This position required her to do a province-wide needs assessment research project in the Deaf Community. At that time there was no service agency for Deaf and hard-of-hearing persons, so statistical data were needed to obtain funding in order to establish such an office. The project gave her an opportunity to meet Deaf people from all walks of life across the province. She encountered signers who had attended the Halifax School for the Deaf in the early 1900s. This led her to initiate research to determine the regional signs unique to the Atlantic Provinces in 1978. Afterwards, she continued to collect and document Maritime region signs. Through the Canadian Cultural Society of the Deaf, a grant was received by the Nova Scotia Cultural Society of the Deaf in 1998. Elizabeth sat on the MSL research committee, but was eventually appointed to coordinate the project and document stories in Maritime region signs. The project had two goals: to have videotaped stories analyzed linguistically by an expert linguist to determine whether or not MSL is a language; and to preserve it.

Her work experience has been varied, covering various disciplines: education, research, social work, administration, public relations, cartographic mapping, accounting, and library work. Since 1991, she has focused mainly on education (ASL, Deaf Culture, tutoring, academic upgrading), research (women with disabilities, accessibility, post-secondary education, entrepreneurship, to name a few), and advocacy, in her efforts to promote greater accessibility, understanding, awareness, inclusion, and services to the members of the Deaf Community of Nova Scotia.

Elizabeth's involvement in organizations, committees, and agencies has been manifold, and has included the Canadian Association of the Deaf (CAD), the Society of Deaf and Hard of Hearing Nova Scotians (SDHHNS), the Nova Scotia Cultural Society of the Deaf (NSCSD), the Deafness Advocacy Association Nova Scotia, (DAANS), and the Halifax Association of the Deaf (HAD). She also spent about six years as a volunteer doing Deaf archival research to assist the author of *Deaf Heritage in Canada*, published in 1996. In 1997 she received an award from the Eastern Canada Association of the Deaf (ECAD) in recognition of her outstanding contribution to the Deaf Community of the Maritime Provinces. In 1993 she was named Deaf Woman of the Year by the Halifax Association of the Deaf. She was also the recipient of a plaque citing appreciation for her five years of work with the Halifax Regional Board of Directors for the Society of Deaf and Hard of Hearing Nova Scotians.

An avid birdwatcher since she was nine years old, Elizabeth enjoys taking an occasional break from her busy schedule to do birding in different parts of rural Nova Scotia. She has also been a birder while travelling in Europe. She takes pleasure in walking, reading, doing Deaf historical research, photographing nature, ink drawing, and travelling. She enjoys being an aunt to her two nieces and two nephews. Elizabeth makes her home in Halifax, Nova Scotia.

DOYLE (SOURS), Gladys Valentine

1898–1996

Devout Church Member, Choir Leader, and Noted Fundraiser for Church Missions.

GLADYS SOURS was born Deaf to Deaf parents, David and Ellen Agnew Sours, at Clinton, Ontario, near Brantford, in 1898. Both David and Ellen Sours had been taught by Samuel Greene, Ontario's first Deaf teacher, and thought very highly of him. He was an American, but when the Ontario Institution for the Education and Instruction of the Deaf and Dumb opened at Belleville in 1870, Samuel Greene came to Canada to became the first Deaf teacher of Deaf students, and was soon nick-named "the Laurent Clerc of Ontario." The Sours family used Sign Language fluently and was very much involved in the activities of the local Church of the Deaf, so a pattern of church work was established for Gladys early in her life. Their interest in hymn signing might well have been fostered by Samuel Greene because he was considered to be one of the most graceful and impressive signers in North America.

Gladys arrived in Toronto as a new bride in 1921, after marrying her Deaf husband, Francis Doyle. He, too, was very active in the church and one of their first projects was to help establish a Church for the Deaf in Toronto, at 56 Wellesley Street East, in 1925. Two years later, in 1927, Gladys set up the Kieuwa Club for the Deaf, "Kieuwa" being an Indian word meaning "meeting place," where she and her husband were both active members for many years. Francis also enjoyed writing the news for the Deaf Community's newsletters, but their main interest was in the church.

Gladys was president of the Women's Association of the Wellesley Street Church of the Deaf for about thirteen years. When Francis passed away in 1957, she opened her home to young Deaf people. She also kept Deaf elderly people and looked after them until 1984, when age forced her to sell her home and move to the Bob Rumball Community Centre of the Deaf.

Gladys loved church music and spent a great deal of her time training choirs to memorize hymns and sign them. She also had a flair for drama and participated in the church's theatrical activities whenever she was called upon to do so. She was probably best known for her tireless efforts in raising funds for mission purposes, mostly through coordinating quilting bees, and making quilts herself. She continued this work until she reached the age of ninety-one. In 1978 Gladys Valentine Doyle was inducted into the Canadian Cultural Society of the Deaf Hall of Fame. In 1994 she was honoured by being named "Deaf Citizen of the Year," a prestigious award which was renamed in 1991 as "The Arthur Hazlitt Citizenship Award." It is presented each year to a Deaf person whose activities (local, provincial, national) have created a positive image of Deafness in the minds of hearing persons.

During her years of residence at the Bob Rumball Elderly Persons Centre, Gladys was very content because there were so many services and activities for her to choose from. She enjoyed the birthday and anniversary special events, trips and excursions, health and fitness program, swimming, the *EPC Newsletter*, and various clubs. She also served as a volunteer for the Deaf-Blind residents by bringing them up to date on all current news at the Centre.

Gladys Doyle was called to her Lord on 4 May 1996, after living a long, productive and fulfilling life for almost a century. She was a prominent figure among early leaders in Canada's Deaf Community and was admired, loved, and respected by everyone who knew her.

JANICE DRAKE was born Deaf, due to maternal rubella, in Exeter, Ontario. She has an older Deaf brother, Gary James Drake, but they have no other known Deaf relatives. She was the fifth child in the Drake family, with two hearing sisters and two brothers, one Deaf and one hearing. As the baby of the family, she was a visual observer who learned a great deal from her older siblings. One of her hearing sisters, Debbie Johnston, works with Deaf children as an educational assistant in an elementary public school in Fort McMurray, Alberta, where Sign Language is used, but not ASL.

Janice's education began at Kent Public School (1969–71) in a self-contained classroom in Charlotte-town, Prince Edward Island, while the family lived at Summerside during her father's military career. She and her brother Gary were in the same class and, from Monday to Friday, were in the care of guardians. On weekends they were collected by their mother and driven home to be with the rest of the family. In 1971 their father was transferred to Trenton, Ontario, and Janice and Gary were both enrolled at Ontario School for the Deaf in Belleville (now Sir James Whitney School). She received her secondary school graduation diploma in 1983 and enrolled at Gallaudet University in Washington, BC, where she earned a Bachelor's degree in Elementary Education. She then attended the University of British Columbia for one year to obtain a Diploma in the Education of the Hearing Impaired before beginning her teaching career at Robarts School for the Deaf in London, Ontario, in 1990. She furthered her education with a Master's degree in Educational Studies from the University of Western Ontario in London in 1999, earning the distinction of being their first culturally Deaf graduate.

While in school, Janice was active in Girl Guides, played softball for three or four years, participated in gymnastics, and in 1982–83, served as Prime Minister for Student Parliament. At Gallaudet University, she held part-time jobs, was an active member of the Phi Kappa Zeta sorority, a representative on the student body government, a stage-crew hand for the production of *The Rose Tattoo*, and administrative secretary for the Gallaudet campus newspaper, *Buff and Blue*.

Within the Deaf Community, Janice has served in many different capacities and on a wide variety of committees at the local, provincial, and national levels. At Robarts School, where she teaches, she has been involved in many camping activities and events such as ASL Literature Week, Samuel Greene Day, and the 1996 Deaf Children's Festival, which was hosted at Robarts for the first time. She has been vice-president of the local Deaf Club, the London Centre of the Deaf (LCD), where she established a Children's program, a Youth program, and a Seniors' (50+) program, as well as organizing LCD's first retreat. She was a project coach for Gateway Camp (Robarts School's summer Deaf Youth Day Camp), and a speaker at Ontario's Deaf Youth Leadership Camp in the summer of 1999. In addition, she was a two-term president of the Ontario Cultural Society of the Deaf.

Janice has been the recipient of numerous well-deserved awards and honours. In 1983 she received the Superintendent's Academic and Leadership Award as well as the Athlete of the Year trophy at her school in Belleville. At Gallaudet University she was given the Charles Ely Award for Women in 1989, and was on the Dean's List in 1987. She has also received recognition from the London Centre of the Deaf for Outstanding Service to the Deaf Community. She is an avid initiator of local programs, and is well known for arranging and organizing educational workshops, as well as social and recreational events and entertainments. In 2001 Janice was appointed educational coordinator at her school. She will assist teachers and support staff in implementing curricula and individual programs.

She is a talented storyteller and has a wonderful sense of humour. Her hobbies and interests during her spare time include reading novels, walking, taking care of her two cats, watching rented movies, and being different and unusual enough to enjoy reading comic books.

1954–

Educational Assistant, Life Skills Counsellor, Facilitator and Intervenor with Deaf Children and Youth, and Outstanding Athlete.

LINDA RUSSELL was born Deaf in York, (Toronto), Ontario. Hers is an extended Deaf family which includes a Deaf brother, Don Russell, his Deaf wife, Ruth, and their four adult Deaf children, Kathy, Darren, and twins, Connie and Bonnie. Her sister Sheila and husband Ken Corbett are also Deaf, although their only child, a daughter, Grace, is hearing. Linda's husband, Elvis Dressler, is Deaf, as are their three children—Lisa, and twins, Justin and Kristen. Many of her Deaf relatives, including her husband, are employed in various capacities at E.C. Drury School for the Deaf in Milton, and at the Bob Rumball Association of the Deaf, also in Milton. Although they have lived elsewhere, Linda and Elvis currently make their home in Milton.

Linda was educated at the Ontario School for the Deaf (now Sir James Whitney School) in Bellevile from 1959 to 1963. She then transferred to the new Ontario School for the Deaf (now E.C. Drury School) in Milton, and was in the first graduating class in 1973. Since then she has furthered her education by taking ASL workshops and acquiring CPR and CPI certification, which she has kept updated every two years since 1994.

Linda and Elvis were married in 1985 and lived in Saskatoon, Saskatchewan, from 1981 to 1991. She was a casual employee at R.J.D. Williams School for the Deaf until it closed in June 1991, supervising children in residence, serving as a teacher's aide in an elementary classroom, acting as an intervenor in work-experience and recreational settings, and being a foster-mother to a fifteen-year-old girl with learning and behaviour problems. For a short time she also worked as a meat-cutter and packer for Chef-Redi Meats in Saskatoon.

After returning to Ontario, Linda found employment as an educational assistant at E.C. Drury School, first in the elementary department, and then in high school. She has also been a part-time skills counsellor in both group and individual settings and has managed risk situations involving aggressive behaviour. She enjoys her job and does well working with others on team projects, as well as being a highly motivated, self-reliant individual.

While she was a high school student, Linda won numerous sports trophies and was an outstanding athlete. She was involved in the residential sports program, and played on several school teams. She and her brother Don were both involved in the World Games for the Deaf, and her interest in sports has never waned. In recent years she has taken up less "physical" sports such as curling and playing darts. Besides sports, her involvement in the Deaf Community has been mainly in the capacity of a volunteer fundraiser. In 1997–98 she was registrar for the Canadian Deaf Festival held in Mississauga, Ontario. In 1998 she was inducted into the Ontario Deaf Sports Association's Hall of Fame.

She is an active member of several organizations of the Deaf and is always prepared to volunteer her expertise wherever it is needed.

In her leisure time Linda joins other Deaf sports lovers in playing darts, golfing, participating in fitness exercises, and helping with organized sports. She also likes to cook, sew, and knit. Above all, she enjoys working with Deaf children and teenagers.

CATHY LUSHMAN was born Deaf to hearing parents in Grey River, Newfoundland. No immediate family members are Deaf but Cathy has six Deaf cousins. Her hearing spouse, Matthew Drinkert (Matt), is an ASL interpreter and mentor to several Deaf clients. Cathy and Matt currently live in Windham, Maine.

Cathy attended the Newfoundland School for the Deaf in St. John's from elementary to high school and was in the first graduating class from the new facility in 1987. She then entered Gallaudet University in Washington, BC, and graduated with a Bachelor of Arts degree in Developmental Drama in 1992. She followed this up with a Master of Science degree in Deaf Education from Western Maryland College in 1994.

Cathy's employment record has been varied. She taught Drama at the Texas School for the Deaf for one year and served as a substitute teacher at the Kendall Demonstration Elementary School in Washington, BC, for a year.

She was a student teacher at the Maryland School for the Deaf in 1996 before taking a permanent position at the Governor Baxter School for the Deaf in Portland, Maine, where she is still employed. Her teaching assign-

ments there have varied from elementary education in 1996, to Deaf adult education in 1997, to head teacher in 2001. She is also in charge of developmental reading assessments of young students.

While attending Gallaudet University, Cathy made the Dean's List twice and was selected to participate in the American Kennedy Centre Festival Competition. Her acting career in Newfoundland included playing the lead role in the Rising Tide Theatre's 1985 production of *Children of a Lesser God*, and playing a role in the 1989 production of *A Man Named Hawk*. In her current position at Governor Baxter School in Portland, she conducts university classes for under-graduates, teaching ASL and Deaf literature. In her leisure hours, Cathy's hobbies and interests include collecting novels and children's books by famous authors, reading, theatrical performing, shopping for clothes, watching movies, and eating out. She is also an outdoor enthusiast who enjoys camping, hiking, kayaking, and boating. In addition, Cathy loves to travel.

DRYSDALE, Joan Gordon

1943–
Warehouse Employee, Tutor, Athlete, and Spokeswoman for the Deaf.

JOAN DRYSDALE, the Deaf daughter of Deaf parents, was born and raised in Halifax, Nova Scotia. She continues to reside there and worked in an IGA warehouse in that city for thirty-seven years. When she was hired it was a Dominion Store but, by the time she retired, it had become an IGA/Superstore. Joan has two hearing daughters, Valerie and Deirdre.

As a child and during her teens, she attended the Halifax School for the Deaf from 1950 until it was torn down in 1961. Her parents, Arthur Gordon Drysdale and Margaret Rose (Hull) Drysdale, had received their education in the same school. Besides her parents, Joan has two Deaf uncles and a few Deaf cousins. She also has a hearing cousin who is a teacher of the Deaf with the Atlantic Provinces Special Education Authority (APSEA). Joan's mother, who is now Margaret Rose Marsh, is at present the eldest member of the Halifax Association of the Deaf which began as the Forrest

Club in 1919. Margaret Rose (Hull) had been their secretary when she was only eighteen years of age.

One of the most memorable events in Joan's life occurred on 8 November 1951. It was a gloomy, rainy day when she stood under a large umbrella among a gathering crowd in front of the Halifax School for the Deaf, waiting nervously for the arrival of the royal limousine in which Princess Elizabeth and her husband, Prince Philip, were touring the city. They were relative newlyweds at that time, having been married only five years. Of course, they are now Queen Elizabeth II and the Duke of Edinburgh. Joan was only eight years old on that special day when she presented a bouquet of flowers to that beautiful young princess who was to be crowned

Queen of Great Britain and the Commonwealth only two years later.

Although her work at the warehouse and the raising of her daughters kept Joan busy in her personal life, she has always found time to be active in the Deaf Community in Halifax. She has served on a number of boards and committees of Deaf organizations and has been a capable spokesperson whenever it was necessary. Joan is athletically inclined and enjoys various sports.

Apart from these activities, Joan has also served as a tutor and is considered an exemplary role model for Deaf women in Nova Scotia and elsewhere. The Halifax Association of the Deaf presented Joan with the John Blois Memorial Award (since renamed Deaf Woman of the Year) for 1983–84. She was also presented with several awards for her long service with her company. In her leisure time, she enjoys cross-stitching, knitting, and other crafts.

DUNN (BARBER), Leslie Jane

1954–
Instructional Teacher Associate, Deaf-Blind Intervenor, and Volunteer.

LESLIE BARBER was diagnosed as profoundly Deaf at the age of fifteen months. Born in Prince Albert, Saskatchewan, to hearing parents, she has no known Deaf relatives. She does, however, have a famous ancestor. Her maternal grandfather was John Tarr of the North West Canadian Mounted Police (NWCMP), who was inducted into its Hall of Fame. Leslie has three hearing children—Danica, Kristina, and Patrick—and the family currently lives in Saskatoon, Saskatchewan.

Leslie received her early education at the Saskatchewan School for the Deaf in Saskatoon. She then acquired a General Office Practice Diploma from the St. Paul Technological Vocational Institute in St. Paul, Minnesota, in 1974. She worked as a data-entry operator for Saskatchewan Government Insurance in Regina, Canadian Data in Vancouver, and the Department of Northern Forests in Prince Albert.

She was married in 1978 and her children were born between 1979 and 1985. After being a housewife and stay-at-home mother to her children for a number of years, Leslie returned to school. She took Adult Basic Education 12 at the Saskatchewan Institute of Applied Arts and Science Technology (SIAST) in Saskatoon in 1994. The following year, in 1995, she took safety oriented first-aid and cardiopulmonary resuscitation, offered by the St. John's Ambulance Association, for which she was recertified in 1999. Between 1995 and 1999 Leslie also earned two other significant certificates: Rehabilitation Worker and Teacher Assistant, both from SIAST at Kelsey Institute. In addition, she holds certification in Professional Assault Response Training from the Canadian Deaf-Blind and Rubella Association.

She has also acquired computer skills and has experienced a variety of types of employment. She is presently working as an intervenor for the Canadian Deaf-Blind and Rubella Association. She has also been a job coach, an ASL instructor, an ASL model, a tutor, and a parenting aide. Her most extensive experience, however, has been in classrooms as a teacher-associate, where she has worked with cognitively challenged students, as well as both Deaf and hearing students. At present, Leslie is employed as a casual Deaf-Blind intervenor and a full-time teacher assistant, working with hearing students in grades one and two, tutoring one-on-one with hearing students in grades three to six, and with three cognitively challenged, hearing, grade eleven pupils.

Leslie's extensive volunteer work has included facilitating leisure activities for the Saskatchewan Abilities Council, tutoring at SIAST (Kelsey Institute), teaching ASL, serving as registrar for the Canada Deaf Curling Championships and the Saskatoon Association of the Deaf, and being an active member of the Saskatchewan Deaf Sports Association, the Saskatoon Deaf Athletic Club, and the Saskatchewan Cultural Society of the Deaf. She is currently serving as a director on the board of the Canadian Association of the Deaf, as well as the Saskatoon Association of the Deaf and the Saskatchewan Association of the Deaf. When she can find any leisure time in her busy life, Leslie's hobbies and interests include reading, spending time with her granddaughter and her new grandson, camping, and skiing.

DZIWENKA (SENGER), Hilda Elizabeth

1945–
Teletypesetter, Administrative Assistant, Computer Operator, and Champion Curler.

HILDA SENGER was born hearing into a hearing family in Saskatoon, Saskatchewan, but became Deaf at the age of three. She attended the Saskatchewan provincial School for the Deaf in Saskatoon from 1954 to 1963. She has no known Deaf relatives but her husband, Marvin Marshall Dziwenka is Deaf. They have three adult hearing children—Yvonne, Susanne, and Benjamin.

Hilda's hearing brother, Tony Senger, is a five-time World Champion arm wrestler who has competed in many international events, and her nephew, Chad Senger, is a competitive body builder. Her husband Marvin, like Hilda herself, is an avid curler.

After graduating in 1963 Hilda found employment as a teletypesetter for the Saskatoon daily newspaper, the *Star Phoenix*, where she worked until she married and moved to Edmonton, Alberta. From 1968 to 1974 she was a teletypesetter for the *Edmonton Journal*. Since March 1979 Hilda has been employed by the government of Alberta, doing computer work and acting as administrative support in the Ministry of Learning where she produces examinations, course outlines, and record books from draft copies for fifty-two trades. She deals with apprenticeships and trade certifications.

The greatest passion of Hilda's life has always been the sport of curling and she possesses a highly impressive record of competitive victories. From 1979 to 1983 she played third and since then has skipped her own rink.

As of 1999, she had won a total of twenty-one curling medals— seven gold, eleven silver, and three bronze.

The following is a rather awesome testimonial to her outstanding prowess as a curler:

Year	Medal	Location
1979—Silver		Port Moody, BC
1980—Silver		Montréal, Québec
1981—Bronze		Winnipeg, Manitoba
1982—Silver		Québec City, Québec
1983—Gold		Edmonton, Alberta
1984—Gold		Toronto, Ontario
1985—Silver		Saskatoon, Saskatchewan
1986—Silver		Ottawa, Ontario
1987—Gold		Winnipeg, Manitoba (*All-Star)
1988—Silver		Montréal, Québec
1989—Gold		Vancouver, BC
1990—Gold		Halifax, Nova Scotia
1991—Bronze		Banff, Alberta
1992—Silver		Ottawa, Ontario
1993—Bronze		Richmond, BC
1994—Silver		St. John's, Newfoundland
1995—Gold		Saskatoon, Saskatchewan
1996—Silver		Kingston, Ontario
1997—Silver		Portage la Prairie, Manitoba
1998—Gold		Winnipeg, Manitoba
1999—Silver		Edmonton, Alberta

EDGAR (BUCHANAN), Eileen Noreeda

1943–
Model Girl Guide, Library Clerk, Educational Assistant, and ASL Instructor.

EILEEN BUCHANAN was born Deaf to hearing parents, Mr. and Mrs. G.R Buchanan, in Nanaimo, on Vancouver Island in British Columbia. Her father was in the Canadian Army at that time and they were stationed there. Eileen is one of three daughters and the only Deaf member of the family, with no other known Deaf relatives. One of her hearing sisters lives in northern BC and the other is in Vancouver, where she works as a professional ASL interpreter. Eileen was married to a Deaf man, Ronald Edgar. She has two wonderful adult Deaf children, a son, Jeff, and a daughter, Jennifer. They all currently live in Vancouver.

Eileen received her education at the Jericho Hill School for the Deaf (JHS) in Vancouver, starting when she was only two and a half years old. In those days, signing was discouraged and all instruction was oral, so her parents and sisters did not learn any Sign Language at that time. Eileen was fortunately able to pick it up by observing older students who were using it. When she graduated she went directly into the workforce.

From 1962 to 1976 she worked as a library clerk at the Vancouver Public Library. Twice, however, she took maternity leave when her children were born, in 1967 and 1970. From 1976 to 1979 she worked at a preschool for Deaf children. In 1979 she started working as an educational assistant at JHS and is currently still employed in that capacity at what is now known as the British Columbia School for the Deaf in Burnaby. She has also been an ASL instructor at evening classes held at various locations in Vancouver and Burnaby.

As a child, Eileen had several particularly enriching experiences. When she was only four years old she joined the Connaught Ice Skating Club, where she learned to figure-skate and took part in several of their ice carnivals, as their only Deaf participant. She was also involved in Brownies, Girl Guides, and Land Rangers, managing on her own without ever having the luxury of an interpreter, but with dedicated support and encouragement from her mother. She earned two significant awards—the All Round Cord, and the Gold Cord. It appears that she was the only Deaf person in British Columbia, and possibly all of

Canada, to have accomplished that achievement. Her successes were featured in the *Vancouver Province* when she was selected as Teenager of the Month, and in other local newspapers in 1960. She also earned two "A" awards and several medals for crafts. In 1999 she was honoured by the Canadian Cultural Society of the Deaf (CCSD) and Deaf/Human Resources Development Canada (DHRDC) as a recipient of one of their Ladder Awards® for her narration in "ASL Storytelling."

Eileen's hobbies involve working at numerous crafts, quilting, scrapbooking, swimming, and camping. Another activity she enjoys is being a clown for special events. She is an expert at creating animals and other unique characters out of balloons. Her grandchildren, family, and friends are vitally important to her. All in all, she has had a satisfying and fulfilling life. Nevertheless, she looks forward to many new challenges in the future.

EDGAR, Jennifer Ann

1970–
Child-Care Counsellor and Teacher of the Deaf.

JENNIFER EDGAR was born Deaf to Deaf parents, in Vancouver, British Columbia. She has a Deaf brother, who is married to a Deaf woman, and they have three hearing children. Jennifer currently makes her home in Burnaby, British Columbia.

In 1973, when she was three years old, she was enrolled at Jericho Hill School for the Deaf (JHS) in Vancouver, and remained there for all her education until she graduated in 1988. During those years, however, she attended various off-campus programs as well, including self-contained classes, classes for Deaf students, and mainstream classes.

From 1988 to 1993 Jennifer attended Gallaudet University in Washington, BC, and she considers it one of the best experiences of her life. In 1990 she joined the Phi Kappa Zeta sorority and participated in several duties as a sorority sister. She worked at The Abbey, assisted with the Tower Clock Yearbook, and served as a student residential advisor. In 1993 she graduated with a BEd degree in Elementary Education.

In 1994, when she entered the workforce, Jennifer's first job was as a residential child-care counsellor at Jericho Hill School for the Deaf, now known as the Victory Hill Residential Program in Burnaby, BC. In 1996 she began taking classes at the University of British Columbia toward a Master's degree in Deaf Education. She started working as a substitute teacher

at the British Columbia School for the Deaf in Burnaby, BC, in 1999.

She graduated in the spring of 2000, with a Master of Education degree in Deaf Education and is presently teaching grades five and six at South Slope Elementary School in Burnaby.

In her youth, Jennifer participated in Brownies and Girl Guides. She attended the Canada Deaf Youth Leadership Camp at Gimli, Manitoba, in 1996, and was also involved in the Encounter Program at the Terry Fox Centre in Ottawa, Ontario. As a student at Jericho Hill School for the Deaf, she won several scholastic awards.

Jennifer's hobbies and interests are varied. She likes working at crafts such as scrapbooking, creating greeting cards, and making Christmas tree ornaments. She also likes to read and is fond of camping and socializing with her many friends. Her most recent interest is in ASL Deaf literature and she eagerly looks forward to pursuing it in her spare time.

Considering her relative youth and her many ambitions, Jennifer's future will doubtlessly include many more interesting experiences and laudable accomplishments.

EGGER (BIRLEY), Marian Alma

1928–
Farmer, Hairdresser, Business Partner, and Volunteer.

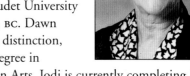

MARIAN MEDLAND was born into a hearing family of six at Dunrea, Manitoba, a farming community near the town of Killarney. Her Deafness went undetected until she was two years old, her family assuming that she was simply slow in developing.

After her Deafness was diagnosed she was sent to provincial residential schools for the Deaf, first in Winnipeg and then in Saskatoon. She graduated just as World War II was ending in 1945, and was one of the first Deaf students to be awarded a scholarship by the Manitoba government to be used for further training and education. Marian decided to become a hairdresser, as opposed to pursuing a teaching degree at Gallaudet College in Washington, BC.

After finishing her training and working briefly as a hairdresser, she and a hearing friend who knew Sign Language went into partnership and established a very successful hairdressing business in Killarney. Later, Marian also worked in a large beauty salon in Regina after marrying her first Deaf husband, Bill Birley, and before their two sons were born—Dale, who is Deaf, and Scott who is hearing.

Marian's present husband, Ralph Egger, is also Deaf. The couple farmed in partnership for many years at Lake Lenore, Saskatchewan, before they retired to the nearby town of Humboldt. Marian has five grandchildren, two step-grandchildren, three great-grandsons, and two step-great-grandsons, the most recent being a pair of twins. Two of her grandchildren, Dawn Jani and Jodi Birley, are Deaf. Both attended Gallaudet University in Washington, BC. Dawn graduated with distinction, earning a BA degree in Communication Arts. Jodi is currently completing her studies there.

Marian has taught Sign Language in her community and has been an active member of Saskatchewan's various organizations of the Deaf. She volunteered her help with the Students' Signing Club in Humboldt and was a member of the Lioness Club in Lake Lenore, where the Eggers had farmed. As retirees, Marian and Ralph spend their time traveling, camping, visiting their family, and socializing with friends. They both enjoy sports and a number of hobbies.

Marian cherishes many fond memories of her residential school and home experiences which helped to shape her life and open so many fascinating doors for her. She especially recalls the many humorous occurrences that constituted dormitory life and made everyone laugh. Fairly recently, she discovered she has a culturally Deaf cousin, Phyllis Calnon, of Branch, Michigan, who was educated at the School for the Deaf in Michigan. Marian and Phyllis now communicate regularly and enjoy a close friendship.

EHRLICH, Christine M.

1964–
Educator, Educational Coordinator, Traveller, and Proponent of Deaf Equality.

CHRISTINE EHRLICH was born hearing to hearing parents in the Kitchener-Waterloo area of Ontario. She became Deaf before her first birthday from the side-effects of medication prescribed for an ear infection. She has no known Deaf relatives and currently makes her home in Belleville, Ontario.

Christine received her early education at E.C. Drury School for the Deaf in Milton, graduating in 1983. She then enrolled at Gallaudet University in Washington, BC, and graduated with a Bachelor of Science degree in Business Administration. Before entering the workforce, she travelled extensively in Africa and South America, particularly in Kenya and Guyana. She joined an international team of volunteers to travel to Guyana to work with local people on community-based projects, from school improvement to rainforest preservation. On returning to Canada in 1991, she was an instructor at Mohawk College in Hamilton, Ontario, working to help Deaf adults build a better future in the working world through the Deaf Empowerment Program.

In 1992 Christine entered the world of banking when she became an employee of the Royal Bank of Canada. Later, however, a major restructuring of the Royal Bank's organization led Christine to consider other career pathways.

In 1991 she was one of the co-founders of GOLD (Goal: Literacy for Deaf Adults), and this sparked her interest in Deaf education. Through her volunteer services with the Ontario Association of the Deaf and the Ontario Interpreting Services Advisory Council, she became involved in working with interpreters. This eventually led her to work as a professional Deaf interpreter herself. She worked on a contractual basis as a research and community developer with the Social, Planning and Research Council (SPRC) in Hamilton, conducting a feasibility study to establish an entrepreneurship program for the Deaf Community living in the Golden Horseshoe area.

When her last contract expired, Christine considered a career change. She decided she would go into full-time teaching and subsequently enrolled at York University's Teacher Training College in Toronto, where she earned a Bachelor's degree in Education. She is currently employed as a high school teacher at Sir James Whitney School for the Deaf in Belleville, Ontario. In addition, she serves as an Ontario ASL Curriculum team member, and is vice-president of the Canadian Cultural Society of the Deaf. She also attends summer sessions to upgrade her professional teaching certification.

Despite her hectic life, Christine finds time to enjoy reading, art, world affairs, and outdoor activities such as skiing, camping, and travelling. She challenges people she meets, old friends and new acquaintances alike, with thought-provoking questions and ideas, encouraging them to think of their values and formative experiences that will help them set goals and dream dreams. For many, she has spurred them on to make those dreams become realities.

ELGAR, Margaret Fern

1955–
Graduate of Carleton University, Strong Advocate for Deaf Women's Issues, and a Lover of New Challenges.

FERN ELGAR was born Deaf to hearing parents, William Nelson and Margaret Olive Elgar, in Arcola, although the family resided in nearby Carlyle, Saskatchewan. Fern had other complications at birth, weighing only two pounds and having a heart murmur that required surgical correction. But she was a fighter and miraculously survived. As a child, she spent a great deal of time in the hospital for various reasons. The cause of her Deafness was maternal rubella, but her family was not aware that she couldn't hear until a close friend made the discovery when she was a toddler. She has no known Deaf relatives but has six hearing siblings, four sisters and two brothers—Robert (now deceased), Anne, Mary Jane, Bill, Jean, and Rena. At present, she makes her home in Fort Providence, Northwest Territories.

When she was five years old, Fern's father took her to be enrolled at the Saskatchewan School for the Deaf in Saskatoon. Fern recalls that her introduction to school life as a residential student was somewhat traumatic, but she soon began to develop both receptive and expressive Sign Language skills. She also was fitted with her first hearing aid and discovered sound for the first time in her life. She was given speech and lip-reading training and remembers that she learned to say only words, never full sentences, and that she had to repeat words again and again until her pronunciation was correct. She also remembers verbal, physical, and psychological abuse.

When Fern was fifteen years old, a move to Regina created culture shock for her as she tried to adjust to a mainstream public school system at a time when the use of interpreters was an unthinkable concept. When her father suffered a stroke, she was left without financial support, but found a Catholic high school that waived her tuition fees. Without any support services, it was a frustrating struggle and a school counsellor suggested that she move to Calgary and enrol at Bishop Carroll High School to pursue her goal of attaining a high school diploma.

When she left high school Fern's first job was a summer project with the Southern Alberta Deaf Centre, located in the old YMCA building in Calgary, where she did research related to the building of a new Deaf centre. When this was done, she kept the office open without an executive director for six months until someone was hired, and then stayed on until December 1980. She later worked for Creative Employment Service as a career counsellor for nearly a year. Other employment followed: a community research project at the University of Calgary, teaching ASL to a teacher of autistic children, working as a teacher aide at Queen Elizabeth Elementary School for the Calgary School Board, and teaching ASL in Didsbury, Alberta, to a Deaf girl, as well as the girl's peers and teachers.

In 1989 Fern was accepted at Carleton University in Ottawa, where she spent eight years and attained a Bachelor of Arts degree in Anthropology with high honours in 1994, as well as a Master of Arts degree in Anthropology in 1997. She holds the distinction of being the first Deaf woman in Canada to acquire both a BA and an MA in Anthropology. Her master's thesis on comparative studies related to residential schools and helped her to grow and understand the topic from two perspectives—residential schools for both Deaf and Aboriginal children. Upon completing her graduate studies, she travelled to Newfoundland before heading to northern Québec where she worked with an Inuit teacher and Deaf children and their families.

While attending Carleton University, Fern worked with the Women's Support Service Centre, made educational videotapes, and worked with Jim Roots for the Canadian Association of the Deaf (CAD) for three summers. She did advocacy related to women's issues and was the founder of the Deaf Women's Action Committee, where she worked to restore funding for women's shelters in Ottawa. She was offered a position at Deaf and Hard of Hearing Services (DHHS) in Calgary as an ASL coordinator, so she moved back to Alberta. There, she liaisoned with the Calgary Police Service regarding persons with disabilities, and was the first Deaf woman to participate for fourteen weeks at the Calgary Citizens' Police Academy. This was an eye-opener for her, but a very educational experience. She also lived for a while in a rustic cabin near Cochrane, Alberta, where she had no indoor plumbing. She enjoyed the secluded lifestyle, chopping wood for her wood-burning stove, and living close to nature. She is now facing another new challenge—life in the small, remote northern community of Fort Providence. This will be a new chapter in Fern's life.

In her leisure time, Fern is an enthusiastic amateur photographer, and the subjects she chooses are nature and people. She likes to dance with friends and is an avid hiker and traveller.

ELIYASSIALUK, Annie

1980–
Prospective Midwife or Day-Care Worker in the Remote North.

ANNIE ELIYASSIALUK became Deaf when she was eighteen months old as a result of meningitis. She has no known Deaf relatives. Her grandfather is the renowned Inuit carver Levi Iumaluk. Annie has a young daughter named Rita, and they make their home in Puvirnituq in northern Québec.

When she was four years old, Annie was sent to McGill University Pre-School in Montréal for a year. At the age of five she returned to her home community at Puvirnituq where she attended the regular, main-stream public school until she was fourteen. Returning to Montréal at the age of fifteen, she attended the MacKay Centre for the Deaf, and from 1995 until 1999, the E.C. Drury School for the Deaf in Milton, Ontario.

Since the birth of her daughter, Annie has been a stay-at-home mother, but she has established a goal to further her education with the hope of possibly becoming a qualified midwife. On the other hand, because she loves children, she may opt for training in early childhood education so she can eventually operate or work in a day-care centre.

She is one of only two Deaf people living in Puvirnituq, the other being a young Deaf boy. Recently, the community has, for the first time, experienced the presence of an ASL interpreter for these two Deaf young people, and they are learning to communicate with them through signs and gestures. Another bonus was that the interpreter was from Ottawa and had Deaf parents, so Annie learned a great deal about other Deaf people and her own identity as a Deaf person.

She is grateful that she had the opportunity to attend the MacKay School in Montréal and E.C. Drury School in Milton, where she learned about Deaf Culture and its distinguishing features. She also learned the differences between her Inuit culture and the "white" culture of her peers. Unfortunately, she was very homesick for her family and community, so she decided to return to her roots when she completed her schooling. Now she misses the Deaf Community in Montréal, and is pondering the wisdom of returning to the south in the future. At present, she is committed to enrolling in early childhood education at Dawson College in Montréal in either the fall or winter session in 2001–02.

Annie is young and ambitious and has many possible career paths open to her in the future, as she leads the way in breaking down the many barriers that presently exist for both Deaf and Inuit youth.

ELLIOTT (GOSSE), Lucinda Jane

1889–1994
Deaf Pioneer in British Columbia.

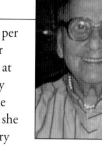

Known as "Lucy" to her family and friends, LUCINDA GOSSE was born Deaf on 1 August 1889, the tenth and youngest child of Stephen and Lucinda (Hennessy) Gosse in Tilton, a small settlement near Spaniards Bay, Newfoundland. Lucy had an older Deaf sister, Diana, and three Deaf cousins: Billy Noseworthy, whom Diana later married; Jonathan Gosse; and Leonard Bishop. They were all sent to the Institution for the Deaf and Dumb, later called the Halifax School for the Deaf (HSD) in Nova Scotia, because no school for Deaf children existed in Newfoundland until the early 1960s. They were residential students who went home only for the summer months.

Lucy's education began in September 1898 and ended in June 1907 when she was eighteen. She was taught orally because she was deemed to have greater "speech potential" than Diana and their cousins who were taught manually. Lucy became quite good at speech and lipreading, but later preferred to communicate with hearing people through writing. Her English was good and she was an avid reader who continued to educate herself until her sight failed at the age of 103. She was proud of the fact that she had met Alexander Graham Bell when he visited the school in Halifax. She also met Helen Keller, the famous Deaf-Blind author and lecturer, and her teacher/companion, Anne Sullivan, when they stayed at the school.

Lucy's mother died in 1907, her father in 1909, and Lucy left Newfoundland the following month. She went to live with Diana and Billy Noseworthy in North Sydney, Nova Scotia, where she found employment in a chocolate factory. In 1911, Lucy, Diana, and Billy Noseworthy, and their baby, Lucy, who was also Deaf, moved to Vancouver, British Columbia. Their cousin, Captain Richard Gosse, owned several salmon canneries along the coast and he gave Billy a job. Lucy hoped he would also find her a job and a place to live, but he insisted she come to live with him and his family because girls of good background did not work or live alone in those days. In November 1912 Lucy, knowing she was not welcome in the home of the Gosse family, solved the problem by finding herself a cheap housekeeping room and a

sewing job that paid $1.50 per week. Later she worked for Purdy's Chocolates, which at that time, consisted of only Mr. Purdy and three female staff members. Eventually, she worked for Pioneer Laundry with a salary of $10.00 per week. She managed to do all of this on her own as there were no advocates nor interpreters for the Deaf in those days.

By 1914 she was living in a rooming house operated by Miss Lily Archibald, a former assistant matron at HSD. Lily's Deaf sister Dolly, who lived with her, had gone to school with Lucy. Through the Archibald sisters, Lucy renewed her acquaintance with Miss Mabel Bigney, one of her former teachers in Halifax. In December 1914, Mabel and Lucy discussed the possibility of starting a small school for Deaf children in Vancouver. At that time the nearest School for the Deaf was in Winnipeg, Manitoba. With Lucy's help, Mabel Bigney started a school with nine pupils in the fall of 1915.

In June 1915, Lucy was married to a Deaf man, Albert Thomas Elliott, a bookbinder by trade, who had come to Vancouver from England in 1906. They had two children—a son, Vince, and a daughter, Delsa. Later there were two grandchildren and four great grandchildren as well.

Albert died on 16 March 1962 in his ninety-first year, and Lucy on 11 March 1994, in her one-hundred-and-fifth year. Both were members of the Plymouth Brethren from 1923 until they died. In 1923 they had met Gottleib Groth, a member of the Brethren, who was fluent in Sign Language and acted as their interpreter at the meetings. It is quite possible this may have been the first religious service of any kind accessible to the Deaf in Vancouver.

Lucy's contributions to Deaf education in British Columbia was recognized when one of the campus houses at the present School for the Deaf in Burnaby was named Lucy Gosse House. Her life story was included in Clifford Carbin's book, *Deaf Heritage in Canada*, published in 1996 by McGraw-Hill Ryerson Limited.

ELLIOT (KERR), Sheilagh

1937–1995
Dedicated Volunteer, Bell Canada Employee, and Proud Mother.

SHEILAGH KERR was born Deaf in North Bay, Ontario. Soon after her birth, she was given up for adoption, and was one of four children adopted by a childless couple, the Bumsteads, from New Liskeard, Ontario. She has no known Deaf relatives but her husband, David Elliot, now deceased, was a Deaf man from Guelph, Ontario, who worked for the Burlington daily newspaper, and later, for a St. Catharines newspaper. Sheilagh and David had four hearing children—three sons, Danny, Shane, and Shawn, and a daughter, Dawn. Danny, who is married and has two children, is a fully qualified ASL interpreter and works at the School for the Deaf in Belleville, from which both his parents graduated. Dawn is a single mother of two and lives in British Columbia, and Shane is married and attends college. Sheilagh was a very proud grandmother who made her home in St. Catharines, Ontario, for many years.

She was educated at the Ontario provincial School for the Deaf at Belleville, now known as the Sir James Whitney School for the Deaf. She was a residential student who went home only for the Christmas and summer holidays, and remained at the school for fourteen years. She then returned home to New Liskeard to work for two years but felt very isolated because there were so few Deaf people in the area. She longed for the fellowship of her Deaf friends. In 1958 she decided to move to Toronto where she could enjoy the activities in the large Deaf Community, as well as improve her education. It turned out to be a wise decision because she was very happy there and was able to secure a good job with Bell Canada.

Before long Sheilagh started dating the man who was to become her husband, David Elliot, from Burlington. He too had attended the School for the Deaf in Belleville, so they had much in common. They were married in 1964 and Sheilagh asked to be transferred to Hamilton so she could live in Burlington and commute to work from there.

In 1969 the Elliots moved to St. Catharines, where David accepted a job with the local newspaper. Their third and fourth children were born in St. Catharines. Sadly, their fourth child, Shawn, drowned in a swimming pool accident when he was eighteen months old. Then, in 1982, David had to undergo heart surgery, but did not survive. He died in October of that year, three weeks after the operation.

Two of Sheilagh's children, Dawn and Shane, spent three summers of their teen years volunteering at the Deaf Youth Camp at Parry Sound, Ontario, where they served as camp counsellors, and greatly enjoyed the experience. Sheilagh was a very active member of the Deaf Community, serving as a board director for the Ontario Association of the Deaf (OAD) and sitting on various committees for the National Festival of the Arts (NFA), as well as the Ontario Festival of the Arts (OFA). She made many volunteer contributions of her time and energy to the St. Catharines Calvary Church of the Deaf and also worked at the Oshawa Deaf Centre, where she was involved in the day program, the Deaf adult lifeskills program, and the literacy skills program, as a contract worker.

Sheilagh was always proud of her achievements as well as those of her three children, who are all fluent in ASL. She kept busy with contract work and, in her leisure time, enjoyed her three cats, one of which was Deaf and was given to her by the local veterinarian. She also liked walking, knitting, and socializing with her friends. Above all, she loved spending time with her grandchildren who were devoted to her. Her death on 3 March 1995 left a profound void in her family and her community. She is deeply missed and lovingly remembered by her children, grandchildren, and her many friends.

EULOTH, Susan Laurie

1967–

Award-Winning Majorette, Canada Customs Law Enforcement Clerk, Sign Language Instructor, and Proud Mother.

SUSAN EULOTH was born to hearing parents in Halifax, Nova Scotia, and has lived in Lower Sackville all her life. Her Deafness was not detected until she was about a year old. Her only Deaf relative is her grandfather, Lester Brown, now in his eighties, with whom Susan has always had a wonderful, warm relationship. He attended the Halifax School for the Deaf and has mixed recollections of his education there. Susan's partner, Donald Doyle, from New Glasgow, Nova Scotia, is also Deaf. Together they are raising Tyler, Susan's wonderful hearing son from an earlier relationship.

Susan began her education at the age of two in a preschool for Deaf children at Ardmore School in Halifax, attending from 1969 to 1972. It was there that she met her close friend Beverly Buchanan. She was then transferred to "out classes" for Deaf students (part of the program at the Interprovincial School for the Deaf, now known as the Atlantic Provinces Special Education Authority [APSEA]) at Burton Ettinger Elementary School until she was eleven. Her parents encouraged her to continue in the mainstream public school system, and she eventually graduated from grade twelve. Susan now marvels at how much she was able to learn without the assistance of an interpreter in any of her classes.

She also considers herself extremely fortunate to have had as her best childhood friend Beverly Buchanan, whose family lived nearby. Beverly now resides in Texas but most of her Deaf relatives are still in Nova Scotia. Susan had the greatest admiration for Beverly's Deaf parents, siblings, and other relatives. They also had a special tie in the fact that Beverly's father, Len Buchanan, and Susan's grandfather, Lester Brown, had once worked together as stevedores in Halifax. Her association with the Buchanans provided Susan with a wealth of experience and knowledge about the local Deaf Community and Deaf Culture. Thus, she grew up developing a deep respect and esteem for Deaf people. She accompanied her Deaf friends to Summer Sounds, a recreational program geared toward Deaf and hard-of-hearing children which included summer camps. She attended Deaf camps until 1980, when she

began to travel around Nova Scotia with her majorette group. She also travelled with her family to the United States and Ontario, but she continued to be invited to attend events in the Deaf Community. Susan had joined the majorettes with her sister, and continued with the hearing group for four years. She won many awards for her performances, including the title "Miss Congeniality." She was comfortable in both worlds, Deaf and hearing.

While she was in high school, Susan was the recipient of an award for the most improved grades. This led to an offer from the Interprovincial School for the Deaf in Amherst (now known as APSEA), for her to travel to Alberta in 1985, along with three other Maritime students (Patrick Davis, Cindy Gent, now Cindy Koskie, and Susan Oram), on a YMCA-sponsored two-week trip. This was a marvelous revelation to Susan, in terms of the scope and influence of the Deaf world, when she met Deaf peers from many other countries.

Susan took a computer training course in Halifax and found full-time permanent employment with Canada Customs as a law enforcement clerk. She has also "team-taught" a Sign Language course with Alan Williams, a Deaf employee, to other Federal government employees, to enable them to learn more about the culture and language of their Deaf colleagues. She was co-chairperson for the Public Service Alliance of Canada (PSAC) Communication Challenge for Deaf employees, and presented monthly workshops throughout Nova Scotia for three years. This program has been discontinued as the number of federal government Deaf employees has decreased.

Susan is proud of her partner, Donald Doyle, who operates his own successful woodworking business and is well-liked, respected, and in great demand for his work in Pictou County, Nova Scotia. She also takes great pride in the achievements of their son Tyler. In her leisure hours she likes spending time with them in various family activities. She also loves to go camping with Deaf friends during summer weekends and enjoys being a mom to Tyler.

EVENSEN-FLANJAK, Aastrid Rosalind

1958–
ASL-Deaf Studies Instructor, Avid Swimmer, Lover of Deaf Theatre, and Active Volunteer.

AASTRID EVENSEN was born hearing to hearing parents, John Henry Evensen, sawmill owner, and Margaret Elizabeth Macdonald (deceased), primary school teacher, in Prince George, in the British Columbia interior. She was their fifth child, joining two brothers, Martin (deceased) and David, and two sisters, Wendy and Heidi. Aastrid was walking and talking at ten months of age when she was stricken with spinal meningitis, a nearly fatal illness. She eventually recovered but was left Deaf, possibly due to the extraction of body fluid from her spinal cord or the large amounts of sulfa medication used to save her life. She is now married to a Deaf spouse, Mijo Flanjak, and they have four hearing daughters, Camille, Jasmine, Lily, and Alyssa. The family has lived in White Rock, BC, for a number of years.

Aastrid was sent to Jericho Hill School for the Deaf and Blind (JHS) in Vancouver at the age of four. Although she was eventually an off-campus student at mainstream elementary and high schools, she remained in the JHS dormitory for fourteen years. There, she became fluent in ASL and was steeped in Deaf Culture. Aastrid then enrolled at Gallaudet College (now Gallaudet University), in Washington, BC, in 1977, but did not complete her degree at that time. She does, however, plan to do so as soon as possible, whenever she can find enough spare time in her busy life.

In 1973 she swam for Team Canada at the World Summer Games of the Deaf in Malmo, Sweden, and again in Bucharest, Romania, in 1977. Although her participation did not yield any medals, it was an exceptional experience for her, and she continued to swim regularly on the Gallaudet campus, winning several awards. She still enjoys swimming as a stress-reducer and leisure activity. She has always had a great passion for theatre and won an award for best supporting actress in the Gallaudet theatrical production of *What*.

Aastrid's employment experience has been varied. At college, she held many different part-time jobs in order to earn enough money to travel to exotic places like Merida, Mexico, Florida, and Cat Island, Bahamas. After a series of other short-term jobs related to Deafness, Aastrid finally found her present job, which she loves. She is an ASL-Deaf studies instructor at Vancouver Community College, where she teaches hearing students three different courses in a ten-month program: visual-gestural communication (VGC), Deaf literature, and ASL literature. For the last few years she has also tutored Deaf children, been an invited presenter on numerous occasions, and has done ASL consulting such as translating English-language scripts into ASL for Deaf actors. In that capacity, she was involved in the production of such videos and plays as *See You in Court, Enough is Enough, My Mother's Tongue*, and the opera *Die Fledermaus*. Once a year, when ASL interpreters apply for COI (Certificate of Interpreting), Aastrid rates their receptive and expressive ASL skills.

She is very active in the Deaf Community, promoting ASL and Deaf Culture. She has served in various capacities with the British Columbia Cultural Society of the Deaf, the Norwest Deaf Outdoor Club, the Canadian Cultural Society of the Deaf, the Deaf Community Foundation, and the Deaf Theatre Club.

Aastrid's present goals are threefold: earn an Instructor' Diploma, complete her BA degree at Gallaudet, and acquire a Master of Arts degree in Deaf Education. She would also love to travel extensively when she can afford to do so.

Her favourite hobbies are gardening and reading to Deaf children as well as to her hearing daughters. She also enjoys walking in the various local parks in her area and likes joining her family in the two pastimes they all love best—camping and boating. No doubt her personal history will have several interesting additional chapters as she pursues her goals.

FALVEY (FLETCHER), Diane Margaret

1957–
ASL and Deaf Culture Specialist, Entrepreneur, Video Producer, and Business Partner.

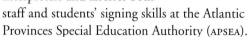

DIANE FLETCHER was born Deaf in Wawa, Ontario. She is a direct descendant of William Fletcher, an Irishman who arrived in Nova Scotia in 1755 and settled in Londonderry. In 1856 Mary Jane Fletcher of Londonderry, a distant relative of Diane's, was one of the first two Deaf pupils taught by William Gray, a Deaf Scottish tailor, in Halifax. Although Mary Jane Fletcher died an untimely death, she was nevertheless registered as Pupil #1 in Book #1 of the Institution for the Deaf and Dumb, which later became the Halifax School for the Deaf. Mary Jane had a younger Deaf brother who died as a child. Diane has no other known Deaf relatives. Her husband, Mike Falvey, is a hearing man and a certified ASL interpreter. They have a hearing daughter, Rebecca, and live in Halifax.

After attending the local school in Wawa for a year, Diane was enrolled at the Metropolitan School for the Deaf in Toronto. Later, she was transferred to the Ontario School for the Deaf (now Sir James Whitney School), in Belleville. She was active in track and field and swimming, was a junior counsellor, and worked for a newspaper in Belleville as part of her graphic arts training. Diane graduated in 1977 and returned to Wawa where she worked for a steel company for a year. She took a year off to travel to British Columbia and Ottawa before returning to Wawa to work for the Ontario Ministry of Resources.

In 1980 she moved to Toronto and worked for the Ontario Ministry of Government Services as a data-entry operator while attending evening classes at York University. She was asked to teach an evening ASL class, and thus began her career as an ASL instructor. After five years of teaching evening courses, she took a full-time position with the Canadian Hearing Society (Toronto Region) as coordinator of its ASL program.

In 1990 Diane moved to Halifax where she taught Deaf Culture and ASL to students in the Interpreting program at Saint Mary's University, and began to expand her classes to include a wide variety of students in different institutions and venues, and at many levels. She was particularly fond of teaching Deaf, hearing, and hard-of-hearing children about their heritage and language, but also found it interesting to work with such groups as recruits in the Halifax Police Force.

In 1994 Diane established a home-based business, Falvey Sign Language Consulting, where hundreds of students have taken her instruction and gone on to become interpreters or work with the Deaf in other

fields. She develops curricula suited to the specific needs of groups such as her "Sign Language for Cops" and "Signs for Northwood Staff." She evaluates Sign Language interpreters and assesses both staff and students' signing skills at the Atlantic Provinces Special Education Authority (APSEA).

Her first experience behind a videocamera occurred when she was asked to record the proceedings at the Deaf Way '89 International Conference in Washington, BC, for the Canadian Hearing Society. In 1990 she was hired to produce a series of stories signed in MSL to benefit interpreter trainees. In 1995 her company produced an eighty-minute documentary, *Maritime Deaf Heritage*, exploring the lives of three famous Deaf Nova Scotian artists—Forrest Nickerson, Christy MacKinnon, and Manton Nickerson.

In 1999 Diane was involved in a pilot project with Human Resources Development Canada (HRDC) which reproduced an information website in ASL on CD–ROM. In 2000 she and her husband, who is also her business partner, produced interpretive videos in Sign Language to facilitate the collective agreement between the Canada Post Corporation and the Canada Union of Postal Workers' contract for Deaf postal workers. She also worked with Pat Boudreault, an LSQ instructor from Montréal, to develop the LSQ version of the same project for Deaf French postal workers. In 2001 she produced a videotape of MSL signs for staff at Northwood Centre for Seniors which caters to Deaf residents on one floor of the building.

Research has played an important role in Diane's work as well. She was a research assistant for a project on Deaf entrepreneurship in Nova Scotia under the aegis of the Deafness Advocacy Association Nova Scotia. In addition, she has done research on Deaf day-care programs in Canada for the Canadian Association of the Deaf.

Diane has been taking university classes with a Bachelor's degree in mind. She has been featured twice on CBC's *Man Alive*, discussing ASL and Deaf Culture issues. She is also involved in several Deaf organizations —the Nova Scotia Cultural Society of the Deaf, where she serves on its MSL research committee; the Society of Deaf and Hard of Hearing Nova Scotians; the Deafness Advocacy Association Nova Scotia; and the Halifax

Association of the Deaf. She has also worked with the Nova Scotia Disabled Persons Commission to develop interpreter policy for the provincial government.

In her rare leisure hours, Diane enjoys gardening, photography, reading, and jogging. She says that "helping people" is part of who she really is.

FARR (DECKER), Susan Elizabeth

1954–
Data-Entry Clerk and Bookkeeper, ASL Instructor, and Deaf Mother of Two Deaf Daughters.

SUSAN FARR was born Deaf into a hearing family in St. Catharines, Ontario. Her parents were not informed of her Deafness until Susan was two years old. Professional advisers suggested that they should get in touch with the John Tracey Clinic in Los Angeles, California, (which has a strictly oral policy) in order to learn how to communicate with their daughter. Instead, they sent her to St. Mary's School for Deaf Children at the age of three and a half years. There, they had to pay a tuition fee of $65.00 per month, which was a large sum of money in the 1950s. Fortunately, her grandparents were able to help with the payments. The Farrs ran a family business, Farr Drainage, which they had purchased from Susan's grandfather.

Susan was married to a Deaf man, Bill Whyte, but they are divorced, and Susan had custody of their two Deaf daughters, Aimee and Ashleigh. She has temporarily given up her custody of Ashleigh until she completes a pending move to Florida. Ashleigh will remain at E.C. Drury School for the Deaf in Milton, where the staff knows her, and where she is comfortable, until she graduates. One of Susan's cousins also has a Deaf daughter, Shinika Reid, who is a student at E.C. Drury School (ECD) in Milton. There are no other known Deaf relatives.

Susan is now married to a kind and caring man with normal hearing, Joe Decker, and they are in the process of making their permanent home in Englewood, Florida.

When Susan was five years old she was sent to the Ontario School for the Deaf in Belleville, and was later transferred to the new School for the Deaf in Milton, Ontario, where she attended from the age of eight until she was seventeen. She realizes now that none of the schools she attended did anything to foster her Deaf identity and heritage. As an adult, Susan has furthered her education and knowledge in various ways, attending classes at Lougheed College in Kitchener and workshops related to Deaf Culture. It was not until she started learning about Deaf Culture and met the Deaf politician Gary Malkowski that Susan began to understand what she had been denied when she was growing up.

Employment-wise, Susan has had a varied career, mainly as an officeworker and bookkeeper. She started out at R & R Chemicals in St. Catharines, and then moved to Kitchener where she worked for a music company. She later landed a job as a data-entry clerk with the Raytheon Company in Waterloo. It was at that time that she married Bill Whyte, who worked for an appliance company, but was often laid off. They moved back to St. Catharines where Susan had gotten a job with General Motors, and worked there as a data-entry operator for fourteen years. Bill worked in the General Motors plant and they lived comfortably, although not always happily. Susan called the Canadian Hearing Society (CHS) and asked about teaching ASL classes, but was advised to take some preliminary Deaf Culture classes at CHS in Hamilton. At that point she had no idea what Deaf Culture actually meant.

When she began to attend the classes, Susan at last found the identity she had been seeking all her life, and began to understand what oppression means. She also realized she was inflicting the same misconceptions on her own Deaf daughters, and decided at once to have them transferred from their mainstream programs to the E.C. Drury School for the Deaf in Milton. This was by no means a simple matter because she met with a great deal of opposition from various sources, but finally, in February 1989, she succeeded. In the meantime, she was working full-time at General Motors, teaching ASL classes at night and coping with a marriage breakdown. In addition, her father died of lung cancer and her younger brother Tom, who was a partner in the family business, was killed in a motorcycle accident.

She was responsible for convincing the Niagara College administration of the need to hire Deaf ASL instructors, helped to prepare a Parent Sharing Kit, and has consistently advocated for ASL as a first language and English as a second language for Deaf children. Susan has been involved in many different political issues related to the Deaf, once leading a political rally in St. Catharines, and encourages her ASL students to write letters to their MPs suggesting solutions to some of the existing problems. She firmly believes that Deaf role models are essential to giving Deaf students confidence and pride in themselves.

Meanwhile, Aimee graduated from ECD, and attended the Rochester Institute of Technology (RIT) in Rochester, New York, where she excelled in her studies, and is preparing to move to Washington, BC, to obtain a Master's degree. Ashleigh continues at ECD. At this time, Susan's life is still a "work in progress," and the same can be said of both her daughters.

FEE (BROOKER), Margaret ("Peggy") Gladys

1934–
Dedicated Telephone Employee, BC Deaf Woman of 1975–80, Curling Enthusiast, and Tireless Volunteer for Organizations of the Deaf.

PEGGY BROOKER was born Deaf into a fourth-generation Deaf family in 1934. Her grandfather, Samuel Hawkins, was one of six Deaf brothers who came from Ireland. Her grandmother, Anna Lenuin, emigrated with her family from Austria to homestead at Lipton, Saskatchewan. Samuel and Anna married and had five Deaf children—Robert, Violet Rose, Christopher, Martha, and Samuel, Jr. Two of Violet Rose's children were born Deaf—Sidney, now deceased, and Margaret (Peggy)—and she also had one son who is hearing, Howard, named after Howard John McDermid, principal of the Manitoba School for the Deaf from 1909 to 1920.

Besides her immediate family, Peggy's Deaf relatives include cousins, uncles, great-uncles, an aunt, a niece, and a great-niece. Among them are Sherry Hawkins-Gabel of Olathe, Kansas, and Hal Pryor Hawkins of Detroit, Michigan, as well as Avonne Brooker-Rutowski and Alexandria Rutowski of Austin, Texas. She also had another Deaf cousin, Ross Bodkin, who died in 1966. She has been married to a Deaf spouse, Ronald D. Fee, for over thirty-five years. Together they have made extraordinary contributions of their time and talents to numerous organizations of the Deaf in areas such as sports, politics, and culture. Two hearing relatives who are ASL interpreters are Janice Hawkins-Williams of Des Moines, Iowa, and Ava Hawkins of Vancouver, BC.

Although her grandfather had homesteaded at Lipton, Saskatchewan in 1905, Peggy's parents were living in Calgary, Alberta, by the time she and her Deaf brother Sidney were born. In 1948 the family moved to the west coast and settled in the Vancouver area. Both Peggy and Sidney attended the British Columbia School for the Deaf and Blind; Peggy, from 1940 to 1953, and Sidney from 1939 to 1951 when he dropped out to join the workforce. While she was a student, Peggy was president of the student council and the Busy Bee Association. She was also awarded the "Best All-Round Athlete of the Year Championship" in 1952. Sidney was an outstanding basketball player, fastball pitcher, curler, and golfer who was inducted into the Northwest Athletic Association of the Deaf (NWAAD) Hall of Fame.

After graduating, Peggy was employed with BC Telephones as a clerical worker and in the Plant Craft Shop from 1954 until her retirement in 1993. Among her awards and honours during that period of her life were two memorable presentations—she was declared a "Telephone Pioneer of America" and "BC Deaf Woman of 1975 to 1980." In addition, she was granted life membership in the Greater Vancouver Association of the Deaf (GVAD).

Peggy knew Ernie Marwick, the first Deaf Canadian to participate in the Deaf World Games in 1959. By asking two of her friends to organize the Canadian Athletic Association of the Deaf (CAAD), she enabled Ernie to represent Canada in Montana-Vermala, Switzerland, in 1959. He had previously participated, as an individual, in Oslo, Norway, in 1955, but Canada had no national Deaf Sports Association at that time. The title of the organization later changed to the Federation of Silent Sports of Canada, and more recently to the Canada Deaf Sports Association. Peggy met her husband, Ronald Fee, who was from Québec, at a Western Canadian Association of the Deaf convention in Vancouver in 1960. There, she introduced him to the CAAD committee.

Both Peggy and her husband love sports, especially curling. Ronald was the founder of several Deaf sports associations—the Federation of Silent Sports, Canada (FSSC), BC Deaf Sports Federation (BCDSF), and the Canada Deaf Curling Championships (CDCC). He was also president of the Canadian Deaf Sports Association from 1992 to 1996. Peggy is a past winner of the Ladies' Curling Championship and the Senior's Mixed Championship.

She ia also a long-time member of the Greater Vancouver Association of the Deaf and has held various offices. In a volunteer capacity, she has contributed significantly to committees trying to improve the (BC) Telus Relay Service and Emergency Communication—(911), raise funds, foster training for medical interpreters, and raise awareness of cochlear implantation practices. Peggy is also involved with the BC School for the Deaf Alumni Association and serves as a director on the board of the Western Institute for the Deaf and Hard of Hearing (WIDHH). For thirteen years she was involved with the Canadian Association of the Deaf and was proud to be chosen senior project leader for "Keeping the Hands in Motion," funded by Health Canada to survey Deaf seniors.

In their leisure time, Peggy and Ronald Fee enjoy their home, their log cabin near Mount Baker, and their pet dog. They do a bit of traveling and work together at renovations to their home and cabin.

FISET, Ghysline ("Gigi") Lisa

1954–
Gymnast, Folk Dancer, Outstanding Athlete, and Sportswoman.

GIGI FISET was born hearing to hearing parents in Trois-Pistoles on the Gaspé Peninsula, but became Deaf at the age of three months from unknown causes. She has four brothers and three sisters, and she currently lives in Montréal, Québec. She has no known Deaf relatives.

Gigi received her elementary education at the Institution des Sourdes Muettes and her high school at Lucien-Pagé. From 1979 to 1982 she was in New York at Danse Folklore and also acted as a folk dance instructor for La Troupe Boischatel. She then enrolled at the University of Montréal where she took up accounting, and later studied graphic arts at Vieux-Montréal College. She was secretary-treasurer of the Association Sportive des Sourds du Québec (ASSQ) for two years and has been its president for fourteen years. She was also central director, francophone director, and manager of the 1987–91 competitions for the Canadian Deaf Sports Association (CDSA), and was CDSA's Dart Commissioner from 1992 to 1998. From January to August 2000 she was CDSA's chief director for the 1st PanAm Track & Field for Deaf Children in Aguascalientes, Mexico, and CDSA's coordinator for the badminton team participating in the Deaf World Summer Games in Italy in 2001.

As an employee, she has worked in the postal department of the Scholarship Office and at the National Bank and was ASSQ's coordinator from 1973 to 1998. She was employed in 1999 by the CDSA as administrative secretary, where she is still working.

In her youth, Gigi won two scholarships in gymnastics as well as two gold medals. She also received a green leader badge in swimming and successfully completed the requirements for the survival program. She participated in the second Québec Deaf Sports Championships in 1972 as a volleyball player, with her team winning four medals—one gold, two silver, and one bronze. In 1978 she participated in the Miss Deaf Canada pageant in Montréal, and during the next four years she won three folk dancing trophies as well as a plaque which honoured her for her outstanding contributions to folk dance. In 1990 she was nominated Volunteer of the Year, and was presented with a lovely floral bouquet and a plaque representing the seventeen associations that benefited from her volunteer services. In 1992 she received a plaque from CDSA as best administrator and, in 1995, she was recognized for her youth leadership by Canadian Deaf Youth Camp. In 1998 the commissioner of the Halifax Darts Association presented her with a floral tribute for her expertise at playing darts.

Gigi became active in sports at the age of five. She was an outstanding runner, skier, rollerskater, high jumper, volleyball player, cyclist, water skier, and dodgeball player, but what she loved best of all, was climbing at a camp in Vaudreuil. She participated in volleyball and swimming competitions with hearing athletes and was part of a group that sang at a telethon. She taught Deaf children to sing during a television show featuring René Simard and Ginette Reno.

Gigi has been an active volunteer in the Deaf Community most of her adult life, holding various offices, teaching folk dance, teaching LSQ classes, and working with Deaf athletes. In her leisure hours, she loves to socialize, swim, jog, cross-country ski, play badminton and tennis, skate, golf, walk, read, and draw. This versatile and active woman will continue to make exemplary contributions to the Deaf Community while providing an outstanding role model for the next generation of Deaf women.

FLEMING (PRESISNIUK), Rita Rose

1937–
Library Assistant and Dedicated Deaf Community Worker.

RITA PRESISNIUK became Deaf at the age of two years. She has no known Deaf relatives except one brother (now deceased) who was Deafened at the age of twelve due to a farm accident. Rita's husband, Jack Fleming, is also Deaf, and they have four adult hearing children—Al, Karen, Gerry, and Brent.

Rita was born at Andrew, Alberta, where she grew up on a farm and attended the Andrew Public School from grade one to grade four. Since there was no provincial school for the Deaf in Alberta at that time, Rita was sent to the Saskatchewan School for the Deaf in Saskatoon, where she attended and lived in residence from grade five to her graduation. After her marriage to Jack Fleming, the couple lived in Edmonton and raised their family there.

Rita worked for the City of Edmonton as an assistant in the Edmonton Public Library System for twenty-five years. During those years, she and Jack were very closely involved in the activities of Edmonton's Deaf Community, particularly the Edmonton Association of the Deaf. Rita has served that organization as secretary and as a director at large. Both she and Jack have received awards of appreciation for their many volunteer services.

As a civic employee, Rita was honoured on several occasions for her work and dedication. In December 1993 she was presented with a certificate recognizing her twenty years of devoted service to the citizens of Edmonton. She had perfect attendance for twenty years.

In November 1998 Mayor Bill Smith presented Rita with a certificate of appreciation for her long service, thanking her for her twenty-five years of dedication and commitment to the people of Edmonton. On the occasion of her retirement, Rita received a letter from the City Council and Administration, congratulating her for her achievements and for having contributed her skills and energy for twenty-five years toward making Edmonton a better place to live. She was given special praise for her contributions to the public library system where she provided high-quality, cost-effective service to the citizens of Edmonton.

Rita is justifiably proud of her achievements, her employment record, and the appreciation and recognition she received from her co-workers, the administration, and the people of Edmonton. She is now enjoying her retirement and continues to contribute to the life of the Deaf Community.

FLEMING, Teresa Lynn

1964-
Deaf Day-Care Director, Educator, Promoter of ASL and Deaf Culture, Presenter, and Deaf Community Leader.

TERESA FLEMING was born Deaf in Edmonton, Alberta, and grew up on a farm with her family in Irma, Alberta. She has three sisters, one of whom is Deaf, Linda Mahe, and a Deaf brother-in-law, Laurier Mahe, as well as two adopted Deaf nieces, Michelle and Kristi Mahe. She also has hearing twin sisters, Lorry and Lotty. Lorry has three children, Shelby, Travis, and Tyler. Interestingly, these boys are third-generation twins as Teresa's father is a twin as well. Lotty is married to Wayne Ewasiw and they have three girls, Shae, Jamie, and Alyssa.

Teresa was educated and lived in residence at the Alberta provincial School for the Deaf (ASD) in Edmonton, graduating in 1982. She went on to Gallaudet University in Washington, BC, to earn a Bachelor of Science degree in Recreation and Leisure Studies in 1988. She has been accepted to pursue a Master's degree in Deaf Education at Boston University and hopes to start her studies when it becomes financially feasible.

Her employment career has been eclectic and has taken Teresa to many different cities in Canada and the US. She has worked in a variety of capacities, from camp counsellor and playground leader to her present position as day-care director of Sign Talk Children's Centre Cooperative in Winnipeg. In fact, she is actually the first Deaf director of that program. She has many years of experience in a bilingual-bicultural day-care setting and has a strong sense of fairness and respect for both the Deaf and hearing communities and their respective language and cultures.

In addition to her early childhood development experiences, Teresa has also developed a strong background in ASL and Deaf Culture, having attended and presented at many workshops and seminars across Canada. She is also a member of many organizations and agencies of the Deaf, and has served in a volunteer capacity on most boards and many committees including athletic and sports clubs for the Deaf. She has developed several "A to Z" and number stories and aspires to be a successful ASL storytelling artist, to travel and explore the world.

Her honours and awards include: Miss Deaf Canada, Miss Deaf Alberta, Most Improved Softball Player at Gallaudet University, athletic and academic awards at ASD, valedictorian at graduation exercises, and outstanding female camper. While studying, she was awarded three scholarships—from Omega Chi Chapter of Phi Kappa Zeta in 1982, from Gallaudet University, Alberta Alumni, in 1982 and from the National Fraternal Society of the Deaf in 1982. She is committed to ongoing professional development, particularly with ASL/Deaf literature. In 1999 she received a Ladder Award® from the Canadian Cultural Society of the Deaf for her outstanding ASL/Deaf story.

FOOT, Karen J.

1959–
Interpreter, ASL Instructor, Coordinator, Artistic Director of Films, and Stage Manager.

KAREN FOOT, deaf since her birth in Kamloops, BC, in 1959, is now a single mother of three children—Vanessa, Melissa, and Jeff. Karen's brother Steve is Deaf, and her son Jeff, who has Down's Syndrome, is hard of hearing, so she has a fairly extensive experiential background on the subject of hearing loss. These influences in Karen's life have impacted her professional career choices.

Karen and her family reside in Surrey, BC. She is currently employed as the supervisor of a Deaf (group home) program, and also works as a freelance Deaf interpreter. Most importantly, Karen is a recognized film director and has several productions to her credit. She was on the steering committee which founded Deaf@vi (Video-In Studios) in 1999, and it has continued to the present time. Karen has recruited Deaf film artists to become Deaf filmmakers since 1989.

In 1998 she received the prestigious Hughes Award for Access to Justice for her ASL video entitled *See You in Court* which was produced for the Greater Vancouver Association of the Deaf with support from the BC Legal Education Fund. Although Karen has resumed her maiden name, she also has film credits listed under her former married name, Karen Skelton.

In 1994–95 she directed the video *Enough is Enough* for the Vancouver Branch of Women Against Violence Against Women. She acted as artistic director and stage manager for the production of *Let Us Grow Together* in 1992, *Challenge* in 1990, and *Night of the Stars* in 1985.

Prior to her involvement with filmmaking, Karen was a camera-person, assistant director, and editor for Roger Cablevision, working on programming for the Deaf, in the early 1980s.

Karen brings to her work a wealth of experience both as a paid employee and as a volunteer. She is a graduate of the Jericho Hill School for the Deaf/Kitsilano Secondary Deaf Program. In addition to her formal education, she has attended many conferences and workshops on a wide variety of topics ranging from first aid/CPR to ASL and Deaf Culture.

Karen has always been active in the events of the Deaf community in Vancouver. She has been president and social director of the Norwest Outdoors Club, co-coordinated youth camps, sat on steering committees, and worked as a camp counsellor. She has also contributed her time and skills to such organizations as the Vancouver and Richmond Association for the Mentally Handicapped and has participated in the work of the Down's Syndrome Society. In April 2000 she became part of a group responsible for the eventual establishment of the British Columbia Alliance of the Deaf (BCRAD) on 6 August 2000, with Karen as president.

Karen's many interests and skills make her a highly respected and valuable member of the Deaf Community in the Greater Vancouver region.

FORD (URSEL), Cora Caroline

1941–
Talented Seamstress, Housewife, Devoted Mother, and Grandmother.

CORA URSEL, an only child, was born Deaf to hearing parents, Margaret and Gustav Ursel, in Winnipeg, Manitoba, in 1941. Although the cause of her Deafness is unknown, it was not a shock to her mother because Deafness was not unheard of on her side of the family. Margaret, a travelling schoolteacher and Gustav, a carpenter, sent Cora to the Saskatchewan provincial School for the Deaf in Saskatoon in the fall of 1947, while they remained in Winnipeg. Soon after, Margaret requested a transfer and followed Cora to Saskatoon one year later.

After twelve happy, fun-filled years making many Deaf friends, Cora graduated from the School for the Deaf in 1960. Later that spring, she was hired by Crest Craft as a seamstress, where she worked very happily with many other Deaf co-workers and friends.

During this time, Cora married Garry Ford, an autobody technician, on 1 August 1964. Four years later they started their family. They have two daughters, Camilla (Cammy) and Corissa, both

hearing. Both are married and Cammy has given Cora and Garry two wonderful hearing grandchildren, Jasmine and Brennan, who bring them tremendous joy.

Cora is a talented and accomplished seamstress and expends her creative energy through quilting, knitting, and crocheting crafts, which she gladly shares with family and friends. Cora's hobbies also include spoiling her grandchildren. She does this by sewing unique outfits for each of them. During the summer months, Cora and Garry enjoy camping in their trailer with family and friends at lakes throughout Saskatchewan.

As a member of the Saskatoon Association of the Deaf (SAD), Cora is proud to have served on various committees and actively participated in many events in support of the local Deaf Community for some forty years.

FORGERON (SAMSON), Mary Barbara

1944–
Skilled Seamstress, Craftswoman, and Champion Athlete.

BARBARA SAMSON was born hearing to hearing parents in Little Anse, Île Madame, a small Acadian community off Cape Breton Island in Nova Scotia. It is believed that she became Deaf in infancy, due to jaundice. Her parents were French-speaking Acadians, and it was her maternal grandmother who first detected Barbara's Deafness which was later confirmed by a doctor. Aside from her mother's sister, who was Deaf, Barbara has no other known Deaf relatives. Her husband, Paul Forgeron, is also Deaf, and they have four adult hearing children who are now all established in successful careers, making their parents very proud of them. Barbara and Paul live in Little Anse, Île Madame, in a house Paul built for the family.

Barbara began her education when she was past eight years of age, after waiting two years for a space in the overcrowded Halifax School for the Deaf. She completed her final year of schooling at the new facility, the Interprovincial School for the Deaf in Amherst, Nova Scotia, now known as the Atlantic Provinces Special Education Authority (APSEA). For the next two years she attended the vocational school, later known as the Atlantic Technological Vocational Centre, where her

main focus was on dressmaking as a trade. It was the sewing teacher at the Halifax school, Mrs. Hummed, who had gotten her interested in sewing. Barbara started out by making children's garments.

She was an outstanding athlete at school, excelling in table tennis, darts, and gymnastics, and was also a member of the girls' baseball, soccer, and volleyball teams. She won four table tennis championships and fourteen prizes in darts competitions. In 1960 she and another Deaf student, Connie Agnew, won the Nova Scotia Gymnastic Association's Senior Award, and her volleyball team won the 1963–64 championship in Cumberland County. Barbara was regarded as a "Big Sister" by the younger girls at school. She gave them advice and guidance but always encouraged them to make their own decisions.

As an employee, Barbara worked for Charles Furrier and later for Fit Rite Clothing. After seven years she started offering alterations and customized sewing services to the Île Madame community in 1971. Her husband Paul works as a maintenance man for the Strait Regional School Board. He is also a highly skilled craftsman in woodworking. Barbara has learned tole painting so she can decorate many of the wooden items he creates. She also does knitting and sewing to offer for sale at their two annual shows, one in Port Hawkesbury every October and the second in Petit de Grat each November. Barbara has taken high school upgrading and she and Paul have learned how to market their skills and products very successfully.

There were fifteen Deaf People in their community during the 1980s so they founded the Île Madame Association of the Deaf (IMAD) in 1982. Barbara served as secretary for a year and as president for four years. The members worked very hard to raise funds to purchase TTYs for local Deaf people and support the club. They got together monthly, played darts every two weeks, and organized social events. Unfortunately, the Deaf Community shrank in size so the Deaf Club had to be disbanded in 1994. Those who are left still meet regularly to socialize.

In her spare time, Barbara likes to camp with her family and sometimes with Deaf friends. She continues her stamp-collecting hobby, which began when she was a child.

FOSTER (OSWALD), Emma Albertina

1926-
Baker, Hospital Support Employee, and Tireless Worker for the Deaf Community.

EMMA ALBERTINA OSWALD was a hearing baby born at Waldersee, Manitoba, in the municipality of Glenella, the thirteenth child of Samuel Oswald and Eva Dilk. Her hearing loss occurred when she was eight months old as a result of scarlet fever. She is the only Deaf member of the Oswald and Dilk families.

Emma was sent to Winnipeg to attend the Manitoba School for the Deaf from 1933 to 1940. At that time, World War II was in progress and the school was taken over by the RCAF as a training centre for the British Commonwealth, so the students were transferred to the Saskatchewan School for the Deaf in Saskatoon. Emma graduated from this school in 1944 and, like most young Canadian girls during the war years, immediately entered the workforce.

She found employment at Bryce's Bakery and later at McGavin's in Winnipeg but, in 1947, two years after the war ended, she left her job to marry Laverne Ormal Foster, a teacher of the Deaf and a respected community leader. Their wedding took place at the Waldersee Lutheran Church in Manitoba. The young couple made their home in Saskatoon where they raised their four hearing sons—Wayne, Harry, Murray, and Colin. Emma also worked in linen services at two Saskatoon hospitals, retiring from the workforce in 1988. She was honoured by the Royal University Hospital with ten- and fifteen-year awards for her devoted service.

Although she was a busy wife and mother as well as a dedicated employee, Emma also took a leadership role in the local and provincial Deaf community. The Saskatoon Association of the Deaf awarded her a twenty-five-year pin and a lifetime membership. The Saskatchewan Cultural Society of the Deaf presented her with an Award of Excellence in 1982. She was one of the founding members of the Saskatoon Deaf Seniors' Club and the Bethlehem Church of the Deaf, which has since disbanded.

Emma's husband Laverne, a prominent member of the Deaf community, was inducted into the Saskatchewan Sports Hall of Fame. He is proud to have a famous celebrity among his kinfolk since his mother was a cousin of Vernon Presley, the father of the late Rock and Roll King, Elvis Aron Presley.

Now retired, Emma and Laverne are both still actively involved in the life of Saskatoon's Deaf community.

1934–
Avid Sports Enthusiast, Valued Civic Employee, and Tireless Volunteer in the Deaf Community.

LEILA McEACHERN was born hearing on a farm near Tatsfield, Saskatchewan. She became Deaf at about three months of age, due to illness. She has two Deaf siblings, a sister and a brother, as well as her maternal grandmother, Elizabeth Jeanotte, who lost her hearing at age five, and attended the Manitoba School for the Deaf. Leila has two adult hearing sons, Bob and Kevin. Although she spent most of her life in Saskatchewan and Alberta, she currently makes her home in Burnaby, British Columbia, where she is enjoying her retirement.

Leila attended the Saskatchewan School for the Deaf in Saskatoon for twelve years, from 1941 to 1953. After graduating, she entered the workforce immediately, moving to Edmonton and taking a job as a clerk-typist with the government of Alberta for three years. She went on to work at the military base at Namao, just outside Edmonton, as a clerk-stenographer from 1956 to 1963. For the next three years Leila became a stay-at-home mother with her two young sons, but she returned to the workforce in 1966, when Bob was three and Kevin was a year old. This time she entered her longest period of employment, as a civil servant at City Hall in Edmonton. She retired from this job in 1989, after twenty-three years of dedicated service.

Leila then moved to Vancouver where she worked for Canada Post for another ten and a half years. She retired in March 2000. Always athletic and sports-minded, Leila has many awards to attest her prowess, particularly in badminton and curling. She played with a badminton team, as the only Deaf member among hearing team-mates, that won a championship in 1962. As a curler with the Alberta Deaf Ladies' Team, she won four gold medals and four silver. Since moving to British Columbia, she has curled with the BC Deaf Ladies' Team, winning a gold medal in 1991, a silver in 1993, and two bronze in 1994 and 1997. In addition to her participation in curling, Leila also served on the committee for the World Games of the Deaf from 1992 to 1997. She was honoured as the recipient of a curling achievement award in Alberta in 1987, and a volunteer award from the Canadian Deaf Festival (CDF), in British Columbia in 1992.

Leila has always been very active in the Deaf Community. While living in Edmonton she served as president and later as treasurer of the Edmonton Association of the Deaf. In 1984 she received an appreciation award from the Canadian Cultural Society of the Deaf (CCSD) for her outstanding service. She was a volunteer worker with the Canadian Team at the World Winter Games of the Deaf held in Finland in 1995, and again with the Canadian Team at the World Summer Games of the Deaf held in Denmark in 1997. She is the current secretary for the Canadian Deaf Curling Championship (CDCC) in Vancouver, and her term runs until 2003. She has served on the British Columbia Deaf Sports Board since 1996 as membership director, and since 2000, she has been a member-at-large on the board of the Greater Vancouver Association of the Deaf.

Leila is proud of her achievements as a Deaf woman, and continues to volunteer the skills and the wisdom of her lengthy experience to Deaf Sports and other agencies and organizations in the Deaf Community.

FRITZ, Caroline Anne

1950–
Administrative Secretary, Business Office Manager, and Dedicated Worker for the Deaf Community.

CAROLINE ANNE FRITZ was born Deaf into a hearing family in Allan, a small community near Saskatoon, Saskatchewan. Some of her family members still live in Allan, and also in Chicago, Illinois, although Caroline now makes her home in Edmonton, Alberta.

Caroline attended the Saskatchewan School for the Deaf in Saskatoon from 1956 until she graduated in 1969. She received a trophy for the highest marks in the school in 1967 and the Senior Ring for best all-round character in 1968. Her favourite subjects were algebra and physical education but she enjoyed every aspect of the residential and academic programs offered at her school. During her senior year she found summer employment at the Allan Potash Mines, where the staff appreciated her cheerful manner and her willingness to learn.

She attended Gallaudet University in Washington, BC, for her preparatory and freshman years, receiving mention on the Dean's List in 1970. She then decided to transfer to a business program at the St. Paul Technical and Vocational Institute in Minnesota, where she earned a General Office Practice Diploma. As her career progressed, she continued to further her education, adding to her qualifications, skills, and knowledge by enrolling in a Deaf literacy program, an automated office systems course, an Internet training program and many workshops, seminars, and lectures related to her work.

Her employment has been varied and interesting, beginning with a position as a civil servant with the government of Saskatchewan. She also worked in the corporate sector in Kamloops, BC, held a clerk II position with the Alberta government, and was an office assistant/clerk at the Western Canadian Centre for Studies in Deafness (WCCSD) at the University of Alberta for two years. There she was recognized for her outstanding organizational skills, her self-motivation, and her ability to communicate with both Deaf and hearing persons. Since 1988 she has been employed as administrative secretary for the Canadian Cultural Society of the Deaf (CCSD) at its headquarters in Edmonton.

Caroline was the first full-time, paid administrative secretary for CCSD. She has also received many commendations for her volunteer service with other organizations. With the Alberta Cultural Society of the Deaf, she served as a bylaws committee member, treasurer, representative, and vice-president. With the Edmonton Association of the Deaf, she has been a member of various committees, and, with the Alberta Association of the Deaf, she was assistant recording secretary. The Association of Visual Language Interpreters of Canada has benefited from her services as a testing proctor; at Grant MacEwan College she contributes regularly as a guest ASL model; for the National Festival of the Arts she has been their newsletter typist; for the Canadian Deaf Festival 2000, she was registration chair; for the XII World Winter Games for the Deaf in Banff, Alberta, she acted as housing and catering coordinator; and she was also a volunteer for the Deaf Children's Festival.

She has been actively involved in assisting with many projects undertaken by CCSD; for example, *The Canadian Dictionary of ASL*, Canadian Deaf Heritage Literature Project, ASL Instructors of Canada (organization and evaluation procedures), and the book *Deaf Heritage in Canada* (researching information). She has also made many contributions to CCSD, apart from her regular duties, which have been recognized and acknowledged in several books, manuals, and other publications. She is well known as a tireless volunteer at Alberta School for the Deaf, helping with student conferences and presenting guest lectures. She has volunteered at Deaf Community bingos, casinos, and social events, as well as for the Sign Language Studies Program's popular event "Deaf Deaf World," and for bingo fundraisers sponsored by the Alberta Chapter of the Registry of Interpreters for the Deaf. Caroline is also known for her mentorship to the many Deaf people who flock to her office asking for advice and assistance.

She credits her close friend, Randy Dziwenka, with encouraging her to become involved in Edmonton's Deaf Community where, over the years, she has volunteered her skills and expertise to dozens of projects at both the local and national levels. She often participates at Grant MacEwan College as an ASL guest model. In June 2001 she was the recipient of the Grant MacEwan College Outstanding Volunteer Award, plus a miniature bear as a personal gift in recognition of her fifteen years of voluntary contributions as a role model, friend, and mentor, as well as her dedication and commitment to the college's ASL/English Interpreter Program and Sign Language Studies Program. In July 2001 Caroline was a volunteer staff member representing the Edmonton Association of the Deaf (EAD) and Calgary

Association of the Deaf (CAD) at a summer camp for thirty-seven Deaf children aged six to fifteen, for which she received a Certificate of Appreciation.

She remains close to her family and in her leisure time pursues many interests and hobbies. Although she has no pets or children of her own, she loves dogs and enjoys those owned by her friends. Caroline acts as an honorary mother/grandmother to several former students from the Alberta School for the Deaf. She is interested in interior design, has always had a great passion for hats, and enjoys photography, outdoor camping, watching figure-skating, playing cards, doing jigsaw puzzles, and travelling. She is also an avid collector of miniature and stuffed bears, as well as memorabilia related to the British Royal Family.

This versatile woman continues to give generously of her time and talents to the Deaf Community at every level—local, provincial, and national.

GABEL (HAWKINS), Sherry Susan

1954–
X-Ray Technician Assistant, Accountant, Department Manager, Dormitory Teacher, Paraprofessional, ASL Tutor and Job Coach, and ASL Assistant.

SHERRY HAWKINS was born Deaf to Deaf parents, Samuel and Lena (Chita) Hawkins, in St. Boniface, Manitoba. She has many Deaf relatives— her paternal grandparents, Samuel and Anna Mary Hawkins (Lennius [Lennon]); her brother, Pryor (Hawkins); two aunts, Violet Rose Brooker (Hawkins) and Martha Annie Bodkin (Hawkins); two uncles, Christopher and Robert Hawkins; two cousins, Sid Brooker and Peggy Fee (Brooker); a second cousin, Avonne Rutowski (Brooker); and a third cousin, Alexandria Rutowski. Her grandfather Hawkins, who was born and educated in Dublin, Ireland, came to Canada and opened his own business, a harness shop, in Rounthwaite, near Brandon, Manitoba, in 1890. It flourished until the advent of tractors made farm horses and harnesses obsolete. Sherry is married to a Deaf man, Dennis L. Gabel, a cabinet installer, and they have two hearing adult children, Luke and Rosa, who are both fluent in ASL. Sherry and Dennis make their home in Olathe, Kansas, US.

Sherry was educated at the Saskatchewan School for the Deaf in Saskatoon for two years and then at the Manitoba School for the Deaf in Winnipeg from 1962 to 1972. In 1974 she went on to attend Johnson County Community College in Overland Park, Kansas, graduating with a diploma in Recreational Leadership in 1976. She is trained in ASL diagnostic assessment and visual storytelling, and was the shared reading project coordinator, as well as being a Deaf mentor to the hearing parents of Deaf children.

Her employment record has been varied and interesting. She worked as an assistant x-ray technician at the Assiniboine Clinic in Winnipeg before moving to Kansas, where she became a dormitory teacher at the Kansas School for the Deaf. She also worked as an accountant at Lee, Overland Park, Kansas, and then at Wal-Mart, where she was a department manager. She returned to the Kansas School for the Deaf in 1987, and has served as a paraprofessional, an ASL tutor and job coach, and an ASL assistant, which includes teaching Deaf studies, ASL diagnostic assessment, and visual storytelling.

Her awards and honours include being named Miss Deaf Canada in 1973, and recognition as Wal-Mart Employee of the Month, as well as Salesperson of the Month.

While living and working in Winnipeg, Sherry participated in Silent Skits, and loved it. When she moved to Kansas, she established a Deaf theatre group in Olathe called Signtastics, with only Deaf actors. They started out with variety shows in order to raise funds for stage plays, and in 1992, began offering a play in February on an annual basis. The group's first production was *Tales of the Deaf Clubroom*, in which Sherry acted. In 1993 they produced *Lover's Leap*, for which she served as publicity director. She acted in *Par for the Corpse* in 1994 and directed *Weekend Comedy* in 1995.

In 1997 she acted in *June Groom*, was in charge of ticket sales in 1998 when they staged *The Odd Couple*, and, in 1999, she directed *The Man with the Plastic Sandwich*. Sherry's husband Dennis designs the stage sets for Signtastics. Theatre has always been their greatest mutual interest and hobby.

GAGNE, Sister Marie Paule SNDD

1933–
Teacher, Sister, Member of the House of Faith, and Pastoral Worker Among the Deaf.

SISTER MARIE PAULE GAGNE is one of the Deaf nuns whose name appears in the special section under "sisters" in this book. She was educated at the School for Deaf Girls (Institution des Sourdes) in Montréal, Québec. When she completed her studies, on 8 September 1954, she joined the religious order of La Congrégation des Soeurs de Notre-Dame des Sept Douleurs (The Sisters of our Lady of Seven Sorrows), which is a community of Deaf nuns.

During her life as a teaching nun, she worked with normal Deaf students for eighteen years and then spent twenty-one years teaching Deaf children with multiple disabilities, including the mentally challenged, whom she educated, little by little, with loving care and patience. At the same time, she became a member of a new pastoral project known as the House of Faith (Maison de la Foi).

This enterprise was the brainchild of Father Gerard Bernatchez CPV. Begun in 1988, its purpose is to provide for the spiritual and moral needs of Deaf youth. The House of Faith project is now led by a team of five—three hearing and two Deaf members. The hearing persons have excellent visual language skills such as French Sign, LSQ, and Pidgin Signs, as well as oral communication fluency in speech and lipreading. The two Deaf members are Sister Marie Paule and Mme. Theresa Kelly.

Sister Marie Paule, along with other House Of Faith members, including the founder, Father Gerard, assists at monthly masses and offers support and encouragement to Deaf children and their parents while preparing them for the sacraments. The project has expanded to include Deaf adults who attend religious retreats, nightly meetings, prayer sessions, and pilgrimages. Sister Marie Paule continues to draw Deaf people from every walk of life to join their friendly table for delicious soups, fresh bread and tea or coffee every month. The pastoral team sponsors beautiful gatherings to bring Deaf and hearing parishioners together to reaffirm their faith and to improve communication among them.

Sister Marie Paule is very active in the House of Faith, doing publicity for organized events and spreading the word of God. Not surprisingly, she is full of energy. Her favourite pastime is ice-skating, which she does regularly, outdoors in the winter and indoors during the summer. She resides in Montréal.

GARDNER (GILLMAN), Mary Josephine

1884–1932
Teacher, Writer, Pioneer Wife and Mother, and Respected Member of her Rural Community.

MARY JOSEPHINE GILLMAN was born hearing to hearing parents in Valley Falls, Kansas. Her father was a noted physician and her mother an accomplished pianist. When she was four years old a severe bout of scarlet fever and possibly paralysis brought her danger-ously close to death. Her father called in medical experts and worked desperately to save her life. He succeeded in bringing her back to consciousness but soon realized she had lost her hearing. Despite all his efforts to reverse her Deafness, he was unsuccessful and initially found it difficult to accept the finality of her hearing loss. As a child, the family fondly called her "Pinkie." As she grew up, she preferred to be known as Josephine.

Josephine's education began in 1892 at the Kansas State School for the Deaf in Olathe, where she remained as a residential student until her graduation in 1904. She immediately took the Gallaudet entrance exams, was accepted, and at the age of twenty-one, began her post-secondary studies at Gallaudet College (now University) in Washington, BC, in 1905, in an era when the patron of the College was William Howard Taft, President of the United States of America. In her third year, she met her future husband, the charming, handsome, and gregarious Harry Gardner. Although Josephine graduated before Harry, she returned for his graduation ceremony when he, as the senior class president, delivered the welcoming address at the graduation exercises. During her college years, Josephine maintained an 8.7 academic average, was popular with her peers, participated in athletic and social activities, and was considered a talented writer.

She occasionally contributed to the Gallaudet student newspaper, *The Buff and Blue*. In 1910 she graduated with a Bachelor of Arts degree and was hired as a teacher at the South Dakota State School for the Deaf, where she taught for the next two years.

When Harry graduated in 1912, he and Josephine were married in Oakley, Kansas, and made their first home in Willows, Colorado. Harry's passion for land led them to the Cayley area of Alberta, Canada, to the homestead he had claimed in 1904. The Gardners were capable, industrious, and respected members of the community. Josephine was the talk of the town when she became the first woman in the Cayley district to drive a car, and also when she had one of her articles published in a national women's magazine.

Josephine and Harry raised three hearing children, Daphne, Charles Gillman, and Mary Jean, who were happy and content in their environment. ASL was the first language in the home and, as they matured, the children all became fluently bilingual. While busy tending to her own family, Josephine became concerned about a neighbouring uneducated and naive Deaf girl of about twelve years of age, and spent considerable time tutoring and helping her, a reflection of her compassionate nature. She was a devoted and loving mother who instilled in her children her own fondness of literature and nature, while raising them to become worthy and successful citizens. They have wonderful memories of growing up on the farm where their mother's great warmth and faith sustained the family.

In 1931 Josephine became too ill to continue managing their home in High River and, through a friend, was invited to a private facility in Calgary where she could receive the physical and spiritual care she sought. She passed away peacefully on 6 April 1932, in her forty-eighth year, and was buried in High River, Alberta. Her favourite poet was William Wordsworth, about whom she wrote in 1910, "In the heart of a retiring and lonely worshiper of Nature, this author (Wordsworth), creates a feeling of peace and calm happiness." Perhaps this is also a fitting tribute that can be applied to Josephine Gardner's influence on her family and the prairie community in which they lived.

GAUNA (GRAVELLE), Kristine

1967–
Window-Dresser, Computer Specialist, Research Assistant, LSQ/ASL Deaf Interpreter and Devoted Mother.

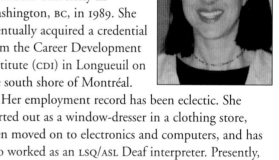

KRISTINE GAUNA was born hearing in Sacramento, California, and became Deaf at the age of eighteen months due to spinal meningitis. She came to Canada in 1991 after meeting her Canadian husband at Gallaudet University, and deciding to move to Montréal. There are no known Deaf relatives on her side of the family, but her Deaf husband, Alain Gravelle, comes from a Deaf family and both of his parents, two brothers, three great-aunts, and two great-uncles are Deaf. Kristine and Alain have three hearing children— Amanda, Alison, and Anisa—all of whom acquired LSQ and ASL as their first language. The family currently makes its home in St. Hubert, Québec, and Kristine is presently a foster mother to a Deaf boy.

Kristine was educated at various schools because her father was a member of the US Airforce and the family moved often. She attended schools in Alaska, Hawaii, and Nebraska—Sustina Elementary and West Anchorage High School in Anchorage, Hawaii School for the Deaf and Blind in Honolulu, and Nebraska State School for the Deaf in Omaha. After graduating, she attended Daytona Beach Community College in 1988 before enrolling at Gallaudet University in Washington, BC, in 1989. She eventually acquired a credential from the Career Development Institute (CDI) in Longueuil on the south shore of Montréal.

Her employment record has been eclectic. She started out as a window-dresser in a clothing store, then moved on to electronics and computers, and has also worked as an LSQ/ASL Deaf interpreter. Presently, she is involved in an exciting project as a research assistant to Dr. Laura Ann Petitto at McGill University who is conducting a study on child language acquisition.

Kristine's involvement in the Deaf Community consists of frequenting the Centre des Loisirs des Sourds de Montréal, mainly to participate in children's activities. Since her children are very young, she is mainly interested in family activities.

Kristine likes to spend time with her family doing outdoor activities such as camping, hiking, and taking nature walks. She is also an avid reader.

GAUTHIER (KOHLMAN), Mary Joan

1926–
Laundress, Library Assistant, and Homemaker.

MARY KOHLMAN was born Deaf into a hearing family at Grasswerder, Saskatchewan, which was part of the "Dust Bowl" during the "Dirty Thirties." She has no known Deaf relatives. When she was eight years old her family decided to leave the drought-stricken area at Grasswerder and move to a better farming region at Goodsoil in the northern part of the province.

At the age of twelve Mary was sent to be educated at the Saskatchewan provincial School for the Deaf in Saskatoon, where she remained from 1938 to 1946. At that time the school offered mainly an oral program but Mary learned to communicate fluently in ASL from the Deaf adults she met at the school and in the community. Her studies included practical courses in hairdressing, bookbinding, cooking, and sewing. She also played volleyball and basketball and enjoyed bowling with her peers.

After graduating, Mary found employment in the laundry department of St. Paul's Hospital in Saskatoon where she worked as a uniform presser. She eventually married a Deaf man, Gaston Gauthier, and they moved to Edmonton, Alberta. For the next three years she worked at the Royal Alexandra Hospital.

Mary and Gaston have two hearing children— Denise and Brian, both now adults with children of their own. In 1973 Mary decided to return to the workforce and found a job as an assistant at the Edmonton Public Library. She spent the next eighteen years there until her retirement in 1991.

Mary, now widowed, still makes her home in Edmonton and enjoys her six grandchildren. Her daughter, Denise Shalagan, works as an ASL interpreter at the Alberta School for the Deaf. In her leisure time, Mary loves to travel and especially enjoys cruises. She is also active in the Deaf Community.

GELEYNSE (TEES), Karina

1974–
Horsewoman, Stampede Queen and Princess, and Miss Rodeo Canada 1999.

KARINA TEES was born Deaf to hearing parents in Red Deer, Alberta, and had a rural upbringing. Her Deafness was not diagnosed until she was three years old, but she started to speak and lip-read by the time she was four. She attended small-town public schools where she was always the only Deaf student. At the age of thirteen she finally learned ASL and completed her education with the assistance of an interpreter. Through sheer determination, patience, and tenacity she graduated high school at age seventeen, with an honours diploma.

Upon completing high school she went to Trinity Western University for a year in Langley, BC. She returned to Alberta for the summer and became involved with horses again. As an attractive and viva-cious young lady, Karina was encouraged by a friend who had been a Calgary Stampede Queen a year earlier, to try out for the Stampede Queen and Princess Contest. Although she was reluctant at first, she finally allowed herself to be persuaded and was pleasantly surprised when she was selected as "Princess" from among forty contestants. After spending a year with the Calgary Stampede Royal Trio, she made the decision to move to southern California to take up studies in practical veterinary medicine and to work with reining and cutting horses. After the first year, Karina decided veterinary medicine was not for her, so she returned to Canada. She enrolled at Red Deer College in Red Deer, Alberta, where she studied part-time and held a full-time job.

Her experience with the Calgary Stampede gave Karina the confidence and readiness to take on the challenge of another Rodeo Queen pageant. In 1998 she competed in the Rodeo Queen Contest at the Ponoka Stampede in Ponoka, Alberta, and, once again, she was chosen from among several contestants for this honour. Her new title made her eligible for the Miss Rodeo Canada pageant, which she entered in November 1998, during the Canadian Finals Rodeo. There were ten contestants who were judged in several different cate-gories: horsemanship, public speaking, rodeo knowl-edge, personality, interviews, modelling, photogenics, courtly manners, and general appearance. On the final day of the pageant, during the crowning, they first announced the four category winners: Horsemanship, Public Speaking, Rodeo Exam, and the Congeniality Award. In spite of being the last one to know, Karina was thrilled to learn that she had won the Horsemanship Award and the overall contest. She emerged as the new Miss Rodeo Canada in front of more than 15,000 spectators at Skyreach Centre in Edmonton, Alberta, at the Canadian Finals Rodeo, on Friday, 13 November 1998. She was crowned "Miss Rodeo Canada 1999," a remarkable achievement for a Deaf woman competing against nine hearing contestants. She is the first and only Deaf woman ever to do so.

Karina is now married to a professional bullrider, Reuben Geleynse, so she is still involved with rodeo, but as a rodeo wife. She and Reuben raise and train horses, and she has a multitude of hobbies and interests that keep her very busy, mainly outdoors. She enjoys sports but prefers a country lifestyle.

Since she still has most of her life ahead of her, Karina looks forward to further challenges and a satisfying successful career in the field of her choosing. One thing she intends to do is always follow her personal motto, which is "never give up," and to continue being a role model to others.

GIBSON, Heather Anne

1959–

School Vice-Principal and Principal, Educator in Ontario Provincial Schools of the Deaf, Ontario Provincial Schools ASL Curriculum Development Coordinator, ASL Evaluation Program Coordinator, Coach, Author and Co-Author.

Born Deaf and raised in Maple Valley, Ontario, HEATHER GIBSON came from a farming background and was the second eldest of five children, including three Deaf and two hearing, born to hearing parents, Joan and Robert Gibson. She first attended public school in Maxwell, Ontario, then the Ontario School for the Deaf (OSD), now known as E.C. Drury School for the Deaf, in Milton. While living in residence at the Milton school, she attended the Bruce Street Public School. Later, she was transferred back to OSD, where her older sister Shawna and her younger brother James were already in attendance.

She entered Gallaudet University in Washington, BC, in the fall of 1977 and graduated with a Bachelor of Science degree in Physical Education in 1982. She then earned a Master of Arts degree in Deaf Education from Western Maryland College in Westminster in 1984. Heather won the Steve Lloyd Mathis III Award in Deafness, presented by the Western Maryland College Graduate Program, recognizing her as top student with the highest grades. There she coached a hearing women's volleyball team and was the first Deaf person in the history of the college to do so at the university level. She also received a Master of Science degree in the "Teaching American Sign Language" Program from Western Maryland College, in 1994, and completed her Principal Certification in 1995 from the Ontario Institute for Studies in Education in Toronto, Ontario. In 1990 Heather was hired as a bilingual-bicultural grade two teacher at the E.C. Drury School, where she taught grade two for two and a half years.

Heather was vice-principal at E.C. Drury School from January 1993 to June 1999. That September she was hired as Ontario Provincial Schools ASL Curriculum Development Coordinator for the three Schools for the Deaf, located in Belleville, Milton, and London. She is often referred to as the "backbone" of bilingual-bicultural Deaf Education. Her insight, knowledge, skill, and leadership in this field have inspired others and paved the way for bilingual-bicultural education for Deaf students to become a reality. Her many accomplishments are truly inspiring. Heather was the first Deaf female vice-principal in Ontario and the second in Canada. In addition, she recently became the first Deaf person to hold the position of principal in an Ontario School and the second Deaf woman in Canada. She was named "Deaf Person of the Year" in 1998 by the Cultural Society of the Deaf for her exceptional contributions to the Deaf Community, its culture and quality of life. She has also been named "Canadian Deaf Woman of the Year," and was inducted into the "Hall of Heroes" by the Canadian Hearing Society, nominated by the Ontario Association of the Deaf. CBC radio Metro Morning's Andy Barrie interviewed Heather on 7 May 1997.

Heather has authored and co-authored numerous well-received professional articles and curricula, and developed ASL diagnostic assessment tools for first- and second-language users for the Canadian Cultural Society of the Deaf and Ontario Provincial Schools. She has presented many workshops and training sessions at the local, provincial, and national levels and also at the international level, at The Deaf Way in Washington, BC, in 2002. She chairs committees, serves in an advisory capacity, and consults to many organizations and agencies, including York University and the Ontario Ministry of Education. She recently researched ASL classifier acquisition and the results have been published in a monograph commissioned by the Ontario Ministry of Education. Heather was also a founder of the Deaf Children's Festival, which continues to be held in many schools for the Deaf in Canada and the United States.

She was an ASL Evaluation Training and Internship Program coordinator for the Canadian Cultural Society of the Deaf (CCSD) and York University in Toronto. The mandate of the project was to train Canadian Deaf students to become qualified ASL raters and interviewers. Heather worked closely with Ron Hall and Vincent Chauvet, who were the ASL evaluation training and internship program instructors.

While at university Heather was a popular and outstanding athlete. She was on the Canadian National Women's Track Team that went to Romania to compete in the World Games of the Deaf in 1977, and the Canadian National Women's Volleyball team that competed in the World Games of the Deaf in then West Germany in 1981, where she was selected as top female Deaf Canadian athlete. She was a member of Phi Kappa Zeta Sorority, a regular on the Dean's List, and the recipient of numerous awards as well as the prestigious George Allen scholarship. From 1984 to 1990 she was employed as a teacher at the Manitoba School for the Deaf in Winnipeg, where she coached junior high and high school girls' and boys' basketball, volleyball, and badminton teams, preparing them for important championship competitions. She also coached the

Manitoba Men's volleyball team to compete in the Canadian Western Volleyball Tournament.

In Winnipeg, she was also a board member for the Independent Interpreter Referral Service, vice-president of the Winnipeg Community Centre of the Deaf (now known as the Manitoba Deaf Centre) and an evaluator of the bilingual day-care centre for the Winnipeg Foundation and Sign Talk Community Centre Board. She was president of the Manitoba Deaf Sports Association and developed sports programs to enhance the skills and knowledge of athletes at different age levels. She was also a board member of a federal-provincial initiative called "The Deaf Training Program for Deaf Adults in Manitoba," as well as being Sign Language director, now known as ASL director, for the Ontario Cultural Society of the Deaf.

Heather was instrumental in producing a videotape entitled *Bilingual-Bicultural Deaf Education for Your Deaf Child* and will produce a videotape on ASL curriculum. She was an actress in the *Freckles and Popper* series of four videotapes developed for Deaf children aged four to seven. Heather has also coached both junior boys' and girls' volleyball teams at the E.C. Drury School.

When this very busy woman can find time for leisure activities, she participates in athletics and enjoys sports. She also collects antique toys and other artifacts related to the history of Deaf people, and loves to travel. Perhaps her greatest contribution to other Deaf women in Canada is her ability to inspire, to provide stellar role modelling, and to act as a true advocate for them. Heather is married to Craig Gamache and they have two wonderful boys, Thomas and Samuel Gibson-Gamache, who, like their parents, enjoy every new experience in their bilingual-bicultural community.

GOERTZEN (YARMIY), Deborah Lynn

1957–
Behavioural Teacher Assistant, ASL Instructor, and Teacher of the Deaf.

DEBORAH YARMIY was born Deaf to hearing parents, Margaret and John Yarmiy, in Brandon, Manitoba. She has a hearing sister, Susan, and a Deaf brother, Robert. She also has a number of other Deaf relatives—three aunts on her father's side of the family, Mary (Yarmiy) Jones, Hazel (Yarmiy) Martin, and Helen (Yarmiy) Bowen, as well as three Deaf cousins, Gwyn Jones, and Charles and Dean Martin. Her late grandmother, Nellie Yarmiy, was Deaf, as was her great grandfather Abramchuk. Her mother has a Deaf cousin, Judy Neufeld. Deborah is married to a hearing

man, Victor Goertzen, and they have three hearing children, two daughters—Catherine and Belinda—and a son, Jonathan. The Goertzens currently make their home in Niverville, Manitoba.

In 1963, while the Manitoba School for the Deaf (MSD) was closed, Deborah was sent to the Saskatchewan School for the Deaf in Saskatoon, where she lived in residence. Two years later, when the Manitoba school reopened, she transferred to Winnipeg, where she again lived in residence for the next eight years. Her family then decided to move to Winnipeg because her brother was under medical care and it would be easier for him to see the specialist. Following this move, Deborah became a day-student at MSD and lived at home with her family for her last two years of her schooling there. She was involved in many activities: president and treasurer of the Junior National Association of the Deaf, secretary of the MSD Student Council, member of the Yearbook Club, and participant in many school sports, of which volleyball and badminton were her favourites.

During her last four years at MSD, Deborah always had a summer job. She worked as a nursing aide at the Tuxedo Villa Nursing Home, as a home visitor for the preschool program for the Deaf, as a playground leader, and as a bookbinder. When she graduated in 1975 she attended the Preparatory Program for the Deaf at Red River College and took a General Equivalent Diploma Exam. She passed her grade twelve, and was then able to enrol in Child Care Service III, a two-year diploma course. Deborah holds the distinction of being the first Deaf person to graduate from this program. When she completed the course, she took a job as a behavioural teacher assistant at MSD.

She was married in 1980. After seven years in her professional career, she decided to stay at home and raise a family. During the thirteen years she was a stay-at-home mother, she worked part-time in the evenings as an ASL instructor at Red River College and in the Adult Education Program of the St. Vital School Division. She became involved in the ASL Immersion Program, where she taught ASL, provided workshops, and evaluated staff. She also substituted for teachers and teacher assistants at MSD, and trained ASL instructors to use the Vista Sign Naturally curriculum. In addition, she taught ASL as a second-language credit course at St. James Collegiate for one semester, and taught basic signs to a grades one to three group at Linwood School at lunchtime.

She was encouraged by friends to attend the University of Manitoba Weekend College Program, so she applied and was accepted. After five years, with the solid support of a mentor, her husband, and her network of friends, she graduated with a Bachelor of Education degree in the spring of 1998. She and Patricia Jones were the first two students to attend the Weekend College Program, but Patricia took additional summer and weekend courses, so she graduated earlier than Deborah. In the fall of 1998 Deborah was hired by Winnipeg School Division No. 1 to teach ASL as a second-language credit course to high school students in grades nine to twelve. She taught six classes, three per semester, in three different schools. Unfortunately, after the first year, the schools did not have sufficient staff allotment for the ASL program to continue and it was dropped.

In September 2001 Deborah began her third year of teaching grade one at MSD, her alma mater. She feels she has learned a great deal from her varied experiences through the years, and remains devoted to her husband, children, sister, and brother, and their families. Meanwhile, her second career is just beginning. Her only involvement with the Deaf Community now is through her work, which keeps her too busy to allow her to volunteer her services to any of the organizations and agencies.

In her leisure hours, Deborah enjoys such hobbies as sewing, arts and crafts, painting, and going out for coffee with her friends.

GOLDSTEIN (ROSNER), Karyn Ann

1951–
Educator, Civic Leader, Advocate for the Deaf, and Dedicated Volunteer.

KARYN ROSNER was born Deaf to hearing parents in Brooklyn, New York. The cause of her Deafness is undetermined and she has no known Deaf relatives on her side of the family. Her Deaf husband, Martin (Marty) Goldstein, had a Deaf aunt and uncle in Montréal— Alex and Esther Goldstein, now both deceased. Karyn and Marty have two children—a hearing daughter, Gayle, an honours graduate from York University in Toronto who sometimes works with Deaf children, and a Deaf son, Jason, who is currently attending Rochester Institute of Technology (RIT). The Goldsteins make their home in Mississauga, Ontario. Marty is the celebrated author of *Deaf Canadians: An Insight*.

Karyn was educated in mainstream schools on Long Island, New York. After she graduated high school in 1969, she attended Gallaudet University in Washington, BC, where she obtained a Bachelor of Science degree in December of 1973. She went on to earn a Master's degree in Deaf Education from New York University in

February of 1975, and has continued to further her qualifications, knowledge, and skills with summer and in-service courses related to her work, as well as specialty courses in computers and librarianship from the University of Toronto and other institutions. She worked in New York city for two years at the Work Study Program before moving to Edmonton, Alberta. In the spring of 1983 she became a Canadian citizen.

Karyn's early teaching career took place in Alberta, where she began as a preschool teacher in the Deaf and Hard of Hearing Program at Glenrose Hospital in Edmonton. She also taught briefly at the Alberta School for the Deaf in Edmonton before the family moved to Calgary where both she and Marty taught for a number of years before moving to Ontario. Since 1991 Karyn has taught at the E.C. Drury School for the Deaf in Milton, Ontario. Throughout this period she has taken leaves of absence to upgrade her skills in the US. In those settings, she worked as a media specialist (librarian and computer teacher) and gained substitute teaching experience while making many innovative contributions to the existing school programs.

Karyn received "Appreciation" plaques for her volunteer activities in the Calgary Association of the Deaf in 1985 and 1986. She was also honoured with a Certificate of Appreciation and an Award of Merit from the National Congress of Jewish Deaf in 1994. Her volunteer experience has been eclectic. She coordinated the 20th Biennial National Jewish Deaf Congress in the summer of 1994. While living in Calgary, she served on the board of Deaf and Hard of Hearing Services, assisting with the selection and hiring of an executive director, chairing library services, and coordinating workshops for Deaf and hard-of-hearing women. She provided consultation to the Alberta Government TTY Relay Service (now Telus), instructed ASL classes at Mount Royal College and other venues, was president of the Calgary Association of the Deaf, and chaired the evaluation team for the Association of Visual Language Interpreters of Canada for two years as well as chairing its third conference in Edmonton. She was also involved with the Western Canadian Association of the Deaf.

Probably Karyn's most notable civic experience occurred in 1991 when she made headlines in the *Calgary Herald*. She and another Deaf person had been called for jury duty, and Karyn made her appearance at the appointed hour in the company of an ASL interpreter. She was rejected as a potential juror because the presence of an interpreter would increase the jury panel from twelve to thirteen persons. During the lengthy public controversy which ensued, Karyn had the unlimited support and encouragement of every disabled organization and agency across the land.

She has recently completed further computer training and is looking forward to creating a website in the near future.

GRAHAM (TOMLINSON), Suzan Faith

1958–
Horsewoman, Microsoft Specialist, and Computer Technician.

SUZAN TOMLINSON was born Deaf to hearing parents in Toronto, Ontario. She has three Deaf brothers—Philip, Stephen and David—as well as a hearing brother, John, and one hearing sister, Ruth. Suzan's father is the pastor at Maranatha Fellowhip Church for the Deaf in Toronto, where her mother is the church secretary and a Sunday school teacher. Suzan and her Deaf husband, John Ronald Graham, live in Cambridge, Ontario, with their three hearing children—JR, Sam, and Amy.

After graduating from Northern Secondary School in Toronto, Suzan attended Algonquin College to take equine care training, and then Seneca College to learn the art of shoeing horses. After earning the required qualifications, she worked with horses for some time until she met John Graham, who had become a pastor after taking training at a Bible college in Dallas, Texas. They decided to marry and Suzan became a stay-at-home mother while their children were young. They lived briefly in Rochester, New York, where John founded his first church. Eventually, he established two other churches.

When the children were old enough, Suzan returned to school to further her education with a view to a career change. She went to a computer school and obtained her MOUSE certification (Microsoft Office User Specialist). She also earned an A+ qualification as a computer technician and is currently waiting for an opening for permanent employment in this field.

Her involvement in the Deaf Community has been mainly through the church, her father's church as well as her husband's. John is currently the pastor of the New Life Deaf Church in Milton, Ontario, where he and Suzan are both involved in the activities of their congregation and John's ministry.

Recently, John founded an organization called Deaf Alive Revival Evangelism (DARE) which will enable them to travel more, preaching their gospel to the world.

Suzan is a gifted Sunday school teacher, Bible study leader, and workshop presenter on topics related to spiritual life. She travels alone or with her husband when she presents workshops. They have taken their ministry to Australia, Singapore, New Zealand, and the United States. Suzan also preaches for John while he is travelling.

In her leisure time, Suzan enjoys walking her dogs, working on her computer, and reading. She recently began to collect pot-bellied teddy bears.

GRAY (MARK), Cora Elizabeth

1928 -
Homemaker, " Jane-of-all-trades" and Proud Mother and Grandmother

CORA MARK, born in Vancouver, became deaf at the age of eight years. Hers was a sensorineural hearing loss. She attended the School for the Deaf/Blind in Vancouver from 1936 to 1943, but was then sent to a mainstream public school for three years. She found this very frustrating due to communication difficulties and left school at the age of seventeen. Cora has a Deaf sister, now well over eighty years of age, who resides in Victoria, BC.

After leaving school, Cora became a "jane-of-all-trades" working at various types of jobs with hearing co-workers. None of her employment was related to Deafness except her last position which was at the Woodlands Mental Hospital in New Westminster, BC, where she worked with deaf clients. Cora appreciated and enjoyed this job, but eventually had to give it up due to health problems.

In 1950, Cora married Ronald E. Gray of Winnipeg, Manitoba. Together they raised three children — David Edward, Diane Elizabeth and Ernest. At the present time, David is living in Montana, US, Diane in Kelowna, BC, and Ernest in Langley, BC. Among them, their children have presented them with seven lovely grandchildren whom they now have time to enjoy. While living in Vancouver, Cora was an active member of the Greater Vancouver Association of the Deaf.

Cora and Ronald are now retired and enjoying their life of leisure. In September 2000, they celebrated fifty happy years of marriage. They currently reside in Kelowna, BC, near their daughter, Diane. Cora keeps herself busy with the things she loves to do — taking care of her home, cooking and baking. In her spare time she likes to read.

GREEN (CLARKE), Mary

1935–
Dormitory Counsellor and Loyal Public Service Employee.

MARY CLARKE was born hearing into a hearing family in Victoria, Conception Bay, Newfoundland. She became Deaf at the age of seven due to illness. She has no known Deaf relatives, but husband, Bruce Green, a skilled painter and wood carver, is Deaf. Mary and Bruce have five adult hearing children—Bertram, Kenneth, Judy, Glen, and Stephen. The family has always lived in St. John's, Newfoundland.

Mary was sent to be educated at the Halifax School for the Deaf in Nova Scotia because no school for Deaf children existed in Newfoundland until the mid-1960s. She attended the Halifax School from 1945 to 1953, living in residence there. When she left school in 1953 and returned to Newfoundland, she immediately entered the workforce.

Her first job at which she worked for four years was as a domestic worker at the Tuberculosis Sanatorium in St. John's. She left this employment when she and Bruce were married so she could become a full-time housewife and mother. Twenty years later, in 1973, she returned to the world of work, spending one year as a domestic worker at Exxon House before she was hired as a dormitory counsellor at the Newfoundland School for the Deaf in St. John's in 1974. She retired from that position in 2000, after twenty-six years of loyal service.

Mary's honours and awards include a certificate of appreciation from the Newfoundland Association of Public Employees, a twenty-year service award from the government of Newfoundland and Labrador and, on the occasion of her retirement, in July 2000, she was the recipient of a Faithful Public Service Award for her thirty-two years and two months as a provincial government employee.

Mary's involvement in the Deaf community includes serving as president of the St. John's Association of the Deaf, and as chairperson of the Eastern Canada Association of the Deaf's 1973 biennial convention, the first time it had ever been held in Newfoundland. She also participates in the Deaf and hearing Five-Pin Bowling Club.

During her leisure time, the hobbies and interests she enjoys are recreational bowling and walking her dog twice daily for exercise. She does cotton knitting, and loves to design and create costumes and hats for special occasions.

GREGORY (BELL), Evelyn

1916–
Weaver, Day-Care Provider, Preschool Aide, and Foster Parent of Deaf Children.

It is not known whether EVELYN BELL was born Deaf or became Deaf as an infant. Her parents were hearing, as were her brother and three of her sisters, but she has one older sister, Annie Bell Shand, who became Deaf around two years of age. Her late husband, John Archibald Gregory, was also Deaf. Evelyn and John had two hearing children—a son, John Bell Gregory, and a daughter, Donna Evelyn Vann, who both became successful adults. Evelyn currently makes her home in Pierrefonds, Québec.

She was born in Blackburn, England, but spent nearly all her life in Canada, in the province of Québec, and was educated at the MacKay School for the Deaf in Montréal. Her deceased husband John was very much involved with the Montréal Association of the Deaf throughout his lifetime. He also served as a lay pastor at the Montréal Mission of the Deaf, and was employed at Canadair until his death.

As young women, Evelyn and her Deaf sister Annie both trained to become very talented weavers, and worked at that trade for a number of years for the Henry Morgan Stores (now The Bay) in Montréal. For a time, Evelyn also worked at the Mount Royal Hotel. With her husband serving as lay minister, Evelyn was a very active member of the Montréal Mission of the Deaf and, for quite a number of years, acted as its treasurer. Her considerable contribution to the Montréal Association of the Deaf eventually led to her being granted a lifetime membership.

In later years, Evelyn worked as an aide in preschool classes at the MacKay Centre for the Deaf, and for many years she also provided day-care services to hearing children. Perhaps her most notable service to the Deaf Community, however, was her competent parenting of several Deaf children whom she fostered.

GROOM, Jane Elizabeth

1839–1908
Teacher, Missionary, Early Western Canadian Colonist, and Spokeswoman for the Deaf.

JANE ELIZABETH GROOM was born Deaf at Woodgate, near Wem, in England, and had a Deaf sister as well as a Deaf cousin. They were educated at the Institute for the Deaf and Dumb at Old Trafford near the city of Manchester.

For nearly five years after her graduation, Jane taught a day class of Deaf students in the school at Bethnal Green in London, but was replaced by a hearing teacher when Great Britain adopted the oral method of instruction for Deaf children in 1882. She then became an Evangelist missionary among poverty-stricken Deaf people in London's East End, and was determined to try to improve their lot.

After visiting Canada for a year, she decided to expand her missionary work by bringing a group of ten Deaf male British emigrants to settle in the Canadian northwest in 1884. They came to the area then known as

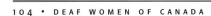

Wolseley, Manitoba, which in 1905 became part of the province of Saskatchewan east of Regina. Jane received kind and courteous assistance from many sources: the Land Commissioner of the Canadian Pacific Railway, the Honourable J. McTavish, a well-known Manitoba farmer named Major Bell and his wife, the Reverend H. Jeslie, and an established Deaf settler, John Parker. She did not intend to establish a colony exclusively for the Deaf, as was being advocated in the US at that time. She helped her colonists find employment on farms and in the communities surrounding Wolseley. Over time, most of them moved away to establish their own homesteads or to go into trades and businesses for themselves.

Jane placed five of her original ten Deaf emigres on the farm of Major Bell, who owned 65,000 acres of land extending a distance of ten miles, in the area that is now known as Indian Head, Saskatchewan. There were eighty cottages on this estate, and Major Bell and his wife took a great interest in their new Deaf employees, making certain they gained the necessary experience and knowledge that eventually would qualify them to acquire good homesteads for themselves. The other five were placed in various trades, as a shoemaker, a saddle and harness-maker, a bricklayer, a cabinet-maker, and a tailor.

Later, Jane returned to England and brought twenty-four more Deaf settlers and their families to Canada, despite media criticism from a number of sources. Daily newspapers in Winnipeg and Québec City were particularly vociferous in their criticism of Jane's plan, suggesting that her "Deaf-mutes" were unsuitable as settlers and would soon become dependent on the country's charity. Nevertheless, Jane Groom was highly respected as a spokesperson for the small Deaf Community that had taken root in the Wolseley area. She had many supporters who soon pointed out to the media that Jane herself was Deaf, and it certainly couldn't be denied that she was highly successful in her efforts at colonization. Her work was backed by many people, both in Canada and in England, and they set up a fund at a bank in London, known as Miss Groom's Emigration Fund, for which subscriptions were solicited. The success of the project proved conclusively that Deaf people, as a whole, are resourceful, ambitious, and eager to succeed. Given the opportunity, they can achieve any goal they are willing to strive for.

Jane Groom died in 1908 and was posthumously inducted into the Canadian Cultural Society of the Deaf's Hall of Fame when it was first established in 1976, along with nineteen other distinguished Deaf Canadians.

Her work provided a nucleus of Deaf persons in Manitoba and Saskatchewan who contributed enormously to Deaf history in Western Canada. The Public Archives Library in Ottawa lists an anonymously authored pamphlet entitled *A Future for the Deaf and Dumb in the Canadian North-West*, which gives an account of Jane Groom's work in the establishment of the pioneer Deaf colony in what was then known as the North-West Territories of Canada.

GROVES-RIVARD, Ruth Alexandra

1943–
Editor, Income Tax Service Provider, and Farming Partner.

RUTH GROVES was born Deaf in St. John's, Newfoundland, but has spent most of her youth and adult life in the province of Québec. She has two known Deaf relatives—her sister, Ina Groves Byrne, and a second cousin, Alexandra Edwards, who is presently a student at the Newfoundland School for the Deaf in St. John's. Ruth's husband, Pierre Rivard, a retired farmer, is also Deaf, and they have two adult hearing children. Pierre has two Deaf sisters, Lise Rivard Turbide and Suzanne Rivard, who are both very active in the Deaf Community, and Suzanne is currently the president of L'Association des Sourds de la Mauricie (La Mauricie Association of the Deaf). Ruth and Pierre currently make their home in St. Maurice, Québec.

Ruth and her Deaf sister, Ina, were sent to the MacKay School for the Deaf in Montréal because there was no such facility for Deaf children in Newfoundland. Ruth spent ten years at MacKay, and Ina, seven years. From the age of five until she was fifteen Ruth attended MacKay School and then lived in Newfoundland until she was thirty-three. At that point she returned to Montréal for five years before she and Pierre were married and moved to St. Maurice. Ina is still in Newfoundland and is married to a hard-of-hearing man, Robert Byrne. They have five hearing children and five grandchildren.

Until his retirement, Pierre Rivard was the successful owner of a farm which was at first a dairy farm, but later featured a beef station and the sale of bulls. Ruth, until she was married, had a career that focused on business with CAE Electronics, where she was the editor of the company's technical publication. Currently, she provides income tax filing services to her clientele in Shawinigan-Sud.

In a volunteer capacity, Ruth served as secretary for L'Association Sportive des Sourds de La Mauricie (Deaf Sports Association of La Mauricie) for five years. She was honoured when the association presented her with an original painting in recognition of her dedication and work as its secretary. Ruth is bilingual and is the La Mauricie region representative for the Québec Association

of the Deaf (CQDA) in Montréal. From 1988 to 1993 she served as chairperson for the organizing committee of the MacKay School for the Deaf Reunion. She is an active member of the Deaf Community who makes many volunteer contributions of time and talent to its various organizations and agencies. She also provided translation from ASL to LSQ (and vice versa) for the Canadian Deaf Darts Championships in London, Ontario, in 2000, and won first place in that competition.

In her spare time, Ruth is an avid sportswoman who enjoys darts, bowling, sandbag throwing, swimming, and pentaque. She also spends a good deal of time on her computer, gleaning information in both French and English. Her main interests are accounting and law, particularly in the area of human rights.

GUILBERT (RONCERAY), Alice Marie

1940–
Educator, Volunteer, and Advocate for the Deaf.

ALICE MARIE RONCERAY was born Deaf in Notre Dame De Lourdes in rural Manitoba in 1940. Although she now lives in Great Falls, Montana, US, she grew up on the Canadian prairies and graduated from the Saskatchewan School for the Deaf in Saskatoon in 1959. Alice still visits relatives in Canada, both Deaf and hearing. She is a cousin of Diane Zimmer and a second cousin of Cheryl Zimmer whose profiles appear in this book.

Since her graduation Alice has led a busy and interesting life with a wide variety of experiences and activities. She has taken an assertive leadership role in the Deaf community wherever she has resided, both in Canada and the US. After graduation she lived in Winnipeg where she was employed by the government of Manitoba. In 1963 she married Derald Guilbert from the state of North Dakota.

The couple moved to the US and raised their two highly successful children—Gisele (BSc in Nursing), and Galen (Bachelor's Degree in Business Administration and Finance), of whom they are justifiably proud. In 1972 she accepted a position as a teacher's assistant at the Montana State School for the Deaf and Blind in Great Falls, where they now live. In addition to her classroom duties, she has also served as a depository manager for the Free-Loan Captioned Media Program.

Alice's work for the Deaf community has been varied and gives her great personal satisfaction. She has served as secretary for the Montana Association of the Deaf (MAD) for over twenty-five years and has been a member of the Montana Registry of Interpreters for the Deaf for several years. She has also been involved in a statewide Telecommunication Committee advocating improvement in TTY distribution and relay services, as well as a committee researching how to establish a Deaf centre. She is an active participant in every event held at the Great Falls Club of the Deaf. In addition to these involvements, Alice was a Junior NAD co-sponsor for seven years, and in 1986, she chaperoned a junior NAD member at the National Junior NAD Convention in Washington, DC.

She has been honoured with awards for her contributions to the Deaf community, most notably in 1985 when she was recognized for her work by being presented with the Montana Association of the Deaf Award, and again in 1987 when she was given special recognition for her outstanding contributions to the MAD Convention and School Reunion. Her capabilities and dedication are exemplary.

HALL (ULMER), Betty Jean

1939–
Clerical Associate, Enthusiastic Bowler, Deaf Volunteer, and Fond Grandmother.

BETTY ULMER was born hearing to hearing parents at Lorlie, Saskatchewan. She became Deaf at the age of five due to a painful and traumatic incident when she was accidentally pushed by playing children into hot ashes that severely burned her feet. She has three hearing sisters and two hearing brothers. She also has an older Deaf sister, Ilene, who lost her hearing at nine months of age as a result of a fall from her high-chair. Betty's husband, Carlyle Hall, is Deaf. There are no other known Deaf relatives. Betty and Carlyle have two adult hearing children and two hearing grand-children. They have made their home in Saskatoon, Saskatchewan, for many years.

Betty's sister Ilene was sent to the Saskatchewan School for the Deaf in Saskatoon, but when their parents took Betty to be enrolled two years later, they were told she had sufficient residual hearing to function in a main-stream public school if she were fitted with a hearing aid.

Betty found this extremely frustrating because the amplified background noises made it hard for her to discriminate speech. As a result, school was very diffi-cult for her. When Ilene graduated she introduced her sister to all her Deaf friends and, before long, Betty became very comfortable among Deaf people.

After graduating high school in Regina, she took a six-month business training course and was able to find immediate employment as a billing clerk for a plumbing company. When she married Carlyle they moved to Saskatoon where he found permanent employment. Betty worked at the Saskatoon Star-Phoenix as a teletypesetter for a while and greatly enjoyed the job.

The couple eventually moved to Edmonton where Betty worked for the government of Alberta as a keypunch operator for about five years. It was during this period that she became involved in various organizations for the Deaf, particularly the Deaf Women's Auxiliary which presented her with an award of recognition in 1975.

Later, when they moved back to Saskatoon, Betty served in various capacities in the Deaf Community there, and was recognized for her contributions with an award from the Saskatoon Association of the Deaf in 1987 and one from the National Festival of the Arts in 1988. She was a founding member of what is now known as Saskatchewan Deaf and Hard of Hearing Services, and was on the board for twelve years.

As an employee, she was a clerical associate with SaskTel for twenty years, enjoying her job and the many friendships she established with her co-workers. In May 2000 Betty accepted an offer of an early retire-ment package and is currently a contented retiree, spending as much time as possible with her beloved grandchildren in Saskatoon and Calgary.

She enjoys weekly bowling outings with her friends and long evening walks with her husband. Betty is a gregarious and outgoing person who enjoys visiting her friends to chat over coffee or to play cards. She and her husband both like to attend organized social events in the Deaf Community.

HANDLEY (PRESTON), Shirley Marline

1950–
Home-Care Attendant, Child-Care Worker, and Business Office Assistant.

SHIRLEY PRESTON was born Deaf to hearing parents in Regina, Saskatchewan, and was their only child. She has no known Deaf relatives, but her paternal grandmother, Eveline Preston, lost some of her hearing at the age of twenty-four during the 1919 influenza epidemic. In 1972 Shirley married a hearing man, but they later divorced and she raised their two daughters, Angela and Amanda, on her own.

Shirley started preschool with hearing children, and because the Saskatchewan School for the Deaf in Saskatoon was overcrowded at the time, she was sent to

a mainstream public school in Regina. In 1958 the Prestons moved to Edmonton, hoping to enrol Shirley at the Alberta School for the Deaf (ASD). However, it was deemed more appropriate for her to attend hard-of-hearing classes in the public school system, which she did from 1959 to 1965. She learned to sign at Cross of Christ Lutheran Church for the Deaf and was finally accepted at ASD in 1965. In 1969 she also attended some classes at W.P. Wagner High School, where she took a nurse's aide course and studied child care as well as foods and fashion. When she graduated in 1971 she took the Gallaudet entrance exam, but decided she would rather remain in Edmonton, where she was the first Deaf person to be hired at ASD as a child-care attendant in the dormitory. She also taught Sign Language to several teachers.

After her divorce Shirley volunteered at her daughters' schools, helped with Brownies and Girl Guides, and taught many hearing children to sign and fingerspell. She also upgraded her qualifications by training as a home care attendant and graduated from the Employment Preparation Program sponsored by Deaf Career Connections in 1995. Since then she has been employed as a Jane-of-all-trades at the national headquarters of the Canadian Cultural Society of the Deaf in Edmonton, assisting the administrative secretary, Caroline Anne Fritz.

Shirley is proud of her Deaf heritage and credits her mother, Edith Preston, with being her greatest inspiration when she worked with the Association for the Hearing Handicapped, now known as the Connect Society, to open the first preschool for Deaf and hard-of-hearing children in the basement of Cross of Christ Church in 1962. Shirley is also proud of her daughters, who are now successful adults—Angela works as a store manager at West Edmonton Mall, and Amanda is an elementary education student at the University of Alberta.

She has always been very active in the Edmonton Association of the Deaf, the Alberta Cultural Society of the Deaf, and the Edmonton Deaf Bowling Club, serving as a volunteer in many different capacities. For her countless contributions, Shirley has been honoured with a number of awards and certificates of recognition and appreciation. She continues to offer her time and talents to activities taking place within the Deaf Community in Edmonton.

HARDY (MONTGOMERY), Paula Clyde

1932–
Sunday School Teacher, Missionary, and Teacher of the Deaf and Hard of Hearing.

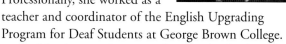

PAULA MONTGOMERY was born in Linden, New Jersey, US. In the 1950s, she was a religious leader among Deaf parishoners in South Carolina and Oklahoma, and also spent considerable time as a missionary in Jamaica, serving in Kingston, Newport, Spur Tree, and Knockpatrick from 1957 to 1969.

When she came to Canada, Paula joined the Evangelical Church of the Deaf in Toronto, Ontario, and became a Sunday school teacher for Deaf children as well as hearing children of Deaf parents. At present, Paula and her husband are members of Grace Deaf Church (GDC) in Richmond Hill, Ontario, where their son, Dean Hardy, is pastoring. She continues as a Sunday school teacher at GDC, and has become involved in the church's Deaf Mothers monthly meeting. For ten summers (1970 to 1980) Paula was a Bible teacher and chief cook at Ontario Summer Bible Camps for Deaf Children at Parry Sound, Ontario. She and her husband became foster parents to a Deaf-Blind boy whom they took into their home at Richmond Hill, and were houseparents in group homes in Toronto and Woodbridge from 1974 to 1988.

Paula also taught ASL to hearing teachers at George Brown College in Toronto and eventually became a teacher of Deaf and hard of hearing students there. Since 1979, in her spare time, Paula has carried out many responsibilities with Deaf Women for Christ, an

organization of which she was a co-founder. She also served on the Advisory Board of Ontario Interpreting Services and has been a "retreat" speaker in Edmonton, Alberta. Professionally, she worked as a teacher and coordinator of the English Upgrading Program for Deaf Students at George Brown College.

Paula's education began at the Maryland School for the Deaf in Frederick and progressed to the South Carolina School for the Deaf in Cedar Rapids, from which she graduated in 1951. She then earned a diploma in General Business Administration. After moving to Canada, she upgraded her qualifications at George Brown College with a certificate from their Instructor Effectiveness Program.

Her work has been recognized and greatly appreciated nationally and internationally, as can be attested by her numerous awards, mainly from Cultural Societies of the Deaf and Quota Clubs—the Hall of Fame Award (Humanitarian), the Mentor Award (Religious Song—All-round performance), a second Mentor Award (Songwriting), the Bronze Award (Songwriting), Deaf Woman of the Year Award (Education), and International Deaf Woman of the Year Award (also Education).

During the summer Paula visits her mother in Princeton, West Virginia, and continues to do short-term missionary work in Jamaica. She and her husband, Jim Hardy, were houseparents in a group home in Woodbridge, Ontario, for fourteen years.

Most of the children in the home were from Ontario but a few were from British Columbia and Manitoba. She continues to be a mentor, role model, and inspiration to all Deaf women in Canada whose lives she touches.

HARGREAVES (WOJCICHOWSKY), Mary

1932–
Photograph Retoucher, Bookkeeper, and Dedicated Volunteer for the Deaf.

MARY HARGREAVES, the second daughter of Stella Harasinski and Joe Wojcichowsky, was born hearing at Bonne Madone, Saskatchewan. Due to spinal meningitis, Mary became Deaf at the age of four and a half years, according to a Mayo Clinic report. She has no known Deaf relatives.

Her parents sent her to the Saskatchewan School for the Deaf in Saskatoon in 1939, and she remained there as a residential student until she graduated in 1950. She would travel to her home only at Christmas, Easter, and for the summer holidays, but she was always happy to spend time with her family. At school, she was a good athlete and was involved in sports. She also enjoyed the practical courses offered at the school, such as home economics and photo developing. When she graduated, she was immediately hired by Thams Photo Studio in Saskatoon, where she worked for eighteen years. She was married to Alfred Hargreaves in 1958 but they divorced fifteen years later.

In 1968 Mary had decided to move to the west coast where she found employment at ABC Photocolour, one of the largest photolabs in Vancouver, BC, where she worked as a photo retoucher for a short time but became a full-time bookkeeper and worked in that capacity until her retirement on 31 October 2000. Mary used a combination of writing and fingerspelling to communicate with the fifty other staff members and the company's clients. Sometimes her boss would interpret for her.

In the Deaf Community, Mary has always been an exemplary role model for her peers. She served on the board of the Greater Vancouver Association of the Deaf for over fifteen years. She also acted as treasurer of the International Year of the Disabled, was a board member of the Western Institute for the Deaf and Hard of Hearing and one of their chief fundraisers, participated in the Deaf Women's Auxiliary group, and was a board member of the BC Deaf Sports Federation. In addition, she was involved with the World Games for the Deaf, the National Fraternal Society of the Deaf, the Greater Vancouver Deaf Curling Club, and the Western Canada Deaf Curling Club. She also provided services for the Deaf at the Independence '92 Conference at the interpretation service booth.

For her many contributions, Mary has been honoured with awards from the Canadian Cultural Society of the Deaf in 1987, and the Western Institute of the Deaf in 1986 and 1988. She was also selected as the 1987 Canadian Deaf Rater of the Year. She enjoys her retirement and continues to do volunteer work. In her leisure hours she likes to participate in outdoor activities.

HARTE (VARSLAVANS), Edith

1940–
Latvian Emigre, Clerical Worker, and Activist in the Deaf Catholic Community.

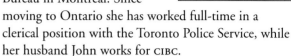

EDITH VARSLAVANS was born Deaf to hearing parents in Latvia during World War II. Her parents had both been educators, her father having been a principal and her mother, a teacher when they fled with their three children to a refugee camp in Germany. Edith has a Deaf brother and a hearing sister. It was in Germany that Edith first attended a school for the Deaf. In 1950, after the war had ended and the family had spent five years in refugee camps, they emigrated to Canada and settled in Montréal. Other than her Deaf brother, Edith has no Deaf relatives. She has a Deaf husband, John Harte, an alumnus of the old School for the Deaf in Halifax and the MacKay School for the Deaf in Montréal. John has worked for the Canadian Imperial Bank of Commerce (CIBC) for many years. Edith and John are the proud parents of two hearing adult children, Andrew and Laura, who are both very proficient in ASL as it was their first language. Edith and John currently make their home in Brampton, Ontario.

When the Varslavans family arrived in Montréal, Edith was sent to a French School for the Deaf—L'Institution Des Sourdes et Muetes, where she was placed in a special class of Deaf children of varying ages so that a teacher, with the help of a teacher-assistant, could teach them English. It was the first time at that school that anyone had ever taught English Deaf students, so it was a rather unique experience for Edith who did very well, learning quickly and easily. There were about four hundred French students in the school, so the English pupils were greatly outnumbered.

Edith left school after completing the tenth grade and entered the workforce. She held various jobs, but spent many years doing clerical work for the Underwriters' Adjustment Bureau in Montréal. Since moving to Ontario she has worked full-time in a clerical position with the Toronto Police Service, while her husband John works for CIBC.

While living in Montréal, Edith was very active in a Deaf Club known as Club L'Epée. She was also a typist for the Federation of Silent Sports of Canada (FSSC) for some time. From 1960–1973 she was a well-known activist with the International Catholic Deaf Association of Montréal (ICDA), Chapter #58. Since moving to Ontario, Edith has become involved in her local Deaf community there.

Although she enjoys her work with the Toronto Police Service, Edith looks forward to retirement in the not-too-distant future. She is eager to pursue her many hobbies and interests, and to offer her services as a volunteer to the various organizations and agencies that advocate for the rights of Deaf people. She has a wealth of experience as well as many talents and skills to share.

In her spare time Edith likes to collect stamps, research her family tree, read, garden, and bake. She enjoys walking and is an enthusiastic traveller. Her immediate goal is to improve her computer skills.

HEATH (GOODWIN), Jean Elizabeth

1916–
Federal Civil Servant, Devoted Grandmother, and Dedicated Volunteer.

JEAN GOODWIN was born Deaf into a hearing family at Davidson, Saskatchewan, where her parents farmed. Despite their many attempts to restore her hearing, they finally accepted the fact that her Deafness could not be cured. When she was eight years of age she was sent to Winnipeg to attend the Manitoba School for the Deaf. In 1931, after the Saskatchewan School opened, she was transferred to Saskatoon. There, she worked on the school newspaper, enjoyed sports, and participated in theatre and dance performances until her graduation in 1937. In 1940 Jean was

voted "Carnival Queen" by the local farmers in her hometown of Davidson. This was certainly a "first" for a Deaf woman. While in Saskatoon, Jean had become a close friend of Maureen Donald whose father (Chief of Police in Saskatoon) helped her secure a loan that enabled her to accompany Maureen to a Western Canada Association of the Deaf Convention in Winnipeg in the same year.

Jean did not return to Saskatchewan but stayed in Winnipeg for one year before going to Ottawa, where she worked as a civil servant from 1942 to 1954. She became a very good friend of Polly and David Peikoff, a well-known Deaf couple who were popular advocates for the Deaf and a great inspiration to her. On her wedding day in 1954, it was David Peikoff who walked Jean down the aisle.

She married Ross Heath from Nova Scotia and they settled in Winnipeg where their hearing daughter, Bonnie Jean, was born in 1955, and their second hearing daughter, Geraldine, (now deceased) in 1957. Ross had attended the Halifax School for the Deaf, and at age fifteen, hitchhiked to Toronto. He was an accomplished athlete, especially in curling, and the Ross Heath Cup is named after him. Their daughter Bonnie Jean (now Dubienski) was the founder and executive director of the Independent Interpreter Referral Service in Winnipeg, and started the first interpreter training program there in 1982. She has held many prestigious positions and was nominated Woman of the Year by the YMCA-YWCA. She has a son, Stephen, attending Georgia Southern University on a tennis scholarship, and a daughter, Katherine (Katie), who recently won a bronze medal for a science project involving devices for the Deaf, hard of hearing, and Deaf/Blind. Jean and Ross' daughter Geraldine (Gerry) shared her father's passion for curling and was an active volunteer. She worked at the Manitoba School for the Deaf for many years, prior to her death in 1993.

Jean was very active in Winnipeg's Deaf community, working as a volunteer for the Winnipeg Community Centre of the Deaf, the Manitoba Deaf Senior's Club, the Church of the Deaf, and the Kiwanis Centre of the Deaf (now known as Deaf Centre Manitoba). For her many contributions, she was awarded various certificates of appreciation. In 1997 she participated in the Deaf Literacy Program. For recreation, she greatly enjoys five-pin bowling and her favorite hobby is sewing. However, her greatest pride has always been in her husband (now deceased) and family, all of whom were involved with the Deaf community.

Now in her eighties, Jean continues to be active as a volunteer and is grateful for her fulfilling and rewarding life. She credits her many successes to her loving family and her wide network of wonderful friends. Her two grandchildren, Stephen and Katie, have become the thrill of her life and she has a wealth of beautiful memories to sustain her. It is her sincere hope that future generations of Canadian Deaf women will be as richly blessed.

HENSHAW (RANGER), Joyce Matilda

1941–
Group-Home Parent, Dedicated Volunteer, and Natural-Born Mother.

JOYCE RANGER was born Deaf into a Deaf family in Reston, Manitoba. Besides her Deaf parents, she had two Deaf brothers, Larry and Tom Ranger. Her husband, Gordon Henshaw is also Deaf. Gordon and Joyce have three hearing sons—Steve, James, and Douglas—and the family currently lives in Cambridge, Ontario. Joyce has many other Deaf relatives in her extended family, and she counts among her kinfolk the Nickersons, the Masters, the Eramchuks, the Zimmers, the Ladyshewskis, the Fasullos, the Desroaches, and the Smalls. All of them are intermingled in one way or another through marriage.

Joyce grew up in rural Manitoba and, because the Manitoba School for the Deaf in Winnipeg was being used for military purposes during World War II and did not reopen until 1965, she was sent to be educated, along with many other Deaf children from Manitoba, to the Saskatchewan School for the Deaf in Saskatoon. After graduating in 1958 Joyce moved to Ontario, where she met Gordon Henshaw. They were married in 1961. Although Joyce worked for Canada Post for eight years, she is best known for her many contributions to the Deaf Community, particularly Deaf and multihandicapped children.

For ten years Joyce and her husband operated a very successful group home on the Ontario Mission property in Milton, north of Highway #401. It was during this period of her life that Joyce's brother, Larry Ranger, and his wife were tragically killed in a motor vehicle accident, leaving two Deaf children. Joyce and Gordon took them into their home and raised them with their own boys. They were the first of several children raised by Joyce and Gordon. When they left the group home at the Ontario Mission, Joyce began working in various capacities at E.C. Drury School for the Deaf in Milton. Eventually she settled into a position in the Drury Program where she looks after about ten clients, teaching them home economics and life skills, including budgeting. She also takes them on outings to such places as Niagara Falls, the Ontario Science Centre, the Metro Zoo, to a summer cottage, and the US.

Every summer Joyce and Gordon have gone to the Ontario Camp for the Deaf at Parry Sound, where Joyce is well known as the "Kitchen Mother" because she not only works in the kitchen, but she also "mothers" all the children who attend the camp. Children seem to flock around her, clamouring for advice, hugs, and motherly talks, simply because she is a natural-born mother.

Deena McNeil of Compassion of Canada once described Joyce Henshaw as having "that heroic quality of character that enables an individual to win a struggle against great odds." Joyce has obviously turned her Deafness into an asset because it has given her the opportunity to help so many others. She keeps very busy as a member of the Ontario Mission of the Deaf at Willowdale, the Ontario Association of the Deaf, the Ontario Cultural Society of the Deaf, the Gospel Deaf Fellowship Church, the evangelical church of the Deaf (where her brother, Tom Ranger, is pastor), and the Blair Community Church. She also currently serves as president of the Ontario Bowling Association of the Deaf (OBAD). Joyce has received many awards and certificates in recognition and appreciation of her compassionate and dedicated services.

In her leisure hours Joyce likes to work at various crafts and is particularly skilled at creating stuffed bears of different kinds. She is an expert needlewoman who enjoys sewing. In the summer of 1984 she and Gordon had a wonderful trip to Europe and, in 2001, they went to Costa Rica for their fortieth anniversary. She looks forward to more travelling in the future.

HERAUF (BOURQUE), Constance ("Connie") Cecilia

1946–
Insurance Policy Typist, Computer Coder, Skilled and Creative Craftswoman, and Lyrical Signing Performer.

CONNIE BOURQUE (Herauf) was born with a profound hearing loss into a hearing family in Regina, Saskatchewan. She has no known Deaf relatives and the cause of her Deafness has never been determined. She has a hearing adult son, Joel Bourque, who is a social worker with the Edmonton Public School Board and works in a group home on weekends. Connie has made her home in Edmonton, Alberta, since 1968.

She was educated at the Saskatchewan School for the Deaf in Saskatoon from 1952 to 1964. During her final school year she began working as a dietary aide at St. Paul's Hospital in Saskatoon and continued that job until she moved to Edmonton, where her first employment was as a teletypesetter for the daily newspaper, the *Edmonton Journal*. From 1979 to 1983 she worked for the Royal Insurance Company of Canada as a senior policy typist. When the company moved its office to Calgary, Connie took a position with the Canadian Indemnity Insurance Company, doing data entry as well as policy typing. After twelve years she changed jobs again, and is currently employed with the Axa Pacific Insurance Company, where she does mainly computer coding. Connie loves her present job and plans to stay with it until she is eligible for retirement.

Apart from her day job, Connie keeps very busy and usefully employed in her sewing and craftsroom at home, which often resembles a miniature flower shop because it contains all the hobby supplies she needs for her ongoing crafts projects. She creates unique items, many of which she sells.

Until fairly recently, Connie's residual hearing was sufficient, with the use of a powerful hearing-aid, for her to communicate and function reasonably well in the hearing world. In the last five years, however, it has diminished progressively. She has begun to renew her signing skills, with all her family doing likewise to facilitate communication with her as she grows older and her Deafness becomes more profound.

Connie has always been a music lover. A few years ago she started signing the lyrics of certain songs she enjoyed. This hobby grew and her family now writes out the words for her so Connie can work out the signs and appropriate body language. When the speakers of a sound system are behind her she can hear the beat and rhythm of the music sufficiently well to synchronize the signed lyrics with it. She enjoys this pastime immensely and has performed publicly at numerous family gatherings, weddings, and other social functions.

The pleasure Connie derives from music also led her to becoming a good dancer, a pastime she still enjoys. Her natural creativity led her to the many hobbies and interests that give so much special meaning and satisfaction to her life.

HESSDORFER, Lorie Gaye

1964–
Successful Businessowner and Outstanding Role Model.

LORIE HESSDORFER was born Deaf into a hearing family in Saskatoon, Saskatchewan. Doctors felt that she might be triply disabled, possibly being Deaf, Blind, and having cerebral palsy. It turned out that she is Deaf and has cerebral palsy, but has normal sight. Her family was encouraged to move into the city of Saskatoon where she would have access to a School for the Deaf, a Centre for Children with Cerebral Palsy, and the CNIB, if it were needed. She credits all her successes to the help and encouragement she received from her loving and supportive parents and two sisters, Janet and Debbie. Lorie also has five nieces, and a nephew who has Down's Syndrome. At the age of thirty she became a great-aunt, and has two great-nephews and one great-niece. Lorie makes her home in Saskatoon.

Although she has no known Deaf relatives, Lorie does have a well-known ancestor—her great-great-grandfather, Damase Carriere, a skilled buffalo hunter, was killed in the 1885 Riel Rebellion. His nephew was the noted Métis leader, Gabriel Dumont, who was associated with Louis Riel in early western Canadian history. Lorie's research of her ancestral roots indicates that hers is the thirteenth generation of a French-Canadian family that came from France around 1600. She is particularly proud of her Métis origins, and her favourite pastime is researching her family background.

Lorie was educated at the R.J.D. Williams School for the Deaf, graduating in 1985. In her last two years she enrolled in a mainstream Catholic school, Holy Cross High School, to earn a grade twelve diploma, graduating in 1984. In 1985 she applied to enter Gallaudet University in Washington, DC. Sadly, Lorie was turned down twice by Gallaudet, but her determination kept her motivated to fight this issue through long distance telephone calls. Eventually, she was accepted to the Gallaudet Preparatory Program in

London, Ontario. In her third year at Gallaudet, she had to withdraw for one year due to a severe bout of mononucleosis. Back home in Saskatoon she was able to assist with the preparations for the final reunion before R.J.D. Williams School for the Deaf closed. The following year she returned to Gallaudet and graduated in 1994 with a Bachelor of Science degree in Accounting.

For over three years Lorie was unable to find employment, but her friend and mentor, Joanne Weber, encouraged her to take courses in entrepreneurship and running a business. In September of 1998 she launched her own business, Oak Tree Bookkeeping Services, with an official grand opening taking place in January 1999. She was able to establish this business through financial assistance from Deaf and Hard of Hearing Services in Saskatoon, several Métis and Aboriginal agencies, and the Cerebral Palsy Association. She is proud to have secured a contract with a major oil company, and her business is doing well. At first Lorie used interpreters to communicate with potential clients. She now uses mainly technological methods such as fax and e-mail. She has been recognized for her outstanding leadership skills with the 3M Award and was granted a certificate of appreciation by Canadian Deaf Youth Leadership (CDYL). The Canadian Cultural Society of the Deaf (CCSD) presented her with a Golden Defty Award, and she has won recognition in bowling, curling and good sportsmanship. She is a very active member of many local organizations and agencies for the Deaf, Métis, and cerebral palsied.

Lorie's favourite pastime is genealogical research, but she also enjoys travelling, reading, and cross-stitching. She bakes excellent cookies, which she always shares with others.

HICKMAN (PRUS), Pola

1917–
Deaf Volunteer and Tireless Advocate for Deaf Rights and Accessibility.

POLA HICKMAN was born hearing into a hearing family during World War I in Warsaw, Poland. She became Deaf at the age of five due to a severe bout of scarlet fever, which damaged not only her hearing but her memory as well. She had to be retrained in all the simple skills she had mastered before her illness, like walking, eating, and drinking. It is possible that there was a Deaf relative in the Prus family, someone who succumbed to scarlet fever at the age of eleven.

In 1926 her father came to Canada to try to make a new life here, and a year later he brought his family from Poland to settle in Kitchener, Ontario. Pola was enrolled at the Ontario provincial School for the Deaf in Belleville. She was twelve years old when she was introduced to an adult Deaf woman living nearby in Waterloo, Emily Lucille Bennet Maynihan, who became her mentor. Between 1930 and 1933, when the Ontario School for the Deaf (now known as Sir James Whitney School for the Deaf) adopted an oral philosophy, Pola lost her interest in education. The new policy stressed speech at the expense of broader learning, and Pola decided to stay home instead of returning to school. Emily supported that decision but took her to the public library and said, "This is your university." From that day onward, Pola spent a great deal of time at the library studying many topics and reading for information. The highlight of her library learning became the appreciation and enjoyment of poetry. Emily also counselled that Pola must be a leader in the Deaf Community, and this led to her becoming a volunteer and exemplary role model to hundreds of Deaf children with hearing parents.

Pola eventually married Frank Hickman, who was also Deaf, and they raised two fine hearing sons, David and Rodney, who learned to communicate with their parents in Sign Language, and have become respected and successful adults. Currently, Pola makes her home in Breslau, Ontario.

She recalls that when she had her first child, her mother felt she should raise the boy because Pola was Deaf. To this, Pola replied that God had blessed her with motherhood despite her Deafness which showed that He approved of her raising her own son. When she sees her two sons today, she smiles at the memory. She also recollects the old belief that because Deaf people were unable to hear (and in many cases, to speak intelligibly), they were naturally unable to think. She has spent her lifetime breaking down these barriers, to show the larger society that Deaf people can do anything their hearing counterparts can do, except hear. Despite her many years of effort, Pola realizes there is still much to be done. She was secretary-treasurer of the International Catholic Deaf Association, a pastoral worker, president of the Waterloo Regional Community of the Deaf, worked with Deaf seniors, and tutored hearing parents of Deaf children.

Pola worked as a volunteer with the Canadian Hearing Society (CHS) for forty-four years to create a more realistic public awareness of Deafness. In 1998, when Pola was eighty years old, the CHS honoured her by renaming their Kitchener Resource Centre on Frederick Street "Hickman Resources." Pola attended the grand opening celebration to cut the ribbon with Kitchener Mayor Carl Zehr, and even managed to teach him a few signs through an interpreter. Now well into her eighties, Pola continues to volunteer her time and skills to CHS, as well as other agencies and institutions that offer services to the Deaf Community. She has been the recipient of the Order of Ontario and several other prestigious awards. In 1997 the Canadian Hearing Society in Kitchener described her thus: "By your actions, you have shown concern for the welfare of others and demonstrated a generous and caring spirit."

HILTON (BUCHANAN), Helen Joyce

1954–
Data-Entry Operator, Website Specialist, and Avid Motorcyclist.

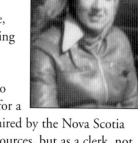

HELEN BUCHANAN was born Deaf into a Deaf family in Halifax, Nova Scotia. Her parents were Josephine (Polly) and Leonard Buchanan, who is now deceased. Polly, Helen's mother, was one of the first Deaf persons to attend Gaelic College in St. Ann's, near Baddeck on Cape Breton Island, to learn the art of weaving in the 1940s. Helen also had two younger Deaf sisters, Beverly, who lives in Texas, and Carolyn, who died of breast cancer at the age of thirty seven. Carolyn's husband, Wade Fitzgerald, is a hearing man and their three children are all hearing, although Wade has a Deaf sister, Linda Keating. Helen's Deaf aunt and uncle, Malcolm and Geraldine (Gerry) Buchanan, live in Moncton, New Brunswick. Helen's husband, Chris Hilton, is hearing, as are their two sons, Cody and Jarad. She also has a Deaf aunt, Joyce Kay, living in Delhaven, Nova Scotia.

Helen attended the School for the Deaf in Halifax for one year before the opening of the Interprovincial School for the Deaf in Amherst, now known as the Atlantic Provinces Special Education Authority (APSEA), in 1961. She completed her education there in 1971, and went on to train as a keypunch data-entry operator at the Atlantic Technological Vocational Centre. After completing her training, she worked for several corporations—Blue Cross, National Sea Products, Medical Services Insurance (MSI), and the Nova Scotia Department of Supply and Services—for a total of twenty-two years. Repetitive use of her wrists led to carpal tunnel syndrome, and it took four years of physiotherapy after surgery before she was able to return to the workforce. By this time, however, she had decided on a career change.

She attended a one-year program at Henson College, Dalhousie University, learning how to develop, edit, and maintain a website. She volunteered her new skills to the provincial government for a year before she was finally hired by the Nova Scotia Department of Natural Resources, but as a clerk, not as a website specialist. Her hope is that she will advance and move into a position where she can put her training to use.

Since her teens, Helen has loved the freedom and pleasure of riding motorcycles. In her early years she rode around the province with a group of bikers. She also owned several foreign-made motorcycles before she was able to indulge in her first Harley-Davidson, which she rode until she became pregnant with her first son, when she reluctantly sold it. She owned another Harley briefly in 1998 but it too was sold when she needed to focus all her attention on being a good mother to her two growing boys.

Helen and Chris went into breeding and raising Doberman Pinscher dogs for sale, but the enterprise did not last long. The purebred puppies required a surgical procedure to their ears in order to make them stand erect, followed by massage to make them firm. This was very tedious and time-consuming work, so the Hiltons gave up dog-raising.

In her leisure hours, Helen makes stained-glass Tiffany lampshades and suncatchers, works on her family tree, reads, and gardens. Motorcycling, of course, will always be her favourite pastime.

HOLEWA (BODEN), Linda Diane

1950–
Postal Clerk, Member of a Volume Electronic Mail Team, and ASL Model.

LINDA BODEN was born Deaf due to maternal rubella to hearing parents in Camrose, Alberta. She has no known Deaf relatives, but her husband, Klaus Holewa, is Deaf. Linda and Klaus have two adult hearing daughters, Krista and Klara. The family currently lives in Edmonton.

Linda was educated at the Alberta School for the Deaf in Edmonton, as a residential student, from 1956 to 1969. She then attended Gallaudet College (now Gallaudet University) in Washington, DC, for two years

from 1969 to 1971. Upon withdrawing and returning to Alberta, Linda found employment with Canada Post, where she continued to work for twenty-one years, both in Edmonton and in Calgary, until she was granted medical retirement in 1995.

During her years with Canada Post. Linda was selected to become a member of a special four-person team that manned the Volume Electronic Mail (VEM) site in Calgary. This was a new technology at the time, and it provided electronic transmission of multi-point messages. The Calgary site was one of eight located in major mail processing plants across Canada. The team was responsible for processing data sent from a central computer in Ottawa. It provided one-stop shopping for mail services—printing, stuffing of envelopes, sorting, and distribution could all be taken care of in only moments by the VEM team. The service has been particularly useful for direct-mail advertising and charitable fundraising. Linda's team received high praise for its productivity and pride in achievement. Two concessions had to be made to create accessibility for Linda—Canada Post provided her with a TTY and a Phone Flasher so she could receive incoming calls, just like her three hearing counterparts. Through Linda's perseverance and dedication, Canada Post Corporation has come to realize that, with appropriate technology, there are few postal jobs that Deaf people cannot do. Hence, this job market is gradually opening more and more doors to Deaf workers.

Linda has always been a very active member of the Deaf Community in both Edmonton and Calgary. She was one of the founders who incorporated the Alberta Association of the Deaf (AAD) into a nonprofit charitable agency in 1972. She also served as president of the Alberta Cultural Society of the Deaf (ACSD) for six years, during which it became the first provincial branch to receive a registry number. In addition, she worked as a volunteer for the World Winter Games of the Deaf held in Calgary, and for the Deaf Children's Festival held in Edmonton in June of 1994. While living in Edmonton she also served as an ASL model for the Sign Language programs at Grant MacEwan Community College. In July 2000 Linda served on the registration committee for the Canadian Deaf Festival held in Edmonton. She was also one of the Deaf staff members at the first Deaf summer camp sponsored by the Edmonton Association of the Deaf (EAD) and Calgary Association of the Deaf (CAD) at Pigeon Lake in July 2001. This involved thirty-seven Deaf children, aged six to fifteen, from various parts of Alberta, and was an enriching experience, for which Linda received a certificate of appreciation.

In her spare time, Linda is an avid genealogist, likes to read, and enjoys outdoor camping.

HOPKINS (CROWELL), Nancy Elaine

1941–
MSL Instructor, Dressmaker, Collector, and Craftswoman.

NANCY CROWELL was born Deaf to hearing parents at Newellton, Cape Sable Island, Shelburne County, Nova Scotia. She grew up, and spent most of her youth there. Nancy has a Deaf brother and her husband, Andrew Hopkins, is also Deaf. They have an adult hearing daughter, Melody Anne. Nancy and Andrew make their home in Waterville, Nova Scotia.

From 1948 to 1958 Nancy attended the Halifax School for the Deaf, where she was a diligent student who achieved good grades and received numerous awards and school prizes. She did exceptionally well in weaving, sewing, knitting, cooking, and embroidering, as well as in her academic courses.

Nancy has always been a very active member of the Deaf Community, volunteering her time and effort to assist with social and recreational activities, as well as serving in various capacities with organizations and agencies of the Deaf. She has been involved in the Halifax Association of the Deaf (HAD), the Canadian Cultural Society of the Deaf (CCSD), the Nova Scotia Deaf Sports Association (NSDSA), the Nova Scotia Cultural Society of the Deaf (NSCSD), the Valley Association of the Deaf (VAD), and the Coordinating Council on Deafness of Nova Scotia (CCDNS), now known as the Deafness Advocacy Association Nova Scotia (DAANS). In 1990 she served on the host committee of the Canadian Deaf Curling Championships held in Halifax. She has won many CCSD awards for her crafts and handiwork.

In her spare time, Nancy teaches Maritime Sign Language (MSL) classes at her church and in schools, and works as a dressmaker. Her special hobbies are embroidery and rug braiding. She has a passion for antiques, collects old Deaf schoolbooks and pictures of classmates, and likes to visit historical museums. For relaxation, she walks on the beach and collects interesting pieces of driftwood. She still keeps score for the Eastern Bowling Association of the Deaf every May at its provincial tournaments which include New Brunswick and Nova Scotia. Nancy is also a dog lover and an avid bird watcher.

HOWSE (ANDERSON), Frances Elizabeth

1936–
Weaver and Maintenance Lady.

FRANCES ANDERSON was born hearing to hearing parents at Channel, Port Aux Basques, Newfoundland. She became Deaf at the age of five, due to illness. Her brother and sister-in-law are Deaf and her husband, Charles A.L. Howse, who does maintenance carpentry, is also Deaf. Frances and Charles have two adult hearing sons, David, who lives in Montréal, and Don, who is in Ontario. Frances and Charles currently make their home in St. John's, Newfoundland.

Frances attended the Halifax School for the Deaf from 1944 to 1952. Her favourite subject was weaving, and she became quite proficient at it. In fact, she worked for some time with the Jubilee Guilds as an accomplished weaver.

When Frances and Charles married and settled down to raise a family, she was out of the workforce for a number of years, being at stay-at-home housewife and full-time mother. In 1970 she returned to work

and accepted a position with K-Mart, where she served as the store's "maintenance lady" until 1990, when she retired. During her twenty years of employment with K-Mart, Frances was the recipient of two awards for her dedicated service and loyalty to the company.

Frances' involvement in the Deaf Community has varied. She is a former president of the St. John's Association of the Deaf (SJAD) and is presently an active member of the Newfoundland and Labrador Association of the Deaf (NLAD). She has also participated in Bible study for the Deaf.

In her leisure hours, Frances enjoys such hobbies as plastic canvassing, knitting, cotton crocheting, basic sewing, baking, and travelling.

HUNTLEY (GALLOP), Elizabeth Ann

1953–
Educator, Program Coordinator, and Interpreter Trainer.

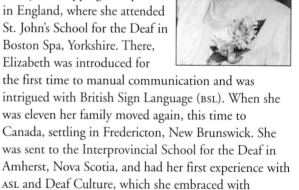

ELIZABETH GALLOP was born in Hobart, Tasmania, Australia. She became Deaf at fifteen months of age due to illness. She has no known Deaf relatives, but her Deaf husband, Harold "Buddy" Huntley, an alumnus of the Moline School for the Deaf and Hard of Hearing, is a prominent member of the local Deaf Community. Elizabeth and Buddy make their home in Coal Valley, Illinois, US. They have two adult hearing children, Barry and Rosemary. Elizabeth is proud to count among her hearing kinfolk the notable Australian painter and artist, Herbert Gallop, who is her paternal grandfather. An art gallery in Wagga Wagga, Australia, bears his name. Years ago, one of Elizabeth's hearing sisters worked closely with the Deaf in Winnipeg, Manitoba.

Because of her family's rather nomadic lifestyle during her youth, Elizabeth's education became a some-what global experience. She was enrolled at St. Mary's Oral School for the Deaf in Portsea, near Melbourne, when she was only two and a half years old. When she was five her family moved to Corvallis, Oregon, where she attended a regular mainstream school with no special class for Deaf students and no interpreter. Elizabeth recalls this as one of the worst educational

experiences of her life. At age nine she moved again with her family to Chipping Campden in England, where she attended St. John's School for the Deaf in Boston Spa, Yorkshire. There, Elizabeth was introduced for the first time to manual communication and was intrigued with British Sign Language (BSL). When she was eleven her family moved again, this time to Canada, settling in Fredericton, New Brunswick. She was sent to the Interprovincial School for the Deaf in Amherst, Nova Scotia, and had her first experience with ASL and Deaf Culture, which she embraced with pleasure and enthusiasm. Elizabeth has many happy memories of her days in Amherst, where she feels her world opened up like a flower bursting into bloom.

Finally, the Gallop family moved west to Manitoba which at last became their permanent residence. Elizabeth attended the Manitoba School for the Deaf in Winnipeg and has a host of wonderful memories of the years she spent there. After graduating, she attended Gallaudet College (now Gallaudet University) in Washington, DC, for two years. There she met her future husband, Buddy, who has several honours to his credit. He was co-founder of the Blackhawk Chapter of the Illinois Association of the Deaf in 1976, and the founder of the Moline School for the Deaf and Hard of Hearing Class Reunion, an event which he has hosted twice. For seven years he was a board member of the Illinois-Iowa Centre for Independent Living.

When Elizabeth and Buddy married, they settled in Illinois to begin their life together. After being a full-time mother and homemaker for several years, Elizabeth completed her post-secondary education at Black Hawk College in Moline, part of Northern Illinois University in DeKalb, where she was a member of the Phi Theta Kappa Honour Society, earning a teaching certification in Pre-Elementary Education. In 1994 she attended Northern Illinois University and graduated with a Bachelor of Science degree in Special Education for the Deaf and Hard of Hearing, enabling her to teach kindergarten to grade twelve.

Elizabeth's employment history is interesting. She worked for four years at the farm implement company, John Deere; taught ASL classes, part-time, at Black Hawk College; served as a substitute teacher for Deaf and hard-of-hearing students in Moline schools; and taught ASL and Deafness-related classes, part-time, at Black Hawk College. She is presently employed full-time at Scott Community College in Bettendorf, Iowa, in the interpreter training program, where she has served as both coordinator and instructor. She considers it pure joy to work with the students and her colleagues, and loves every minute of it.

She is a member of various organizations, including the Conference for Interpreter Trainers (CIT), the Illinois Teachers for the Deaf and Hard of Hearing (ITHI), the Illinois-Iowa Centre for Independent Living, and the Gallaudet Alumni Association. In their leisure hours, Elizabeth and Buddy enjoy travelling and browsing around antique shops. She strongly believes that Deaf women are capable of doing anything they set their minds to, contributing to both the Deaf and hearing communities.

HUSSEY, Barbara Lyn

1975–
Teacher, Advisor, Caseworker, and Youth Leader.

BARBARA HUSSEY was born Deaf into a multi-generation Deaf family in Burnaby, BC. Her parents, David and Hester Hussey, and her sister, Leslie Hussey, are all Deaf, as are some of her distant cousins. Barbara acquired her early education at the Jericho Hill School for the Deaf (mainstream off-campus classes) in Vancouver, BC, from 1980 to 1991. She then attended the Model Secondary School for the Deaf in Washington, DC, before entering Gallaudet University. There she obtained a BA degree in Elementary Education (Summa Cum Laude) in 1998 and an MA degree in Deaf Education–Elementary (with honours) in 1999.

While attending Gallaudet University, Barbara was twice mentioned in *Who's Who in American Colleges and Universities* and twice made the Dean's List. In 1995 she won the Agatha Tiegel Hanson award for "Outstanding Freshman of the Year" and the "Student Body Government Volunteer of the Year" award. She became a member of the Phi Alpha Pi Honour Society at Gallaudet, and vice-president of the Phi Kappa Zeta sorority. Barbara has superior communication skills and is a creative and innovative teacher.

In 1997 and 1998 she acquired student teaching experience at several schools in the Washington area,

which she valued highly, particularly at the Sidwell Friends School where she could demonstrate her progressive ideas. Her ultimate student teaching assignment, however, took her to the Southeast Asian Institute for the Deaf in the Philippines for three months in 1999. There she taught English, following a more traditional curriculum, but was able to introduce dialogue journals to the school for the first time. She also participated in promoting the development of interdisciplinary thematic units and the establishment of learning centres.

From 1994 until she graduated from Gallaudet, Barbara held several interesting part-time jobs—working as a leader for the BC Deaf Youth program, as a gameroom assistant at Gallaudet, as a caseworker for Deaf children for two government ministries in Vancouver, BC, and as a residence advisor at Gallaudet. From these positions, she gained confidence and developed excellent employment skills and attitudes.

To date, Barabara classes her trip to China as the most memorable event in her life. She travelled with her parents to join her sister Leslie, who was teaching at the Dalian School for the Deaf. The experience had an enormous impact on her but, more importantly, she was able to compare the Chinese program with her own very different teaching experience in the Philippines, where most of the schools were still using Signed English. This was a most unusual situation for a young woman who had been accustomed to ASL all her life.

Barbara currently makes her home in Minneapolis, Minnesota. She teaches at the Metro School for the Deaf in that city.

HUSSEY (JOHNSTON), Hester Judith

1950–
Teacher, Counsellor, Youth Worker, and Foster Parent.

HESTER JOHNSTON's Deafness was not discovered until she was two years old and the cause remains unknown. She was born into a hearing family in Kamloops, BC, the youngest of three children. She was educated at Jericho Hill School for the Deaf in Vancouver, BC, from age five to seventeen, living in the dormitory. Although the school had an oral philosophy and tradition at that time, she learned to sign from her friends in the residential program and soon accepted ASL as her native language. At home the Johnston family communicated with her through home signs, gestures, and drawings, so she could take an active part in conversations. During her last year at Jericho Hill she was fortunate to have the opportunity of living with a Deaf family, from whom she learned a great deal about the identity, values, culture, language, and folklore of the Deaf.

Hester eventually married David John Hussey and together they raised two lovely Deaf daughters, Leslie Louise and Barbara Lyn. Over the years, they also acted as foster parents to five Deaf adolescent girls. As a couple, Hester and David have served as group-home workers and residence staff for Deaf children, teens, and adults.

While her husband's main interest is in Deaf sports, Hester loves to work with Deaf people who need her help and guidance. She acquired an Early Childhood Education Certificate from Douglas College and a certificate from the Justice Institute of BC which qualified her to work with troubled teens. As a family, the Husseys travelled to China on a study tour and met Deaf Chinese people, developing a deep respect and admiration for them and their country. When their daughter Barbara went to the Philippines to do one of her student teaching practicums at a school for the Deaf, David and Hester visited her and saw many beautiful sights as they toured the school and the surrounding countryside.

From 1979 to 1993 Hester worked with Deaf children and their families in a variety of ways —teaching, supervising, planning projects, co-coordinating programs, and hosting summer camps. In 1993 she became a child-care counsellor for the Special Education Department in Vancouver and, in 1997, a part-time auxiliary child-care counsellor at the Victory Hill Residence. She was also a proprietary care worker for a Deaf-Blind man who lived in her home. From 1999 to 2001, Hester worked with the Jericho Individual Compensation Program, interviewing clients regarding their experiences at Jericho High School and preparing their testimony for a panel of lawyers who adjudicated compensation amounts. This was particularly challenging because communication was not always easy and the issues they discussed were sensitive ones. She and her husband have always been active members of the Deaf community, volunteering endless hours of their time and expertise.

David is of British descent and has Deaf relatives in England on his mother's side of the family. His great-grandfather was a neighbour and playmate of Sir Winston Churchill, and one of his female ancestors could have (but didn't) marry the noted British poet, Percy Bysshe Shelley. A penchant for teaching and working with children and young people seems to run in Hester's family. Several of her relatives were teachers and now both of her daughters are also educators.

Hester has spent nearly all her adult life working with Deaf people of all ages and at all levels of communication. She and David reside in Burnaby, BC, and have many hobbies and interests but continue to find time to devote to the Deaf Community.

HUSSEY, Leslie Louise

1973–
Honour Student and Born Teacher.

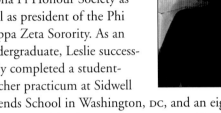

LESLIE HUSSEY is a member of an extended Deaf family. Her parents, her sister Barbara Lyn, and many of her paternal cousins are Deaf. She also has an aunt who is hard of hearing.

Leslie was born to David and Hester Hussey, in Burnaby, BC, in 1973. She began her education at Jericho Hill School for the Deaf at the age of five in 1978. She completed her schooling (grades five to twelve) at Kitsilano Secondary School, where she was the first Deaf student to master a four-year French-language program. In 1997, Leslie graduated, Magna Cum Laude, from Gallaudet University in Washington, DC, with a BA in Elementary Education. The following year she completed, with Honours, an MA in Deaf Education.

Throughout her growing-up years, Leslie aspired to become a teacher, often "playing school," where she taught her sister and their Deaf cousins. She loved being part of a Deaf family and appreciated the fluent, open flow of communication. In the summer she worked as a camp leader in the Deaf Youth Program. In high school she was chosen "Premier Student" by her peers at a Western Canada Tournament of the Deaf.

During Leslie's Gallaudet years, her name appeared in *Who's Who in American Colleges and Universities*, and she was a member of the Phi Alpha Pi Honour Society as well as president of the Phi Kappa Zeta Sorority. As an undergraduate, Leslie successfully completed a student-teacher practicum at Sidwell Friends School in Washington, DC, and an eight-week overseas teaching internship program at Dalian School for the Deaf in Liaoning Province in China.

Since her graduation, Leslie has been employed as a teacher of the Deaf for the middle school grades at the Florida School for the Deaf and Blind in St. Augustine, Florida. Her sister is also a teacher and her parents have always been involved in various roles with Deaf youth— as foster parents, group-home workers, and residence staff—so her background is steeped in traditional ASL and Deaf culture. It is a wonderful legacy on which to build a successful and satisfying life and career.

Leslie has a lifetime ahead of her to be a role model who inspires others, and to become a leader among Deaf women wherever she chooses to live.

HUTCHINSON (BELISLE), Lucille Edith

1947–
Jane-of-all-Trades at R.J.D. Williams School for the Deaf, Fundraiser, ASL Instructor, and Dedicated Volunteer.

LUCILLE BELISLE was born Deaf to hearing parents at Willow Bunch, Saskatchewan. She has a Deaf sister, Lydia Storey, and a late Deaf brother, Michael Belisle. Her husband, Robert C. Hutchinson, is also Deaf, and they have two adult hearing sons, Jamey and Rod. Lucille and Robert currently make their home in Saskatoon, Saskatchewan.

Lucille received her education at the Saskatchewan School for the Deaf in Saskatoon (later renamed the R.J.D. Williams School, which is now closed). She recalls travelling by bus back and forth to her farm home at Willow Bunch, near the US border, from Saskatoon, for holidays and summer vacations from 1953 to 1964 when she graduated. For the first three years, her older sister Lydia travelled with her. Her Deaf brother Michael, who died of a massive heart attack in 1998, at the age of forty-one, also attended the school in Saskatoon. Lucille is very grateful to her hearing family for having sent their Deaf children to such a wonderful school where they received a good general education, developed good communication skills, and acquired many other useful talents.

After graduation, Lucille was hired by the government of Saskatchewan as a laundress at the school she had attended. When the laundry services were discontinued, she became a general service worker, and later a parental care supervisor. Following the closure of the school, Lucille began teaching ASL classes at the Saskatchewan Institute for Applied Arts and Science Technology, (SIAST), as well as other venues throughout Saskatoon, instructing city staff members wherever needed. She also teaches a Sign Language course to employees on the University of Saskatchewan campus.

Within the Deaf Community, Lucille has played a major role as a volunteer. She was on the committee that organized the 50th Reunion of the Saskatchewan School for the Deaf in 1983 and later, the 60th Reunion as well. She upgraded her skills by going to Grant MacEwan College in Edmonton to study ASL structure and Deaf Culture. She has been very active in the Saskatoon Association of the Deaf and the Saskatchewan Cultural Society of the Deaf, acting as a successful fundraiser as well as serving on their boards and some committees. She has also been a board member of Saskatchewan Deaf and Hard of Hearing Services and continues to participate fully in all activities taking place within the Deaf Community.

Lucille is proud to have been honoured and recognized for her many contributions with awards and certificates of appreciation and merit. She has entered crafts and hobby tournaments at Deaf festivals of the arts and, in general, has kept herself well occupied in her productive and satisfying life.

Lucille and Robert have been happily married since 1968. He was a long-time employee at the University of Saskatchewan in the technical/medical artworking laboratory. They are proud of the two fine sons they raised. Lucille is now a contented, retired homemaker, enjoying her various craft hobbies when she is not too busy with events in the Deaf Community.

JACKSON, Jennifer Anita

1976–
Teacher Assistant, Project Researcher, Editor, Caseworker, Division Leader, and Law Student.

JENNIFER JACKSON was born Deaf to Deaf parents in North York (Toronto), Ontario. Her father, Rod Jackson, of Toronto, was a 1971 graduate of Gallaudet College (now Gallaudet University) in Washington, DC. Her mother, Mary Ryan, is an alumnus of Cabra School for Deaf Girls in Dublin, Ireland. Mary came to Toronto in 1972 and married Rod Jackson in 1974. Jennifer has a Deaf sister, Lucia Jackson, who is currently studying at York University. She also has numerous other Deaf relatives on both her mother's and her father's side of the family. Her mother has served on the board of the Ontario Association of the Deaf (OAD), as has her sister. Jennifer's mother also volunteers her time to do office work for that organization and has been a board member of the Canadian Hearing Society (CHS). Her other Deaf relatives are very active in their local Deaf Communities. Jennifer currently makes her home in Toronto.

She began her schooling at Clairlea Public School in Toronto, attending for one year before spending the next three years at Clarke School for the Deaf in Northampton, Massachussetts. She then returned to Ontario and attended mainstream public schools in Oakville—St. Michael's and St. Matthew's. The family then moved to Stittsville, near Ottawa, where she attended St. Paul's and then Holy Trinity High School. Finally, for grades eleven and twelve, she went to Sir James Whitney School for the Deaf in Belleville, Ontario. She and her sister Lucia then attended mainstream classes at Dante Alighieri Academy with ASL interpreters. Since graduating high school, Jennifer has completed a BA Honours degree in Political Science,

Law and Society at York University in Toronto, where she was a member of the Dean's Honour List. Since 1999 she has studied Law at Osgoode Hall Law School in Toronto, and is a LL.B. candidate for 2002. Her legal experience, to date, includes editing, researching, and proof-reading citations in articles and footnotes submitted for publication in the *Osgoode Hall Law Journal*. She has also been a caseworker and division leader in the Community and Legal Aid Services Programme.

In 2000 Jennifer was the Anglophone Delegate of Canada to the United Nations' Beijing +5 International Seminar and Training for Young Women with Disabilities, held in New York City as a follow-up of the 1995 conference in Beijing, China. She was also the 1999 delegate for Canada at the World Federation of Deaf Youth Leadership Camp in Brisbane, Australia. From 1997 to 1999 she worked as a teacher-assistant in American Sign Language courses taught in the Deaf Education Department at York University in Toronto. Prior to that she was a project researcher assessing the literacy needs of Deaf, Deafened, Hard of Hearing and Deaf-Blind Youth in Ontario.

Jennifer also has a number of other extracurricular activities to her credit. She participated as a panelist in various disability awareness discussions and workshops hosted by York University's Office for Persons with Disabilities. She assisted in the instruction of written English to Deaf students of LINC (Language Instruction for Newcomers). She was a regular participant in coordinating social events hosted by various organizations of the Deaf (such as OAD), served as secretary of OAD and was a director on the board of Goal: Ontario Literacy of Deaf People (GOLD).

Apart from her studies and involvement in the Deaf Community, Jennifer's hobbies and interests include reading, biking, swimming, long-distance walking, sampling new foods, collecting books, writing letters, telling stories, and looking at photographic works, especially those depicting people.

This intelligent and ambitious young woman is an inspiration and outstanding role model to Canada's present generation of Deaf teenaged girls now approaching adulthood.

JAMES, Ada Mary

1870–1965
Alumnus and Teacher of the Ontario Institution for the Deaf and Dumb, now Known as Sir James Whitney School for the Deaf.

ADA JAMES was born hearing to hearing parents, Samuel and Maria James, who had emigrated from England and settled in Ontario. They were living in St. Thomas, in Elgin County, at the time of Ada's birth, and Samuel James provided for his family through casual work as a painter. Ada had three siblings—a sister, Mabel, and two brothers, Saul and Lewis. When she was five years old, Ada contracted a severe case of scarlet fever which left her profoundly Deaf. Her parents consulted a series of medical specialists and other professionals, but were finally told Ada would never hear again. They were advised to have her try an assistive listening device that was popular at that time—an "audiphone"—but, unfortunately, it did not enable Ada to hear.

When she was eleven years old, in 1881, she entered the Ontario Institution for the Deaf and Dumb in Belleville (now known as the Sir James Whitney School for the Deaf). This was her first real experience with formal education. At home, she had been taught the alphabet, simple arithmetic, knitting, and sewing. Her teachers soon found her to be a very intelligent girl and a quick learner. By 1887 she was at the top of her class and was one of the most popular students in the school. She became a teacher and was employed at her alma mater for a total of thirty-nine years, from 1891 to 1898, and 1899 to 1931. She was considered an outstanding educator and was noted for the extra-curricular activities she provided for her students, particularly in social-recreational events and the performing arts.

Ada's tenure at the Ontario School for the Deaf was fraught with uneasiness because of the constant controversy over oralism versus manualism. The oral system of teaching was adopted as policy throughout the school in 1912, and Deaf teachers were being phased out of the program. By 1931 Sign Language had officially disappeared from all classrooms and the hiring of Deaf teachers was no longer sanctioned. Thus, Ada was obliged to take early retirement, although she was the last Deaf teacher to leave the school. One of the most memorable highlights of her teaching career occurred in 1914, when the Duke and Duchess of Connaught and their daughter, Princess Patricia, spent an hour at the Belleville School as part of a royal tour. Ada James trained and led a large group of students in signing "God Save the King" during the reception, which took place in the newly opened girl's residence. The royal entourage was duly impressed.

Although she was an active member of the Ontario Association of the Deaf (OAD), very little opportunity existed for a Deaf woman of that era to hold office or influence decisions, so Ada contributed her talents by organizing social and recreational activities. While OAD, with predominantly male control, focused on Deaf issues such as Canada's immigration policy and driving regulations, the organization completely overlooked the role of women in its own ranks. It was not until 1941 that OAD finally issued an official complaint about the treatment of Deaf teachers at the Belleville School.

By the time Ada James passed away in 1965, women were taking their rightful place in the various organizations of the Deaf, and many were holding executive positions. They provided strength and determination in the ongoing controversies that surrounded the education policies being dictated for Deaf children in Ontario, particularly at the Belleville School, where the memory of Ada Mary James has been preserved to this day.

JASPAR (FESCHUK), Mary

1930–

ASL Instructor, Community Volunteer, Caregiver, Photographer, Picture Framer, and Business Woman.

MARY FESCHUK was born Deaf into a hearing family at Meath Park, near Prince Albert, Saskatchewan. She has no known Deaf relatives, but her husband, Peter Jaspar, of Prince Albert, is Deaf, and they have two adult hearing children. Their son Don now resides in Calgary, Alberta, and works for a world relief organization, Samaritan's Purse. Their daughter Annette and her husband Graham live in Prince Albert with Mary's two hearing grandchildren, Connor and Kate. Annette and Graham both work for the Saskatchewan Department of Social Services, and Annette is also a freelance ASL interpreter. Peter Jaspar is an alumnus of the French School for the Deaf in Montréal, Québec, where he received all his education except for one year at the Saskatchewan School for the Deaf in Saskatoon. At school, he was trained to be a printer, but his father owned the Magnet Grocery Store in Prince Albert, and Peter became an experienced grocery delivery man for his father's store, where he worked for sixteen years. His chief employment, however, was as a warehouse clerk for the Co-op, working there for twenty-eight years before he retired. Mary and Peter have made their home in Prince Albert since before they were married in 1954.

Mary received her education at the Saskatchewan School for the Deaf in Saskatoon, and trained at a downtown photography studio during the last two years before she graduated. She then returned to Prince Albert and was employed at various jobs before she became an entrepreneur and started working as a photographer from her home. This venture into self-employment lasted twenty years, from 1960 to 1980. She also set up a home-based picture framing business in 1970, from which she retired in 2000. In addition to owning and operating her own business, Mary also became an ASL instructor, attending classes and work-shops, as well as teaching and doing private tutoring, from 1980 until the present time.

She has been an active member of the Prince Albert Association for the Hearing Impaired (PAAAHI) since its inception in 1982, serving as treasurer and member of the social committee. She was a director on the board for Services for Hearing Impaired (now Saskatchewan Deaf and Hard of Hearing Services [SDHHS]), from 1986 to 1990. Prior to 1990 she was involved with the Saskatchewan Association of the Deaf (SAD), the Saskatchewan Coordinating Council on Deafness (SCCD), the Saskatchewan Cultural Society of the Deaf (SCCSD), and various Catholic retreats for the Deaf.

Mary has been the recipient of many awards and honours. In 1974 she was presented with the Canadian Cultural Society of the Deaf's Golden Defty Award for her photographs. She also received local trophies for her photographs at the Prince Albert Exhibition. Other honours bestowed upon her were for excellence in picture framing, and in recognition of her many valued contributions to organizations for the Deaf and hard of hearing, particularly SDHHS, PAAHI. and SCSD. As a bowler, she has also received many trophies, shields, and pins since joining her first league in 1948. Now, fifty-four years later, she still hasn't missed a bowling season.

This versatile woman finds time in her busy life to participate in her favourite sport, ten- and five-pin bowling. She enjoys doing jigsaw puzzles and word-finds, and likes to play cards. She has been the principal caregiver for her aging mother while waiting for nursing-home placement, loves baby-sitting her grand-children, reading, watching television, travelling, and socializing with friends. She is held in high esteem by all her friends and former students.

JENKINS, Olive M.

1870–1958

Dormitory Supervisor and Counsellor, Dedicated Volunteer in the Deaf Community, and Avid Bridge Player.

OLIVE JENKINS was born hearing to hearing parents, one of the three children of David and Mary Pengelly Jenkins of Swansea, Wales, in Great Britain. She had a brother, Fred, and a sister, Edith. At the time of her birth in 1870, her family was living in Coquimbo, Chile, South America. Olive became Deaf at the age of eight, but the cause of her Deafness was not recorded. In 1882 the Jenkins family left Chile and moved to Canada, settling on the west coast in Victoria, BC. She had no known Deaf relatives, was never married, and spent most of her life in Winnipeg, Manitoba.

Because there was no school where Deaf children could be educated in British Columbia at that time, nor was there such an institution in either Alberta or Saskatchewan, Olive had to be sent to the Manitoba Institution for the Education of the Deaf and Dumb in Winnipeg, Manitoba (later changed to the Manitoba School for the Deaf), which was at that time located on the corner of Portage Avenue and Sherbrooke Street. She arrived in Winnipeg in 1891 and was a member of the graduating class of 1905. After completing her education, she took a position at the school she had attended, working in the residence as a dormitory supervisor and counsellor, a position she held for nearly forty years.

Olive Jenkins was widely known in all Deaf Communities across Western Canada. A great many of the most outstanding Deaf Canadian women from both eastern and western Canada grew up under her care and guidance. She was associated with the Manitoba School for the Deaf for nearly fifty years, first as a pupil and later as a staff member. Her devotion to her work contributed significantly to the education, social skills, employability status, interests, and hobbies of all the Deaf girls who grew up under her supervision. She was sometimes thought of as a strict disciplinarian, but was always respected and admired by all her young charges. She encouraged thrift and economy, insisting that the girls mend and take good care of their clothes, recycling worn items rather than discarding them. Many of them even became expert at darning the holes in their worn socks.

Olive was also renowned in the Deaf Community of Winnipeg. She was active in the Winnipeg Church of the Deaf's Ladies' Aid Society, raising large sums of money through the sale of her candy and fancy work. She was known far and wide for her wonderful skills at candy-making, embroidering, and other crafts, and continued her fundraising activities until her eyesight began to fail. She was chairperson of the McDermid Scholarship Fund, a tireless volunteer with the Western Canada Association of the Deaf (WCAD), and a lifetime member of the Winnipeg Community Centre of the Deaf (WCCD).

Olive was a talented bridge player who was famous for her regular bridge parties. She was an outstanding cook and party organizer, which made her a popular hostess among Deaf bridge players in the community.

She passed away peacefully in her sleep at Grace Hospital in Winnipeg on 13 May 1958, in her eighty-fourth year, mourned and sadly missed by all who had known her. She had suffered a severe stroke in February, from which she never recovered. In keeping with her wishes, Olive's remains were cremated and her ashes were scattered to the four winds.

JENSEN, Shauna Lynne

1961–
Entrepreneur, Businesswoman, Craftswoman, and Skilled Horsewoman.

SHAUNA JENSEN was born hearing in Drayton Valley, Alberta, but became Deaf before her third birthday. Her eldest and youngest brothers are also Deaf, but they have no other known Deaf relatives. Shauna has been with her hearing partner, Ray Nickason, for seventeen years and they have three hearing children—Matthew, Jonathan, and Haley. Ray owns and operates his own business which provides parts, servicing, painting, and the restoration of horse and livestock trailers. They currently make their home at Entwistle in rural Alberta.

Shauna was a member of the 1979 graduating class at the Alberta provincial School for the Deaf in Edmonton (ASD). Since then she has had varied employment experiences, working as a cake decorator in Wetaskiwin, near Edmonton; as a chambermaid at Sunshine Village, a popular skiing resort near Banff; as a cleaning woman at the Michener Centre in Red Deer; and as a teacher's aide at Elnora School, where she worked with a Deaf student.

The year after she finished high school, in 1980, Shauna was honoured by being chosen Miss Deaf Alberta. This boosted her confidence and self-esteem. Currently, she is self-employed, owning and operating her own business, a company that sells equine-wear and dancing outfits. She also offers custom sewing, and can produce all types of costumes, equine accessories, and upholstered items.

Shauna's greatest love is horses, and she often shows her prized equines at local horse shows. To date they have won more than one hundred rosettes, all with high marks. One of her lifelong dreams has been to show her horses in a competition of the Canadian National Quarter Horse Show, held annually in Red Deer, to see how they would fare in that type of setting. Perhaps some day soon her wish will be fulfilled.

Although Shauna is a busy woman, running her own business, taking in extra sewing, and being a mother to her three offspring, she still finds time to garden, a pastime she enjoys. She also collects antiques and loves ski-dooing in the winter months. Because she lives some distance from Edmonton, it is difficult for Shauna to be involved to any extent in the Deaf Community, or to help out with the activities of the many agencies for the Deaf. Nevertheless, she enjoys visiting her many Deaf friends in Edmonton whenever possible. Shauna is an exemplary role model for younger Deaf women who are considering starting their own home-based businesses.

JICKELS (LYONS), Janice ("JJ")

1952–
ASL Program Technician, Multicultural Coordinator of Medical Interpreting Services and Courses, Co-Founder of "ASL Way" and Canada DeafCom, Author of the Guidebook for "ASL Signing Naturally," TV Host, Advocate for Deaf Rights, and Staunch Promoter of ASL.

JANICE LYONS, or "JJ," as she prefers to be known, was born Deaf to hearing parents in Vancouver, BC. She is the youngest of three daughters and the only Deaf member of her family. Her hearing uncle, Ken Lyons, was the first captain of HMS Lord Selkirk, which, in 1970, escorted the British Royal family on a river cruise while they visited Canada. Since 1973 she has been happily married to a Deaf man, Bruce Jickels, who works as a lathe operator at a local sawmill. Before starting their family, Bruce and JJ enjoyed many out-door activities, including four-wheel driving. In 1978 JJ was one of the founding members of the 4x4 Club, which she served in various positions. At that time she drove a 1969 Bronco. Together, she and Bruce have raised three lovely hearing daughters—Jennifer, Jessica, and Jaclyn. In 1988 all three girls became involved in the movie industry. They appeared in *We Are No Angels*, with Jessica in a major role, and in *Deep Sleep*, as well as *Deadly Intentions*. Jessica has appeared twice on *Sesame Street*, one episode being about a family with Deaf parents, which involved Bruce, Jennifer, and Jaclyn. This led to opportunities for the girls to model and appear in several commercials, as well as the TV series *MacGyver* and *Street Justice*. JJ herself appeared on the TV program *Danger Bay*, and Bruce, JJ, and Jennifer were all involved in the production of the movie *Love is Never Silent*. The Jickels family currently lives in Ladner, BC, a small town near Vancouver where many movies have been shot.

JJ was educated at Jericho Hill School for the Deaf in Vancouver, BC, from 1957 to 1969. When she left school, she immediately entered the workforce as a key-punch operator for Canadian Pacific Airlines, and did a variety of other data processing jobs. Her greatest interest, however, was in teaching and promoting ASL. In 1986 she began to teach ASL at night school, as well as in a group home and a hearing-ear dog program. In 1990 she became the program technician for the Douglas College Program of Sign Language Interpretation, and coordinated ASL classes for their Continuing Education Program. She also did freelance interpreting in a variety of settings, and soon realized the dire need for Deaf interpreters. She enrolled in the program and became the first Deaf woman in Canada to receive a diploma as an ASL/English interpreter in 1998. Currently, she is in the process of completing her ASL Instructor's Certificate.

JJ's contributions to the ASL and interpreting needs of the Deaf Community have been extensive. In 1987, in conjunction with another Deaf woman, she helped establish Sign Language Instructor's Feedback, which later became ASL Way. She attended many workshops for Sign Language Instructors of Canada, (SLIC), and was co-chair of the planning committee for its 1992 conference held in Richmond, BC. She also wrote the guidebook for "ASL Signing Naturally, Level 1," which is now used by ASL instructors across the province of BC. In addition, she worked on a number of informational videos, including *The Role of the Interpreter in Therapy*, as well as several educational videos. JJ was instrumental in helping to develop important assessment and screening tools for ASL students and interpreters, including the BC Provincial ASL Mastery Exams, the Sign Language Competency Interview,

Post-Secondary Interpreter Screening, and Medical Interpreting Screening. She also made a significant contribution to the establishing of Canada DeafCom Inc., which administers the Sign Language Competency Interview. JJ has been an interviewer and rater for Canada DeafCom since its inception and is currently the board president.

Following the historic 1997 *Eldridge* decision, the Medical Interpreting Service (MIS) for BC was established at the Western Institute for the Deaf and Hard of Hearing. JJ is its multi-cultural community coordinator and is responsible for providing information about the service, developing materials to educate consumers and ensuring them of access to qualified interpreters. She is a regular presenter of workshops to the Deaf Community, interpreters, and health-care providers, and, in 2000, did a presentation on medical interpreting at the Association of Visual Language Interpreters of Canada (AVLIC) conference in Edmonton. At present, Jennifer works with her mother as the dispatcher for MIS. JJ also works as a Deaf interpreter with both Deaf and Deaf-Blind clients in medical, judicial, and mental-health settings, while continuing to contract her services to Douglas College.

JJ is a former host of *The Deaf Program* for Shaw Cable, and in 1984 she helped coordinate and film the Deaf Women's Conference in Vancouver. She is a long-standing member of the Greater Vancouver Association of the Deaf, and has served as editor of their newsletter. She is also active in the BC Cultural Society of the Deaf, AVLIC, and the Westcoast Association of Visual Language Interpreters. Her goal is to improve services for all Deaf persons.

When this busy woman has leisure time, she enjoys being with her dogs, gardening, boating, and camping. She also looks forward to the day when she will be able to spoil her many grandchildren.

JONES (WAITT), Patricia Irene

1952–

Teacher, Champion Athlete, and First Deaf Woman to Graduate from the University of Manitoba.

Patricia Waitt was born in Montréal, Québec, to loving hearing parents, Rudyard and Rita Waitt. She became Deaf at five months of age due to illness. She has a hearing sister, Penny; two hearing brothers, Norman and Thomas Waitt; and a Deaf husband, Gwyn Jones, who has fourteen known Deaf relatives, including in-laws. Patricia and Gwyn, who is supervisor of the boys' and girls' dormitories at the Manitoba School for the Deaf, have three adult hearing children—Bronwyn, Selwyn, and Meghan—as well as a hearing granddaughter, Alexandra, and a grandson, Aidan, who are the joy of their lives. While Patricia was growing up, her father, Rudyard Waitt, was a wing commander in the Royal Canadian Air Force, so she was accustomed to moving around with her family to the many different cities across Canada where he was posted. She and her husband currently make their home in Winnipeg, Manitoba.

Patricia received most of her early education in mainstream public schools in Ottawa, but was sent to the Manitoba School for the Deaf for junior and senior high school when her father was stationed in Winnipeg. She then spent two years at Gallaudet College (now Gallaudet University) in Washington, DC, but decided to marry in 1973 rather than complete a degree there. About twenty years later, when her children were old enough, Patricia enrolled at the University of Manitoba, and became the first Deaf woman to graduate from the Faculty of Education with a BEd degree in 1996. Her attendance, and her outstanding achievement of a 3.9 grade point average, were made possible by the provision of qualified ASL interpreters for all her classes. Since graduating she has been employed as a teacher at the Manitoba School for the Deaf (MSD), her alma mater.

During her attendance at MSD, Patricia was involved in many athletic activities, capturing school championships in curling, basketball, volleyball, and track and field, where her record for the sixty-yard dash continues to stand. She also served as vice-president, secretary, and social convenor for the school's student council from 1965 to 1970, and as president of the Drama Club from 1967 to 1969. After she was married, Patricia was secretary of the Winnipeg Deaf Athletic Club (WDAC) from 1973 to 1976. From 1981 to 1985 she was president of the Winnipeg Women's Auxiliary, and is currently chairperson of the MSD elementary department's monthly meetings, as well as a representative for Principal Advisory Communication Technology.

Patricia and Gwyn celebrated their twenty-fifth wedding anniversary in 1998, and enjoy their busy life with their family and many friends in the Deaf Community. Her lifelong dream of becoming a teacher has been fulfilled. Patricia's motto is: "It's never too late to learn—We keep learning until the day we die." During her leisure hours, Patricia's hobbies and interests include sewing, cooking, gardening, working around the house, and on her computer, but most of all, she loves to spend time at their lake cottage with her family.

Her greatest interest has always been to work with Deaf children, encouraging them to achieve higher learning, and to improve education and technology for them. She coordinates the student teacher program for the University of Manitoba's Faculty of Education, and when she has time, she likes to read mysteries and history.

HEATHER JOYCE was born in Halifax, Nova Scotia, where she continues to make her home. At the age of six, it was discovered she had a significant hearing loss, which continued to worsen for several years. She has no known Deaf relatives, although some family members have lost some degree of hearing as they age. Heather primarily uses her vision to communicate with the hearing world, through speech and speechreading with the support of her hearing-aid, and using her TTY. She has excellent speech and talks easily with hearing colleagues and friends. She also knows some Sign Language, which she uses with Deaf people.

Heather's education began at St. Catherine's School in Halifax, which she attended from primary to grade nine. While she was in grade seven, FM systems first became available in the public schools, and she received her first one, on loan, from the Atlantic Provinces Special Education Authority (APSEA). For grades ten to twelve, Heather attended Armbrae Academy (Halifax Ladies' College). Upon graduation, she had to relinquish the use of the assistive listening device. She enrolled in Dalhousie University in Halifax, but had difficulty hearing the lectures without the help of the FM system. One of her geology professors, in an attempt to make things easier for her, obtained a grant towards the purchase of one. The Nova Scotia Department of Community Services then contributed the remainder, so she was able to get her own personal listening system. This made the difference that allowed her to complete her education. To this day she still finds it useful to have her own system for meetings and lectures at work.

Graduating from Dalhousie in 1986 with a BSc in Geology, Heather started her working career with the federal government and in the private sector on a contractual basis. In 1988 she found employment with Canadian Hydrographic Services (CHS), a branch of the Department of Fisheries and Oceans. Six months later she was offered a permanent post, through the Employment Equity Program, which was established to attract more women and persons with disabilities who had a science background into the workforce. By 1991 Heather was one of the two female hydrographers out of about thirty in the Maritimes region, formerly known as the Scotia-Fundy region.

The job of a hydrographer can involve going to sea. After the data is collected in the field, it must be compiled into charts so it can be used by mariners. These charts need to be maintained continuously. The biggest portion of Heather's work is done in an office, although going to sea is probably the most exciting aspect of her job. She has sailed mainly in the coastal waters of Newfoundland and Nova Scotia, and at times been the only woman on the ship. When she first started hydrography, assistive devices that worked properly on ships were hard to come by, so relying on colleagues and crew members appeared to work best for emergency situations. It requires teamwork, open communication, and making certain everyone on board understands how to help. Cooperative teamwork enables the staff to assist Heather and she in turn, can be of help to them.

Recognizing that she is working in a nontraditional career for women, Heather finds it challenging, stimulating, and rewarding, and enjoys her work. She is modest about her achievements. She chose hydrography as her profession and is accomplished in her field. When she has time to relax, she likes to walk, read, and garden. She also does lap swimming and has taken up ocean kayaking.

LOREEN JUHASZ was born in Lethbridge, Alberta, into a hearing farm family residing in the nearby town of Del Bonita. She became Deaf at the age of nine months due to serious illness. She has no known Deaf relatives, and currently makes her home in Edmonton, Alberta. When Loreen was a child there were four Deaf people living in Del Bonita, which was a most unusual circumstance for a small village with a population of approximately one hundred. It certainly worked to Loreen's advantage because she was able to acquire ASL skills from one of these Deaf persons, a woman named Rebecca Shade Dalton, who still lives in Lethbridge.

Loreen was educated at the Alberta School for the Deaf (ASD) in Edmonton, where she was a residential student from 1964 to 1977. She was a conscientious pupil and, in 1970, the teachers of the Junior Wing presented her with a special award for her efforts. During her final year at ASD, Loreen was the recipient of two prestigious awards—a Dormitory Leadership Award and the Lil Kroker Award for her high standing in the Gallaudet entrance exams. While attending school in Edmonton, she spent weekends and holidays at home with her family at Del Bonita. Loreen was an enthusiastic 4-H Club member and in 1975 won the First Year Feeder Award. In high school she served as student council secretary in 1974–75, and as treasurer in 1976–77.

Loreen then attended Gallaudet College (now Gallaudet University) in Washington, DC, from 1977 to 1983, graduating with a Bachelor of Science degree in Home Economics. On returning to Alberta, she found employment as a relief and weekend staff member for Community Living Support Services in Edmonton. After five years at this casual job, she found full-time employment with Alberta Education as a dormitory counsellor at ASD, from 1986 until 1989. Currently she is working as a classroom teaching assistant at ASD, a position she has held since 1989.

Loreen has always been very actively involved in the local Deaf Community. She served as secretary for the Alberta Association of the Deaf (AAD) for ten years. She also made a considerable contribution to the Alberta Deaf Sports Association, acting as its secretary and vice-president in 1994, and president from 1995 to 1997.

In addition to her contributions as a volunteer to the Alberta Deaf Sports Association in general, she also worked specifically for the Edmonton Deaf Women's Slo-Pitch organization, as president in 1991–92 and manager from 1992 to 1994. When the twelfth World Winter Games of the Deaf were held in Banff in 1991, Loreen worked tirelessly on the Games Preparation Committee. She was involved with Team Canada in Switzerland in 1999 and in Italy in the summer of 2001. She did not actually attend the 2001 Games, but worked with Jo-Anne Robinson's committee, as its "attire chairperson." She is also an active member of the Edmonton Deaf Fellowhip Church where she helps with the planning of children's programs.

In her spare time Loreen enjoys sewing and quilting. She is an avid sports fan and likes to watch games like football, hockey, and many others. She is also a devoted pet lover and is the proud owner of two lovely cats, Bambi and Faline.

KAKEE, Katysie

1955–
Weaver, Craftswoman, and Deaf Children's Mentor.

KATYSIE KAKEE was born hearing to a young single mother in the Nunavut wilderness and became Deaf at the age of five months. She is the mother of two boys, but lost a third son who died at the age of seventeen. One of her remaining sons, Tommy, was adopted by her as an infant. There are no known Deaf relatives in Katysie's extended family. She has four brothers and three sisters who are all hearing.

She was educated orally in the public school system and presently makes her home with her two boys at Pangnirtanq in the recently created Nunavut Territory. She has worked at the Weaving Shop in the Co-op store in Pangnirtanq since 1974.

Katysie communicates well with Inuit home signs and is now learning ASL (American Sign Language). At present, she is involved with two families who have Deaf children, a four-year old girl and a twelve-year old boy. While learning ASL, she is also teaching it to these children and providing them with an adult Deaf role model. Their parents often seek her advice on raising their Deaf children.

Because of the isolation of her community and the great distances between settlements, it is difficult for her to meet other Deaf adults, but she is a strong person whose efforts are recognized. She has recently been consulted about the "home signs" she used with her family when she was growing up. This will lead to important research as to whether or not an Inuit Sign Language ever existed.

Katysie is a talented weaver who is doing contract work for the Co-op, but also freelances and does other crafts as well. Her hobbies are knitting, fishing, and sewing sealskin boots and shoes. Her goal is to locate all Deaf persons in the Nunavut Territory and to see that their services are improved to include TTYs, computers, and better education. Katysie has an excellent reputation for her handcrafts and the Inuit garments she creates. She is considered one of the likeliest future advocates of the Deaf in northern Canada.

KALK (KAZEN), Sharon

1948–
Curling and Bowling Champion, and Inductee into the Northwest Bowling Association of the Deaf Hall of Fame.

SHARON KAZEN was born profoundly Deaf to hearing parents, in Snohomish, Washington, US. Her family lived on a dairy farm where Sharon helped to milk cows, and grow crops such as corn, peas, and potatoes during her summer vacations. She has a brother who is also profoundly Deaf. Her husband, William Kalk, is a Deaf man, and they have two hearing children. Since 1971 the Kalk family has lived in Burnaby, on the British Columbia lower mainland.

Sharon received her early education in mainstream public schools in Seattle, Washington, attending Summit School, University Heights School, and John Marshall Junior High School. From 1965 to 1968 she attended Washington State School for the Deaf in Vancouver, Washington. There she was a cheerleader, played on the volleyball team, was an outstanding bowler, and participated in track and field events.

Sharon is well known for her bowling achievements. In 1983 she was a member of the team representing the

Pacific Coast Deaf Women's Bowling Association that won the championship in Reno, Nevada. Her team members were Patti Dobie, Linda Archibald, Marilyn Loehr, and Marion McKenzie. They set a new record handicap of 80 per cent of 200 (3060). In 1990, Sharon, with teammates Linda Prue, Diane Sanregret, and Anne Valliers, won the Labatt's Blue Light National Classified Bowling Championship. This was a combination of ten-pin, five-pin, and candlepin bowling. Sharon and her team won the Ten-Pin National Championship, finishing with a 12–3 round robin record. She was the only Deaf participant in the tournament.

Sharon's curling prowess is also commendable. In the early 1980s, she skipped a championship rink representing British Columbia with teammates Janice

Sigurdson, Gerry Bain, and Judy Hussey. They won the bronze medal in Deaf Curling Championships in Montréal, Québec, and also in Québec City in 1982.

In March 2000 the Northwest Bowling Association of the Deaf presented Sharon with a plaque citing her outstanding achievements as an officer/bowler and inducting her into their Hall of Fame in Spokane, Washington.

Apart from her involvement in ten-pin bowling and curling, Sharon's hobbies and interests include photography and outdoor camping.

KANJI, Salma

1966–

Outreach Worker, Coordinator, Presenter, Born-Leader, and Advocate for the Deaf.

SALMA KANJI was born Deaf, to hearing parents, in Kampala, Uganda, Africa. She has no known Deaf relatives, but her Deaf husband, Al-Nasir, has an older brother, Amin, who is Deaf. Al-Nasir, a Gallaudet University graduate with a Bachelor of Science degree in Business Administration, was the first Deaf person hired by the Royal Bank of Canada, in Calgary, in 1988. He is a strong advocate for the employment of Deaf workers. Salma and Al-Nasir currently make their home in Calgary, Alberta.

Salma's family emigrated to Canada in 1972, leaving Uganda because of the civil strife there, and settled in Vancouver. After overcoming the initial culture shock, she was sent to Jericho Hill School for the Deaf, where she attended for two years before the family moved to Calgary. Salma received her High School Diploma from Queen Elizabeth Junior and Senior High School in 1985. She then attended the Gallaudet Alternative Preparatory Program in London, Ontario, for one year, focusing on general studies, but decided to return to Calgary rather than attend Gallaudet University at that time. In 1986 she enrolled in the social work program at Mount Royal College and graduated with a diploma in 1989. She then married Al-Nasir Kanji and, in 1999, decided to further her education and qualifications by taking management development.

Since 1988 Salma has been employed in a number of interesting positions. She has been an assistant counsellor, an assistant coordinator, and a workshop presenter. In addition, Salma was a summer camp coordinator for the Calgary Association of the Deaf and the events coordinator for the Alberta Deaf Celebration in 1999–2000. She has provided residential roommate support and is currently employed as an outreach worker. Over the years she has successfully supervised and managed a wide range of clients and projects. She consistently provides objective leadership and communication between the community and the corporate sector.

For her continuous interest, achievement, and dedication, Salma has been recognized by various authorities and agencies. In high school she received two awards for her outstanding academic performance, as well as a citizenship certificate. Deaf and Hard of Hearing Services presented Salma with awards for her outstanding contributions as a board member and, in 2000, she was named "Member of the Year" by the Calgary Association of the Deaf. In 2001 she was chosen as chairperson of special events for the 14th World Congress–Federation of the Deaf to be held in Montréal, Canada, in 2003, a position that is bound to bring its own rewards. She enjoys new challenges and is very involved in the activities of the Deaf Community in Calgary. She sees herself as a leader among multicultural Deaf women and encourages others to have vision, to analyze themselves, set goals, and be confident enough to take risks. She says that motivation and community involvement are the key factors.

In her leisure hours Salma likes to garden, shop, and travel. She is a dog-lover, and became the first pet-owner in her family when she adopted Pepper, a silky terrier. She took a puppy training course, and has developed a very close relationship with her dog. Salma is constantly seeking ways to enhance and expand her supervisory, managerial, and leadership skills.

ELIZABETH KASS, the eldest of seven children, was born with normal hearing in Dubuque, Iowa, US. She attended parochial schools until 10 April 1944 when, at the age of ten and a half, she became Deaf virtually overnight due to unknown causes. This, of course, changed her life. At that time, she had never met nor seen any Deaf person and had no idea that there were others like her. Although she felt some concern as she contemplated her future, her faith made her trust that God would take care of her.

In September of the same year, just a few days after her eleventh birthday, she began attending Ephpheta School for the Deaf (now closed), in Chicago, Illinois, where she was first introduced to Sign Language. After graduating from the eighth grade in 1947, she attended four years of high school at St. Rita's School for the Deaf in Cincinnati, Ohio. When she graduated in 1951 she would have liked to attend Gallaudet College (now Gallaudet University) in Washington, DC, but in those days, government funding for this purpose did not exist. With six younger children in the family to support, her parents simply could not afford to send her.

Elizabeth, who is known as Betty to her family and friends, found employment with a news agency in Dubuque, where she did secretarial work for three years.

Not knowing any other Deaf people in her hometown, she decided to move to Chicago in 1954. She spent four years there working for a large insurance company. Although she enjoyed her work and was happy to be socializing in Chicago's large Deaf Community, she began to feel that there must be more to life than what she was experiencing. After some time of reflection and prayer, she reached the decision to devote her life to working for God and His people.

Thus, early in September 1958, she left Chicago for Montréal, Québec. Because she had not been one of the former pupils of the Institution for Deaf Girls, where the congregation of Little Sisters of Our Lady of Seven Dolors was located, she was obliged to spend a year there before entering the religious community. During that year, she had the opportunity to learn French and Québec Sign Language (LSQ). On 1 September 1959 she entered the congregation as a postulant. She received the Holy Habit on 14 September 1960 and pronounced her vows on 15 September 1962, taking the name Sister Mary of Calvary. Just a few years later the government of Canada requested that all religious adherents use their family names to avoid confusion in identity since Sisters from different communities often had the same names. She has since been known as Sister Elizabeth Kass, the same as before she took her vows in 1962.

Following the profession of her vows, Sister Elizabeth taught English-speaking pupils at the French Institution for Deaf Girls. When the Québec government required them to move to MacKay School for the Deaf, she was assigned to teach English as a second language to the older French pupils at the Institution, going from one class to another. One year, she had 120 pupils out of a total of 400 who were attending the Institution at the time. During the final eighteen months before the Institution closed and the girls were moved temporarily to the Institution for Deaf Boys, Sister Elizabeth was asked to replace a hearing Sister in the audiovisual room. She also did all the printing and photocopying for the staff. Later, at the Institution for Deaf Boys, she taught special classes in French. During the second year she replaced one of the teachers who was on maternity leave. When this teacher returned Sister Elizabeth left the Institution for Deaf Boys and began teaching some mentally challenged young Deaf adults elsewhere. At this time she was also doing pastoral work, visiting older Deaf people in their homes, hospitals, and group homes. She spent many of her summers working at a Catholic camp for Deaf children, mainly in the arts and crafts building during her latter years there.

It was while she was at the camp that she received a call to go into town to see her superior, but was not told the reason. When she met with her superior, she was shown a letter with a request from St. Mark's Catholic Community of the Deaf in Edmonton, Alberta, asking for Sisters who knew Sign Language to do pastoral work in the community, and she was asked if she was interested. Sister Elizabeth asked for time to think and pray about it. A week later she gave an affirmative answer, saying that she would give it a try, even though she had never been to western Canada, and did not really know anyone there.

And so, in October 1983, at the age of fifty, Sister Elizabeth took up the challenge of moving west, where she now lives with the Sisters of Providence in Edmonton, happily doing pastoral work with St. Mark's Catholic Community of the Deaf. For eighteen years she has helped to prepare the Sunday liturgy, adapted readings, prepared for baptisms, first communions and other sacraments, prepared Sunday bulletins, and helped put out newsletters. She also teaches religion at the Alberta School for the Deaf (ASD), visits people in homes and hospitals, teaches crafts, and performs many other duties. In her leisure time, she enjoys reading, working on various crafts, and occasionally photography as well.

KELLY, Theresa

1926–

Sister of a Deaf Religious Order, Teacher, Spiritual Leader, and Member of the House of Faith.

THERESA KELLY became Deaf at the age of two and a half years as a result of a severe bout of spinal meningitis. She was born in New York City into a large family of eleven children, seven boys and four girls. Their parents were simple, sturdy Catholic folk of Irish descent whose ancestors had come to America from Dublin. They all accepted her Deafness and she was well-loved and cared for by each of her family members. Theresa was the only Deaf child and there are no other known Deaf relatives. She has seven hearing nephews and a hearing niece who are all members of the New York City Police Force, in keeping with the tradition of early Irish immigrant families.

Theresa was sent to St. Joseph's residential School for the Deaf when she was only three and a half years old. Her mother hastened to learn fingerspelling so she could communicate with her small daughter, and the two of them remained very close in their affection for each other until Mrs. Kelly passed away on Theresa's forty-eighth birthday, on 10 March 1974. When she was old enough, Theresa attended four years of high school and six months of college before she took a job as an office clerk with *Commonwealth Magazine*, where she was the only Deaf employee among fifteen hearing staff members.

It was during that period that Theresa's boyfriend tragically died of a serious illness, leaving her so devastated that her thoughts turned to dedicating the rest of her life to a religious order.

Upon investigating, she was appalled to learn that American convents were not accepting Deaf novitiates. At one time the Sisters of Charity in Cincinnati, Ohio, had a few Deaf members, but they were no longer accepting new entrants who were Deaf. Thus, it happened that Theresa applied to a community of Deaf nuns in Montréal, Québec, where she was accepted. Her family worried about her leaving the country and culture of her birth to go so far from home, but they soon realized she had found her true vocation and were greatly consoled to see her feeling happy and contented with her religious life.

After taking her final vows, Theresa was assigned to teach Deaf English students for four years before they were transferred to the MacKay School for the Deaf. She later became their plastic arts teacher, a position she held for the next thirty years of her sisterhood. The lifestyle of nuns had changed drastically during those three decades, and Theresa found herself uncomfortable with many of the new policies, especially the discontinued practice of wearing full habits and the prevailing lack of focus and direction for the future.

Upon prayerful reflection and much serious consideration, she decided not to continue renewing her vows annually and to become, instead, a part of the lay community, where she felt she would have a better opportunity to advocate for the Deaf.

Theresa is now a member of the House of Faith and the Association of Clerc of St. Viator, where she ministers to Deaf young people and addresses the needs of Deaf persons of all ages and from every walk of life. She currently makes her home in Vimont, Laval, Québec.

KENEALEY, Shirlee Anne

1947–
IBM Keypunch Operator, Personnel Classification Assistant, and Proud Grandmother.

SHIRLEE KENEALEY was born hearing into a hearing family, in London, Ontario. She has a hearing brother who is five years her senior. The family moved to Winnipeg when Shirley was an infant. When she was almost two years old she became very ill with spinal meningitis and almost died. Her father, who worked as a mechanic at Modern Dairies, came home from work one day and called for Shirlee. When she did not reply, her parents became concerned and took her to a doctor. They discovered then that Shirlee was profoundly Deaf as a result of the meningitis. She has no known Deaf relatives and currently makes her home in Abbotsford, British Columbia.

The doctor who diagnosed Shirley's Deafness suggested that her parents investigate schools for the Deaf, which they did. Eventually, they enrolled her at the Saskatchewan School for the Deaf in Saskatoon. Shirley is grateful to them for choosing the Saskatchewan school rather than the Manitoba School, which she feels would not have been the best place for her. She became a residential student, living in the dormitory, and travelling home only for the Christmas and summer holidays. Life in the dormitory gave her invaluable exposure to ASL and Deaf Culture. Before she started school, she had been in the habit of constantly screaming which was nerve-wracking for everyone in the household. By the time she went home for her first Christmas, her screaming had stopped completely, much to the amazement and relief of her parents.

When Shirlee left home to attend school her mother missed her sadly because the house was too quiet. The family's doctor advised her to get a job to keep herself busy and her mind occupied. Thus she became an employee of Stall Sportswear, where she was a sewing-machine operator. When Shirley was fifteen the family moved to Vancouver and enrolled her at Jericho Hill School for the Deaf, where she attended until she graduated in 1967. She trained as an IBM keypunch operator and found a good job with the Tahsis Company, where she worked for five years before she married and started her family. Her two hearing daughters, Yvonne and Claudia, learned ASL before they could speak and became fluent signers.

When her daughters were no longer dependent upon her, she took computer and bookkeeping courses and found a job with the Correctional Service of Canada, as a classification assistant in the personnel department. She continued to work there for twelve years. In addition to her work, Shirlee has been involved with the National Advisory Committee for Persons with Disabilities. She also worked as a volunteer for three years, spending time with a Deaf girl who was frustrated because her parents had never learned to communicate in Sign Language.

Shirlee's hobbies and interests include walking, bowling, and helping to organize activities and events in the Deaf Community. She has three pets—two cats and a dog. One of the cats, Wiley, is Deaf, which makes him very special to Shirlee, since they share the same affliction. When she wants to get his attention, she stamps her feet on the floor so Wiley can feel the vibration, or she flicks the lights on and off. In certain situations, she and Wiley are both isolated from the rest of the family and household. Shirlee does not feel Wiley would make a good protector for anyone. Besides enjoying her pets, she is a loving grandmother of four fine grandchildren.

KENNEDY (McKISSICK), Marilynn Dee

1956–
Educational Assistant, and Co-Founder of Sign Talk Children's Centre.

MARILYNN MCKISSICK was born hearing into a hearing family, in Ottawa, Illinois, US. At about four months of age she became very ill with a high fever and pneumonia which brought her close to death. She survived but became profoundly Deaf as a result. She has no known Deaf relatives, but is married to a Deaf man, Gerard Kennedy, and they have two hearing children, Shannon and Rosalie. Her father, who was a civil engineer, hired a Deaf man to work with him for the Illinois Department of Highways. This gentleman taught her father ASL so that he could communicate with Marilynn. Marilynn and Gerard Kennedy currently make their home in Belleville, Ontario.

Marilynn was educated at the Illinois School for the Deaf and Gallaudet College (now Gallaudet University), in Washington, DC. She came to Canada in 1983. While residing in Winnipeg, Manitoba, she helped to establish the Sign Talk Children's Centre (STCC) with support from Winnipeg's Deaf Community in 1987. It was designed specifically for Deaf children and hearing children of Deaf parents so both oral English and ASL are primary modes of communication among both staff and children. Marilynn was a child-care worker

and ASL consultant at STCC and her daughter Shannon was one of the first children enrolled in the program. Marilynn and her family moved to Ontario in 1988. Her comment on the success of the Sign Talk Children's Centre is that she planted the seed and the seed blossomed beautifully with the support of the parents and the Deaf Community.

In Ontario her employment has been varied. She has worked in the preschool program at the Bob Rumball Centre of the Deaf in Toronto and, for a few years, was employed by the Canadian Hearing Society in its Interpreter Apprentice Program, also in Toronto. She has been teaching ASL classes in various places since 1983 and at present works as an educational assistant at Sir James Whitney School for the Deaf in Belleville.

During her leisure time Marilynn's hobbies and interests include drawing, working at various crafts, attending a fitness club, rollerblading, and cross-country skiing.

KOSKIE (GENT), Cindy Lynn

1967–
Basketball Enthusiast, Community Counsellor, and Coordinator of the Shared Reading Project.

Cindy Gent was born Deaf in Rivers, Manitoba, to hearing parents, Mary Ann and Arthur Henry Gent. Her parents did not realize she was Deaf until she was about three years old. She was then fitted with hearing aids. With the diagnosis, her family understood why she had been a frustrated child since birth. The cause of her Deafness is unknown and she has no Deaf relatives. Her husband, Marvin Sutherland Koskie (Mar), is Deaf and has numerous Deaf kinfolk. They have two children—Dinnah Ann, who is attending first grade in a French Immersion school, and Eric Arthur, who is in a bilingual/bicultural day-care centre, (Sign Talk Children's Centre).

Because her father served in the Canadian military, Cindy's family moved quite often to accommodate his various postings. When she was an infant, the family spent three and a half years in Germany before returning to a posting in Canada at Trenton, Ontario. Cindy was enrolled at the Ontario provincial School for the

Deaf in Belleville in an oral program. In 1977 her father was transferred to Cold Lake, Alberta, and Cindy entered the Alberta provincial School for the Deaf (ASD) in Edmonton. There, at the age of ten, she was first introduced to Sign Language (ASL). She remained at ASD for seven years before moving to her father's next posting to Summerside, PEI, in June of 1984.

Cindy attended the Atlantic Provinces Resource Centre for the Hearing-Handicapped (now Atlantic Provinces Special Education Authority) in Amherst, Nova Scotia, for one year and then enrolled at Three Oaks Senior High in Summerside for two years, for grades eleven and twelve. When she graduated, she was accepted at St. Mary's University in Halifax where she completed the first year of a Bachelor of Arts degree before the family was transferred again, this time to

Winnipeg, Manitoba. She took her second year of the BA program at the University of Manitoba but, instead of completing her degree, she and Mar decided to get married. Mar works part-time as an educational interpreting consultant and does contract work teaching ASL classes and doing Deaf interpreting.

Cindy's employment career began with the job of house manager at a group home. When her children were toddlers she stayed at home and taught evening ASL classes. She now holds two positions with the Society of Manitobans with Disabilities—as a community counsellor and coordinator of its Shared Reading Project. She greatly enjoys the challenge of both jobs.

In 1985 Cindy played on the Canadian basketball team at the Deaf Olympics. She has been on the board of Sign Talk Children's Centre since 1997 and the Manitoba Deaf Association (MDA) since it was founded in 2000.

In her leisure time, Cindy likes to go camping, water-skiing, and downhill skiing. Her favourite pastime, however, is spending time with her husband and children.

KOSKIE (SUTHERLAND), Elizabeth ("Bessie") Margaret

1917–1975
Fundraiser, Respected Volunteer in the Deaf Community, and Church Steward.

BESSIE SUTHERLAND was born Deaf into a hearing family at Clandeboye, Manitoba. She was the fourth of six daughters (Mary, Grace, Mabel, Bessie, Florence, and Shirley) born to Walter Sutherland and Elizabeth McBain. She had aunts and uncles who were hard of hearing, and a cousin, George Sutherland, who was Deaf. Her Deaf husband was Anthony (Tony) Koskie, and they had three Deaf children—Carol, Bruce, and Marvin (Mar). The family home on Parkview Street in Winnipeg, Manitoba, was always filled with love, trust, and happiness, not only for the Koskies, but also for everyone who passed through its doors. Bessie and Tony were married in 1945 at St. George's Anglican Church in Wakefield, near Clandeboye. The wedding reception was held on the lawn of Bessie's home, which was a combination of the Sutherland store and residence in Clandeboye, well known for its home cooking and home-made ice cream. They settled in Winnipeg and raised their family there.

Bessie was very active in the Deaf Community, particularly with the Winnipeg Community Centre of the Deaf (WCCD). In 1942 she joined the Women's Auxiliary and served as its secretary in the early years. During the 1960s she was sales and entertainment chair and, from 1968 until her death, she was treasurer. She quickly became known for her outstanding ability as a fundraiser, and was appreciated for her contribution in that capacity. She and her husband attended and supported functions and activities in the Deaf Community, but the needs of their family always came first. Deaf children who grew up in that era will never forget Bessie's wonderful impersonation of Santa's helper every Christmas. At the national level, Bessie was involved in the Western Canadian Association of the Deaf, playing an important role on the Convention Planning Committee.

Another significant part of Bessie's life was her role in the Winnipeg Evangelical Church of the Deaf, later called the Winnipeg Church of the Deaf, where she was active in the Ladies' Circle and the Board of Stewards. She was instrumental in helping to establish Camp Kakepitay on church-owned lakeside property near Vermilion Bay, Ontario. She assisted with fundraising as well as daily maintenance, cleaning, and cooking.

She was an enthusiastic sports fan and, like her father, loved curling, first with the Fort Garry Ladies' Curling Club and later with the Winnipeg Deaf Curling Club and the Western Canada Deaf Curling Association. She also won many bowling trophies and loved to perform Scottish Highland dances such as the Sword Dance and the Highland Fling. She was a member of the Manitoba Cultural Society of the Deaf (MCSD) and the Canadian Cultural Society of the Deaf (CCSD) and, in 1972, she was the recipient of CCSD's Golden Defty Award. One of her many creative successes was an outstanding quilt she made from recycled materials.

Bessie died on 30 October 1975, just prior to the opening of the Kiwanis Centre of the Deaf (now Deaf Centre Manitoba), a project which had been dear to Bessie's heart. She was an excellent adviser and a loving, caring person who is remembered with great affection by all who knew her. She was buried at St. George's Anglican Church in Wakefield, Manitoba, where she and Tony had been married thirty years before.

KOSKIE (OYE), Linda Kiyoko

1953–
Counsellor, Outreach Worker, Presenter, and Tireless Volunteer in the Deaf Community.

LINDA OYE was born hearing into a hearing family in Winnipeg, Manitoba. She became Deaf at the age of eighteen months due to illness. She has no Deaf relatives in her immediate family, but she is married to a Deaf man, Bruce Koskie, who comes from a Deaf family with numerous Deaf relatives. Linda and Bruce make their home in Winnipeg, where she has been tirelessly involved in the life of the Deaf Community for many years.

At the age of five Linda attended a mainstream public preschool program for a year, but was enrolled at the Deaf and Oral Day School on Wellington Avenue when she was six. She was then transferred to the new Manitoba School for the Deaf (MSD) on Shaftsbury Avenue in Tuxedo, where she received the rest of her education until March 1972, when she left to attend St. Paul's Technical Vocational Institution in St. Paul, Minnesota. She took a nine-month business office course and was employed as a keypunch operator at Manitoba Data Services for fourteen years. She left that job and entered the Deaf Human Service Training Program under New Careers, where she trained for two and a half years, under the sponsorship of the Winnipeg Church of the Deaf, to become an outreach worker in the Deaf Community. Since then, her education has been ongoing and self-achieved as she explores the myriad needs in her local community and seeks viable solutions.

While attending MSD Linda was secretary of the student council and the Red Cross Committee. She was also involved in the drama club, the volleyball, basketball, and baseball teams, and was the recipient of several merit certificates as well as the prestigious Ralston Shield Award. She has been active in Japanese dancing in the Manitoba Buddhist Church, which her family attends, and recalls a special birthday Buddha celebration and concert where she was the only Deaf child among many hearing peers. She also danced with the Japanese group on a TV program and volunteered at the Japanese pavilion in summer festivals. More recently, she was named Miss Deaf Congeniality and was a contestant for Miss Deaf Manitoba in a Miss Deaf Canada pageant.

Linda's contributions to the Deaf Community in Winnipeg are manifold. She has served in various capacities as a volunteer for the Manitoba Cultural Society of the Deaf (MCSD) to enhance the cultural life of the Deaf Community both locally and nationally. At the Winnipeg Community Centre of the Deaf (WCCD), she has held many offices— recreation director, community action director, Christmas dinner party chairperson and committee member, member of the WCCD News committee, member of the Silent Shadow Drama Club, WCCD picnic chairperson and committee member, Deaf Provincial Organization chairperson, and Life and Learning Workshop chairperson. For all of her efforts, Linda was presented with the Most Outstanding Board Member Award by the WCCD. She has also been a generous volunteer at the Winnipeg Church of the Deaf, holding the positions of secretary, convenor, chairperson, and coordinator. In addition, Linda has served on the Sign Talk Children's Centre Board, the Deaf Literacy Steering Committee, the Deaf Poetry Society, the Kiwanis Centre of the Deaf (now Deaf Centre Manitoba), and the Manitoba School for the Deaf Advisory Council. Currently, she holds membership in seven organizations and agencies for the Deaf as well as the Manitoba Japanese-Canadian Citizen's Association and the Manitoba Japanese Cultural Centre, in keeping with her bilingual and bicultural background.

As an outreach worker, Linda established the Deaf Resource Library in 1990, gave presentations on a Deaf Cultural and medical model, counselled Deaf women with children, and both Deaf women and men on Deaf mental health and abuse issues. She is a devoted advocate for the inclusion and acceptance of the Deaf in all facets of life. Occasionally, she works as a substitute at the Sign Talk Children's Centre, and with Deaf Aboriginal children as a youth-care worker at the Kai-naguin (Get Sign Language) Group Home (also known as the Craig Street Group Home). This versatile and energetic woman continues to be a highly respected asset and resource in Winnipeg's Deaf Community.

Her personal hobbies and interests include reading, crewel work, jigsaw puzzles, volleyball, travelling, cooking, playing cards, and word searches. She is also an avid bowler. At the age of twelve she participated in the Youth Bowling Council, winning the Manitoba provincial trophy. She was also the only Deaf bowler chosen to play at the national level in the Canadian Youth Bowling Council in Vancouver, BC, and won fourth place.

KOVI, Anna Annika

1948–
Hungarian Emigre, Proud Canadian, and Mother of Three Successful Adults.

ANNA KOVI was born Deaf to hearing parents, Sandor and Rozalia Katz, in Budapest, Hungary. She has several Deaf relatives in Hungary and two of her three children are Deaf. Her daughter Nancy, who is hearing, is a graduate of Concordia University in Montréal and works as an ASL interpreter. Her son Alvin, who is Deaf, works in Johannesburg, South Africa, helping to develop their Deaf Community and establish organizations of the Deaf. Anna's third child, Tamara, who is Deaf, has a BA degree in English from York University in Toronto and is attending Gallaudet University in Washington, DC, for a second degree in Secondary Education, with a view to graduate studies in Deaf Education. Anna currently makes her home in Montréal.

As a young child in Budapest, Anna attended a School for the Deaf for five years. This was during a period in history when there was a great deal of unrest, preceding the historical uprising of 1956. Many Hungarian immigrants to Canada had fled from the Communist regime in their homeland. Anna's father refused to accept or participate in Communist politics and escaped to Vienna, Austria. Anna recalls that when she was eight years old, she saw Hungarian soldiers fighting against the Russians for several months between October of 1956 and January 1957.

Her relatives sided with the Communists, believing it was the only way they could be assured of a better

and safer way of life. Anna's father fled to Canada while Anna and her mother moved to Geneva, Switzerland, and then spent six months in Genoa, Italy. After three years of being separated from him, Anna and her mother finally rejoined her father in Montréal, Québec and Anna was enrolled at the MacKay Centre for the Deaf. She remembers how sorely she missed her relatives in Hungary, especially her three Deaf cousins.

A decade passed and Anna became a wife and mother of three lovely children of whom she is justifiably proud. As an adult, she has participated in the Deaf Community in numerous ways. For many years she volunteered on the Social Committee for the Montréal Association of the Deaf (MAD) and is currently one of its board directors. She regularly visits Deaf friends and relatives in Europe and the United States.

Anna's working career has focused on her training and skills as a data-entry operator. She has worked in that capacity for the Royal Bank of Canada, Air Canada, and Federal Express (Fedex).

In her leisure time, Anna enjoys gourmet cooking, reading, swimming, and cycling. She is also an enthusiastic world traveller and appreciates spending time with her family.

KROSCHINSKI (MOUALLEM), Noha

1955–
Talented Hair Stylist and Jane-of-all-Trades.

NOHA MOUALLEM was born hearing in Kab-Elais, Lebanon. At nineteen months of age she fell three storeys, striking her head on a concrete surface. Miraculously, she survived the fall, but the head injury left her profoundly Deaf. She moved to Canada with her mother in 1958 and settled in Edmonton, Alberta, where Noha still makes her home. Arabic is the language spoken in her family's household, where a very traditional Lebanese lifestyle is maintained.

Noha's education began in the Edmonton public school system where she was taught to speak and speechread English, receiving no instruction in Sign Language. In 1970 she was enrolled at the Alberta provincial School for the Deaf (ASD), where she lived in the dormitory even though her home was in

Edmonton, to enable her to learn ASL more quickly and absorb the Deaf Culture. This was not an easy transition for her because she was coping with three different worlds— the traditional Lebanese culture and language; the English-speaking, hearing culture; and the Deaf world of ASL as a member of the Deaf Community. Today she is proud of her Deaf heritage and fully accepts herself as a Deaf individual. Noha is actively involved in all aspects of the Deaf Community.

She has several Deaf relatives—a sister (Iyshie Mouallem), an aunt (Fatima Mouallem), and a hard-of-hearing cousin, (Saad Mouallem). She has a hearing husband, Kelly Krochinski, who is a professional driver and accomplished Olympic weightlifter. They have two hearing children, Quinton and Zaina.

Noha's employment has been varied. She has worked as a dental assistant, volunteered at the University of Alberta's Western Canadian Chair of Studies in Deafness (WCCSD), and been an employee of the Royal Bank of Canada. While attending ASD, Noha was a part-time student in a vocational program at Victoria Composite High School where she trained in beauty culture.

In 1973 she entered a hairdressing competition in Vancouver and placed third out of five for her unique style. She also placed first in the Miss Deaf Canada Pageant in 1976.

When she married Kelly in 1990, they both agreed to respect each other's differences and to accept all three worlds that Noha lives in. They do not interfere with each other's traditions and beliefs. Their son, so far, has learned very little ASL, but their daughter is becoming quite fluent in both ASL and Signing Exact English (SEE).

In 1996 Noha returned to school, enrolling in an upgrading program at Alberta Career Computer. She is now attending on-site placement, doing job searches and workshops. She hopes to find a part-time administrative position which would allow her to make use of her training and many natural talents.

KURZET, Modela Jan

1970–
Youth Leader, Instructor, and Noted Canadian Actor.

MODELA KURZET was born Deaf to Deaf parents, the only child of Irene and Jacob Kurzetkowski, in Gdansk, Poland. The family emigrated to Canada in 1983 and settled in Toronto, Ontario, where Irene and Jacob, who are both artists, continue to reside. Modela's boyfriend, Humberto Silva Jr., is Deaf, and she and Humberto currently make their home in Los Angeles, California.

Before the family left Poland, Modela attended the School for the Deaf in Wejherowie. When they arrived in Toronto, she was enrolled in the Greater Toronto School for the Deaf, where she attended for one year before transferring to Danforth Technical School where she was a student from 1995 to 1998. She then took acting classes at the New School of Drama, and later took further training as an actor at the Granton Institute of Technology.

Her working life has been focused almost entirely on an acting career, both in film and on videotape, often working on projects related to Deafness. In 1986 she acted as anecdotist, or spokeswoman, for the Canadian Hearing Society's production of the video *Deaf Communication*. The following year, in 1987, she participated in EPS #26—*War of the Worlds (or No Direction Home)* directed by Johnny Roni for CBC Television. In 1991 Modela was lead actor in *Signs of Friends*, a Labatt's Beer Commercial directed by Gord Olan for Westside Productions and, in 1995, she was in the cast of the movie *Mrs. Winterbourne*, directed by Richard Benjamin for the Tri-Star Sony Pictures Entertainment Company. Also in 1995, Modela served as youth leader and instructor for the *Signs of Summer*

Program directed by Michele Pinet for A Show of Hands Theatre Company. Later in the same year she was principal actor in the film *Ghosts*, directed by Steven Rumbelow for the Renegade Motion Picture Corporation.

Modela has appeared in media photographs and press releases with the noted American Deaf actress, Marlee Matlin, as well as with Shirley MacLaine and Ricki Lake. In 2000 she was lead actor in the videotape *Interacting with the Deaf and Hard of Hearing*, directed by Larry Fugate for the Los Angeles Police Department to be used as a visual aid in its training program. In 1991 the Toronto Association of the Deaf awarded Modela a certificate of appreciation and thanks for her valuable efforts and support. She was among the 6,000 Deaf people who reportedly showed up for an all-day outing at Disneyland in Anaheim in March 2000, where she was photographed by the press in the company of Minnie Mouse. In 2001 Modela was principal actor in *U.S. Navy* (Public Service Announcement), a commercial directed by Rob Lieberman for his production firm, Lieberman Company. Modela has been lauded as an extraordinary actor by directors and critics. She communicates mainly through an interpreter.

In Canada, she was a member of the Toronto Association of the Deaf and is currently involved with the Deaf Entertainment Foundation and Guild in Beverly Hills, California. In addition, she is a staunch supporter of the Greater Los Angeles Deafness and

Media Awards. She continues to maintain a home in Toronto and sometimes accepts acting assignments there. Also, she frequently visits her parents and many friends in Toronto.

In her leisure hours, Modela likes to garden, landscape, and do interior decorating, mainly with the use of plants. She enjoys international travel and is always interested in international ethnic cuisine.

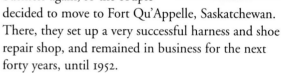

LABELLE (McGREGOR), Flora
1877–1963
Wife and Helpmate of a Popular Deaf Businessman.

FLORA MCGREGOR was born hearing to Scottish immigrants, Donald and Ann McGregor, in Toronto, Ontario. She became Deaf at the age of two years as a result of a severe spinal fever and all attempts to restore her hearing failed. She had no known Deaf relatives.

Flora grew up in Toronto but received her education at the Ontario Institution for the Education and Instruction of the Deaf and Dumb (now known as Sir James Whitney School for the Deaf) in Belleville, Ontario, from 1885 to 1895, when she graduated with honours. There she met the man who was to be her future husband, the handsome and ambitious Noah Labelle, who attended the Institution from 1884 to 1893. Both Noah and Flora were outstanding students. Noah was born Deaf to French-Canadian hearing parents in St. Albert, near Ottawa, Ontario. Following his graduation from the Belleville Institution, Noah operated his own shoe repair shop in St. Albert for two years before taking a job in a brush factory in Toronto. Later, he worked at Adam's Harness Shop and, in 1902, he travelled extensively in the eastern US, in search of better employment but did not succeed in finding any.

Noah Labelle returned to Toronto and renewed his acquaintance with Flora McGregor. They were married on 29 December 1903 at her parents' home in Toronto, where the bride was attended by her sister, Mary, and the groom by his brother, Alexander. Miss Gussie Ogilvie provided sign interpretation for the bridal pair. Flora and Noah spent their honeymoon in Ottawa and Montréal and then moved to Winnipeg, where Noah

had found employment with the Great West Saddlery Company.

They remained in Winnipeg from 1904 until 1912. Noah longed to operate his own business again, so the couple decided to move to Fort Qu'Appelle, Saskatchewan. There, they set up a very successful harness and shoe repair shop, and remained in business for the next forty years, until 1952.

Flora and Noah were both very popular and well liked by the citizens of the village of Fort Qu'Appelle. With the advent of modern tractors and other farm machinery, the use of horses began to decrease, thus affecting the harness industry. The Labelles continued to provide shoe repair services and were active in the life of the small community.

Flora Labelle passed away peacefully in 1963, at the age of eighty-six. Noah was four months short of his 100th birthday when he died in 1976. They were both mourned and missed by all who knew them in the farming community of the Qu'Appelle Valley. One of their oldest friends, a farmer named Jim White, composed a commemorative poem dedicated to them, which he titled *The Harness Shop*. It was published some time after their deaths. It captures the essence of a small-town business in the early twentieth century, frequented by adults and children alike, who took great pleasure in observing the talents and personalities of the Deaf proprietors.

LAMONTAGNE (BIGRAS), Lysette Marie-Andrée

1943–
Input Operator, Film Editor, Documentary Technician, and Dedicated Volunteer.

LYSETTE BIGRAS was born hearing, into a hearing family, in Hull, Québec. She became Deaf at the age of four years, due to illness. She has no known Deaf relatives. Her hearing father, Jean-Yves Bigras, was well known as a director, producer, and animator for Radio-Canada TV, and the producer of three French-language movies. He was also an actor in French theatre. Lysette's husband, Peter Lamontagne, is a Deaf man, and they reside in Longueuil, Québec. Both Lysette and Peter are very actively involved in the Deaf Community as volunteers.

Lysette was educated at L'Institut des Sourdes de Montréal, a school for Deaf girls, where she received her high school diploma. She also took a course to become a bilingual typist and received her diploma in 1963. In 1964 she completed the requirements for certification as a data processor, receiving a diploma from International Data Processing.

Lysette has had an interesting and varied working career. She was an input operator for Bell Canada and worked for Blue Cross Health Insurance for some time. She then started editing films for a film company and became a freelance film editor, contracting to various film companies. At the present time, Lysette is working as a technician with documentary books for the library at the University of Québec in Montréal, a job she has held for the last thirty years, and enjoys immensely.

In the Deaf Community, Lysette and Peter have both served in many different capacities. Lysette has been president, treasurer, and member of the Board of Directors for the Le centre Québécois de la déficience auditive (CQDA). She also represented Québec as a delegate at national conferences and continues to live by her motto, "It's never too late to learn!" Peter has served as treasurer for the Montréal Association of the Deaf and president of the Federation of Silent Sports of Québec. He has also been on the committee for the Canadian Deaf Curling Championships.

Lysette has officially been recognized for her many contributions to Deaf organizations, agencies, and issue-related causes. She has received certificates citing her dedication and fidelity from the Canadian Cultural Society of the Deaf (CCSD), the Canadian Association of the Deaf (CAD), the Montréal Metropolitan Association of the Deaf, and the Association of Hearing Impaired Adults. She continues to support many Deaf causes and participates in most events and activities taking place in the Deaf Community.

LAMPITT-BAXTER, Julie Rose

1957–
Gifted Performer, Skilled Fundraiser, ASL Instructor, Survivor, and Positive Thinker.

JULIE LAMPITT-BAXTER was born Deaf in Kamloops, British Columbia. She was raised by her hearing grandparents and lived part-time with her hearing mother. She has no known Deaf relatives. She is exceedingly proud of her hearing son, Darryl, affectionately known as "DJ," who is an avid figure skater. Julie currently makes her home in Vancouver, BC.

She was educated at the Jericho Hill School for the Deaf (JHS) in Vancouver from 1962 to 1975. During her latter years at JHS, she was transferred to an off-campus program, which involved attending several mainstream public schools in the Vancouver area. She graduated from Kitsilano Secondary School in 1975. That summer she joined the leadership program for Deaf youth in Parry Sound, Ontario. While attending high school, she was recognized as the school's top fundraiser, and so began her lifelong passion for fundraising. She also took up horseback riding and dancing lessons. Over the years she explored baton-twirling, ballet, tap, and modern dance. All of these experiences laid the groundwork for her passion for the performing arts.

Julie's first job was as an office clerk, and she quickly realized that sitting at a desk all day was not her forte. She joined the Canadian Theatre of the Deaf (CTD) and enjoyed performing on their BC tours, but the main highlight for her was the troupe's participation in the National Festival of the Arts in 1976. In 1978 she entered the BC Cultural Society of the Deaf's pageant and was selected as Miss Deaf British

Columbia. Over the years that followed, she explored various jobs until she finally settled on teaching ASL. This has been her career for over twenty years, and she is currently an ASL instructor at Vancouver Community College (VCC).

Teaching ASL has allowed Julie to satisfy her love of language, to promote Deaf Culture, and to meet many interesting people. She has a thirst for learning and participates in as many educational workshops as she possibly can. She has many hopes and dreams and would like to find interesting ways to promote and preserve Deaf Culture and history. Her combined interests in the film industry, photography, and Deaf history have led her to capture certain Deaf events on videotape. This passion began in her youth when her grandfather recorded family events with his movie camera and encouraged her to use it at an early age. She feels Canada's many outstanding Deaf leaders should be immortalized on film, and she recognizes how many valuable Deaf mentors and role models have given her inspiration and encouragement throughout her life.

As a survivor of sexual abuse, Julie has learned that positive thinking is the key to coping and success. It has given her a chance to redeem her self-esteem and accept the challenges of new experiences and ideas. She firmly believes that "what goes around, comes around." If we are caring and open with others, we will, in return, gain the respect and support we need.

In her leisure time, Julie is almost constantly involved in advocacy for the Deaf, participating in most Deaf Community events and volunteering her time and skills to many organizations and agencies of the Deaf, either as a director or a member. Apart from these activities, her hobbies and interests include gardening and growing flowers, reading, watching movies, camping, canoeing, and horseback riding. She used to do tap, modern, and ballet dancing, but now her greatest interest is studying ASL and attending different workshops.

LANDREVILLE, Nancy ("Nano")

1975–
Seasoned Traveller, Dedicated Worker for the Deaf, Researcher, and Editor.

NANCY LANDREVILLE was born Deaf to hearing parents at Le Gardeur, a rural area of Québec, where she grew up on a farm. She has a Deaf brother, Benoit Landreville, but no other known Deaf relatives. Nancy currently makes her home in Montréal.

She received her high school education at Polyvalente Lucien-Pagé, graduating in 1993. She then attended the Human Sciences Program at Cegep du Vieux-Montréal for two years to earn a college diploma, and is also a graduate of the Computer Graphics Program at College Ahuntsic. Her life has been filled with exciting opportunities and experiences, and each one has added to her confidence and maturity.

When Nancy was six years old she tried artistic skating, but didn't stay with it because it was not really to her liking. At age ten she started karate, which she liked much better, but had to give it up to help her father on the farm. When the farm was eventually sold, she registered with a women's softball team where all players were hearing. After playing with the team for two years, she decided to switch to a Deaf team for the next two years. When she was eighteen Nancy was elected president of a women's softball team. She organized many fundraisers to enable the team to participate in the Canadian Softball tournament in Vancouver in 1994. Since then she has played ice hockey with a hearing team and, due to her efforts as goalie, the team won a championship. Since 1992, she has visited eight European countries and in 1996 went to Mexico with three friends. She has also travelled extensively in the United States and western Canada. In 1999 she represented the Canadian Association of the Deaf in the Youth Internship International Program (YIIP), which took her to Venezuela for six months to provide information and support to Deaf adults trying to improve access and services in their communities. Later, she was the French Deaf Women's delegate at the United Nations' Beijing Plus Five Conference in New York, by invitation from the World Deaf Federation (WDF).

Much of Nancy's early inspiration came from her Deaf brother's Deaf girlfriend, Lyne Noiseaux, a confident and talented young woman Nancy greatly admires. Lyne encouraged Nancy to get to know herself and to trust her instincts. Lyne promised her that each new venture she tried would give her increased poise and self-confidence. For two years Nancy worked as a French teacher and illustrator with Deaf adults at Centre Alpha Sound, where she strived to boost the morale and self-confidence of the attendees. She is a member of many organizations of the Deaf and has contributed significantly to a wide variety of Deaf Communities.

Nancy is also involved in the activities of Montréal's Deaf Community. She was a member of a research team on Deaf bilingualism at the University of Québec at Montréal (UQAM) in 1999 and, in 2000, worked as a multi-media editor. Currently, she is employed by the Royal Bank of Canada.

Nancy strongly encourages young Deaf women to have confidence in themselves, to establish their own identity, to strengthen their personalities, and to do this in a step-by-step manner as they experience life to the fullest.

LAPIAK, Jolanta Agnieszka

1972–
Founder of "Deaf World Web" and "Handspeak" Websites, Artist, Photographer, Swimming Record-Holder, and Gold Medalist.

JOLANTA LAPIAK was born profoundly Deaf to Deaf parents of Polish-Russian ancestry in Wroclaw, Poland. She has a younger brother who is hard of hearing and several Deaf aunts, uncles, and cousins. Some of them live in Canada but most are in Poland. She attended a preschool for Deaf children and was then enrolled in the School for the Deaf in Gdansk, completing her first grade in 1980. Shortly before serious labour unrest led to the Solidarity Movement in Poland, the family fled to Austria as refugees, and eventually emigrated to Canada, settling in Edmonton, Alberta, in 1981.

Jolanta attended the Alberta School for the Deaf and graduated in 1990 with the honour of receiving the Governor General of Canada Medal for her excellent academic record. She then enrolled at Gallaudet University in Washington, DC, where she earned a BA degree in Psychology, graduating in 1994, summa cum laude.

Two years after arriving in Canada, Jolanta joined an Edmonton swim club which eventually led her to some remarkable accomplishments as a national swimmer. She won all eleven events in which she competed at the Canada Summer Games in Vancouver, BC, in 1984. She later participated in the World Games for the Deaf in Los Angeles in 1985 and in Christchurch, New Zealand, in 1989, winning a bronze in Los Angeles and a silver and gold in Christchurch. She holds the world record for the Deaf in the 200-metre. butterfly plus eight other Canadian swimming records for the Deaf. For the opening of Calgary's 1988 Winter Olympics, Jolanta was chosen to be one of the torchbearers who carried the Olympic torch in the cross-Canada event that ended at the Olympic Stadium in Calgary.

In 1995 Jolanta founded the Deaf World Web (DWW), an award-winning website that has been featured in many publications. She then launched the most popular section of DWW—*Sign Language Dictionary On Line*, and continues to add new features and sections. Her dream is to become a travelling photojournalist and/or a netbroadcaster, as well as a mixed media artist and art healer. She initiated *Alberta Deaf News* in 1997, a popular newsletter for the Alberta Association of the Deaf, and worked on *CAD Chat*, a publication of the Canadian Association of the Deaf. She was employed as communications and information officer for the Canadian Association of the Deaf in Ottawa from 1998 to 2000 and is vice-president of the World Federation of the Deaf Youth Section for a four-year term ending in 2003. In April 2000, through Jolanta's efforts, the DWW section that was launched as the *Sign Language Dictionary On Line* became *Handspeak*, an independent offspring of DWW.

When she travels, Jolanta immerses herself in the Sign Languages and unique features of Deaf Culture in other nations and pursues her interest in photography and the arts. At home she enjoys painting in watercolours and practising other art forms. Her goal is to study for an advanced degree in anthropology, the arts and/or multimedia.

LAPIAK (TURKAWSKA), Zofia Julia

1949–
Shoemaker, Canadian Certified Bookbinder, and Notable Polish Emigre.

ZOFIA TURKAWSKA was born Deaf to hearing parents in Bartniki pow Milicz, Wroclaw, Poland. She has three Deaf sisters; a Deaf husband, Kazimierz (Kazio); a Deaf daughter, Jolanta; and a hard-of-hearing son, Joachim.

Zofia attended a school for the Deaf from 1958 to 1968, and transferred to a vocational school from 1965 to 1968, with a view to obtaining certification as a bookbinder in Jelcz, which is the location of a large military base and bus-manufacturing plant. She and Kazio had met and dated when she was only fifteen years old. It was a serious courtship and Kazio wanted to marry her, but Zofia thought it best to focus on completing her education and acquiring the coveted certificate that would qualify her for a better future.

When they married in 1968, Zofia, at age nineteen, became a housewife and worked on a farm in Ratowice, as well as working with about twenty other Deaf people making shoes in a shoe factory in Wroclaw. She worked two shifts daily for about six months before she quit and took up bookbinding, which became her career from 1969 to 1980. Her long-held dream of becoming certified in bookbinding did not materialize. Though she had paid the application fee and received a letter of confirmation for an interview on 24 June 1980, it happened to be the exact date that the family had already planned to flee Poland to escape Communism and its influence. Zofia, with her daughter, Jolanta, who was eight years old at the time, and Zofia's youngest unmarried sister, Anna, left Wroclaw and travelled to Vienna, Austria, by train in that summer of 1980 that was so rife with political unrest in Poland.

Zofia had visited her cousins in Edmonton, Alberta, in 1978, and was greatly impressed with the city, the province, and the country. Back in Poland, Zofia and Kazio discussed the possibility of emigrating to Canada. Kazio went to Italy to arrange his own escape from Communism with the intention of sponsoring the immigration of the rest of the family later. He was unsuccessful, but learned from the experience, and was given advice. Back in Poland the plan changed, and that is why Zofia, Jolanta, and Anna escaped to Austria first, so that Kazio could stay behind to sell their property before he joined the family. A month later, Kazio also fled Poland and joined his family in Vienna. After Zofia, Anna, and Jolanta had spent fourteen months in Vienna, and Kazio, thirteen, they were granted a sponsorship to Edmonton where they surprised all their relatives when they contacted them. Kazio and Zofia found jobs at once, and Jolanta was enrolled at the Alberta School for the Deaf (ASD). A few years later, their second child, a son, was born. They named him Joachim.

After working for fourteen years at an Edmonton book bindery, Zofia finally realized her lifelong dream— she was granted a Canadian Bookbinding Certificate in 1995. She and Kazio have both worked hard to make a good home for their children, and have become involved in Edmonton's Deaf Community. They are justly proud of their family, particularly Jolanta, who is now an adult and very active in promoting Sign Languages and Deaf Culture, besides being a keen student, continually furthering her education, and adding to her knowledge. Zofia has never regretted her move to this country, where the family has thrived and prospered. She is proud of her work as a bookbinder and is highly respected and skilled at her trade.

LAWRENCE (GELDART), Kathern Bernice

1947–
Educator, Artist, Poet, Drama Teacher, Gymnastics Coach, Sports Enthusiast, and Champion Curler.

KATHERN GELDART was likely born Deaf, although her Deafness was not discovered until she was two years old. She was the fourth child born to hearing parents, Eva Beatrice Cormier and Everett William Geldart, in Moncton, New Brunswick. She has five hearing siblings, three older than herself, as well as a younger sister, Rosemary, and a younger brother, Darrel. She is the only Deaf member of the family and has no known Deaf relatives. Kathern and Rosemary were always very close, and developed home signs which they used to communicate with one another. In 1977 Kathern married a Deaf man, Ross Lawrence, and they raised his two hearing children from his previous marriage, Darcy and Loretta, who are now both married and living in British Columbia. Loretta presented them with their first grandchild in 1998, a hearing boy named Jeremy. Kathern has made her home in Edmonton, Alberta, since 1975.

She began her schooling at the age of seven, when her father, mother, and grandfather Cormier took her to Halifax, Nova Scotia, and enrolled her at the Halifax School for the Deaf. She noticed at once that the children there used signs that were different from her home signs. She recalls being welcomed to the school by an older student, Joan Drysdale, who offered her a lollipop and invited her to come and play with the other Deaf children. She soon adjusted to residential school life and has many happy memories of it. In 1961 the school in Halifax was demolished and a new facility, the Interprovincial School for the Deaf, was established in Amherst, Nova Scotia. By then Kathern was a teenager, but she attended for four years before she enrolled at Edith Cavell School near her home in Moncton, and later completed her high school studies at Moncton High School. This was an outstanding achievement in an era when interpreters and notetakers were unheard of. Kathern then attended Gallaudet College, now Gallaudet University, in Washington, DC, where she obtained a Bachelor of Arts degree in English in 1972. She went on to take Graduate Studies at Western Maryland College, in Westminster, Maryland, where she completed the requirements for her Master's degree in Deaf Education.

Kathern's employment experience began with summer and part-time jobs, both before and while she attended Gallaudet and Western Maryland College.

She spent her entire professional career as a teacher at the Alberta School for the Deaf (ASD) in Edmonton, Alberta. There, she has worked with all levels—primary, intermediate, junior, and senior high. She was an English and language arts teacher at the upper levels and is fondly remembered for her many drama presentations, skits, and Christmas concert contributions. Having trained as a gymnast, she also coached gymnastics, as well as volleyball, and initiated numerous school projects and events. She did a great deal of work as the ASD archivist and, on the occasion of the school's fortieth anniversary, spearheaded the research and eventual publication of its forty-year history.

As a member of Edmonton's Deaf Community, Kathern's contributions have been mainly in the recreational area. She was very involved with the Alberta Deaf Sports Association, as an active member, president, and secretary. She was an avid curler who successfully competed in several Canadian Deaf Curling Championships and served in various capacities on the executive of the Alberta Deaf Curling Association, now known as the Edmonton Deaf Curling Association. As a professional, she was a member of the Association of Canadian Educators of the Hearing Impaired (ACEHI) and on the newsletter committee of the provincial branch. She played racquetball and curled with hearing teams to expand her skills and gain new experience. Artistically, Kathern entered literary contests in national Deaf festivals and won recognition for her poetry and artwork, including the prestigious Defty Award. She attended classes and became a passionate water-colourist with at least forty paintings to her credit.

Kathern retired from teaching on 30 June 2001 and plans to pursue a different career in eastern Canada. Her leisure activities and interests include quilting, painting, reading children's classics, stamp collecting, and scrapbooking. As she prepares to move back to her home province, Kathern leaves behind, in the province of Alberta, and particularly in the city of Edmonton, not only the fondest of memories, but an impressive twenty-six-year legacy of personal achievement and public contribution.

LeDREW-SHARPE, Barbara Sophie

1965–
Banking Officer, Business Office Employee, Nursing Assistant, ASL Instructor, and Community Volunteer.

BARBARA LEDREW was born Deaf to Deaf parents in St. John's, Newfoundland. She has numerous Deaf relatives besides her parents—her brother, Paul LeDrew, an instructor at George Brown College; her mother's brother and sister; her father's sister; and her husband, Eugene Sharpe, who works as an administrative support clerk for the federal government, with Public Works Government Service of Canada. She and Eugene also have two Deaf children, Gregory and Jessica. Eugene's sister Denise Jacobs is a teacher at the Newfoundland School for the Deaf, and Barbara's mother Gwen also worked there for many years before her retirement. Barbara, Eugene, and their children currently make their home in Chamberlains, Newfoundland.

Barbara's education began at the Newfoundland School for the Deaf in St. John's in 1971. She received a certificate of completion in 1985, and went on to take St. John's Ambulance training in lifesaving, first-aid, and CPR. In 1986 she enrolled at the College of Trades and Technology in St. John's, from which she graduated with a certificate in Vocational Education as a Nursing Assistant in 1987. She followed this up with a continuing education certificate in Microsoft from the Cabot Institute of Applied Arts and Technology in 1988. For the next two years she took courses in computer awareness, employment skills, teaching ASL, and upgrading in mathematics and English. In 1991–92 she attended George Brown College in Toronto, graduating with honours in Communication Skills, and earning credits in Deaf Futures and Wordperfect Computer Skills.

Barbara's work experience has been varied and interesting. During her teens she was a volunteer at the Salvation Army Grace General Hospital, where she delivered and removed patients' trays, took patients to the x-ray department, and performed many other errands in every part of the hospital. The staff appreciated her for her friendliness, self-motivation, reliability, and consistency. In 1987 she spent four months as a nursing assistant at the Children's Rehabilitation Centre, but was unable to pursue this career further because of the testing methods and the restrictions on interpreter involvement. She brought the issue of fair testing to a national level by taking her case to the Newfoundland Human Rights Commission. Because the examination procedures followed the national guidelines, the provincial Human Rights Commission was unable to assist her. Faced with formidable bureaucratic barriers, she gave up her cherished dream of becoming the first Deaf Canadian registered nursing assistant, and went on to study business office practices and computer competency.

After brief stints in the offices of the St. John's Association of the Deaf and the YMCA-YWCA, Barbara established herself in a banking career, first with the Toronto-Dominion Bank in Barrie, Ontario, and then with the Bank of Nova Scotia, where she was employed for eight years. Currently, Barbara is a stay-at-home mother to Gregory and Jessica. In the evenings, when Eugene is at home with the children, she teaches ASL at College of the North Atlantic, and is an ASL tutor at Academy Canada. Since September 2000 she has been president of the Parent-Teacher Association at the Newfoundland School for the Deaf.

In her leisure time Barbara enjoys hobbies and interests which include collecting antiques, stamps, and coins, cross stitching, knitting, country woodcrafts, tole painting, and gardening.

LEHMAN (LAMBERT), Thelma Louise

1938–
Seamstress, Government Clerk, and Talented Craftswoman.

THELMA LAMBERT was born Deaf into a hearing family in North Star, Alberta. She has a number of Deaf relatives—two second cousins, a niece, a nephew, and her sister-in-law, Hilda Parser. Her hearing niece, Darlene Karran, is an ASL interpreter. Her husband, Joseph "Earl" Lehman, a retired heavy-duty mechanic, is hard of hearing. Thelma and Earl have three hearing children—two daughters, Debra and Cindy, and an adopted son, Dustin. Cindy knows ASL and usually interprets for her mother and for other Deaf seniors who know her well. The Lehmans have made their home in Edmonton, Alberta, for many years.

When Thelma was born on 4 March 1938 she weighed only three pounds. It was a bitterly cold winter and they kept her warm by placing her on the open oven door of the wood stove in the farm kitchen. She thrived and grew up on the farm with her three sisters and two brothers, although her Deafness was not detected until she was at least two years old. The family's dog seemed to accompany her everywhere, and when she was called, the dog always came with her, so her parents and siblings had no reason to suspect that she could not hear, nor did anyone realize that the dog was such a great blessing.

It was a neighbour who first suggested that Thelma was Deaf. Her parents were overwhelmed because they had never seen nor heard of anyone who was Deaf. They took her to a doctor who confirmed that she was, indeed, Deaf, due to maternal rubella, and suggested that she be sent to a school for Deaf children. It was wartime and the Manitoba School for the Deaf was being used by the military so the pupils had to be sent to other schools, causing overcrowding in Saskatchewan,

and there was no such school in Alberta at that time. Therefore, it took a while before Thelma could be enrolled at the Saskatchewan School for the Deaf in Saskatoon, so she spent her time on the farm, assisting with chores and riding horses.

In 1944 Thelma and her mother travelled by train from Grimshaw, Alberta, to Edmonton, and then to Saskatoon. There were so many soldiers on the train that Thelma had to sit on her mother's lap most of the way. When they arrived in Saskatoon they went directly to the School for the Deaf, and that was where Thelma remained, as a residential student, until 1956, going home to her family only during the Christmas and summer holidays.

When she graduated, Thelma moved to Edmonton and found employment as a seamstress for the Hudson's Bay Company (now The Bay). In 1958 she married Earl Lehman and continued working until she was pregnant with their first child. When Debra was born, in 1961, Thelma became a full-time, stay-at-home mother. Cindy was born in 1965 and Dustin was adopted in 1979. When she returned to the workforce, Thelma found employment with the Alberta government as a clerk. She was reclassified as a clerk II, and continued working for the government for twenty-six years, receiving a pin and citation for her dedication and long service.

Her leisure-time hobbies are crafts and sewing. She often does craft shows with her Deaf sister-in-law, Hilda Parser. They both enjoy these events because they like meeting new people and making new friends.

LETOURNEAU, Charmaine, OC (Order of Canada)

1947–
Educator, Administrator, Adviser, Mentor, Advocate, and Spokesperson for the Deaf.

CHARMAINE LETOURNEAU, born in Lloydminster on the Saskatchewan/Alberta border, was hearing at birth but became Deaf at an early age due to illness. Her family lived in the rural community of Smith in northern Alberta, and she was the only Deaf child. At the age of five she was sent to Montréal, Québec, to begin her education at the MacKay Centre for the Deaf. She remained there for four years but returned to her home province when the Alberta School for the Deaf opened in Edmonton. She attended the new school until she graduated in 1965. She spent the next five years at Gallaudet University in Washington, DC, taking preparatory courses and completing a BA degree with a major in Psychology and a minor in Literature. Later, she added to her professional qualifications by attending sessional classes at the University of Alberta to earn a Professional Diploma after Degree in Education and a Graduate Diploma in Elementary Education.

Charmaine's professional career has focused on the field of education and learning while she pursued various roles as a classroom teacher, ASL instructor, workshop presenter, drama coach, librarian, school vice-principal, curriculum developer and coordinator, program evaluator, and school administrator. She currently holds the position of assistant principal at the Alberta School for the Deaf in Edmonton.

Throughout her lifetime, Charmaine has held offices in nearly every organization of the Deaf at the local, provincial, and national levels. She has been one of the strongest advocates to bring equality, accessibility, acceptance, and inclusion to all Deaf Canadians and she has fostered pride and esteem in Deaf Culture, in ASL/LSQ, and in the concept of a bilingual/bicultural approach to educating the Deaf. She has mentored students, founded the Western Canada Tournament of the Deaf, served on many advisory boards and committees, sat on task forces, developed curricula, assisted in coordinating local, provincial, national, and international events, created position papers, and initiated countless projects and programs. She continues to be an eloquent spokesperson on issues related to the Deaf and has contributed immensely to a better quality of life for all Deaf Canadians.

Charmaine is proud of her Aboriginal ancestry and heritage and was given two prestigious awards in recognition of her public leadership role—one by the North Peigan Blackfoot Confederacy and the other by the Institute for the Advancement of Aboriginal Women. She has also been the recipient of many outstanding service awards, certificates of appreciation, and other distinctive honours from organizations of the Deaf and other community agencies. In 1987 she was declared "Deaf Albertan of the Year" and in 1989 was chosen as CAD's "Deaf Citizen of the Year." In 1996 CCSD created the "Charmaine Letourneau ASL/LSQ Award" in her honour, to be presented to students from all Schools for the Deaf in Canada for excellence in ASL/LSQ. She was inducted into the CCSD Hall of Fame in 1998. In 2001 she was named to the prestigious Order of Canada, the highest public honour any Canadian can hope to achieve.

Charmaine shares her south Edmonton home with her dog, Tippy, and her cat, Cally. She enjoys her many friendships and loves reading, doing family genealogical research, and various handicrafts when she can find time for these hobbies in her busy life.

LEWIS (GUEST) (FITZAKERLY), Sarah

1840–1919
Member of an Influential Deaf Family.

SARAH FITZAKERLY was born in England on 3 June 1840. She had a Deaf sister, Margaret, who later became Margaret Widd, wife of Thomas Widd, the Deaf founder of the Protestant Institution for Deaf Mutes in Montréal. This was the forerunner of today's well-known MacKay Centre of the Deaf.

Sarah and Margaret Fitzakerly grew up in Yorkshire, near Sherwood Forest, where England's legendary Robin Hood had supposedly roamed. Their father, Timothy Fitzakerly, worked as a horticulturalist on the palatial estate of the Duke of Newcastle in Worksop, Yorkshire. The girls were sent to be educated at the Yorkshire Institution for the Deaf and Dumb in Doncaster. Sarah entered the school in 1847 and remained there until she graduated. Her sister Margaret married Thomas Widd, and Sarah became Mrs. Guest, but was soon widowed.

When she was twenty-seven years old and newly widowed, Sarah Guest agreed to accompany her sister and husband to Canada when the Widds decided to emigrate in 1867. They settled in Montréal and Thomas Widd immediately set about establishing a Protestant School for Deaf children in a city which was predominantly French-speaking and Catholic. Meanwhile, Sarah's father, Timothy Fitzakerly, had also emigrated to Canada and settled on a farm near Brussels, Ontario.

Always in delicate health, Sarah was unable to enter the general workforce, but she did serve as matron of the Protestant Institution, which her brother-in-law Thomas Widd had so recently founded, for eleven years, from 1870 to 1881. She then moved to Toronto, where she eventually met her second husband, Norman Vickers Lewis, who had become Deaf as a result of a bout of scarlet fever when he was four years old. He had been educated at institutions for the Deaf and Dumb in Toronto and Hamilton, and at the age of thirteen, had been apprenticed to the *Toronto Daily Globe* to learn the printing trade. He worked as a printing foreman for some time before he opened a small enterprise of his own in 1885, and began publishing a semi-monthly magazine for Deaf Canadians, *The Silent Nation*.

On 24 March 1882 Sarah Guest (nee Fitzakerly), the British-born widow, became the bride of Norman Vickers Lewis, the Canadian entrepreneur, who was twelve years her junior. They continued to reside in Toronto, where Norman was very much involved with his printing business. Sarah's sister and her husband, Margaret and Thomas Widd, had meanwhile moved to Los Angeles, where they founded the Ephphatha Mission, later renamed the Episcopal Gallaudet Mission. Due to Sarah's failing health, she and Norman decided to follow the Widds to California, settling in Los Angeles in 1886, at 2225 Vermont Street. Again, Norman worked for several printing companies before he established his own business in an annex, which he had added to their house. His first printing job was the *History of the Los Angeles Association of the Deaf*. Later he published a magazine which he called *Philocophus*, which means "Deaf mute's friend."

Unfortunately, the move to California did not improve Sarah's health and she died in 1919. Norman became involved in the Episcopal Gallaudet Mission and printed and published its newsletter *The Church Messenger*. He remarried two years after Sarah's death, and became an avid collector of coins, stamps, and badges. He died in 1934 at the age of sixty-nine. Most of Sarah's influence on the Deaf Community was indirect, achieved largely because she was the wife of a notable Canadian Deaf husband, Norman Lewis, and the sister-in-law of a well-known Deaf activist, Thomas Widd. Nevertheless, she was a true pioneer in the history of Deaf Canada.

GEORGINA SCOTT was born hearing into a hearing family in Penhold, Alberta. She became Deaf at the age of two but the cause was unknown. Her late hearing brother, Dennis George Scott, a prisoner of war and decorated veteran of World War II, was a very prominent Albertan who was recognized in several ways for his many contributions. He was a recipient of the Alberta Achievement Award, presented to him by Premier Peter Lougheed and, in 1977, the Silver Jubilee Medal. In 1981 he was granted the most prestigious honour of all—he became a member of the Order of Canada. Georgina has a third cousin who is Deaf, David Poffenroth. Her husband, Frank Gilliam Lilley, is also Deaf. They have two adult hearing children—a son, Frank Jr., and a daughter, Deanna. Frank Sr. is a retired journeyman painter, an avid downhill skier, a golfer, and a computer buff. Georgina and Frank also have five wonderful grandchildren whom they enjoy immensely. The Lilleys currently make their home in Calgary, Alberta.

Georgina was educated at the Manitoba School for the Deaf in Winnipeg from 1937 to 1940. She was past seven years of age when she left home by train to attend school at such a great distance from her home. Understandably, she was apprehensive, but she soon made friends and enjoyed the residential and academic components of her school life. During World War II, when the Winnipeg School was taken over by the RCAF, Deaf pupils from Alberta were sent to the MacKay School for the Deaf in Montréal, Québec, and that is where Georgina finished her education, from 1940 to 1947. The three-day train trip across the country soon became quite enjoyable, and all the Deaf children who travelled together had fun. Georgina recalls that their food was served to them as if they were royalty.

When she left school and joined the workforce, her employment varied. She worked in a knitting factory where she made sweaters using a serger, and was a helper in a bakery. She also once had a unique job covering caskets for a casket manufacturer. What Georgina is best known for, however, is her long history as an ASL instructor at Mount Royal College (MRC) in Calgary, where she taught for eighteen years until her retirement in April 1996. For ten weeks following her official retirement, she taught ASL to Aboriginal people at the Gleichen Reserve near Cluny, Alberta. She still teaches short ASL immersion classes when she is called upon to do so, and has earned the distinction of being the eldest ASL instructor in Canada. While she mostly developed her teaching skills on her own, she did take some training as well, at the University of New Brunswick.

During her many years at MRC, her love of teaching and her commitment to bridging the gap between the Deaf and hearing cultures impressed her students, who thought she was wonderful. It was a joy to be in her class. Her course of instruction was part of MRC's Faculty of Continuing Education and Extension Program. She loved every moment of the many years she spent there. Georgina felt she learned as much from her students as they learned from her, and her own endless patience served as an example of what they needed in order to master ASL effectively. She soon realized that some students, on entering the program, thought they could learn ASL in a few easy lessons, but she made certain they knew from the outset that it was going to require a lot of hard work and a great deal of patience. It was always a personal triumph for her when students completed her course and were able to sign.

Georgina has been a member of the Calgary Association of the Deaf for many years and has also volunteered with Deaf and Hard of Hearing Services. She belongs to the Calgary Deaf Senior's Club, where she goes to play whist, bingo, and "cingo"—the "c" meaning "Calgary." She also volunteers at bingo fundraisers for the Calgary Association of the Deaf. Sometimes she joins other Deaf women for coffee in a cafe or mall food court, but she especially enjoys being around young people. She sees them as our future.

Georgina and Frank have been married for fifty years and have had a good life together. Their daughter Deanna works for Deaf and Hard of Hearing Services (DHHS) in Calgary and manages its interpreting services. Frank Jr. is a coordinator of payroll operations for Petro-Canada, also in Calgary. Both Deanna and Frank Jr. enjoy spending time with members of the Deaf Community. In May 1992 Georgina was presented with the Distinguished Faculty Teaching Award by her colleagues at MRC.

In her spare time, besides enjoying her family, particularly her grandchildren, Georgina likes to do embroidery, work at Wonderword puzzles every morning, read, and cook. She is also fond of computer games and e-mail. She and Frank go to as many Deaf conventions as possible and attend most events and gatherings in the Deaf Community.

LISA LOMAX was born Deaf in Saint John, New Brunswick, although her hearing loss was not discovered until she was a year old. Her Deafness is congenital, on the paternal side, as her hearing father has five known Deaf relatives. Lisa also has a Deaf cousin, Sharon Mortimer.

When she was two and a half years old Lisa started preschool, attending three times weekly, with several other Deaf children. Her mother took a basic Sign class in order to be able to communicate with her daughter, and has continued to use fingerspelling and Sign Language ever since. In 1975 Lisa was transferred to a day class at Glen Falls Elementary School where there were about fifteen Deaf students. In 1979 she was enrolled at the Interprovincial School for the Deaf in Amherst, Nova Scotia, which later became the Atlantic Provinces Resource Centre for the Hearing Handicapped (APRCHH), and is now known as the Atlantic Provinces Special Education Authority (APSEA). She remained there as a residential student from 1979 to 1986. In 1986 she returned to Saint John to attend Forest Hills Junior High School where there were a few other Deaf students. In 1988 she returned to Amherst to study printing and graphic arts at the Atlantic Technological Vocational Centre, graduating in 1990.

Lisa was employed as a custodian with the Saint John Public School Board, after working at various odd jobs. She now holds down two positions: housekeeping at a hotel during the day and doing custodial work for the Saint John School Board at night. She also had the exciting experience of performing in three movies. In the summer of 1985, parts of the movie *Children of a Lesser God* were being filmed in Saint John, and Lisa was cast in a minor role that required her to dance at a school prom. She was thrilled to meet the Deaf actress Marlee Matlin, who played the lead and later won the Best Actress Oscar for her performance. Lisa's second acting role was in the Deaf sex-education videotape, *Loving Yourself*, produced in 1989 in Halifax. In 1998 the movie *In Her Defense* was being filmed in Saint John and Lisa was again cast in a minor role with Chris Shay, another Deaf actor from Saint John. The movie featured Marlee Matlin and Michael Dudikoff.

Lisa's extensive collection of memorabilia related to the late Princess Diana has attracted media attention and was featured in a local newspaper and on television. Her interest in the British royal family began when she was a young girl watching the royal wedding of Diana and Charles on television in 1981. Her hope is that some day she will be able to travel to England to visit the museum at Althorpe where Diana is buried. Lisa has met two members of the Royal Family—Queen Elizabeth II, in 1984, at Mount Allison University, in Sackville, New Brunswick, and Prince Charles, during his 1996 visit to Saint John. She was always impressed with Princess Diana's involvement with the Deaf in England and her interest in British Sign Language (BSL).

Lisa is a very active athlete, attending a fitness club for workouts. She also enjoys biking, walking, swimming, and kayaking. Within the Deaf Community, she likes to attend social events and educational workshops. She continues to live in Saint John and has done some volunteer work for the Saint John Association of the Deaf. She does canvas sewing and loves to travel. While she was in high school her class visited the Alberta School for the Deaf in Edmonton on a student exchange in 1988. She has also been to Montréal and Boston and, in 2001, attended the Canadian Hearing Society's Mayfest in Toronto. One of her greatest delights is to take care of her nephew and nieces.

LONSDALE, Mary Kathleen

1878–1936
Outstanding Teacher of the Deaf and Tireless Worker for Deaf Causes.

MARY LONSDALE was the Deaf daughter of William Thomas Lonsdale, of Headingly, Manitoba, who was one of the earliest advocates to urge the Legislative Assembly of the Manitoba Government to take responsibility for the establishment of a provincial School for the Deaf in Winnipeg. Mary had a Deaf sister, Alice, born in 1885, and a Deaf brother, Herbert, born in 1887. Mary was enrolled at the school which existed in 1888 in the Fortune Block in downtown Winnipeg. Her father, William Thomas Lonsdale, with three Deaf children to be educated, was a member of the original delegation which successfully petitioned the Liberal government of that day, under Premier Thomas Greenway, to appropriate the sum of $20,000 for the construction of a provincial institution, and another $5,000 for its maintenance. This was the origin of the Manitoba Institution for the Deaf and Dumb, which later became the Manitoba School for the Deaf.

Mary received all her basic education at this school from which she graduated in 1902, and her sister Alice in 1905. Both had been students in the school's first department of articulation which focused on oralism. Mary then attended Gallaudet College in Washington, DC, and became a teacher of the Deaf. She returned to her alma mater where she taught briefly in 1911. When the Manitoba Institution for the Deaf and Dumb legally changed its name in 1912 to the Manitoba School for the Deaf, she took up a full-time position there, which she held until her death in 1936. At the beginning of her professional career, she taught in the old school building situated at Portage Avenue and Sherbrooke Street, where she had been one of the first pupils to enroll in 1888.

The classes she taught were generally made up of primary grade students who had difficulty learning. Mary also devoted much of her time to teaching a Deaf-Blind pupil, Billy Moug. She was considered a teacher of exceptional ability whose patience and perseverance nearly always assured success in her students.

Mary was also untiring in her efforts to improve conditions for the Deaf. She was an active member of the Western Canadian Association of the Deaf (WCAD), the Ladies' Aid of the Winnipeg Church of the Deaf, and the McDermid Memorial Committee, which looked after a scholarship fund set up in memory of Duncan Wendall McDermid and his son, Dr. Howard John McDermid, both of whom, in turn, were hearing superintendents of the Manitoba School for the Deaf from 1890 to 1920. Among the first WCAD elected officers for the 1923–1926 term were David Peikoff as president and Mary Lonsdale as first vice-president.

The changes that took place in educating the Deaf during her professional career made her work more stressful, but she was constantly cheerful and projected a positive attitude. She never failed to be courteous and loyal to her family, the Deaf Community, and the school where she taught. She was considered a peacemaker, both as a student and as a teacher, and was a loyal citizen devoted to her country and the British Empire in which the Dominion of Canada played an important role in her day.

When she passed away on 1 October 1936 all who knew her felt bereft and saddened by the great loss of an outstanding and dedicated teacher and community worker. In November 1937 a portrait of her was donated by a former staff colleague, Miss Mae Young, and placed in the school library in memory of Mary's devotion to the school she had loved. Many tributes have been paid to her by numerous well-known educators and members of Manitoba's Deaf Community. She had an understanding heart and a true Christian spirit which endeared her to her pupils, colleagues, and wide network of friends.

MACALISTER (SLATER), Brenda Louise

1952–
Deaf-Blind Educator, Consultant, Coordinator, Presenter, and Outstanding Role Model.

BRENDA SLATER was born Deaf to hearing parents in Vancouver, British Columbia. She has no known Deaf relatives, but her husband, Ian Macalister, a mechanic and machinist journeyman, is Deaf. Brenda and Ian have two adult hearing children, Sean and Mandy. Because her family had moved to Ontario when she was a toddler, Brenda spent her years from the age of four until she was thirteen at the Ontario School for the Deaf and Blind in Belleville. Her family then returned to BC and she attended Jericho Hill School for the Deaf and Blind in Vancouver until she graduated. Brenda and Ian currently make their home in Burnaby, British Columbia.

For eleven years, from 1970 to 1981, Brenda was employed as an electronic production worker. Since 1998 she has been significantly involved as the coordinator of the Volunteer Intervenor Program for the Deaf-Blind under the sponsorship of the Canadian National Association of the Blind (CNIB) and the presenter of workshops on Deaf-Blind issues.

She is a member of the BC Association of the Deaf-Blind (BCADB) and took leadership training in Seattle, Washington, in 1993. She also took training in 1996 in group facilitation for the Nobody's Perfect parent group, sponsored by the BC Ministry of Children and Families. This prepared Brenda for her present career as a training specialist to develop community and employer awareness of the issues faced by Deaf-Blind persons. She was hired by the Mainland-South Coast District of the CNIB because she is Deaf-Blind herself, knows the Deaf-Blind Community, and understands the Deaf-Blind language and culture. She matches volunteers with the necessary communication skills to Deaf-Blind clients who then decide how they will use the volunteer's services. The intervenor's role is mainly to communicate information to the client so that he/she can then make personal choices and decisions.

Because Deaf-Blind people have varying degrees of auditory and visual challenges and use different types of communication, Brenda works hard to ensure that all clients can communicate through a medium with which they feel comfortable. Creating an inclusive environment is her principal goal. She is proud to be a role model for the Deaf-Blind community. Her belief is that in the future, with changing public attitudes and new adaptive technologies, more and more Deaf-Blind people will be taking post-secondary education and seeking employment.

Brenda has served as a volunteer for many organizations and agencies at both the executive and committee level. She was vice president of the Greater Vancouver Association of the Deaf (Women's Group) (GVAD), has presented at the University of Washington State Medical Centre in Seattle, served on the board of directors for the Canadian National Society of the Deaf-Blind (CNSDB), chaired a Well-Being Program Workshop Planning Committee, and held several offices in the BC Association of the Deaf-Blind.

Brenda has done research on accessibility for Deaf-Blind students at universities and colleges, served as an outreach worker, and acted as a volunteer ASL instructor for the CNIB. She is an independent, successful woman who provides proof of what can be accomplished when accessibility challenges are overcome. Although she leads a very busy life, she finds time to grow jade plants and to knit. She enjoys outdoor activities such as camping, boating, fishing, hiking, and swimming. Brenda is an outgoing and gregarious person who likes to go shopping and socializing with friends. Travelling is also one of her major interests, and she is currently very excited about the prospect of acquiring a new guide/hearing dog because it will increase her independence.

MacDONALD (BOUDREAU), Mary Elizabeth ("Betty")

1952–
Hair Stylist, Data-Entry Operator, Deaf Catholic Coordinator, and Deaf Literacy Practitioner.

BETTY MACDONALD was born Deaf, although her hearing loss was not discovered until she was three months old. Her hearing family lived in New Waterford, Cape Breton, Nova Scotia, where she grew up. She has no known Deaf relatives. She is married to a hearing man, David MacDonald, and they have two adult hearing children, Allan and Colleen. Betty and David make their home in Dartmouth, Nova Scotia.

Betty's education began at the Halifax School for the Deaf and was completed in 1970, at the new Interprovincial School for the Deaf in Amherst, now known as the Atlantic Provinces Special Education Authority (APSEA). She then decided to become a hairdresser and took a twelve-month training course in Sydney. Despite the difficulties of learning without an interpreter, she did well, and completed the course requirements readily. She was hired as a shampoo girl, but was never allowed to actually use her hairdressing skills on any of the clients, so she decided to set up her own business. By the end of the year she had attracted quite a well-established clientele, thanks to her mother who took telephone calls and booked appointments for her. After Betty moved to Dartmouth, however, it was not easy because no TTY relay service was available in those days. After seven years she decided it was time for a career change.

Betty enrolled at a business college in Halifax to take a six-week course to become a data-entry operator. This worked out well for her and she was hired almost immediately by Sears, where she remained happily employed for the next eleven years. She was then laid off due to restructuring of the company. At first she was devastated but later Betty came to realize that the lay-off was the best thing that could have happened. She entered the Deaf Academic Upgrading Program at the Nova Scotia Community College, Halifax Campus, and, in due course, this changed her whole life.

In June 1997 she received her high school equivalency diploma with honours, which boosted her self-esteem and gave her new confidence. She became a part-time coordinator of a Deaf literacy program, and is still working in that capacity. She has also been the Deaf Catholic coordinator since 1997, and for two years worked as a teacher assistant at APSEA. In addition, she worked as a job coach for Deaf teenagers at APSEA for one year. At Nova Scotia Community College, she taught Maritime regional signs to interpreter training students as well as level III science (grades nine and ten) to Deaf upgrading students, and tutored both Deaf and hearing students there. She also conducted Deaf needs assessment research in Nova Scotia. Betty continues to expand the Deaf literacy program in the province.

An active member of the Deaf Community, Betty has been involved in many committees, organizations, and agencies. Among them are the International Catholic Association of the Deaf (ICAD), the Halifax Association of the Deaf (HAD), the Deafness Advocacy Association Nova Scotia (DAANS), and the Society of Deaf and Hard of Hearing Nova Scotians (SDHHNS). She helped organize a Deaf parents' support group, and since 1997 has represented SDHHNS on the Halifax Regional Municipality Advisory Committee for Persons with Disabilities. Betty has extraordinary insight and understanding of Deaf Literacy issues. In recognition of her enormous contributions, the Halifax Association of the Deaf presented Betty with the prestigious John Blois Memorial Award, naming her the Deaf Woman of the Year in 1982–83, a well-deserved honour.

In her spare time she skates, bowls, and enjoys many other sports. She is constantly involved in community events and activities, and loves to work with children. This truly amazing woman is highly respected and admired for her energetic approach to life. She is a good listener who offers unconditional support and encouragement. Ironically, it took a depressing job lay-off to bring out Betty MacDonald's latent capacity for extraordinary leadership and selfless service to her community.

GLADYS BLAIS was born hearing to hearing parents in Thurso, Québec. She became Deaf at six months of age due to spinal meningitis. She had no known Deaf relatives on her side of the family, but her husband, Peter Henderson MacDougall, a postal worker and lay preacher, was Deaf. She had a hearing sister, Ethel Blais, who lived in Toronto and worked at the Doubleday Book Company, and a hearing brother, Ted, who was a highly successful businessman in Malarctic, Québec.

Peter and Gladys had two hearing sons—Peter (Jr.), who worked as a researcher in the parliamentary library after completing a degree in political science and journalism at Carleton University, and Jamie, who is currently a professor in the Psychology Department at McGill University, and the founding president of the Canadian Deafness Research and Training Institute in Montréal. He was formerly the psychologist and director of research at the MacKay Centre (for Deaf and disabled children) in Montréal. He also worked at the National Technical Institute of the Deaf in Rochester, New York, as a research associate and associate professor. He recently won the "2000 Community Service" awards from both the Canadian and American Psychological Associations for his work with the Deaf.

Peter (Sr.) had a Deaf sister, Elsie MacDougall, who was married to a Deaf man, Colin MacLean. Peter, Elsie, Colin, and Gladys all attended the School for the Deaf in Belleville, Ontario. Gladys and Peter, with their children, made their home in Ottawa, where Peter worked for the Postal Service and Gladys was a devoted housewife and mother.

When Gladys and Peter were first married they lived in Limoges, Ontario, near the MacDougall family farm. Gladys worked on the farm but, when they moved to Ottawa, she became very actively involved in the Deaf community. She was especially helpful to a number of troubled Deaf children whom she invited to her home, and often advised them on many aspects of their lives. Both Gladys and Peter regularly attended Deaf Club socials, and were devout members of the Ottawa Church of the Deaf. They had many wonderful friends in the Deaf Community, including the Brighams, McPeakes, Mr. Huband, and Gladys's best friend, Ruth Routliffe and her husband Colby,

whose daughter Adele is an ASL interpreter in Toronto.

While she attended the Belleville School for the Deaf, Gladys was considered an oral phenomenon, and often told her children about her Sunday outings, by horse and buggy, into the town of Belleville where she was expected to show off her oral skills as an example of the school's success in teaching Deaf children to speak and speechread. Later, however, she came to realize that she had been taught very little else. Her education had focused entirely on the development of oral skills. Furthermore, she also recognized that her oral talents had been developed, not through the school, but through the dedication of her mother, whom she adored. Mrs. Blais (Wigney) invented her own methods of teaching speech and speechreading, which were evidently highly successful.

When her mother died one winter month, Gladys was not sent home from school to attend her funeral, but was kept in Belleville until the summer vacation. To the end of her days, she never really got over this harsh blow—days which were spent at the Bob Rumball Centre in Toronto. Bob was a frequent guest at the MacDougall home in his early days in Ottawa, and it was a great comfort to her to have both Bob and her family at her side at the end of her days.

Although Gladys never tried to steer Jamie into the field of Deafness in his studies, she was pleased when he made that decision, encouraging him to help the Deaf in having ASL recognized and accepted. Peter (Sr.) was by no means as oral as Gladys, but he was also a vigorous proponent of ASL as the language of instruction and communication for the Deaf.

In her spare time Gladys's favourite hobbies were gardening and sewing. She was also renowned for her culinary talents, and people came from far and wide to sample her creative cuisine. There is no doubt, however, about what she did best, and that was to practice her natural gift of being an outstanding mother and a warm, loving human being. She left her mark on all whose lives she touched and will forever be missed by her children, grandchildren, and her wonderful network of remaining friends.

MacGREGOR (FRIESEN), Alvina Irene

1945–
Singing Leader, Sunday School Teacher, Teacher Aide, Skilled Seamstress, and Occasional Preacher.

ALVINA FRIESEN was born hearing into a hearing family at Steinbach, Manitoba. At the age of two years she became Deaf following a severe bout of scarlet fever. Her husband, James MacGregor, an autobody repairman, is also Deaf. They have a niece and a great nephew who are Deaf but their own two adult children, Debbie and Sean, are both hearing. They also have a hearing grandson, Brett, who is the joy of their lives. Alvina's hearing sister, Rose Plett, now deceased, learned to sign and became a minister to the Deaf and Alvina's niece, Sharon Plett is an ASL interpreter in the United States. Alvina and James currently make their home in Winnipeg, Manitoba.

Alvina received her education at the Saskatchewan School for the Deaf in Saskatoon, and at the Day School for the Deaf in Winnipeg. She then worked in a garment factory as a seamstress from 1961 to 1963 and later found employment in two print shops. The first was Sanford Evans where she was a staff member for three years—1963 to 1966. She then spent two years, 1966 to 1968, at Universal Printing. For the next twelve years she was a housewife and stay-at-home mother, but she returned to the workforce in 1980 and found employment at "Granny's" until 1988. Since then she has

worked as a teacher's aide at the Manitoba School for the Deaf.

When her husband took up scuba diving in 1974, he needed a partner, so Alvina joined him a year later, becoming the first female Deaf diver in Winnipeg. In 1976 she became involved in ice-diving and took an advanced course that qualified her to dive in search of bodies and weapons for forensic purposes. She learned how to swim in murky waters and how to bring a sinking boat to the surface. On one of her many dives, she found a Canadian National Railways pickaxe of historic significance. Alvina's diving activities continued until 1990.

Apart from her current job, Alvina has many interests she enjoys. She is a highly skilled seamstress who fashions clothes for herself, her family, particularly her beloved grandson, and others. She is a talented signer of songs and leads the singing in her church. She also teaches Sunday school and on occasion preaches when the regular pastor is unavailable. This very versatile woman is a perfect role model for younger Deaf women in her community.

MacINNIS, Susan Michelle

1968–
Deaf Student Activist, Data-Entry Operator, Actor, Storyteller, and ASL Instructor.

SUSAN MACINNIS was born Deaf to hearing parents in Middle Musquodoboit, a rural village in Nova Scotia. She was educated at the Interprovincial School for the Deaf in Amherst from the age of four until she graduated in 1987. She then obtained qualifications for keypunch data entry from the Atlantic Technological Vocational Centre (ATVC) in Amherst, where she was president of the student council.

In 1989, buoyed and inspired by the "Deaf President Now" revolution at Gallaudet University in Washington, DC, which had taken place in 1988, Susan and about twenty-five other Deaf students met and came up with twenty-five complaints and issues, including the poor quality of instruction for Deaf students, the instructors' lack of fluency in ASL/MSL, and the restrictions on off-campus life for Deaf students. Wanting to resolve these problems, they met with Phyllis Cameron, the director of the Atlantic Provinces

Resource Centre for the Hearing Handicapped (APRCHH), now known as the Atlantic Provinces Special Education Authority (APSEA). The discussion was not productive, so the students decided to walk out in protest the next day.

The students' action was supported by the Deaf Community and Deaf leaders in Halifax, but was easily thwarted by the hearing administration and, to some extent, by the media. Although it was intended that the planned protest remain secret until it was launched, a press release was sent to the media so the event would receive publicity. Unfortunately, reporters called the school to verify the facts, and thus, the administration became aware of the plan, and was able to suppress it to a large degree. Although the students went ahead with the original plan, and some improvement was realized, there was not nearly as much reaction as they had hoped for. Despite the fact that the movement was not too successful, and that Susan and the students were left feeling powerless and oppressed, the experience boosted Susan's self-esteem and confidence. Eventually, the students returned to their classes to complete their studies.

Susan has worked for eleven years as a data-entry operator, and is pleased to note that the Bank of Nova Scotia, where she is currently employed, is becoming much more "Deaf-friendly." Many of her co-workers are learning to sign in order to improve communication between Deaf and hearing staff members. Susan's favourite task, however, is teaching ASL to Deaf children.

She felt honoured to be chosen to play the role of a Deaf daughter in the popular video entitled *Loving Yourself.* The intent of that production was to help Deaf teenagers become more aware of issues related to sex, such as teen pregnancy and sexual abuse, as well as relationships with family and friends and the need for open communication.

This was a memorable experience for Susan. She has a unique gift for storytelling, a keen sense of humour, and loves to tease people.

MACKIE, Robyn Dawne

1970–
Skier, Teacher, Camp Counsellor, and Traveller.

ROBYN MACKIE was born Deaf after her biological mother contracted rubella during her pregnancy. Her adoptive family fetched her from Edmonton and took her home to Calgary, Alberta, where she grew up. They named her Robyn Dawne Mackie.

When she reached school age, Robyn attended the Deaf Program at Queen Elizabeth Elementary School and later, Queen Elizabeth Junior/Senior High School. She achieved a fully mainstreamed education with only one other Deaf student in the program in grades ten, eleven, and twelve. After graduating from high school she entered Mount Royal College, transferring to a university program two years later. In 1998 she completed a BA degree in Anthropology and was the first Deaf student to graduate from the University of Calgary.

Robyn was a member of the Alberta Ski Team for Persons with Disabilities and competed in slalom, giant slalom, and downhill events. She joined the Deaf Canadian Alpine Team for the World Winter Games of the Deaf held in Banff in 1991, where she did quite well but was unable to finish the giant slalom. She was a ski racer from 1988 to 1992 but finally decided to withdraw due to lack of sponsorships.

In 1989 Robyn competed in the Alberta Deaf Pageant and placed third among four contestants. She is currently a literacy teacher for the Deaf at Bow Valley College and has been an ASL instructor for quite a number of years. She has many years of experience as a camp counsellor and has even trained young hearing people as camp leaders at a YWCA summer leaders-in-training camp. She has appeared in a Telus TV commercial and has won two prestigious scholarships—the "Steven Wilkins" and the "Pan Canadian." Robyn is proud of her accomplishments which also include a CCSD Award for second place in poetry writing.

Robyn loves to travel and recently visited Nepal with its world-renowned Himalayan Mountains in September 2000. She took two journeys to Australia, one in 1995 and the other in 1999, when she and her husband attended the World Congress of the Deaf in Brisbane. In 1997 Robyn visited a few countries in northern Europe and cheered for the Canadian team at the World Summer Games of the Deaf in Denmark.

In 1999 she married Dean Stuber who is also Deaf, a graduate of Gallaudet University, an expert in computer information systems, and president of the Calgary Association of the Deaf. He has also held several other offices in organizations of the Deaf. Robyn and Dean live in Calgary, Alberta, with their two cats, Auburn and Blake.

MacKILLOP (HULME), Doris

1926–
Dormitory Houseparent, CNIB Intervenor, Foster Parent, and Group-Home Operator.

DORIS HULME was born hearing to hearing parents in New Waterford, Cape Breton, Nova Scotia. She became Deaf at the age of two and a half years due to spinal meningitis. She has no known Deaf relatives, but her husband, Donald John MacKillop, now deceased, who was a printing instructor and house-parent, was Deaf, and his father and grandfather were both hard of hearing. Doris and Donald had three hearing children—Carol Ann, Donna Lee, and Donald John, Jr. They lived in Atlantic Canada and Ontario throughout their marriage but Doris currently makes her home in Surrey, British Columbia. She has eight grandchildren and two great grandsons. Her son's wife, Heather, is Deaf, and they have five daughters.

Doris was educated at the Halifax School for the Deaf for eleven years, and then at Centennial College. Her employment record has been interesting and varied. She worked briefly as a sewing machinist and, after moving to Amherst, Nova Scotia, was a houseparent at the Interprovincial School for the Deaf for three years. When the family moved to Toronto, Doris found a job as a reader for a clipping service and worked there for over six years. She left that position to look after a foster child and to operate a group home with her husband Donald in Georgetown, Ontario. They had been there for eleven years when Donald passed away, and Doris moved back to Toronto.

Doris did volunteer work at the Ontario Mission of the Deaf for a while, but soon found full-time employment as head of housekeeping at the new Bob Rumball Centre of the Deaf, where she worked for more than

three years before being hired to work with Deaf-Blind people at the Canadian National Institute for the Blind (CNIB) as an intervenor. She remained in that position for over nine years until her retirement in 1991.

Doris' involvement in the Deaf Community as a volunteer has been extensive and impressive. Positions she has held are as follows: secretary of the Halifax Association of the Deaf, secretary of the Eastern Canada Association of the Deaf, secretary and president of the Canadian Association of the Deaf, treasurer of the Canadian Coordinating Council of the Deaf, president of the National Fraternal Society of the Deaf, secretary and president of the Women's Association of the Evangelical Church of the Deaf, secretary of the board of trustees for the Evangelical Church of the Deaf, secretary of the Ontario Camp of the Deaf, member of the Advisory Board of the Canadian Hearing Society, and chairperson of the National Fraternal Society of the Deaf's convention held in Toronto in 1979, which was attended by 1,000 people.

Another interesting distinction achieved by Doris was that she and Jim Kvarnberg, who now resides in Edmonton, were the first Deaf persons to send a message to each other on the teletype, which was the forerunner of the modern TTY.

Doris' hobbies and leisure time activities include knitting, quilting, reading, photography, spending time with her family, and travelling.

MacKINNON (MAXCY), Christine ("Christy") Rosalie

1889–1981
Artist, Illustrator, Storyteller, and Teacher.

CHRISTY MACKINNON was born hearing into a large family on a farm in Beaver Cove, in the parish of Boisdale, overlooking the beautiful Bras d'Or Lakes on Cape Breton Island, Nova Scotia. She became Deaf at the age of two years after a siege of whooping cough, which she and her sister barely survived. The illness left Christy Deaf and Mary Sarah, "Sadie," with some residual hearing. They had an older Deaf sister, Mary Catherine, who attended the Halifax School for the Deaf for only a few years. They also had five Deaf cousins, including Mary Ann MacLean, who spent a

total of sixty-one years at the Halifax School for the Deaf as a student, administrative assistant, and teacher.

Christy's father, known as Professor Joseph D. MacKinnon, was a local schoolmaster in a one-room school house in Boisdale. He was renowned in Cape Breton for his scientific knowledge about farming practices, and was a noted Gaelic scholar who published a Gaelic dictionary.

When his wife died in childbirth in 1892, Joseph began taking Christy to school with him because there was no longer adequate supervision for her at home. Thus, at the age of three, she was exposed to her father's lessons with his older students, and was able to pick up knowledge as well as useful skills. However, in 1900, when she was eleven years old, the decision was made to enroll her at the Institution for the Deaf and Dumb, later known as the School for the Deaf in Halifax. She was unhappy and homesick at first, but eventually made some friends and settled down to become a capable and talented student. Before long, her family and teachers all began to recognize her outstanding artistic ability, so she was enrolled at the renowned Victoria School of Art and Design founded by Anna Leonowens, an English teacher at the king's court in Siam (now Thailand) from 1862 to 1867, who was a vocal supporter of women's rights and abolition of slavery, and a prominent citizen of Halifax for more than twenty years. The school is now known as the Nova Scotia College of Art and Design (NSCAD). Christy's attendance was an adjunct to her regular academic program at the School for the Deaf, and other Deaf students also took courses there.

After graduating from high school in 1908, Christy continued studying at the Victoria School and undertaking assignments commissioned by local citizens. In 1912 she was awarded a scholarship to study at the Boston Museum of Fine Arts, so she moved to the United States. From 1915 to 1919 she lived in New York city where she continued studying art and working as a freelance illustrator.

In 1920 she returned to Canada to teach art at the Halifax School for the Deaf, her alma mater. Eight years later, in 1928, George Bateman, principal of the school at that time, expressed in his annual report his deep regret at losing her as a teacher because she had resigned and was about to be married. She commanded an unusual degree of respect and affection among staff and students, and was a skilful, devoted teacher. She was also an officer of the Forrest Club, forerunner of the Halifax Association of the Deaf, serving as its vice-president from 1920 to 1924, secretary from 1924 to 1926, and treasurer from 1927 to 1928, when she resigned to be married. On 21 August 1928, Christy married a Deaf printer, John Maxcy, from New York and moved back to the United States. Until 1948 Christy worked as an illustrator for the famous toy firm of F.A.O. Schwarz in New York City. Some years later, she and John retired and moved to Sutton Mills, New Hampshire, where she continued drawing and painting. When John died in 1952 Christy moved to Natick, Massachusetts, to live near her Deaf sister Sadie Theriault. It was there that she began recording and illustrating the memories of her childhood.

It was not until Christy's death, at the age of ninety-one, that her niece, Inez MacKinnon Simeone, began to develop her aunt's illustrations and diary notes into a book. Hundreds of drawings as well as written materials had been bequeathed to Inez by her aunt, and these became the foundation for a book. Through Inez' efforts, some of Christy's work was posthumously published in a book entitled *The Silent Observer*, a fitting testimony to Christy MacKinnon's enormous talent. The beautiful story and illustrations in this volume reveal the author's keen sense of humour, her courage and compassion, and the breadth of her perception.

Christy MacKinnon was a remarkable woman. When she died in 1981 she left a rich literary and artistic legacy for future generations. In her lifetime she had met and rubbed shoulders with many illustrious individuals, including Alexander Graham Bell and Helen Keller. She retained these childhood friendships into her adult life, and over the years came to know various internationally renowned artists, illustrators, and publishers.

Nevertheless, she remained a simple and loyal friend and colleague without pretension or vanity. Although *The Silent Observer* may appear to be a children's book, it has been read and enjoyed by people of all ages. Today, Christy MacKinnon's work lives after her, as do the enduring and affectionate memories she left within the hearts of her co-workers, friends, family, and students.

MARY ANN MACLEAN was born Deaf in McLeanville, Cape Breton, Nova Scotia, the eldest of eleven children, five of whom were Deaf. She also had two Deaf cousins. Mary was one of the very few Deaf women who had a lengthy association with the School for the Deaf in Halifax. She was a student from 1893 to 1902 in what was then known as the Institution for the Deaf and Dumb. She then worked as a clerk in the principal's office from 1902 until 1931 and taught sewing to the senior girls from 1931 to 1954, spending a total of sixty-one years at the school. She had entered the school at the age of nine and left at the age of seventy. In total, she had worked at the school for fifty-two years when she retired.

Mary Ann is remembered for her unselfish service to the Halifax School. She was well known for the wonderful social events and parties she organized, especially at Hallowe'en, and for the dramas she staged, of which the most memorable was *David Copperfield*. Although she was Roman Catholic, she acquired the services of a Deaf minister, Reverend Light, from Boston, who came to Halifax once a year for thirty years to visit the school, meet the Deaf people in the community, and minister to the Protestant Deaf. Reverend Light and Mary Ann instituted Bible study classes, which continued for many years. She was regarded unofficially as the goodwill ambassador to the Deaf in central and western Canada, making Deaf people there more aware of the Eastern Canada Association of the Deaf (ECAD) in the Atlantic provinces.

Within the Deaf Community, Mary Ann held many important positions and volunteered her services to a variety of causes. She was an associate editor of ECAD's bi-monthly newsletter *The Deaf Herald*, which was published until 1955. She was the first treasurer of the Halifax Association of the Deaf (HAD), then known as the Forrest Club, and held the offices of treasurer, secretary, vice-president, and president during the years the club remained active. After her last year in office, in 1940, she became one of the club's permanent trustees. She was also treasurer of the Eastern Canada Association of the Deaf for thirty-eight years. In every office she held, she served faithfully and well. On her retirement in 1954, she was presented with flowers and a sizeable sum of money at a banquet held in her honour, which was attended by both principals under whom she had served—George Bateman and K.C. Van Allen. Forrest Nickerson, who was then president of the Halifax Association of the Deaf, lauded her for her years of commitment and dedication. The school's Board of Directors presented her with a Scroll of Honour, and the staff wished her well, presenting her with a lovely travelling case.

Mary Ann had some famous relatives. Her Deaf sister Adeline became Sister Mary Adeline of the Sisters of Charity of Mount St. Joseph in Indiana. She had been a brilliant student at the Halifax School for the Deaf and later spent many years at the Glockner Penrose Hospital in Colorado Springs, Colorado, using her outstanding artistic skills to produce beautiful scrolls and certificates, and also spent some time in New Mexico. One of Mary's Deaf cousins was Christine "Christy" MacKinnon, author and illustrator of the beautiful book entitled *The Silent Observer*, who had also been a student at the Halifax School for the Deaf for eight years, and later returned to her alma mater as an art teacher.

Mary was posthumously inducted into the Canadian Cultural Society of the Deaf 's Hall of Fame. After her retirement she spent her final years in Regina, Saskatchewan, with her ninety-five-year-old mother, her sister, and a brother until she died peacefully in 1960. Her cousin Christy MacKinnon wrote a fine tribute in her memory, lauding her unselfish mission on behalf of Deaf people and her fifty-five years of indispensable service to her Deaf Community. She cited Mary's intuitiveness and her integrity while recalling her as a "big sister" to whom Deaf folks, including Christy herself, flew for help when they were in trouble. She was admired for the swiftness of her fingerspelling and her ability to communicate with strangers by writing notes.

MADDISON (BAGNELL), Mary Elizabeth

1949–
ASL Instructor, Teacher Assistant, and ASL Facilitator.

MARY BAGNELL was born hearing, to hearing parents in Sydney, Cape Breton, Nova Scotia. She became Deaf as a result of spinal meningitis, which she contracted on her fifth birthday. She was the youngest of three children, and has an older brother and sister who both have normal hearing. She has no known Deaf relatives, and her husband, Michael Elroy Maddison (Roy), is a hearing man. They have two hearing sons—Troy, whom they were fortunate enough to adopt when he was eleven days old, and Todd, who is their biological son. Michael works in the forest industry and the family lives in Port Alberni on Vancouver Island, in British Columbia.

Mary began her formal education at the Halifax School for the Deaf in 1956 and continued to attend there until 1961, when the new Interprovincial School for the Deaf opened at Amherst. She was transferred and attended there from 1961 to 1968. An attempt was made to place her in a mainstream public school in Sydney, but was unsuccessful without the services of an interpreter, so she returned to Amherst and attended the Atlantic Technological Vocational Centre, graduating in 1970 with IBM and Lithography Certificates. Over the years Mary has broadened her knowledge and qualifications by taking various college courses related to human resources.

She was raised in a hearing environment and no one in her family learned to sign. In that era, during the 1950s and early 1960s, signing was discouraged, and families were urged to direct their Deaf child's focus toward speech and lipreading. Mary realizes now that this was wrong, but she did manage to develop excellent lipreading skills and fluent speech. Despite their earlier sentiments, her entire family is now very supportive of the Deaf Community and Deaf Culture. Mary considers herself most fortunate to have a caring family and a wonderful husband to whom she has been married for thirty years.

Her first job was as a teacher assistant with a class of seven Deaf students in a mainstream public school, under the direction of a qualified teacher of the Deaf. She worked in that capacity for seven years, from 1972 to 1979, before taking the next six years off to start her family. In 1985 she returned to work as a teacher assistant in the local school district, in a class of special needs children. At present, she works as an ASL facilitator at an elementary school where there are two Deaf children in a primary classroom, in an integrated setting, with the support of their own interpreter. She also travels to the west coast of Vancouver Island once a week to an elementary school where she serves in a supportive role to a Deaf boy and his aide. In addition, she teaches ASL in both schools. She has also been an ASL instructor at the college level in Port Alberni for many years.

Mary has many fond recollections of growing up in Sydney, Nova Scotia, but also remembers the humorous incidents created by the building in which she and her family lived. Her father was an embalmer and undertaker, so they lived above the funeral home in private quarters. Mary often received alarmed looks from people when she mentioned where she lived, and when her Deaf friends came to visit her, they were always apprehensive about the possibility of the corpses rising from their resting places.

Mary has a full and happy life, and in her leisure time likes to walk around the local track and take aerobics classes. She enjoys working at various crafts, reading good novels, and using her computer.

MAHE, Linda

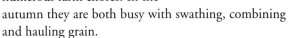

LINDA MAHE was born Deaf to hearing parents in Edmonton, Alberta. She was raised on a farm at Irma with one Deaf sister and two hearing sisters who are twins. Linda's Deaf sister is Teresa Fleming, who now resides and works in Winnipeg, Manitoba. Linda and her husband have two adopted daughters—Michelle and Kristi who are Deaf and are currently attending the Alberta School for the Deaf (ASD) in Edmonton.

Linda herself was educated at ASD from 1967 to 1980. After graduating she went directly into the workforce, taking a job in the housekeeping department at the University of Alberta Hospital.

In 1982 Linda married Laurier Mahe and became a farmer's wife. It was fortunate that she had grown up on a farm and was familiar with what needed to be done. She and her husband work well together as a team, cultivating the land, sowing crops, hauling grain, baling hay, raising livestock and poultry, and making their farm as productive as possible. Sometimes Laurier takes on part-time jobs in the Alberta "oilpatch" and Linda helps him with such chores as painting colour codes on the pipes.

The benefits of Linda's poultry-raising are twofold. She produces eggs for local marketing and sells the birds for their meat. At calving time in the early spring, she assists Laurier with the births and looks after the newborns which often require special care if they are weak or if the weather is very cold. During the summer months Linda operates the hay baler and drives the tractor for numerous farm chores. In the autumn they are both busy with swathing, combining and hauling grain.

Linda believes she has a "green thumb" because she is a very successful gardener. Every fall the harvest from her large garden provides her with many hours of pleasure pickling, making jams and jellies, bottling tomatoes, and freezing the rest of the produce for winter consumption. Her berry bushes and apple trees are a source of healthy nutrition for her family. She grows strawberries, raspberries, and saskatoons to be frozen, eaten fresh, or turned into delicious desserts, syrups, jams, and jellies. She also makes and bottles her own salsa from her garden produce.

Although living in rural Alberta somewhat isolates her from the Deaf Community, Linda keeps herself busy and profitably occupied. She enjoys her daughters when they are home on weekends and holidays, and her partnership in farming provides her with a great sense of accomplishment and satisfaction.

MANCHUL (MANN), Agnes Anne

AGNES MANN was born Deaf to hearing parents on a farm at Lemberg, Saskatchewan. She has some distant cousins who are Deaf but no known Deaf relatives in her immediate family. Her husband, Walter Manchul, a carpenter, painter, and welder, is Deaf. Their only child, a hearing daughter, Janice Caroline Manchul, works as an ASL interpreter. Agnes has a younger hearing brother, Jim, to whom she was very close when they were children. Agnes and Walter make their home in Edmonton, Alberta.

Agnes was sent to the Saskatchewan School for the Deaf in Saskatoon in the fall of 1946. During her first year she had a number of illnesses that kept her out of the classroom for all but two months. She contracted diphtheria and scarlet fever and also developed rheumatic fever. She was much healthier during the rest of her thirteen years at the school in Saskatoon. She studied hairdressing, typing, sewing, and cooking as well as her academic subjects. After she graduated in 1959, she spent two years at home before attending Business College in Regina.

Although Agnes had a severe vision loss as well as her hearing loss, she did well at school. She often relied on her friends to get around and to prevent her from sustaining serious injuries by falling or missing stairs and other hazards. Growing up on the farm gave her a variety of rich and wholesome experiences from which she learned about the world around her, and she soon developed a tactile sense that would serve her for life.

Agnes also developed an adventuresome spirit and a cheerful, positive outlook which eventually led her to a successful career. She worked for Regina Tent and Awning, repairing tents and tarpaulins for several months and then headed to Winnipeg to look for work. She was hired in the Winnipeg garment district where she sewed for Jacob's Fashions, but later moved to Saskatoon to take employment with Denham's Tent and Awning Company. In the fall of 1966 Agnes moved to Edmonton, where she worked in two different garment factories before she married Walter Manchul in 1968. After their daughter Janice was born, Agnes was a stay-at-home mother for a while, and Janice soon became a very proficient interpreter for her parents.

Having been diagnosed with Usher's Syndrome at an early age, and eventually losing much of her peripheral vision, Agnes enrolled in a CNIB course to obtain her Literary Braille Transcription Certificate and was rather surprised at how readily she developed this new skill. In 1983, when the Materials Resource Centre of Alberta Education needed someone to transcribe school textbooks into Braille, Agnes applied for the position, even though her husband was doubtful that she would be able to do it. With Janice to interpret for her, Agnes went to be interviewed and was offered the job. Her first paycheque convinced Walter that his wife had launched herself into an interesting and rewarding career. She sometimes used a hand-held magnifier and had access to large-print computer software. To enhance her vision she wore reading glasses and, when she could not see fine print, she simply enlarged it on a photocopier. She communicated with co-workers through Sign Language and written notes. As a result, thousands of blind and visually challenged students have benefited from her work.

In 1996 Agnes attended the Reaching Out Conference in Toronto, which was sponsored by the Canadian National Society of the Deaf-Blind. She entered one of her sewing projects in the crafts competition and was awarded first prize. An enthusiastic quilter, Agnes made a bedspread which she designed to depict the entire Braille alphabet from A to Z. The pillow shams repeated the letters ABC and XYZ. When her co-workers saw her project, they arranged for Agnes to meet the Deputy Minister of Education, Dr. Leroy Sloan, who admired her work and complimented her on achieving first prize.

Agnes's two favourite hobbies are reading and sewing. She reads Braille materials and most of her sewing, which includes beautiful original tablecloths, quilts, curtains, and children's clothing, is done through her highly developed sense of touch. She also enjoys travelling and has done so quite extensively. She was acting president of the Edmonton Deaf-Blind Society from 1995 to 1998, and is also involved in Edmonton's Deaf Community. The successes and accomplishments of this skilful and versatile woman make her an enviable role model for all Canadian women, whether they are Deaf, Blind, hearing, or sighted.

MARGO (THOMPSON), Joyce Bettina

1923–
Business Office Clerk, Civil Servant, and Outstanding Volunteer in the Deaf Community.

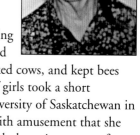

JOYCE THOMPSON was born in Regina, Saskatchewan, the only child of hearing parents. It is not known when she became Deaf, but her parents suspected it was a result of a traumatic fall into an open cellar when she was nineteen months old. She has no known Deaf relatives except a cousin, Russell Thompson, who was a long-time resident of the Manitoba Deaf Centre in Winnipeg. Joyce has a Deaf husband, George Margo, and they have four hearing adult children, three girls and one boy—Sharon R. Holme, Sandra J. Bello, Dorothy R. Margo, and David C. Margo. Joyce and George currently make their home in Toronto, Ontario.

As a young girl, Joyce helped her father on the family farm whenever he needed her. In the summer holidays during World War II she drove a team of two horses with a hay rake and, occasionally, a team of six horses with a harrow. She also took turns with her father to drive the tractor to get the grain crops cut before threshing time. She stacked hay, stooked sheaves, shovelled grain, milked cows, and kept bees after she and four other Deaf girls took a short beekeeping course at the University of Saskatchewan in Saskatoon. She now recalls with amusement that she was never permitted to wear slacks or jeans to perform any of these chores.

Joyce was educated at the MacKay School for the Deaf in Montréal for one year before the Saskatchewan School for the Deaf opened in Saskatoon, and she completed her studies there in 1942. She then attended Bible College in Regina, as a special student, from 1942 to 1946, and worked as a volunteer in its office after her class each day, doing typing and mimeographing, which was the forerunner of modern-day photocopying. She also worked temporarily in photography studios in Regina and Toronto before taking a permanent position for two years with Coutts Hallmark in Toronto as an office assistant. She then worked for the Toronto Real Estate Board and was a part-time employee at the Post Office during the Christmas rush. From 1970 to 1987 she was a civil servant with the Ontario Ministry of Consumer and Commercial Relations.

Joyce's volunteer work with organizations and agencies related to Deafness has been extensive and interesting. She has served as both president and secretary of the Women's Association of the Evangelical Church of the Deaf in Toronto and contributed significantly over many years to the group's quilting activities. She worked in the Gift Gallery at the Bob Rumball Centre for the Deaf from 1987 to 1990, and for eight years, during the 1970s, was a provincial director of the Ontario Cultural Society of the Deaf (OCSD). She assisted with a three-day National Cultural Tournament sponsored by the Canadian Cultural Society of the Deaf (CCSD), combined with the 41rst biennial convention of the Ontario Association of the Deaf (OAD), held at the Belleville School for the Deaf in 1974. She participated in the National CCSD Cultural Conference at the Winnipeg Community Centre of the Deaf in 1975, as well as the Third National Cultural Tournament and Defty Awards Night in Vancouver in 1976. She was the Miss Deaf Canada Pageant Director from 1976 to 1978, and served as registrar for the Miss Deaf Canada Talent Pageant later held in Niagara Falls.

Joyce's daughter, Dorothy Margo, worked briefly at the Western Institute of the Deaf in Vancouver, spent two years with Connect Counselling Services of the Canadian Hearing Society in Toronto, and was the first person to work at the Woodfield Supportive Housing Agency for the Deaf and hard of hearing. Since 1994, she has been working in Chicago, Illinois, as a freelance ASL interpreter.

Joyce is well known for her infectious smile, her rhythmic singing in church, and her extensive travels. She loves drama and theatre, and many of her fondest recollections are of the roles she played in dramas produced at the Saskatchewan School for the Deaf in Saskatoon. She once played the lead in *Snow White and the Seven Dwarfs*, for which one of the Deaf teachers, Esther Paulson (Deer), who was talented in art, designed and created all the dwarfs' masks as well as the rest of the costumes. In 1939, wearing a beautiful, borrowed, long blue gown and hand-made tiara, Joyce played the part of Queen Elizabeth (now known as the Queen Mother) with a boy who played her husband, King George VI, re-enacting the royal tour, complete with the Queen's trademark hand-waving, which had passed through Saskatoon earlier that spring. She also participated in other drama productions, and still enjoys Deaf pantomime. Her favourite pastimes are reading and working on crossword puzzles.

MARK (SKINKLE), Rosanne Lily Mary

1966–
Bank Clerk, Classroom Assistant, Miss Deaf Canada Title-Holder, and Proud Mother.

ROSANNE SKINKLE was born Deaf, to Deaf parents, Mary Wilson and Glenn Skinkle, in Belleville, Ontario. She is a third-generation Deaf family member. Other Deaf relatives are her grandmother, Lily Roberts, her grandfather, Fred Gwalter, and her uncle, Freddie Gwalter. Her husband, Scott Mark, is also Deaf, and they have a beautiful daughter, Rexana, who is a fourth-generation Deaf member of Rosanne's family. Rosanne, Scott, and Rexana currently make their home in Belleville, where Rexana will attend Sir James Whitney School for the Deaf when she is old enough. All of Roseanne's family members are alumni of the School for the Deaf in Belleville.

After graduating from Sir James Whitney School in Belleville in 1985, Rosanne attended the Ontario Business College in Kingston. Subsequently, she worked at the Bank of Montréal in Peterborough and Belleville from 1986 until 1998. She then took a position as a classroom assistant at Sir James Whitney School, and is still employed there. She loves working with Deaf children, encouraging them to set goals, strive for success, and to communicate in ASL.

In 1992 Rosanne was chosen Miss Deaf Canada at a pageant held in Vancouver and sponsored by the Canadian Cultural Society of the Deaf (CCSD). She also won the Best Talent Award twice, once in a Miss Deaf Ontario pageant, and once in a Miss Deaf Canada

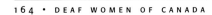

pageant. Her poem, entitled *My Shadow*, is a poignant explanation of how Deaf people feel when they are involved in the hearing world, how they react against injustice, and long for understanding.

Rosanne's involvement in the Deaf Community has been mainly as a fundraiser for different events held at Sir James Whitney School or sponsored by organizations of the Deaf. As a Deaf family, they participate in most events and activities in the Deaf Community.

During her leisure time, Rosanne's favourite hobbies are sewing, painting, and riding horses. She is also an enthusiastic coin collector.

MARTIN, Julie Ann

1964–
Instructor, Workshop Facilitator, ASL Poet, and Storyteller.

JULIE MARTIN was born Deaf in Stevens Point, Wisconsin, US. She now holds dual American–Canadian citizenship but has spent the greater part of her life in Canada. When her family lived in Wisconsin she attended a Deaf preschool program at age three, a Deaf program in a mainstream public school at age five, and the Wisconsin School for the Deaf at age seven. When she was eleven years old, the family moved to Canada and Julie was enrolled at the E.C. Drury School for the Deaf in Milton, Ontario, where she attended until 1982. For the next two years she was in Vancouver, spending one semester at the Jericho Hill School for the Deaf (JHS) and the rest in the JHS Program at Kitsilano Secondary School, until she graduated in 1984. That fall she enrolled at Gallaudet University in Washington, DC, but withdrew in 1987. She eventually earned a BA degree in Sign Communication (renamed American Sign Language) from Gallaudet University in 1994.

Her working career has largely focused on Sign Communication. She has worked as an ASL instructor at St. Clair College of Applied Arts and Technology in Windsor, Ontario, for the Vancouver Public School Board, at Vancouver Community College and for the Deaf Children's Society of BC. She has also been an ASL evaluator and has organized curricula and activities for an ASL program set up for hearing college students. Julie has also participated in and facilitated numerous workshops pertaining to ASL communication and is a qualified interviewer-rater with the Canadian Cultural Society of the Deaf's training.

While attending Gallaudet University, Julie made the Dean's List in 1993 and 1994, but her best known achievements were her ASL poetry performances which were well received and highly commended. During Deaf Literature Week, she was asked by the Deaf Issues Department staff to present her first performance in the spring of 1994. It was the beginning of her career as a performing poet and storyteller in the ASL literature series. Since then Julie has developed new material and has performed solo and as a team with a Deaf partner, John Warren. Together they continue to mesmerize audiences, both Deaf and hearing. Julie feels strongly that it is important to maintain the performing arts in the Deaf Community and to use them to educate the general public about Deaf Culture. With that goal in mind, she and John Warren have teamed up as partners to present ASL literature performances to the public across Canada.

Although she considers herself first and foremost a performing poet and storyteller, Julie has many other interests and hobbies. She enjoys a variety of sports and likes to quilt and attend craft fairs. She also researches ASL linguistics and lexicalized fingerspelling.

Her repertoire of ASL performances includes poetry, skits, personification, and comedy. When she was younger, she had seen the movie, *Brian's Song*, which inspired the development of her special talents and movements with which she entertained her friends in the school dormitory. To date, one of her most memorable presentations is her strobelight-effect "Rubick's Cube" story. The Deaf Community and the hearing public will doubtlessly be seeing more of her in the future. Julie Martin is a talented performer who loves to entertain an audience.

Since 1995 she has been employed as a full-time instructor at Vancouver Community College, where she is responsible for the ASL and lab portion of the ASL and Deaf Studies course, a ten-month full-time study program. Julie is also a long-time member and supporter of the British Columbia Cultural Society of the Deaf, of which she is currently president.

1942–
Proud Former Girl Guide, Skilled Computer Operator, and Dedicated Volunteer in the Deaf Community.

DONNA MAGILL, who has a hearing twin brother, was born Deaf to hearing parents in Saskatoon, Saskatchewan. Her Deaf relatives include a great aunt on her mother's side and a distant cousin in England. She also had a Deaf male relative on her father's side. Donna's husband, David George Mason, a professor at York University in Toronto, is also Deaf. They have three adult hearing children—Sandra, who is a department head of special needs counselling, career and life management, and English as a second language; Peter, who graduated with a BA degree in Sociology in 2001; and Colleen, who is an ASL interpreter in Calgary. Donna and Dave have lived in Edmonton, Alberta, for many years.

Donna was educated at the Saskatchewan School for the Deaf in Saskatoon, later renamed the R.J.D. Williams School for the Deaf. She graduated in 1960 and delivered the valedictory address at the graduation ceremony. Because the school emphasized oralism, she had very little opportunity to learn about Deaf Culture or her Deaf heritage. As a young teenager, however, she regularly met a group of Deaf adults at the Riverdale swimming pool on Wednesday afternoons and they introduced her to the Deaf world. For the next twenty years, she was a housewife, a stay-at-home mother, and a data-entry operator for several corporations, including Imperial Oil, Elan Data Makers, the Alberta government, Medical Services Incorporated, and the City of Edmonton.

In 1982 Donna decided to upgrade her qualifications to include computer competency. For the next dozen years, she took courses for various word-processing systems, orientation, and proofreading, several levels of Word-Perfect certification, and numerous other software-related courses. From 1983 until 1990 she worked as a word-processing operator for Transport Canada. She then transferred to Canada Place where she did word-processing for the Airports Group, as well as for Property and Transition Management. Until her retirement in 1997, Donna transcribed, recorded, revised, and reproduced various types of narrative and tabular material in special formats. She also reformatted text on magnetic diskettes, proofreading to produce high-quality text. In addition, she performed many other duties in the employ of the federal government. Her computer skills in general and her expertise in the field of word processing are very impressive.

Within the community, Donna has always played an important role as a volunteer for many organiza-tions of the Deaf. She was active in the Western Canada Association of the Deaf (WCAD) and at the local level has served the Edmonton Association of the Deaf (EAD) as president, vice-president, and secretary. Locally and internationally, because her husband is a Gallaudet University graduate, she became involved in the Women's Auxiliary of both EAD and the Gallaudet University Alumni Club.

Provincially, she served the Alberta Association of the Deaf (AAD) as treasurer. At the national level, she has been secretary for the Canadian Cultural Society of the Deaf (CCSD). Her very significant contributions have been recognized by both EAD and CCSD with plaques and certificates for outstanding service. She has also been the recipient of other forms of recogni-tion for her dedication and leadership in the Deaf Community, both in Saskatoon and Edmonton.

Years ago she was an aide at the Alberta Hard of Hearing preschool, now the Connect Society, and taught ASL to the parents of Deaf preschoolers for two years. When EAD held fun Sign Language classes for profit, she taught those classes for a period of time. For five months during 1983, when the Universiade Games were held in Edmonton, Donna set up the timetables for the officials and athletes to be picked up and dropped off at various locations. After the Games ended, she typed the manuscript for the book entitled *Proceedings of the FISU Conference—Universiade '83 in Association with the xth HISPA Congress*, for which she received recognition in the Acknowledgements. This was an international publication which was distributed worldwide.

A memorable occasion occurred in the early fifties when Donna, as a Brownie in Saskatoon, carried the flag and led the Brownies, Girl Guides, and their leaders in a parade held in honour of the visit of Queen Elizabeth II and her husband, Prince Philip, the Duke of Edinburgh, during their royal tour of Canada. Being a Girl Guide for ten years during her youth helped Donna become a self-motivated person who works well with others, has respect for others, accepts challenges, and exercises patience and tolerance toward others. Another unforgettable experience took place in April 1996 when Donna shook hands with Hon. Shirley McClellan, Alberta's Minister of Health, after accepting a $50,000 cheque to purchase a van for EAD. In July 1999 she and her husband Dave attended the World Federation of the Deaf Conference in Brisbane, Australia. They have also travelled quite extensively in Canada and the US.

In her leisure hours, Donna enjoys cross-stitching, knitting, and quilting. She reads, travels, swims, and has a special knack for house painting.

McADAM, Elizabeth ("Beth") Marie

1965–
Certified ASL Instructor and Proctor, Literacy Projects Coordinator, and Dedicated Volunteer in the Deaf Community.

BETH McADAM was born Deaf to hearing parents, Mary Claire McAdam and Samuel McAdam, now deceased, in Ottawa, Ontario. She was the eldest of three Deaf sisters. Her siblings are Susan Bedder, who has two daughters, one hard of hearing and one Deaf; and Kerri-Anne Gillespie, who has a Deaf daughter. Beth has three Deaf children—Paul Pierre Bougeois, Samantha (Sammi) Bourgeois, and Bradley (Brad) Bourgeois. All of them are Culturally Deaf and attend the Ontario School for the Deaf (E.C. Drury) in Milton. Beth and her children currently make their home in Toronto.

Beth attended mainstream public schools in Kanata, Ontario, graduating from A.Y. Jackson Secondary School in 1984. She then attended Gallaudet College (now Gallaudet University) in Washington, DC, for one semester, but dropped out due to "culture shock," which is very common among Deaf students who have come though the public school systems and not been exposed to the cultural aspects of a school for the Deaf. She had planned to return to Gallaudet but, instead, married and had three wonderful Deaf children of whom she is justifiably proud.

She received certification for the Canadian Hearing Society's Management Equity Training (MET) courses in 1998, and is currently taking research courses. She is also a certified ASL instructor in Levels I and II, and a certified proctor. Beth worked as administrative assistant for the Canadian Association for the Deaf under the executive director, Jim Roots, in Ottawa, for six months, before accepting a job offer as a literacy instructor for a program called Impact-ASL, located at the Canadian Hearing Society in Toronto. She later became the program coordinator and worked there for ten years before moving to GOLD (Goal: Ontario Literacy for Deaf People), where she serves as projects developer for the Deaf/Deaf-Blind literacy stream.

Beth has served on the board of directors for GOLD, and is currently president of the Ontario Association of the Deaf. She is finding it a very enriching experience to work with its board of directors. She was also the chairperson for Deaf Fest 2001.

In her leisure time, Beth's hobbies and interests include walking her dog, reading, and camping.

McCLELLAND (SODERHOLM), Ritva Paivikki

1948–
Data-Entry Operator, Accounting Clerk, and Civil Servant.

RITVA SODERHOLM was born in Finland and moved to Canada with her family when she was about four years old. Whether she was born Deaf or became Deaf in infancy is unknown. Her family settled in Thunder Bay, Ontario, and Ritva was sent to the Ontario provincial School for the Deaf in Belleville. When she was sixteen, in the summer of 1964, the family moved again, this time to British Columbia, so Ritva finished her education at Jericho Hill School for the Deaf (JHS) in Vancouver. She has no known Deaf relatives, but is married to a Deaf man, Jim McClelland, and they have two hearing daughters. Currently, Ritva and Jim make their home in Port Coquitlam, BC.

After graduating from Jericho Hill, Ritva took a data-entry course and got her first real job with Revenue Canada, as a casual worker during income tax time. Her next employment was with Office Overload, where she was sent on assignments to different companies requiring a data-entry operator. Some of these jobs were interesting and others were boring, but she gained experience and learned different office practices. Her first permanent job was with United Way, then known as the Red Feather Campaign. She greatly enjoyed working there because her duties were varied and the staff members were wonderful. Two years later she was hired by the Medical Services Association, where she worked for two years in data entry.

In 1970 Ritva married her high school sweetheart, Jim McClelland, and they bought a house outside Vancouver. She left her job to become a housewife and full-time mother, their first daughter arriving in 1972 and their second in 1974. She enjoyed this new role and was kept busy taking her girls to swimming lessons, Brownie activities, and social events with other Deaf mothers who had children of similar ages.

When both girls were in school, she started volunteering to work with Deaf children in the area where they lived, and was asked to work at their local school as a substitute teacher-aide. She loved this work, but unfortunately it was only a temporary measure for one year. She did not enjoy her next job in a vegetable warehouse, where she was employed for two years, but it was convenient because she could drop off her girls at school in the morning and pick them up after school. She also had the Christmas and summer vacations off, so she could be at home with her family.

Eventually, Ritva went back to school to learn word-processing and found she enjoyed every minute of it, although she was the only Deaf person in the class and no interpreter was provided. She mostly studied and worked on her own, but liked the challenge. She and Jim and the girls moved to Port Coquitlam, which was closer to Vancouver and for Jim, it eased the stress of long commutes to his job.

When Ritva acquired her word-processing certificate, she worked briefly for the provincial government, but later was hired by the federal government, and remained in that position for twelve years as an accounting clerk. The highlight of her career came in the year 1992–93, when the G–8 Summit was hosted in Vancouver, bringing the presidents of Russia and the United States as well as other world dignitaries together for a meeting. Ritva was assigned to a special project which was exciting and interesting, and earned her a prestigious award and citation from the Deputy Minister of Public Works, Government Services Canada.

She took early retirement in 1998, feeling that twenty years of office work was enough. Nevertheless, she still works part-time, providing support in local group homes, mainly for the Deaf. She and Jim have also undertaken to provide care in their own home for a Deaf person who is cognitively challenged. In addition, Ritva has been involved in the Deaf Community in various capacities for many years. For quite some time, she was secretary for the Greater Vancouver Association of the Deaf (GVAD), and was also a long-time secretary for the Greater Vancouver Curling Club (GVDCC). In 1991, she was chairperson of the Sexual Abuse Prevention Program for the Deaf (SAPPD) when they made the video entitled *Sharing Secrets* in which she played the role of a mother. She found the work demanding, but challenging, and enjoyed every moment, especially the actual videotaping.

When she can find time in her busy life to enjoy leisure activities, Ritva likes to do needlecraft, read, hike, cycle, and travel.

McDERMID (LORENZEN), Mary Ettie

1859–1943
Manitoba's First Deaf Teacher and Wife of Dr. Duncan W. McDermid.

MARY ETTIE LORENZEN was born Deaf to hearing parents, Prussian immigrants Louis and Margaret Lorenzen, near Sarnia, in Lambton County, Ontario. Several attempts were made to reverse her Deafness but none was successful. Hence, she was enrolled at the Ontario Institution for the Education and Instruction of the Deaf and Dumb (now Sir James Whitney School for the Deaf) in Belleville, on 9 February 1871. There she received most of her schooling and was a bright pupil who made excellent progress. She remained at the Institution until 1880, when she was appointed assistant teacher by Dr. D.W. McDermid, a new principal who had been appointed in 1877.

In 1882, Dr. McDermid married Mary, who was considered one of the most efficient and capable teachers in the school. She was also deemed to be the most graceful signer in North America at that time. Duncan W. McDermid, a hearing man of Scottish background, was born and raised in Martintown, Ontario. At the age of twelve he began serving as the Belleville school's visitor's guide, telegraph operator, and clerk. In 1877 he was appointed principal, a position in which he served with distinction for eight years. In 1890 he was appointed superintendent of the Manitoba School for the Deaf (MSD) in Winnipeg, where he served very successfully until his untimely death by drowning in 1909. Mary Ettie and Duncan had two hearing children—a son, Howard, and a daughter, Ruth. It was Howard who replaced his father as superintendent of the Winnipeg school when he died.

When Duncan took up the post of superintendent, Mary Ettie became the school's art teacher, and held that position for the next sixteen years, thus earning the distinction of being the first Deaf person to teach in the province of Manitoba. She and her husband were proponents of a "combined method" of instruction, using both speech and sign. They believed that cognitive development and language acquisition could be best achieved through the manual method, and that speech and speechreading were better left to the students for whom the level of success seemed likely to justify the expenditure of time and effort.

During their tenure at the Manitoba Institution, a number of excellent projects were initiated. One was

the Pharnorth Literary Debating Society which aimed to furnish intellectual stimulation and social entertainment to its members. It included educated people in Winnipeg's Deaf Community and advanced pupils from the school. Another of their initiatives was the publication *The Silent Echo*, an eight-page monthly newspaper.

In 1891 a fire destroyed a portion of the building which housed the school, and the students and staff had to be temporarily relocated to an old, upper-class residence which came to be known as "Bannatyne Castle" because of its ornate structure. Mary Ettie continued teaching at the school until 1906 and was a prominent figure in the Deaf community until her death in 1943. The contributions of the McDermid family to Canada's Deaf history were extensive and significant, especially in Ontario and Manitoba.

McDONALD (BENTLEY), Carol Anne

1947–
Hairdresser, Model, Calendar Girl, Keypunch Operator, ASL Teacher, and Entrepreneur.

CAROL BENTLEY was born in Glenwood, and her Deaf brother, Bradford Starr Bentley, in Brandon, both in southern Manitoba. In 1953, when Bradford was twelve years old and Carol was only five, their parents sent them to Saskatoon to attend the Saskatchewan School for the Deaf. There, they learned to communicate in ASL by observing Deaf adults.

In 1957 Bradford graduated and became a hairdresser in Saskatoon while Carol remained in school until 1963. She enjoyed having a working brother in the city because he would take her out on weekends and look after her. Their mother had often commented on her skills at styling hair, so Carol decided to follow in her brother's footsteps and become a hairdresser. When she took her training there were no interpreters so she had to read lips or ask for written explanations. Fortunately, she was a good lipreader and successfully completed her one-year course at the Scientific Beauty Salon in Winnipeg without much difficulty.

After certification she worked at Mario's Salon in Polo Park for nine years during the late 1960s and early 1970s. During those years she also modelled for Eaton's Department Store. Her photographer once sold a calendar for which she had modelled to the Winnipeg Fire Department and she recalls receiving $25 in payment. She also remembers being dressed as a bunny and modelling nylons for Eaton's in an Easter advertise-

ment that appeared in the *Winnipeg Free Press*. She enjoyed these experiences and learned from them.

In 1973 she left her job as a hairdresser to seek greater challenges in the computer field, enrolling in a ten-week course offering business and data-entry training at Success/Angus College. She then found casual work as a keypunch operator at Manitoba Data Services. Her next position was as a data-entry operator for Air Canada on the night shift, where she remained for two years. She viewed it as a nice experience and appreciated the free travel pass to Las Vegas. In addition to these jobs, she also did casual work in data entry and held a clerical position at Revenue Canada Taxation Centre for nine years.

Currently, Carol operates a cleaning business for homes and offices which allows her to enjoy her independence. She also teaches ASL classes at Red River Community College and St. Boniface Collegiate. She has taught basic level ASL to staff members at Great West Life Insurance and an intensive one-week summer course at the Manitoba School for the Deaf.

Carol has one hearing son, Robbie, who is a lawyer and of whom she is justifiably proud. Her hobbies are plants, pets, cooking, exercising, and surfing the Internet.

McDONALD, Heather Anne

1966–
Avid Sportswoman, Community Support Worker, Sign Language Instructor, and Deaf Youth Researcher.

HEATHER McDONALD was born Deaf into a hearing family at Port Alberni, on Vancouver Island, BC. Her Deafness was not diagnosed until she was about six months old, and the cause remains unknown. Heather had two hearing brothers, one of whom is now deceased, and a hearing sister, but she has no known Deaf relatives. She currently makes her home in Victoria, BC.

In the early 1970s, when Heather's Deafness was dis-covered, her parents, along with other parents of Deaf children founded the Alberni-Clayoquot Association for the Hearing Handicapped. The group wrote many proposals to establish a special class for Deaf and hard-of-hearing children, to provide them with hearing aids, and to hire a teacher to educate them. This organization eventually disbanded because the students were transferred to the Jericho Hill School for the Deaf in Vancouver.

The John Tracey Clinic in California sent monthly lesson packages to help Heather's parents train her. When she was six years old, they enrolled her in a mainstream public school in Port Alberni, where she remained until she was twelve. Heather was then transferred to Jericho Hill School for the Deaf (JHS) in 1978, and received her first introduction to ASL. Heather remembers how shocked she was to learn that Deaf people could actually have professional careers and participate in competitive sports and athletics, just like their hearing peers.

During her final year at JHS, she was selected to play basketball for Team Canada at the World Summer Games for the Deaf in Los Angeles. All players were required to raise the necessary funds to attend. The JHS athletes called the *Vancouver Sun* and, as a result of an article and photographs in that newspaper, they were able to acquire the funding to attend the Games. Her experience in Los Angeles was almost overwhelming when she met so many other athletes from around the world, all using different Sign Languages. However, they soon began to communicate with one another, and she became aware that Deaf people faced the same barriers in every country of the world due to lack of understanding on the part of the hearing population.

After graduating from JHS, and taking an eighteen-month course in computer programming at the Vancouver Vocational Institute, Heather worked for an insurance company. After a while, she decided she needed a break, so she applied for a year's leave of absence and it was granted. She flew to Australia and her travels soon taught her that she was in the wrong career. Her strength lay in working with people, rather than machines and technology. When she returned to Canada, she began volunteering in various capacities in order to get Deaf young people to socialize, make new friends, and share their experiences and dreams.

She also volunteered to serve as workshop coordina-tor for an event called "Silent Weekend," sponsored by the Island Deaf and Hard of Hearing Centre, which was held at Thetis Island near Chemainus, on Vancouver Island. This turned out to be a wonderfully successful occasion, where 141 Deaf and hard-of-hearing campers gathered with their parents, children, and siblings. Mainly, they discussed the frustrations of centuries of Deaf history in which hearing professionals had advised and advocated for the Deaf, without having an appropriate understanding of the realities of Deafness. The presentations were excellent and the discussions were stimulating and rewarding.

Heather took a ten-month training course at Camosun College in Victoria, BC, to become a com-munity support worker, and has worked in that capac-ity in Nanaimo, Coombs, Vancouver, Surrey, and Victoria, providing guidance, developing skills, and offering support to numerous families and individuals. She has also taught ASL and worked as a youth researcher. Heather is currently employed as a support worker with the Capital Regional District, Mental Health Department, in Victoria. She has served on the "Silent Weekend" camp committee for more than four years, was co-facilitator for the "Sign It Up For Fun" work-shops, and has been sports director for the British Columbia Deaf Sports Association for seven years.

Heather is a strong, independent woman who is easy-going but determined and goal oriented; a self-starter who copes with stress by drawing, reading novels, and walking for miles along the beach. She is also an enthusiastic camper and hiker. Above all, she is a splendid role model for other young Deaf women, locally and nationally.

McINTYRE, Lois Arlene

1959–
Coach, Athlete, Rehabilitation Counsellor, and Traveller.

LOIS MCINTYRE, who currently makes her home in Ottawa, Ontario, received her early education in Moose Jaw, Saskatchewan, Winnipeg, Manitoba, and Belleville, Ontario. She then attended Gallaudet University in Washington, DC, where she completed a BA degree in Elementary Education and a Master's degree in Rehabilitation Counselling.

Tennis has long been an important part of Lois' life. While at Gallaudet, she played on the Varsity Tennis Team for four years, two of them as co-captain, and received the Most Dedicated Player and Most Valuable Player Awards. She was also assistant coach for some time, and was given an award for her dedication. Since 1984, she has been an active member of the Canadian Deaf Sports Association, competing as a tennis player in two World Games of the Deaf, in Los Angeles, California in 1985 and in Christchurch, New Zealand in 1990. In 1986 she received an Achievement Award from the City of Belleville for her accomplishments in tennis which included participation in many tournaments both locally and abroad. Lois is still an active tennis player and also enjoys playing squash and curling.

As a member of the Ottawa Deaf Curling Club, she won a silver medal in a mixed bonspiel in Saint John's, New Brunswick in 2000, as well as two earlier Deaf Sportsmanship Awards from her home club in Ottawa. For five years she was sports director for the Ottawa Deaf Sports Club.

The year 2000 was an exciting one for Lois. Besides winning the Silver Curling Medal, she completed a 150-kilometre MS Bike Tour, won first place in the Master's Singles in the International Open Tennis Championships in Basel, Switzerland, played squash, and took a cardio-kickboxing fitness class just for fun.

She has travelled extensively in Canada and the US and has visited New Zealand, France, The Netherlands, Monaco, and Northern Italy. For pleasure, other than her involvement in sports, Lois enjoys working in her darkroom, developing black and white photographs. For relaxation, she reads mystery and adventure books.

She is employed as a counsellor with the Canadian Hearing Society and for many years has been a dedicated advocate for the Deaf, promoting equality, accessibility and inclusion. She often lectures to staff at the many service agencies in the Ottawa area on issues related to Deafness, and has been teaching ASL classes for a number of years. Within the Deaf Community, she was the founder of Ottawa Mayfest and, as its chairperson for four years, raised $17,000 in funding. She also participated in developing videos on the subjects of family violence and self-esteem for Deaf viewers and personally attended the Supreme Court hearing that resulted in the landmark victory in the famous *Eldridge* case on 9 October 1997.

Lois is proud of the fact that her father was instrumental in creating job opportunities for Deaf keypunch operators in Belleville during the early 1970s. At present, however, her greatest excitement deservedly stems from her being chosen as the tennis coordinator/coach for the Canadian Deaf Sports Association which enabled her to coach two young men for the 2001 Summer World Games of the Deaf in Rome, Italy. She was also chosen to be on the Accessible Advisory Council for the city of Ottawa for a three-year term ending in 2004.

McKERCHER, Anne Elizabeth

1942-
Educator, Counsellor, and "Deaf History" Buff.

ANNE MCKERCHER was born Deaf in Petrolia, Ontario, and now resides in Toronto. She has one Deaf daughter, Nicole Andrea.

Anne attended the Ontario School for the Deaf in Belleville from 1953 to 1967. She then went to Washington, DC, where she attended Gallaudet College until 1972, earning a Bachelor of Arts degree. When Anne returned to Ontario, she worked for two and a half years as a counsellor at Huronia Regional Centre for the Mentally Challenged in Orillia. She later entered the Teacher Training Program at Belleville so she could commence her teaching career. In 1981, she also completed her Master's degree in Education at Western Maryland College.

Anne's professional career spanned nearly three decades, beginning with her work as a counsellor and later as a certified teacher. She taught for almost four years at Sir James Whitney School in Belleville before transferring to E.C. Drury School in Milton, where she taught for twenty years.

Although Anne has no Deaf relatives other than her daughter, she does claim kinship to the famous Scottish missionary and explorer Dr. David Livingstone, who explored Africa and devoted his life to ending the slave trade there. According to the research literature, he was Anne's great-great-uncle.

In her leisure hours, Anne loves researching Deaf history, particularly the bygone days of Deaf Communities in Ontario. Her major hobby is collecting Deaf memorabilia, a pastime to which she fondly refers as "Deaf mania."

Anne has contributed significantly to the lives of those who passed through the Deaf education systems at the Milton and Belleville schools during her teaching career. She recently received an award for working with the provincial schools for twenty-five years, a laudable achievement. She is currently teaching at Metro Toronto School for the Deaf where she is happy with her life and her work.

McLAUGHLIN, Linda Teresa

1952–
Educator and Advocate of Bilingual/Bicultural Education and Intervention for Deaf and Special Needs Infants.

LINDA MCLAUGHLIN was born Deaf to hearing parents in North Vancouver, British Columbia. She has two Deaf brothers, Joe and Ron McLaughlin, as well as seven hearing siblings. Joe, who was the first Canadian Deaf principal of the twentieth century at the Alberta School for the Deaf during the late 1980s and early 1990s, is now a vice-principal at the South Slope Elementary School/British Columbia School for the Deaf. Ron is working as an accountant for an Internet company, and has incorporated several start-up companies in San Clemente, California. Linda is married to Harvey Bradley, and they have three children, Harvey Jr., who is Deaf, Carmela, and Amy. They currently reside in Merced, California.

Linda was educated at Jericho Hill School for the Deaf in Vancouver, BC, but attended several mainstream public schools as well—Trafalgar, Cecil Rhodes, Dawson, and King George Secondary. She studied at Gallaudet College (now Gallaudet University) in Washington, DC, graduating with a Bachelor of Science degree in Physical Education in 1976. She obtained a certificate for teaching the Deaf from Sir James Whitney School for the Deaf in Belleville, Ontario in 1977. Linda then went on to acquire a Master of Education degree specializing in Deaf Education from Western Maryland College in Westminster, Maryland. She also earned a credential as a specialist in Special Education from the University of Toronto.

From 1977 to 1988, Linda was an elementary school teacher and coach at the E.C. Drury School for the Deaf in Milton, Ontario. In 1988, she switched from classroom teaching to home visiting, and acquired a job as a preschool educator at the Resource Centre of the E.C. Drury School, which she held for the following decade. Her goal was to provide in-home learning experiences, early exposure to ASL and Deaf Culture, and to bring parents of Deaf preschoolers together for playgroups, field trips, and Deaf Community events. Learning through play and two-way communication was her philosophy for developing a child's early language, emotional, and social experiences. During that period of time, she also taught at the Smithson School in Kitchener, Ontario, working with five preschoolers and conducting home visits with their parents on Fridays. The following year, she volunteered for the Parent-Infant Program at the Learning Center for Deaf Children in Framingham, Massachusetts. Since then she has worked for the Parent/Infant Program/Early Intervention Agency with Deaf preschoolers as well as their parents and siblings. She introduces ideas for parent/infant interaction, storytelling and playgroups. In addition, she has been a part-time teacher at the Horace Mann School for the Deaf in Boston, Massachusetts, with duties ranging from preschool through high school, including working with parents and siblings.

Apart from her job, Linda has many other achievements to her credit. She has attended numerous conferences related to Deafness and wrote a well-received article for the *Bicultural Centre Newsletter* entitled "Time to Change: Open Doors for Deaf Teachers to Teach Deaf Infants." She has always been a prominent member of the Deaf Community, holding memberships in many organizations and agencies of the Deaf. In 1977 she participated in the 13th World Games for the Deaf held in Romania, and was involved in the Ontario Deaf Sports Association for many years. In 1988 she was inducted into the Athletic Hall of Fame at Gallaudet University.

Linda's greatest interest has always been in children and young women. She loves to entertain Deaf children with rich cultural and language stimulation while their parents attend ASL classes or workshops. She collects the drawings of very young children and incorporates them into quilts. She also brings both Deaf and hearing parents of Deaf youngsters into Deaf Community events to help them absorb Deaf Culture.

In her leisure hours, she enjoys swimming, walking, and doing various types of crafts. Linda is an excellent role model and inspiration for younger Deaf women, both in Canada and the United States.

McNAMARA, Mary Jane Anne

1954–
Survivor, Counsellor, and Resilient Role Model.

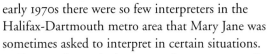

MARY JANE MCNAMARA was born with normal hearing in Halifax, Nova Scotia. At the age of three she lost some degree of her hearing due to scarlet fever, and was fitted with a hearing aid. She was given speech therapy and by age nine had mastered all speech sounds including the difficult sibilants and fricatives. At five, she began attending public school, but was transferred to the Convent of Sacred Heart where the teachers were nuns who wore traditional habits. Because the shape and size of their wimples prevented Mary Jane from seeing their faces in profile, she had difficulty speechreading what they said. It is quite understandable how this would lead to frustration and rebelliousness on the part of a student with a significant hearing loss. Mary Jane was also required to take French and music (singing), which led to further resentment and a feeling of failure.

At age nine she was finally sent to the Interprovincial School for the Deaf at Amherst, Nova Scotia. This was her first introduction to ASL and Deaf Culture. It was also a painful period of her life where she suffered physical abuse until her parents came to her rescue. She was then sent to a mainstream public school in Halifax until she reached grade eleven. Without an interpreter, however, she felt her needs were not being adequately met, so she dropped out of school. Her hearing continued to deteriorate and by age thirty, she had to wear bilateral hearing aids. In the early 1970s there were so few interpreters in the Halifax-Dartmouth metro area that Mary Jane was sometimes asked to interpret in certain situations.

In 1977 she worked as an employment counsellor for Silent Outreach, which was sponsored by the Halifax Association of the Deaf (HAD). While there, she was able to convince HELPLINE (a twenty-four-hour crisis line) to set up a message relay system, which was the only such service available in the Halifax–Dartmouth metro area, around the clock until 1978, when the Interpreter Service for the Deaf, now part of the Society of Deaf and Hard of Hearing Nova Scotians (SDHHNS) gradually took over the system during office hours. HELPLINE continued after-hours until 1991, when Maritime Tel and Tel (MTT) took over the Relay Service.

In 1976 Mary Jane married a hearing African Canadian man and they had a hearing daughter,

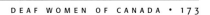

Natalie Anne. Although the marriage ended in divorce, Mary Jane has always made certain Natalie Anne is aware of her black heritage and identity. Later, Mary Jane started living with a Deaf partner with whom she had a hearing daughter, Julie. Natalie Anne and Julie grew up using Sign Language and have taken ASL courses to refine their first language, which was ASL. Entering the Deaf world brought many new experiences into Mary Jane's life, especially when she realized it is not a silent world at all, but quite a noisy one for people who can hear. Her relationship with Julie's father eventually ended, and Mary Jane decided to go back to school where she aquired her Nova Scotia Academic Upgrading Certificate in 1994, and learned to use an ASL interpreter in class.

The year 1989 was a period of major crisis for Mary Jane. Her hearing continued to decline alarmingly and she also came to the realization that she had to do something about her serious drug and alcohol addictions, which had been perpetuated by years of stress and abuse. In 1992 she spent forty-four days in rehabilitation at the Minnesota Chemical Dependency Program for the Hearing Impaired in the United States. All staff members were fluent in ASL and very knowledgeable about Deaf issues. Mary Jane now views herself as a "survivor," a term commonly used in reference to recovered female victims of abuse and addiction.

Mary Jane's involvement in the Deaf Community includes serving as president of the Halifax Association of the Deaf for two years, and as vice-president of the Deafness Advocacy Association Nova Scotia (DAANS). Through attendance at educational workshops, she has acquired certification to counsel, teach life skills, and act as a job coach to others. She considers herself a Deaf oralist, feeling comfortable in both the Deaf and the hearing world. Today, she continues to juggle her work as a presenter to groups, agencies, and employers with her part-time jobs as a photo lab technician, ASL instructor, and tutor to several Deaf preschoolers.

In her spare time, Mary Jane likes to read, cycle, walk by the ocean, practice photography, and cultivate houseplants, for which she has a green thumb. Natalie Anne and Julie have given their mother unconditional love and support throughout the difficult periods in her life, for which she is grateful. She also takes strength and courage from the Serenity Prayer. In November 2001 she received a cochlear implant.

McNICOLL, Helen

1879–1915
Famous Canadian Impressionist Painter.

HELEN MCNICOLL was born hearing into a hearing family in Toronto. She was the eldest of eight children, some of whom were later to show a talent for drawing. Helen, although she became Deaf at an early age due to scarlet fever, exhibited the most promise. Her father, David McNicoll, became the first vice-president of the Canadian Pacific Railway (CPR) in 1903, so the family moved from Toronto to Montréal where the CPR had its headquarters at that time. It was in Montréal that Helen received her first academic art training at the Art Association. Although she was privately tutored, it appears that she managed to have some contact with the city's Deaf Community.

She later studied oil painting under William Brymner, a well-known Canadian painter of the human figure who had studied in Paris. Like most other Canadian artists of great renown, Helen McNicoll supplemented her initial training with study abroad: in her case, at the Slade School of Art in London, followed by a course of instruction at St.Ives in Cornwall, where she directed her attention to the aims of impressionism, particularly the study of light and atmosphere. She became a close friend of Dorothea Sharp, a member of the Royal Society of British Artists and vice-president of the Society of Women Artists. The two women painted together in Yorkshire, Paris, and London. In 1914 Helen was elected as an Associate of the Royal Canadian Academy.

Helen's paintings largely interpreted sunlight and atmospheric effects, which is evident in the titles she chose, such as "Street in Sunlight," "A Sunny Morning," "Sunny September," "The Sunny Vista," and "Sunshine." In many ways, her career as a Canadian painter paralleled that of A.Y. Jackson, one of the famous Group of Seven who had also been tutored by William Brymner before studying in France and England. The Toronto Art Gallery lists Helen McNicoll as one of a group of "notable and deceased Canadian painters," among them the world-class artists Cornelius Krieghoff and Tom Thomson, indicating her stature in the artistic community.

Unfortunately, Helen's career was cut short by her death from diabetic complications, in Swannage, England, in 1915, when she was only thirty-six years old. By 1925 she had been recognized widely through a memorial exhibition of her work, but from 1926 until 1970 she was almost forgotten. Recent exhibitions of Helen's paintings have renewed interest in her as an outstanding Canadian Impressionist. Having spent so many years in England, she painted intimate glimpses of everyday life during the Victorian and Edwardian era, most often depicting women and children. Today she is considered one of Canada's most accomplished women painters, on par with such notables as Sophie Pemberton, Laura Muntz, and Emily Carr.

In 1908 she was awarded the first Jessie Dow Prize by the Art Association of Montréal and in 1914 received the Women's Art Society Prize, acclaiming her work as "a triumphant study in reflected light: pure painting." The eighty-page book *Helen McNicoll: A Canadian Impressionist*, by Natalie Luckyj (1999, Toronto Art Gallery of Ontario), contains reprints of her work and the story of her life. The most recent exhibit of Helen's paintings was shown at the Dundas Street Art Gallery of Ontario in late 1999 and early 2000. Many of her works are part of various private collections across Canada and the United States.

McNUTT, Wendy Dawn

1974–
Website Builder, World Traveller, and Multilinguist.

WENDY McNUTT was born Deaf into a hearing family in Truro, Nova Scotia. She has an older Deaf cousin but no other known Deaf relatives. She currently makes her home in Montréal, Québec.

Wendy attended the Interprovincial School for the Deaf in Amherst for eight years before transferring to a public school with an ASL interpreter in Dartmouth. The family then moved to Danforth, Ontario, where she again attended a public school, also with an interpreter. Finally, she was transferred to the School for the Deaf in Milton, Ontario, where her academic skills improved because all the teachers were fluent in ASL. When Wendy was sixteen it was discovered that she was dyslexic, a condition she inherited from her father's side of the family. She then had a private tutor to help her overcome this learning disability and improve her English skills.

In 1992 Wendy and a hearing friend spent three sum-mer months visiting eight different countries in Europe. Then, in 1994, she was chosen, along with ninety-three other students from across Canada, as a Rotary Exchange Student to spend a year in Argentina. She was the only Deaf person among them. It was a memorable experi-ence because she learned the Spanish language and cul-ture and met some Deaf friends who taught her Spanish Sign Language. She graduated in 1995 and in 1997 was accepted into Saint Mary's University in Halifax, trans-ferring to Dalhousie University in 1998. Although she did not stay to complete a degree, Wendy is the only member of her family who has ever attended university.

As part of the Canadian Society of the Deaf's Youth Internship International Program (YIIP), she worked in Venezuela for six months assisting Deaf adults to improve access and services for their community. Her team worker was Nancy Landreville, a Deaf French woman from Montréal, with whom she formed a lasting friendship. Nancy comes from a strong Deaf background and through her friendship, Wendy soon began to have greater respect for the Deaf world. While they were in Caracas a historic mudslide occurred that worried their parents, but Wendy and Nancy were safe.

On returning to Canada, Wendy decided to move to Montréal and learn Langue Signes de Québécois (LSQ). Being multilingual meant that her signs were sometimes a combination of ASL (American), MSL (Maritime), FSL (French), Spanish Sign Language, and LSQ. She joined the workforce with her first real job when she took employment with an Internet company which maintains a website analyzing worldwide import and export tariffs for Canada Customs. Nearly one hundred countries make use of this service.

Wendy's life is never boring. She enjoys playing ice hockey and baseball, appreciates the visual arts and loves travelling, particularly to learn about society's various subcultures. She is keenly interested in both the Deaf and hearing worlds because she is the only Deaf person in her family and is often the only Deaf person in social groups. Wendy believes that risk-taking strengthens her confidence. Her plan for the near future is to travel around the world exploring different Deaf communities, especially those in Third World countries, and perhaps to write a book that encourages other young Deaf people to take risks and follow their dreams.

1915–1997
Federal Civil Servant, ASL Instructor, and Influential Leader of the Deaf.

ELEANOR MORRISON was born Deaf to hearing parents in Vancouver, British Columbia. She had a Deaf brother, Jack Morrison, to whom she was very close, and her husband, Clarence McPeake, was hard of hearing. At the time of her death Eleanor was living in Ottawa, Ontario, and was very much involved in the Deaf Community there. Jack was living in Toronto and was active in the Ontario Association of the Deaf and the Bob Rumball Centre for the Deaf. Eleanor's work was mainly political in nature, while Jack did most of his work through the church. They frequently visited one another. Sadly, they both died within a week of each other in June 1997.

Eleanor's parents both died tragically when she was twelve years old. She and her brother Jack attended the same schools for the Deaf and formed a deep bond with each other. Their Aunt Hilda and Uncle Sam took them in and cared for them, and they had a close relationship with them. Eleanor and Jack were both in good health and very active in organizations and agencies of the Deaf, until Jack was diagnosed with cancer in 1996. At eighty-two years of age, Eleanor suffered a heart attack and was hospitalized. She was recovering well when she suffered a stroke and two weeks later simply passed away in her sleep when her heart stopped beating. Just before her death, Jack's health worsened and he entered a hospital in Toronto. About a week after Eleanor's death, Jack, too, passed away.

Eleanor McPeake was quiet and unobtrusive as she went about her work in the community. She never sought the limelight, nor did she want anyone to focus any attention on her good works. It was typical of her to think she was not deserving of any honours, even though she was involved in Deaf leadership at every level—national, provincial, local, and personal. Despite her modest character, she was the recipient of the Ontario Community Service Award from the Ontario Department of Community Services as well as a number of other awards and recognition for her contributions.

She was president of the Canadian Association of the Deaf (CAD) for four years and served on its board of directors for nearly twenty years. After leaving the board she continued to serve that organization as a representative from the National Capital Association of the Deaf (NCAD), an organization in which she held numerous offices. She was also very active in the Ontario Association of the Deaf (OAD), as well as the Capital Region Centre for the Hearing Impaired (CRCHI). In addition, she served on the Advisory Board for Bell Relay Service for a number of years, and was a director of the Canadian Hearing Society, as well as the Total Communication Environment movement.

During her working years she was employed as a federal civil servant with Labour Canada, where she remained until her retirement. She taught ASL in five different federal government departments for eleven years and carried this crusade into several public schools and social agencies as well.

It would be a mistake to remember Eleanor only for her work with the many agencies and organizations she served. Her greatest strength lay in her work with people. She was famous for bringing Deaf newcomers gently into the Deaf Community, and was adopted into many Deaf families as an honorary, but real family member.

Eleanor was an enthusiastic world traveller who visited China, Japan, Europe, Hawaii, and the United Kingdom, as well as all the provinces and territories in Canada, often for Deaf causes, but also because she enjoyed seeing new places and experiencing new people. She was always full of stories and snapshots when she returned from these faraway places, and has left her family a rich legacy in the form of souvenir albums dating back to her twenties.

When she passed away a memorial service was arranged as a tribute to her, and was held at the Capital Region Centre for the Hearing Impaired. The room was packed from wall to wall with people who knew and appreciated her importance to the community. The crowd included every generation, from infants to seniors, representing hearing people, Deaf people, and the hard-of-hearing community. She will always be remembered for the countless lives she touched and made better.

MIHALIK (BUCKLER), Barbara Ann Mary

1949–2000
Wife of Twenty-Seven Years, Mother of Three, Sister, Friend, and Inspiration to All Who Knew Her.

BARBARA BUCKLER was born hearing to hearing parents in Montréal, Québec. The exact age when she became Deaf is uncertain, but it was likely when she was two or three years old, as a result of a severe case of whooping cough. She was raised by a foster family from before the age of four. After a lengthy search for her family roots, Barbara was able to contact some members of her extended family. There is no apparent history of Deafness among them, but it is impossible to know for certain. Her husband, Peter Mihalik, was Deaf from birth, but their three children—Jamie William, Teresa Ann Mary, and Jason Peter—all have normal hearing. They have always made their home in Montréal.

Barbara received both her elementary and secondary education at the MacKay Centre for the Deaf in Montréal and followed it up with business office training and computer courses. She was employed by Canada Post as an office clerk, and from 1997 to 2000 worked in the offices of Sun Life of Canada. She was very actively involved in Montréal's Deaf Community and was a member of the Montréal Association of the Deaf for more than twenty years. As social director, she served on countless committees to organize activities, fundraisers, and social events, and was well suited for the job. She was respected and admired in the Deaf Community and possessed great charm and charisma. Always gregarious, she loved being around people in a social environment.

In September of 1995 Barbara was diagnosed with a very advanced stage of breast cancer. Her tumour had already metastasized to some of her bones, making simple daily activities difficult and painful. At her doctor's suggestion she agreed to a radical, experimental breast cancer treatment at the Royal Victoria Hospital in downtown Montréal. It was her best hope for remission of the disease and began with six months of intensive chemotherapy, including monthly stem cell transplants and two bone marrow transplants. This meant she had to be hospitalized for three weeks each month during the first year. The final stage involved intensive radiation daily to the sites affected by the malignancy.

When Barbara arrived at the hospital to begin the treatment the nurses had prepared for her by borrowing flash cards from the MacKay Centre and setting up a large marker board so they could write to her. Before long they realized all their preparation had been unnecessary because Barbara possessed the uncanny ability of communicating through facial expression, body language, and simplified signs. She then taught the nurses some basic signs and reminded them to speak slowly, clearly, and distinctly so that she could speechread effectively. Whenever doctors or nurses spoke to her through their face masks, she would reach up and pull the masks off their faces. Her indefatigable spirit and ability to put everyone at ease made her popular throughout the oncology ward and, often, she was sent to depressed cancer patients to give them a morale booster. She instilled in them the belief that living for today was a small victory that would give them the strength to live for tomorrow.

Barbara fought valiantly for her life, kept a positive outlook, and never lost her infectious smile. Thirteen months later she went into partial remission. Her hair grew back, she regained physical strength, and she resumed a normal life, returning part-time to her office job. Fifteen months later the cancer returned more aggressive than ever and metastasized to her spine. She continued to fight with every ounce of energy she possessed, but eighteen months later she sadly passed away in the presence of her loving and devoted family. Her lifespan, from 24 November 1949 to 22 April 2000, totalled less than fifty-one years.

Barbara's story is not fiction, but sober reality. She was one of the statistical "one in seven" Canadian women affected by breast cancer. She was also a woman who remained optimistic no matter what life threw in her direction. Through her pain and suffering she made everyone around her understand that life is precious and every second should be embraced. She embodied all the strengths most people could only hope for when faced with such adversity.

Her trademark was a happy face. She drew them everywhere—on her children's lunch bags, on her doctor's medical notes, in the margins of her recipe books, and in her personal journal. For Barbara, they represented the key to facing life's obstacles—a happy smile, with courage and determination. She will remain an inspiration to all who knew her and her brave smile will never be forgotten.

MITCHELL (EDWARDS), Ellen Marion

1906–
Seamstress and Skilled Craftswoman, Lady's Companion, and Beloved Elder in the Deaf Community.

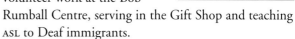

ELLEN EDWARDS was born hearing into a hearing family in Montréal, Québec, in 1906. She became Deaf at the age of four, due to illness, and has no known Deaf relatives on her side of the family. Now in her mid-nineties, Ellen has been married and widowed twice. Both husbands, Carl Mergler and Andrew Mitchell, were Deaf. Carl Mergler was a highly respected and well-loved lay preacher in the Deaf Community during the 1940s and lectured on Christianity locally and in Ottawa. Ellen and Carl had two daughters, Ellen Junior (now deceased) and Janet McConnell. She also has grandchildren and great-grandchildren who adore her. At present, Ellen makes her home at the Bob Rumball Centre for the Deaf in Toronto, Ontario.

Although she was born in Montréal, Ellen spent the first eleven years of her life in New York city in the United States. The family moved back to Montréal and, in her senior years, Ellen moved to Toronto. She received her education at the MacKay Institute for the Deaf (now the MacKay Centre) in Montréal. Her first husband, Carl Mergler, had a hearing brother, J.K Mergler, and a nephew, Bernard Mergler, who were both prominent lawyers in Montréal. Ellen and Carl's two daughters both worked in the Deaf Community. Janet was a teacher of the Deaf at the MacKay Centre and an interpreter for mainstreamed Deaf students. Two of her grandchildren also work as teachers of the Deaf.

After Carl's death Ellen worked for some years as a seamstress for Harley Baby Clothes and later became a

lady's companion to Miss May Cunningham, a former Deaf teacher at the MacKay Institute who had retired and was living in Oakville, Ontario. In more recent years, Ellen did volunteer work at the Bob Rumball Centre, serving in the Gift Shop and teaching ASL to Deaf immigrants.

Ellen has been recognized in various ways for her many contributions to her community. Perhaps the most significant tribute appeared in the *Toronto Star*, lauding her for her handicrafts as well as her wonderful family—two daughters, seven grandchildren, and fourteen great grandchildren. One of her granddaughters, Glenna Lea McConnell, who is a teacher of the Deaf and a folk-singer, recently completed a CD which she dedicated to her grandmother. She has also written a song entitled, *Beauty and Grace*. Glenna's CD is also on CD–ROM and includes the story of Ellen's life, as told in ASL by her daughter Janet at Ellen's ninety-fifth birthday celebration.

Because of her great age and her popularity in the Deaf Community, many gatherings have been held in Ellen's honour. Her mind is still sharp but, sadly, her vision is failing, which makes conversation with her more difficult. This remarkable woman remains cheerful and optimistic, an incredible role model for all Deaf women in Canada.

MONAHAN (WALLIS), Leah Jane

1948–
Administrative Assistant, Data-Entry Operator, and Public Affairs Assignment Contractor.

LEAH WALLIS was born hearing into a hearing family at Westlock, Alberta. She became Deaf at the age of two months due to illness. She was an only child who was raised by her grandparents, and has no known Deaf relatives. She is married to a Deaf man, Wayne Monahan, who has been a truck driver for well over twenty years. Since 1999 he has operated his own trucking business, Freightliner, and drives from coast to coast in Canada. Leah and Wayne have two adult hearing sons, Bob and Jason. They make their home in Edmonton, Alberta.

Although none of Leah's relatives has ever worked with the Deaf, she does have hearing family members

who have made notable contributions to their communities. Her grandfather, Reginald Wallis, was appointed a special constable for the Game Enforcement Branch of the RCMP in Fort Assiniboine, Alberta. Her grandmother, Rebecca Wallis, performed the duties of a local midwife and also often assisted at the deaths of members of pioneer families. This usually involved duties that are performed at funeral homes today. Many babies were born in the Wallis home, attended by Leah's grandmother and Nurse Hyde, and some of them still reside in the Fort Assiniboine area today. Minor court cases were also held in the Wallis home, with all the necessary dignitaries in attendance.

Leah was educated at the MacKay School for the Deaf in Montréal from 1952 to 1955. She then transferred to the newly opened Alberta School for the Deaf (ASD) in Edmonton, where she remained from 1955 to 1966. She took computer courses at Alberta Vocational College (AVC), now renamed Norquest College, attended an extensive eight-week hands-on training course in computer technology at the Office of the Future Training School, and studied business administration and accounting at Alberta College.

Leah's employment experience has been varied. She has mainly worked as a data-entry operator, but has also done general office work, and even worked in a hospital laundry in Lethbridge for a while. In Edmonton she was a clerk-typist for Supplies and Services and in Calgary was employed with Shell Canada, the Provincial Traffic Court, the Canada Immigration Centre, and United Parcel Services (UPS). She left UPS in 1998 and received an Achievement Award from the company in 1999 for her steadiness, regular attendance, and dedication to her job. She has been an asset to all her employers, and while she was with Shell Canada, undertook its public affairs assignments on a contractual basis. She obtained her class V driver's licence, and has always owned her own vehicle, a useful plus for some of her jobs.

While living in Calgary Leah held various positions in organizations of the Deaf and was an active member of the Deaf Community. She is now contented to stay at home more, and to spend time on her own interests and hobbies.

In her spare time Leah enjoys working at various crafts, especially those involving embroidery, crocheting, and knitting. She also likes to do puzzles. Whenever possible she loves to ride in the big truck with her husband, and they both enjoy camping, hiking, and travelling. She is contented and happy in her present employment as a housekeeper at the Airway Motel in Nisku, near the Edmonton International Airport, where her son Bob supervises the housekeepers.

MONCRIEFFE, Dawn Marie

1968–
Athletic Role Model and World-Class Runner.

DAWN MONCRIEFFE was born Deaf as a result of maternal rubella in North Lambeth, England. Her family emigrated to Canada and she grew up in Winnipeg, Manitoba, where she attended the Manitoba School for the Deaf after a short stint at Mulvey Public School. She has no known Deaf relatives and currently makes her home in London, England.

From a very early age Dawn showed promise as an outstanding runner. This put her in continuous contact and gave her ongoing experience with different coaches and groups of runners, as well as individual world-class competitors. In fact, while attending the Manitoba School for the Deaf, she showed such enormous potential that her physical education teacher, Larry Stuart, referred her to Wayne Goulet, the president of the Manitoba Deaf Sports Association, when she was only thirteen. Wayne wasted no time in getting her into a proper track club so she could begin serious training.

Filled with vigour and enthusiasm, Dawn rapidly developed her outstanding skills, despite communication problems with her hearing coach. Wayne Goulet continued to offer Dawn advice and support in order to boost her self-confidence among the hearing peers with whom she competed in inter-city and inter-provincial meets. Finally, in 1985, at age seventeen, she qualified for the World Games for the Deaf in Los Angeles, California, where she came in fourth in the 800-metre event. It was her first experience as a runner at the international level.

In 1987 Wayne Goulet left Winnipeg to pursue his own career goals. This left Dawn in a somewhat rudderless state, without the stability of his support and encouragement. She decided not to participate in the World Games for the Deaf in New Zealand in 1989. Instead, she opted to upgrade her education, and moved to Toronto. There she joined the Toronto Olympics Club where many world-class athletes train. One was the well-known Deaf sprinter Rohan Smith, whom Dawn had met in Vancouver, BC, in 1984. Rohan introduced her to such notables as Ben Johnson, Donovan Bailey, Angela Taylor, and others from York University who were enrolled in the training program.

While she was on a short vacation in Jamaica, Dawn trained on her own and later qualified to compete in the 800-metre run at the Canadian Track and Field Championships in Montréal in 1991. It was an exciting event with thousands of spectators watching the meet on live television. Dawn did not make the finals but did increase her personal best by four seconds.

At the World Games for the Deaf in Bulgaria in 1993, Dawn captured three medals—a gold for the 1,500-metre and two silvers for the 800-metre and the 3,000-metre races. The temperature was a gruelling forty-three degrees centigrade, so dehydration was her major concern. Possibly, had the weather not been a factor, Dawn might have done even better.

She returned home and decided to continue her pursuit of higher education, but she also continued training. She passed the entrance exams for both Gallaudet University in Washington, DC, and the National Technical Institute for the Deaf in Rochester, New York. However, at that point, the Canadian government cut back financing for Deaf students wishing to attend college or university, so she was unable to honour either acceptance. She decided to leave Canada and return to England, the country of her birth.

Dawn now lives in London, England, where she trained vigourously at Battersea Park with the British Miler Club and a coach who sets high, strict standards

for his trainees, in order to prepare for the Canadian team participating at the 2001 World Games for the Deaf held in Rome. There, she won a bronze for the 1,500-metre event, but the heat prevented her from doing well in the five- and ten-kilometre races. She plans to run in the 2002 Deaf World Championships being held in Germany. She and her partner, Nick Busk, plan to spend a few months in Australia during the winter of 2001–02 for competition and training, and Dawn is already preparing for the World Games for the Deaf to be held in Australia in 2005. She and Nick plan to marry in July 2002. Dawn would like to enter Melrose College in California to train as a fashion designer which, next to running, has been one of her main interests since her late teen years.

Dawn has always been interested in clothes and has developed excellent taste in fashion. She has a flair for creating clothing for various age groups and hopes to become a designer for children's clothing and maternity wear. She also has a keen interest in interior home design. Her dream is to go into partnership with her sister to design and create maternity wear for the Canadian and American market. She is currently awaiting acceptance of her application to the Melrose College of Design.

MOORE (GORDON), Peggy Anne

1958–
Data-Entry Operator, Business Office Clerk, Deaf Activist, Invoicing Clerk, and Freelance ASL Instructor.

PEGGY ANNE GORDON was born hearing but became Deaf in infancy due to rubella, high fever, and ear infection. Her Deafness was not diagnosed until she was two years old, her parents and their doctor believing she was too indolent and stubborn to listen and speak. She has no known Deaf relatives, but her husband, Barry Joseph Moore, her best friend and mentor, is Deaf. They have two hearing children, a daughter, Amy, and a son, Mark. The Moores currently make their home in Mississauga, Ontario.

Peggy Anne was educated at the Metro Toronto School for the Deaf (MTSD), in an elementary oral Deaf program, from 1960 to 1972, when she was chosen to be the valedictorian at her graduation ceremony. She then attended Northern Secondary school from 1972 to 1976 in a program for Deaf and hard-of-hearing students attending mainstream classes. She entered the workforce after graduating and has held a variety of positions, from data-entry operator to business office clerk, and has studied stock options—buying and selling—at the Toronto Stock Exchange. She decided

to be a stay-at-home mother for a while but, when she applied for a position with the Canadian Hearing Society and was offered the job, she re-entered the workforce and has never looked back.

Peggy Anne credits her dear friend and mentor, Florence, with helping to make her the person she is today, by encouraging her to attend Deaf Culture workshops. Most of all, she is grateful to her husband, who actively encouraged her to go out and explore the world while he worked in the daytime, and stayed at home with the children many nights and weekends. Because she was educated orally, she had learned the hard way, struggling through high school, using only speech and speechreading as her mode of communication, and missing a great deal of what was being said. She had no social life with other Deaf students because she lived quite a distance from the school, so she grew up in a state of confusion, not knowing who she really was.

Attending her first workshop in Deaf Culture in 1988 greatly impacted and changed her life. Peggy Anne then embarked on a long journey of self-discovery and sought to find her place within the Deaf Community. Being hired by the Canadian Hearing Society opened a whole new world for her and enriched her experiences, not only through promotions within the workplace, but also through contact with other Deaf staff members. She soon became involved with the Ontario Association of the Deaf (OAD) and the Deaf education movement. She began to realize what a rich culture, language, and heritage she had forfeited by attending an oral school program. But she does not blame her parents for making that decision as they were unaware of other options and took advice from professionals who advocated oralism. When her mother attended a brief presentation on Deaf Culture, she realized how her daughter had been deprived of her true identity and language. Peggy Anne long ago forgave her, and they have a close, loving relationship.

When Peggy Anne attended a reunion at her former school (MTSD), she was asked to present and her former teachers were shocked to see her giving her presentation in ASL instead of spoken English. She explained what she had missed in her youth and told them that all Deaf students are entitled to clear communication from their teachers. They were astonished to see what a strong person she had become. She got involved in political rallies and organized workshops for OAD, but finally had to resign to focus on her health and family. She started training to become an ASL instructor. The time she spent doing that, while looking after her family was very valuable to her.

Peggy Anne started teaching ASL in 1990 and was offered a job as a Sign Language Coordinator, a position she still holds today. When a volunteer position came up with the Ontario Cultural Society of the Deaf (OCSD) she was appointed ASL director. She is now in her third term with the OCSD board and loving every minute of it. Peggy Anne Moore has had an interesting journey of self-fulfilment and identification. She is finally reaping the benefits that have made that journey worthwhile and extremely rewarding.

MOORES, Alma

1957–
Dedicated Volunteer, Curling Fan, and Fundraiser.

ALMA MOORES was born Deaf at Flower's Cove, a small rural village on the Northern Peninsula of Newfoundland. Her Deafness was not detected by doctors until she was three months old. She has no known Deaf relatives, and currently makes her home in Halifax, Nova Scotia.

Alma's education began at the Newfoundland School for the Deaf (NSD), which was temporaily set up at Fort Pepperel, in Pleasantville, a suburb of St. John's, where she attended from 1964 to 1965. In 1965 NSD moved to the Torbay complex of the old Royal Canadian Air Force barracks near the St. John's airport. Alma remained there until 1971. She then returned to Flower's Cove where she was sent to the local public school for grades six to eleven. It was when she was in the eleventh grade, at the age of sixteen, that Alma became seriously ill and was eventually diagnosed with juvenile rheumatoid arthritis. This changed her entire life.

She had always dreamed of becoming a teacher of the Deaf and, until her illness, had also been an enthusiastic athlete, participating in soccer, broomball, softball, and floor hockey. After she was diagnosed with arthritis, Alma had to start taking sixteen aspirin tablets each day, which not only sapped her energy and stamina, but also interfered with her academic advancement.

Alma enrolled at the Atlantic Technological Vocational Centre (ATVC) in Amherst, Nova Scotia, where her Deaf classmates were encouraging and supportive, but she could not understand their ASL signs which were different from her Newfoundland signs. Nevertheless, she wanted to remain at ATVC with her friends and explored different courses for two years until graduation. It was at that time in her life that she fully accepted ASL as her language and Deaf Culture as her heritage. As the years passed, Alma longed to obtain a high school diploma which would qualify her for a good job. She eventually earned a Nova Scotia Academic Upgrading Certificate which gave her high school equivalency.

Several attempts at joining the general workforce met with disappointment so Alma finally settled for becoming a babysitter, which she greatly enjoyed. Alma prefers to keep busy and in touch with other people.

She decided to become a volunteer with the Society of Deaf and Hard of Hearing Nova Scotians. This organization serves the Deaf, the hard of hearing, the late-Deafened, and the Deaf-Blind. Alma has been with the society since 1989 and her volunteer contributions to its programs have been manifold. She is an active member of the Halifax Association of the Deaf (HAD), and was its secretary for two years. She was also a Nova Scotia Deaf Curling Association delegate to the Canadian Deaf Curling Championships for two years. In addition, Alma worked hard to help raise funds for the Nova Scotia Deaf Curling Association to send curlers to the Canadian Deaf Curling Championships in Edmonton, Alberta, and Winnipeg, Manitoba.

Volunteer work and attending Deaf social activities give meaning and purpose to Alma's life. In her leisure hours she is an avid reader, does some oil painting, reads horoscopes, does crossword puzzles, and surfs the Internet.

MORRIS (BODRUG), Dora

1905–1987
Gardener, Artist, and Skilled Craftswoman.

DORA BODRUG was born Deaf into a hearing family who emigrated to Canada from the Ukraine to settle in the farming community of Dallas in Manitoba. She was twelve years old at that time. Later, in 1919, a Deaf sister, Rosalie, was born in Dallas, Manitoba.

The Bodrug family eventually moved to the Matlock district where Dora spent most of the rest of her life after attending school for one year at the Manitoba School for the Deaf in Winnipeg. During her childhood family members created "home signs" in order to communicate with her, but she never really had an opportunity to learn ASL, nor was she able to speechread. Therefore, she was not able to communicate fluently either with other Deaf people or with the hearing world. There is no doubt that Dora, with her many talents, could have done a great deal more with her life had she been persuaded to stay in school longer, but it was embarrassing for her to be placed with children much younger than herself, so her decision to leave school is quite understandable.

She was a remarkable woman who lived a productive and interesting life in her rural community. Dora married a hearing man, Stephen Morris of Libau, Manitoba, around 1928 and lived with his family, but was unhappy with all the hard work and no pay so she eventually separated from Stephen and never saw him again. She returned to Matlock with their three children—Jane, Steve, and Alice. Around 1942 she met and lived with another hearing man, Cliff Kazmerchuk. When she expressed a desire for a little house of her own, Cliff built one for her on the lot next to his.

Despite her lack of formal education and her difficulty with communication, Dora was a respected and admired member of the Matlock community and contributed much to the life of the village through her various skills. Matlock has a large population of summer residents who own cottages in the area and many of them depended on Dora for their fresh raspberries. Until she was past eighty years of age, she grew berries and vegetables which she delivered and sold to the cottagers on the west shore of Lake Winnipeg. She kept a neat and attractive yard and garden which the local residents enjoyed visiting. At the age of eighty-two she was still cutting her own grass and looking after her property. The outbuildings in her yard were gaily decorated with handpainted flowers, birds, and animals. In her spare time Dora knitted, crocheted, and sewed tiny replicas of local birds with precise details as to colour, shape, size, and markings.

Dora was a talented craftswoman who sold her various creations such as ornaments, afghans, cushions, and braided rugs to her many rural customers. She enjoyed her independence and was always willing to lend a helping hand to her neighbours. Her children, all hearing, grew up and married. Alice had only one son, while Jane had six children—three boys and three girls—and now has seven grandchildren. Steve had two daughters and now has five grandchildren. This makes a total of twelve great-grandchildren for Dora. Ever cheerful and busy, Dora was admired by all who knew her and was greatly missed in the Matlock community when she died peacefully in 1987. She was very proud of the many accomplishments of her niece and nephew, her sister Rosalie's Deaf children, Angela Stratiy and Robert Petrone.

1950–
Coordinator, Employment Counsellor, Rehabilitation Practitioner, and Social Worker.

ELEANOR MORSE was born Deaf to hearing parents in Saint John, New Brunswick. She has two Deaf cousins. Her husband, Philip Taylor, is a Deaf man from California, and they have a hearing son, Mark. They currently make their home in Halifax. A cousin on Eleanor's father's side of the family, the late John Elvin Shaffner, who died on 28 June 2001, was the Lieutenant-Governor of Nova Scotia from 1978–84. In more recent history, her cousin Alexa McDonough is the leader of the federal New Democratic Party (NDP), and was for some years a provincial MLA as well as leader of the NDP in Nova Scotia.

Eleanor's education was eclectic. She taught herself to speechread and took speech therapy with a private therapist for ten years. After spending two years in a private nursery school in 1954–56, she took grade one in an oral program at the Boston School for the Deaf in Randolph, Massachusetts. That part of her education was paid for by the State of Massachusetts. The next year she returned to Rothesay, New Brunswick, where she attended Rothesay Elementary School for grades two to six (1957–62). On Saturdays she met with a private tutor to keep pace with her class.

Later, she attended the Interprovincial School for the Deaf, now known as the Atlantic Provinces Special Education Authority (APSEA), in Amherst, Nova Scotia, for two years (1962–1964). From 1964–66 she was back home and attended grades eight and nine at the Rothesay Junior High School, again with a tutor. She then took grade ten by correspondence courses through the New Brunswick Department of Education with a full-time tutor. In 1967–68, in preparation for entrance to Gallaudet University in Washington, DC, she received tutoring from a retired principal at the St. Vincent's Convent, as well as studying grade eleven physics at St. Vincent's Girls' High School.

Eleanor entered Gallaudet University in the summer of 1968 to learn American Sign Language, because it differed from her native Maritime Sign Language (MSL).

She completed her studies in sociology-social work in December 1973 and received her BA degree in May 1974. Eleanor was married on 6 April 1973, and she and Philip lived in Washington, DC, for a few years. Their son Mark was born there on 18 January 1974, and Eleanor was a full-time mother for a while. On returning to New Brunswick in May 1976, she found employment coordinating a new pilot employment outreach program with the Saint John Deaf and Hard of Hearing Services (SJDHHS), which was the first such program in Canada.

However, in 1977 she left her work to join Philip who had been accepted into a Bible college in Missouri. When she returned to New Brunswick the following year, there was no job available, so she decided to upgrade her qualifications at Dalhousie University in Halifax. For her BSW internship, she supervised some Deaf students who researched and documented Deaf-related resources that were found in libraries in Nova Scotia for the Coordinating Council on Deafness of Nova Scotia, now known as Deafness Advocacy Association Nova Scotia.

Since completing her BSW there, in 1981, she has been steadily employed. She was an employment counsellor for Silent Outreach, once part of the Society of Deaf and Hard of Hearing Nova Scotians in Halifax, before moving to Edmonton, Alberta, where she held several very responsible positions. Her first employment in Alberta was as a job placement counsellor with the Western Industrial Research and Training Centre. She then worked as a rehabilitation practitioner at Lauderdale House, a group home for Deaf adults with disabilities who need to develop life skills in order to become employable and live independently. She then became placement coordinator at Grant MacEwan Community College, making intern arrangements for Deaf students with multiple disabilities and providing support to host companies, as well as other important duties. Later, she was a residential counsellor at two different group homes, one for the province of Alberta during weekends, and the other for Catholic Social Services during the week. In due course she became coordinator of a computer-training program for sixteen Deaf students and four staff members whom she supervised for a year.

In the fall of 1990 she and her family moved back to New Brunswick, where she worked as a case manager for the New Brunswick Department of Social Services for six months. Her responsibilities involved assessing parents of children with disabilities for requests for medical equipment, supplies, and services and also doing home assessments for runaway youth living away from home. Afterwards, she taught ASL and provided interpreting services. In addition, she assessed clients for Vocational Rehabilitation For Disabled Persons (VRDP) sponsorship eligibility for their education. She also provided crisis intervention counselling. She has been a registered social worker since 1990. In 1997, she moved to Halifax to take a job as an employment services coordinator with the Teamwork Cooperative.

Eleanor's involvement with the Deaf Community has also been varied and interesting. In Edmonton she was treasurer for the Alberta Association of the Deaf (AAD), where she managed a budget of $350,000. While in Saint John she was involved with the Saint John Association of the Deaf and served on the board of directors for the Saint John Deaf and Hard of Hearing Services. In Halifax she has been active in the Halifax Association of the Deaf (HAD), the Nova Scotia Cultural Society of the Deaf (NSCSD), the Society of Deaf and Hard of Hearing Nova Scotians, and the Nova Scotia Deaf Sports Association (NSDSA).

In her leisure time, Eleanor enjoys crafts, researches the Morse genealogy, watches movies, and walks Mimi, her Boston terrier. On long weekends and holidays she enjoys going back to her home in Quispamsis, New Brunswick.

MOYER, Sonya Theresa

1950–
Psychiatric Attendant and Computer Clerk.

SONYA MOYER was born Deaf into a hearing family in Medicine Hat, Alberta. She currently makes her home in St. Albert, a suburban community north of Edmonton, with her hearing son Ryan. She has no known Deaf relatives, but has a cousin-by-marriage who is well-known in Canada's sports community— Lance MacDonald, a former National Hockey League player with the Calgary Flames.

Sonya was educated at the Alberta School for the Deaf in Edmonton from 1955 to 1970. She was one of its original pupils when it opened. After graduating, she attended Gallaudet College (now University) in Washington, DC, where she received a BA degree in Psychology in 1975.

From 1976 to 1983 Sonya worked in the US as a psychiatric attendant at Centre State Hospital in the state of Indiana. When she returned to Canada she found employment with the Royal Canadian Mounted Police (RCMP), in Edmonton, as a computer clerk. She also became actively involved in organizations in the Deaf Community, serving on various committees.

Sonya, openly lesbian, attended a lesbian weekend class at the University of Alberta, where she met her partner (now former partner) Liz Broad. Liz had abso-lutely no knowledge of Deafness, ASL, or Deaf Culture, but she was immediately attracted to Sonya's friendly nature and warm personality. They fell in love and Liz was not at all bothered by Sonya's Deafness because she was determined to learn to communicate with her fully and with ease. On a hot and humid day in August 1991, Sonya became the first Deaf lesbian in Canada to marry a hearing partner.

The service for their spiritual union took place at the Unitarian Church of Edmonton, which has a lengthy history of gay and lesbian marriages. There were sixty guests in attendance, both Deaf and hearing, straight and lesbian. Sonya taught Liz to sign and together they made a home for themselves and Sonya's son Ryan.

Liz worked as a registered nurse with Alberta Health Care and attended ASL classes at Grant MacEwan Communnity College, where she completed level II. As the years passed she learned to understand Sonya better and became more familiar with Deaf Culture and the Deaf Community. Sonya and Liz have since parted amicably.

MULLEY-ROSE, Brenda Arlene

1960–
Champion Figure Skater and Provincial and Federal Civil Servant.

BRENDA MULLEY was born hearing to hearing parents in St. John's Newfoundland. She became Deaf at the age of three due to illness. She has no known Deaf relatives, but her father was president and vice-president of the Parent-Teacher Association at the Newfoundland School for the Deaf. Her family often invited Deaf students from the school to private and public events and functions. Brenda's hearing husband, Bob Rose, was the number-one salesman in Canada in 1997 and again in Atlantic Canada in 2001. Brenda and Bob currently make their home in Mount Pearl, Newfoundland.

Brenda is fluent in ASL and is active within the Deaf Community. She was recently elected to a two-year term as president and is a past vice-president of the Newfoundland and Labrador Association of the Deaf. She was also host chairperson of the Eastern Canada Association of the Deaf's (ECAD's) 41st Biennial Convention held in St. John's in July 2001.

She was educated at the Newfoundland School for the Deaf in St. John's. After graduating she attended Prince of Wales College for two years. In 1979–80 Brenda took courses in cartographic and photogrammetry technical surveying at Cabot College. In 1989 she also obtained a Business English Diploma from Avalon Community College.

Her employment record is varied and interesting. Brenda gained valuable experience with her father's contracting business, where she assisted with office duties for twelve years, doing bookkeeping, looking after payrolls, and working with business and income tax statements. She also had summer jobs with the provincial Department of Forestry and Lands, where her major duty was drafting and updating old maps. Her first government job was as a file and mail clerk with the Department of Social Services, but she soon advanced to a clerk-accountant position.

In 1986 she moved to the federal government's employ as assistant draftsperson at the Forestry Research Centre, and then worked as a records control clerk in the office of Statistics Canada (Census) at Taxation Centre.

Brenda became the first Deaf training assistant for three Deaf people who were in training for an initial classified assessment. It was her responsibility to help them learn and understand the taxation operation manual. Since 1986 she has worked with Revenue Canada, now Canada Customs and Revenue Agency, in St. John's in various capacities.

In her youth, Brenda was a member of the St. John's Figure Skating Club, excelling in precision and synchronized skating. She is the holder of ten provincial championship medals, nine gold and one silver, which she accumulated over a period of ten years. Since 1992 she has been involved with an adult precision skating team.

Besides her interest in skating, Brenda's hobbies and pastimes include many sporting activities, swimming, camping, moose hunting, fishing, crafts, reading, and flower gardening. She is a member of the former Torbay Senior Ladies' Fastball League and participates in the Deaf Curling League.

NADON-YUEN, Judy Susan

1959–
Athlete, Accounting Clerk, Instructor, and Cultural Leader.

Born JUDY SCHNITZLER in Saskatoon, Saskatchewan, she became Deaf at the age of two and attended R.J.D. Williams Provincial School for the Deaf until 1970. She was transferred to St. Philip Elementary School which she attended up to the seventh grade. She then went to Holy Cross High School for five years, where she completed her grade twelve with honours in arts. After graduating, Judy went to Minnesota for her professional training as a data processor, data-entry operator, and computer operator.

Returning to Canada with her newly acquired credentials, Judy found employment with the Potash Corporation of Saskatchewan, where she worked as a data-entry operator and accounting clerk for the next eighteen years. She married Richard Nadon, but was widowed in 1990. In 1995 she married Allan Yuen, and their son Val was born in 1997. The family now resides in Calgary where Judy has held several jobs—at Bow Valley College where she worked with a Deaf quadriplegic client as well as doing some teaching, at Trimac Transportation Systems as a data-entry clerk, at Friday Personnel as an accounts payable/data-entry clerk, and at Sunterra Quality Food Market as an accounting clerk. Currently she is a homemaker.

Judy had a great deal of involvement with the Deaf Community in Saskatchewan, serving on the board of Saskatchewan Deaf and Hard of Hearing Services and the Sask-Tel Special Needs Advisory Panel, co-editing *Saskatoon Deaf News*, coordinating Deaf Dance Workshops, and co-chairing the 1988 National Deaf Festival of the Arts. She was president of the Saskatchewan Cultural Society of the Deaf for a year and served as provincial director for a year, as well as being a member of the Advisory Committee on Programming for the Hearing Impaired at Saskatchewan Institute of Applied Arts and Science Technology (SIAST—Kelsey Campus). In addition, Judy was a board director for the Canadian Association of the Deaf (Saskatchewan representative) from July 1994 to July 1996, and represented the Canadian Association of the Deaf for Transport Canada during that period.

Judy has also had considerable experience as an instructor of ASL and Deaf Culture, teaching classes at R.J.D. Williams School, the Royal Bank of Canada, and SIAST. She was a presenter at Deaf Culture and Leadership workshops in Saskatoon and attended similar workshops and conferences in Washington, DC, Ottawa, Vancouver, and Niagara Falls.

Judy's athletic accomplishments are also very noteworthy. She was a member of the Saskatchewan track and field team at the 1977 Canada Summer Games in St. John's, Newfoundland, and at the 1976 Provincial Summer Games in Swift Current, Saskatchewan, where she was awarded a gold in discus, a silver in shotput, and a bronze in javelin.

Other honours include an Award of Merit for her many contributions to the Saskatchewan Cultural Society of the Deaf, a Canadian Cultural Society of the Deaf (CCSD) Distinguished Cultural Service Award, a Holy Cross High School Leadership Award, an Outstanding Female Track and Field Award, an Outstanding Contribution to Athletics Award, an MVP Badminton Award and a Graduation Proficiency in Art Award.

Having accomplished many achievements in her community in Saskatchewan, Judy now enjoys her life as a wife and mother in Calgary.

NAGY (DIAKIW), Patricia Eugenia

1940–

Farm Wife, Support Group Founder, and Member of Numerous Organizations and Agencies for Deaf and Hard-of-Hearing Persons.

PAT DIAKIW was born hearing to hearing parents in the rural community of Cudworth, Saskatchewan. At the age of three she lost a significant degree of hearing as a result of a severe case of double mumps and drainage in her ears. At the age of six doctors removed her tonsils and adenoids in the hope of improving her hearing, but that did not happen. She has three relatives who were born Deaf—her paternal grandfather and his two brothers, John, Peter, and Onefrey Diakiw. Pat always had a special bond with her grandfather, who used home-invented sign language and wore a constant smile. She was married to a man with normal hearing who was a lifelong farmer in the Wakaw district. Pat has three adult children—Karen, Kevin and Sandra—all married, as well as nine grandchildren, all with normal hearing. Pat has now retired from farming and remarried. Her husband is Mervyn Hunchak, a late-Deafened man, and they presently make their home in Saskatoon, Saskatchewan. They are both very involved in a support group for hard-of-hearing and late-Deafened persons.

When Pat was nine years old she was fitted with her first hearing aid, a sixty-five-dollar body model. Now, more than fifty years and many hearing aids later, she is still a hearing-aid user, wearing two behind-the-ear models. She is also a natural and avid speechreader. When Pat was young, she was always very self-conscious about wearing her aid, but saw its benefits and began to wear it regularly. When her children were small she taught each of them to speak and enunciate clearly to facilitate her speechreading.

In the 1990s, after a busy family reunion in Cudworth, Saskatchewan, Pat noticed her hearing loss was becoming more severe, and she became depressed. Her daughter contacted a hard-of-hearing support group in Regina and Saskatoon. They provided advice and encouragement to help Pat cope. She was soon confident enough to start a support group and hold informational meetings in her own rural community of Wakaw with help from the Hard of Hearing Association of Saskatoon (HHAS) and grants from the Department of Health and Welfare for the New Horizons Outreach Program. Pat took classes and workshops in Saskatoon to sharpen her skills and became more involved in the hard-of-hearing community. She is now a board member of Saskatchewan Deaf and Hard of Hearing Services (SDHHS) and was a member of the Saskatchewan Late-Deafened Persons Association (SLPDA), which is now dissolved.

She is presently the president of the Hard of Hearing Association of Saskatoon (HHAS), which is a branch of the Canadian Hard of Hearing Association (CHHA). She is also a member of several organizations of the Deaf in Saskatoon, and she and her husband

love to socialize with other members at many of their events. They are learning and studying ASL, enjoying closed-captioned TV, and using their TTY, e-mail, and fax machine to communicate. Pat is constantly striving to create greater public awareness and understanding of the realities of hearing losses.

She is now an outgoing, well-adjusted, confident woman who has no regrets about her Deafness. She has received loyal support from family and friends, as well as from the organizations which she serves. As a result, she says her life has become fuller and richer, and she now is an active and enthusiastic leader of a newly formed support group called Listen Up—Saskatoon. Because she is so deeply involved in the work, she has little leisure time for her interests and hobbies. When time permits, she enjoys travelling and spending time with her family.

NEMEROFF (HALL), Thelma Louise
1913–1984
Keypunch Operator, Bible Study Participant, and Dedicated Activist for Deaf Causes.

THELMA HALL was born hearing into a hearing family in Montréal, Québec, where she lived her entire life. At the age of five she was stricken with meningitis, and, as a result, became Deaf. She had no known Deaf relatives, but her husband, Archibald ("Archie") Nemeroff, is a Deaf man. Thelma and Archie had three hearing sons, all of whom received a university education—Robert Dickson, a successful word processing plant designer, residing in Washington State, US; Howard Nemeroff, a tax lawyer in Montréal; and David Nemeroff, currently between jobs and residing in Florida. At present, Howard is on the executive of the Canadian Deafness Research and Training Institute. Thelma and Archie made their home in Montréal throughout their marriage.

Thelma was educated at the MacKay School for the Deaf, now known as the MacKay Centre, in Montréal. Upon completion of her schooling there, she attended a business college in Westmount, Québec, where she earned certification as a keypunch operator, a very common career choice for Deaf women of that era. She also attended Vanier Junior College in St. Laurent, Québec, where she studied English literature.

She worked as a keypunch operator for a number of years with the Sun Life Assurance Company and CIL Industries. After 1952 she left the workforce and became a full-time housewife, stay-at-home mother, and advocate for the Deaf.

Throughout her lifetime, Thelma was a powerful activist, promoting Deaf issues and volunteering her services to organizations and agencies related to Deafness. From 1954 to 1984, at the local level, she was a very active member of the Montréal Association of the Deaf (MAD), serving as its secretary for more than twenty-five years. She was also chairperson of the organizing committee for MAD's twenty-fifth and fiftieth anniversary celebrations. She was involved with the Canadian Association of the Deaf (CAD) at the national level, serving as its secretary from 1975 until she became ill in 1984. Also at the national level, Thelma served the Canadian Cultural Society of the Deaf (CCSD) as secretary from the time the organization was founded in 1980 until her illness in 1984. In addition to her work with organizations and agencies in the early 1970s, Thelma participated in Bible study groups for Deaf people under the guidance of a local minister, Frank Vann. She was a pioneer in lobbying the National Film Board of Canada to develop closed captioning for its films. Once she had succeeded in achieving this goal, she introduced the captioned films to different Deaf audiences such as seniors and youth groups throughout Montréal, much to their delight. She also became involved in the plight of several Deaf immigrants and helped them to establish themselves and their families in the Montréal community.

Her death, due to cancer, on 9 October 1984, was a blow to the Deaf Community, and a sad occasion for all who had known her. On 17 August 1992, Jim Roots, executive director of CAD, sent a touching letter to Archie and his sons, indicating that a plaque formally recognizing Thelma's enormous contributions to that organization had just been unveiled at CAD headquarters at 2435 Holly Lane in Ottawa. Readers who visit the CAD office will see it prominently displayed there. Its

inscription reads: "The Head Office of the Canadian Association of the Deaf is furnished in memory of Thelma Nemeroff, in grateful recognition of her many years of work on CAD's behalf." Thelma's photograph is included on the plaque. The plaque will serve as a continuous testimonial to future Deaf generations about the outstanding contributions made by this remarkable woman to her Deaf peers across Canada.

Thelma was a voracious reader who often finished a lengthy novel in one day's sitting.

NESBITT, Tara Dawn

1981–
Champion Swimmer, Dedicated Student, and Aspiring Social Worker.

TARA NESBITT was born Deaf to hearing parents, Judy and Ron Nesbitt, in Pointe Claire, Québec. The cause of her Deafness is unknown, and she has no known Deaf relatives. She grew up in Oakville, Ontario, and has fond recollections of summer vacations at the family cottage at Cloudy Lake, a seven-hour drive north of Toronto, where she virtually lived in the water. Swimming has always held great importance in her life. She is currently a student at the Rochester Institute of Technology (RIT) in Rochester, New York, where she was undefeated during her freshman year in all college-level swimming competitions. During her sophomore year she was defeated only once.

Tara joined the highly rated Oakville Swim Club when she was thirteen years of age and before long she was turning in times that were only fractions of seconds behind those recorded by the Canadian Olympic swim team. This did not surprise her parents who recall her dog-paddling in the family bathtub as a tiny infant. In fact, her swimming prowess may be at least partly inherited, because her father was at one time a member of the Canadian National Swim Team. Although he never tried to push Tara in the direction of competitive swimming, he is obviously proud of her incredible achievements to date.

Several Canadian universities recruited her and, because of her fierce sense of patriotism, Tara would have preferred to remain in Canada. She chose, however, to attend RIT because of its proximity to the National Technical Institute for the Deaf (NTID), which would offer her more social opportunities than she would have had in her homeland. She started her third year in the fall of 2001, majoring in social work and environmental studies, with a view to becoming either an international or environmental social worker. She is

also working as an English peer tutor at NTID. During her school years at home, Tara was always an honour student. Since entering RIT, she has consistently been on the Dean's list, as well as being named "Athlete of the Week" four times during her freshman swimming season there and once during her sophomore year.

Tara's swimming accomplishments are impressive. While swimming with the Oakville Club, she regularly placed in the top fifty in Canada in the 50-metre freestyle and 100-metre backstroke. In 1997 she represented Canada at the World Summer Games of the Deaf in Denmark, winning a total of six medals—four golds, one silver, and one bronze. In 1998 she broke the Oakville record in the 100-metre backstroke in the 15–17 age category, and still holds that record.

During her freshman year at RIT, 1999–2000, she broke and still holds four individual records—the 50-yard backstroke, 100-yard backstroke, 200-yard backstroke, and the 200-yard individual medley. She ended that season with a record of 26-0, and went on to compete in the NCAA division 3 Championships in Atlanta, Georgia, in the 100-yard backstroke, 200-yard backstroke, and 200-yard individual medley.

She also competed in the World Summer Games of the Deaf in Italy in July 2001 where she won two gold medals in the 100-metre backstroke and the 200-metre backstroke, a silver in the 400-metre individual medley, and a bronze in the 200-metre individual medley.

While swimming competitively in Oakville, Tara was the only Deaf member of the team and sometimes felt quite isolated from her teammates who could not communicate with her by signing. At RIT, however, there are several other Deaf swimmers on the team, so there are fewer communication barriers. Most of them are capable speechreaders and many of the hearing swimmers are learning to sign.

Tara travelled with a friend to Botswana, Africa, during the summer of 2000 and did volunteer work at a school for the Deaf. She has also given some thought to competing in the Ironman Triathlon some day. She has always been focused and goal oriented, ready to take on challenges. In view of her ambitions, capabilities, and personality, she will no doubt be adding many exciting triumphs to her life story as she continues to pursue her goals.

NEUMANN (PUGH), Marilyn Fay

1941–
Proud Mother, Rehabilitation Support Worker, and Deaf-Blind Intervenor.

MARILYN PUGH was born Deaf to hearing parents at Osoyoos, British Columbia. She was one of five children, and the only Deaf person in the family. The cause of her Deafness was deemed to be maternal rubella. She has no known Deaf relatives, but is married to a Deaf man, Hugh Neumann, and they have three hearing daughters—Carla, Faye, and Debra. They also have five beautiful grandchildren whom they adore. Marilyn and Hugh make their home in Edmonton, Alberta.

When Marilyn was only five and a half years old she left the security and comfort of her family and home to become a residential student at Jericho Hill School for the Deaf (JHS) in Vancouver. She missed her two sisters and two brothers, and they missed her. Visits home were few and far between and she longed for Christmas, Easter, and summer vacations so she could rejoin her family. Nevertheless, she remained at JHS until she graduated in 1961 and, for the most part, enjoyed school and dormitory life. During her senior years she also attended Vancouver Vocational Institute (VVI) where she developed skills in key punching, book-keeping, and sewing. These were trade skills aimed at making Deaf students more readily employable. At that time, however, labour strikes were widespread in BC and jobs were scarce.

In 1964 Marilyn decided to move to Toronto, Ontario, where she would be acting as maid of honour at a good friend's wedding. She looked for work but managed to find only casual employment here and there, and soon realized jobs were as hard to come by in eastern Canada as they were back home. Her stay lasted only about a year before she returned to BC.

In 1966 Marilyn met Hugh Neumann, formerly of Edmonton, Alberta, at a Deaf baseball event. It was almost love at first sight, and they were married in August 1967. By then, they had moved to Edmonton, where Hugh could find work. Although Marilyn registered in a government progressive skills program, she soon became a housewife and stay-at-home mother of three lovely daughters. In 1977 the Neumanns built their own home, and she was kept busy. By the early 1980s she knew it was time for her to rejoin the workforce. Because times had drastically changed, she returned to school for further training. Subsequently, she worked in the printing industry for over four years before she found employment as a rehabilitation support worker with individuals requiring assistance in the community. This job led her to her current position as a Deaf-Blind intervenor in a group-home setting, providing daily home and/or community support where needed. She enjoys her job and works well with people, but is also looking forward to retirement so she can spend more time with her husband and their family.

Their eldest daughter, Carla, is married, and has one son. She is currently working at Grant MacEwan College in the ASL-English Interpreter and Sign Language studies programs, having become a professional interpreter in 1995. Faye has two children and currently works for Remax Real Estate. The baby of the family, Debra, has two children and plans to be married soon. She and her partner live and work in Edmonton.

Marilyn's involvement in the Deaf Community includes working at fundraisers for the Association of Canadian Registered Intepreters of the Deaf (ACRID) and as a volunteer helper for activities sponsored by the Edmonton Association of the Deaf (EAD).

In her leisure hours Marilyn enjoys such hobbies as sewing, knitting, crocheting, arranging dried flowers, and painting.

NICHOL, Joyce Eva

1956–

Data-Entry Operator, Mature Student, and Dedicated Home-Care Worker.

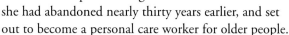

JOYCE NICHOL was born in Fredericton, New Brunswick, the eleventh child in a family of twelve, and lived in Harvey, a nearby rural community. Her Deafness was not discovered until she was two years old when her father realized she could not hear the honking of the car horn. She has no known Deaf relatives and the cause of her Deafness was not determined. She grew up on a farm where she was always surrounded by livestock and many other animals, so life was often hectic. She sought peace and relaxation by riding her horse, bareback, to a nearby brook. There, she could sit on the bank and enjoy nature's beauties in solitude. Currently, Joyce makes her home in Halifax, Nova Scotia.

When her Deafness was recognized, her father taught her to speak and read lips. She was sent to the Ontario School for the Deaf, now known as Sir James Whitney School, in Belleville, for one year. She was then enrolled at the Interprovincial School for the Deaf, now known as the Atlantic Provinces Special Education Authority (APSEA), in Amherst, Nova Scotia, where she spent the next eleven years. Joyce has always felt she learned more from her siblings, particularly two of her sisters who are registered nurses, than she ever learned at school. She looked up to her sisters as role models and longed for a career in the medical/health field similar to theirs. Her brother, however, suggested that such a goal would be impossible for her to achieve, so she took his advice and trained as a data-entry operator at the Atlantic Technological Vocational Centre in Amherst. She then entered the workforce and took employment on a contractual basis with different employers, including the RCMP and the Department of Justice.

In 1982 Joyce took time off to be a stay-at-home mother for her two hearing daughters, Jennifer and Leeann. In 1990 she enrolled in the Women in Transition Training Program which had been established to assist women returning to the workforce. On completing the training she was unable to find permanent work for nine years. She decided she was tired of data entry and contractual work and finally, in 1999, Joyce decided it was time for a major career change. This time she was determined to pursue the goal she had abandoned nearly thirty years earlier, and set out to become a personal care worker for older people.

Accompanied by an interpreter, she arrived for an appointment to be interviewed, causing some dismay on the part of the interviewer who had not realized Joyce was Deaf. Nevertheless, the interview went quite well and Joyce was accepted into the program, to train in the field of home care rather than the personal care training she had hoped for. In 2001, after completing the requirements, she found employment with Northwood Home Care in Halifax, and has been kept very busy serving her growing roster of Deaf and hearing clients. Her ultimate goal is still to become a personal care worker. She has completed the required 200 hours of home care work in order to take further training and achieve her ambition as soon as a Sign Language interpreter is made available to her.

She loves her work and is delighted to have the opportunity to make people comfortable and happy while building a professional career in the field she had dreamed of three decades ago. In July 2001 she was a Deaf facilitator for a CPR course with Deaf participants. Through the Canadian Heart and Stroke Foundation, she is now training to become an instructor to teach CPR and first aid to Deaf people.

During her leisure hours she likes to crochet, hike, ride horseback, play darts, listen to music, and dance. She has Bambi, her pet chihuahua, who thinks his mission in life is to sit in her lap and be her guard dog. Her two cats, Jerry and Candy, also provide her with constant pleasure, and one of them even gives her "high fives" with her paw.

NICKERSON (DIETRICH) (ZIMMER), Lucille May Anne

1937–
Special-Needs Assistant, Residential Counsellor, Role Model, and Widow of the Late Forrest
Curwin Nickerson, Founder of the Canadian Cultural Society of the Deaf.

LUCILLE ZIMMER was born Deaf at Shoal Lake, Manitoba, into a multi-generation family of Deaf siblings and relatives, currently totalling nearly thirty in number. She was the second child of eleven, five of whom were Deaf, born to hearing parents, John and Elizabeth Zimmer. She has a Deaf sister and three Deaf brothers. The other Deaf relatives are cousins, second cousins, nieces and nephews, and many in-laws. Her first husband, Milfred Dietrich, was a hearing man, but her second husband, the late Forrest Curwin Nickerson, was a Deaf artist and poet from Atlantic Canada, who is nationally and internationally recognized as the founder of the Canadian Cultural Society of the Deaf.

One of Lucille's Deaf brothers, Gerald, teaches at the School for the Deaf in Burnaby, British Columbia, and another, Rick, is an instructor in Deaf Studies and ASL in the Interpreter Training Program at Red River College, in Winnipeg. Her Deaf sister, Jean, now retired, taught English as a second language to Deaf adults at George Brown College in Toronto. Lucille has two adult hearing children, Wayne and Beverley, from her first marriage.

Lucille's family grew up on a farm and, with five Deaf children, they soon developed "home signs" which were later replaced with ASL after they attended school. She gratefully credits her parents for having the foresight, courage, and wisdom to send their Deaf offspring to a school for Deaf children where they developed excellent communication skills and received a good education.

The Manitoba School for the Deaf in Winnipeg was being used for military purposes during World War II, so all Deaf students from Manitoba had to be sent elsewhere. Thus, when the eldest Zimmer child, Jean, was ready to be enrolled at the Saskatchewan School for the Deaf in Saskatoon, her mother could not bear to send her off alone, so Lucille was enrolled with her sister and, as a result, began her education before she had reached her fifth birthday. Between 1949 and 1954 she missed many weeks of school due to repeated bouts of rheumatic fever, but she was always able to catch up and maintain an excellent academic standing.

When she finished school Lucille worked temporarily as a microfilmer for a private firm before becoming a full-time filming clerk for Manitoba Medical Services in Winnipeg. In 1957 she married Milfred Dietrich

and, after a brief attempt at farming near Dropmore, Manitoba, they moved to Winnipeg where Milfred was hired as a bus driver for Winnipeg Transit, and Lucille became a stay-at-home mother to their children.

When Wayne and Beverley were old enough, Lucille returned to the workforce, alternating as a casual clerk with the Manitoba Education Department's school broadcasts and the government of Canada's Taxation Data Centre. During this period, Lucille also attended evening classes at Red River Community College, obtaining a High School Equivalency Diploma as well as completing several trimesters in child care services, with exceptional grades in all her course work.

In 1980 she was offered job training under the Federal Manpower Program at the Manitoba School for the Deaf. For the next six years she trained in various capacities—as an assistant in a special-needs classroom, a counsellor for a special-needs boy in the dormitory, an aide in a preschool classroom, and a helper with linen services in the dormitories. After nearly twenty-five years, her marriage resulted in legal separation, and she was divorced from Milfred Dietrich in February 1987.

On 1 July 1987, Lucille married Forrest Nickerson, but sadly, they had only a few happy months together. Forrest became seriously ill in January 1988 and was diagnosed with colon cancer which had metastasized to other body organs. On 16 June 1988, he passed away at their home, in the presence of Lucille and his daughter Cindy, who had come to offer moral support to Lucille and assist with his care. The family laid him to rest in Chapel Lawn Memorial Gardens in Winnipeg.

As his primary care-giver during his illness, Lucille finally achieved her childhood dream of being a nurse. At the age of ten she had been told that nursing could never be a career option for a Deaf person because of the inability to hear with a stethoscope and to communicate adequately with hearing staff and patients.

Following Forrest's death Lucille continued to work at the Manitoba School for the Deaf as a residential counsellor until her retirement. She continues to serve Winnipeg's Deaf Community in various capacities and enjoys socializing with her many Deaf friends. Her hobbies include sewing and reading.

NIXON, Marilyn Olive

1949–
Educator, Summer School Supervisor, Work Experience Program Coordinator, and Dedicated Employee.

MARILYN NIXON was born Deaf in Regina, Saskatchewan. Her mother and her brother Bob are both hard of hearing, so her Deafness is possibly due to genetic causes. Marilyn currently makes her home in Austin, Texas, where she has lived and worked for seventeen years.

As a young child Marilyn attended Wetmore Public School in Regina for three years. In 1957 she was enrolled at the Saskatchewan School for the Deaf in Saskatoon, where she attended as a residential student until she graduated in 1968. She then went to Gallaudet College, now Gallaudet University, in Washington, DC, graduating in 1973 with a Bachelor of Arts degree in Sociology. Marilyn then returned to the Saskatchewan School for the Deaf in Saskatoon and worked as a dormitory counsellor for three and a half years, while attending summer sessions at Western Maryland College to pursue a Master's degree in Deaf Education. She also acquired teacher certification and, in the fall of 1977, was the first Deaf teacher hired by the Calgary Board of Education to teach Deaf children at Queen Elizabeth Elementary School in Calgary, Alberta.

After two years in Calgary, Marilyn returned to Western Maryland College to complete her Master's degree in Deaf Education. In the fall of 1980 she moved to Winnipeg where she taught at the Manitoba School for the Deaf for four years. In 1984 she accepted a position in Austin, Texas, as a middle school teacher at the Texas School for the Deaf (TSD). In the summers of 1999 and 2000 Marilyn coordinated and supervised the early childhood education and elementary summer school program. Currently, she is coordinating the Work Experience Program at TSD, working with high school students. Her current assignment, as job-training teacher, gives her a new avenue to nurture work skills, foster good habits, and attitudes among older students to help them prepare their long-term goals after their graduation from high school.

Marilyn loves children and sees their misbehaviours as opportunities to teach them the difference between right and wrong. She sets high expectations in her classroom and, in an age when job loyalty is rapidly diminishing, her supervisors are pleased with Marilyn's dedication and loyalty to TSD. She has worked on many committees, coached the varsity girls' basketball team for five years, sponsored the Academic Bowl team (a knowledge contest), and sponsored the Junior National Association of the Deaf organization. She helped senior classes prepare for their graduation and provided junior peer assistance leadership. She is always prepared to lend a hand, wherever it might be needed. She provides motivational leadership and is considered an exceptional teacher by all who know her. She gives new teachers support and encouragement and is always a confident, reliable team player.

During her leisure hours, Marilyn enjoys travelling, reading, taking care of her dogs and cat, and attending TSD athletic games and events.

NOTLAND (TOMENCHUK), Olga Frances

1926–
Homemaker, Photo Finisher, and Farmer.

OLGA FRANCES TOMENCHUK was born on Christmas Day in 1926 at Poplar Bluff, a small Saskatchewan community near the Manitoba border. She attended the Saskatchewan provincial School for the Deaf in Saskatoon from 1932 to 1945. Her eldest sister, Mary Robinson (nee Tomenchuk, and now deceased), attended the same school. After graduating, Olga became a photo finisher, taking training courses, and working in that field for ten years.

She fondly remembers her former teachers and values the education she received at the school in Saskatoon, crediting her wonderful instructors there for her skills in dressmaking and other talents they helped her develop. She also recalls the many hours the women spent knitting sweaters, mitts, and berets for the soldiers who fought in World War II, and the beautiful quilts they created and donated to the Red Cross for the war effort.

In 1957 Olga married Alf C. Notland and became a farmer's wife and partner. They both worked hard and raised their two hearing daughters, Alva Cecile (now deceased) and Silva May, who has pursued a career as an ASL interpreter. After more than forty years of happily married life, Olga and Alf enjoyed their retirement in Calgary. Sadly, Alf battled Parkinson's Disease for eight years until he passed away on 23 November 1998. He is deeply missed by his wife and daughter. Olga continues to reside in her condo and enjoys the community life there as well as the activities in the Deaf Community and her church.

She has many hobbies, which include cooking, needlework, dressmaking, knitting, and crocheting. She is a devout Christian and demonstrates her faith in everything she does. Her daughter Alva, prior to her sad and sudden death in 1989, was very talented at performing religious and gospel music in ASL. Olga's love for Jesus brings peace and serenity into her life.

NOWOSAD, Patricia Susan

1949 1992
Pioneer Canadian Deaf Performing Artist.

PATRICIA NOWOSAD, called "Pat," is well known as one of the first female performing artists in the Canadian Theatre of the Deaf. She was a native of Vancouver, British Columbia, born hearing to hearing parents, Roy and Jean Nowosad. She had four hearing sisters, and became Deaf at the age of two. After a three-year attendance at the Jericho Hill provincial School for the Deaf in Vancouver, she was transferred to Ladner, British Columbia, to complete her elementary and high school education in the mainstream public school system. Her parents felt this was best for her, since she would have to deal with the hearing world sooner or later. Thus, Patricia learned to communicate perfectly with both the Deaf and the hearing. She was loved dearly by her family, especially her four sisters, and was always very close to her parents. Her sisters are all married—Shirley Ann Fee, Louise Jean Scott, Nancy Mildred Dunlop, and Janet Eileen McCormick. Pat was an extremely independent person with a deep need to prove she could do things on her own.

The Canadian Theatre of the Deaf came into existence in 1975, although it was then known as the British Columbia Deaf Mime Troupe. One of the first four Deaf Canadian aspiring performers was Pat Nowosad. She had always been fascinated with Marcel Marceau so she studied mime before she joined the troupe in 1975. Another female troupe member was Maryann Chmiel. Before long, they became an established professional touring company affiliated with the Canadian Cultural Society of the Deaf (CCSD).

As performers, the troupe received rave reviews as they attempted to break down some of the barriers between the Deaf and hearing worlds. Unfortunately, the group's financial future became so uncertain that despite their prestigious international status and reputation as Deaf performers, individual members began to pursue other career interests.

Pat worked for several corporations and at the E.C. Drury School for the Deaf in Milton, Ontario, for several years. She was also the recipient of numerous awards for her contributions to the Deaf Community, as well as her talents as a performer.

Sadly, she passed away in 1992 at the age of forty-three years, greatly missed and always remembered by her parents, sisters, and her daughter, Ursula.

SHARLENE NYE-PETRONE was born hearing to hearing parents, Joan and Lawrence Nye, in Hamilton, Ontario. She became Deaf at the age of two as a result of being stricken with meningitis. Her great-aunt, Elsie Goodall, is Deaf, but she has no other known Deaf relatives on her side of the family. She is married to a Deaf man, Robert Edward Petrone, who has numerous Deaf relatives, including his late father, Edward Petrone, his mother, Rosalie Petrone, his sister, Angela Petrone Stratiy, and his deceased aunt, Dora Morris. Robert is a Gallaudet graduate in Social Work, and has a Master of Education degree in Deaf Education from Western Maryland College. After eight years of teaching at the Manitoba School for the Deaf in Winnipeg, he moved to Ontario and has been a high school teacher at E.C. Drury School for the Deaf in Milton since 1990. Sharlene and Robert have three hearing children, two from his previous marriage, Shay and Byron, and a new baby boy, Tyrone. They presently make their home in Cambridge, Ontario.

When Sharlene's Deafness was discovered, her parents took Sign Language courses in order to learn to communicate with her. They also worked as volunteers for the Canadian Hearing Society and, for five years, from 1983 to 1988, they ran the lease-to-purchase program which allowed Deaf persons to obtain TTYs and closed caption decoders at affordable prices.

After two years at Queensdale Preschool in Hamilton, Sharlene was educated at the former Ontario School for the Deaf, now called E.C. Drury School, in Milton, for fourteen years. While she was a student she was the recipient of many different awards including the Superintendent's Award, the Communication Award, and the Good Conduct Award. When she graduated in 1989, she enrolled at Gallaudet University in Washington, DC, to pursue a Bachelor of Arts degree in Biochemistry. She had always been interested in science, but had never anticipated she would one day major in biochemistry. After graduating from Gallaudet, she attended Western Maryland College to take up graduate studies. There, she obtained a Master of Science degree in Deaf Education.

Upon completing her studies Sharlene applied for a position as a high school science teacher at her alma mater, E.C. Drury School for the Deaf in Milton. She was offered the position and accepted, so the school has more or less become her second home. She has spent more than eighteen years there as a student and a teacher. As a staff member, she has served as graduation chairperson, student parliament advisor, yearbook advisor, Class of '99 and '01 advisor, and coach of the school's soccer team. She also met her husband, Robert Petrone, at E.C. Drury School because both of them are faculty members there.

While attending Western Maryland College (WMC), Sharlene was involved with the Western Maryland College Association, working with students to create and implement a professional/social organization for Deaf education students. She was also an active member of the by-laws committee, and worked with candidates who were applying for staff positions at WMC. She is currently chairperson of school events at E.C. Drury School.

In her leisure hours, Sharlene's hobbies are interior decorating, knitting, working at country crafts, and travelling.

NYITRAI (STONE), Kathryn ("Kathy") Evelyn

1948–
Residential Counsellor and Teacher Assistant.

KATHY STONE was born Deaf into a hearing family at Yorkton, Saskatchewan. She had a Deaf uncle, her mother's brother, Chester Scoville, who is now deceased, but was a former student at the Manitoba School for the Deaf in Winnipeg. Kathy has no other known Deaf relatives and her two adult children, Arnall and Amanda, are both hearing. Kathy currently makes her home in Edmonton, Alberta.

She was educated at the Saskatchewan School for the Deaf in Saskatoon, from which she graduated in 1968, and was chosen to present the valedictory address at the graduation ceremony. She had been taught orally, so her presentation was given orally and interpreted in ASL by Mr. Chapman. Kathy was an excellent student and was awarded the Senior Ring for the year 1967–68. She participated in many school activities in her teen years and was especially active in the school's Youth Bowling Club. She recalls winning a bowling championship in 1968 where their Deaf team competed against hearing teams in a hearing league.

When she left the Saskatchewan School for the Deaf, Kathy attended Gallaudet College (now Gallaudet University) in Washington, DC, from 1968 to 1973. She majored in biology and received a BA degree. While there, she received an award for having the highest grades during her preparatory year. Many years later she took correspondence courses for a year in childhood development through Athabasca University in Alberta.

Kathy's employment began with a job as a housekeeper at the Duck Mountain Provincial Park in Saskatchewan. After moving to Alberta she spent nineteen years as a residential counsellor at the Alberta School for the Deaf (ASD), while it had a residential program. When the residence closed in 1993 Kathy began working as a teacher assistant at ASD, and that is still her position today.

For many years Kathy and her children lived in Spruce Grove, just outside Edmonton. During that period of her life, when Arnall and Amanda were young, she was kept very busy with their school and recreational activities, because they were involved in hockey, soccer, softball, and swimming. Until they were in their teens, she was assisted in their sporting activities by her former husband, Gabor. She also had to commute to her work at ASD. This made it virtually impossible for her to be active in the Deaf Community in Edmonton.

When Kathy moved to the city she became a member of the Edmonton Association of the Deaf (EAD), and enjoyed volunteering and assisting in any way she could. She has taken ASL training and become a member of the Alberta Cultural Society of the Deaf (ACSD). Everyone who knows Kathy refers to her as a lady with a heart of gold. She is generous with her time and energy, and is always willing to help out where help is needed. Her colleagues at ASD, over the many years of her employment there, commend her highly for her willing assistance and generosity. She is held in high esteem by both staff and students. On 27 November 2001, Kathy was presented with a certificate in recognition of her exemplary work by the Edmonton Public School Board. The nomination was initiated by the teachers and students at ASD.

Kathy's hobbies and interests include cycling, knitting, crocheting, working at various crafts, gardening, swimming, and bowling. She is a kind and gentle woman who is an outstanding role model for the next generation of Deaf women in Canada.

OLSON (COLE), Marlene Anne ("Mac")

1941–
Farming Partner, Ceramics Creator, Informal Sign Language Instructor, and Computer Enthusiast.

MARLENE ANNE COLE was born into a hearing family that lived in the rural community of Asquith, near Saskatoon, Saskatchewan. The cause of her Deafness is unknown and she has no Deaf relatives. She is married to Elmer Olson who is Deaf and they have two hearing daughters—Elmira, who lives in Edmonton, and Sheri, who lives in Saskatoon. Three other children died in infancy.

Marlene was a student at the Saskatchewan School for the Deaf in Saskatoon from 1947 to 1960. There were three girls in the school with the name "Marlene" so, in order to distinguish between them, Marlene Anne Cole was given the nickname "Mac" which was derived from her initials. She started school when she was four and a half years old, which made it hard for her to leave her family. Because of her young age, she soon forgot her family members between her trips home for Christmas. Marlene remembers playing a lot of sports, including basketball, gymnastics, and softball. She loved all her friends and her classes, but remembers how mean the punishments were.

Following her graduation from the School for the Deaf, Marlene worked at Dowding's Florist Shop in Saskatoon for thirteen years, which she enjoyed. Her boss and the staff taught her how to arrange flowers for different types of special occasions. In 1966 she started dating Elmer Olson, whom she had known at school, and who had been in her graduating class. He was working as a goldsmith for Logan Kennedy Jewellers in Saskatoon at that time. Marlene and Elmer were married in 1967 and built a house on a farm they developed, south of Saskatoon on Highway #11. They raised cows, chickens, and pigs, and Marlene cooked

meals while the men worked in the fields every summer.

When Logan Kennedy retired in 1982, Elmer bought his jewellery business, and is still the owner. Marlene took ceramics classes and purchased a kiln to do her own firing. For years she taught other Deaf women the art of ceramics and hosted Sign Language classes attended by her neighbours. She offered the ceramics classes in her basement and the group took turns going to different neighbours' homes for the sign lessons, serving refreshments and turning the events into social outings which they all enjoyed.

Marlene's leisure hours are filled with various hobbies and interests. She likes crocheting, quilting and working on the computer. She also does the accounting for Elmer's business. Sometimes she meets friends for coffee and a visit. She has been a member of the Saskatoon Association of the Deaf (SAD) since she graduated from the School for the Deaf and has served on various committees.

PARADIS (DAIGNEAULT), Jeanne d'Arc

1945–
Assistant Editor, Long-Time Customer Services Representative for *Reader's Digest*, and Proud Wife and Mother.

JEANNE D'ARC PARADIS was born Deaf in Rivière-Du-Loup, Québec, into a large family with three hard-of-hearing brothers and four sisters, two hearing and two Deaf—(herself and Esther). Hers is a hereditary hearing loss and she has several relatives who are hard of hearing—her mother, an aunt, an uncle, and her grandmother. Her Deaf sister, Esther Paradis-Larivière, an ex-nun, is now married to a Deaf husband, Claude Larivière, and they have an adult hearing son.

Jeanne d'Arc's husband, Jacques Daigneault, is Deaf and they have two daughters, Isabelle and Nadia, who each have only a slight hearing impairment. Isabelle works for 911 (Alert-Santé), and loves her job, which accommodates her hearing needs by providing her with a personal telephone line. Nadia is in the process of completing a teaching degree. Whether she will teach Deaf or hearing students has not yet been decided.

Jeanne d'Arc and Jacques make their home in Anjou, Québec, and Jacques works as a barber. Neither Isabelle nor Nadia have any children at present, but their parents look forward to enjoying grandchildren in the future.

Jacques has owned his own barber-shop in Beloeil, Québec, for thirty-five years. It is situated in the house

where he was born, and he is well known in the community. His customers are mostly hearing people, but they manage to communicate with him quite readily.

Jeanne d'Arc is the assistant editor of the French newspaper for the Deaf Community, *Revue Voir Dire*, which is published bi-monthly in Montréal and covers a wide variety of topics. Like most other Deaf girls born into French families in the province of Québec, she attended the Institute for Deaf Women on St. Denis Street in Montréal from age fourteen to eighteen. She received her earlier education in mainstream public schools with hearing children, which presented the obvious systemic difficulties.

On completing her education, Jeanne d'Arc began working as a customer services representative for *Reader's Digest* in Montréal, where she was the only Deaf employee for over thirty years, from December 1964 until June 1996. That summer she was among the 103 people who were laid off from their jobs, which she found hard to accept. She had become fluently bilingual during her years with *Reader's Digest*, and had given that company excellent and dedicated service.

After losing her job, she was asked to teach a French course to Deaf people at Centre Alpha-Sourd and became very active in the Deaf Community, serving as vice-president of Montréal's Deaf Community Centre, secretary of Centre Alpha-Sourd, and secretary of Regroupement des Organismes des Sourds du Québec (ROSQ). In 2003, ROSQ will host an international congress, so there are busy months ahead for Jeanne d'Arc.

When she has any leisure hours, she enjoys spending time with her family and many friends. Her hobbies are reading and writing, as well as velo and rollerblading.

PARKER, Betty-Lou

1959–
Deaf Lifeguard, Talented Swimmer, Aquatic Instructor, and Highly Motivated Role Model.

BETTY-LOU PARKER was born Deaf to hearing parents in Walkerton, Ontario. She has a younger Deaf sister, Beth Parker, who is involved in newsletter reporting, and a hearing cousin, Jennifer Roe, who works as a classroom assistant at Robarts School for the Deaf in London, Ontario. Betty-Lou also works at Robarts School and makes her home in London. Her sister Beth, in 1999, contributed interesting stories about Betty-Lou to *Deafnation News* and *Deaf Canada Today*. These articles have broadened the Deaf Community's understanding and appreciation of Betty Lou's unique accomplishments, explaining how she has made quick water rescues possible.

Betty-Lou was educated at E.C. Drury School for the Deaf in Milton, Ontario, from 1965 to 1974, and at Robarts School for the Deaf in London, from 1974 to 1979, earning a high school diploma. Further education took the form of earning an impressive array of certificates and credentials to qualify for the National Lifeguard Service. She is also a licensed aquatic instructor.

While taking her water safety training, Betty-Lou worked at odd jobs. She was a talented swimmer and lifeguarding soon became her goal. She was apprenticed to Donna Forster and Paul Carroll, who are both highly rated hearing lifeguards. She took Bronze Medallion and Bronze Cross courses, Red Cross leadership training, first-aid, and CPR certification, and water safety training before she applied and was hired for the lifeguarding position at Robarts School. Although the courses were difficult, her positive attitude and determination helped her to succeed. She has always been keenly motivated and is a positive thinker who has the support and confidence of family members and friends.

When Betty-Lou took the lifeguarding position, her mentor, Donna Forster, made certain she had TTY access for emergency calls. She also contacted the Royal Life-Saving Society of Canada (RLSSC) to inform them of Betty-Lou's Deafness. That was how she happened to find out that Betty-Lou was the first Deaf lifeguard in Ontario. There is a strong possibility that she might also be the first in Canada, but no records exist to verify this claim. Nevertheless, she is a wonderful role model for Deaf children and adults alike. They recognize her outstanding skills and qualifications, and can aspire to take as much pride in their own achievements as Betty-Lou has taken in hers during her twelve years of service.

At the Robarts School she started out as a residential counsellor, but is currently working as a classroom assistant who helps special-needs students, an ASL instructor, an aquatic instructor, and a pool lifeguard. Her volunteer activities in the Deaf Community include serving on various committees—Deaf Children's Festival, Deaf Concerns, World Deaf Olympics Funding, Robarts School Interpreters, and Internal Review of Employment Equity. She has also acted as convenor for the Canadian Deaf swimming championships. From February to June 2001, she acted as a supervisory team leader.

When she can find leisure time in her busy life, this talented and dedicated woman pursues her favourite hobbies—interior design and refinishing antique furniture.

If any young Deaf women were interested in becoming lifeguards, Betty Lou Parker would be the right person to consult.

PARSER (LEHMAN), Hilda Amanda

1925–
Talented Craftswoman and Active Senior in the Deaf Community.

HILDA LEHMAN was born hearing into a hearing family in a rural Mennonite community near Tofield, Alberta. She was the eldest of five children and the only girl. She and one of her brothers, who is hard of hearing, both lost a significant degree of their hearing at an early age due to a severe bout of measles and high fevers. Hilda's loss was greater than her brother's, but they were always close to each other because of their mutual affliction. She has no other known Deaf relatives but her brother is married to a Deaf woman, to whom she has always been close.

Hilda's deceased husband, Alfred Parser, was a charming Deaf Frenchman from Montréal. They had four hearing children, one daughter and three sons. The eldest, Darlene Karran, is an ASL interpreter who works at the Alberta School for the Deaf (ASD), and Consulting Services under the Edmonton Public School Board. The three boys are also fluent in ASL, and they are a very close-knit family. Alfred passed away in 1996, but they made their home in Edmonton for many years, and Hilda continues to reside there in her condo, with her small Yorkshire terrier for companionship.

Because there was no school for Deaf children in Alberta at that time, Hilda was sent to the Manitoba School for the Deaf in Winnipeg when she was eight years old. This was a difficult decision for her parents. Because they did not know Sign Language and only used gestures to communicate with Hilda, it was a frightening experience for her as she did not understand where she was going nor why. Nevertheless, with the encouragement of their family doctor, who knew Hilda was a bright child and needed to learn to interact and communicate with other Deaf children, the family reluctantly let her go.

She recalls meeting other Deaf children on the train who were communicating in Sign Language, causing her to feel lonely and left out. As it happens, despite the family's sacrifice when they sent her off to school, it was the best thing they could possibly have done for her. She was soon accepted and loved being among her Deaf friends in the residential school environment.

Because the Lehmans were poor, struggling farmers, they could not afford the train fare to bring Hilda home for the Christmas holidays, so she did not see them again until the following summer. She loved them all dearly, but was anxious to get back to school in the fall where there was Sign Communication all around her. Although her mother and brothers did learn some signs, they relied mainly on fingerspelling, and her father never did learn to communicate with her except through gestures.

One of Hilda's fondest recollections of her youth is the day her father brought home a Deaf horse they named Erma. She formed a strong bond with Erma and rode her constantly, always looking forward to seeing her on her visits home from school. During World War II the Manitoba School for the Deaf was taken over by the military, so she had to complete her education at the R.J.D. Williams School for the Deaf in Saskatoon, Saskatchewan. She then returned to Winnipeg and found employment in a bakery. A year later she moved to Edmonton, where she met and married Alfred Parser.

Hilda and Alfred ("Fred") lived in Toronto briefly, but soon returned to Edmonton to a drier climate due to Fred's chronic sinus condition. Their children were all born in Edmonton, and Hilda is now the proud grandmother of five granddaughters and one grandson. Because she grew up with four brothers and then raised three sons, she is pleased to have so many female grandchildren, but she loves them all equally.

Hilda is a talented craftswoman who has supplied a variety of her hand-made items for sale at craft shows and stores for more than fifteen years. Sometimes, she and her Deaf sister-in-law collaborate in these enterprises. She is very independent and has travelled extensively, mostly with her husband, but occasionally with other Deaf women, and once with a church group to the Holy Land and Greece. She is active in the Deaf Seniors' Club and keeps herself fully occupied with her hobbies and other interests.

PARSONS, Amy Louise

1982–
Born-Leader, Camp Counsellor, Model Student, and Avid Traveller.

AMY PARSONS was born deaf to hearing parents in Halifax, Nova Scotia. Her father's family has been part of the Black community in Lucasville, Nova Scotia, for many years, and her great-grandfather served in the No. 2 Construction Battalion, the first and only true Black battalion in Canadian military history, formed during World War I. Amy has no known deaf relatives, but has a multitude of deaf friends. Her parents opted for a Total Communication approach when her deafness was diagnosed, and Amy began to sign at two years of age and continued to expand her skills. Today she is flexible in her communication, using speech, lipreading, and some signs with hearing friends, and ASL with deaf friends. Amy currently makes her home in Beaver Bank and Wolfville, both in Nova Scotia.

Her formal education began at the age of four, in day classes for deaf children at Harbourview School in Dartmouth, Nova Scotia, where Total Communication was used, with teachers signing and speaking simultaneously. Five years later she entered her neighbourhood school as part of the Atlantic Provinces Special Education Authority's (APSEA's) mainstream program, with an interpreter. Amy was the first elementary-level student to receive interpreter funding under the APSEA program. Through grades seven to twelve she was part of school teams such as track, softball, and basketball.

She continued her schooling in this manner until she graduated from Millwood High School in Lower Sackville, Nova Scotia, where she was elected by her peers as valedictorian of the class of 2000, and delivered the valedictory address at the ceremony. Her advice to her peers was not to consider their graduation as the end, but to look upon it as the starting block in the game of life. In her final year of high school she was picked as editor of the 1999–2000 school yearbook.

While attending high school Amy gained a variety of employment experiences: part-time as a clerk in the local library, a produce clerk in a supermarket, and an administrative assistant for the Society of Deaf and Hard of Hearing Nova Scotians. Since 1989 she has attended the Elks' Deaf Camp in Harvey, New Brunswick, as a camper and then as a counsellor, providing a splendid role model for younger deaf children. She is presently a student at Acadia University in Wolfville, Nova Scotia, and loves it. Living in residence gives her an opportunity to meet new and interesting people from all walks of life who make her feel accepted as a vital part of the academic community. She uses an interpreter and notetaker in her classes.

On campus, Amy was elected to the Students' Representative Council (SRC), the governing body of the Acadia Students' Union (ASU), for 2000-01. She was then elected to represent the Student's Union (ASU) on the Acadia Board of Governors for 2001–02. She has also been involved with the university's Sensory Motor Instructional Leadership Experience (SMILE), where local children with disabilities interact with university students in the local pool one morning a week. Amy has found it a very rewarding experience.

She has travelled extensively in Canada and, in March 2000, visited five European countries. She keeps busy and enjoys reading in her leisure hours, so she is never bored. Her philosophy is that today's accomplishments will lead to tomorrow's successes. Her goals are to finish her Bachelor of Arts degree and continue to work toward her PhD. For her personal motto, she has adopted this quote from one of her role models, Dr. Irving King Jordan, the first deaf president of Gallaudet University: "Deaf people can do anything except hear." In view of her young age, the deaf community across Canada can expect to reap the benefits of Amy's successes far into the future.

FRANCES LUCILLE FORD was the only child of William Waller Ford and Isabelle Medd Doughty. She was born hearing in Bowling Green, Kentucky, but became Deaf in infancy due to a severe case of measles. In 1917 she was enrolled in the Kentucky School for the Deaf in Danville where she was educated until her graduation in 1931.

Shortly after graduating, the very popular Miss Ford was attending a social event at a Deaf Club in Detroit, Michigan. There she was told about "Eddie" Payne, a young Deaf Canadian who had recently successfully passed the required tests to earn an airplane pilot's license in what is now the city of Windsor (at that time called Walkerville), Ontario. The story fascinated her and she was eager to meet this unique young man.

Soon afterward, the same Deaf Club sponsored a beauty contest and Frances was selected as the winner. At the social gathering which followed, she had the happy privilege of finally meeting Edward Thomas Payne who promptly invited her to join him on one of his flights. She accepted his invitation and they departed on what was Frances' first experience in the air. They both claimed that while they were soaring among the clouds, romance blossomed between them. They were married at Eddie's mother's home in a beautiful wedding ceremony in South Walkerville on 4 June 1932, followed by a honeymoon trip to Toronto, Niagara Falls, and London.

The happy young couple settled in South Walkerville and raised two fine children—a son, William, who later became an Alberta MLA, and a daughter, Lynn. Edward Payne was believed to have been the first licensed Deaf male pilot in North America, and possibly even in the world. He continued flying such aircraft as the Reid Rambler, Gypsy Moth 60, Taylor Cub, and the Piper Cub until the advent of radio communications at the end of World War II.

Frances and Edward were popular and very active in their South Walkerville community. Frances possessed great beauty and charm and was a highly successful homemaker and hostess whose name often appeared in the society columns of local newspapers. Edward was employed as a linotype operator with the Walkerville daily newspaper, *The Border Cities Star*. He, too, was very popular, especially among his co-workers at the newspaper and his fellow pilots at the Border Cities Aero Club. They were occasionally visited by Frances' relatives and friends from Kentucky.

Throughout her life Frances remained popular not only in the Deaf Community but also among her hearing peers. She was proud of her accomplished husband and her two children, whom she loved unfailingly, and was strengthened by her abiding faith in God.

When Edward Payne died in 1973, Frances left Windsor, Ontario, and relocated in Alberta where she resided for the next twenty-eight years among her expanding family which, at the time of her death, included nine grandchildren and thirty-six great-grandchildren. Her son Bill was an MLA for Calgary-Fish Creek from 1979 to 1993. He sponsored successful legislation recognizing ASL as an official language in Alberta, as well as a successful motion that cleared the way for Deaf persons to be called to jury duty. In addition to his work in the provincial legislature, Bill chaired a $1.2-million fundraising drive to endow the Western Canadian Chair of Studies in Deafness (WCCSD) at the University of Alberta in Edmonton.

Frances Payne spent the last years of her life at the Intercare Southwood Care Centre in Calgary, where she died peacefully in her sleep at the age of eighty-nine years on 14 January 2001. She is sadly missed and fondly remembered by her devoted family and many friends.

PEIKOFF (NATHANSON), Pauline Pearl

1913–
"Walking Alumni Encyclopedia," Office Assistant, and Tireless Volunteer.

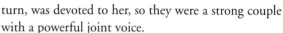

PAULINE (known to her family and friends as "Polly") PEARL NATHANSON was born Deaf in Winnipeg, Manitoba, where she was educated at the School for the Deaf from 1921 to 1930. She then attended Kendall School for a year before entering Gallaudet College in Washington, DC, in 1931. In 1932 she married David Peikoff and they returned to Canada, settling in Winnipeg where David became a partner in Central Press, a commercial printing business. He had earned his BA degree from Gallaudet College in 1929, majoring in English and Journalism. During his under-graduate days he also worked at the *Washington Post* newspaper, so he had an excellent background for his entrepreneurship in the printing business.

After four years, however, David and Polly, with their two hearing daughters, moved to Toronto where they remained for the next twenty-four years. David worked as service manager for the Sealy Mattress Company, a business that was owned by Polly's family. David became a prominent activist and advocate for the Deaf and hard of hearing, holding prestigious offices in many organizations, several of which he founded. There is a common saying that "behind every successful man there stands a woman" and, indeed, this was certainly true of David and Polly Peikoff.

Although she was the wife of Canada's best-known Deaf political activist, Polly's contribution to his work was largely "behind the scenes." She devotedly supported her husband in all areas of his advocacy in Canada as well as in the US, while David was president of the Gallaudet Alumni Association from 1954 to 1961 and after their move to Washington, DC, in 1961. She was shy of publicity and willingly worked quietly and efficiently in her husband's shadow. David, in turn, was devoted to her, so they were a strong couple with a powerful joint voice.

When they moved to Washington, Polly took with her, to the Gallaudet Campus, the same quiet dedica-tion and energy she had always exhibited in Toronto. Together, she and David helped establish the Gallaudet Canadian Club in 1967, with fifty members. Polly worked in the Gallaudet Alumni Office for twenty-three years, where she fondly became known as "the walking encyclopedia" for her wide knowledge of alumni affairs. She assisted her husband, who was director of development, and Jack Gannon, who was director of alumni relations. She was well known for organizing alumni reunions and, even after she retired, continued to serve in a volunteer capacity.

Her greatest honour was achieved on 23 October 1986 when the Gallaudet Alumni Association announced the establishment of the Polly Peikoff Service to Others Award. This tribute honours her as a woman with a "can-do" attitude who quietly and unobtrusively dedi-cated her life to serving others. She is seen as a powerful role model for all Deaf women both at home and abroad. She now makes her home in Laurel, Maryland, US.

PENNER-ZIMMER, Patricia ("Gail")

1949–
Champion Swimmer, Keypunch Operator, Sports Enthusiast, Scuba Diver, Bowling Champion, and Draftsperson.

GAIL PENNER was born hearing in New Westminster, BC. She became Deaf at eighteen months of age after having adenoid surgery. She then went to live with her maternal grandparents, Stinson and Blanche Mercer, who raised her on a farm at Rosedale, BC. In 1954, when she was five years old, she was sent to Jericho Hill School for the Deaf and Blind in Vancouver. Her grandparents took her home to the farm on certain weekends, and worried about her constantly, but were pleased with her progress. Gail was the eldest of five children—a sister, a stepsister, and two stepbrothers, all of whom are hearing. She has no known Deaf relatives, but is married to a Deaf man, Gerald C. Zimmer, an alumnus of both the Saskatchewan and Manitoba Schools for the Deaf, a Gallaudet graduate, and currently a teacher at the Burnaby South School which houses the British Columbia School for the Deaf. She also has two hear-ing cousins, Barry and Danny McMillan, who had the privilege of being photographed by the media while escorting Prime Minister Trudeau and Prince Charles through their father's fish cannery in Vancouver on separate occasions. Gail and Gerald have three hearing children—Amanda, Alexander, and Anna. They make their home in Burnaby.

While attending Jericho Hill School, Gail joined the swim team and competed against other high schools and swim clubs, winning many ribbons and two sportsmanship awards. She also participated in other sports such as basketball, volleyball, fencing, field hockey, baseball, and bowling. With her classmates, she also enjoyed roller- and ice-skating. At the World Games for the Deaf held in Washington, DC, in 1965, she was a member of the Canadian Deaf Swim Team that won gold in the medley relay and bronze in the backstroke. She later competed in Belgrade, Yugoslavia, and in Malmo, Sweden, where she won a bronze medal in the medley relay.

In the meantime, she decided to further her education by taking a keypunch operator's course, which led her to a job with BC Tel (now Telus) where she worked for three years. She and a close friend then decided to escape to Europe for nine months, backpacking through Scotland, England, Czechoslovakia, Yugoslavia, Greece, and Italy, visiting schools for the Deaf wherever they could. On their return, Gail landed a job at Foremost Data Centre, where she worked for the next four years. She decided to upgrade her education with the intention of registering at Gallaudet College (now Gallaudet University), but her plan did not materialize. She was hired again by BC Tel, acquiring promotions from keypunch operator to accounts payable, then to billing control and verification, and eventually to financial analyst. She had been taking courses in drafting at the BC Institute of Technology

and in 1994 became a draftsperson in outside field operations for BC Tel. She has held that position for twenty-eight years and still loves it, always learning new technologies and keeping abreast of new ideas.

As a young woman, Gail took scuba-diving lessons and became certified, passing on the techniques to the young people at Deaf Youth Leadership Camp when it was hosted by Vancouver in 1976. Another highlight of her youth was the pleasure of being crowned Miss Deaf Canada in Vancouver in 1976. She participated in tennis championships and won twice in ladies' doubles, went cross-country skiing at Madonna Di Campiglio in the Alps of northern Italy when she attended the World Winter Games for the Deaf in 1983, and was a member of the Canadian bowling team in Denmark in 1997 and in Rome in 2001. She has been very actively involved in the BC Deaf Sports Federation and the BC Cultural Society of the Deaf.

Gail has been an active member of the Greater Vancouver Association of the Deaf (GVAD) for many years, and was involved in the membership committee, acted as social director, typed its newsletters, and assisted with the children's Christmas party. She has also served as its volleyball chairperson and prepared its tennis schedules.

Gail's hobbies include sewing, art, crafts, knitting, crocheting, cross-stitching, coin and stamp collecting, and solving jigsaw puzzles. She also loves pottery-making, rollerblading, hiking, alpine skiing, and swimming. She is eager to take up kayaking as well. Her extensive travels have given her a global perspective on life and, with her myriad skills and talents, Gail is an excellent mentor and role model for young Deaf Canadian women.

PERRY (WIENS), Deborah Anne

1957–
ASL Instructor, Residential and Community Support Worker, and Business Office Clerk.

DEBORAH WIENS, born into a hearing family in Montréal, Québec, became Deaf at six months of age due to illness. Her mother has had an adult-onset hearing loss for over twenty years, but Deborah has no other known Deaf relatives. She is married to a Deaf man, P. Michael Perry, who is an autobody repairman, and they have two Deaf sons, Clint and Colin. Clint will be taking an automotive paint course, and Colin hopes to take a General Education Diploma (GED) and has taken part in filmmaking and web design. Deborah and Michael currently make their home in Cloverdale, BC.

Deborah was educated at the MacKay Centre for the Deaf in Montréal, where she was valedictorian when she graduated. She then added other credentials to her qualifications as a mature student. She is a certified first-aid practitioner through the St. John's Ambulance Society and a graduate of the ASL Instructors' Certification Program at Douglas College in New Westminster, BC. In addition, Deborah has participated in various educational conferences and workshops for the purpose of professional development.

Her employment history has been interesting and varied. From 1975 to 1979, she worked for the Royal Bank of Canada in Montréal, Statistics Canada in Ottawa, Employment and Immigration Canada in Ottawa, and the Ottawa Public Library. Since 1979 she has served as an ASL instructor in several venues, beginning in Ottawa, Ontario, and continuing in New Westminster, BC. She has also worked as a secretary for the Vancouver Church of the Deaf, coordinator's assistant for the Kiwassa Neighbourhood Service Agency in Vancouver, and one-to-one resource person for Social Services and the Handicapped Resource Centre and Insurance Corporation of British Columbia. She has done private ASL tutoring, acted as a life-skills instructor, and worked as an office clerk for Employment and Immigration Canada and the Burnaby Emergency Physicians' Association. In Toronto, Ontario, she was a job-training coach at the Bob Rumball Association for the Deaf and, in Abbotsford, BC, she was a residential careworker. Deborah is currently employed full-time as an adult support worker with the Delta Community Living Society in Tsawwassen, BC.

Deborah's involvement in the Deaf Community consists mainly of her countless hours of volunteer work with the Vancouver Church of the Deaf and the Kiwassa Neighborhood Service Agency. In her leisure hours Deborah pursues numerous hobbies and interests, which include a variety of arts and crafts, needlepoint, interior decorating, gardening, crocheting, and sewing.

PETRONE (BODRUG), Rosalie

1919–
Homemaker, Garment Industry Worker, Skilled Seamstress, and Volunteer for the Deaf Community.

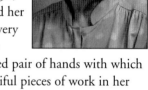

It is a unique coincidence and a source of pride for ROSALIE PETRONE that she shares her 14 December birthdate with her only daughter, Angela Stratiy. Mother and daughter were born twenty-eight years apart—Rosalie in 1919 and Angela in 1947. Both were born in Manitoba.

It is not known exactly when Rosalie became Deaf but it was likely at a very early age because she seems to have spent her entire life within the Deaf community and Culture. She and her Deaf sister Dora were raised in the farming community of Dallas, Manitoba, where their parents settled as immigrants from the Ukraine. Dora came to Canada with her parents while Rosalie was born in Dallas.

She attended the Manitoba School for the Deaf in Winnipeg from 1931 to 1940 and then the Saskatchewan School for the Deaf in Saskatoon for an additional year. She then worked as a housekeeper for a family in a private Winnipeg home for one year before taking a job as a seamstress at the Northern Shirt Factory.

In 1943 she married Edward Petrone, who was also Deaf. Together they raised two fine Deaf children—Angela and her younger brother Robert, who was born in 1955. Edward and Rosalie enjoyed forty-eight years of married happiness before she was widowed. After their children became teenagers, Rosalie worked in the garment industry in Winnipeg for the Allan Company, the Hercules Company, and Kaplan's until 1969 when she began her fourteen-year career as seamstress at the Manitoba School for the Deaf.

After retiring from the workforce in 1983, she lived in Calgary for four years before settling in Edmonton in 1990, to be near her daughter and her grandsons of whom she is very fond and justly proud. She possesses a remarkably gifted pair of hands with which she has crafted many beautiful pieces of work in her lifetime.

She continues to be active in Edmonton's Deaf community, particularly with the Canadian Cultural Society of the Deaf, for which she has received recognition in the form of awards. The achievement which gives her the greatest pride and satisfaction is her role as the mother of two highly successful Deaf offspring—Angela Stratiy of Edmonton and Robert Petrone of Milton, Ontario. Angela, in particular, has made innumerable and highly significant contributions to the Deaf community locally, provincially, nationally, and internationally.

Rosalie, now in her eighties, continues to enjoy sewing, often completing alterations in a matter of hours. For new garments and more complex items, she rarely requires more than a day or two. One of her fairly recent creative projects was the sewing of two flags for the Canadian Cultural Society of the Deaf, one in English and the other in French. More recently she made a flag for the Youth Canada Tournament of the Deaf, held in Edmonton, Alberta, 12–17 May 2001.

She is happy and contented among her many Deaf friends in Edmonton and still drives her car, a skill she acquired in Winnipeg when she was sixty years old.

She does not go on lengthy trips, but likes the independence of driving herself to do her shopping in nearby stores.

PETTYPIECE, Marguerite Mabel

1939–
Outstanding Speed-Skater, Avid Curler, and Retired Grandmother of Five.

MARGUERITE PETTYPIECE was born hearing into a hearing family in Boissevain, Manitoba. She became Deaf at the age of two due to illness. Her Deaf great-uncle, Clarence Pettypiece, was the first president of Winnipeg's Silent Hockey Club in 1912, when it was part of the city's Independent Amateur Hockey League. He was also very active in Winnipeg's Deaf Community.

Marguerite has two Deaf daughters, Kyra Zimmer and Sarah Rabu, who received Bachelor of Education degrees from the Faculty of Education at the University of Manitoba's 122nd Spring Convocation in 2001. Both of them graduated with a 4.0, straight-A, average. Marguerite was among the group of more than thirty Deaf friends and relatives who proudly attended their convocation. The university provided Kyra and Sarah with ASL interpreters for all their courses. They were also assisted by their classmates who shared their notes with them. Only one concession was made—they were exempted from the music requirement for their BEd degrees.

Kyra and Sarah both have Deaf husbands, Rick Zimmer and Marty Rabu. Kyra and Rick have a Deaf son, and Sarah and Marty have four hearing children. Marguerite is proud of her grandchildren as well as their parents. Kyra teaches in a Deaf literacy program and her husband Rick teaches ASL/English interpreting at Red River College (RRC). Sarah's husband Marty works for Boeing while Sarah teaches grade two at the Manitoba School for the Deaf.

Marguerite was educated at the Saskatchewan School for the Deaf in Saskatoon, where she completed grade ten before returning to Manitoba to join the workforce. She was employed by the Manitoba government for twenty-five years and in the private sector for ten years. She retired in 1999 and has made her home in Winnipeg for several decades. She has always been very active in the Deaf Community, especially in Deaf sports.

As a young girl, Marguerite was an outstanding speed-skater, for which she received numerous medals and trophies. In 1957 she ranked as Saskatchewan's top intermediate female speed-skater. Since 1980 she has also curled on many rinks with different skips, doing her share toward winning an impressive array of six gold and seven silver medals, from 1980 to 1998, at Canadian Deaf Championship bonspiels held in major cities across the country, from St. John's, Newfoundland to Vancouver, British Columbia.

In addition to her athletic awards, Marguerite received citations of appreciation from her employers before she retired, and several lunches were held in her honour. In her leisure hours she spends time with her daughters and their families, and enjoys such hobbies as reading and socializing over coffee with her friends.

PHILPOTT, Evelyn Ethel

1945–

Outstanding Food-Service Worker, and Dedicated Employee of the Government of Newfoundland and Labrador for Thirty-Three Years.

EVELYN PHILPOTT was born hearing to hearing parents at Cottle's Island, Newfoundland. She became Deaf at the age of one year due to illness. Evelyn has a younger sister, Joy Philpott, who is Deaf, a Deaf nephew, Glenn Barker, and a Deaf cousin, Roy Philpott. A hearing cousin, Denika Philpott-Lewis, works as an ASL interpreter for the Newfoundland Coordinating Council on Deafness (NCCD). Evelyn also has two hearing sisters and one hearing brother. She currently makes her home in St. John's Newfoundland. At the Eastern Canada Association of the Deaf's (ECAD's) 40th Biennial Convention held in Wolfville, Nova Scotia, she met a Deaf man from Ontario, James Macalpine, whose Deaf wife had passed away several years before. They have since become close friends.

Evelyn received one year of schooling at the MacKay Centre for the Deaf in Montréal, in 1959–60. This bright, talented woman has spent her entire adult life becoming self-educated. Her parents were very apprehensive about sending her away to school but, after five years of staying at home, Evelyn took a job-training and basic life-skills program at Hoyle's Home in St. John's. She then went directly into the workforce, joining the staff at the old Newfoundland School for the Deaf in Torbay for four years, from 1965 to 1969, as a food-service worker.

After one year working at the E.C. Drury School for the Deaf in Milton, Ontario, she returned to the Newfoundland School for the Deaf in Torbay for the next seventeen years, 1970 to 1987. Thus, she had

become an official of the Department of Education and a civil servant of the government of Newfoundland and Labrador. She continued to work in that capacity when she moved to the new School for the Deaf in St. John's in 1987, and continued for thirteen more years until her retirement in November 2000. When she retired, Evelyn was honoured with a Public Service Award for longevity, thirty-three years as a provincial government employee.

The Newfoundland Association of Public Employees also presented Evelyn with a certificate of appreciation on the occasion of her retirement in 2000. Throughout her many years as a distinguished food-service worker, Evelyn provided excellent role modelling for the students. She encouraged them to try unfamiliar foods and to eat properly.

Evelyn's involvement in the Deaf community includes membership in the Newfoundland and Labrador Association of the Deaf, where she enjoys playing dingo and attending card parties. Every second Wednesday evening, she plays skipbo with her friends, and also attends a monthly Bible study class for the Deaf.

In her spare time Evelyn does a variety of home cooking and baking, likes doing printed cotton embroidery, walking, and shopping. Recently, she enjoyed travelling to Nova Scotia to attend ECAD's 40th Biennial Convention in Wolfville.

PHILPOTT, Joy Elsie

1954–

Data-Entry Operator, Pay-Coding Clerk, Enthusiastic Curler, and Mature Student.

JOY PHILPOTT was born Deaf in Cottleville, Notre Dame Bay, Newfoundland. She has an older Deaf sister, Evelyn, who recently retired from the Newfoundland School for the Deaf (NSD) in St. John's, after working there for thirty three years in food services. She also has a Deaf nephew, a Deaf cousin, and a hearing niece who is an ASL interpreter. Joy is temporarily making her home in Halifax where she is upgrading her academic qualifications.

She was educated at NSD, where teachers used SEE rather than ASL as the language of instruction. Although

Joy is fluent in ASL, her first language, she has always felt that English, her second language, needed upgrading. After graduating from NSD in 1973, Joy trained at the Atlantic Technological Vocational Centre in Amherst, Nova Scotia, to qualify as a data-entry operator. She worked at that job for many years and later became a C4 pay-coding clerk at the Insurance Processing Operation Centre with Human

Resources Development Canada in St. John's, Newfoundland. In the summer of 2000 she was presented with a wristwatch and a certificate of appreciation for her twenty-six years of employment with the federal government.

Joy was always frustrated by her lack of a high school diploma, which she felt prevented her advancement and promotion on the job, so she made the decision to return to school. She had the full support and encouragement of Keith Clarke, her supervisor, and Tony Tilley, learning coordinator at the Information Technology Centre, who developed a learning plan. Searching for a program where ASL was the language of instruction took some time. Financial support was approved for her to enter the Deaf Academic Upgrading Program at Nova Scotia Community College in Halifax, from January 2000 to June 2001.

Joy acknowledges that her education as a mature student has been the result of team effort. Coupled with her own initiative and determination were the efforts of her friends and co-workers who created the opportunity and made financial support possible. She especially credits Keith Clarke, Rudy Rumsey, and Marina Mercer with being persistant on her behalf. During the 2000–2001 academic year, Joy carried a full course load, including English, mathematics, science, social studies, and computer literacy. She estimates that another two or three years of study will earn her the coveted high school equivalency diploma. This has become her cherished goal.

Prior to returning to school, Joy was an avid athlete and an accomplished curler who participated in the Canadian Deaf Curling Championships for twelve consecutive seasons, from 1988 to 1999. She enjoyed meeting old and new friends in each of those championships, but has had to put her curling career on hold, temporarily. She was also an enthusiastic cyclist, iceskater, rollerskater, and cross-country skier. Meanwhile, her lifelong dream is becoming a reality. Her plan is to return to Newfoundland upon completing her studies in Halifax.

PINK (McLAREN), Linda Patricia Mary

1944–2001
Keypunch Operator, Bank Employee, Microfilmer, and Private Day-Care Operator.

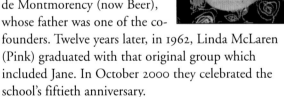

LINDA McLAREN was born hearing to hearing parents in Montréal, Québec, but became Deaf at the age of five, due to meningitis. She had no known Deaf relatives, but her husband, Garnet Pink, a long-time employee of the Department of National Defence, is Deaf. They had two hearing children, now successful adults, of whom they were justifiably proud—a daughter, Jennifer Badeen Pink, who is a specialist working with brain-injured persons, married to a wonderful man, Alex Badeen, and a son, David Pink, who is a location manager in the film industry in Vancouver, BC. Linda and Garnet have made their home in Ottawa since 1974. Linda could also proudly claim kinship to Daniel Petrie who directed and produced the internationally acclaimed movie *Children of a Lesser God,* which was filmed in Nova Scotia. Linda had two hearing sisters—Frances, who is a missionary nurse in Kenya, Africa, and is married to Walt, and Diane, who lives in Toronto with her husband, Heinz.

Linda received her education at several schools in Montréal, beginning with Priory School which was a private facility for hearing students. She then attended the Montréal Oral School for the Deaf before she went to Queen of Angels Academy, also for hearing students, where she finished her academic high school studies, along with her friend, JoAnne Stump. The Montréal Oral School for the Deaf opened in 1950, with five little "pioneer" pupils, one of whom was Jane de Montmorency (now Beer), whose father was one of the co-founders. Twelve years later, in 1962, Linda McLaren (Pink) graduated with that original group which included Jane. In October 2000 they celebrated the school's fiftieth anniversary.

Following her graduation, Linda attended O'Sullivan Business College, where she took courses that qualified her as a keypunch operator and office clerk. Subsequently, she was employed at Air Canada for three years and with the Bank of Nova Scotia for ten years. She also had a part-time job as a microfilmer and ran a private day-care business in her own home for ten years.

Linda and Garnet were actively involved in the National Capital Association of the Deaf from the time they moved to Ottawa. Over the years she was a regular volunteer for many of the activities sponsored by the Ottawa Deaf Club, where she was highly respected and recognized for her contributions and dedication.

In her leisure hours, Linda enjoyed various hobbies. She was keenly interested in most arts and crafts and was an avid collector of porcelains, dolls, and angels in particular. She also liked to read and travel. Sadly, Linda fought a difficult but courageous battle against bone cancer, and appreciated the support of her family and her wide network of friends in the Deaf Community. She passed away, surrounded by those who loved her, on 23 July 2001.

PIPER, Dellalee Bernadine

1964–

Advocate for Deaf Children and Youth, Athlete, Poet, ASL Instructor, and Aspiring Teacher of the Deaf.

DELLALEE PIPER, born in Calgary, Alberta, became Deaf at the age of eighteen months due to complications from a bout of German measles. She grew up with four adopted sisters and one brother, all with normal hearing. Her parents were involved with the Deaf Community while she was in school and helped with Scout Cubs for Deaf boys. Her closest sister, Deloris Piper, to whom Dellalee gives credit for helping her establish her Deaf identity, is a certified ASL interpreter now living in Vancouver, British Columbia. Dellalee was married to a Deaf man, and they had two hearing sons, Delvin and Delby. She is presently living with a hearing partner, Kevin Sinasac, and they have a hearing daughter, Kirbylee. Dellalee, Kevin, and the three children currently make their home at Lake Country, British Columbia.

Dellalee began her education at several mainstream public schools in Calgary, beginning from the time she was five years old in 1969 until she was twelve, in 1976. She was then enrolled at the Alberta School for the Deaf (ASD), in Edmonton, where she attended until she graduated in 1982. At first she was a residential student, but a year later her family moved from Calgary to Edmonton and she became a day student. Everyone in her family learned to sign. At ASD, Dellalee felt she had finally found her identity as a Deaf person and was able to grow, learn, and thrive. She soon became involved in acting, signing her poetry, signing Christmas carols for seniors in nursing homes, playing on ASD's sports teams, and becoming a Deaf Girl Guide of Canada.

She was chosen as Miss ASD at a pageant in 1981, attended Deaf Leadership Camp at Prince George, BC, in 1981, was involved in ASD Camp Breakaway in 1982, and was president of the graduation committee in 1982. She taught ASL in a summer program and worked with Deaf children at a summer day camp. Following her graduation from ASD, she attended Alberta College from 1982 to 1984, won the Dr. G.H. Villet Award, and participated in the Edmonton Deaf Festival with her poetry and stories. She then moved to Banff, Alberta, for work experience and was employed at Sunshine Village, Panorama Resort, and Moraine Lake. In the summer of 1984 Dellalee attended the Deaf Festival of the Arts in Edmonton, and was chosen as second runner-up in the Miss Deaf Canada Pageant.

She moved back to Calgary where she attended Career College to take courses in accounting and computer work, while teaching ASL as a volunteer to staff at a life insurance company. She also played on the Deaf women's slo-pitch and volleyball teams and was secretary for the Western Canada Deaf Summer Games hosted in Calgary in 1987, at which her volleyball team won first place. In 1988 she attended the Canadian Deaf Summer Games in Toronto to play co-ed volleyball, and the team won a gold medal. While living in Calgary she was married and divorced.

In 1992 Dellalee moved to Whistler, BC, with her present partner, where she taught ASL and was named "Employee of the Month" by the Whistler Resort Association twice in one year. They moved to Slocan, BC, where their daughter was born and Dellalee became an advocate for Deaf children and youth, travelling to Trail, Castlegar, Nelson, and Grandforks to teach Deaf Culture, Deaf values, and ASL. They later moved to the Okanagan, where she has continued the same type of work for the Okanagan School District, going into schools to expose students to Deaf Culture, ASL storytelling and poetry, in addition to working with the Deaf Children's Society of BC. She teaches ASL as a second language at a high school, and attends Douglas College, taking classes toward becoming a certified ASL instructor. She will then pursue a degree in Deaf Education. In addition to her work as a Deaf advocate, she serves on the committee representing the Okanagan in the Deaf Community Foundation of BC, is secretary for the Okanagan-Thompson Association of the Deaf, and sits on its committee for medical interpreter services.

Dellalee has been the recipient of many awards, honours, and recognitions for her contributions to the

Deaf Community, and has had her share of media attention. Her fondest memory is that of winning the Miss Deaf Alberta title in Calgary, in 1983–84, when she signed her poem "I'm Proud to be Deaf," for the talent portion of the contest.

In her leisure time, Dellalee's hobbies and interests include reading, writing poetry, spending time with her family, camping, swimming, skiing, hiking, cycling, and travelling. Her dream is to travel to other countries to teach Sign Language and Deaf Culture, and to help the Deaf in any way she can. Above all, she loves to entertain children, and they, in turn, greatly enjoy her many talents.

PIZZACALLA (WOJCIK), Helen Vera

1955–
President of the Canadian Cultural Society of the Deaf, Published Co-Author and Collaborator, Presenter, Mentor, Performer, and Educator of the Deaf.

HELEN WOJCIK was born Deaf to Deaf parents, Nicholas Wojcik and Ruth (Morton) Wojcik, in Kitchener, Ontario. She has several Deaf relatives—her sister, Norma Steele, her brother, Danny Wojcik, an uncle, Frank Wojcik, and an aunt, Wanda Aubey. She also has a famous hearing forebear, an ancestor on her mother's side of the family, Robert Morris, who was a congressman for the state of Pennsylvania and one of the signers of the American Declaration of Independence on 4 July 1776. He also served as a United States senator, representing Pennsylvania from 1789 to 1795. Helen's spouse, Mario Pizzacalla, is Deaf, and they have two hearing children, Roman and Lisa. The Pizzacallas currently make their home in Thorold, Ontario.

Helen's education began at the Ontario School for the Deaf in Belleville, where she attended for three years before transferring to the new provincial School for the Deaf in Milton (now E.C. Drury School) on 23 April 1963, as one of its first students. She graduated in 1971 and went on to Gallaudet University in Washington, DC, where she earned a Bachelor of Science degree in Business Administration in 1976. After many years of working in business offices, she went back to school, obtaining an Ontario Teacher's Certificate in Deaf Education from York University in Toronto in 1993.

Although Helen is probably best known for her lengthy involvement with the Canadian Cultural Society of the Deaf (CCSD), (as vice-president from 1991 to 1996 and president since 1997), she has achieved many other outstanding accomplishments. In 1990 she served as treasurer for the highly successful National Festival of the Arts and, since that same year, has also been a dedicated Sunday school teacher at St. Catharines Church of the Deaf. She collaborated with Joanne Cripps in the authorship of the publication *Cross-Cultural Mediation Programs for the Culturally Deaf*, which deals with conflict resolution based on mediation principles and cultural understanding of the Deaf Community. Also with Joanne Cripps, she co-developed the popular handbook *Strategies for Deaf Presenters*, published and copyrighted in 1998, which highlights improvement of interpersonal skills and the effectiveness of public presentation for Deaf individuals.

Helen has presented on conflict resolution on numerous occasions, including the National Conference on Peacekeeping and Conflict Resolution (NCPCR) held in Minneapolis, Minnesota, and at Carleton University in Ottawa. She was also one of the first mentors in the Ladder Awards® contest for ASL stories in the publication *River of Hands*, as part of the Canadian Deaf Heritage Project for the preservation of Deaf literature.

Her employment history includes business office experience at University of Waterloo, computer programming at R.W. Hamilton, an industrial distributor, and nearly ten years as a programmer-analyst with CBC Computer Systems. Since 1993 she has been a high school teacher at E.C. Drury School for the Deaf in Milton, her alma mater.

In 1982 she and her husband Mario were presented with the Golden Defty Cultural Award for the Performing Arts by CCSD. Mario and Helen have performed comedy skits for special events in Deaf churches, clubs, schools, and on many Deaf Community occasions since 1976. They have had a family tradition of taking a special Spring Break ski trip since 1984, which has taken them to ski resorts in Banff, Jasper, Whistler, Québec, the New England states, Switzerland, Austria, Italy, and, most recently, Albertville, France, in 2001.

Helen also contributed to this book by writing the Foreword.

PROCYK (MORRISON), Jean Haddow

1925–
Well-Known and Faithful Member of Edmonton's Deaf Community.

Jean Morrison was born prematurely due to maternal illness in Hardisty, Alberta. She was Deaf at birth and was the only Deaf member of her family which included a sister, now living in Holden, Alberta, and three brothers, all deceased. Jean was married to a Deaf man, Joseph Nicholas Procyk, who worked as a window cleaner for Muttart Home Builders for nineteen years, and then as a handyman at St. Stephen's College on the University of Alberta campus until his retirement at the age of sixty-three. Jean and Joseph made their home in Edmonton, Alberta, where Jean continues to reside. Joseph died on 22 December 1987. Jean's hearing niece, Maureen Tiedman, a former Royal Lepage Real Estate saleswoman, had a TTY for business use, so she could communicate with Deaf customers. She also knew Sign Language and had many Deaf people among her clientele.

Jean was sent to the Manitoba School for the Deaf in Winnipeg when she was nine years old, as there was no school for Deaf children in Alberta at that time. She remained there from 1935 to 1941, when she was transferred, at the age of fifteen, to the MacKay Institute for Protestant Deaf-Mutes in Montréal, Québec. In 1945, when she was nineteen, Jean graduated and returned to her home in Hardisty, where she remained, unemployed, for a year. She then moved to Edmonton and took room and board with her brother and sister-in-law while she worked in downtown Edmonton cafes for three years. Eventually, she was hired to work as a kitchen staff member at the Alberta School for the Deaf (ASD). She continued her employment there for sixteen years, retiring at the age of sixty-four, when she was honoured with a certificate of appreciation from Alberta

Education. Jean was popular among staff and students at ASD for her friendly attitude and cheerful personality.

Two months before Jean was to marry Joseph Procyk, when she was only twenty-two years old, she was sent to the Ponoka Mental Hospital in southern Alberta to undergo sterilization surgery. The step was taken because her brother did not want her to have Deaf children. At that time the procedure was approved by a provincial Eugenics Board, and was routinely performed on many young people who were deemed, by the board, to be unfit to procreate. The surgery was funded by the government of Alberta, and led to widely publicized lawsuits during the 1990s. Jean was unaware of the purpose of the surgery and only learned what had been done to her when she and Joseph were trying to start a family. They both loved children and were understandably devastated and heartbroken.

Jean has always been a very vibrant, faithful, and active member of the Edmonton Association of the Deaf (EAD), never missing any of their activities. She was presented with a twenty-five-year membership certificate in 1976, and a forty-five-year certificate in 1996. She travels everywhere by public transit, on the Edmonton Transit Service (ETS), and is affectionately referred to as "the walking information centre for ETS."

Jean's hobbies and interests include shopping, watching television, knitting, sewing, and travelling. Most of all, she loves attending seniors' events at the EAD Community Centre, where she has established a wonderful circle of friends.

RAYNER (BRIGGS), Helen Isabelle

1920–
Bookbinder, Traveller, and Fifty-Year Member of the Regina Association of the Deaf.

HELEN BRIGGS was born hearing into a hearing family at Spalding, Saskatchewan, but apparently became Deaf at the age of two as a result of scarlet fever. She has no known Deaf relatives, but her husband, John Rayner, was also Deaf.

Helen attended a country school near her home with her older brother, Stewart. Their teacher, Miss Scott, soon discovered that Helen was Deaf and appealed to government authorities on her behalf. As a

result, Helen was sent to the MacKay School for the Deaf in Montréal, Québec, in September 1930 because there was no such school in Saskatchewan at that time.

Helen recalls boarding the train rather apprehensively, carrying a beautiful doll in her arms. She soon discovered that there were numerous other Deaf Children on the train, also heading to Montréal to attend MacKay School. She was delighted to meet Joyce Thompson (now Margo) and the two little girls became fast friends, a relationship that has lasted a lifetime, even though Helen lives in Regina and Joyce in Toronto.

At MacKay School for the Deaf, Helen was taught to sign, read, and write by a dedicated teacher, Miss Anderson. A year later, the Saskatchewan provincial School for the Deaf (later known as the R.J.D. Williams School, which is now closed) opened in Saskatoon. Helen was enrolled in the fall of 1931 and continued her education there for the next eight years.

After leaving school she stayed on the farm and helped her mother for some time but, in 1943, she decided to go to Regina to look for work, since it was wartime, and workers were in great demand. For a while she provided home care for welfare babies but later, in 1943, she found a job as a bookbinder with Commercial Printers. There she met John Rayner who was to become her husband.

John and Helen were married in 1947 and both continued working at Commercial Printers until they retired—John in 1983 and Helen in 1985. They enjoyed being retirees, travelling to Arizona for the winter months for several years. John was an avid golfer and Helen liked sight-seeing during their travels.

John's death in 1989 was sad event for Helen, but she finally sold their house and moved into a condominium in 1993. She still enjoys travelling, but most of all she loves socializing with her many friends in the Deaf Community. She was honoured in 1994 with a recognition of her fifty years of membership in the Regina Association of the Deaf.

REID, Sandra Jeanne

1957–
Teacher, Sports Enthusiast, ASL Instructor, Volunteer, and Role Model.

SANDRA REID was born Deaf to hearing parents, John and Barbara Reid, in London, Ontario. She has two hearing sisters, Marilyn Reid and Susan Belton, who have both been involved in working with the Deaf. Marilyn was a residential counsellor at Robarts School for the Deaf in London, and is presently a regional director of the Canadian Hearing Society for London/Sarnia. Susan also worked as a residential counsellor at Robarts School, and was an advisor for Gallaudet preparatory students there. While she was growing up, Sandra's parents were very much involved in activities and organizations related to Deafness. Her father served as treasurer and president of the London Association for Deaf and Hard of Hearing Children. He was also a board member and president of the London branch of the Canadian Hearing Society. Sandra's mother was a volunteer library assistant at Robarts School for the Deaf.

Sandra has no known Deaf relatives, but her Deaf husband, Kenneth (Ken) Alfred Bradley, has a Deaf brother, Chris Bradley, and a Deaf sister, Barbara Bradley. Ken received his education at several local schools in Ontario and at the Davison School in Atlanta, Georgia, which is a private oral school for Deaf students. He has always been an outstanding athlete, particularly in hockey and slo-pitch, and has organized many tournaments at provincial, national, and international levels. Sandra and Ken have two hearing sons, Sean and Alex, and the family currently resides in Edmonton, Alberta.

Sandra attended E.C. Drury School for the Deaf in Milton, Ontario, from 1963 to 1973, when she was transferred to the new Robarts School for the Deaf. She was one of the first three students to graduate from Robarts in 1975. She then attained a Bachelor of Arts degree in Mathematics at Gallaudet College (now Gallaudet University) in 1980, and a Master of Education degree in Deaf Education from Western Maryland College in Westminster, Maryland, in 1981.

Sandra has spent her entire professional career as a teacher at the Alberta School for the Deaf (ASD) in Edmonton, teaching a variety of subjects, mainly at the junior and senior high school level. She has also been an ASL teacher at Jasper Place High School and Grant MacEwan College. She has been involved in countless projects and extracurricular activities with both staff and students at ASD, as a committee advisor, trip coordinator, events organizer, leadership provider, counsellor, and professional advisor. She also has been a successful fund-raiser for ASD and Deaf Community needs. In addition, she has been involved with the Canadian Cultural Society of the Deaf (CCSD) in numerous capacities, with American Sign Language Instructors of Canada Evaluation (ASLICE) and American Sign Language

Instructors of Canada (ASLIC), and with every other organization and agency of the Deaf in Edmonton.

Sandra has received many awards and honours, ranging from a proficiency scholarship to athletic trophies and appreciation certificates. She is very active in the Deaf Community and has held many top positions in various organizations. She is close to her family, is interested in interior design, enjoys reading and watching TV, and is the owner of an eighteen-year-old cat. She keeps busy researching her family tree, watching her boys play hockey and lacrosse, and travelling. She has made two trips to Scotland, Ireland, and England, and looks forward to similar excursions in the future. Above all, Sandra is a cheerful, competent, and highly respected role model for the young people with whom she works.

RENAUD, Michelle Elizabeth

1975–
Camp Counsellor, Groundskeeper, Assistant Instructor, Horse Trainer, and Gifted Horsewoman.

MICHELLE RENAUD was born profoundly Deaf into a hearing family in Guelph, Ontario. The cause of her Deafness is unknown and she has no Deaf relatives. She took her first riding lessons at the age of ten, and has spent her entire life around horses. They are her greatest passion, and her parents were glad to make her happy. Her mother, Dee Renaud, worked as a teacher's aide and library clerk at E.C.Drury School for the Deaf in Milton, Ontario, from 1982 to 1992.

Michelle attended preschool at Smithson School in Guelph for three years but at the age of six was enrolled at E.C. Drury School in Milton, where she remained until she graduated in 1993. She studied computer graphics and design for three years at the Rochester Institute of Technology in Rochester, New York, and took a correspondence course in pet grooming from Montréal. Presently, Michelle is studying animal health care to become a veterinary assistant, through a program based in Toronto. When she was thirteen years old Michelle was chosen, along with twelve other students, to receive the Junior Ontario Citizen of the Year Award in 1988, for her outstanding volunteer work with disabled riders at the Sunrise Equestrian Centre. Since then she has been the recipient of two gold medals for the Canadian Dressage Championship held in British Columbia in 1992 and in Ontario in 1993. She has also won many ribbons in horse shows at the local, provincial, national, and state levels.

When she joined the workforce, Michelle spent many years at the Sunrise Equestrian Centre in Toronto, first as a groundskeeper, then as an office and stable assistant, later, as a camp counsellor for five years, then as assistant program director, and, finally, as a horse trainer. At present, she is employed at Horseback Adventures in Waterloo, Ontario, as its animal health care manager, stable manager, and trail ride guide for approximately fifty horses. It took a long time for her to realize this dream because she was refused this type of employment on the basis of her Deafness. With the help of a good hearing friend, whose difficult stallion Michelle was able to manage with ease, she eventually convinced potential employers that her skills, ability, and qualifications were what mattered, not her hearing status. The staff at Horseback Adventures finally agreed to try her on a temporary basis. When they realized how good she was with the horses, they soon gave her a full-time job. She is now one of their most trusted and respected employees.

Michelle's success with difficult horses has become legendary. She understands them and can analyze their body language, their eccentricities, and their needs. She has worked with many animals besides horses and, since she was a young girl, people have trusted her to look after their pets and livestock. She is sensitive to the abuse and neglect some people exercise with their animals and is a very outspoken critic of such practices. Through extraordinary efforts she has saved three orphaned Canada goslings, a pregnant ewe, that was later named "Michelle," after her benefactress, and has rescued several horses from being sent to the meat factory because others considered them unmanageable. She is an animal lover who currently owns two dogs, two ferrets, and a one-year old Clydesdale-thoroughbred cross foal.

Michelle has many dreams—to teach riding to Deaf people through the Canadian Therapeutic Riding Association, to train horses of her own, and to start her own private horse-training business. This gifted and versatile woman is an outstanding role model to all Deaf women in Canada who are struggling to break down formidable barriers in order to realize their dreams.

RICHARDS (CROCKER), Janet R.

1951–

Records Classifier, ASL Instructor, Avid Defender of Animal Rights, and Initiator of Newfoundland's Annual Silent Walk for ASL Support.

JANET CROCKER was born hearing to hearing parents in Creston, Placentia Bay, Newfoundland. She became profoundly Deaf at six months of age due to illness. Janet has two Deaf siblings—her sister, Judy Shea, who was the first Deaf teacher at the Newfoundland School for the Deaf and is still there after twenty-six years, and her brother, Dale Crocker. They have one Deaf cousin, Bradford Crocker. Janet is married to a hearing man, Bob Richards, and they have two adult hearing sons—Mayo, who is presently a student at Memorial University of Newfoundland, in St. John's, and Oral, who is living in St. John's. At present, Janet and Bob make their home in South River, Newfoundland, with their two dogs and three cats.

Because there was no school for Deaf children in Newfoundland until the 1960s, Janet received her early education as a residential student, at the MacKay School for the Deaf in Montréal and the Interprovincial School for the Deaf in Amherst, Nova Scotia, returning home to Newfoundland only during the summers. Her sister and brother attended the same schools. They enjoyed their years there, among other Deaf students where there were no barriers to communication. After the Newfoundland School for the Deaf was established in Torbay, Janet completed her education there, graduating in 1969. Since then she has attended several community colleges where she furthered her knowledge and expanded her skills by taking numerous courses such as sewing, keypunching, operating IBM machines, cooking, filing, and becoming computer competent.

After working at odd jobs for a while, Janet finally found employment with Public Works and Government Services Canada in St. John's, and has continued working there for the past fourteen years in their Records Section. She is highly thought of by her co-workers and loves the easy, friendly atmosphere of her workplace.

She is also a certified ASL instructor in her spare time, teaching privately as well in a public facility, Cabot College, in St. John's. In addition, she is very active in the Newfoundland/Labrador Association of the Deaf, advocating for Deaf rights, and in the Newfoundland Deaf Sports Association, networking with sister groups across the nation. Janet has been the recipient of awards of appreciation from both of these organizations.

She is well known for other issues and causes she embraces. She was the initiator of Newfoundland's Annual Silent Walk in support of ASL as an official language and is also an avid defender of animal rights, constantly raising funds and public awareness in aid of theSociety for the Prevention of Cruelty to Animals (SPCA) and other organizations. She is regarded as a crusader for the many charitable organizations she supports.

In her spare time, Janet loves to dance, and it has become her favourite means of relaxation. All hearing people who know her feel they have learned a great deal about the realities of Deafness from associating with her, and she greatly enjoys socializing with both Deaf and hearing peers. Her other hobbies and interests are sewing, floss embroidery, collecting antiques, travelling, cooking, and cycling.

ROBERTS (MEASNER), Laurel Ann

1956–

ASL Instructor, ASL Rater and Interviewer, ASL Literacy Consultant, and ASL Outreach Initiator.

LAUREL MEASNER was born hearing into a hearing family in Regina, Saskatchewan. She became Deaf at eighteen months of age, due to spinal meningitis. She has no known Deaf relatives on her side of the family, but her husband, Kenneth Wayne Roberts, is Deaf, and has a Deaf sister and niece. Laurel and Kenneth have two hearing children, Randall and Jennifer, and currently make their home in Trenton, Ontario.

Laurel was educated at the Saskatchewan School for the Deaf in Saskatoon until 1974, and graduated from Walter Murray Collegiate in 1975. She was accepted to attend Gallaudet College, now Gallaudet University, at the age of fifteen, but decided to follow a different pathway and became involved in the Deaf Community instead. She also took up data processing and worked at Page Credit Union in Regina for eight years until she was married and moved to Milton, Ontario, where she was employed for five years at the Halton Community Credit Union. She also worked briefly as an accounting clerk in the Suzy Sher Head Office in Mississauga.

Laurel's contributions to the Deaf Community have been manifold. She was the co-founder and, for several years, a provincial director of the Saskatchewan Cultural Society of the Deaf (SCSD). She has also been a member and served in various capacities with numerous other organizations and agencies of the Deaf: Regina Curling Association of the Deaf, Western Canadian Deaf Curling Association, Canadian Deaf Curling Association, Regina Association of the Deaf, Canadian Cultural Society of the Deaf, National Festival of the Arts Committee, Belleville Association of the Deaf, and the Ontario Cultural Society of the Deaf. In 1978 she was Miss Deaf Saskatchewan in the National Festival of the Arts and, in 1981, during the "Year of the Disabled" her ASL handshapes appeared on a float in the Regina City Parade. Hers was the first women's rink from Saskatchewan to compete in the Canadian Deaf Curling Championships in 1982.

As an ASL professional, she began by teaching various courses at Regina Community College and was a teacher aide at Sheridan College in Oakville, Ontario. She then taught levels I and II courses in "Signing Naturally" for the Canadian Hearing Society and Sir James Whitney School for the Deaf in Belleville. Laurel has been a moderator/panelist for ASL workshops, a presenter/organizer at many special events, the coordinator of a Family Learning Weekend, an ASL interviewer/rater, an ASL tutor, a recruiter and trainer of Deaf mentors, and

the coordinator of outreach ASL and Deaf mentor programs. She is currently employed at Sir James Whitney School for the Deaf in Belleville as its ASL instructor and makes home visits to preschool families in eastern and northern Ontario. Since 1993 Laurel has coordinated and developed outreach ASL programs, and has produced materials and curricula to offer ASL to parents of Deaf children.

In addition to enabling families to learn ASL, her objective is to empower them and provide cultural information. The families learn strategies and techniques for helping their Deaf children acquire language, enhance communication, and develop social and emotional skills. The program also includes interactive activities, storytelling, and conversational interaction. Laurel is entirely dedicated and committed to families. She received her ASL Instructors of Canada Certificate in 2000.

For her outreach efforts, she was nominated for the Amethyst Award for Outstanding Achievement in the Ontario Public Service. She has also been the recipient of a Distinguished Cultural Service Award from the Saskatchewan Cultural Society of the Deaf. She was one of the first ASL raters and interviewers to receive a certificate from York University, Toronto, Ontario. One of her most important accomplishments has been her provision of a positive Deaf role model and Deaf mentor to individuals, families, and communities. She exhibits strong leadership, is highly motivated and passionate, and provides inspiration.

In her spare time, this busy woman enjoys such hobbies and interests as curling, gardening, photography, canning and preserving produce from her garden, and collecting data for her family history.

ROBINSON, Jo-Anne Marie

1949–
Educator, Outstanding Athlete and Coach, Champion Swimmer, Nationally and Internationally Recognized Figure in Deaf Sporting Events, and Avid Genealogist.

JO-ANNE ROBINSON was born Deaf to hearing parents in Vancouver, British Columbia. She has two hearing siblings—a brother, David, and a sister, Patricia, but no known Deaf relatives. Jo-Anne has made her home in Edmonton, Alberta, for nearly thirty years.

She received her early education at Jericho Hill School for the Deaf, Dunbar School, and Lord Kitchener School, all in Vancouver, and graduated in 1967 from Jericho Hill School for the Deaf. She then attended Gallaudet College, now Gallaudet University,

in Washington, DC, where she obtained a Bachelor of Science degree in Physical Education in 1972. The following year she received her Diploma/Teaching Certificate in the Education of the Deaf from the University of British Columbia and, in 1975–76, completed the requirements for a Master of Education degree in Deaf Education at Western Maryland College.

As a student, Jo-Anne was the recipient of several scholastic honours at Jericho Hill School for the Deaf, but her most notable achievements were in swimming. She became involved in competitive swimming at an early age, and was the only Deaf member among hearing peers in a local swim club. She won medals in several swim meets in British Columbia while competing against hearing swimmers in her age group. At the 1965 Tenth World Summer Games for the Deaf she won four gold medals, setting a Deaf world record in each case. She was recognized for this accomplishment by the mayor and the City of Vancouver, as well as the Federation of Silent Sports of Canada. In 1966 she was runner-up for the American Deaf Athlete of the Year Award and, in 1967, named Best Female Swimmer of the Year at Gallaudet College. She continued competitive swimming until 1970, winning gold, silver, and bronze medals in Yugoslavia, and the Deaf Athlete of the Year Award in 1969. The next year she was declared Junior Athlete of the Year by the British Columbia Sports Federation, and Best Female Swimmer of the Year at Gallaudet College.

Scholastically, Jo-Anne was the recipient of a Phi Kappa Zeta and a Gudelsky Scholarship. She also received an Alberta Deaf Sports Award in recognition of her contributions to sports in Alberta and was runner-up for Executive of the Year at Air Canada. She has been awarded numerous other sports and swimming recognitions, was inducted into the Hall of Fame by the Canadian Cultural Society of the Deaf, into the Gallaudet Swimming Hall of Fame, and was named the Most Outstanding Deaf Athlete of the Twentieth Century in the year 2000.

Her employment began with part-time jobs while she attended Gallaudet College and Western Maryland College, but Jo-Anne has spent her entire teaching career at the Alberta School for the Deaf (ASD) in Edmonton, Alberta. She has taught there at all levels, and was the school's computer expert and coordinator for many years, as well as the initiator of a variety of school projects and events. She has also participated in the activities of the Deaf Community in various capacities as a volunteer, and has made enormous contributions locally, provincially, nationally and internationally, mainly in the field of sports. She is considered a Gestuno expert and has presented workshops on that subject several times. Other workshops and presentations have been related to computer topics, disabled sports, and coaching. She is also a published co-author of three sports-related articles, and co-editor of this book.

Jo-Anne's hobbies and interests include researching her family tree, gourmet cooking, and travelling. She has mentored and encouraged countless students during her years at ASD, and has spent several decades of her life tirelessly promoting Deaf Sports across Canada, while holding various positions in the Canadian Federation of Silent Sports. She has also been committed to the Coaching Association of Canada, preparing a manual to enable hearing coaches to deal more effectively with Deaf athletes, and coordinating Coaches' Workshops for the Deaf. She was the first Canadian elected to Le Comité International des Sports des Sourds (CISS), and her voluntary services have been recognized world-wide by all affiliated National Deaf Sports Associations. Jo-Anne has dedicated herself to stimulating and maintaining international interest and participation in World Sports for the Deaf, has edited newsletters, been a technical delegate for CISS swimming events, and was twice "Chef-de-Mission," at the World Summer Games for the Deaf held in Rome in 2001, and the World Winter Games of the Deaf held in Davos, Switzerland, in 1999.

Deaf Sports at the local, national, and international levels owe an enormous debt of gratitude to Jo-Anne Robinson for her global vision, dedication, tenacity, wisdom, and guidance, and her selfless contribution of time and energy. Today, her high ideals and demanding standards are reflected in all organized athletic events for Deaf competitors.

ROGERSON (BRYSON), Helen Amelia

1930–2001
Descendent of a Historical Deaf Family, Seamstress, Volunteer, Presenter to the Queen.

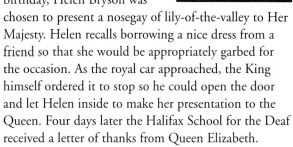

HELEN BRYSON was born Deaf to hearing parents in Dartmouth, Nova Scotia. Her family has an interesting background in the early Deaf history of the province. Helen's great grandfather, George Tait, a Scottish carpenter who had emigrated to Canada in the nineteenth century, was Deaf. It was in response to his suggestion that William Gray, a Deaf Scottish immigrant tailor, set up the first class for Deaf children in Halifax. George Tait married Cynthia Amelia Tupper, a hearing woman from Stewiacke, Nova Scotia, who had three Deaf brothers. One of them, John Carl Tupper, was a teacher of the Deaf at the Halifax School for the Deaf for eight years.

Cynthia and George Tait had a large family, and their sixth hearing child, Rachel Amelia, married Alexander Collier Bryson. They were Helen's grandparents, and Helen well remembers her grandmother, Rachel, who would talk with her using a British two-hand manual alphabet, the same as she did with George, her father. Helen's husband, Robert Rogerson, was a Deaf man from South Maitland in Hants County, Nova Scotia, and they had four hearing children. Robert died in 1972.

Helen Bryson was educated at the Halifax School for the Deaf from 1936 to 1946. Her fondest memory of those ten years occurred on her birthday, 15 June 1939. It was the year of Canada's first cross country royal tour, when King George VI and his Queen Consort, Elizabeth, who is now fondly referred to as "the Queen Mother" and is more than 100 years old, toured Canada from coast to coast shortly after the King's coronation. They were the parents of Britain's present queen, Elizabeth II. Every-where they went, school-children gathered to catch a glimpse of the royal couple, and such was the case at the School for the Deaf in Halifax.

Because it was her ninth birthday, Helen Bryson was chosen to present a nosegay of lily-of-the-valley to Her Majesty. Helen recalls borrowing a nice dress from a friend so that she would be appropriately garbed for the occasion. As the royal car approached, the King himself ordered it to stop so he could open the door and let Helen inside to make her presentation to the Queen. Four days later the Halifax School for the Deaf received a letter of thanks from Queen Elizabeth.

When Helen left the school in 1946 she worked as a seamstress, first for Simpson's Department Store and later for Wood Brothers, a Halifax clothing store. In 1950 she left the workforce to marry Robert Rogerson and raise a family. Widowed in 1972, Helen went back to work as a seamstress at the Cole Harbour Regional Rehabilitation Centre for sixteen years until her retirement in 1995. She had six grandchildren and six great grandchildren.

In 1998 Helen decided to move to Belleville, Ontario, to be closer to her family. She enjoyed working at a variety of crafts, and was a dedicated volunteer at the Belleville General Hospital where she photographed newborn infants, and met many new friends. Sadly she died on 30 November 2001, and will be greatly missed by all who knew her.

ROY, Julie Elaine

1948–
Educator, Collaborator on the First and Second LSQ Dictionary in Québec, and Pedagogical Advisor.

JULIE ELAINE ROY was born Deaf to hearing parents in Montréal, Québec, where she still makes her home. The cause of her Deafness was thought to be placentia previa, and was not discovered until she was about four years old. Some of her family members have lost significant degrees of hearing as a result of aging, but Julie Elaine has no known culturally Deaf relatives. Her only sister, Marie-José Roy, was a former interpreter for the Deaf, and her great-uncle, Pierre Dansereau, a renowned Montréal ecologist, became quite Deaf in his old age.

Julie Elaine's education began at a school on the military base where her father was stationed in Valcartier, Québec, and she attended there from 1953 to 1955. She was then sent to L'Institution des Sourdes-Muettes, a school for Deaf girls, later known as L'Institution des Sourdes de Montréal, and replaced in 1981 by École Gadbois, in honour of the Gadbois sisters who became nuns and taught Deaf girls. She also received private tutoring, from Mrs. Hélène Manta until 1968, to obtain her High School Diploma, and English tutoring from Miss Nell Morrison from the fall of 1968 to the spring of 1969. She then attended the MacKay School for the Deaf, now known as the MacKay Centre for the Deaf, for several months before enrolling at Gallaudet College, now Gallaudet University, in Washington, DC, in the summer of 1969. She graduated with a BA degree in history in the spring of 1973, and obtained a Master's degree in Deaf Education from Western Maryland College in 1975.

From 1974 until 1992 Julie Elaine taught at the Polyvalente Lucien–Pagé (High School), in self-contained classes. There were 2,000 students in the school and about 100 of them were Deaf. Her teaching assignments were mainly in history, geography, and Deaf studies. Since 1992 she has been employed at Cégep du Vieux Montréal as pedagogical advisor. Her tasks include the coordinating of services such as interpreting, note-taking, homogeneous classes, and tutoring for Deaf and hard-of-hearing students attending colleges.

Julie Elaine's greatest achievement to date was her collaboration with a Deaf colleague, Raymond Dewar, and a hearing LSQ interpreter, Paul Bourcier, in 1981, to co-author *Langue des signes québécoise (LSQ)*, the first Canadian textbook in which 800 signs used by the francophone Deaf Communities in Québec were illustrated. With the tragic and untimely death of Raymond Dewar in 1983, she and Paul Bourcier carried on to complete the second book of 1,700 LSQ signs in 1985. Paul presently works at Cégep du Vieux Montréal as a pedagogical advisor, with the same type of duties as Julie Elaine's. In the past, he taught at Polyvalente Lucien-Pagé. He has served as vice-president and interim president for the Association of Visual Language Interpreters in Canada (AVLIC), and is a freelance interpreter in his spare time.

Julie Elaine's honours and citations in recognition of her contributions and achievements are many. She was the recipient of the Lieutenant-Governor's award, while attending L'Institution des Sourdes-Muettes in 1961 and, in 1990, she was presented with an Education Award celebrating the fiftieth anniversary of women's right to vote in Québec. The following year, in 1991, she received a distinctive Prize of Honour from the Alliance des Professeurs de Montréal, the Montréal Teachers' Alliance under the Centrale des Syndicats du Québec (CSQ).

In her leisure hours, Julie Elaine enjoys reading in both English and French, and doing crossword puzzles in French.

RUSSELL, Kathileen ("Kathy") Doreen

1970–
Teacher, Athlete, and Enthusiastic Volunteer.

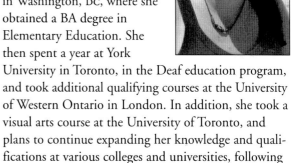

KATHY RUSSELL was born in Brampton, Ontario, to Deaf parents, Ruth Ratzliff and Don Russell. As an infant, after having several ear infections, Kathy showed less and less response to sound. By the age of two years, it became obvious she was Deaf. Besides her parents, she has numerous other Deaf relatives—her Deaf siblings are her younger brother, Darren, and her twin sisters, Connie and Bonnie. Her Deaf aunts and uncles are Linda Russell and Elvis Dressler, and Sheila Russell and Ken Corbett. She also has three Deaf cousins—Lisa Dressler and twins Kristin and Justin Dressler, all children of Linda and Elvis Dressler. At present, Kathy lives in Cambridge, Ontario.

Kathy was educated at E.C. Drury School for the Deaf in Milton, Ontario. Although, for the most part, she was mainstreamed, with support services from E.C. Drury, she spent most of her free time with her Deaf peers at the school since her public high school was on the same campus. With so many Deaf relatives and her rich campus experience, Kathy's life has been steeped in Deaf Culture and tradition. After graduating, she attended Gallaudet University in Washington, DC, where she obtained a BA degree in Elementary Education. She then spent a year at York University in Toronto, in the Deaf education program, and took additional qualifying courses at the University of Western Ontario in London. In addition, she took a visual arts course at the University of Toronto, and plans to continue expanding her knowledge and qualifications at various colleges and universities, following a philosophy to which she subscribes, that "life is an ongoing learning process."

Kathy's first "real" job was with the Ontario Association of the Deaf (OAD), where she served as community development coordinator from June 1993 to August 1994, assisting with the revision of by-laws, doing general secretarial work, and representing OAD at various meetings and events inside and outside government-supported functions, acting as staff counsellor and assisting with the Deaf Youth Leadership Camp in Stayton, Oregon. Her first teaching position was at Robarts School for the Deaf in London, Ontario, in 1995, where she taught grades four, five, and six, and then from 1996 to 1999, preschoolers who were between two and four years of age. In September 1999 she transferred to the E.C. Drury School in Milton where she teaches various subjects including English, mathematics, and the arts in grades six to eight. She is very active in many extracurricular activities, but one of her most notable contributions was the production of *The Deaf Grinch Who Stole Christmas, the Nativity, Hanukkah, Kwanzaa, and Everything Else*. Kathy wrote the script, directed the play, and involved over 100 students in staging it for an annual Christmas concert.

Her contributions to the Deaf Community and its organizations have also been impressive. She edited the *Deaf Burlington Association Newsletter*, was sports director and newsletter editor for the London Centre of the Deaf, served as secretary and daily newsletter editor for the Deaf Canadian Festival held in Mississauga in 1998, founded and coordinated a Deaf Youth leadership Camp in 1999, and contributed to the establishment of a Canadian Deaf Youth Camp to run concurrently with the Canadian Deaf Festival held in Edmonton, Alberta, in 2000.

Kathy has always been interested in sports and athletics, and has made many contributions to Canadian Deaf volleyball, badminton, slo-pitch, and ball hockey. She was coordinator/player of women's volleyball for the Deaf World Summer Games held in Rome in 2001. The last time the Canadian Deaf Sports Association sent a women's volleyball team to the Deaf World Games was in 1985, in Los Angeles, and Kathy was determined to bring the sport back to Deaf athletes in Canada.

In her spare time, Kathy pursues many interests and hobbies which include the graphic design of flyers for Deaf Community functions, photographing people, nature, and interesting man-made objects, and playing volleyball in various leagues and tournaments. This versatile and ambitious young woman will probably be making her mark in many future events of great importance. In the meantime, she is providing outstanding leadership and a positive role model to Deaf teenaged girls, the future Deaf women of Canada. Her favourite quote is an ancient Tibetan proverb—"Our hands exist so that our soul does not remain silent," a fitting tribute to past, present, and future generations of Deaf people everywhere.

RYALL (HEAVENOR), Linda May

1949–
Champion Swimmer, ASL Literature Specialist, ASL Instructor, Computer Instructor, Presenter, Project Developer, and "Deaf Wilderness Woman."

LINDA HEAVENOR was born Deaf as a result of maternal rubella in Powell River, BC. She has no known Deaf relatives, but her husband, Gordon Douglas Ryall, is hard of hearing. They have four hearing children—Benjamin, William, Rachel, and Marshall—all of whom have learned ASL. The family currently lives in Oshawa, Ontario.

Linda attended public schools on Vancouver Island until she was ten years old. She was then enrolled at Jericho Hill School for the Deaf and Blind (JHS) in Vancouver, where she lived in residence for eight years, graduating in 1968. During her attendance at JHS, she was involved in sports, student council, and the swim club.

After graduating, she took IBM training to obtain a certificate in Business Administration. Later, she upgraded her English and math skills in order to take the Gallaudet entrance exam. Linda was twenty-five years old when she entered Gallaudet University in Washington, DC. After two years, in 1977, she decided to get married instead of completing her degree, and began raising her family.

When her children were older, she started attending ASL training workshops in Edmonton, Saskatoon, and Regina. She also took computer training and obtained a diploma in Microsoft Computer Business Applications (MCBA). In 1996 she studied ASL linguistics and structure and attended ASL workshops sponsored by the Canadian Cultural Society of the Deaf.

Linda's employment career gave her a wide variety of experience, from being a competitive swimmer and lifeguard to holding data-entry positions with several corporations. Her main focus, however, was on ASL, as an instructor, coordinator, and workshop presenter.

Having lived in several locations, Linda has been involved in the Deaf Communities in Vancouver, BC, at Gallaudet University, in Windsor, Ontario, in Regina,

Saskatchewan, and currently in Oshawa, Ontario. When she was fifteen years old she participated in the World Summer Games for the Deaf in Washington, DC, winning two gold and one bronze medal, and again in the World Summer Games for the Deaf in Belgrade, Yugoslavia, in 1969, where she earned two silver medals in swimming. Her first victories in Washington led to her being invited to ride on a float displaying her medals in the Powell River annual parade. She was also presented with a large trophy by her hometown, which she later donated to JHS to be awarded for excellence in swimming. In the ensuing years, Linda continued to be involved in competitive swimming, water safety instruction, and lifeguarding.

She has had wide and varied experience in Deaf Culture and organizations of the Deaf. She participated in the first Canadian Deaf Youth Camp at Parry Sound, Ontario, served as treasurer of the Regina Association of the Deaf, was secretary of the Durham Deaf Club in Oshawa, and also of the Toronto Deaf Curling Club. She was the first certified ASL instructor in Saskatchewan and organized and coordinated ASL workshops, often being the presenter as well. She developed projects, taught computer skills to the Deaf, and was involved in Deaf Adult Education. While living in Regina, she was also an active member of Sign Language Instructors of Saskatchewan and president of the Regina Cultural Society of the Deaf from 1990 to 1992.

Linda has been the recipient of at least fourteen prestigious awards and certificates for her swimming and curling prowess, as well as for outstanding merit, recognition, and appreciation in several others areas. She was chosen Miss Deaf Vancouver and competed in the Miss Deaf Canada pageant in 1974, winning a bronze medal for second runner-up. Her most recent honour came in April 2001, when she was awarded a Certificate of Teaching Excellence by Durham College in Oshawa for her outstanding success in ASL instruction.

Besides her membership in the usual organizations of the Deaf, Linda is also an active member of Deaf Women Against Violence Everywhere (DWAVE). For one week in August 2001, Linda was one of five Deaf women to attend the course, "Canadian Outward Bound Wilderness School-Women of Courage," in Burk's Falls, Ontario. The group consisted of two instructors (one Deaf and one hearing), two interpreters, and the five Deaf students. It was an exhilarating experience, and they now refer to themselves as "Deaf wilderness women."

RYALL (SIEVERT), Shelley Lynn

1964–
Leader in the Deaf Community, Data-Entry Clerk, Business Entrepreneur, and Spokeswoman for Deaf Literacy.

SHELLEY SIEVERT was born Deaf to hearing parents in Halifax, Nova Scotia. She has a Deaf brother, Paul Sievert, two hearing sisters, Joan Weatherbee and Valerie Sievert, and two Deaf cousins, Tina Cross and Miriam Gardner. Her Deaf great grandparents were educated at the Halifax School for the Deaf, and were active members of the Maritime Association of the Deaf. Shelley is married to a Deaf man, Bob Ryall, who has two Deaf sisters, Glenda and Karen, and a Deaf brother, Gordon, whose wife, Linda, is also Deaf. Shelley and Bob have two hearing daughters, Angela and Clara. The Ryalls currently make their home in Oshawa, Ontario.

Shelley was raised in Amherst, Nova Scotia, where she attended the Interprovincial School for the Deaf, but was sent to a public, mainstream high school to take some subjects with an interpreter. She graduated in 1982 and went on to the Amherst Technological Vocational Centre (ATVC) to train as a data-entry operator. Later, after moving to Ontario, she took further training at Durham College, and obtained a certificate to become a teacher in an adult education program. Shelley has been involved with Goal: Ontario Literacy for Deaf People (GOLD), a literacy program for Deaf adults, and has taught various school subjects using ASL, with its unique grammatical structures and syntax, as the language of instruction.

Her employment history has been varied and interesting. While living in the Maritimes, Shelley worked for Blue Cross Health Insurance in Moncton, New Brunswick. After moving to Ontario in 1987, she worked for the Insurance Crime Prevention Bureau in Etobicoke before moving to Oshawa. There, she worked briefly with the provincial Health Department and in the Taxation Office before she married Bob Ryall and became a stay-at-home housewife and mother for a few years. Before returning to the workforce, Shelley attended Deaf Culture and linguistic workshops and trained to teach "Signing Naturally," levels I and II. She has been teaching hearing adults at Durham College for nine years and has also established her own business which markets her family literacy programs. She is a team leader with ASL instructors, organizing meetings, developing curricula, collecting feedback, and finding solutions for any complications that might arise between Durham Deaf Services and Durham College. She has also worked with children through Silent Voice, in an eight-week summer program as a counsellor and instructor.

In addition to her paid employment, Shelley has done extensive volunteer work, particularly in the field of Deaf literacy. Her services were recognized, with special honours for her commitment and dedication, by Durham Deaf Services in June 2000. She was president of the Durham Deaf Club from 1993 to 2001, and is constantly advocating for Deaf rights and improved interpreter services. She has a hearing-ear dog named Stoney, and has presented workshops on that subject. Her greatest passion, however, is her outreach work with families, especially parents with Deaf, hard-of-hearing and nonverbal children. She fosters ASL communication in the home and community, and also teaches small groups of Deaf adults who are language-challenged, thus enhancing their life skills.

In her rare leisure hours, this busy woman enjoys various hobbies and interests which include outdoor activities such as walking, biking, and camping. At home she likes to sew and is working at becoming computer literate. She also swims and participates in Deaf bowling tournaments.

SAAB (DOLA), Roda Emily

1940–1999
Scholar, Figure Skater, Wife, and Mother.

RODA SAAB was born Roda Nuuvuka on 28 September 1940, in the Inuit community of Payne Bay (now called Kangirsuk) in northern Québec. When Roda was very young she moved with her mother, Mary Tukkipih, to Quautag, another Inuit community in northern Québec. She continued to live with Mary until she was nearly eight years old but, meanwhile, a sad tragedy, which had a profound effect on the rest of Roda's life, had befallen the family.

Like all others who lived in the remote northern settlements at that time, Roda's family were nomadic people who lived in an igloo and used a team of huskies to pull their sled and provide transportation. These dogs were not domesticated as pets and were left outside overnight to bury themselves in the snow for warmth. They were always cold and very hungry in the morning, so they had to be thrown some meat or fish before it was safe for people to emerge from their igloos and approach them.

Roda was three years old when her cousin, who was also three, failed to heed Mary's warnings not to go outside before the dogs were fed. He ventured out of the igloo where, in a hungry frenzy, the huskies attacked him as if he were prey. As Roda and her mother watched in horror, he was instantly disembowelled by the vicious pack.

It is believed that the shock of this gruesome spectacle resulted in Roda's Deafness. From that day onward she never again responded to her mother's voice or any other sound. Sometime before her eighth birthday, in 1948, she became very ill and was taken to the Royal Canadian Naval Hospital at HMCS Stadacona in Halifax, Nova Scotia, where a vigilant nurse observed that she never reacted to any kind of noise. Back at home, before her illness, Roda had never chattered or shouted while playing with other children and had made no attempt to use her voice. It became evident that Roda was profoundly Deaf.

She was taken away from her family and declared a ward of the federal government. She was also given the new surname "Dola." In September 1948 Roda Dola was enrolled at Halifax School for the Deaf where she stayed until 1957. She was taught by the oral-aural method, which involved learning to speak and read lips, but this was extremely difficult for her. She was very successful at learning to type, weave, and sew. She loved to skate and was encouraged to join the Bluenose Figure Skating Club to improve her skills. There were at least four other Deaf skaters in the club—Lois Hennigar (Nickerson), Jeannie MacNeil, Ethel Harris (Boudreau), and Connie Agnew (Legge).

In the winter of 1957, after about six years of training, Roda had perfected nearly all fancy skating figures and become a solo performer in figure skating. She won the senior novice solo competition. Her performance displayed such rhythm and grace that it brought her considerable applause and congratulations.

Roda liked to put her hands on the piano while it was being played so she could feel the vibrations of the music. Wooden floors also yielded certain vibrations. On the skating ice, however, she had to depend on her eyes to learn timing and movement by following the instructor's flashlight, watching others, and using her imagination.

In the fall of 1957 Roda was sent to Halifax Ladies' College, a private girls' school, which was informally known as "Ladies' College" (now Armbrae Academy), where she was the only Deaf student but excelled academically. In 1960 she left Ladies' College to attend Gallaudet College, now Gallaudet University, in Washington, DC. According to *Deaf Heritage in Canada* by Clifford Carbin, published in 1996, Roda was the first Deaf female resident of Nova Scotia to enrol at Gallaudet College.

Roda eventually married, moved to Ottawa, worked for a number of years, and raised three hearing children. She was very good at telling jokes and singing songs in Sign Language. Sadly, she passed away on 23 December 1999 at the age of fifty-nine. Her ashes were sent home to her northern community to be buried beside her mother in Quautag. Despite the tragic events of her early life, Roda (Dola) Saab is considered to have been a very accomplished and successful Deaf Canadian woman.

SANDERS, Beverley Viola

1940–
Floral Designer, Homemaker, and Worker for the Deaf Community.

BEVERLEY was a hearing baby born into a hearing family in Weyburn, Saskatchewan, and was raised on her parents' farm there. She became Deaf at the age of two and a half years as a result of a serious ear and throat infection. Her Deaf husband, Mervin Sanders, was born Deaf due to maternal rubella. They both attended the Saskatchewan provincial School for the Deaf in Saskatoon for their entire education and were married in 1964.

Beverly and Mervin now make their home in Regina where Mervin was a barber for seven years before getting a better job as a shop technician with Saskatchewan Government Telephones. Together they raised two daughters—Viola who is hearing, and Julie, who is Deaf. Both girls are married and Viola has two children. Neither Beverley nor Mervin had any known Deaf relatives, but their younger daughter, Julie, is married to a Deaf man, Todd Maryniak. Julie and Todd have no children.

Beverley worked as a floral designer at the Avenue Flower Shoppe in Regina for seventeen years and at Gale's Florist's for twenty-four years. At the same time she was also a homemaker and mother. Mervin retired in May 2000, and Beverley in July 2000. Both are now enjoying their leisure time.

Beverley keeps very busy with her involvement in the Deaf Community. She is currently president of the Regina Association of the Deaf and secretary of the Regina Deaf Athletic Club. She has also served with other local agencies of the Deaf in various capacities and enjoys the many social activities that are part of Regina's Deaf Community. Beverley loves to work on committees and has made many significant contributions to the delight and enjoyment of her Deaf friends and peers. Her greatest pleasure is to see everyone happy.

SANDFORD, Robyn Barbara Janet

1957–
Ballet Dancer, Actor, Poet, Published Author, Educator, Curricula Developer, and Presenter.

ROBYN SANDFORD was born Deaf into a hearing family in Peterborough, Ontario. The cause of her Deafness is unknown and she has no Deaf relatives. She is the niece of Janet Churchill and granddaughter of Luella May Springstead, both of Oakville, Ontario, and a cousin of Paul Churchill of Gaithersburg, Maryland, US. It was these three hearing relatives who raised Robyn and they all take great pride in her multitude of achievements. Robyn is the mother of two happy, healthy hearing children, Byron and Deanna, and they currently make their home in Burlington, Ontario.

Although she went to kindergarten in Oakville, Ontario, under the Halton Public School Board, Robyn received her basic education at E.C. Drury School for the Deaf in Milton (formerly the Ontario School for the Deaf), where she was one of the first pupils when the school opened, and continued to attend from 1963 to 1976. When she graduated, she attended Gallaudet College (now Gallaudet University) in Washington, DC, where she excelled, and her name appeared on the Dean's List as well as in *Who's Who Among Students in America's Universities and Colleges*. She became a member of the Phi Kappa Zeta Sorority and, in 1980, was one of thirteen Canadians among 247 graduating students when she obtained a BA degree in Psychology. She then went on to acquire a Master's degree in Deaf Education at Western Maryland College in Westminster in 1981. She received a Specialist Certificate as an educator of the Deaf from the University of Toronto in 1985, and additional qualifying credentials from York University in Toronto, Ontario, in 2001.

As a child, Robyn was an avid ballerina who competed with hearing dancers and won many awards. For a time the judges were unaware that she was Deaf. At Gallaudet she was a member of the Modern Dance Group, but resigned in favour of returning to her first love, which was ballet. She became the first Deaf member of the Washington City Ballet Company, and holds the distinction of being the first Deaf ballerina in Ontario, possibly in Canada.

Robyn's professional employment also created a "first" when she became the first Deaf teacher in Ontario to be hired by her alma mater where she had earlier been a student. At E.C. Drury School for the Deaf she has taught at many age and grade levels, and was involved in the Bilingual-Bicultural Pilot Program. She was an actor for the Bi-Bi videotape that was produced as part of that program, and also worked in the preschool home visiting program. She has worked tirelessly to develop an ASL curriculum suitable for nursery to grade twelve, and was involved in team research, which led to the publication of her article entitled "Clever Nose," by the Ontario Ministry of Education. She has also written ASL poetry that will be published for use in preschool education, and has researched *The Joy of A to Z Storytelling* for grade four classes. She is now researching Deaf definitions and other terms used nationally in Deaf education, and is a regular presenter of ASL literary material. Culturally, she is noted as an expert signer of poetry, music, and prose directed toward young children, and has been a staunch promoter of such CCSD projects as the collection of ASL and Deaf literature, *River of Hands*, and the Ladder Awards®. She has won recognition for her ASL storytelling by being presented with the prestigious Ladder Award®.

Robyn is very active in the Deaf Community and has served in many capacities for various organizations of the Deaf, particularly the Canadian Cultural Society of the Deaf (CCSD) and the Ontario Society of the Deaf (OCSD). She has been involved in *The Canadian Dictionary of ASL* project since 1982, a CCSD enterprise which is nearing completion and will be published by the University of Alberta Press. She has also played the roles of "Deaf God" and "Deaf Eve" in a film entitled *Grist*, soon to be released in Toronto.

Robyn's interests are so diverse that they keep her very busy. When she has leisure time, she enjoys such hobbies as reading, watching suspense movies, looking for antiques, travelling, swimming, aerobics, fishing, camping, hiking, skiing, and gardening.

This versatile woman continues to educate, entertain, and bring pride and joy into the lives of Deaf people, particularly children.

HEATHER SHAND is the adopted Deaf daughter of Deaf parents, Annie Bell and James Shand of Montréal, Québec. She is married to James Burton Roth who is Deaf, and they currently make their home in Bothell, Washington, US. Both were married before and, between them, have nine children—three Deaf girls, four Deaf boys, and two hearing girls. The Deaf girls are Priscilla, who is a student at Gallaudet University; Cinbrella, also at Gallaudet; and Shandella. They are fifth-generation Deaf members of the family, and Priscilla is now the mother of a Deaf son who is a sixth-generation Deaf family member.

The Deaf boys are Cynan, Jesse, Jim Jr., and Robert, and the two hearing girls are Vanessa and Heidi. Heather Saunders-Roth has a Deaf sister, Muriel Murray, who lives in Montréal, and James Roth has a Deaf sister, Linda Chapman, who lives in Langley, BC. Heather's deceased first husband, Amos Saunders, was instrumental in establishing the Northern California Independent Living Program (NCILP). He had a Bachelor of Arts degree in Political Science and was a certified paralegal. Of historical interest is the fact that Amos Saunders was the great nephew of Mabel Hubbard, the hard-of-hearing wife of Alexander Graham Bell.

Heather was educated at the MacKay Centre for the Deaf in Montréal and has held numerous jobs in Canada and the US. She has worked for the Royal Bank of Canada, a photo-finishing company called Fotomat. a business called Dynamatic, the JC Penney Company, and HD's Unique Alterations and Repairs. Art and design are her forte.

She is also a motorcyclist, and may have been the first female "Deaf biker" in Canada. She made headlines in the US when she biked alone from Tucson, Arizona, to Sturgis, South Dakota, in 2000, for which she was given recognition by the Deaf Bikers of America. At present, she is secretary for the Northwest Deaf Biker Association in the state of Washington.

As a student at the MacKay Centre, Heather was involved in many student activities and clubs such as the YWCA Oral Student Group, a Jewish Deaf club, and others. In 1974 she was recognized by the Canadian Cultural Society of the Deaf (CCSD) for her artistic talents, receiving the Golden Defty Award for her painting, a bronze award in drawing, and a gold award in sewing at CCSD's Festival of the Arts. As an adult living in Montréal, she socialized often with French Deaf people and even interpreted for them from English to French. She was a gregarious person who travelled often, and stopped frequently to visit Deaf communities and their clubs.

On her way to California in 1980, she met Amos Saunders, and they decided to get married. She attended California State University at Chico and was an art major until she left school when her third child was born. She has since revived the Chico Deaf Club. When she lived in Tucson, Arizona, she was vice-president of the Deaf Ladies' Crafter's Guild.

Heather has lived in various parts of the United States, and has been recognized for several unique feats. When Shandella was nine months old, she began choking on a toy she had put in her mouth. Heather applied CPR skills she had learned at Girl Guides in Montréal, while Amos called 911. Later, she was honoured by the Butte County Forest Service for miraculously saving the child. When her children were attending a mainstream program at Magee Middle School in Tucson, Arizona, she found out that her daughter and seven of her friends were plotting to run away, so she hastily informed the principal who took immediate action by calling the other seven parents, and, thus, a potential disaster was averted. For her part in it, Heather was honoured by the school officials.

In her spare time, Heather enjoys cooking, sewing, knitting, designing garments, and photography. She also likes to go camping and is an avid collector of Indian relics. Heather is particularly grateful to her adoptive parents, James and Annie Shand, who were wonderful Deaf role models and gave her so many opportunities to become the talented, sociable, outgoing, fun-loving person she is today.

SAWCHUK (LONG), Lois Elizabeth

1916–1991
Skilled Seamstress, Tailor, and Craftsperson.

LOIS ELIZABETH LONG was born in Newkirk, Oklahoma, US. Details of her early life are sketchy but it seems likely that some type of hemorrhaging led to her Deafness during early infancy. It is believed that she was cared for by Aboriginals from a nearby reservation and that they saved her life. Her father's family was of British origin, but her mother had grown up at Collingwood, Ontario. She missed her Canadian family, who by then were living in Alberta, so when Lois was eleven months old, the Longs decided to move to Canada. In September 1916 they arrived in Calgary by train and from there they travelled to the rural community of Delia in a wagon with a team of horses. With them were their two small daughters, Lena and Lois. Their firstborn, a son, had died at birth. Three more children were born at Delia—Wendel (who died at an early age), Ivan, and Phyllis. They were a close-knit family and demonstrated a great deal of love and patience toward Lois, who would often wander down to her uncle Fred DeMott's farm to play in the hay. Because she was Deaf they couldn't call to her, so it was sometimes difficult to find her.

While living on the farm at Delia, Lois attended Starland School with her older sister, Lena, and was a good student. Eventually, she was sent to the Manitoba School for the Deaf in Winnipeg, where she attended for ten years. However, there was no money to send her to Gallaudet College in Washington, DC. Her fondest hope was to become a nurse or midwife. In those days she could not be accepted into such a training program due to her Deafness, so she learned how to sew and tailor clothing instead. For five years she held an annual dressmaking show which was a popular event in Delia.

In 1943 Lois married Steve Sawchuk and moved with him to Edmonton, Alberta. The couple spent forty-six happy years together and raised two fine daughters, Betty and Jeanette. Steve was a published poet and the Canadian Cultural Society of the Deaf (CCSD) has a copy of his book of poetry. Lois worked in a garment factory, tailoring military uniforms during World War II. After the war ended in 1945, she made uniforms for railway personnel. Business slowed down so she quit her job in 1958 and the family moved to Calgary, where she worked in a drycleaning plant but eventually had to give it up due to low wages. In 1963 her husband Steve was involved in a serious car accident and was hospitalized for twenty-eight months. He was paralyzed from the waist down. She took care of him at home for as many years as she could. Steve died in 1991, just four months before Lois.

Apart from the jobs she held, Lois was always busy sewing at home for other people. In her lifetime she created 280 wedding ensembles and many individual cocktail gowns. Occasionally, she was called upon by frantic brides to complete outfits that had been left unfinished by other seamstresses and often she had to work within restrictive deadlines, but she always saved the day and finished the work on time. She often entered contests at the Calgary Stampede and won many prizes and awards. She was an etremely talented woman, and the bridal gowns she created were always very unique because she trimmed them with sequins and beads. Each one was not only a true work of art, but also a labour of love, because she took so much pride in her work. Her hands were never idle and she always had sewing, quilting, and crocheting projects in progress.

She spent her last years at the Bethany Care Centre in Calgary because she suffered from arthritis and could no longer take care of her own property. Throughout her lifetime she enjoyed many hobbies and recreational activities. She had a passion for riding horses, curling, baseball, and hockey. She also hooked rugs, made baby quilts, created ceramics, and did crewel work. Hers was a productive and interesting life. She passed away peacefully in 1991, missed and admired by everyone who knew her.

SCOULAR (MALONEY), Donna May

1945–
Long-Time Federal Civil Servant and Deaf Community Worker.

DONNA MALONEY was born Deaf into a hearing family in Vancouver, BC. She has no known Deaf relatives, but both her former and her current spouses are Deaf. She has three adult hearing daughters and currently makes her home in Richmond, BC. Her daughters sometimes volunteer as interpreters.

Donna was educated at Jericho Hill School for the Deaf in Vancouver, followed by a preparatory year at Gallaudet University in Washington, DC. She then took business courses at the Vancouver Vocational Institute for six months and entered the workforce rather than committing to a four-year university degree program.

Her employment history is varied and interesting. When her daughters were old enough to be in school she became a federal civil servant and worked for eighteen years with the Public Service Commission of Canada, from 1980 to 1998. She advanced from a data-entry clerk to acting supervisor, then human resources assistant, and, at times, acting officer of the Commission. Donna moved to finance/supplies in 1998, managing the TB vets' database for two years. At present she is unemployed, but is very busy and active in the Deaf Community.

Because she likes doing advocacy work, Donna has served in many organizations of the Deaf in various

ways. Currently, she is president of the Greater Vancouver Association of the Deaf. She is also secretary-treasurer of the Canadian Association of the Deaf and secretary of the World Congress of the Deaf (sponsored by the Canadian Association of the Deaf). She has contributed in various roles to the Deaf Women's Group and, from 1995 to 2000, was secretary of the Jericho Hill School Alumni. She was also president of the Western Institute for the Deaf for one year. In every one of these organizations, Donna was an eloquent spokesperson for equality and accessibilty for the members of the Deaf Community.

In her leisure hours, Donna spends time with her family, surfs the Internet, and watches good movies. She also likes outdoor activities such as camping, swimming, walking, and enjoying the scenery. What Donna enjoys most, however, is her volunteer work, promoting better understanding and improved interaction between the Deaf and hearing communities. She is a born leader, but is also a supportive and confident team player.

SELLMAN (DOLMAT), Irene A.

1965–
Business Office Administrator, Charity Canvasser, Deaf-Blind Intervenor, and Church Community Volunteer.

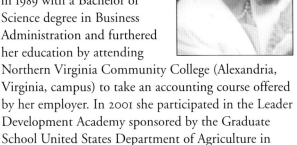

IRENE DOLMAT was born Deaf into a hearing family in Montréal, Québec. The cause of her Deafness was maternal rubella, and she has no known Deaf relatives. Her husband, Daniel Sellman, is a Deaf man who has three Deaf siblings—two brothers, Alan and Dave, and a sister, Lynn. Although Irene has no famous Deaf connections, her hearing cousin, Natalie Watson (Pilcow), was once a research assistant to a graduate student at McGill University, who was studying possible differences in brain hemisphere activity between Deaf and hearing children. Also, her hearing grandfather, Dolmat, was mayor of Botowo, Poland, before World War II. Irene and Daniel currently make their home in Silver Spring, Maryland, US.

Irene was educated at the Montréal Oral School for the Deaf and MacKay Centre, graduating in 1983. She spent the next year in the Gallaudet Alternative preparatory Program in London, Ontario, and then enrolled

at Gallaudet University in Washington, DC. She graduated in 1989 with a Bachelor of Science degree in Business Administration and furthered her education by attending Northern Virginia Community College (Alexandria, Virginia, campus) to take an accounting course offered by her employer. In 2001 she participated in the Leader Development Academy sponsored by the Graduate School United States Department of Agriculture in Washington, DC. She received a program leader plaque.

Irene's employment history has been interesting and varied. Her job with the Federal Deposit Insurance Corporation (FDIC), in Washington, DC, has allowed her some flexibility. She has worked in the Division of Supervision, in the Administration Section, since 1997. Prior to that, she was in the Division of Finance, Travel

Reimbursement Section, from 1989 to 1997. She was the recipient of Special Service Achievement Awards in 1990, 1992, 1994, and 1997. She received STAR Awards (Special Thanks and Recognition) in 1998, 1999, 2000, and 2001. In addition, she was granted prestigious Certificates of Appreciation as Combined Federal Campaign Keyworker in 1999 and 2000. She was a canvasser for the US Savings Bond Drive in 1999.

Irene's contributions to her community are many. She was a member of the Metro Deaf-Blind Service Centre in Rockville, Maryland, from 1997 to 1999. She gives freely of her time to nonprofit organizations such as Deaf-Blind organizations, and is an active member and volunteer of the Open Bible Deaf Church in College Park, Maryland, where she teaches Sunday school and has been on two summer missions—Jamaica in 1996, and Russia in 2001.

In her spare time, Irene enjoys her latest hobbies, membership in the Majic Stampers Club, Maryland, US, and decorative landscaping.

SELLNER (PATERSON), Jean Winnifred

1909–1972
Deaf Teacher and Specialist in Domestic Arts and Sciences.

JEAN PATERSON, although she lived in British Columbia, was educated at the Manitoba School for the Deaf from 1918 to 1929. Because British Columbia, Alberta, and Saskatchewan did not have any established provincial schools for Deaf children at that time, most students travelled (sometimes thousands of miles) by train to Winnipeg to be educated. Jean was one of them.

The Western Canada Association of the Deaf (WCAD) established the McDermid Scholarship Fund (masterminded by David Peikoff) in 1930 to help raise funds for Deaf individuals from the four western provinces who wished to attend Gallaudet College, now known as Gallaudet University, in Washington, DC. Jean Paterson was one of the first recipients of this scholarship following her 1929 graduation from the School for the Deaf in Winnipeg.

Records indicate that she was also the first female resident of British Columbia to attend and graduate from Gallaudet University with a Bachelor of Science degree in 1934. This was accomplished in an era when a university education, even for a hearing woman, was considered to be much less important than marriage, a home, and a family.

After graduating from Gallaudet, Jean returned to Canada and secured a teaching position, a rare feat in that day and age for a Deaf person, even in a School for the Deaf, where nearly all teaching staff members were hearing. She was hired by the Saskatchewan Provincial School for the Deaf in Saskatoon, which had opened in September 1931, and continued her employment there from 1934 to 1940 as a teacher of the domestic arts and sciences which were particularly important for girls in most Schools for the Deaf of that era.

Jean Paterson was married on 10 August 1940 to Hubert Joseph Sellner of Comfrey, Minnesota. He was a 1937 graduate of Gallaudet College who was a mathematics teacher first, and then switched to teaching carpentry. Together, Jean and Hubert left Canada to make their home in the US, where Hubert held a teaching position at the Minnesota School for the Deaf in Fairbault. Jean also taught for one year as an industrial arts teacher. For the next two years, she did substitute teaching in the home economics classes as well as other general classes. Jean and Hubert had two hearing sons, Robert, now deceased, and Patrick.

The family left Minnesota in 1953 and moved to El Cerrito, California, when Hubert acquired a teaching position at the California School for the Deaf in Berkeley. Jean did substitute teaching at the school, and both of them were very active members of the Deaf Community. For many years Hubert was secretary and treasurer of the East Bay Club for the Deaf (EBCD) in Oakland, California, until the building which the club owned was sold during the early 1980s. Jean's greatest passion was her art, and she also loved home decorating. She was very creative and produced quantities of work which she sold at her own art shows two or three times a year. At Gallaudet she had been a member of the Phi Kappa Zeta sorority and was always very active in sorority events.

Jean and Hubert are both deceased—Jean passed away in 1972, and Hubert in 1995, both in Brookside Hospital in San Pablo, California. Their remains are interred at St. Joseph's Cemetery in San Pablo. They are sadly missed, but are fondly remembered by all who knew them, especially their son, five grandchildren, and one great-grandson.

SHAND (BELL), Annie

1914 –

Weaver, First Deaf Canadian Woman to Adopt a Deaf Child, and First Female President of the Montréal Association of the Deaf.

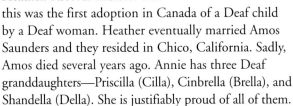

Annie Bell was born hearing in Verdun, Québec, a suburb of Montréal. Her Deafness, at the age of two, resulted from a severe bout of whooping cough. She has a Deaf sister, Evelyn Gregory, and three hearing siblings, a brother and two sisters.

In 1922, when she was eight years old, she was enrolled at the MacKay School for the Deaf in Montréal where she was educated until she graduated in 1934. Following her graduation, Annie became a highly skilled weaver.

For several years she worked at her weaving trade for the Henry Morgan stores in Montréal (now known as The Bay). In 1940 she returned to the MacKay School for the Deaf as an assistant teacher of weaving, a position she held until 1967. During this period of her employment, Annie was the very popular leader of an informal club, known as the MacKay Deaf Ladies' Sewing Group, at her alma mater. Later, she continued working there as a dormitory counsellor, also teaching weaving, until her retirement in 1979 at age sixty-five.

On 2 September 1942 Annie Bell married a very fine Deaf man named James Wilson Shand. They made their home in Montréal where she continued her employment at the MacKay School for the Deaf. James was a Canadian who had been educated at two well-known oral schools in the US—the Wright Oral School in New York, New York, and the Clarke School in Northampton, Massachusetts, even though he was from Montréal.

In 1957 Annie and James adopted a Deaf daughter, Heather. Records indicate that this was the first adoption in Canada of a Deaf child by a Deaf woman. Heather eventually married Amos Saunders and they resided in Chico, California. Sadly, Amos died several years ago. Annie has three Deaf granddaughters—Priscilla (Cilla), Cinbrella (Brella), and Shandella (Della). She is justifiably proud of all of them.

Annie Shand was always a very busy and popular woman in the Deaf Community in Montréal. In 1944 she was the first female to be elected president of the Montréal Association of the Deaf (MAD), formerly known as the Montréal Deaf Association (MDA). Annie's beloved husband James passed away in 1985 and she moved to the Ottawa/Hull area. In 1989 she was the recipient of a notable award of appreciation for her contributions and services to the Deaf Community, both in Montréal and Ottawa/Hull.

Now well into her eighties, Annie continues to keep busy working at her various crafts, volunteering, and travelling. She is a cheerful and well-loved member of the Deaf Community who continues to make her home in Hull, Québec.

SHEA (CROCKER), Judy Davina

1948–

Academic Teacher, ASL Instructor, Driver Education Instructor, and Dedicated Volunteer in the Deaf Community.

JUDY CROCKER was born hearing to hearing parents in Corner Brook, Newfoundland. She became Deaf as a result of spinal meningitis before she was four years old. She has a Deaf sister, Janet Richards, a Deaf brother, Dale Crocker, and a Deaf cousin, Bradford Crocker, who is at present attending Gallaudet University in Washington, DC. Judy is married to a hearing man, William Shea, a surveyor and senior instrument man, who is also a member of a country music band.

Judy and William have four hearing children, two daughters—Janet, who is presently working with IBM in Columbus, Ohio, as an advisory Information Technology (IT) specialist, and Michelle, who is a paralegal/ legal secretary with the Newfoundland Legal Aid Commission in St. John's—and two sons, Billy and Adam. Judy's father, Joseph Crocker—JX 299593—was a World War II veteran, as was her father-in-law, Michael Francis Shea—JX 181698. Both served in the armed forces of the United Kingdom because Newfoundland did not become a province of Canada until after the war. The Sheas currently make their home in St. John's, Newfoundland.

Judy received her early education at four different schools for Deaf students, She attended the Halifax

School for the Deaf for three years, the MacKay School for the Deaf (now the MacKay Centre) in Montréal for three years, the Interprovincial School for the Deaf in Amherst for four years, and, finally, the Newfoundland School for the Deaf in Torbay for three years, graduating in 1968. She obtained a Bachelor of Science degree in Home Economics from Gallaudet College, now Gallaudet University, in Washington, DC, in 1973, the first Newfoundlander to do so.

In 1976 she attended the driver education program offered by the Department of Highways, and acquired certification as a driver education instructor. Judy also holds an Education Certificate from four different institutions—Nova Scotia Teachers' College in Truro, the University of Moncton in Moncton, New Brunswick, Western Maryland College in Westminster, Maryland, and the Memorial University of Newfoundland in St. John's. In addition, she holds an ASL Instructor Training Certificate from Avalon Community College in St. John's.

All of Judy's employment experience has been in the field of education. Prior to teaching at the Newfoundland School for the Deaf, she had been a driver education instructor for the provincial Department of Highways for two years, a related subjects teacher at the Atlantic Technological Vocational Centre in Amherst, Nova Scotia (no longer in use), a home economics teacher at the Atlantic Provincial Resource Centre for the Hearing Impaired in Amherst for six years, and, from 1989 to the present time, an ASL instructor at the College of the North Atlantic and at Memorial University in St. John's. Her main teaching position, however, has been as an academic junior high school teacher at the Newfoundland School for the Deaf in St. John's, where she has taught since 1979.

Judy's volunteer activities are many. Besides the extracurricular events in which she participates at her school, she is a former president and secretary of the Newfoundland/Labrador Association of the Deaf and sat on the Mayor's Advisory Committee in St. John's. She is also a former president and current treasurer of the Newfoundland Coordinating Council on Deafness, was president of the Newfoundland Deaf Sports Association, has been a member, vice-president, and recently elected treasurer for a two-year term of the Newfoundland and Labrador Council of Educators of the Deaf, is a member of the Canadian Association of Educators of the Deaf and Hard of Hearing, and is a proctor and ASL rater for the Association of Visual Language Interpreters of Canada. Judy formerly served as vice-president of the Eastern Canada Association of the Deaf and was the founder of Dingo, a Newfoundland/Labrador Deaf version of Bingo. Judy belongs to other organizations and agencies too numerous to list here. She has also been the recipient of several appreciation awards in recognition of her contributions to her community and her school.

Although leisure time is a rare commodity for Judy, she enjoys such interests and hobbies as recreational curling, reading, walking, ice-skating, and travelling. She also likes working at crafts, especially cross-stitching and paper tole.

SHEMI, Orly

1974–
Dressmaker, Fashion-Designer, Alterationist, Counsellor, Tutor, and ASL/ISL Instructor.

ORLY SHEMI was born with a significant hearing loss into a hearing family in Israel. They emigrated to Canada in 1991. The cause of Orly's Deafness is undetermined and she does not know any Deaf relatives, although she may have some Deaf cousins. Her parents, two sisters, and a brother are all hearing. Orly currently makes her home in Montréal, Québec.

Her education began at the age of five at Niv. Solad and Shalva elementary schools. Later, she took her high school education at Ironi A Haifa and Unim High Schools in Haifa and Kfar-Saba, Israel. After coming to Montréal in 1991, she spent two years in the Cycle II program at the MacKay Centre for the Deaf, advancing to the IPL program (Individual Paths for Learning). In 1999 she graduated in Fashion Design from the International Academy of Design. She also took ASL instructors' training at a Vista Training program in Vermont, US.

Orly's first job in Canada was as a day-camp counsellor for hearing children in Montréal, during the summer of 1992. The following year she worked with a Deaf, partially sighted child at the MacKay Centre for the Deaf, pursued a work-study project at Shari's as a hairdresser, and another as a sewing machine operator at l'Esprite garment factory. Further work-study projects included a stint as a dressmaker's assistant at Shoshi Studio, child-care attendant at the MacKay

Centre and at Canadian National Railways (CNR), dressmaker and alterationist with the Caromio Company, and volunteer counsellor for teenagers at Camp Massawippi, the MacKay Centre Camp, where she also tutored Deaf students. From 1999 to 2001 she worked with the Deaf Buddies Program at the MacKay Centre for the Deaf and was again a leader at Camp Massawippi. In 2000–2001 she led an ASL play group and acted as a substitute teacher of the Deaf.

Orly has made many volunteer contributions to her community. Both in Israel and at the MacKay Centre, she was student-council president. She has often helped to organize dinners, parties, dramas, and games for over a hundred people, planned and arranged travel itineraries for Deaf teenagers in Israel, presented

lectures on Deaf Culture, and participated in a leadership convention in Victoria, BC, with other Deaf youth from across Canada. In addition, she also collected and organized supplies to be shipped to Cuba. More recently, she was offered a position to act as a counsellor to Jewish Deaf children at Camp Kesher in Pennsylvania and to instruct them in Israeli Sign Language (ISL).

In her spare time, Orly enjoys baby-sitting, ice-skating, writing, reading, sewing, travelling, and playing volleyball, as well as other team sports. She is a fascinating woman of incredible talents who serves as a wonderful role model for all Deaf Canadian women, particularly those under thirty, who are establishing their careers goals for the future.

SHERRIFF (HAYES), Cheryl Lynn

1958–
Competitive Swimmer, Water Polo Player, and Tae Kwon Do Expert.

CHERYL HAYES was born Deaf in Saskatoon, Saskatchewan. She was taken into foster care as an infant and was later adopted by her foster parents. She has no known Deaf relatives but is married to a Deaf man, Harry Sherriff, who is known to his friends as "Buster." Cheryl and Buster have two hearing children, a daughter, Tanya, and a son, Tyler. The Sherriffs currently make their home in Edmonton, Alberta.

Cheryl attended the Saskatchewan School for the Deaf in Saskatoon from 1961 to 1977. She then took high school upgrading classes at Alberta College in Edmonton for two years, from 1977 to 1979. She took some computer courses but soon lost interest and decided that an office career would be too confining for her.

She had started swimming competitively at the local level at the tender age of four. When she was only nine years old, as a member of the Saskatoon Kinsmen Goldfins swim team, she began competing at the international level. In 1973 she swam for Canada's team at the 12th World Summer Games for the Deaf in Malmo, Sweden. There, she won two medals, a silver and a bronze. In 1975 she competed in the First Pan American Games for the Deaf in Venezuela, where she captured five medals, four gold and one silver. The Saskatoon Board of Trade presented her with an award in recognition of the national honour she had achieved.

The Harry Bailey Aquatic Centre in Saskatoon is named after a prominent local swimmer and coach who was inducted into the Hall of Fame in 1973. He was also Cheryl's swim coach and trainer. When the Aquatic Centre opened, Cheryl was given the honour

of swimming the length of the pool, in lieu of a ribbon-cutting ceremony, to declare its official opening on 14 April 1976.

At the age of eighteen, in 1977, she brought home two silver and two bronze medals from the 13th World Summer Games for the Deaf held in Romania, and then retired from competitive swimming. Throughout her swimming career, she brought home 222 ribbons, seven trophies, five plaques, one medal-plaque, two trophy-plaques and twenty-nine medals. She was also mentioned in two of Bob Ferguson's books, *Who's Who in Canadian Sports*, in 1975 and 1977, and is the only Deaf athlete named in either book.

The year 1977 was memorable for Cheryl for other reasons than her swimming achievements. She received a formal invitation from the Minister of State, Fitness and Amateur Sport, on behalf of the government of Canada, to attend a state luncheon in Ottawa on October 15 in the Ballroom of the Skyline Hotel, being held in honour of Her Majesty The Queen and His Royal Highness The Duke Of Edinburgh. This was a very exciting event for Cheryl. She was also invited to Rideau Hall to be presented with a medal by the Governor General, Jules Leger, commemorating the twenty-fifth anniversary of Queen Elizabeth II's accession to the throne. Meeting the Queen and Prince Philip was an unforgettable experience, despite Cheryl's initial nervousness.

After deciding against an office career, Cheryl found employment with the Value Drug Mart Association. She works in a warehouse and enjoys the physical activity much more than sitting at a computer all day. She is in charge of bin maintenance for the Prescription Department, and takes on other responsibilities as well.

In addition to her remarkable feats as a swimmer, Cheryl enjoys playing water polo for which she has received local recognition. She is active in Tae Kwon Do and earned a yellow belt in 1980, and a green belt in 1981. This talented and determined woman seems to have achieved the impossible despite the barriers she faced in taking instruction, and the isolation she faced as the only Deaf person among her many hearing counterparts, although some of her friends did learn basic signs.

Cheryl is too busy to become actively involved in Edmonton's Deaf Community, but she maintains her membership in the Edmonton Association of the Deaf (EAD). She loves Harley Davidson motorcycles, enjoys art, and likes to travel. She is a cat fancier and the proud owner of two lovely Siamese felines, her favourite breed.

SHINKAWA, Esther Mayumi

1966–
Counsellor, Project Coordinator, Community Outreach Worker, and Video Producer.

ESTHER was born Deaf to hearing parents and has a Deaf sister and a Deaf cousin. She resides in Surrey, BC, and has always been a tireless advocate for the Deaf, particularly Deaf women, in her province.

Esther received her high school education in a mainstream public school where she earned two fine arts awards during her last two years (grades eleven and twelve). She then received a BA in Psychology from Gallaudet University in Washington, DC, in 1990, and has had a challenging and varied employment history since her graduation.

In 1993 Esther was appointed as a rape crisis counsellor and program coordinator for Deaf and hard-of-hearing women at Women Against Violence Against Women (WAVAW). In that capacity, she was involved in the production of the ASL video *Enough is Enough* in 1995, for which over half of the crew and actors were Deaf, and in the production of another ASL video, *See You in Court*, produced by Wild Ginger Productions of White Rock, BC.

In addition to her several years of peer counselling she has done outreach work, giving presentations on Deafness-related issues to hearing women's organiza-tions. She has also served on the board of the Deaf Women's Group (part of the Greater Vancouver Association of the Deaf) from 1991 to 1993, and was one of the founding members of The Bright Place for Deaf Women of BC, (incorporated in 1998). Its purpose is to advocate for Deaf women and provide educational activities, programs, and services. Esther was a board member until January 2000 and was hired to act as the project coordinator for the group's first major program—"Creating Change for Deaf Women of BC." She is currently one of five Deaf recipients of training scholarships for digital video production at Video-In, which is the group's second program for Deaf people. She is also a member of the Wired Women Society (Vancouver chapter).

Esther is detail oriented and has strong inter-personal communication skills with diverse groups of individuals, both Deaf and hearing. She continues to be a valuable asset to the Deaf communities on BC's lower mainland.

SHORES-HERMANN, Patricia Anne

1961–
Teacher, Public Relations Promoter, and Capable International Spokeswoman for the Deaf.

PATRICIA SHORES was born Deaf to hearing parents, Nellie and Wallis Shores, at Boksburg in South Africa. She has two brothers—John Branton Shores, a Gallaudet graduate of 1981, who is Deaf, and William (Bill) Wallis Shores, a corporate lawyer, who is hearing. John's wife, Heather, is Deaf, and they have a hearing son, Kent. Bill's wife is Sandra, and they have two hearing children, Jane and Thomas. Jane, Kent, and Thomas are very important to Patricia and she enjoys her role as an aunt. She is married to Roland Hermann who comes from a Deaf family, and whose parents and sister are Deaf. Patricia and Roland have made their home in Schaffhausen, Switzerland, since 1991.

Patricia attended St. Vincent School for the Deaf in Johannesburg, Transvaal, South Africa, from 1963 to 1976. She worked hard and was among the top students in her class each year. School activities included art, flower arranging, and pottery classes. Patricia was very active in school sports, track and field, gymnastics, and swimming. She played tennis at the Zoo Lake Tennis Club and swam at the Northeast Swimming Club which is the famous preparatory swimming school for the South African Springboks. She was also a Girl Guide in a hearing troop, played field hockey, and was a leader at St. Vincent School. While in South Africa she had a close and loving relationship with her maternal grandparents, now deceased, but was born after her paternal grandparents had passed away.

When she was fourteen, in 1976, Patricia's family emigrated to Canada. They settled in Edmonton, Alberta, where both Patricia and John were enrolled at the Alberta School for the Deaf (ASD). When she graduated, in 1979, she had the honour of being chosen as valedictorian. She then attended Gallaudet College (now Gallaudet University) in Washington, DC, where she obtained a Bachelor of Arts degree in Secondary Education and International Studies, focusing on Western Europe, in 1985. She followed this up with summer courses at the University of Alberta in Edmonton to obtain her Alberta Teaching Certificate. She was one of the first Deaf teachers to teach hearing children with an interpreter in the Edmonton Public School System. She began her professional career as an educational counsellor for the Western Canadian Chair of Studies in Deafness (WCCSD) at the University of Alberta, and continued her studies at the University of New Brunswick in June 1987.

In 1985 she married Roland Hermann. They lived in Edmonton for two years, then in Toronto, until their move to Switzerland (Roland's homeland) in 1991. While they lived in Toronto, Patricia served as the first Deaf manager at the provincial level of the Canadian Hearing Society (CHS), where she focused on the development of Sign Language services within the province of Ontario, setting up the first teacher training program and establishing minimum standards for ASL instructors.

During her post-secondary years, Patricia earned many distinctions. She served as president of the Gallaudet Student Body Government in 1983–84. She was also listed in *Who's Who in American Universities and Colleges* and received a sorority recognition as the recipient of an Outstanding Student Certificate in the spring semester of 1981. In 1982 she was chosen Miss Deaf Canada at a pageant held in Toronto. Following that event, she embarked on a two-month tour of Canada to promote public awareness and open people's minds regarding Deafness.

Patricia's employment has varied and has given her the opportunity to gain experience and expertise in teaching, educational management, and developing teaching materials in the areas of culture and language. Her ongoing task, however, is promotion—striving to gain recognition of Deaf persons in the larger society. This requires all her skills—teaching, researching, lobbying, presenting, and attending many meetings. Presently, she is employed as a lecturer in the Hochschule für Heilpädagogik (HFH) in Zurich, Switzerland. She has two main responsibilities there, coordinating and directing the Swiss German Sign Language Interpreter Training Program (DOLA) and the Swiss German Sign Language Teacher Training Program (GSLA). She also teaches English as a second language in junior and senior high school vocational and academic programs. At this time, Patricia is the only Deaf person in Switzerland hired in a leadership capacity for this academic training program.

Her involvement in the Deaf Community includes promotion of Sign Language recognition and serving on the board of GS MEDIA, which focuses on Sign Language research and literature. She also helps her husband with his political, theatrical, and social activities. In 2001 she was recognized internationally in *Who's Who Among Professional Educators* for her academic contributions in Switzerland. She initiated the first

European Conference for Deaf Sign Language teachers, instructors, and trainers in the interpreter-training field, held in October 2001. Her dream of returning to university to complete a doctorate has had to be put on hold due to the time constraints of her present work, but is not forgotten.

Her hope is to give something back to her parents, her late father, Wallis, and her mother, Nellie, for the sacrifices they made in leaving their families in South Africa during their middle years to give their children better opportunities to contribute to society, prosper, and succeed. She is grateful to her extended family, her teachers, neighbours, and friends for the love and

caring support that made Patricia who she is today. Her gratitude also extends to Canada for accepting her family, and to all leaders in the Deaf Community for providing the inspirational leadership and political/social activity that helped to shape her ideals.

In 1999 Patricia lost her beloved father after a long battle with cancer, leaving her mother, brothers, and their wives and families, all in Edmonton; herself and Roland in Switzerland, and extended family members in South Africa.

In her leisure time, which is very limited, she reads, travels, walks with the family dog, Lola, cooks, and gardens.

SIGURDSON (GABRIEL), Sylvia Olof

1939–
Champion Curler, Data-Entry Operator, and ASL Instructor.

SYLVIA SIGURDSON was born Deaf to hearing parents in Gimli, Manitoba. She has a Deaf brother, John Sigurdson, who lives in Vancouver, British Columbia, and works as a tile installer. She also has a hard-of-hearing niece, Donna McLeod, who lives in Lockport, Manitoba, and works in the human resources office of the Canadian Wheat Board. Like her aunt Sylvia, Donna is very much involved in Deaf curling. Sylvia has a hearing son, Calvin, who is in his first semester at the University of Manitoba, pursuing a degree in English Linguistics. He is now in his fourth year of the ASL/English interpreter's program at Red River College in Winnipeg, and is studying Deaf history there as well. Sylvia has always made her home in Winnipeg.

She was educated at the Saskatchewan School for the Deaf (SSD) in Saskatoon. The Manitoba School for the Deaf on Shaftesbury Boulevard was not in operation during World War II, but was being used by the Royal Canadian Air Force as a wireless training school, and did not re-open until 1965. Like all other Deaf students in Manitoba, Sylvia had to be sent out of the province for her schooling. She remained at SSD as a residential student until she graduated in 1957.

When she entered the workforce, Sylvia got a job with Manitoba Health, where she has continued to work as a data-entry operator for over forty years. She was fortunate to be offered keypunch training through a company-sponsored, ten-day course. In addition to her day job, Sylvia has taught ASL immersion for the past ten years in Sturgeon Creek.

Besides working full-time and teaching ASL, Sylvia is kept very busy during the winter months as an avid

curler with the Deaf Curling Club. She has also been involved in the Deaf Community, and has won numerous medals, awards, and plaques for her contributions. As a curler, she has accumulated a most impressive record of successes:

1979—Vancouver, first prize		All-star as 2nd
1980—Montréal, first prize		All-star as 3rd
1981—Winnipeg, second prize		All-star as 2nd
1986—Ottawa, first prize		All-star as 3rd
1988—Montréal, first prize		All-star as 3rd
1989—Vancouver, second prize		All-star skip
1990—Halifax, second prize		
1991—Banff, second prize		All-star skip
1992—Ottawa, first prize		All-star skip with no loss.
1996—Kingston, first prize		All-star skip
1997—Portage La Prairie, first prize		
1998—Winnipeg, second prize		
1999—Edmonton, first prize		All-star skip and sportsmanship team with no loss.

Her rink has won the Canadian Deaf Curling Championship nine times, and won second place five times. She has been an all-star eleven times, five times as skip. She also entered the Manitoba Scott Tournament of Hearts three times—in 1983, 1984, and 1985—but did not win for Manitoba.

Because she is such a busy woman, Sylvia has very little time to enjoy hobbies, but when she does have spare time on her hands, she enjoys reading.

SJOLIN (RIVARD), Lillian Mary

1926–
Farming Partner, Cat Fancier, and Skilled Craftswoman.

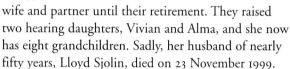

LILLIAN RIVARD was born Deaf to Deaf parents in Lampman, Saskatchewan. Her father was Albert Rivard, also born in Lampman, who was educated at the old Manitoba provincial School for the Deaf in Winnipeg. Her mother was Frances Knight, born at Roche Percée, Saskatchewan, and educated first at the old School for the Deaf in Regina, Saskatchewan, and then at the Manitoba School for the Deaf in Winnipeg. Albert and Frances had married in 1925, and Lillian was born a year later. She was their only child.

Lillian was the first pupil to arrive at the new Saskatchewan provincial School for the Deaf in Saskatoon in the fall of 1934. She was small for her age and very timid about leaving her parents and home to travel to the city. She was accompanied on the trip by Mrs. Rachel Christie, a very active Deaf volunteer from nearby Prince Albert. The wee girl was very nervous and shy about meeting other Deaf children. She now recalls, however, that Mrs. Christie gave her a large bag of candy to take her mind off her fears and make her feel at home and comfortable.

Lillian married Lloyd Sjolin in 1953 and became a farmer's wife and partner until their retirement. They raised two hearing daughters, Vivian and Alma, and she now has eight grandchildren. Sadly, her husband of nearly fifty years, Lloyd Sjolin, died on 23 November 1999.

Lillian has always been a pet lover (especially cats) and has numerous hobbies that keep her occupied. She enjoys sewing and quilting, but crocheting is her favourite pastime. She also does fancy beadwork and is proud of her home and flower garden. Lillian Sjolin currently resides in Kinistino, Saskatchewan, about thirty minutes from Humboldt.

SKIRVING (BEEHAN), Louise Annette

1958–
Science Technician and ASL Instructor.

LOUISE BEEHAN was born into a hearing family in St. John's, Newfoundland. The cause of her Deafness was not determined and she has no known Deaf relatives.

She attended the Newfoundland School for the Deaf in St. John's from 1964 to 1976. While she was a senior student there she was selected to participate for two years in the 4-H Club summer program, which led her to develop a keen curiosity and a love of nature and outdoor life. When she graduated, the St. John's Association of the Deaf presented Louise with an award for attaining the highest marks in her graduating class. In 1976 she attended the Atlantic Technological Vocational Centre for one year in Amherst, Nova Scotia, before transferring to the Nova Scotia Institute of Technology in Halifax. There, she enrolled in a challenging medical laboratory technology program, from which she graduated in 1979.

She was hired by the Memorial University of Newfoundland Medical School as a science technician in a research laboratory, where she worked side by side with her future husband, Paul Skirving. Louise married Paul, a hearing man, in 1985. They have three hearing children—Mary Louise, born in 1989, Douglas, born in 1991, and Peter, born in 1994. The family currently resides in St. John's. In 1989 Louise was hired by the Newfoundland School for the Deaf as a science technician/ instructor, and continues to work there in that position. As a valued staff member, she is always eager to assist with school projects and special events, and provides an excellent Deaf role model for the students.

In 1995 Louise's husband Paul was accepted into the Medical School at Memorial University of Newfoundland. Life became extremely busy for Louise during the next four years while Paul concentrated on his studies. She took on extra responsibilities as a working mother, chauffeur, and household manager. She was very proud of her husband's accomplishments when he graduated as Paul Skirving, MD, in 2001. He now practices medicine in the St. John's area, and is the first family physician in Newfoundland who is fluent in ASL. He has also volunteered for many years as religious interpreter for their parish church. Before entering medical school, Paul was the pastoral worker for the Deaf in the Archdiocese of Newfoundland where he coordinated and taught religious studies at the Newfoundland School for the Deaf.

Louise is very proud of her children's successes in the annual Kiwanis Music Festival. Despite being unable to hear them play the piano and sing, she delights in watching their performances and is thrilled with their achievements.

Louise has two hearing sisters—Patricia Hawksley, an ASL interpreter, and a teacher at the Newfoundland School for the Deaf, whose husband, Fred Hawksley, is an associate drama professor in the Faculty of Education at Memorial University, and has collaborated with her in writing and directing award-winning theatre performances at her school, and Margaret Peddigrew, who has worked as an interpreter in Newfoundland and Labrador for over twenty years, and whose husband, Robert O. Peddigrew, is the executive director of Newfoundland and Labrador's Medical Care Plan (MCP). Louise can also claim a famous hearing cousin, Leonard

J. Cowley, who was deputy minister of fisheries and oceans before he died suddenly at the age of forty-nine, and has a Canadian Coast Guard vessel named after him.

Louise has been teaching ASL at the College of Trades and Technology (Adult Division) for twelve years, and has also been an ASL instructor at the Newfoundland School for the Deaf. As a member of the Newfoundland and Labrador Association of the Deaf (NLAD), she volunteers her time and skills in their fundraising efforts, particularly the "Silent Walk," and other special events.

Louise enjoys outdoor activities such as camping, walking, bird watching, and cross-country skiing. She especially enjoys country life with her family at their summer cottage, and likes to read and cook. Her favourite beverage is Twining's Irish Breakfast tea, and she carries her own tea bags wherever she goes.

SMITH (MILLS), Nora Florence

1918–1997
Administrative Secretary, Editor, Honour Student, and Volunteer Worker for the Deaf.

NORA MILLS was born in London, England, in 1918 and held dual Canadian/British citizenship. She lived most of her life in Winnipeg, Manitoba, where she was a tireless worker in the Deaf Community and was admired and respected by her peers, both Deaf and hearing.

In her youth, Nora attended the Manitoba School for the Deaf where she was an honour student and was presented with the prestigious Weagant Medal and Bar for her exemplary academic achievements. During her school years she worked with Deaf adults who were members of the Winnipeg branch of the Western Canadian Association of the Deaf (WCAD), becoming a very active member of that organization early in her life.

When she graduated, Nora attended evening classes at the Manitoba Commercial College to qualify for an office job. She managed to achieve this without the benefit of interpreters, and within six months was hired by the Manitoba Department of Education for a clerical position. She spent the following thirty-nine years as an employee of the Manitoba government— eighteen with the Department of Education, and twenty-one with the Correspondence Branch. When she retired in 1980 she had advanced to the position of administrative secretary. Gary Doer, who is now Premier of Manitoba but was at that time president of the Manitoba Government Employees' Association (MGEA), presented her with a special lifetime membership in MGEA, a framed certificate, an MGEA pin, and a Manitoba government pin.

In 1977, on the twenty-fifth anniversary of the accession of Queen Elizabeth II to the throne, Nora was one of ten Deaf Canadians to be awarded a certificate and medal by the government of Canada. This was one of her proudest achievements.

Throughout her working years, Nora found time to serve the Deaf Community in various capacities, particularly the Winnipeg Community Centre of the Deaf (WCCD) where she held nearly all the executive positions at different times. She was president of the Women's Auxiliary for two years and editor of the *WCCD Newsletter* from 1964 to 1978. The Western Canadian Association of the Deaf (WCAD) also benefited from Nora's contributions when she served on two local committees for conferences and acted as secretary for three years.

Her Deaf husband, William Henry Smith, known in the Deaf Community as "Bill," was also very active in the Winnipeg Community Centre of the Deaf and the Western Canada Association of the Deaf. In the latter part of his life, he was seriously ill for a number of years. When Nora devoted all her time to caring for him, her services to the organizations of the Deaf had to be curtailed. Nevertheless, she was held in high esteem by everyone who knew her and her dedication did not go unrecognized.

She held two lifetime memberships—one in the Manitoba Government Employees' Association and the other in the Winnipeg Community Centre of the Deaf. She was also the proud recipient of some distinctive awards for her skills at signing hymns and for her competence in writing newsletters, awarded to her by the Canadian Cultural Society of the Deaf (CCSD). Norah was noted and admired in her church for the way she signed hymns and, in 1973, won the Bronze Award for Hymn Signing at CCSD's National Festival of the Arts, followed in 1974 with a Gold Award for General News Publications and a Silver Award in 1976, also for General News Publications.

Until her death on 14 March 1997, at the age of seventy-nine, Nora (Mills) Smith was a member of the Manitoba Deaf Seniors' Centre. In passing, she left a very fine legacy of dedication, efficiency, and loyalty to future generations of Deaf Manitobans and Deaf Canadians, and was an outstanding role model for all Deaf women in Canada.

SMITH (CHARLEBOIS), Paulette Anita Marie

1958–
Role Model for Deaf Children, Activist, and Lobbyist.

PAULETTE CHARLEBOIS was born Deaf in Shellbrook, Saskatchewan, to hearing parents. She has a Deaf sister, Monique Bowman, a hard-of-hearing spouse, Ray Smith, and two hard-of-hearing sons, Corey and Duane. Her daughter, Rachel, is hearing and Paulette has a hearing sister, Lorraine, who works with Deaf-Blind adults in a group-home setting. Her husband is a businessman, owner of Avanti Tile and Terrazzo in Saskatoon, Saskatchewan, where he and Paulette make their home. The Charlebois family claims kinship to the well-known Canadian Métis leader, Louis Riel, whose mother was Julie Lagimodiere, second-youngest daughter of Marie-Anne (Gaboury) Lagimodiere, one of the first white women on the western prairies. Paulette's mother is Carmen Lagimodiere.

Paulette obtained her education at the Saskatchewan provincial School for the Deaf in Saskatoon. She then took a one-year business and bookkeeping course at Red River Community College in Winnipeg and worked for a few years in a dental laboratory and printing company prior to the birth of her children. In the early 1990s she went back to school, attending Grant MacEwan Community College in Edmonton to study ASL and Deaf Culture. She has worked as an ASL instructor and Deaf role model for the Saskatoon Catholic School Board since 1995.

Paulette's interest in ASL, Deaf studies, and Deaf Culture has led her to a wide variety of experiences. She participated in the organizing of a workshop on bilingual-bicultural education, focusing on the role of Deaf teacher-aides in this type of program. She has also coordinated ASL summer immersion programs in Saskatoon.

Paulette has been significantly involved in organizations and agencies in the Deaf Community, serving on the entertainment committee of the Western Canada Association of the Deaf, fundraising for the Canadian Deaf Curling Championships, chaperoning candidates in Miss Deaf Canada competitions, sitting on the board of Saskatchewan Deaf and Hard of Hearing Services, and helping to evaluate interpreters for the Association of Visual Language Interpreters of Canada (AVLIC). Her efforts are always aimed at learning and improvement, and her tenacity is admirable. She is extremely versatile, and has participated in two movies for Saskatchewan Deaf and Hard of Hearing Services (SDHHS), *Pay the Price* and *Not My Problem*.

In 1990–91 Paulette worked full-time as an ASL role model for the hearing child of a Deaf mother and in 1995 was employed as an ASL instructor for six months at Vancouver Community College, where she planned the course, selected materials, taught, and evaluated students' progress. She was among the group of protesters and activists who lobbied the provincial government to keep the R.J.D. Williams School open in 1991, and was involved in the student strike at that school in 1973 when the student body fought for the use of Total Communication.

Paulette has won several Canadian Deaf Curling Championship trophies and in 1978 was the second runner-up in the Miss Deaf Canada Pageant. She continues to take a keen interest in the Deaf Community and to volunteer her time and energy toward making good things happen. She has been treasurer of the Saskatchewan Deaf Children's Society (a new club) since August 1998.

Paulette's leisure hobbies and interests include camping, golfing, curling, and walking, but her favourite pastime is cross-stitching.

SNODDON, Kristin Anne

1974–
ASL and Literacy Consultant, Program Coordinator, and Student of Deaf History and Culture.

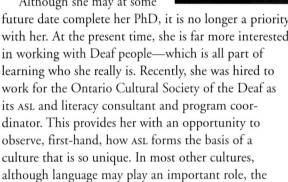

KRISTIN SNODDON was born hearing to hearing parents in Orillia, Ontario, and has no known Deaf relatives. When she was in kindergarten, at the age of five, she became profoundly Deaf due to spinal meningitis. Her parents decided to have her continue her mainstream public school education, and she did so, in Beaverton, Ontario, in classes where she was the only Deaf student. She did not learn to sign, other than to use the manual alphabet, until she became an adult.

At the age of fifteen Kristin underwent cochlear implantation at the Hospital for Sick Children in Toronto. She had never seen any culturally Deaf adults and had no idea how they lived, worked, and coped with their Deafness. The implant was not successful and eventually had to be removed along with an infected mass that could have been life-threatening. The entire experience left Kristin with many doubts and questions about who she really was and where this experience might lead her. Unknown to her at that time, her journey into Deaf Culture and the Deaf Community had begun.

Kristin earned an Honours BA degree with distinction, specializing in English, from the University of Toronto in 1997, and the following year she completed a Master's degree in English at the same university. It was the childhood cochlear implant issue that first led her to become involved with organizations of the Deaf, but that is no longer her main interest. Her discovery of ASL and Deaf Culture has guided her along many new paths and she feels there are probably some very exciting opportunities in her future. She is very close to her family and is delighted that her mother and sister are learning to sign. She has become an eloquent and influential spokesperson in promoting ASL, Deaf pride, and Deaf Culture and she now views Deafness as a desirable state rather than a pathological one requiring correction.

Although she may at some future date complete her PhD, it is no longer a priority with her. At the present time, she is far more interested in working with Deaf people—which is all part of learning who she really is. Recently, she was hired to work for the Ontario Cultural Society of the Deaf as its ASL and literacy consultant and program coordinator. This provides her with an opportunity to observe, first-hand, how ASL forms the basis of a culture that is so unique. In most other cultures, although language may play an important role, the focus is usually multi-faceted.

Kristin considers her personal history important only because it holds so many paradoxes. She was raised in the "hearing world," without exposure to the "Deaf world." When she met other Deaf people and started signing, she felt "reborn." Acquiring two university degrees in English had its purpose for her. Before learning ASL she communicated mainly in writing and felt her English had to be as precise as possible. Now that she is learning ASL, the new language has become just as essential to her. Kristin is fully aware that because she is learning and growing as a Deaf person, her history is far from finished. In view of her youth and ambition there is no doubt that many new discoveries, challenges, and successes still lie ahead.

SNOW (FITZPATRICK), Mary Theresa

1923–
One of the First Three Female Deaf Houseparents at the Newfoundland School for the Deaf and Loyal, Active Member of the Deaf Community.

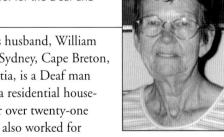

Mary Fitzpatrick was born Deaf to hearing parents, into a large family in St. John's, Newfoundland. She has a Deaf brother, John Fitzpatrick, who became a Christian Brother at Les Clercs de St. Viateur, now known as Mission Centre in Montréal, Québec. He also worked as a residential houseparent and was a long-time teacher of developmentally delayed Deaf students. Her hearing brother, Michael Fitzpatrick, was a lawyer and judge for a total of fifty years in Cornwall, Ontario.

Mary's husband, William Snow, of Sydney, Cape Breton, Nova Scotia, is a Deaf man who was a residential houseparent for over twenty-one years. He also worked for twenty years as a commercial printer. Now, as a retiree, he enjoys woodworking and woodcrafts and is a very successful vegetable gardener. Mary and William have two hearing daughters—Ann Marie Gaulton, a residential nurse at the Newfoundland School for the Deaf, and Eileen Blanchard, a receptionist for Petro-Canada. They also have six hearing grandchildren. Their son-in-law, Barry Gaulton, is a shipping agent for Geopetroleum, and one of their granddaughters, Giselle Gaulton, is an aspiring young chef at the Allegro Italian Kitchen in Edmonton, Alberta.

Mary was educated at the Halifax School for the Deaf from 1931 to 1941. When she left school, she returned to Newfoundland and became a stay-at-home house-keeper and substitute mother for her four younger sisters after their mother died, remaining at home for twelve years. In 1964, when the first Newfoundland School for the Deaf opened at Fort Pepperell in Pleasantville, St. John's, Mary became one of the first three Deaf female houseparents to be hired. She continued working in that capacity when the school was moved to Torbay in 1965, and then to St. John's, where she worked until her retirement in 1987. She received a certificate of appreciation for her dedicated twenty-three years of service from the government of Newfoundland and Labrador on the occasion of her retirement.

Mary has always been an active and loyal member of the Newfoundland-Labrador Association of the Deaf, and has conducted their monthly Deaf Bible study activities. She was also the first elected female vice-president of the Caribou Silent Club, which was the first organization of the Deaf in St. John's. Prior to her retirement, she enjoyed recreational five-pin bowling with the Deaf Bowling League, and still loves a game of Skipbo every second Wednesday evening.

Mary is a talented dressmaker who sewed beautiful clothes for her two daughters when they were younger. She now works at a craft known as plastic canvassing, and does wool and floss embroidery. She also likes to bake and is a good knitter. When the weather is suitable, Mary enjoys walking for exercise.

SNOWDON (MORRISON), Lena May

1881–1979
Monoline Typesetter, Newspaper Compositor, and Lifetime Member of the Eastern Canada Association of the Deaf.

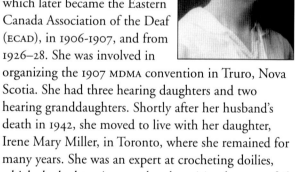

LENA MORRISON was born Deaf in Glenholme, Nova Scotia, and died in Moncton, New Brunswick, at the age of ninety-eight. She left the Institution for the Deaf and Dumb, later known as the Halifax School for the Deaf, in 1898.

For about seven years until her marriage in 1911, Lena worked as a monoline typesetter for *The Morning Chronicle* and *The Evening Echo*, both Halifax newspapers of that day. At the time it was believed that she was the only Deaf female compositor in Canada (Source: *Deaf Heritage in Canada*). She married Harold Sigmond Snowdon, a tailor, who was born Deaf in Wood Point, New Brunswick, but was raised in River Hebert, Nova Scotia. He attended the Institution for the Deaf and Dumb in Halifax from 1891 to 1899. They lived in Moncton for many years. He predeceased Lena in 1953, so she was a widow for more than twenty-five years. She also had two older Deaf sisters, Georgie and Edith Morrison.

Georgie Ella Morrison, the eldest of the three Deaf Morrison sisters, attended the Halifax School for the Deaf (HSD) from 1882 to 1891. In 1900 she married John J. Dunlap, a Deaf upholsterer from Truro, Nova Scotia, who had graduated from HSD in 1881, and had a Deaf grandfather and a Deaf sister. Georgie was vice-president of the Maritime Deaf Mutes Association (MDMA), which later became the Eastern Canada Association of the Deaf (ECAD), in 1906-1907, and from 1926–28. She was involved in organizing the 1907 MDMA convention in Truro, Nova Scotia. She had three hearing daughters and two hearing granddaughters. Shortly after her husband's death in 1942, she moved to live with her daughter, Irene Mary Miller, in Toronto, where she remained for many years. She was an expert at crocheting doilies, which she had to give up when her vision began to fail. In 1967 she died in Toronto, and was buried in Truro, Nova Scotia.

Edith Morrison, after attending HSD from 1887 to 1898, worked as a dressmaker for a number of years and married William S. Bellefontaine, a Deaf tailor from West Chezzetcook, Nova Scotia, who had attended HSD from 1896 to 1904. They lived in Halifax for many years and were active in ECAD and the Forrest Club, which later became the Halifax Association of the Deaf. Edith was one of two vice-presidents of ECAD between 1908 and 1911. She was also on the Forrest Club's executive committee for one year, 1919–20.

Edith was also involved in the Forrest Club's women's group, which they called the "Sewing Circle" but later changed the name to the "Fireside Circle" to better reflect the spirit of social entertainment rather than the mere business of sewing. Shortly after her husband's death in 1959, Edith moved to Moncton to be near Lena, and died there in 1969.

Lena was an active member of the Moncton Association of the Deaf for many years and also the Eastern Canada Association of the Deaf, which granted her a lifetime membership. She was vice-president of the Maritime Deaf Mutes Association (later ECAD) from 1924 to 1926.

The May-June 1974 issue of *The Deaf Canadian*, volume 3, reported that Lena Morrison Snowdon, the last surviving member of her immediate family and long-time resident of the City of Moncton, was the honoured guest at a party to celebrate her ninety-second birthday on 18 June 1973. She was at that time residing in one of the towers of the Moncton Senior Citizens' Centre, and it was apparently her first birthday party in all of her ninety-two years of life. The celebrated event was a gift from her neighbours and friends. Leonard Jones, the mayor of Moncton, presented Lena with a brooch and a copy of *The History of Moncton*, on behalf of the City. Lena received several telegrams from notable Canadians in high office.

In July 1979 Lena was expected to attend the Eastern Canada Association of the Deaf's convention in Moncton as an honoured guest and one of the eldest members. Unfortunately, she was too fragile to make the short journey to attend the banquet. She passed away peacefully later that year on 30 December 1979, just a year and a half short of a full century of living.

SPINK-MITCHELL, Christine

1949–
Hairstylist, Mentor, Counsellor, ASL Instructor, Storyteller, and Researcher.

CHRISTINE SPINK, born in Edmonton, Alberta, to hearing parents, became Deaf at the age of three years and nine months, due to influenza/meningitis. She has one Deaf relative, a cousin, Loretta Wall, who resides in Winnipeg. Christine's Deaf spouse, Len Mitchell, is highly respected in the Deaf Community and is currently involved with the World Federation of the Deaf. He is employed at the Manitoba School for the Deaf as an educational interpreting consultant and bilingual-bicultural officer. Christine's basic education was acquired at the MacKay Centre in Montréal in 1955 and at the Alberta School for the Deaf from 1956 to 1966.

Upon leaving school, she enrolled at the Marvel Beauty School in Edmonton to train as a hairstylist. This was a monumental challenge as there were no interpreters and she had to use speechreading, gesturing, and writing to communicate. However, her hearing colleagues were wonderful mentors who broke down language barriers and included her in all their fun. She readily passed the provincial hairstyling examination and had no trouble finding work because she had already established a good reputation with her entries in several hair show competitions.

By 1976 she knew she needed a greater challenge, so she enrolled at Gallaudet University in Washington, DC, a promise she had made to her friend and role model, Charmaine Letourneau, when they were both students at Alberta School for the Deaf. In 1981 she received a BA degree in Sociology, followed by a Master's degree in Counselling in 1983. She did her counselling internship at Alberta College in Edmonton and taught ASL classes in the evenings. While at Gallaudet, she supported herself by providing hairstyling services on campus, teaching ASL classes, working in the media library, counselling adult education students and working for two summers with Family Learning Vacation, where she taught ASL to hearing parents of Deaf children.

Christine was the winner of the first Miss Deaf Canada Pageant, chosen in 1973. Being honoured in this way boosted her self-confidence and gave her courage. She became the founder of the Alberta Cultural Society of the Deaf in 1974 and has held many of the executive positions in the Edmonton Association of the Deaf at one time or another. She worked as a counsellor at Lauderdale House, a group home for multihandicapped Deaf adults, and as a counsellor for Deaf adults under Family Services. In addition, she was one of the pioneer teachers in the Interpreter Training Program at Grant MacEwen Community College. She is also the holder of an ASLPI Certificate from York University in Toronto— (American Sign Language Proficiency Interview as rater and interviewer).

Christine and her husband Len moved from Edmonton to Winnipeg in 1987. She has held many important positions in that city—"ASL on Wheels," which involved teaching ASL to staff and their employers in their workplaces, being self-employed and offering contract counselling services, and working as a school counsellor, ASL specialist, workshop presenter, and coordinator of programs and events for the Deaf. Her most recent team project is the study of ASL literature and its application to bilingual/bicultural literacy.

Christine is also one of Canada's most noted ASL storytellers. As an ASL storytelling promoter and mentor, she contributed significantly to the success of the Ladder Awards®, an ASL literature and Deaf Heritage literature project sponsored by the Canadian Cultural Society of the Deaf (CCSD). Through her mentorship, several ASL storytelling winners of the Ladder Awards® had their

stories published on CD–ROM and videotape by CCSD with For the Record Productions with financial support from Human Resources Development Canada.

In 1995 Christine was the recipient of the Deaf Woman of the Year Award from the Quota Club, and appeared on CBC Radio's *Morningside* with Peter Gzowski. She is an active member of the Calvary Temple Church of the Deaf and the Calvary Women's Fellowship, and a leader in songs of worship and praise. She enjoys reading, doing crafts, and writing poetry when she has leisure time. Like Helen Keller, she believes that when God closes one door, He opens another. As her mother always said, she believes in watching for open doors and taking advantage of the opportunities they offer.

ST.LOUIS (RICHER), Murielle Odile Marie

1934–
Skilled Seamstress, LSQ Instructor, and Promoter of LSQ and ASL as Languages of Instruction.

MURIELLE RICHER was born hearing to hearing French-Canadian parents with a large family at McLennan in northern Alberta's Peace River Country. She has four hearing siblings and one Deaf and one hard-of-hearing sister. There are no other known Deaf relatives. The cause of her Deafness was a bout of scarlet fever when she was eighteen months old. Her father was an Albertan but her mother came from Québec and both had been raised in a French-Canadian cultural background. The family farmed at Donnelly and moved to the village of McLennan when Murielle was nine years old.

When she was six, her parents pondered the question of her education and it was decided that, because of her family background, she should be sent to a French school. Accordingly, Murielle joined several other Deaf youngsters from northern Alberta to make the long journey to Montréal by train. At the end of the first day they were joined in Edmonton by a large group of Deaf children from across Alberta, and two appointed supervisors to escort them on their three-day journey to Montréal. There was no provincial School for the Deaf in Alberta at that time.

Murielle was one of five girls in the group of about sixty Alberta students sent to Institution des Sourdes, which was operated by the Sisters of Charity of Providence. For the next thirteen years, she travelled back and forth to her home in Alberta every summer and spent all the shorter school holidays with her aunt in Montréal. Her education was strictly an oral one, and students were forbidden to sign. If they broke this rule, they were punished by having to wear mittens.

During the long summer train rides, however, there were no such restrictions and they all communicated happily and freely with each other by signing. In 1954 Murielle graduated and returned to McLennan where she became a very proficient seamstress and provided many elegant garments for her local clientele.

In 1956 she left home again to settle in Sudbury, Ontario, and live with her uncle's family. She soon found employment as a diet cook at St. Joseph's Hospital. She also renewed her acquaintance with Roger St. Louis, whom she had met in Montréal and who was now working as a barber. Before long, Roger and Murielle were married and raising seven hearing children. They now have several grandchildren and some of their family members work as sign interpreters and teachers of the Deaf. As a couple, Roger and Murielle began to campaign for access and inclusion of Deaf Francophones in the public education system and they succeeded in opening programs for Deaf people at Cambrian College, as well as initiating the first full-time LSQ interpreting program, which was then transferred to the new Boreal College.

Eventually, Roger volunteered to teach LSQ classes at Centre Jules Léger, administered by the University of Ottawa. His perseverance and determination led to the acceptance of LSQ as a legitimate language with its own grammar, syntax, and lexicon. Both Roger and Murielle were full-time LSQ instructors in several northern Ontario cities from 1989 to 1997. They became involved with the Review Board for Post-Secondary Education of the Deaf in Ontario, the provincial reviewing of LSQ interpreters for certification, intervention services for Deaf-Blind Persons, and a number of other agencies that advocated for Deaf Francophones in Ontario. With the support of three MPPs, they succeeded in bringing in legislation that declared ASL and LSQ to be the official languages of instruction in all education programs for Deaf persons in Ontario. Murielle has deservedly been honoured for her outstanding contributions to the Deaf Community with numerous awards, certificates, and medals.

STINSON-RILEY, Kathleen Victoria Fleming

1900–1989

Teacher and Pioneer in the Education of the Deaf, Influential Volunteer, and Devout Church Worker.

Available research documents confirm few details about KATHLEEN STINSON's early family circumstances, but there is no doubt that she had a profound influence on the history of Western Deaf Canada during her eighty-nine years of life. She attended the Manitoba School for the Deaf from 1908 to 1918, and then went to Gallaudet College (now Gallaudet University) in Washington, DC, from 1919 to 1922. Her first year, 1918–19, was spent at the Kendall School for the Deaf which offered preparatory courses for students who wanted to meet the necessary requirements for admission to the College.

Back in Canada, after graduating from Gallaudet, she taught at the Manitoba School for the Deaf from 1922 to 1924, where the eminent David Peikoff was one of her Deaf colleagues, and they both taught manual classes. On 8 July 1923, the Ladies' Aid Society of the Winnipeg Church of the Deaf was established, and Kathleen was one of the founding members. This group later provided strong fundraising support for the establishing of the Winnipeg Community Centre for the Deaf (WCCD).

Kathleen returned to the US to teach at the Montana State School for the Deaf from 1924 to 1929. She returned to Canada to become one of the original Deaf teachers at the Saskatchewan Provincial School for the Deaf in Saskatoon where she taught from 1931 to 1943. This was during a period when the school was actively paving the way to implement a strictly oral policy and all the Deaf teachers constantly felt pressured to leave. Kathleen Stinson was the last experienced Deaf teacher at the school when she resigned in 1943.

While teaching in Saskatoon, Kathleen and another Deaf teacher, Esther Paulson, arranged a meeting at their home on 10 May 1932, which ultimately led to the birth of the Saskatoon Association of the Deaf (SAD). The six people who attended this initial meeting served as temporary officers of an organizing committee that later established the Saskatoon chapter of the Western Canada Association of the Deaf (WCAD). Kathleen was secretary of the founding committee. She was also instrumental in establishing *The WCAD News* in 1936. Following the 1935 Triennial Western Canada Association of the Deaf Convention in Saskatoon, Kathleen, as first vice-president, suggested that some kind of newsletter be published by the organization as a means of keeping in touch with the membership between conventions. The first issue, subsidized by a loan of ten dollars from the first editor, Harold Norman Phillips of Winnipeg, was printed in May 1936, and sold for twenty cents per copy to members and fifty cents per copy to non-members. With the September/October issue in 1987, after a fifty-two-year record of continuous publication, *The WCAD News* became *The Deaf Reporter*.

Kathleen Stinson was married twice. In August of 1943, shortly after she left the Saskatchewan School for the Deaf, she became the third wife of the Reverend A.H.J. Staubitz, an American minister who had been ordained in Kitchener, Ontario. When he retired in 1956 after thirty-two years of pastoral work, mostly in the US, the couple moved to Silver Creek in New York State. A mere eighteen months later, the Reverend Staubitz passed away at the age of seventy-three. Kathleen then returned to Canada and later married George Riley. They were very active in the fellowship of the Vancouver Church of the Deaf where she had significant influence on all congregational events. A young hearing minister from Manitoba, Reverend Donald Hume, was taught ASL by Kathleen and George Riley when he took charge of their congregation, so that he could effectively minister to his Deaf parishioners.

Kathleen Stinson (Staubitz) Riley left a lasting imprint on many members of the Deaf Community in western Canada when she passed away in 1989, at eighty-nine years of age. She will always be fondly remembered as a teacher, a tireless worker for Deaf causes, and a devout religious leader.

STOREY (BELISLE), Lydia Susan

1939–
Commercial Sewing Machine Operator, Dietary Assistant, and Deaf Volunteer.

LYDIA BELISLE was born Deaf to hearing parents in Willow Bunch, Saskatchewan. She had three hearing siblings—Theresa, Laura, and Gerard—and two Deaf, a sister, Lucille, and a brother, Michael, who died of a massive heart attack in 1998. The family knew very little about Deafness and had no information about the education of Deaf children, so Lydia was nine years old before she was enrolled her at the Saskatchewan provincial School for the Deaf in Saskatoon. She has always been grateful to her parents for having sent her to the school. She enjoyed her years there (1948 to 1957) and felt it changed her life to be among Deaf peers. The academic program, coupled with the residential aspects of the school, provided her with a good practical background to seek future employment.

When she graduated in 1957, Lydia trained for two weeks to become a crest-maker with Crest Craft Limited in Saskatoon. Pleased with her work and her attitude, the company hired her immediately as a full-time sewing machine operator. She worked for the company for twenty-six years until it went out of business in 1983. For the next seven years she was employed as a dietary assistant in the kitchen of the school she had attended, renamed as the R.J.D Williams School for the Deaf. When the school closed in 1991, Lydia once again became a commercial sewing machine operator and was employed by Western Embroidery, where she is still working at present.

Lydia is married to a Deaf man, John Storey. They have three hearing adult children and several hearing grand-children. John is now retiring from his job as a watch and clock repairman which kept him employed for forty-eight years. They have both been very actively involved in the life of Saskatoon's Deaf Community and have received various forms of recognition for their countless contributions. John became a member of the Saskatoon Association of the Deaf in 1953 and Lydia in 1957. Both have been granted honorary lifetime memberships for their exemplary involvement.

Lydia has also contributed a great deal of time and effort to the Canadian Deaf Festival, for which she has been recognized by the Canadian Cultural Society of the Deaf. In her leisure time, she loves swimming and lawn bowling for exercise and recreation. At home she enjoys gardening, sewing, and quilting.

She is also very supportive of John's work with Saskatchewan Deaf and Hard of Hearing Services, Saskatchewan Deaf Sports Association, Saskatoon Deaf Athletic Club, Saskatoon Deaf Catholic Club, Saskatoon Deaf Seniors' Club, Western Canada Association of Deaf, and Western Canada Deaf Reunion. Together they are a busy couple who are valued and respected by the Deaf Community.

STRATIY (PETRONE), Angela Jean

1947–
Educator, Deaf Interpreter, Consultant, Program Chair, Author, Businesswoman, Presenter, Producer, Director, Performer, Comedian, and Proud Deaf Canadian. *"Laughter-is-the-Best-Medicine"*

ANGELA PETRONE was born Deaf into a Deaf family in Winnipeg, Manitoba. Her mother (Rosalie Bodrug Petrone), father (Edward Petrone), aunt (Dora Bodrug Morris) and brother (Robert Petrone) were all Deaf. Her father and aunt are now deceased but her mother resides in Edmonton and her brother teaches at E.C. Drury School for the Deaf in Milton, Ontario. Angela currently makes her home in Edmonton with her three hearing sons, Micha, Drury and Conrad.

Her early education began in a mainstream public school (Isbister) in Winnipeg and progressed to the Saskatchewan School for the Deaf in Saskatoon, from which she graduated in 1965. Angela recalls this period in her life as completely "black or white" (with no allowance for any "grey" areas), a time filled with "don'ts and can'ts." When she entered Gallaudet University in Washington, DC, she underwent a complete metamorphosis, entering a new and exciting phase of her life, to which she fondly refers as "The Brave New Deaf World," where there were no barriers to success and Deafness took pride of place.

Her keen interest in drama soon had her involved in various Gallaudet plays. She played the role of

"Knowledge" in *Everyman* which led to her winning the "Best Actress" award in 1969, as well as a scholarship to attend a summer session at the National Theatre of the Deaf (NTD) in Waterford, Connecticut. The following year, she played "Nurse Rebecca" in *The Crucible*. Throughout her college years, she was affectionately known as "Rye Whiskey" the saloon singer. She graduated from Gallaudet with a BA degree in English Literature in 1970, and in 1975 obtained a Master's degree in Deaf Education from Western Maryland College.

Since then, Angela's life has been a continuous series of successes in many fields and her contributions to the Deaf Community, locally, provincially, and nationally, have been many. She has been employed as an educator—at the North Dakota School for the Deaf in Devil's Lake, North Dakota, the Manitoba School for the Deaf in Winnipeg, Manitoba, the Alberta School for the Deaf in Edmonton, Alberta, as a substitute teacher, and Grant MacEwan Community College (GMCC), now known as Grant MacEwan College in Edmonton, Alberta.

She has been the initiator of many educational innovations and has an impressive list of achievements to her credit. Her greatest pleasures as a teacher often came from her involvement in theatrical productions, at which she excelled. When she taught ASL at Red River Community College in Winnipeg and the University of Alberta in Edmonton, she was the mainstay behind the spring and Christmas plays from 1970 to 1986, and helped to establish student clubs, councils, and organizations.

Meanwhile, Angela participated in countless extracurricular activities and became an exemplary role model in promoting heightened public awareness of ASL and its influence on Deaf Culture, Deaf history, Deaf pride, and Deaf challenges. She has been a powerful advocate for change in such areas as interpreter training, evaluation, and certification; closed captioning for TV programming, videos and films; more and better resources and materials for Deaf education; the development of bilingual-bicultural education programs; and above all, to create pride in the capacity of Deaf people to laugh, to be entertained, and to enjoy their unique forms of comedy and humor. She has also provided ASL consultation.

Forrest Nickerson is known as the "Father of Deaf Culture," and Angela was his "backbone," perhaps better known as the "Mother of Deaf Culture" in the founding of the Canadian Cultural Society of the Deaf (CCSD) in 1970, in which she played many leading roles. She was the managing director of the Canadian Theatre of the Deaf, initiator of the Miss Deaf Canada Pageant, coordinator of the National Festival of the Arts, and later president and then executive director.

Another responsibility Angela undertook was to serve as the coordinator of the ASL Instructors of Canada Evaluation and Training Program and assisting with *The Canadian Dictionary of ASL* before she finally retired from CCSD in 1999. While living in Winnipeg, Angela was a member of the Winnipeg Community Centre of the Deaf (WCCD) from the time she was an infant. Her parents were firm believers that the Deaf Club was important because Deaf people attended events there in order to learn from other Deaf people. Her father made sure that when she returned from Gallaudet she would help others, so she became very involved in WCCD again, acting as president, founding member of the TTY Committee, president of the Women's Auxiliary, and variety show director. Now she is secretary of the Edmonton Association of the Deaf, and her heart is still with the Deaf Club. As her father always said, it is the centre of everything for Deaf people, providing service, assistance, counselling, entertainment, therapy, and all the other things that are not accessible to the Deaf anywhere else.

Angela is currently employed as curriculum developer, coordinator, and instructor for the ASL/English Interpreter Program, the Sign Language Studies Program, and the ASL (noncredit) Evening Program at Grant MacEwan College (GMCC) in Edmonton. In 1990 she was the first Deaf Program Chair of the GMCC Interpreter Training Program. Angela is also an entrepreneur with her own business, Deaf Utopia, which markets her performances and workshops. She has produced videos on various topics. Her first public video release was *Pursuit of ASL: Interesting Facts Using Classifiers*, produced by Dr. Marty Taylor, Interpreting Consolidated, in 1998. Another video, *You Think Deaf People Have Problems?*, was released in December 1999. It features Angela Petrone Stratiy's one-woman comedy show giving a humorous perspective on hearing people based on her own research, and shows how Deaf people survive in the hearing world.

Angela is the author of several professional articles, was a consultant for *The Canadian Dictionary of ASL* with Carole Sue Bailey, Kathy Dolby, and Hilda Campbell, co-edited *Deaf Women of Canada* with Jo-Anne Robinson, and Hilda Campbell as author, and has acted as an adviser for many Deaf causes, projects, and events. In addition, she is an inspiring guest lecturer and public speaker. Angela has received local and national recognition for her many contributions to Canada's Deaf Community. She has received several very prestigious honours, awards, and certificates including being inducted into the Canadian Cultural Society of the Deaf (CCSD) Hall of Fame in 1998 and receiving the Association of Visual Language Interpreters of Canada Award of Excellence in 1992, CCSD Founder's Order of Honour in 1980, Winnipeg YWCA Woman of the Year Nominee in 1980, and Quota International Deaf Woman of the Year in 1979.

Her greatest passion in life, however, is her unmistakable success as Canada's first and only Deaf female standup comedian, for which she has received rave reviews in both the Deaf and the mainstream media. Deaf Canadians everywhere will continue to enjoy and benefit from Angela's many talents, interests, and creative instincts. She continues to enjoy travelling for her ASL-Deaf Culture workshops, her one-woman comedy show, and her duo-comedy act with Bob Whitford.

STUMP-NELSON, JoAnne Mary

1943–
Versatile Educator, Deaf Advocate, and Volunteer.

JOANNE STUMP was born Deaf into a hearing family in Montréal, Québec. She has no known Deaf relatives, but her spouse, Norman Nelson, a retired teacher, is Deaf. Like JoAnne, he is a strong advocate of justice and equality for Deaf persons. They have two adult children—Paul, who is Deaf and Rebecca, who is hard of hearing—and two granddaughters.

JoAnne received her early education at Clarke School for the Deaf in Massachusetts and her High School Diploma from Queen of Angels Academy in Dorval, Québec. At Gallaudet University in Washington, DC, she earned a BA degree in Sociology with a minor in Psychology and then went on to Western Maryland College to train as a teacher of the Deaf, where she was one of the three first Deaf students in the Deaf Education Program when it opened in 1970. In 1976 she obtained an MA degree in the National Leadership Training Program at California State University in Northridge and was the first Deaf Canadian to be invited into that program. Two years later she earned another MA credential in Special Education, also from California State University. In 1991 she received her Diploma in Educational Technology from McGill University in Montréal, Québec. JoAnne has continued to add to her qualifications and knowledge by taking courses in educational technology, bilingual teaching methods, and literacy training. She has also attained certification in Sign Communication Proficiency Interview Training (SCPI).

Her career as an educator has provided JoAnne with a wealth of diversity in experience—Sign language instructor, diagnostic testing coordinator, specialist in Deaf studies, computer specialist, coordinator of a resource centre, life skills instructor, and regular classroom teacher of the Deaf at various grade levels. In 2000 and 2001, Joanne taught ASL at summer sessions at the University of Vermont. She is currently employed at the MacKay Centre for the Deaf and is a member of several professional organizations. Apart from her teaching, she has participated in other interesting activities. In 1972 she met with the Bell Pioneers to distribute old teletypewriters in the Montréal area. She was also president of the Montréal Telecommunications of the Deaf Association from 1972 to 1988.

JoAnne has been the deserving recipient of numerous awards, scholarships, and honours, including honorary membership of Phi Kappa Zeta. She continues to be a member of many organizations of the Deaf, and has served in an executive capacity in the Canadian Association of the Deaf, Montréal Association of the Deaf, Canadian Deaf Sports Association, Canadian Coordinating Council of Deafness, Bell Relay Service Advisory Council, National Fraternal Society of the Deaf, Canadian Cultural Society of the Deaf, and Montréal Teacher's Association.

JoAnne has travelled to northern Québec on four occasions to different Inuit villages to participate in annual six-day family workshops attended by Deaf Inuit children and their families. She and her husband Norman focus on storytelling to create Deaf awareness and Deaf identity. They find it challenging and hope the children will grow up to become good Deaf role models for future generations of Deaf Inuit children.

JoAnne and Norman make their home in LaSalle (Montréal), Québec, and are well known for their efforts to improve access and inclusion for Deaf people everywhere. JoAnne attends conferences and forums and speaks out eloquently on all issues related to Deafness in general. In particular, she promotes openness in communication and cultural diversity. She considers herself to be in a double-minority situation because she lives where French is the dominant spoken language and she is first of all Deaf, and secondly she uses ASL which is based on the English language. Her work as a spokesperson for the Deaf Community is laudable and well appreciated, and will doubtlessly be ongoing for many years to come.

In her spare time, JoAnne enjoys travelling, beach-combing, horticulture, crafts, collecting antiques, photo-graphy, and genealogy. She also likes to read novels, watch captioned movies and TV programs, work on her computer, and surf the Internet. She is proud of her Irish ancestry and the many stories her Irish mother shared with her, passing on her wisdom, and urging her daughter to be a strong woman who will allow no barriers to stand in her way.

SULLIVAN, Heather ("Dawn")

1973–
Computer Programmer, Lab Assistant, and Supervisor.

DAWN SULLIVAN was born Deaf to hearing parents in St. John's, Newfoundland. She has no known Deaf relatives and the cause of her Deafness is undetermined. Dawn currently makes her home in Manuels, Newfoundland.

She was educated at the Newfoundland School for the Deaf in St. John's from 1978 to 1993. Following her graduation, she attended Gallaudet University in Washington, DC, to obtain a Bachelor of Science degree in Computer Information Systems in 1998. While attending Gallaudet, Dawn was on the Dean's List and was named "President's Scholar." She was also a member of the Phi Alpha Pi Honour Society, served as corresponding secretary for the Delta Zeta Sorority, and represented it on the Student Council, played intramural basketball, was a member of the Election Week Committee, and served on the Finance Committee. In addition, she performed many volunteer services such as ushering at the 1996 and 1997 commencement exercises, cleaning the Washington Women's Shelter, and ushering at the Gallaudet University Theatre. On Net Day in 1997, she volunteered to wire the computer network at a Model Secondary School of the Deaf.

Dawn's employment history is varied and eclectic in nature. She has worked as an administrative clerk in the Government Service of Canada, has taught ASL to a Deaf client who was developmentally delayed, and offered French tutorials to students learning to read and write French at Gallaudet University. She also wrote an unpublished "how-to" book entitled *Winning the Job Market*, aimed at college audiences, about the successful pursuit of experiential education and career opportunities. While she was a student at Gallaudet, she worked as an assistant in the computer lab, troubleshooting problems for computer users. She became a lab supervisor and trained four other assistants while she continued solving problems, installing and upgrading hardware and software, establishing schedules, and completing time-cards for lab assistants.

During the summer of 1997, back home in St. John's, she worked in the Information Technology (IT) Division of the provincial Department of Forest Resources and Agrifoods, which led to a permanent job there when she graduated. She enjoys her work as a "Jane-of-all-trades" with regard to the computer system—designing, coding, testing, documenting, coordinating, developing, training users, consulting with directors and managers, and converting materials to a format acceptable to posting on the website.

In her spare time, Dawn designs web pages. For recreation, she plays table tennis and enjoys bowling and skiing. She likes to travel and plans to do more of it in the future. As a craftswoman, she prefers cross-stitching and tole painting. This talented and ambitious young woman has a bright future in which to achieve her many goals in life.

SUTHERLAND (NICHOLSON), Annie Ethelwynne ("Winnie")

1896–1965
Artist, Clerical Worker, Homemaker, and Tireless Worker for the Deaf.

ANNIE NICHOLSON, who preferred to be called "Winnie," was born Deaf into a hearing family near Dauphin, Manitoba. She had no known Deaf relatives. Her siblings, a sister, Grace, and brothers, Arthur, Kenneth, and Raymond were hearing as were their parents. Winnie's Deaf spouse, George William Sutherland, whom she married in 1926, came from Fort Chipewyan in what is now northern Alberta, but until 1905 part of the Northwest Territories. Winnie and George both attended the Manitoba School for the Deaf in Winnipeg and made their home in that city after they were married.

Prior to settling down to married life, however, Winnie attended Gallaudet College in Washington, DC, and returned to Winnipeg to work for some time at Trader's Trust. After marrying George Sutherland she became a full-time homemaker but provided a strong leadership role in the Deaf Community. Together, she and George raised three fine hearing children—two daughters, Jane, who now lives in Kingston, Ontario, and Shelagh, who lives in Winnipeg, and one son, Dr. Ian Sutherland, who lives in Winnipeg. George had a Deaf sister, Barbara Sutherland, who worked closely with Winnie on her many projects aimed at improving the quality of life for Deaf persons in Winnipeg. Winnie's three children eventually presented her with ten grandchildren, all hearing, many of whom are involved in medicine or other "helping" professions.

Winnie's eldest daughter, Jane, trained in Pittsburgh to become a teacher of the Deaf and taught in Pittsburgh and Winnipeg before she married and moved to Kingston, Ontario, where she continued to provide counsel and support for many Deaf persons. Signing was the first language that she and her sister and brother learned, so all three were comfortable among both Deaf and hearing people.

Winnie's greatest success was her campaign to provide a church and a full-time pastor for Winnipeg's Deaf Community. She helped to raise the necessary funds in many innovative ways and the Winnipeg Church of the Deaf soon became a reality. She was also very active in the Winnipeg Community Centre of the Deaf and was elected the first president of the Women's Circle in the new church. She possessed artistic talents and loved to paint and create beautiful things. The Winnipeg Art Gallery once displayed one of her still-lifes for several months. She often used her creative skills in food preparation and her fancy open-face sandwiches were highly popular at teas and receptions.

Winnie's parents were a prominent business couple in Winnipeg. They saw to it that she received a musical education, endless exposure to cultural refinements, opportunities to travel, and role modeling in leadership as well as an academic education. Her family were all fluent signers, as were her three children. Because communication was never a barrier, their home was always a popular gathering place for Deaf people of all ages. When she died in 1965, Winnie Sutherland left behind a powerful legacy within the Deaf Community for which she will always be remembered with the greatest love and respect.

SWANSON (HENDERSON), Blanche

1897–1979
Farm-Wife and Partner, and Alberta Deaf Pioneer.

BLANCHE HENDERSON was born hearing into a hearing family in Kingsville, Ontario. When she was five years old, in 1902, her family moved west to the Okotoks area in Alberta. While travelling by train to their new home, Blanche contracted a severe case of scarlet fever which was followed by ear infection and mastoiditis. The result was that she became Deaf. She attended public schools in rural Alberta where she was always the only Deaf child enrolled. Unfortunately, her education had to be terminated after the fourth grade because of the distance to school and the necessity of crossing a river on a railroad bridge. Nevertheless, Blanche loved to read, and always kept a good dictionary at her side. Consequently, she developed an excellent vocabulary that belied her lack of formal education. She was a very intelligent and extroverted woman, with a wonderful sense of humour. Her children recall that during difficult times, of which there were many in rural Alberta, she always had faith that things would work out favourably, and they usually did.

Her husband-to-be, Alexander David Swanson, was a graduate of Gallaudet College (now known as Gallaudet University) in Washington, DC. He was born in Scotland and became Deaf at the age of nine months due to the after-effects of a smallpox vaccination.

In 1881 he emigrated to Canada with his family, and they settled in Manitoba, but later moved to Ontario where he attended the Ontario Institution for the Deaf and Dumb (now Sir James Whitney School for the Deaf) in Belleville, from 1885 to 1895. He then went to the Kendall School in Washington for a year to prepare for his entrance to the college. He was a student at Gallaudet from 1896 to 1901, when he graduated with a Bachelor of Arts degree. His instructors encouraged him to become a teacher of the Deaf. He decided instead, to return to his family who had meanwhile moved to Alberta. He then homesteaded a section of land in the Spruceville district, near what is now the town of Lacombe. He farmed during the summers and worked in lumber camps during the winters until 1921, when he rented out his farm and went to Indiana to work as a linotype operator.

When Alexander Swanson returned to Alberta for a visit with his family in 1925, he met Blanche Henderson, and immediately began a courtship with her. They were married on 1 June 1926, when he was nearing fifty years of age, and Blanche was twenty-eight. At first they lived on rented land in the Lakeside area but, following the birth of their first child, Ronald, they moved to the farm at Spruceville. They eventually had three more children—all hearing, two sons, Alexander Gordon and William, and a daughter Elizabeth, whom they called Betty. In order to make sure their children learned to speak properly, they hired a hearing man to work on the farm so they would be exposed to English speech. Unfortunately, the hired man, Karl, was Norwegian and spoke English with a thick Norwegian accent. Ronald, the eldest child, learned to speak

Norwegian fluently and to speak broken English with a strong Norwegian accent. Blanche, whose speech was fairly good, constantly had to correct the children's pronunciation. Because both Blanche and Alexander were avid readers, their home always had an abundance of reading material. Thus, they were able to instill a love of reading and learning in all four of their offspring.

The Swansons were progressive farmers and took great pride in their efforts. Frequently, local farmers went to them for advice. Even at the height of the Great Depression (also known as "The Dirty Thirties"), both Blanche and her husband were resourceful enough to provide adequately for their growing family. Both were devoutly religious and, during the Depression, their social conscience prompted them to hire several Deaf people, including George Young, Harry Likiforuk, Fred Bouder, Mike Goulet, and Bill Ewasiuk. Blanche also had a hired girl who was Deaf, Ethel Slaughter.

When Alexander died of cancer in 1943, Blanche sold the farm west of Lacombe and moved to another farm on the edge of the village of Bentley, Alberta, so her children would be close to a high school as they were all of school age, from eight to fifteen. This farm became her home for the next thirty-seven years. She had many friends, both Deaf and hearing, and had frequent visitors who stopped in for tea and conversation. Laughter was the order of the day, especially with her hearing friends who communicated with her in writing, often sharing a good joke or a humorous anecdote. She was an avid gardener and her visitors always went home with bouquets of whatever flowers were in bloom. She enjoyed sewing, knitting, crocheting, and tatting, and fashioned many beautiful garments for her children and grandchildren.

Blanche lived the last few years of her life in Calgary so she could be near her daughter Betty. She died of heart failure on 31 December 1979, at the age of eighty-two, and was buried in an Okotoks cemetery near other members of the Henderson family. During her lifetime she held the respect and admiration of all who knew her. When she passed away, she left her children a legacy of tolerance, humour, and the strength of faith.

SWEDICK, Theresa Anne

1952–
Deaf Activist, Collector of Celebrity Autographs, Correspondence, and Memorabilia, and Fan Club Member and Organizer.

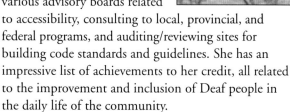

THERESA SWEDICK was born Deaf into a hearing family in St. Boniface, Manitoba, the eldest of four children. The family was raised in three Manitoba towns—Rivers, Churchill, and Beausejour. She has a Deaf uncle, Ernest Kohare, and is a relative of Ed Schreyer, the former Premier of Manitoba and one-time Governor General of Canada. Although her parents are now deceased, a number of her family members still live in the Beausejour area. From 1958 to 1965 Theresa was educated at the Saskatchewan School for the Deaf in Saskatoon. When the Manitoba School for the Deaf opened in Tuxedo (Winnipeg), she attended there until 1969.

With enough residual hearing in her left ear to appreciate music, Theresa became an avid Elvis Presley fan at the age of six. As an adult, she was successful in ensuring that twenty-five of Elvis Presley's thirty-four feature films included closed captioning on home video. She has corresponded with (and met many) celebrities from the world of entertainment, and famous people in politics and other walks of life. She became a lobbyist for improved television programming and was able to appeal to those on her lengthy list of celebrity correspondents to support her crusade. Most of them responded in a positive and encouraging manner.

After leaving school Theresa furthered her education by taking a one-year course in office and business training at Red River Community College. The next year she followed this up with a training program to become a keypunch operator. From 1988 to 1990 she participated in the New Career Deaf Training Program to become a human services worker and, in 1997, she trained as a universal design accessibility consultant at the University of Manitoba's Barrier Free Institute. She has been employed in various capacities by the Manitoba government, and/or the government of Canada since 1978, and has assisted with accessibility audits and projects for the City of Winnipeg.

Theresa's extensive volunteer activities have included her steady lobbying for captioning improvements, serving on numerous boards and committees of organizations and agencies in the Deaf Community, providing input at public hearings, serving on various advisory boards related to accessibility, consulting to local, provincial, and federal programs, and auditing/reviewing sites for building code standards and guidelines. She has an impressive list of achievements to her credit, all related to the improvement and inclusion of Deaf people in the daily life of the community.

She was also the recipient of two distinguished awards presented to her in 1997 for her involvement in what is now referred to as the "Flood of the Century"— the Manitoba Access Awareness Award from the Manitoba government, and the Premier's Volunteer Award. Both were in recognition of her efforts to keep the members of the Deaf Community informed of events resulting from the devastation of the flood.

Theresa's list of famous international contacts is much too lengthy to be included here. Suffice it to say that it comprises the names of dozens of celebrated persons in the entertainment and recreation industries, political figures, family members of entertainers and performers, and other individuals who rank among the "rich and famous." She has organized and run a fan club herself and is a member of many others.

Theresa's personal achievements have been many, but she ranks these among her most notable: her involvement as an extra in *Street Legal*, closed captioning on *Elvis Presley* home videos and for such productions as *Wanted: Dead or Alive*, *ET: The Extra-Terrestrial*, and *Snow White*, plus the captioning of many TV programs as well as the provision of ASL interpreters for events such as the Pan Am Games and the daily press conferences during the Flood of the Century. She is currently involved with developing and implementing the City of Winnipeg's Sign Language Interpreter Policy which was announced on 26 February 2001.

TAYLOR (HAZELL), Lynda Jean

1952–
Bookkeeper, Avid Curler, and Expert Farming Partner.

LYNDA HAZELL was born Deaf to hearing parents in Virden, Manitoba. She was the last of eight children and has a Deaf sister, Helen, who was the seventh child in the family, so their Deafness may have resulted, at least partially, from genetic causes. Helen Stover, Lynda's elder Deaf sister, now lives in Kentucky and works for the First National Bank. They have no other known Deaf relatives. Lynda is married to a Deaf man, Kenneth Taylor, who has a hard-of-hearing brother, William Taylor. Kenneth has been a grain and cattle farmer all his life. As his wife, Lynda has become an expert partner, familiar with every aspect of their farming operation. They have two hearing sons, Jason and Duke, and the family make their home on their farm near Stony Plain, Alberta.

Lynda was educated at the Saskatchewan School for the Deaf in Saskatoon from 1959 to 1973. She attended a technical-vocational school in St. Paul, Minnesota, for a year (1974–75), where she trained as a bookkeeper. Her first employment was as a furrier at Fur Town and HFC in Saskatoon. She then became an office clerk for five years at a Credit Union in Regina, Saskatchewan, but left to be married in 1980.

While living in Saskatoon and Regina, Lynda was a very active member of the Saskatchewan Cultural Society of the Deaf (SCSD) and of the Western Deaf Curling Association (WDCA). In 1980 she was on the team that won first place in a Mixed Championship Bonspiel in Regina. She was one of the co-founders of the Regina Cultural Society of the Deaf and served as a provincial director from 1977 to 1979. In Alberta, she has been a member of the Edmonton Association of the Deaf (EAD), Edmonton Deaf Curling Association (EDCA), and Alberta Deaf Sports Association (ADSA) for a number of years.

Both Lynda and her husband have always been avid curlers. She participated in the Canadian Deaf Curling Championships (ladies' team) and won second place in Winnipeg in 1981. After her two sons were born, Lynda started curling again and also played with hearing teams in afternoons and evenings for seven years. Kenneth, too, curled with hearing teams in order to maintain his skills.

In 1997 Lynda and Ken Taylor were instrumental in setting up Deaf teams and coordinating them with hearing teams at the Shamrock Curling Club in Edmonton, to curl just for fun. Their Deaf team won the 1997 championship. Lynda also participated in ladies and mixed curling with the Canadian Deaf Curling Championships held in Saskatoon, Saskatchewan, Winnipeg, Manitoba, Kingston, Ontario, and Edmonton, Alberta. She played on a ladies' team in Saskatoon in 1995 and 1996, came second in Winnipeg, with a mixed team, in 1997, and third in Edmonton in 1999, also with a mixed team. She continues to be an enthusiastic curler in both Deaf and hearing leagues.

When Lynda married Kenneth in 1980, they moved to the farm at Stony Plain, near Edmonton, and have lived there since. She is a full partner as a farmer, operating all the machinery and participating in all the seasonal work. She has expert knowledge of both the cattle and grain industries, and understands the production and marketing techniques of the beef, grain, and hay which their farm yields.

In her leisure time, Lynda enjoys working at puzzles, cycling, and walking. In the winter months, she and Kenneth still both love to curl.

TAYLOR, Norma Jean

1960–
Skater, Sportswoman, Educator, and School Administrator.

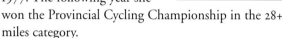

NORMA JEAN was born profoundly Deaf to hearing parents, Walter and Joan Taylor, in North Battleford, Saskatchewan, in 1960. Her hearing loss was not detected until she was about eighteen months old. Her family moved to Saskatoon where she was able to attend the R.J.D. Williams School for the Deaf. When she reached the high school level, she transferred to mainstream schools for grades eleven and twelve, which she took at Walter Murray Collegiate and Holy Cross High School. The transition was difficult because she had only part-time access to an interpreter, but she managed, with determination, to graduate in 1979.

After earning a BA degree in Elementary Education from Gallaudet University in Washington, DC, in 1985, she taught Deaf students in Wetaskiwin, Alberta, before she was hired by the Canadian Hearing Society in Toronto as a coordinator of Impact-ASL Program. In 1988 she became a faculty member and coordinator for the College Preparation Program for Deaf and Hard of Hearing Students at George Brown College in Toronto. She was later promoted to its Deaf Education Centre as chairperson, a prestigious appointment as she was the first Deaf chairperson in the Ontario College System.

In 1996 Norma Jean assumed the principalship at the Manitoba School for the Deaf in Winnipeg. It boasts a bilingual/bicultural program where ASL is the language of instruction and English is taught as a second language. She is a strong advocate of this method of educating Deaf children. The appointment made her the first Deaf woman in Canada to hold such a position.

As a child, she took up speedskating and joined the Saskatoon Lions' Speedskating Club in 1971, skating competitively both nationally and internationally and winning numerous medals and awards. In addition to her skating honours, she was also named High School Cross-Country Running Champion for the City of Saskatoon in 1977. The following year she won the Provincial Cycling Championship in the 28+ miles category.

Norma Jean is married to a Deaf husband, Abbas (Ali) Behmanesh, and they have two hearing children, Magara and Melinda. Despite her impressive and demanding employment history, she has always found time for involvement in the activities of the Deaf Community. She has been a board member of the Canadian Cultural Society of the Deaf and the Ontario Association of the Deaf. She has also chaired committees related to the training and program standards of interpreter services. In addition to her formal educational qualifications, she has attended many conferences, workshops, and seminars to broaden her perspective and generate inspiration.

In 2001 Norma Jean accepted the position of System Principal for Deaf and Hard of Hearing Programs with the Calgary Board of Education in Calgary, Alberta. Her mandate is to forge stronger bonds with the parent communities and the community agencies, in order to further the best interests of all Deaf and hard-of-hearing students.

In her spare time she enjoys scrapbooking and is an avid reader. This efficient and capable woman will doubtlessly continue to be an exemplary role model for all Deaf women in Canada, for many years to come.

TAYLOR, Ruby Belle

1932–
Weaver, Dedicated Public Service Employee, and Dormitory Counsellor.

RUBY TAYLOR was born Deaf into a hearing family in Springdale, Newfoundland. The cause of her Deafness was undetermined and she has no known Deaf relatives. She has a Deaf husband, Hammond Taylor, who is a TTY repairman, maintenance worker, horticulturist, and former scuba diver. He also holds the distinction of having been the first licensed Deaf driver in Newfoundland, and is well known for having founded the Caribou Silent Club in St. John's. Ruby and Hammond have one adopted daughter, Vonita, who is hard of hearing. They have always made their home in St. John's.

Ruby was educated at the MacKay Centre for the Deaf in Montréal from 1947 to 1951. Although Newfoundland had united with Labrador to form Canada's tenth province in 1949, there was no school for Deaf children established until the early 1960s. Therefore, all Deaf pupils had to be sent either to Halifax or Montréal for their schooling.

Ruby became an accomplished weaver and, when she returned to Newfoundland, worked for the Jubilee Weaving Guild for two years. When the Newfoundland School for the Deaf finally opened in 1964, she immediately found employment there as one of its three female Deaf houseparents—along with Mary Snow and Juanita Clouter—thus becoming a public service worker for the government of Newfoundland and Labrador. She continued to work in that capacity until she retired on 31 March 1989. She was presented with a certificate of appreciation for her twenty-five years of faithful service.

Ruby's participation in the activities of the Deaf Community in St. John's includes being a long-time member of the Newfoundland and Labrador Association of the Deaf (NLAD), attending the monthly Deaf Bible study meetings, being a five-pin bowler in Deaf bowling leagues in the past, playing skipbo with a group of five Deaf retired women, and participating in card games of 120s/45s.

In her spare time she enjoys such hobbies and interests as floss embroidery, quilt making, crocheting afghans, knitting slippers, cotton knitting, and going for long daily walks. She and her husband enjoy traveling together. At home, they like to make jam and bottle pickles.

TEBOW (CHAIKOWSKI), Susan ("Sue") Sophia

1951–
Employment Counsellor, Instructor, Champion Curler, and Cancer Survivor.

SUE CHAIKOWSKI was born Deaf to Deaf parents, Joseph and Marjorie Chaikowski, in Winnipeg, Manitoba. She has a Deaf sister, Rita Bomak, a Deaf brother-in-law, Kenneth Bomak, and two Deaf nieces, Sally and Cathy Bomak. She has no children of her own but enjoys her sister's family and makes her home in Winnipeg.

Sue received her education at two provincial Schools for the Deaf—Saskatchewan (in Saskatoon) and Manitoba (in Winnipeg). This happened because the Manitoba School was closed to Deaf students and used by the RCAF during World War II, and later as a Normal School for training teachers. It did not reopen as the School for the Deaf until 1965 when the teacher training program was moved to the Faculty of Education at the University of Manitoba. During those years (1940 to 1965), Deaf students from Manitoba were sent to Saskatchewan.

Following her graduation from the Manitoba School for the Deaf, Sue worked as an employment counsellor for Deaf and Hard of Hearing Services and as an instructor for Deaf landed immigrants (newcomers to Canada). She also worked for Canada Post from 1975 to 1989. What brought her the greatest fame, however, was her outstanding achievement as a curler. When she was only eighteen years old, in 1970, she won her first zone championship in the Manitoba Junior Curling League. Since then her curling successes have been exemplary.

Following is a list of her triumphs in the Canadian Deaf Curling Championships covering the years from 1982 to 1994:

1982 Gold Medal
1983 Silver Medal
1984 Bronze Medal
1985 Gold Medal
1986 Gold Medal
1987 Silver Medal
1988 Gold Medal
1993 Gold Medal
1994 Gold Medal.

In addition to the above record, Sue played third on a rink skipped by Bernice Telford of the Charleswood Ladies' Curling League when it won the Investors Syndicate Trophy in 1984.

In 1995 Sue was shocked when she was diagnosed with breast cancer and had to undergo a mastectomy to remove twelve lymph nodes, ten of which were cancerous. While she was in hospital, friends and family showered her with attention, gifts, and cards. She made a remarkable recovery. The surgery was followed by Adriamycin chemotherapy treatments and Zofran pills to prevent nausea. She lost her hair and most of her appetite. Again, her parents, sister Rita, and a wide network of friends provided her with unconditional love and emotional support. The treatment was successful and a close watch was kept to make sure the cancer had not spread to other body organs. Six years later, her cancer is still in remission and the prognosis is good. She is now affectionately known as "Superwoman" and continues to curl and play darts.

In 1997 Sue was the first woman to be elected as chairperson for the Canadian Deaf Curling Championships at Portage La Prairie, Manitoba. Curling talent obviously runs in the Chaikowski family because her younger sister, Rita Bomak, also has achieved a most impressive personal record of curling victories.

THÉBERGE (WILLANS), Carole

Lawyer, Federal Department of Justice Counsel, and Advocate for the Hard of Hearing.

CAROLE WILLANS was born in Ottawa and acquired a profound bilateral hearing loss due to an accident at the age of four years. She has no known Deaf or hard-of-hearing relatives and is married to Normand Théberge, is a lawyer in private practice. They have two children, Daniel and Caroline, and the family currently makes its home in Gatineau, Québec. Daniel has worked as a summer student for the Canadian Hard of Hearing Association and for the Outaouais Hearing Association. He is currently treasurer of the Canadian Hard of Hearing Association's Branch in Outaouais (Hull, Québec).

By the time Carole's hearing loss occurred, she had already become fluently bilingual in French and English. With a great deal of effort on the part of her parents and herself, she managed to keep both languages, although she took all her education, until university, in French. Her mother always claimed that there was nothing Carole couldn't do, and that has also been Carole's belief throughout her lifetime.

Carole considers herself to be hard of hearing and not Deaf. She has two powerful hearing aids that enable her to make some use of her residual hearing, and her speechreading skills have been honed with constant use and practice. She relies heavily on her visual ability to read body language, facial expressions, and other situational and context clues.

She studied civil law (Québec law) at the University of Ottawa, articled in Hull, and started working in a private practice firm in 1981. After nine years she left private practice and, thanks to her then mentor, Marilyn Dahl, worked for a year as executive director of the Canadian Hard of Hearing Association (CHHA). Working at CHHA, where her hearing loss was not only

accepted, but an asset, was quite an eye-opening experience for Carole.

In 1992 she joined the federal Department of Justice as a counsel in the Criminal Law Policy Section and has worked there ever since. Her job is to provide policy advice to the Minister of Justice in respect of the criminal law pertaining to persons with disabilities, the safety and security of seniors, prostitution involving children and youth, street prostitution, prize fighting, and the use of official languages in court. At work, Carole relies on a portable FM system and sometimes real-time captioning. She uses a regular telephone with powerful amplification, and sometimes a TTY. Her employer has been wonderfully open to her accommodation needs. Wanting to give something back, Carole acts as chairperson of the Department's Advisory Committee on Employment Equity and Persons with Disabilities, and presides over the federal Interdepartmental Consultation Committee on Persons with Disabilities. Her favourite volunteer involvement, on a list too extensive to include here, is her position on the National Board of Directors of the Canadian Hard of Hearing Association where she represents the province of Québec.

Carole has been honoured as the recipient of several awards: the 125th Anniversary Commemorative Medal awarded by the Governor General of Canada, the Marilyn Dahl Award of Merit by the Canadian Hard of Hearing Association, and several leadership and instant awards at the Justice Department. She is also the co-editor of several newsletters and magazines related to hearing loss.

MONA THRASHER was born with normal hearing, the first child of a Portuguese father, Bill Thrasher, and an Alaskan Inuit mother, Alice, in a bush camp on the Mackenzie Delta between Aklavik and Inuvik, on 24 February 1942. Bill Thrasher was the son of a whaler and captain of the legendary mission boat *Our Lady of Lourdes*, which carried supplies from Tuktoyaktuk to the northern settlements of Holman, Coppermine (renamed Kugluktuk), Sachs Harbour, and Cambridge Bay. Bill's father had come to the Arctic from Portugal in the late 1800s. Mona has no known Deaf relatives, and currently makes her home in Yellowknife, Northwest Territories.

When Mona was ten years old she left her family's log cabin to attend the Aklavik Roman Catholic Mission School for the next seven years. She returned to her home during July and August, when the school was closed, and remained in the residence throughout the rest of each year. In her thirteenth year, Mona was Deafened as a result of an unfortunate accident. However, she returned to the Mission School where, despite her Deafness and the new difficulties with communication, she continued her education. Because there was no way for her to learn to sign, she has always communicated mainly through written English, speech, and speechreading.

In her early teens, Mona's artistic talents were recognized and encouraged by all her teachers, but particularly by Father Adam, Bishop Denis Croteau, and an instructor named Bern Will Brown. At the age of eighteen, Mona was invited by Father Adam to paint the "Stations of the Cross" in the Igloo Church in Inuvik, which was newly built at that time. She completed the fourteen murals, each two and one half by three feet, in just over two months.

All her paintings are a reflection of the memories of her childhood in the High Arctic. Her technique is to work from pencil sketches on canvas, over which she paints in oils, using mainly shades of blue and white to show the semi-darkness and the harshness and frigidity of the climate in the region where she grew up. Since her first commission from Father Adam, Mona Thrasher has completed more than 800 works in oils and pastels. Each painting captures the essence of her native Inuvialuit culture—polar bears, seals, igloos, dog teams, northern lights, kayaks, and various hunting and fishing expeditions. She is a true Northener who is familiar with many regions, but particularly the Mackenzie Delta, where the Inuvialuit and Dene cultures meet. She rarely portrays the vast barrenness of the land without some type of human activity, and her choice of colours reflects the Arctic winters that prevail for nine months of the year. All her works have a life-like quality that stems from her imagination and strength of composition.

Mona is a highly disciplined artist who often needs only a week or two to complete a canvas. Her early works were displayed in the Inuvik parish hall and sold through the efforts of Father Adam and Bishop Croteau. Today she is the established "artist-in-residence" at Northern Images in Yellowknife, where she moved in 1990.

Mona Thrasher is a splendid role model, not only for Deaf women in Canada, but also for all Inuvialuit women in Canada's remote northern settlements. With no formal art training, the canvases of this highly talented woman promote greater knowledge and understanding of the land, its people, and their unique way of life, both past and present. Her very heart and soul seem to guide each of her brush strokes.

TOO, Brenda

1976–
Deaf Educator, Athlete, Counsellor, and Promoter of ASL and LSQ.

Born in the city of Montréal, it is not clear exactly when BRENDA TOO became Deaf because her Deafness was not diagnosed until she was five years old. She has no known Deaf relatives and currently makes her home in North York, Ontario.

Brenda was educated at the Montréal Oral School for the Deaf and the La Salle Catholic Comprehensive High School in La Salle, Québec, before obtaining two university degrees, among other educational credentials. She acquired a BA degree from McGill University in Montréal and a BEd degree from York University in Toronto, as well as Teacher of the Deaf certification and a College Diploma (DEC), the latter from Dawson College in Montréal. Brenda served four student practicums, two in Ontario provincial Schools for the Deaf and two in public schools. In addition, she has volunteered and held part-time jobs with such institutions as the Downs Syndrome Association, La Salle Youth Centre, Step by Step Program, MacKay Centre for the Deaf, and YMCA.

Brenda has always been an avid sports enthusiast and has won prestigious recognition for her athletic talents, especially in badminton. In 1992, while she was still in high school, she was the recipient of the Most Valuable Player Award from the Badminton League. This was only a year after she had been awarded the title of Most Improved Player. She also tried out for the badminton team for the Deaf World Games in Italy in May 2000.

Brenda is fluent in both American Sign Language (ASL) and Québec Sign Language (LSQ), and volunteered her services to act as secretary of the executive board of American Sign Language of Montréal, a position she held for over a year. In 1998 she held a paid position with this organization, contacting agencies, promoting awareness, and obtaining sponsors. She also participated in the French Immersion Programme at Trois Riviéres, worked at the MacKay Centre for the Deaf in Montréal as an assistant recreational program coordinator, and at Securiplex in Lachine, as an office clerk.

In her leisure hours, Brenda plays volleyball and badminton and enjoys biking. She is also fond of outdoor activities, arts, crafts, and reading for pleasure.

TROFIMENKOFF (CRAWFORD), Lezli-Jo

1960–
Counsellor/Therapist, Farrier, Homemaker, and Self-Employed Entrepreneur.

LEZLI-JO CRAWFORD was born hearing to hearing parents at Imperial, Saskatchewan, the eldest of three children, two girls and one boy. She was raised on a grain farm at Simpson, Saskatchewan, and lived there most of her life. She became Deaf at twelve months of age due to spinal meningitis. She attended Metro School for the Deaf in Toronto from 1964 to 1967, living there with her mother and sister while her father remained on the farm. He visited them during the winter and they visited him during the summer. This family separation was very difficult for all of them so they decided to enroll Lezli-Jo at the Saskatchewan Provincial School for the Deaf in Saskatoon, renamed R.J.D. Williams School for the Deaf, where she remained until she graduated in 1977. Once again her mother, sister, and brother lived with her in Saskatoon and her father remained on the farm. They went to the farm every weekend, and Lezli-Jo enjoyed being there and riding horses in her spare time. This arrangement was certainly easier than the long and costly trips back and forth to Toronto.

Lezli-Jo eventually attended Gallaudet University in Washington, DC, earning a Bachelor of Science degree in Home Economics with specialization in Child Development and Family Life. Because of her life-long love for horses, she then attended a four-month training course at Olds Agricultural College in Alberta to become a qualified farrier, a career choice rarely made by women. Lezli-Jo had always owned horses and enjoyed riding them. When she married her Deaf husband, Kenton Trofimenkoff, the horses had to be sold because the couple made their home in the city of Saskatoon, where Kenton is a postal carrier. They now have two hearing sons, Shane and Travis. Lezli-Jo has no known Deaf relatives, but Kenton has a Deaf brother, Earl, of Saskatoon, Saskatchewan, who has two Deaf children—Warren Trofimenkoff of London, Ontario, and Valerie Trofimenkoff who is living with her Deaf mother, Patricia Jones in Toronto. Kenton also has three Deaf cousins—Todd McQuait of Regina, Saskatchewan, Samuel Rezansoff of Saskatoon, and Barry Reiben of Veregin, Saskatchewan.

Lezli-Jo has had a variety of employment experiences. She worked as a counsellor/therapist with emotionally disturbed Deaf children and as a vocational rehabilitation counsellor with Deaf and hard of hearing adults. She was also a parental care supervisor at R.J.D. Williams School for the Deaf and has worked as a farrier. When her boys were young, she became a full-time homemaker.

In 1998–99, Lezli-Jo took a self-employment training course with a view to becoming an entrepreneur. She became the owner of her own business, a company that sold baking mixes to clubs and schools for fund-raising purposes. Unfortunately, she has had to close her business to take care of her husband, during a brief illness, and to look after their two young boys. Lezli-Jo and Kenton are presently living in Saskatoon with their two sons. Nevertheless, Lezli-Jo has dreams and hopes that she might once again own horses in the future.

In addition to her work with Deaf children and adults, Lezli-Jo has also taught ASL classes and served as president of Sign Language Instructors of Saskatoon for several years. While attending Gallaudet University, she made the Dean's List during her first and third year. She was also first runner-up for the Miss Deaf Canada pageant held in Montréal in 1984. Considering her rather complicated life as a Deaf child, Lezli-Jo Trofimenkoff has achieved some highly commendable goals in adulthood.

TROFIMENKOFF (JONES), Patricia ("Patti") Jane

1949–
Creative Dancer, Guidance Counsellor, and Teacher of the Deaf.

PATTI JONES was born Deaf into a Deaf family in Plainview, Texas. The members of her family who are Deaf include her parents, Boyce Neely Jones and Mary Ruth Fincher; an aunt, Jodell Lawrence; an uncle, Carl Fincher; a cousin, Cindy Perry; a sister, Kathy Jo Jones; and a brother, Samuel Elton Jones, who was married twice. He has three daughters from his first marriage—Lori, Heather, and Amy—who are living in Utah. His present wife is Allison. Patti's sister Kathy Jo was the first Miss Deaf Texas and first runner-up for Miss Deaf America. In the early 1990s, her cousin, Cindy Perry, was Miss Deaf Texas. Patti has two Deaf children, Warren and Valerie. Her sister Kathy Jo, a graduate of Gallaudet University in Washington, DC, is a school counsellor for both Deaf and hearing students at T.H. Rogers School in Houston, Texas. One of Patti's hearing cousins, whose parents are Deaf, is a certified professional interpreter.

Patti's education began at Texas A&M Consolidated School in College Station, Texas, where she finished seventh grade before transferring to the Texas School for the Deaf in Austin. She remained there until she graduated in 1969 as valedictorian and the recipient of several scholarships. She then enrolled at Gallaudet College (now Gallaudet University) in Washington, DC, and graduated in 1974 with a Bachelor of Arts degree in Sociology-Social Work and a minor in Deaf Education.

Patti moved to Canada when she married in 1974 and settled in Saskatoon, Saskatchewan. She earned a Saskatchewan Teaching Certificate in Deaf Education at the University of Saskatchewan in 1978, and later obtained an Ontario Teaching Certificate at York University in Toronto, in 1995. She taught at the Saskatchewan School for the Deaf (renamed R.J.D. Williams School), from 1974 until the school closed in 1991. Since then Patti has taught at E.C. Drury School for the Deaf in Milton, Ontario. She is a guidance counsellor for high school and adult education programs, and does some teaching as well—drama, physical education, and mathematics.

Patti is a talented dancer who created and led the Saskatchewan Interpretive Dance group from 1974 to 1991. She also established the very popular Dancing Hands Troupe in Milton in the spring of 1992. Patti's other involvements in the Deaf Community include several positions in the Saskatoon Cultural Society of the Deaf, long-time member of the Saskatchewan Cultural Society of the Deaf, director on the board of the Canadian Cultural Society of the Deaf, member of the Saskatoon Association of the Deaf and the Saskatchewan Association of the Deaf. In addition, she was a member of the Task Force on Deaf Education in Saskatchewan from June 1988 to March 1989, when the issue of keeping the R.J.D. Williams School for the Deaf open was a hot topic. She directed the Deaf cast that produced the national film on drugs and alcohol for the Deaf—*Pay the Price*—in 1990. She also directed the signing choir that performed at the 1989 Jeux

Canada Games and in 1991 at the World Winter Games for the Deaf in Banff, Alberta. She acted as hostess on *Deaf Talk Show* on Cable 10 in Saskatoon, and has coached Deaf students competing in International Creative Arts for the Deaf since 1982. Recently, she co-directed a Deaf cast in a soon to be released film, *One Family—Many Faces*, which was sponsored by the Trillium Foundation, and is designed for use in peer mediation for the Deaf in North America. She has served on numerous boards in Ontario, in an advisory capacity, and is a member of the Ontario Cultural Society of the Deaf.

Patti has been the recipient of several prestigious awards for her work. In 1999 she received the Halton Award for her outstanding contribution in promoting a safe and healthy community in the Halton Region. In 1990 she was named Saskatchewan Deaf Citizen of the Year, and has received other certificates of appreciation as well. Her Dancing Hands Troupe has been featured on TV several times and in a documentary film. The group has performed across Canada and the US and plans to travel to Europe in the near future.

Patti currently makes her home in Etobicoke in the Greater Toronto area. In her leisure hours she enjoys such hobbies as reading, shopping, collecting interesting art, and travelling, especially in Europe. Above all else, Patti loves to dance and to spend time with her son and daughter.

TURNER (CURRIE), Colleen ("Colly") Cecilia

1970–

Animal Lover, Talented Canadian Artist, Book Illustrator, and Mural Painter.

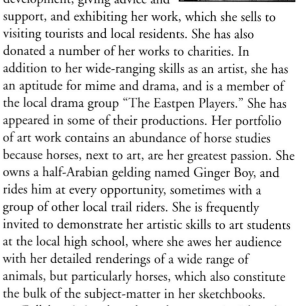

COLLEEN CURRIE was born Deaf as a result of maternal rubella, to hearing parents in Fredericton, New Brunswick. She was the fifth of six children in the family of Lewis and Norma Currie. She has no known Deaf relatives, but is proud to be a descendant of an uncle who is a Korean War veteran, and an aunt who served in the Canadian Forces during World War II. Colleen is married to a Deaf man, Kirk Roderick Turner, an expert in small motors who works as a skilled labourer. Colleen and Kirk have a hearing daughter, Jessica Ashley Currie-Turner, with a second child due in late 2001. They live at Eastport, on Newfoundland's Bonavista Bay.

Colleen received her education in several schools. At the age of three she was enrolled in a preschool on Charlotte Street in Fredericton, where she attended with a small group of other hearing-impaired children. She was sometimes considered a loner because she seemed to prefer being by herself, drawing pictures, instead of being gregarious and cultivating a circle of friends. From the time she could hold a pencil or crayon, she was always scribbling and doodling, often on the walls of her home, much to the dismay of her mother. "Colly," as she is affectionately called, also spent three years at the School for the Deaf in West Hartford, Connecticut, where she showed promise in the visual arts and won awards for her work. She later studied jewellery design and pencil sketching at a community college in New Brunswick, but was frustrated by the insurmountable barriers to communication.

Since living in Eastport, Colly's artistic career has been aided and encouraged by the local resident artist, Walter Pinsent, owner of an art studio. He has guided her development, giving advice and support, and exhibiting her work, which she sells to visiting tourists and local residents. She has also donated a number of her works to charities. In addition to her wide-ranging skills as an artist, she has an aptitude for mime and drama, and is a member of the local drama group "The Eastpen Players." She has appeared in some of their productions. Her portfolio of art work contains an abundance of horse studies because horses, next to art, are her greatest passion. She owns a half-Arabian gelding named Ginger Boy, and rides him at every opportunity, sometimes with a group of other local trail riders. She is frequently invited to demonstrate her artistic skills to art students at the local high school, where she awes her audience with her detailed renderings of a wide range of animals, but particularly horses, which also constitute the bulk of the subject-matter in her sketchbooks.

Colly's artistic talents have drawn provincial media attention, both in community newspapers and on CBC television. She has also exhibited at the national level at Canadian Deaf Festivals in Mississauga, Ontario, in 1998, and in Edmonton, Alberta, in 2000, where, in both cases, she took top spot in her category. Also in 2000, she was recognized by the committee of the

Eastport Peninsula Canada Day Celebrations for her cover illustration of a commemorative book, *The Eastport Peninsula: A People of the Sea and Soil*, which she repeated in a matching wall mural. In 1999 she was honoured for her work as an illustrator of Deaf and ASL literature, receiving the prestigious Ladder Award® sponsored by the Canadian Cultural Society of the Deaf. It provided her an opportunity to work with other renowned Deaf illustrators and attend a two-day workshop in Toronto, where the awards were presented. Her dream is to succeed as an artist in the tradition of the late, beloved Forrest Curwin Nickerson, founder of the Canadian Cultural Society of the Deaf, who was a noted artist and fellow Maritimer.

Colly's hobbies and interests, apart from her art and her love of horses, are reading, swimming, taking daily walks, caring for her pet animals, visiting art galleries, and travelling. She was particularly awed by her experience in western Canada when she visited Edmonton during Festival 2000, travelled to Calgary, and had her first glimpse of the world-famous Calgary Stampede.

One of her favourite causes, which she shares with other Newfoundland horse artists, is the preservation of the Newfoundland Pony. She is remarkably adept at transforming any horse and rider either into serious art or a simple cartoon. The versatility of her skill is also evident in the expansion of her subject-matter to include ships, seascapes, and natural scenes. It has been said by those who know her well that Colly's Deafness gives her an unusually keen visual awareness, and that she relies on her art as an alternative form of expression.

UNDERSCHULTZ (FREEMAN), Diane Elizabeth

1964–
Accounting Clerk, Human Resources Worker, and Capable Volunteer in the Deaf Community.

DIANE FREEMAN was born hearing into a hearing family at Rimbey, Alberta. She became Deaf at the age of two and has no known Deaf relatives. She married a Deaf spouse, Grant Underschultz, and they have two hearing children, Karl and JoBeth. Diane and Grant currently make their home in Edmonton, where Grant has served in executive positions for various organizations of the Deaf, and has many outstanding achievements to his credit in Canadian Deaf sports.

Diane was educated at the Alberta Provincial School for the Deaf in Edmonton, graduating in 1985. Part of her high school program was completed at J.P. Wagner Composite High School. She is at present attending Grant MacEwan Community College in its Human Resources Management Program; she completed her accounting studies there in 1989. She has also attended numerous workshops, courses, and seminars related to her field of employment.

Diane's working life has been varied and interesting. Her first job was with Employabilities as office clerk and bookkeeper. She was then hired by Scotia Bank as a senior deposit accounting clerk and worked there for a number of years. Since 2000 she has been employed at All Weather Windows as a human resources assistant. In addition, she has also had varied volunteer experiences, serving the Connect Society, the Premier's Council, and the Interpreter Advisory Committee.

As a volunteer within the Deaf Community, Diane has played many roles. In 2000 she was chairperson for the Deaf Children's Festival and master of ceremonies for the Canadian Deaf Festival. She has been both president and treasurer of the Alberta Cultural Society of the Deaf, a member of the Edmonton Association of the Deaf, and treasurer of the Alberta Deaf Sports Association.

During her school years she served on many committees, participated in various unique events and was granted numerous awards and honours for her dedication, performance, and willingness to improve herself. During the year of Alberta's seventy-fifth birthday, in 1980, the Edmonton Public Library published a book entitled *Seventy-five and Growing*. A poem written by Diane when she was a teenager appears on page eighteen. The title of the poem is *Sweet Alberta*. She was an outstanding student and was the graduation president for her class in 1985.

With Diane's many skills and talents, as well as her boundless energy, determination, ambition, and enthusiasm, her interesting life history is far from finished.

UNGAR, Michele Angela

1969–
Licensed Physiotherapist and Health Columnist.

MICHELE UNGAR was born with a profound hearing loss in one ear and a moderate-to-severe loss in the other. Her parents and older sister are Deaf so she was raised in the cultural atmosphere of a Deaf family in their Toronto home, although she was always encouraged to participate in both the Deaf and the hearing communities. From the third grade onward, Michele was educated in mainstream public schools. She attended Gallaudet University in Washington, DC, for one year and became interested in sports and sports medicine. This led to her desire to become a physiotherapist, but Gallaudet offered no training program so she returned to Canada.

Seeking an accredited physiotherapy training facility, Michele was proud to be accepted into the Rehabilitation Medicine Program at the University of Toronto where, for the first two years, she was completely overwhelmed by the staggering communication difficulties she faced in the labs and clinics. No interpreters were available at that time, so Michele decided to focus entirely on the elective courses required to complete her degree, until such time as she could have all the assistive resources needed for her to return full-time to the physiotherapy courseload.

She persuaded the University of Toronto to do everything possible to accommodate her needs. By her fourth year, ASL interpreters were provided and demonstrations were videotaped and captioned. Meanwhile, Michele was supplementing her income by teaching ASL classes at the Bob Rumball Centre for the Deaf. During the summers she served internships at various hospitals and clinics. In the spring of 1996 she graduated with a Bachelor of Science (Honours) degree in Physical Therapy, becoming the first Deaf physiotherapist in Canada. She then passed the rigorous national physiotherapy licensing exams with ease.

Her professional career has been varied, but one highlight was her role as Team Canada's Physiotherapist at the 1997 Summer World Games for the Deaf in Copenhagen, Denmark.. She currently makes her home in Red Deer, Alberta, where she works for the Alberta government in a large long-term care facility for clients with developmental disabilities. Her work consists mainly of consulting, patient assessment, and supervision of four therapy assistants.

In 2000 Michele began writing a column on health-related issues for *Deaf Canada Today*. Her hobbies are cycling, hiking, backpacking, snowboarding, and travelling.

UPTON (DUFFLEY), Theresa Marie

1966–
Health-Care Aide, Coordinator of Sign Language Services, Counsellor, and ASL Instructor.

THERESA MARIE DUFFLEY was born profoundly Deaf, due to undetermined causes, to hearing parents, Adeline and Phillip Duffley, in Saint John, New Brunswick. She has no known Deaf relatives, but her father and grandfather each had a significant hearing loss as they aged. Her great-aunt also experienced a substantial hearing loss in her twenties. Theresa is married to a Deaf man, Scott Upton, a full-time, self-employed pressman and desktop publisher who attended E.C. Drury School in Milton, Ontario, Sir James Whitney School for the Deaf in Belleville, Ontario, and Gallaudet University in Washington, DC. Theresa and Scott have two hearing children, Jason and Ashley, who are both fluent in ASL. The family currently lives in Kingston, Ontario.

When Theresa was three years old, her father was president of the Parents' Association for Deaf Children in Saint John. She received her early education in mainstream public schools in Saint John— at Princess Anne School (1969–1974), Hillcrest School (1974–1977), and Forest Hill Elementary and Junior High School (1977–1980). She was then sent to Sir James Whitney School for the Deaf in Belleville, Ontario, where she completed her education from 1980 to 1985. She enrolled at St. Lawrence College in Kingston, where she took a two-year nursing course and was awarded a health-care aide certificate in 1987.

Her studies were similar to those of a registered nurse's aide, but did not include the administration of medications. Theresa's was an untraditional career choice because, at that time, it was deemed that Deaf women were not capable of performing health-related services in clinics, hospitals, or nursing homes. This made her somewhat unique in breaking down some of the barriers faced by all Deaf people when it comes to career planning.

Theresa's employment experience began with a summer job in the health-care field at Rideau Crest, a nursing home for seniors in Kingston. She then spent a year at the Providence Manor Nursing Home and two years at the Fairmount Home for the Aged, until 1988. In 1990 she was hired by the Canadian Hearing Society (CHS) in Kingston and worked there as a counsellor, ASL instructor, and coordinator of ASL Services until 1995. Since then she has been employed as an ASL instructor by CHS, Queen's University, St. Lawrence College, and the Brockville Board of Education in Brockville, Ontario. She has also worked with Miller, Rundle, and Associates, a new business in Kingston, where she provides counselling, teaches ASL, and gives presentations to companies that employ Deaf or hard-of-hearing staff. In the spring of 2001 she began taking a course in neuro-linguistic programming which will assist her in her work when completed.

Theresa attends workshops related to Deaf issues and volunteers her assistance to Deaf women in crisis—a service at which she excels. She has also volunteered for some Deaf sports activities such as the Canadian Deaf Slo-Pitch Championship in 1990 and various Deaf Darts tournaments in Ontario. In 1990 she assisted with the Kingston Regional Association of the Deaf's thirtieth anniversary celebration and later helped with the E.C. Drury School Reunion for 1980–85 graduates. She is known for her willingness to participate and serve in the Deaf Community in any way she can.

When Theresa can find spare time in her busy schedule, she enjoys sewing and doing various crafts. She is quite skilled at translating songs and poetry from English to ASL, especially Christmas carols, and is an avid ASL storyteller. She likes to sign her stories and poems on videotapes, which may at some future date be considered for publication.

VAUGHAN, Vanessa Rea

1969–
Actor, Artist, Writer, Filmmaker, Director, Producer, Entrepreneur, and Workshop Presenter.

VANESSA VAUGHAN was born Deaf in Toronto, Ontario. She obtained a Bachelor of Fine Arts degree from York University with special honours and is well known in the Canadian Arts community. Her film and television work and her art exhibits have earned her a prominent place among the most notable.

Vanessa's successes are as manifold as her talents. She is a bold entrepreneur, currently self-employed, owning her own business, Handscape Media, of which she is the founder and creative producer. Her company promotes and markets art and drama workshops using Sign Language and works with fellow Deaf artists on film and video projects. She was a 1993 Gemini Award nominee for her leading role as Alexander Graham Bell's love interest in the dramatic television miniseries, *The Sound and the Silence*. She has also co-starred with Kiefer Sutherland in *Crazy Moon*.

Her many honours and accomplishments include an Ontario Arts Council First Film and Video grant; being chosen to do the cover artwork for the publication *Tales of Survival: Anthology of Deaf Women's Stories*; being selected as one of eight Canadian artists for the *Deaf Artist's Curriculum*, developed by the Curriculum Foundation to be used as an educational resource guide; and the selection of her short film, *Edda's Song*, for broadcast on the Women's Television Network (WTN) and on all international Air Canada flights.

Vanessa's interest in a film career began in a David Suzuki *Nature of Things* documentary featuring Deaf children learning to communicate. Since then she has never looked back and has continued to foster her dreams and goals as a writer, actor, director, and producer in the national film industry. Recently, she was listed in *Who's Who in Canada*. She is versatile and venturesome, with many special skills and interests. She was the arts and entertainment editor for Canada's national newspaper of the Deaf, *Deaf Canada Today*, focusing on events and developments in the world of the arts within the global Deaf Community.

Her paintings have been exhibited in several public venues. Vanessa's passion for water, the Canadian landscape, and the cottage experience are evident in her art. Her colourscapes are bold and bright, but have a sense of silence in the vastness of each scene. She has also

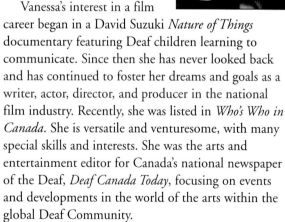

done numerous private portrait commissions, and her many film, television, and theatre credits speak for themselves.

In her leisure time Vanessa enjoys the great outdoors, rowing, canoeing, and swimming. She continues to explore the vast possibilities of ASL as one of the most fascinating forms of visual art.

VIRGIL (McEACHERN), Pearl Doreen

1924–2001
Egg Sorter, Librarian, and Respected Role Model.

PEARL MCEACHERN was born Deaf to hearing parents in North Battleford, Saskatchewan. Among her Deaf relatives were her grandmother, Elizabeth Flanagan of Tatsfield, Saskatchewan; her brother, Lloyd McEachern of Calgary, Alberta; and her sister, Leila Fredland of Burnaby, British Columbia. Pearl's husband, Owen Virgil, deceased in 1994, was a Deaf man who was born in Portage la Prairie, Manitoba, and attended the Manitoba School for the Deaf in Winnipeg. Pearl and Owen had five hearing children, one of whom is deceased—Diane Galley of Fort Saskatchewan, Alberta. Their remaining offspring are Bonnie Berg, Juliette Charney, Robert Virgil, and Yvonne Tjernstrom. Throughout their marriage, Pearl and Owen made their home in Edmonton, Alberta.

Pearl and her two Deaf siblings were educated at the Saskatchewan School for the Deaf in Saskatoon. Pearl was at least nine years old before she was enrolled at school while Lloyd and Leila began their education at six years of age. Pearl attended from 1933 to 1943. When she arrived in the city of Saskatoon, after living nine years in rural Saskatchewan, she was quite awed when she saw the tall buildings and the busy streets. Pearl did not understand at first why she had been sent there, but her Deaf grandmother explained she was there to learn to read and write.

Pearl soon adjusted to her new environment and was eager to learn. She was pleased to be taught how to crochet, and her first crocheted items—brightly coloured round mats—were works of art. At bedtime she and her five dormitory colleagues would play until very late, and she was often the leader in the games they played and the fun they had.

One of Pearl's favourite humorous recollections occurred on a Sunday afternoon when her friend, Helen Briggs of Regina, took her to visit her aunt in a Saskatoon hospital. It was the first time Pearl had ever seen a city policeman wearing a traditional buffalo coat and hat. She thought he looked very large and menacing, and was afraid he intended to put her in jail. As she grew older and accustomed to the sights of the city, she realized how naive she had been as a child, and it always made her laugh.

As a young woman, Pearl was employed as an egg sorter at McDonald's Consolidated for four years. Later in life she worked as a librarian for fifteen years until her retirement.

She liked to keep busy and her hands were never idle. She was skilled at many crafts and was always occupied with numerous knitting, crocheting, and sewing projects.

During her lifetime Pearl was an active member of the Deaf Community, cheerfully contributing her time and skills wherever she could. Sadly, her involvement had to stop while she fought a courageous battle against cancer, but she remained a respected and admired role model among her wide network of friends.

On 20 August 2001, her struggle ended. Pearl passed away, greatly missed by her son and daughters, in-laws, sister and brothers, twelve grandchildren, seven great-grandchildren, and countless friends. The memories of this courageous woman will always be revered in Edmonton's Deaf Community.

VLUG, Leanor Henrietta

1945–
Educator, Editor, Coordinator, and Volunteer.

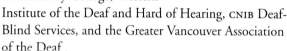

Born LEANOR LINDSAY in Los Angeles, California, Leanor Vlug has lived and worked on both sides of the American-Canadian border. She became Deaf at ten years of age and received a mainstream education in Los Angeles, graduating from Hollywood High School before enrolling at Gallaudet College in Washington, DC. She graduated from Gallaudet with a BA in History in 1967.

After graduation Leanor married a Deaf fellow-student, Henry Vlug, a Canadian whose family had emigrated from The Netherlands to reside in Powell River, BC. The young couple moved to Canada where Henry continued his studies at Simon Fraser University and the University of British Columbia.

While Henry pursued a career as a teacher, the Vlugs lived in Vancouver and later in Washington, DC, where both their daughters were born (Kaaren in 1974 and Margaret in 1976). In 1980 they returned to Canada and Henry worked for three years for the Greater Vancouver Association of the Deaf before he entered Law School in 1983.

Leanor is not aware of any Deaf ancestors, but she does know that her (hearing) great-grandfather was a judge in El Paso, Texas, and a pioneer in El Paso society. This would seem to be a fitting background for her current status as the wife of one of Canada's well-known Deaf lawyers.

While her husband furthered his education, Leanor earned a Master's degree in Adult Education in 1994 and has held various positions as an instructor and coordinator with Vancouver Community College, Western Institute of the Deaf and Hard of Hearing, CNIB Deaf-Blind Services, and the Greater Vancouver Association of the Deaf.

Leanor has been honoured for her work with a number of awards. In 1992 she was granted the Canada Medal for Volunteerism as well as the Canadian Association of the Deaf's Arthur Hazlitt Citizenship Award. The Western Institute for the Deaf presented her with a Certificate of Appreciation for her volunteer services from 1986 to 1992. Her name also appears on the Greater Vancouver Association of the Deaf's Honour Roll for her editorial services, as well as her contributions as a board member. During her college days, Leanor was a member of the Gallaudet Honour Society—Phi Alpha Pi.

Currently, Leanor is a founding member and secretary of the Bright Place for Deaf Women, the first incorporated society for Deaf women in BC. She continues to be an exemplary role model for all Deaf women in Canada and abroad.

WAIT (ROULT), Donna Vera

1939–
Born Teacher, School Administrator, and Drama Enthusiast.

DONNA ROULT was born Deaf to hearing parents in Stratford, Ontario. She has a Deaf brother, two Deaf nieces, several Deaf cousins, and her great-great grandmother was also Deaf. Her Deaf spouse, Mark Alton Wait, is now deceased but was very active in Deaf sports and athletics, as well as other organizations of the Deaf. Donna has three adult hearing children. Her Deaf brother currently works at the Maryland School for the Deaf. Donna, too, makes her home in the US at Stuarts Draft, Virginia.

As a child, Donna became interested in drama and her aunt sometimes took her to the Shakespearean plays at Stratford, which kindled her passion for theatre. In 1944, after her family moved to Scarborough, she was enrolled at the Ontario provincial School for the Deaf at Belleville, from which she graduated in 1958. She was an avid reader and enjoyed sports, storytelling, and socializing with her friends. There were no interpreters and certainly no captioned TV programs or movies, but she recalls that everyone loved dormitory life and thought it was great fun.

Donna is grateful that Dr. David Peikoff encouraged her mother to learn ASL so she could communicate with her daughter. She also credits him with having a profound influence on her own attitude because in those days there were no Deaf teachers or other adult Deaf role models for students to pattern themselves after. The Peikoffs became close friends of the Roult family.

During the summers Donna sometimes worked for a textbook publishing company. She also helped on archaeological digs under the guidance of the Royal Ontario Museum and was the first Deaf person to register at the W. Thornton Modeling Agency in Toronto. Despite strong objection from the Ontario Ministry of Education, she enrolled at Gallaudet University in Washington, DC, and completed a BA degree in History in 1963 and a Master's degree in Deaf Education in 1964. Her desire to return to Canada to teach was thwarted by the ruling that she would have to take courses in speech and audiology and teach in the public school system. Thus it came about that she accepted a teaching position at the Minnesota School for the Deaf, where she taught for three years. She met an Italian man whom she married, and they lived in Italy for several months. There she learned the importance of total immersion while she was learning Italian, and was able to apply this philosophy to her teaching style.

When her marriage ended, Donna moved to Maryland where she obtained a teaching position. She then met Mark Alton Wait and became a wife and mother. She worked at the Maryland School for the Deaf as a family services specialist and teacher for over twenty years. When an opportunity arose for Donna to become elementary principal at the Mississippi School for the Deaf, the family moved. After three years in that position, Donna was needed at home because Mark had been diagnosed with cancer. Since his death, she has taught English and supervised the high school department at the Virginia School for the Deaf.

Donna has received several prestigious awards and honours—Most Promising Actress, Teacher of the Year, Employee of the Year, Recognition of Service to Deaf Women in Mississippi, Recognition of Service to Children (essay writing), Service to the State of Maryland, and other academic awards while she was a student. Everyone who knows Donna acknowledges that she is a born teacher who loves her job.

WALKER, Laura Dawn

1961–

Fashion Illustrator, Talented Artist, ASL Instructor, and Experimenter with Art Media.

LAURA WALKER was born Deaf into a hearing family in Swan River, Manitoba. She has a hearing brother and sister who have given, along with their parents, unconditional support and encouragement to Laura. She has no known Deaf relatives and the cause of her Deafness is undetermined. Laura makes her home in Toronto, Ontario.

Laura received her education at several schools. In Detroit, Michigan, she attended the Lutheran School for the Deaf for seven years before transferring to Balmoral Hall School for Girls in Winnipeg, a private school which she attended for three years. She then attended the Manitoba School for the Deaf to complete her high school, and took a few art classes at Shaftesbury Public School, which is located across the street. Laura enrolled at Gallaudet University in Washington, DC, and graduated in 1984 with a Bachelor's degree in Studio Art. During her Gallaudet attendance she was selected as runner-up in a photography competition and made the Dean's List in her junior year. She then moved to Toronto and spent two years studying at the Ontario College of Art and Design.

When she began her professional career as an artist and fashion illustrator, she soon became well enough known to sell her illustrations to such fashion magazines as *Flare*, *Wedding Bells*, and *Domino*. Her newspaper clients include *The Globe and Mail* and *The Toronto Star*, and her list of retail clients is most impressive, including Harry Rosen, Holt Renfrew, Ira Berg, Ports International, Creeds, and Queen's Quay. In addition to her fashion illustrations, Laura created the logo for the Canadian Council on Rehabilitation and Work (CCRW) and consulted five Deaf illustrators for the book called *River of Hands*, a Deaf Heritage project completed in January 2000, which was sponsored by the Canadian Cultural Society of the Deaf.

Although she continues to work professionally as an artist/fashion illustrator, and has her own studio in Toronto, she is expanding her various forms of expression to include self-portraiture, still life, logo design, and drawing. She experiments with felt markers, charcoal, pastels, water colour, and other media. She also uses Adobe Illustration and Adobe Photoshop on her Macintosh computer, and is contemplating taking a few sculpting courses. She has received special recognition for her work from the Ontario College of Art and Design and a Merit Award at the *Studio Magazine* Annual Awards sponsored by *The Toronto Star*.

In the fall of 2001 Laura became involved with art workshops to expose Deaf students to her work in twenty schools across the province of Ontario. The program is sponsored by the Deaf Artists' Association of Canada (DAAC). She formerly worked for the Impact ASL Program with the Canadian Hearing Society (CHS) in Toronto and taught classes in mathematics and pre-employment to Deaf and hard-of-hearing adults. In the evening, once a week, she teaches level I and II ASL classes to hearing learners at CHS.

In her leisure hours Laura loves to cook, collect old prints, swim, and travel. She lives with her precious border collie, Fido, and daily practices her personal motto: Believe that everyone is equal, and never give up your talent.

WARD (SMOLNICKY), Shauna Rae

1968–
ASL Instructor, Rater and Interviewer, Youth Mentor, and Foster Parent.

SHAUNA SMOLNICKY was born Deaf to hearing parents in Calgary, Alberta. Her only Deaf relative was her maternal great-grandmother but she has a Deaf husband, Owen Victor Ward, and a Deaf foster son. She and Owen are also closely involved with a Deaf client and have mentored a Deaf teenager for over three years.

When she was three years old, Shauna's family moved to Ottawa where her father worked for IBM. There she attended Centennial School, where she was allowed to use ASL. When she was eight, the family returned to Calgary and Shauna was enrolled in a mainstream oral program at Stanley Jones School where she was quite unhappy.

From the age of twelve until she was eighteen, Shauna attended Queen Elizabeth School in a large mainstream program with fifty Deaf students. She had never met nor seen a Deaf teacher until Marty Goldstein arrived at Queen Elizabeth and soon became her mentor. After graduating in 1986 Shauna was encouraged by several people, but particularly by one interpreter, to enrol at Gallaudet University, even though that had never been a part of her plan for her future. Fortunately, she followed this good advice and graduated with a BA degree in Sign Communication (ASL) in 1992.

When she returned to Calgary, Shauna met Owen Ward and they have been together ever since. She taught ASL evening courses for the Calgary Board of Education and Mount Royal College, and in 1994 they moved to Edmonton where she taught evening ASL classes at Grant MacEwan Community College and acted as a resource person in the development of "Signing Naturally" materials and curricula. She also worked part-time at different group homes that had Deaf residents. She and Owen became involved in the local Deaf Community where she was secretary for the Alberta Deaf Sports Association and editor of its newsletter.

In 1996 they moved once again—this time to Sudbury, Ontario, where Shauna accepted employment as a laboratory assistant at the Cambrian College ASL/English interpreter training program, and later became an instructor. Once again they became closely involved in the Deaf Community, with Shauna serving as vice-president of the Sudbury Association of the Deaf. They remained there for two years, returning to Calgary in 1998, where Shauna is currently a support worker and Owen works with a mentally challenged Deaf client. Together they completed the necessary foster parenting workshops that qualified them to become foster parents to their Deaf foster son.

In the summer of 1999 Shauna obtained a certificate from York University in Toronto, Ontario, and the Canadian Cultural Society of the Deaf. This gave her the necessary qualifications to be an ASL rater and interviewer. She has been secretary of the Calgary Association of the Deaf (CAD) since 1999 and is currently secretary of the Alberta Cultural Society of the Deaf (ACSD) and the Alberta Association of the Deaf (AAD). Owen is very active in all aspects of advocacy for the Deaf. Shauna's immediate plans include a return to school to further her education so she can explore new interests. In fact, after observing the summer program, ASL Immersion 2000, in Winnipeg, Shauna has already decided to establish a similar one in Calgary.

In July 2001 Shauna was a volunteer staff member representing CAD at a Deaf summer camp held at Pigeon Lake, Alberta. The attendees were thirty-seven Deaf children aged six to fifteen from various parts of the province. She found it a very enriching experience and received a certificate of appreciation for her participation. This is the type of involvement in the Deaf Community which Shauna most enjoys. She looks forward to many similar opportunities in the future.

WARICK, Ruth Patricia

1948–
Newspaper Reporter, Magazine Editor, Assistant Professor, Published Author, Advocate for the Hard of Hearing, Researcher, and Post-Secondary Disability Advisor.

RUTH WARICK was born with a severe hearing loss in Kipling, Saskatchewan. She has a Deaf brother, Dennis, who teaches at the Alberta School for the Deaf in Edmonton, but has no other known Deaf or hard-of-hearing relatives. She lived in Saskatchewan most of her life but today makes her home in Vancouver, British Columbia.

Ruth was educated in mainstream public schools at a time when resource rooms and itinerant supports were unheard of. Caring teachers made it possible for her to succeed and she became very resourceful at learning on her own. In 1966 she graduated from Marian High School in Regina and, immediately after, attended the University of Regina. In 1969 she obtained a BA degree and, in 1970, a BA Honours degree. Thereafter, she entered the workforce, but even while she was working full-time, her love of learning led her to pursue part-time studies to complete a Master of Arts degree in 1983 and a Master of Education degree in 1990 from the University of Regina. Ruth is presently working on a doctoral degree in Educational Studies at the University of British Columbia. It was not until she began her present studies that the services and supports of a disability office became available to her. Meanwhile, she has learned to adjust her learning style and study practices to better suit her needs in certain courses.

Her professional career and volunteer background have been eclectic. Ruth's employment has included many challenges, from being a reporter for *The Regina Leader-Post* to her present position as an advisor at the Disability Resource Centre at the University of British Columbia. In the intervening years, she worked for the Saskatchewan government with the Public Service Commission, as well as directing Women's Services for Advanced Education and Manpower, and was assistant professor of professional programs and coordinator of community programming at University of Regina Extension.

As a volunteer, she has chaired the BC Family Hearing Resource Centre and the National Women's Reference on Labour Market Issues. She is the current editor of *Listen/Ecoute*, the national magazine for the Canadian Hard of Hearing Association, of which she is a past president, and sits on the editorial board of *Communique*, put out by the Canadian Association of College and University Student Services. Ruth is also a board member of the Canadian Association of Speech-Language Pathologists and Audiologists and serves on the Steering Committee of the Institute of Hearing Accessibility Research at the University of British Columbia.

She has been honoured by many prestigious agencies and organizations. Among these honours were a graduate scholarship from the Social Sciences and Humanities Research Council of Canada, an Award of Merit from the Institute of Public Administrators of Canada, and an Award of Excellence and Promotional Awards from the Canadian Association for University Continuing Education. She was a YWCA Woman of the Year nominee in 1983 and was selected to participate in the Governor General's Canadian Studies Conference in 1987.

In addition to these achievements, Ruth has authored and/or co-authored eight publications. As her research activities continue, more of her findings will doubtlessly be published. She can be credited with many earlier achievements, too numerous to be included here. She has also made many presentations and continues to do so locally, nationally, and internationally.

WEBER, Joanne Catherine

1959–
Educator, Program Developer and Coordinator, Consultant, and Developer of Professional Materials.

JOANNE WEBER was born Deaf at Wilkie, Saskatchewan. She currently makes her home in North Battleford, Saskatchewan, with her two daughters, Anneliese and Paula, but has spent much of her professional life in and around Saskatoon.

She has achieved an impressive list of university credentials, beginning with a general BA degree from the University of Saskatchewan in Saskatoon in 1980. This was followed by a Master's degree in Library Science from the University of Alberta in Edmonton in 1984. In 1985 she received a BA Honours Certificate in English from the University of Saskatchewan, followed by a BEd degree with distinction. She then did a year of graduate study at Gallaudet University in Washington, DC, which qualified her for certification in Deaf Education by ACEHI (Association of Canadian Educators of the Hearing Impaired).

In 1977 Joanne won the Saskatchewan Junior Citizen of the Year Award and in 1981 received a Saskatchewan Library Bursary. The Saskatchewan Cultural Society of the Deaf presented her with an Award of Merit in 1989 and, in 1995, she was a nominee for the YWCA Woman of the Year Award in the field of business and the professions.

At present, Joanne owns and operates two businesses, eClear Consulting, with a hearing partner, and The Lang Tree. The focus of eClear is instructional design and training in the areas of entrepreneurship, career readiness, employment, and life skills. It also offers design and implementation of information management systems for small businesses and nonprofit organizations. The Lang Tree focuses on parent-teacher services for the Deaf and hard of hearing. From 1997 to 2000 Joanne was employed at North West Regional College, where she supervised four employees and was the official coordinator of literacy and university programs. Prior to that she gained professional experience in a number of interesting jobs—consulting, training, resource-room teacher, regular classroom teacher, adult-education teacher, and teacher of the Deaf at R.J.D. Williams School for the Deaf in Saskatoon.

She is also the author of two articles published in professional journals—"Language Lab: A Pilot Project at R.J.D. Williams School for the Deaf in Saskatoon," *ACEHI Journal*, 1997, and "Teacher Support in Mainstreaming Deaf and Hard of Hearing Students in Rural Saskatchewan: A Pilot Project," *CAEDHH Journal*, 1997 (Canadian Association of Educators of the Deaf and Hard of Hearing).

In her varied career, Joanne has initiated, developed, and coordinated many innovative and creative programs, and developed and produced practical resource materials to assist teachers and other professionals in implementing them. She has also provided consultation, trained and supervised personnel, and worked tirelessly to achieve equality for Deaf and hard-of-hearing persons. One of her most interesting endeavours has been the creation of The Lang Tree consulting business, which she continues to own and operate. She has developed materials and provided workshops, seminars, and classes related to The Lang Tree philosophy and methods. She has also furthered her knowledge and enhanced her skills by attending selected conferences and workshops. In addition, Joanne is a motivational speaker who has done several signed speaking engagements about her own life as well as Deaf education and Deaf Culture.

In her leisure hours she enjoys yoga, swimming, and cycling, but spends as much time reading as she possibly can. She is also a published poet and is currently working on her first novel involving a Deaf character.

1969–
Nature and Animal Lover, Veterinary Assistant, Kinesiologist, Seasoned World Traveller, and Jane-of-All-Trades.

HEATHER WESTERLUND, second child of Lloyd and Maxine Westerlund, was born Deaf at Holy Cross Hospital in Calgary, Alberta. She was brought up on a farm about 230 miles from Calgary, near Oyen, Alberta. She has an older Deaf brother, Shane, but no other known Deaf relatives.

Heather's education began at the age of five at Stanley Jones School in Calgary, where her brother, Shane, was already in attendance. She transferred to Queen Elizabeth School briefly, but eventually, both Heather and Shane were enrolled at the Alberta School for the Deaf (ASD) in Edmonton, where they lived in residence and went home on weekends for four years. Heather sadly missed her parents and her farm home and was quite unhappy, so her mother moved to Edmonton to make a temporary home for the family. She soon became involved in ASD's Parents' Association, helping to raise funds for many projects and provide practical solutions to a variety of policy issues. Heather's life became much happier. She enjoyed living as a family again, with her father visiting them as often as he could.

She liked school and was a hard-working, diligent student. In addition to her studies, she took jazz dance lessons for eight years, winning a silver medal in 1986. She also belonged to their local 4-H Beef and Horse Club for about fourteen years and won numerous trophies. In her final year she competed with her brother Shane, and they tied for the Grand Championship. Heather was athletic and sports-minded, participating in basketball, volleyball, badminton, and skiing, occasionally winning awards. During high school her work-experience program included stints at a veterinary clinic and an equine centre, both of which she enjoyed. She graduated from grade twelve in 1988.

Although she passed the Gallaudet entrance requirements, Heather decided to remain at home. She taught ASL classes in Edmonton for a while and capably assisted her father in all his farming activities. Agriculture has always been her major interest and she has honed her skills to perfection under her parents' guidance. In 1989 she worked for two months at Pax Natura Ranch near Edmonton and took courses at Lakeland College in Vermilion, which she found difficult without an interpreter. Subsequently, she attended Red Deer College and earned a diploma in kinesiology. In the summer of 1998 she enjoyed working as a trail guide in Banff National Park, and is currently employed in a summer job at the Rangeland Veterinary Clinic at Consort, Alberta, as an assistant.

Travel has greatly enriched Heather's life and given her a global persepective. She has visited countries in Europe, toured Australia and New Zealand and, in 1994, spent six months working on a dairy and pig farm in Sweden as part of an international rural exchange program. In addition, she has travelled widely in Canada and the United States, including Hawaii. In 2000 she enrolled in Animal Health Technology at Olds Agricultural College in central Alberta. The first six months of classes were held at the Southern Alberta Institute of Technology (SAIT) in Calgary. In March 2001 the focus shifted to the Olds campus. When her studies are completed, Heather will either return to work on the family farm or take employment as a veterinary assistant. Either way, she will be working at something she loves.

Heather has many interests. As a young girl, she took tap-dancing lessons, learned to figure skate, and was a baton twirler and majorette. She has experienced bungee jumping, sky-diving, parachuting, parasailing, white water rafting, and scuba diving. She also took class IA driver training and obtained her licence in 2000. This qualifies her to handle the loading, unloading, and driving of cattle and grain trailers for farm work.

Her greatest pleasure has always come from assisting her parents on the farm. She handles all modern farm equipment with ease and loves to ride and train horses. She is also very knowledgeable about cattle, can doctor them when they are ill, and assists when calving problems arise. Because she spends so much time at the farm, it is difficult for her to become involved in the Deaf Community on a regular basis. She and her brother Shane remain best friends and continue a close relationship. During her school years she was very active in all cultural and recreational events and has maintained many of her early relationships with Deaf friends.

Throughout her life Heather has enjoyed challenges and is always eager to develop new skills and acquire more knowledge. She has an abiding love for rural settings and appreciates the joys of farm and outdoor life. Her history is by no means complete and, in view of her relative youth, there will doubtlessly be many exciting chapters added in the future.

WIDD (FITZAKERLY), Margaret

1836–1909

Alumna of the Yorkshire School for the Deaf in Doncaster, Devout Protestant, Residential School Matron, and Teacher of the Deaf.

MARGARET WIDD was the Deaf wife of Thomas Widd, a Deaf Englishman who was the founder of what is now known as the MacKay Centre for the Deaf in Montréal, now the oldest school for the Deaf in Canada. Margaret and Thomas Widd saw a need for an English Protestant institution in Montréal, even though two French Catholic Schools already existed. They had emigrated from England, together with Margaret's Deaf sister, the widowed Sarah Guest, who later married Norman Vickers Lewis, a Deaf printer and publisher who operated his own business in Toronto, Ontario.

Margaret and Sarah grew up in Yorkshire, England, where their father, Timothy Fitzakerly, worked as a horticulturist on a palatial estate owned by the Duke of Newcastle. Both Margaret and Sarah were educated at the South Yorkshire Institute for the Deaf and Dumb in Doncaster. Timothy Fitzakerly also emigrated to Canada with the rest of his family in 1867, and settled on a farm near Brussells, Ontario. The Widds settled in Montréal.

Margaret's husband was hired as assistant editor of *The Daily Witness*, a Montréal newspaper with a wide circulation, in which he published his opinions about the needs of Deaf students with an English Protestant background. He felt they were being indoctrinated into the Catholic faith at the existing schools. Both Margaret and Thomas Widd were energetic in their dedication to this cause and, before long, the publicity resulting from the newspaper articles and subsequent letters to the editor captured the attention of several wealthy philanthropists. They held public meetings, established a society, and elected a fundraising committee.

In 1869, the Protestant Institution for Deaf-Mutes and the Blind was incorporated by the Legislature of Lower Canada (now the province of Québec). In 1870 the society rented a house with ample grounds and enough space to accommodate twenty students. In September of that year the new school welcomed its first eleven pupils, nine boys and two girls, with Thomas Widd as principal and Margaret Widd as matron and assistant teacher. Their teaching methods were entirely manual, using natural signs, writing, and a combination of the American one-handed fingerspelling alphabet and the British two-handed version.

Under Thomas Widd's supervision, the boys learned to perform carpentry and gardening tasks to help maintain the house and grounds, while the girls, under Margaret's guidance, learned dressmaking, sewing, mending, and household management to supplement their academic education. By 1875 enrolment had increased so significantly that a new building was required.

Joseph MacKay, a wealthy Scottish immigrant, offered to donate property and fund the construction of a new school. In due course, the MacKay Institution for Protestant Deaf-Mutes became a reality. It opened in 1878 on the same site where the present MacKay Centre is situated.

At last Margaret and Thomas Widd had realized their dream. Unfortunately, due to her husband's poor health, both of them had to resign their positions and they eventually moved to Los Angeles, California. Their legacy has continued to serve Deaf pupils from across Canada for well over a century. Many students from the western provinces, before provincial schools were established, were sent to Montréal to be educated.

In Los Angeles, Margaret and Thomas Widd continued to be influential in the Deaf Community. They were devout Protestants and established the Ephphatha Mission for the Deaf, which was later renamed the Episcopal Gallaudet Mission. They were also active members of the Los Angeles Association of the Deaf.

Margaret Widd passed away peacefully on 11 February 1909, in her seventy-third year. She was laid to rest in the Angelus-Rossedale Cemetery in Los Angeles, California.

WILLIAMS, Joanne Elizabeth

1953–
Craftswoman, Avid Bowler, Deaf Community Volunteer, and Business Office Employee.

JOANNE WILLIAMS was born Deaf into a hearing family in Montréal, Québec. She has no known Deaf relatives, and now makes her home in Lachine. She has three hearing sons—Michael, Jim, and Chris.

Joanne was educated in Montréal, spending three years at the Montréal Oral School for the Deaf, from 1959 to 1962. She then attended Herbert Symonds Public School from 1963 until 1969, and finished her schooling at the MacKay Centre for the Deaf from 1969 to 1973.

Joanne has worked for several employers, starting with the Gillette Company. She then took a job with the Royal Bank of Canada and later with the Best Western Motel in Dorval.

She has been actively involved in the Deaf Community in Montréal throughout her adult life, volunteering her time and effort in many ways. For twelve years she served as a director on the board of the Montréal Association of the Deaf and has participated in many social, cultural, and recreational events, helping out in any way she can.

During her leisure time, Joanne enjoys her family and works at a variety of crafts at which she is very talented. She is an excellent bowler and has competed in a mixed league at Laurentian Lanes in Montréal for thirty years. She has numerous bowling trophies to attest to her prowess in that sport. She is also a member of the Darts Club, which she attends three times a week at the Legion Hall in Lachine. This is her second year playing darts and she has met many new friends at these events.

Joanne and her partner, Michel, have been enjoying the summers and weekends at their trailer in the Laurentian Mountains since 1998. There, they play darts, horseshoes, and sandbags, and often participate in tournaments. In March 2001 they had a wonderful ten-day trip to Myrtle Beach, South Carolina. Although she is quiet and unassuming, Joanne is a strong pillar of the Deaf Community in Montréal and is admired and respected by her peers.

WILLIAMS (MILLHAM), Myrtle Elsie

1907–1998
Outstanding Craftswoman, Advocate for Deaf Education, Loving Wife, Mother, and Helpmate.

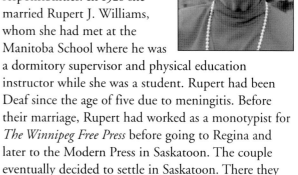

MYRTLE MILLHAM, only daughter of Albert and Elsie Millham, was born on a farm at Hazelcliffe, Saskatchewan, a village that no longer exists. She had seven brothers with whom she competed for attention during her childhood. Her parents became concerned when, at the age of two, she made no effort to speak and did not respond to sound. A doctor eventually confirmed that she was profoundly Deaf, probably as the result of scarlet fever in early infancy.

Myrtle attended the first Saskatchewan provincial School for the Deaf, at that time situated in Regina, for one year before it closed in 1916. She was then sent to Winnipeg to complete her education at the Manitoba School for the Deaf, which changed location several times before the new building on Shaftesbury Boulevard was completed. She was a good student, a competitive athlete, and an outstanding needlewoman who excelled in many types of handwork. She loved figure skating, played ice hockey in a girl's league, and was a member of the Winnipeg Snowshoe Club.

Following her graduation, Myrtle returned home to assist her mother with the farm responsibilities. In 1928 she married Rupert J. Williams, whom she had met at the Manitoba School where he was a dormitory supervisor and physical education instructor while she was a student. Rupert had been Deaf since the age of five due to meningitis. Before their marriage, Rupert had worked as a monotypist for *The Winnipeg Free Press* before going to Regina and later to the Modern Press in Saskatoon. The couple eventually decided to settle in Saskatoon. There they raised two hearing daughters—Audrey, a counsellor for the Deaf, and Joan, a teacher of the Deaf.

Myrtle and Rupert shared strong feelings about educating Deaf children so, with the support of the Western Canadian Association of the Deaf, they initiated a campaign for a new school to be built in Saskatoon.

Their efforts eventually paid off and the Saskatchewan School for the Deaf opened near their home in 1931, with Rupert as the dean of residence, a position he held until his retirement in 1963. Myrtle was always there to lend her support and assistance, helping with the Girl Guides and the St. John's Ambulance first-aid program. Both she and Rupert were also involved in the Western Canada Association of the Deaf as two of its founding members. Rupert died in 1973. Nine years later, in 1982, the school was renamed in his honour, to become the R.J.D Williams School for the Deaf (closed in 1991).

As she aged, Myrtle's eyesight began to fail but she continued to create beautiful pieces of handwork until she suffered a stroke in 1994. She then moved to Luther Sunset Home where she died peacefully in 1998 at the age of ninety.

WINTER, Cheryl Anne

1957–
Deaf Theatre Enthusiast, Information Officer, Athlete, and Video Producer.

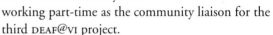

CHERYL WINTER was born Deaf into a hearing family in Fredericton, New Brunswick. She has no known Deaf relatives. Her education began with preschool in Halifax, Nova Scotia, for two years. She then attended the Metro School for the Deaf in Toronto before moving to Edmonton, Alberta, where she completed her schooling in the mainstream public system. She spent the next two years in a liberal arts program at Gallaudet University in Washington, DC, and then took her BSc degree in Business Administration and Marketing at California State University at Northridge in the San Fernando Valley.

Cheryl's Deaf husband, Terry Gardiner, has a BA degree in Sociology (Social Work) from Gallaudet University, a Diploma in Deaf Education from the University of British Columbia in Vancouver, and a British Columbia Teacher's Certificate. He is now employed as a teacher of the Deaf at the British Columbia School for the Deaf (BCSD) in Burnaby. Cheryl and Terry have two hearing children, Brandon and Shanna, with whom they make their current home in Burnaby, BC.

While living in Edmonton, Cheryl worked as a research assistant in the Department of Educational Psychology at the University of Alberta before taking a position with the Canadian Association of the Deaf in Toronto, where she remained for three years. She next worked as a data-entry clerk for the Public Service Commission in Vancouver, and then with the Deaf Children's Society of BC as an information officer. Since the late 1980s, Cheryl has been upgrading her skills and knowledge by attending workshops, classes, and seminars in Deaf studies, the sociolinguistics of ASL, and two levels of photography. Earlier, she was awarded two scholarships, one of which she was unable to use due to job commitments. She completed her training in video production, and produced her first video in 1999 as part of the first DEAF@VI project in Vancouver, BC, and presented it at the first annual video screening of local works by Deaf artists and producers in the same year. She is now in her second year of working part-time as the community liaison for the third DEAF@VI project.

Cheryl has also volunteered her time and expertise to the Deaf Community in several ways—as a member of committees for the Canadian Deaf Festival, the Bell Relay Service Implementation, and the Closed Captioning Consumers group. Cheryl loves theatricals and was involved in the Gallaudet University Troupe and the American Theatre of the Arts during her university years. She played tennis with hearing competitors in local, provincial, and inter-provincial tournaments, and participated in the tennis tryouts in Edmonton in 1980, where she was selected as a member of the Canadian Deaf National team to participate in the World Summer Games for the Deaf in Cologne, Germany, in 1981. She still enjoys tennis but no longer plays competitively.

She has also edited newsletters for the Ontario Deaf Sports Association, the Canadian Association of the Deaf, and the Deaf Children's Society of BC. Cheryl has presented papers on several issues related to Deafness and has received recognition for her dedication and loyalty. In 1991 she was a member of the Canadian Deaf National team for the World Winter Games for the Deaf held in Banff, Alberta, where she looked after the team's apparel, took photographs, and served as a driver.

In her leisure hours, Cheryl enjoys photography, scrapbooking, hiking, and travelling, but most importantly, she likes spending quality time with her family.

WITCHER, Pamela Elizabeth

1975–
Research Assistant, Program Coordinator, Artist (Painter, Poet, and Actress), ASL Teacher, and Interpreter.

PAMELA WITCHER was born Deaf to Deaf parents in Montréal, Québec. She has a Deaf brother, three Deaf uncles and several Deaf first and second cousins. One of her cousins is involved with the Canadian Association of the Deaf and another is currently attending Gallaudet University. Pamela is quadralingually fluent in ASL (American Sign Language), LSQ (Langues des Signes Québécoise), English, and French.

She received her early education at the MacKay Centre, West Hill High School, and Wagar High School from which she graduated in 1993. She then earned a degree in Collegial Studies from Dawson College. She was awarded honours for her higher than average academic achievements, and went on to McGill University where she earned a Bachelor of Social Work degree in 1998. During 1997 she was awarded full reimbursement to attend the Deaf Women United Conference in Rochester, New York. She has participated in the International Women's March and is a keen advocate for women and Deaf women's issues.

While attending McGill, Pamela worked as a research assistant and lab manager in the School of Communication Science and Disorders. She also taught a class entitled, "ASL: Learning and Theory." From 1993 to 1998 she worked as an assistant after-school program coordinator at the MacKay Centre, working with Deaf children and teenagers. After graduating she worked for a year as the centre's after-school program coordinator, operating three recreational programs simultaneously. In 1999 she was under contract as an actress, performing the role of the Deaf psychic in *Someone is Watching*. Since 1998 she has also worked for CommunicaSigne,

interpreting between ASL and LSQ in various settings such as conferences, festivals, and meetings. As a volunteer, she served on the board of the Québec Cultural Society of the Deaf for one year.

In addition to her other successes, Pamela is a published poet and author: *Now That You're Gone* (1993); *Youthanthology*, "Deaf Like Me" (1995); *Deaf World Web* and *Deaf Montréaler*, "Human Abuse;" *The Tactile Mind* (2001); and a book of photographs—*Missy's One Day Album* (to be published).

In her leisure hours she is fond of rowing, cross-country skiing, hiking, backpacking, and mountain biking. Her hobbies include travelling, reading, writing poetry, oil painting, black-ink drawing, watching international movies, and attending dance shows. As well, Pamela enjoys intellectual group discussions on a variety of topics. In the future she hopes to travel and work in Third World countries. In addition, she hopes to go to graduate school to continue her academic studies and work in the mental health field as a counsellor and consultant.

Pamela believes in a holistic approach to life and struggles with the reality of being a woman in a patriarchal society, particularly in Deaf patriarchal communities. She also struggles to accept the existing oppression among various groups within the Deaf Community in Canada. In view of her youth, Pamela has many exciting years ahead of her in which to attain her goals and dreams.

WOOD, Lois Marian

1957–
Community Support Worker, Respected Caregiver, and Enthusiastic Pet Lover.

LOIS WOOD, the second of four children, was born profoundly Deaf, due to maternal rubella, into a hearing family in Vancouver, British Columbia. At the age of three she was fitted with hearing-aids. Her parents ordered a correspondence course from the John Tracey Clinic in California so they could train her orally at home. She has no known Deaf relatives, and currently makes her home in Victoria, BC.

When Lois was five years old she was enrolled at Jericho Hill School for the Deaf in Vancouver, where

she was taught orally. Signing was not allowed at that time. Her family lived in Quesnel, BC, so Lois was a residential student, and was surprised to see the children signing to each other in the dormitory. Because they all missed her, Lois's family moved to Vancouver and lived in a house across the street from Jericho Hill School (JHS) for twenty years. After four years at JHS,

Lois was sent to a mainstream public school to complete her education. These were extremely difficult years for her because she had to lip-read what was being said, and most of that was guesswork. There were no interpreters or notetakers in those days.

When she graduated and joined the workforce, Lois was employed full-time by the City of Vancouver as a clerk-typist from 1978 to 1992. With support and encouragement from her parents, she then enrolled in an associate arts degree program at Seattle Centre Community College in Seattle, Washington, where she attended for three years. Subsequently, she obtained a Mental Health Worker Certificate from Malaspina University-College in Duncan, BC, and first-aid/CPR certification, to become a qualified community support worker, from Camosun College in Victoria, BC. Lois worked as a respite caregiver in her own home for three years. Since 1996 she has worked as a community support worker for the Island Deaf and Hard of Hearing Centre (IDHHC) in Victoria and Nanaimo, BC.

In addition to her formal education and training, Lois has attended several important workshops related to care-giving, mental health issues, and behaviour management. She has also presented workshops on mental health issues, stress and anger management, and legal rights. One of the most meaningful experiences of her life occurred while she was a student in Seattle, when she worked part-time as a personal care-provider for a thirty-two-year-old woman named Erin Eyer at the family's residence in Greenbank, Washington. Erin has multiple disabilities including a heart condition, behavioural problems, and cognitive challenges. She is legally blind and cannot speak. Erin's parents consider

Lois the finest person who ever tried to work with their daughter. The two women have since become close friends in a sister-like relationship. Erin herself provided a testimonial declaring that others had attempted to change her through kindly pretenses, but kindness was never a pretense with Lois. She gave Erin equality and love, and shared her life as a sister. Erin expresses her infinite and limitless love and respect for Lois Wood, and she continues to visit her for a week or two every six months at her home in Victoria.

As a volunteer, Lois has served the Deaf Community in numerous ways. Since 1999 she has been a member of the Advisory Committee for Medical Interpreting Services of BC, worked on the World Deaf Timberfest Committee, helped to raise funds for the Dogwood Deaf Women's Slo-Pitch team, and was secretary for the Canadian Deaf Youth Leadership Camp in the late 1970s. She has always been an ardent fan at Deaf athletic events, especially bowling, basketball, and slo-pitch, and has attended World Winter and Summer Games for the Deaf.

In her leisure hours this busy woman's greatest interest is in her family of pets. She is the proud owner of a twelve-year-old cocker-spaniel named Andy, and two three-year-old Himalayan cats, a breed that is half Persian and half Siamese. She calls the male Wanekia, a First-Nation word for "life of creation," and the female Amitola, a First-Nation word for "life of a rainbow." She loves her work with IDHHC, and is happy and contented with her life. Lois enjoys gardening, doing Tai Chi, walking, socializing with friends, and travelling. She is keenly interested in natural healing, and is delighted to live near the Pacific Ocean on beautiful Vancouver Island.

WOOD (McGUFFIN) (DICK), Marjorie, CM (Centennial Medal), OC (Order of Canada)

1903–1988
Author and Advocate for the Deaf-Blind.

MARJORIE DICK was born in Rainier, Oregon, but moved to North Vancouver, British Columbia, with her parents when she was seven months old. In the third year of her life she contracted a severe case of measles which left her Blind and with a marked degree of hearing loss. By the age of seven she had become both Blind and Deaf. She was sent to day-schools in Seattle, Washington, for several years but her real education did not begin until she went to Salem, Oregon, at the age of twelve, to attend the state residential School for the Deaf. She learned very quickly, making up for all the years she had lost, and soon gained

confidence and self-esteem. Marjorie became very popular among the students for her ability to invent and tell amusing and interesting stories. Among her many hearing, sighted relatives were several well-known and respected citizens, including her cousin, the Honourable Walter S. Owen, who served as British Columbia's Lieutenant-Governor during the late 1970s and early 1980s.

On 2 September 1922, determined to have a home and family of her own, Marjorie married a Deaf man,

Albert F. McGuffin, who worked in a casket factory for forty-five years to support her and their three hearing children—two girls, Doreen and Marjorie (Jr.), and a boy, Warren. Because she could not read to her children, Marjorie began inventing interesting stories to tell them. This skill eventually led her to a literary career. Marjorie and Albert had been married thirty-six years when Albert died at age seventy-eight. She later married Eric A. Wood and continued to live in the Vancouver area where she had spent most of her life.

It was not until she was nearly thirty years old that Marjorie registered with the Canadian National Institute for the Blind. Later she also became a member of the Canada Council of the Blind, which was organized in Winnipeg in 1940 and now has more than 5,000 members across Canada. She learned Braille and took formal training as a writer through a correspondence course from the University of Chicago. In 1952, she produced the first issue of *Dots and Taps*, a Braille magazine which she bound with household string and from which sixteen copies were made. This publication is said to have been a turning point in the history of Deaf-Blind persons in Canada.

Marjorie had more than thirty articles published in newspapers and children's magazines, but is probably best known for her book entitled *Trudging Up Life's Three-Sensed Highway*, which was published by the Versatile Publishing Company in 1978, with a foreword written by her cousin, Lieutenant-Governor W.S. Owen. She had won the Women's Press Club Award in 1958 and was awarded the Centennial Medal in 1967. The Canadian Council of the Blind honoured her with the Merit Award in 1968 when the National Institute for the Blind presented her with a scroll for her outstanding service to the Deaf-Blind in Canada.

In 1976 she was selected as the first recipient of the Arthur Napier Magill Distinguished Service Award. Shortly after returning home from Toronto where she had received this honour, Marjorie was astonished to learn that she had been appointed a Member of the Order of Canada in recognition of her many contributions to the welfare of all Deaf-Blind Canadians. The investiture took place at Government House in Ottawa and was presided over by Jules Leger, then Governor-General of Canada. Her eldest daughter, Doreen Crawford, accompanied Marjorie on this unforgettable trip.

Despite the loss of both sight and hearing at an early age, Marjorie McGuffin Wood lived a very full and productive life. She died in the Vancouver General Hospital at the age of eighty-five on 18 November 1988. She will always be remembered as someone who broadened the horizons of Deaf-Blind Canadians, strengthened their ties of friendship, and altered their scope of communication and employability.

WOODCOCK, Kathryn PhD, OMC, PEng

1956–

World's First Deaf Woman with a PhD in Engineering, Canada's First Deaf Hospital Vice-President, Author, and Professor.

KATHRYN WOODCOCK developed a hearing loss that was not diagnosed until she was thirteen years of age. She received a mainstream public school education, excelling in all academic areas. Her Deafness progressed gradually and she did not learn to sign until she was thirty, managing to get along through speechreading. After graduating from high school she decided to follow in her father's footsteps and become an engineer. She enrolled at the University of Waterloo and earned a Bachelor's degree in Applied Sciences and Systems Design Engineering. Kathryn was one of only four women in a graduating class of fifty-five.

She then spent a year working for Xerox Canada and eighteen months at St. Mary's General Hospital in Kitchener. She next became a vice-president of Hospital Services at Centenary Hospital in Scarborough. This was a remarkable achievement because she was, at twenty-four, one of five vice-presidents responsible for 600 staff members and a $19-million budget. Her administrative duties included food services, maintenance, housekeeping, power plant, security, parking, and purchasing. She was also the senior management champion for occupational health and safety and active in the Ontario hospital industry, serving on collective bargaining and health and safety committees and making presentations about ergonomics, safety, and accessibility.

From 1983 to 1988 she combined her full-time work at the hospital with classes at University of Waterloo, where she earned a Master's degree in Engineering (Systems Design). Then, in 1996, she completed a PhD in Mechanical and Industrial Engineering at the University of Toronto.

Kathryn's professional life has been a series of successes and varied experience. After leaving health care, she developed a career in academia and research. She is currently an associate professor of occupational and public health at Ryerson University in Toronto. Previously she was a manager in the Prevention Division of the Workplace Safety and Insurance Board, an adjunct professor of systems design engineering at Waterloo, and an assistant professor at Rochester Institute of Technology (jointly with the National Technical Institute for the Deaf in Rochester). She also consults for clients in Canada and the US.

She is well known for her impeccable research skills and is a published author of many professional papers and articles. Kathryn is also a gifted lecturer and is frequently an invited presenter. She was the first Deaf board president of the Canadian Hearing Society in Ontario, is a founding member of the Canadian Deafened Persons Association (CDPA), has been active in the Association of Late-Deafened Adults (ALDA), and, among many other honours, has been the recipient of the Ontario Medal of Good Citizenship. Her book, *Deafened People: Adjustment and Support*, was published by University of Toronto Press in 2000. One of the few books available on acquired Deafness, it incorporates original research by her husband, Miguel Aguayo. In her spare time Kathryn enjoys the company of her lovely young daughter, Ruby.

WOODWARD, Helen

1951–
Educator, ASL Instructor, Community Worker, Performer, and Artist.

HELEN WOODWARD was born hearing into a hearing family in Brampton, Ontario. She became Deaf at the age of five due to spinal meningitis. Although she has several relatives with severe hearing loss, including grandparents and uncles, Helen is the only one in her family who uses ASL.

She was educated at the Ontario provincial School for the Deaf in Bellevile, graduating in 1970. She then attended Gallaudet University in Washington, DC, completing a BA degree in English in 1975. Helen furthered her education and qualifications by taking graduate studies at summer sessions at Western Maryland College, earning a Master's degree in Deaf Education in 1983. She is currently employed as a teacher of the Deaf by the Ontario Ministry of Education and Training at the E.C. Drury School for the Deaf in Milton, and makes her home in Cambridge, Ontario.

Helen has always been a very active participant in the life and work of the Deaf Community at all levels— locally, provincially, and nationally. She is a current member and past president of the Ontario Cultural Society of the Deaf, has served on the national board of the Canadian Cultural Society of the Deaf as cultural director, co-chaired the National Festival of the Arts in 1990, has taught local Bible study groups, is a member of the Cornerstone Community Church in Cambridge, and has taught ASL evening classes for several years.

Helen has been recognized and honoured for her contributions to the Deaf Community with an Appreciation and Outstanding Help Award from the Ontario Cultural Society of the Deaf. In 1984 she was the recipient of the coveted Golden Defty Award at the National Festival of the Arts for Best Overall Performing Artist for her singing, using ASL.

Helen says that the highlight of her life has been the unexpected discovery that she can draw. It all began with a teaching assignment in art that left her apprehensive and concerned. Nevertheless, with the help of God and the patience of her pupils, Helen was led to this remarkable path of self-discovery. She has since developed unique skills in drawing with coloured pencils and has supplemented her natural talent with a few courses and private lessons.

Her art has now become more than just a hobby. She has a studio in her home and is excited by the possibilities that lie ahead in this field. She is also a member of the Colored Pencil Society of America.

In her leisure hours Helen loves to read, but she has very little spare time. Her newfound artistic talents and dedicated services to the Deaf Community continue to expand her horizons and bring new and exciting challenges into her life.

WOOSNAM (SMITH), Marjorie Mary Elsie

1917–
Talented Seamstress, Craftswoman, Outstanding Homemaker, and Beloved Mother.

MARJORIE SMITH was born in Clandeboye, Manitoba. She became Deaf shortly before she was three years old, due to illness. She is married to a hearing man, Joseph Ross Woosnam, who worked for the CPR for nearly forty years. They had four hearing children, three daughters and a son—Penelope Anne (Penny), Brenda Lynn, Rosemary (now deceased), and Ross Glenn. Their second daughter, Brenda, communicates well with the Deaf, and went to Africa to set up a school in Nigeria, where she worked with Deaf children for fourteen years before returning to Canada in 2001. Besides working for the CPR, Joseph has been a member of the Royal Canadian Legion for fifty years and worked for the Legion on a voluntary basis for decades. For his contribution, he was presented with the Canada Good Citizen medal and the Meritorious Service Award. In addition, he is well known as a creator and collector of lead soldiers, and has been featured on television and in newspaper articles. He also has two famous relatives—Dan Woosnam, the golfer, and Phil Woosnam, the soccer player. Marjorie and Joseph presently make their home in Vancouver, BC.

Marjorie was educated at the Manitoba School for the Deaf in Winnipeg, from 1925 to 1935. She recalls it as being a wonderful place, where she enjoyed both the academic and the residential programs and acquired many lasting friendships. When she graduated she went directly into the workforce, first as a housekeeper, and later as a dry-cleaner. She considers her greatest achievement to be her success as a mother and homemaker. Although she is now in her eighties, Marjorie still enjoys canning, preserving, baking, and sewing. She is an expert needlewoman and for many years made clothes for other people. She still sews for her family, particularly her grandchildren. She was also very skilled at making chenille bedspreads and bathroom accessories.

At the present time, Marjorie's view of a good life is to stay at home and have her family over for dinner. When a Deaf seniors' club, the Happy Hands Club, was established in 1990, she took on the presidency, and has contributed since then in other capacities as well. She feels it is important for Deaf people to keep in touch with each other as they get older.

Marjorie's greatest passion is watching sports on television. There is nothing she likes better than watching a Canucks hockey game.

YOUNGS (LIEBMAN), Ilene Bonnie

1952–1997
Teacher, Researcher, and Activist.

ILENE LIEBMAN was genetically Deaf, born in Brooklyn, New York, to Deaf parents, Samuel and Marsha Liebman. Marsha had a Deaf brother, Abraham Glazer, and Samuel had one Deaf brother, Israel, and one hearing brother, Abe. Ilene had three Deaf sisters—Louise, Sheila, and Brenda—a Deaf niece and nephew and a Deaf brother-in-law. She was married to Macklin Youngs, who is also Deaf, as are their two children, Megan and Vance. Her hearing brother-in-law, Len Aron, is superintendent of the Washington State School for the Deaf. Her sister Brenda Aron works at the same school as an ASL specialist. Her sister Sheila Wadler teaches at Lexington School for the Deaf in New York, while her sister Louise works as a computer programmer. Her husband, Macklin Youngs, is vice-principal of the Secondary Department at the provincial School for the Deaf in Milton, Ontario.

Ilene received a public school education at PS 47, an oral day-school in Manhattan, and Canarsie High School in Brooklyn. She won the prestigious ARISTA award when she graduated, an honour reserved for those who consistently achieve straight As. She then attended Gallaudet University in Washington, DC, graduating with a BA degree in Psychology/Social Work in 1976. Later, she received her Master's degree in Deaf Education from Western Maryland College at Westminister, Maryland. While at Gallaudet she was listed in *Who's Who in American Colleges and Universities*.

She worked as a residential counsellor for the Deaf in Trenton, New Jersey, before coming to Canada to teach elementary level students at the MacKay Centre for the Deaf in Montréal, Québec. She also taught English as a second language to Deaf French adults before leaving to take up a new position at the E.C. Drury School in Milton, Ontario. There she immersed herself in the bilingual/bicultural nursery program and became the first home-visiting teacher to use the Bi/Bi approach in teaching Deaf infants and preschoolers.

Ilene then became involved in bilingual/bicultural research which she completed before her sad death in 1997 following a valiant four-year battle with cancer.

Her work was published as *Seize the Moment: A Pilot Case Study of a Toddler's Natural ASL*, and was supported by the Ontario Ministry of Education and Training. After her untimely death, the Bi/Bi Research Fund was established by the Ontario Cultural Society of the Deaf to encourage other Deaf and hard-of-hearing scholars to continue the work and to provide follow-up to Ilene's findings and conclusions.

Ilene Youngs will always be remembered as a passionate activist in support of the education and literacy of Deaf children.

ZARUBIAK, Twyla Maria

1968–
Banking Official, ASL Instructor, and Spokeswoman for the Deaf and Hard of Hearing.

TWYLA ZARUBIAK was born three months prematurely, weighing only two pounds, at St. Paul's Hospital in Saskatoon, Saskatchewan. As a result of the premature birth she was diagnosed with a severe hearing loss. Encouraged by her family to be as versatile as possible, she was undaunted by the usual barriers to communication with which Deaf people are faced. Today she is the proud possessor of a BSc degree from Gallaudet University in Washington, DC, where she majored in Economics and Finance.

Twyla has also had a wide variety of work experience, beginning with summer jobs as a park attendant, a maintenance worker, a dog groomer, and a clerical worker, and leading to several interesting positions with the Royal Bank of Canada, in Saskatoon and in Regina. She has been a personal property security officer, a reconciliation loan clerk, a PTB/night deposit clerk, a proof clerk, and a customer services representative. She continues to upgrade her skills and qualifications by attending workshops.

In her personal life, Twyla's accomplishments have also been varied. She was a second runner-up in a Miss Deaf Canada pageant, and won a Miss Congeniality Award as well as awards for highest scholastic achievement, highest average, and for being valedictorian. Her leadership qualities and superior interpersonal skills

have made her an excellent role model for other young Deaf people.

While at Gallaudet University she was a member of the Alpha Sigma Theta sorority and acted as newsletter editor and fundraising director. She also assisted with the Gallaudet yearbook, helped in a soup kitchen for the homeless, and performed household and yard chores for the elderly.

She is fully bilingual in ASL and English and teaches ASL classes. She is a board member for Saskatchewan Deaf and Hard of Hearing Services (a director for southern Saskatchewan), and the Regina Association of the Deaf. Her hearing sister, Darla Thorstad, is a special needs teacher who uses basic Sign Language with her pupils in order to convey concepts that help them master the English language more readily. Twyla was selected to serve on a diversity committee with one other staff member for the Royal Bank.

In August of 2001, Twyla married a hearing spouse, Martin Chartrand. In her leisure time she reads, travels, and gardens, but what is closest to her heart is her involvement in the activities of the Deaf Community. Twyla has many Deaf friends who are very dear to her.

ZIMMER (RONCERAY), Diane Marie

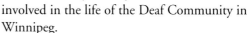

1945–
Data Processor, Proud Deaf Mother, and Deaf Community Volunteer.

DIANE RONCERAY was born Deaf at Treherne, Manitoba. She has a Deaf husband, Lawrence Zimmer, a Deaf daughter, Cheryl Zimmer, and a Deaf cousin, Alice Guilbert. Her husband has numerous Deaf relatives.

Diane was educated at the Saskatchewan provincial School for the Deaf in Saskatoon, graduating in 1963. She was sent to Saskatoon because the Manitoba School was not in operation at that time. She and her husband live in the Whyte Ridge area of Winnipeg, Manitoba, where they raised their Deaf daughter, Cheryl, and hearing son, Kevin. Cheryl is married to Brian Brozeit and works at Red River Community College as an instructor in the Deaf studies program. She was one of the first Deaf persons to receive a Bachelor of Education degree from the University of Winnipeg so her parents are deservedly proud of her. Kevin, the general manager of Ibex in Winnipeg, is unmarried and travels extensively. Both Diane and Lawrence take keen pride in the accomplishments of their children.

After graduating in 1963, Diane became a data processor and has been employed as a processing clerk at Cancercare for twenty-four years. Her husband has been employed at Boeing, Canada for twenty-six years in its Winnipeg plant, where he did much to improve the corporate views about hiring Deaf employees. Diane and Lawrence are now both looking forward to their retirement, and are still very actively involved in the life of the Deaf Community in Winnipeg.

Diane was correspondence secretary for the Canadian Cultural Society of the Deaf in 1981–82, and recording/correspondence secretary in 1983–84. She was presented with an Appreciation Award for her outstanding service in 1982. She has also been secretary for the Manitoba Cultural Society of the Deaf and participated enthusiastically in all events and activities generated by the many organizations and agencies of the Deaf Community. Her greatest and most highly respected contribution was her typing of the manuscript for the late Forrest C. Nickerson's acclaimed publication *A Deaf Artist's Trail*, a labour of love for which she volunteered.

In her leisure time, Diane enjoys researching her family tree and spending time with her husband and children. She is always a willing volunteer when help is required in the Deaf Community.

ZIMMER (ERICSON), Edith Irene

1941–
Dedicated Office Worker and Retired Homemaker.

EDITH ERICSON was born Deaf, due to maternal rubella, in Minnedosa, Manitoba. This was during World War II, when the Manitoba School for the Deaf was being used by the RCAF as a Wireless School. In view of these circumstances, she was sent to the Saskatchewan provincial School for the Deaf in Saskatoon.

Edith has no known Deaf relatives on her side of the family, but her husband, Dennis Joseph Zimmer, comes from a multi-generation Deaf family in the Winnipeg area. He was also the first Deaf person to be employed by Boeing of Canada, which influenced the hiring of many more Deaf people by that corporation at its Winnipeg plant. Edith and Dennis make their home in Winnipeg. They have no children.

Following her graduation from the Saskatchewan School for the Deaf, Edith worked for nearly four decades with Manitoba Hydro. She started her clerical job on a manual typewriter, advanced to an electric

model, then to a magnetic card machine, and finally to a computer which she continued to use until her retirement.

On 6 January 2000 the company and staff held a retirement party in her honour to recognize her many years of dedicated service. Since retiring, Edith has been assisting a Deaf/blind person as a volunteer.

Edith enjoys bowling once a week with other retired ladies and attending certain activities in the local Deaf Community. In her leisure time she relaxes by working on puzzles and keeps busy with her housework. Her husband Dennis is more involved than Edith as a volunteer with the various organizations of the Deaf. Edith is very happy and contented in her retirement.

ZIMMER, Susan Marie

1955–
ASL and ESL Teacher and Deaf Volunteer.

SUSAN ZIMMER was born Deaf in Winnipeg, Manitoba, and has a Deaf spouse, Robert Zimmer. They have two Deaf daughters, Laurie and Dana, and many Deaf relatives among Robert's extended family.

Susan was educated at the Manitoba School for the Deaf (1965–1974) and at Red River Community College (1974–1976). While attending the provincial School for the Deaf, she was presented with the prestigious Ralston Award. She has also been honoured as Miss Deaf Canada, and was the owner of Gus, the first hearing-ear dog in Manitoba. When Gus passed away in 1993 she replaced him with her second hearing-ear dog, Lira.

Susan's employment has focused mainly on the field of education—teaching ASL and ESL to immigrants, working with Downs Syndrome children, and as an early childhood specialist at the Sign Talk Children's Centre (STCC). In fact, she was a member of the parent group that established STCC.

As a member of Winnipeg's Deaf Community, Susan has been kept busy with her many involvements as a volunteer with the STCC board, Women's Auxiliary of the Deaf, Camp Kakepitay, Winnipeg Community Centre of the Deaf, Winnipeg Church of the Deaf, Deaf Youth Camp, and ASL Immersion program. She also assists with and participates in the community's social and recreational events.

Although her life is a busy one, Susan finds time to spend with her husband and daughters, enjoying family camping, hiking, and fishing trips. She loves children and is dedicated to working with them. In her spare time she cooks and does crafts and gardening. For exercise she prefers to take long walks.

SISTERS (DEAF NUNS)

A Unique Group of Dedicated Deaf Women.

No history of Deaf Women in Canada would be complete without mentioning the significant contribution made by those who dedicated their lives to their church. Although several stories throughout the text of this volume profile deeply religious women who served their churches in different ways, the authors have not focused on any specific religious order with Deaf adherents.

This section provides historical information about such a Roman Catholic Community. The first known Deaf Sister in Canada was Margaret Hanley of Montréal who was born in Kingston, Ontario. In 1859, at the age of seventeen, she entered the Community of the Daughters of Charity, commonly known as the Sisters of Providence at Montréal. She pronounced her vows shortly before her death on 16 March 1860 at the Hospice St. Joseph, taking the name Sister Marguerite du Sacre Coeur. The second Deaf Sister was Marie Olive Mondor of Joliet, Québec, who made her vows with the same religious community in 1862 and became Sister Come de la Providence. She died in 1933 at the age of ninety-one. One other Deaf woman joined this community before it stopped taking Deaf candidates. She was Elise Routhier, who entered the

community at the age of twenty-eight and later became known as Sister Priscille. She was eighty-three when she died in 1933.

Among the elderly women for whom the Sisters of Providence provided care were some for whom communication was difficult because they had hearing problems or could not speak. In 1848 Father Charles Lagorce began teaching Sign Language. The Superior and foundress of the Sisters of Providence, Mother Emilie Gamelin, encouraged the Sisters to attend his classes. One of the most eager to learn was an eighteen-year-old novice named Sister Albine Gadbois, who made her religious profession in 1849 and became Sister Marie de Bon Secours.

In 1850, she was assigned to a boarding school and was in charge of the English classes. It was there that she became the part-time teacher of an eight-year-old Deaf girl named Margaret Hanley, whose father had brought her to the nuns to be cared for after her mother had died. Sister Marie de Bon Secours was very successful in teaching Margaret to read, write, and pray. At the beginning of the year 1851, another Sister was assigned to the school, permitting Sister Marie de Bon Secours to have more time to teach Margaret and

Fiftieth Anniversary of the founding of the Sisters of Our Lady of Seven Dolors.

another Deaf girl, Georgina LaVallee, the daughter of a friend of the Gadbois family. Three other Deaf girls came to join them that first year. This is considered the beginning of the Sisters of Providence's work with the Deaf. In 2001 they celebrated the 150th anniversary of this significant aspect of their contribution to the history of the Deaf in Canada.

Many readers may not be aware of a religious community in Canada where Deaf Sisters served in many different capacities during the late nineteenth and early twentieth centuries. This congregation was founded in Montréal in 1887 by the Sisters of Providence at the request of Father Francois Xavier Trepaniér, who was the first chaplain of the Institution des Sourdes-Muettes (Institution for Deaf Girls). This congregation, made up entirely of Deaf Sisters, was based on a similar religious congregation in France which Father Trepaniér had visited during a trip to Europe. This religious order, called Little Sisters of Our Lady of Seven Dolors, was established at the Institution for Deaf Girls operated by the Sisters of Providence, of which Margaret Hanley, Georgina LaVallee, and Marie Olive Mondor were the first three pupils. Although directed by the Sisters of Providence, this congregation has its own rules and constitutions. In 1974, the word "Little" was removed from the name of the congregation.

At the establishment of this new community on 1 April 1887, nine Deaf postulants were admitted. Of these, five persevered to make their vows in 1890 and became the first five foundresses. They were: Catherine Beston (Sister Marie de Bon Secours), Rosalie Geoffroy (Sister Francois Xavier), Alexina Bolvin (Sister Francois de Sales), Emelie Montpellier (Sister Marie Ignace), and Eugenie Lemire (Sister Marie Victor).

Although most of these Sisters were former pupils of the Institution of Deaf Girls, there were also some from the United States and of these several were Franco-Americans. A total of 149 Deaf women have entered this congregation since its foundation. Of this number, eighty-seven persevered to take their vows. The largest number of Deaf Sisters at any one time was sixty-four in 1959. The Deaf Sisters of Our Lady of Seven Dolors (sometimes translated into English as Seven Sorrows) provided assistance in the classrooms, supervised students, took care of the sick, aged, and blind at the institution, looked after the sacristy, worked in the sewing rooms and infirmaries, helped in the kitchen, and did whatever else was required of them.

With the gradual takeover of the education of Deaf students by the provincial government, the Deaf girls were obliged to move to another school along with Deaf boys. When this took place, the Sisters of Our Lady of Seven Dolors and the Sisters of Providence at the institution moved to Our Lady of Providence's residence, which had been constructed especially for them. For some of the older Sisters it was an extremely difficult adjustment as they had lived at the institution for fifty years or more, first as students and later as nuns. Among the younger Sisters, some continued to teach, but most went into social and pastoral work.

One of these was Sister Elizabeth Kass of Dubuque, Iowa, who had entered in 1959. After spending twenty-five years in Montréal, she began her present service as a pastoral worker with St. Mark's Catholic Community of the Deaf in Edmonton, Alberta. Among other things, she teaches religious education to students at the Alberta School for the Deaf, has written many articles, and has been an outspoken advocate for the Deaf. Others who became pastoral workers after 1976 were Sister Helene Lebrun and Sister Germaine Landry, who continue to serve the Deaf in Montréal.

The early growth of the Congregation of Sisters of Our Lady of Seven Dolors seems to have been directly related to the success of the Institution des Sourdes Muettes as a residential school for Deaf Girls. Most of those who joined this community had been students at the school, and were inspired by the example of the Deaf Sisters who assisted them in their education. Once the school closed, and the Deaf girls were being educated elsewhere, the influence of the Deaf Sisters began to diminish and it became increasingly difficult to attract new recruits to enter the order. There have been no new members since 1965, and the Deaf Sisterhood appears to have come to the end of an era.

Sisters of Our Lady of Seven Dolors, both Canadian and American, all of whom were Deaf and served in Canada:

Adele Aube, Cecile Ayotte, Jeanne Beauvais, Blanche Belanger, Rosanne Berube, Adelina Bouchard, Delphine Bouchard, Eva Boulanger, Marie Bourassa, Victorine Bourassa, Annie Campbell, Virginia Capler, Marie-Reine Cloutier, Albertine Cyr, Jeannine Dagenais, M. Madeline Denis, Marie-Jeanne Desjardins, Aldea Dupuis, Ouida Erd, Marie-Paule Forcier, Adele Fournier, Marie-Paule Gagne, Marie-Blanche Gagnon, Ursule Gendron, Louisa Holmes, Ida Hughes, Elizabeth Kass, Clara Labelle, Hortense Lafond, Yolande Laliberte, Germaine Landry, Marguerite Laplante, Rosalie Larochelle, Yvonne Larochelle, Regina LaSalle, Helene Lebrun, Renelle Lebrun, Georgette Leduc, Margaret Lefoley, Beatrice Leger, Stephanie Lessard, Cecile Marcoux, Katherine Molley, Dora Moss, Rosarie Nolet, Diana Ouellette, Claudia Pauze, Bernadette Pelletier, Jacqueline Pepin, Juliette Pepin, Lydia Perrier, Eva Perron, Laurette Preville, Carmen Proulx, Mary Jewel Reid, Odelide Sabourin, Josephine Scannell, Genevieve Smith, Zelia Therrien, Fernande Thibault, Therese Tremblay, Therese Turcotte, Fleurette Tull, and Micheline Veilleux.

References

Most of the material in this book was drawn from archive collections, records of organizations of the Deaf, transcripts, letters, newspapers, newsletters, various journals, personal interviews, resumes, reminiscences, and family lore. There are, however, several sources that should be mentioned since readers may want to refer to these publications.

Carbin, Clifton, *Deaf Heritage in Canada* (Whitby, ON: McGraw-Hill Ryerson, 1996).

Crawford, Isabel, *Kiowa: A Woman Missionary in Indian Territory* (Lincoln, NB: University of Nebraska Press, 1998). (Reprinted from the original 1915 edition, entitled *Kiowa: History of a Blanket Indian Mission*.)

Cripps, Joanne S., *Quiet Journey: Understanding the Rights of Deaf Children* (Owen Sound, ON: The Ginger Press, 2000).

MacKinnon, Christy, *The Silent Observer* (Wreck Cove, NS: Breton Books, 1993).

Stanley-Blackwell, Laurie, *Compassionate Observer: Cape Breton's Christy MacKinnon*, The Journal of the British Deaf History Society, vol. 2, 1 (August 1998), BDHS Publications, Feltham, England.

Wood, Marjorie McGuffin, *Trudging up Life's Three-Sensed Highway* (Vancouver: Versatile Publishing, 1978).

Additional sources are *Deaf Canada Today*, OAD News, *Vibes* (the Canadian Hearing Society's journal), *Gallaudet Today*, CAD Chat, and *Dots and Taps* (a quarterly journal published by the CNIB), which was the brainchild of the late Marjorie McGuffin Wood.

Photo Credits

Pg. 1B, *Manitoba Echo*, April 1939, Vol. XLVI, No. 7

Pg. 8, Canadian Mute—Ontario School for the Deaf—Sir James Whitney Archives, Belleville, Ontario

Pg. 13B, courtesy of Margaret Dunn

Pg. 27, credit to Cindy Wilson, *Telegraph-Journal/Times Globe*, [Saint John, NB]

Pg. 37A, Canadian Mute—Ontario School for the Deaf—Sir James Whitney Archives, Belleville, Ontario

Pg. 46, Cultural Horizons, Canadian Cultural Society of the Deaf

Pg. 50, Western Canada Association of the Deaf

Pg. 53, American Baptist Historical Society, Valley Forge Archives Center

Pg. 99, courtesy of Jean Gardner

Pg. 103B, Royal National Institute for the Deaf Library, London, England

Pg. 121, Canadian Mute—Ontario School for the Deaf—Sir James Whitney Archives, Belleville, Ontario

Pg. 123, Winnipeg Community Centre of the Deaf

Pg. 139, Canadian Mute—Ontario School for the Deaf—Sir James Whitney Archives, Belleville, Ontario

Pg. 148, Canadian Mute—Ontario School for the Deaf—Sir James Whitney Archives, Belleville, Ontario

Pg. 151, Western Canada Association of the Deaf

Pg. 157B, NS Archives and Records Management, Halifax

Pg. 159, NS Archives and Records Management, Halifax

Pg. 167, Winnipeg Community Centre of the Deaf

Pg. 173, Art Gallery of Ontario, Toronto, Ontario

Pg. 186, courtesy of Howard Nemeroff

Pg. 218, courtesy of Jacqueline Belmore

Pg. 222, courtesy of Betty Halverson and Hilda Parser

Pg. 224, courtesy of Maureen Donald (individual photo)

Pg. 235, courtesy of Gordon and Christina Ayles, Moncton

Pg. 243B, courtesy of Bill Swanson (son)

Pg. 250, Photo credit: Antoine Mountain

Pg. 264, MacKay Centre for Deaf Children, Montreal

Pg. 275, Courtesy of Sister Elizabeth Kass